AMAZON

A RIVER'S JOURNEY FROM THE ANDES TO THE ATLANTIC

THOMAS PESCHAK

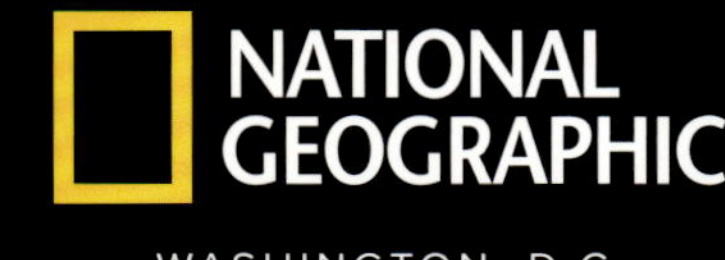

WASHINGTON, D.C.

AM
AZ
ON

A waterfall plunges off an ancient granite *tepui* (mesa) in Colombia's Chiribiquete National Park, home to the drainage basins of the Mesay and Cuñare Rivers, which flow into the Caquetá, a major tributary of the Amazon River.

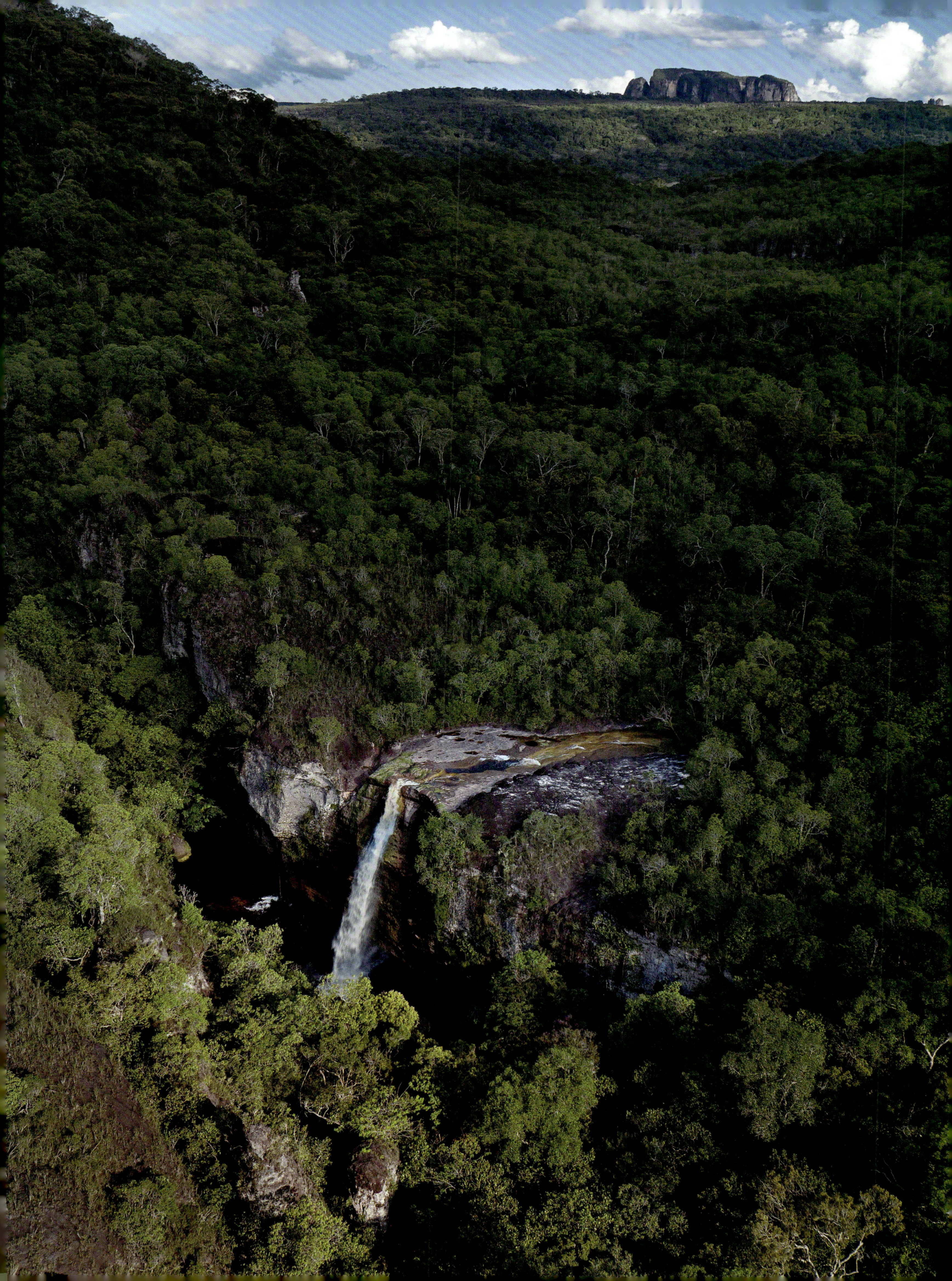

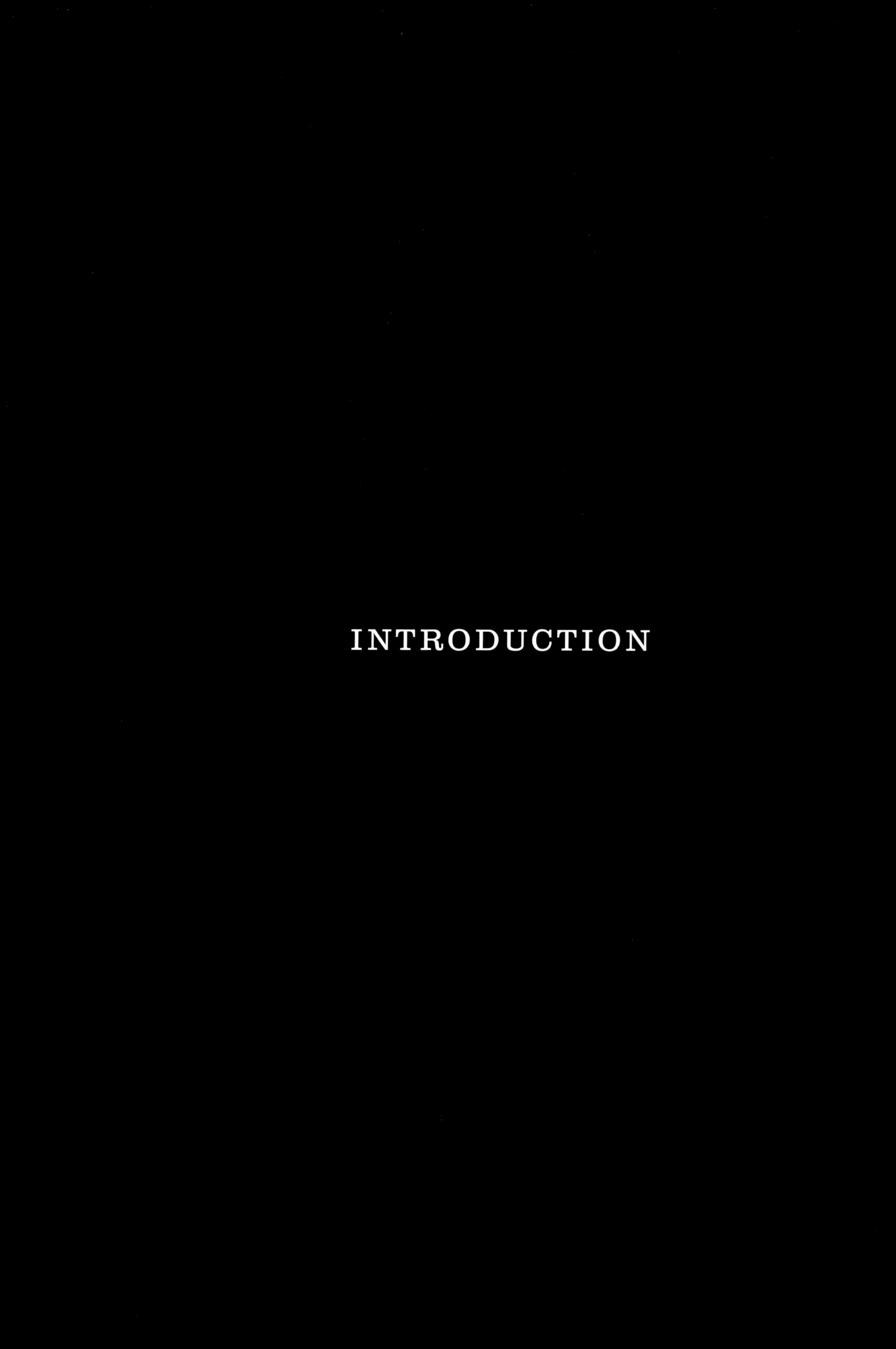

INTRODUCTION

FROM SEAFOREST TO RAINFOREST

MY ARMORED FASHION CHOICES have me on the verge of collapse. I am layered up with thick combat pants, two long-sleeved shirts, gloves, a head net, and a pair of snakebite gaiters. I will do whatever it takes to protect myself from enemies, both real and imagined. The ferocious sting of bullet ants, a whopping 4 out of 4 on the Schmidt sting pain index, has been described as "walking across hot coals with a three-inch [7.5 cm] nail embedded in your heel." The potentially lethal fer-de-lance, an easily excitable pit viper with inch-long (2.5 cm) fangs, is almost invisible against the leaf litter and responsible for most of the snakebites in South America. The bite of a female phlebotomine sand fly carrying a protozoan parasite could easily infect me with disfiguring leishmaniasis and require months of intravenous chemotherapy to cure. With every labored step in the stifling heat, I ask myself again and again what the hell I'm doing deep in the Amazon rainforest.

For 25 years, I have explored and documented our planet's wildest seas and most remote coastlines—first as a marine biologist researching the Great African Seaforest of giant bamboo kelp and later as a photojournalist specializing in ocean stories. I am well versed on how to avoid getting bitten by a great white shark, crushed by a feeding humpback whale, entangled in kelp, or stung by a venomous lionfish. I paid my dues exploring remote coral atolls, wading in lagoons so thick with sharks their fins breach the surface like sails of a flotilla. And after more than 50 expeditions, 20 *National Geographic* magazine print feature stories, and eight books, I was at ease and in sync with the ocean and its creatures. But I am a neophyte in the jungle.

WHAT IS AN OCEAN PHOTOGRAPHER doing here in the first place? How did I go from seaforest to rainforest? What possessed me to trade my comfortable ocean life for the Amazon? After almost two decades of traveling up to 300 days a year on assignment for National Geographic and conservation groups like the Save Our Seas Foundation and the Manta Trust, I was mentally, physically, and creatively burned out. I felt like I was repeating myself, and for someone who prides themself on pulling off pioneering firsts, this was a hard pill to swallow. It was either time to give up being a photographer or find a new challenge that would reinvigorate and reaffirm my love for the natural world and storytelling.

Around the same time, I came across a little-known fact: 434 dams had been built right across the watershed of the Amazon River and another 463 were in various stages of planning. I knew that dams at this scale are a death knell for freshwater biodiversity; they block animal migrations and disrupt the critical flow of nutrients and sediments downstream. The waters of the Amazon also play a crucial role for millions of people, with fish often being the only affordable protein source.

Decades of overfishing have dramatically reduced fish populations, and some larger predatory fish are now threatened. Additionally, unregulated aquarium fish collecting has resulted in some smaller species becoming rare. Plastic pollution has also become a major issue. A recent study found that 80 percent of freshwater fish species sampled in a tributary of the Amazon had ingested plastic particles. A 300-plus percent increase in the price of gold has resulted in an epidemic of small gold mines like a rash across the region. It is now estimated that more than 100 tons of mercury are poured into the Amazon and its tributaries each year, and 90 percent of fish caught by villagers downstream from mining clusters are contaminated. And in recent years, climate change has brought severe drought to the region, resulting in the lowest river levels recorded in 120 years.

It quickly became clear that the aquatic biodiversity of the Amazon River faces as many—if not more—conservation challenges as marine ecosystems. When the rainforest burns and the landscape lies blackened and scorched, global headlines abound. But when the world's most biodiverse freshwater system is under siege, silence ensues. For decades, the rainforests—the lungs of the Amazon—and terrestrial biodiversity have overshadowed the mighty river. In comparison, the world's greatest freshwater habitat—the circulatory system that feeds this mighty forest—has been neglected by science and storytelling.

Sandwiched between the Andes and the Atlantic Ocean, the Amazon River flows for 3,975 miles (6,400 km). If superimposed on a map of the United States, the river would begin in Tucson, Arizona, and the mouth would sit at National Geographic headquarters in Washington, D.C. The river's watershed—approximately the size of Australia—is the lifeblood of the region. It teems with numerous veins and capillaries. The aquatic web consists of more than a thousand tributaries, tens

With the Amazon River and its tributaries in dire need of a spotlight, I launched into an ambitious plan to shift the world's focus from the trees to the river and its aquatic underworlds.

of thousands of smaller rivers, and hundreds of thousands of shallow streams. Collectively, this network funnels up to 11 million cubic feet (311,500 m^3) of water into the Atlantic Ocean every second and makes up 20 percent of the world's fresh water annually. To mimic such an incomprehensible volume, you would have to shower continuously for 50 years just to match one second of outflow.

Unlike ocean biodiversity, which (apart from the deep sea) has been exhaustively photographed and documented, the aquatic and underwater worlds of Amazonia and its little-known creatures are only rarely, if ever, documented. The Amazon is the most diverse and productive freshwater habitat on Earth, and the three different river types—white water *(várzea),* black water *(igapó),* and clear water (also called *igapó)*—flow across South America.

From source glaciers and high-altitude streams to floodplain lakes, palm swamps, and mangroves, the habitats are as varied as they are unique. They host iconic and astonishing biodiversity. To date, 2,320 species of fish have been discovered, but the real number is estimated to exceed 6,000. Aquatic reptiles and mammals are also well represented, with six species of caimans, four species of anacondas, 16 species of turtles, two species of freshwater dolphins, a giant otter, and the near-mythical Amazonian manatee.

Novel and superlative behaviors go hand in hand with this outstanding diversity. For instance, the six-foot-long (1.8 m) dorado catfish holds the record for the longest freshwater fish migration in the world, an epic journey that crosses nearly the entire width of South America. The adults travel more than 7,200 miles (11,580 km) from the river's estuary to spawn in the Andes. This is nearly four times the length of the longest Pacific salmon migrations.

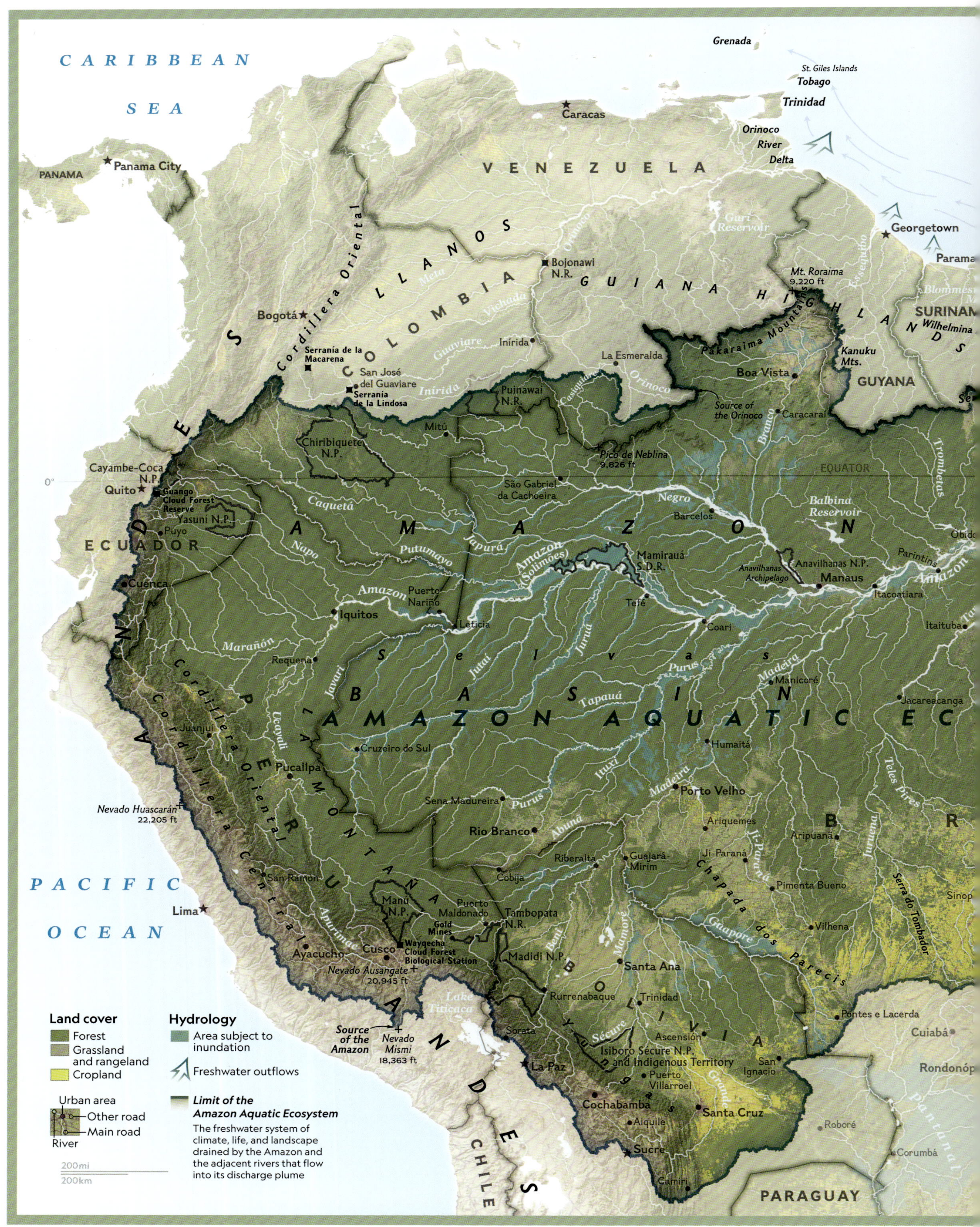

CARIBBEAN SEA
PACIFIC OCEAN
VENEZUELA
COLOMBIA
ECUADOR
PERU
BOLIVIA
GUYANA
SURINAM
PARAGUAY
CHILE
PANAMA
LLANOS
GUIANA HIGHLANDS
ANDES
AMAZON
BASIN
Selvas
AMAZON AQUATIC EC
LA MONTAÑA
Cordillera Oriental
Cordillera Central
Chapada dos Parecis
Serra do Tombador
Yungas
EQUATOR
Land cover
Forest
Grassland and rangeland
Cropland
Hydrology
Area subject to inundation
Freshwater outflows
Urban area
Other road
Main road
River
Limit of the Amazon Aquatic Ecosystem
The freshwater system of climate, life, and landscape drained by the Amazon and the adjacent rivers that flow into its discharge plume
200 mi
200 km

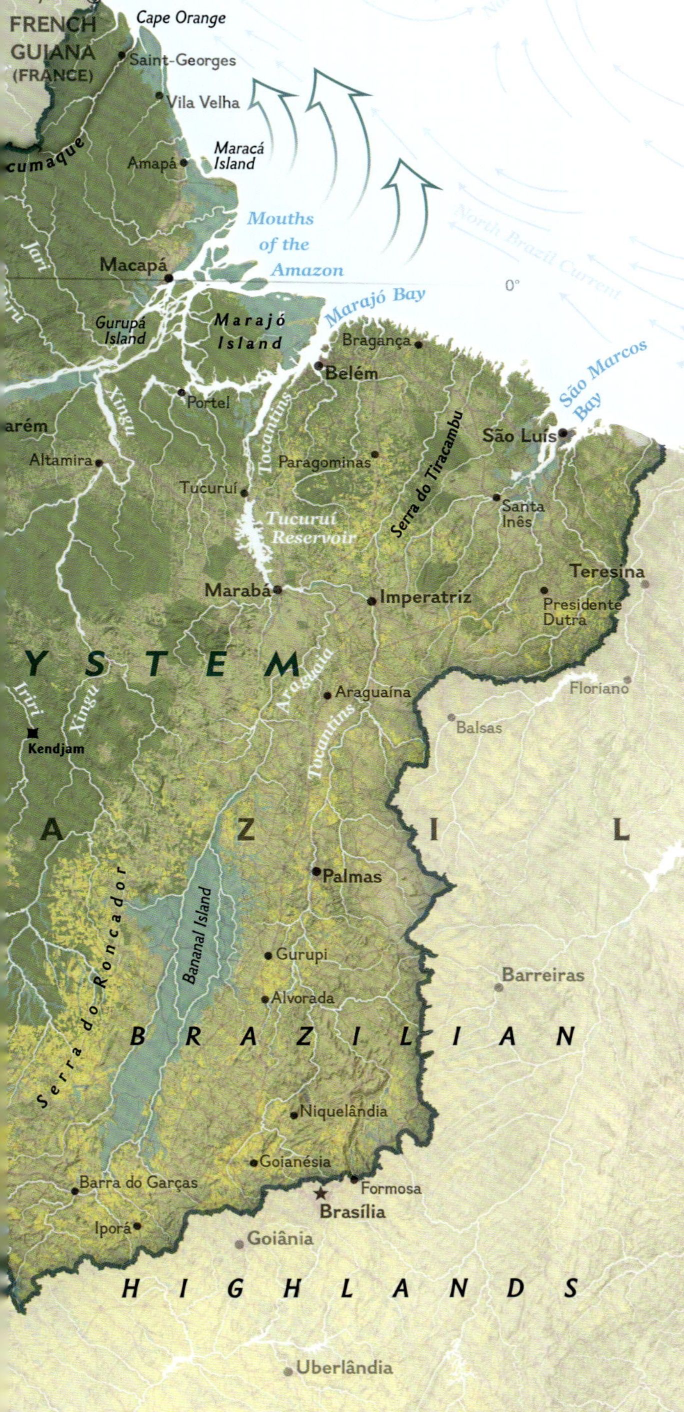

THE AMAZON AQUATIC ECOSYSTEM

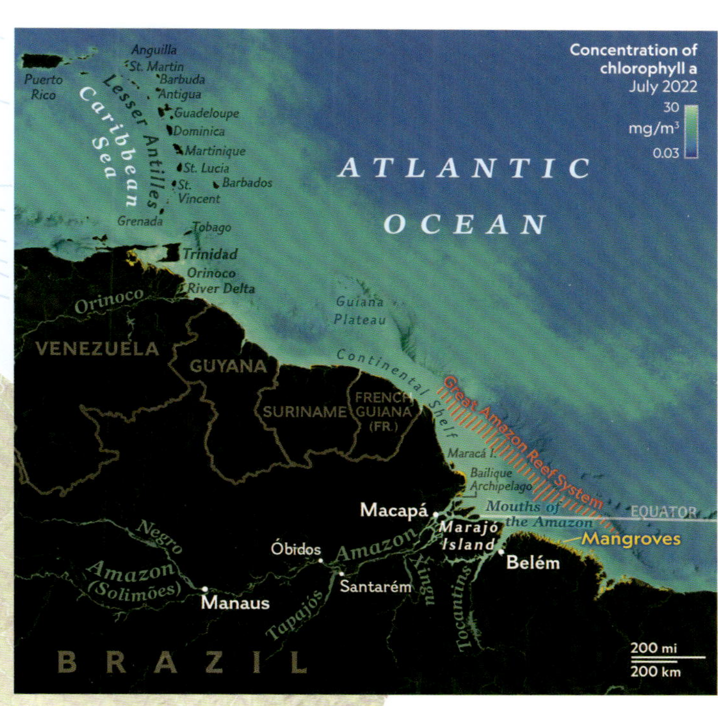

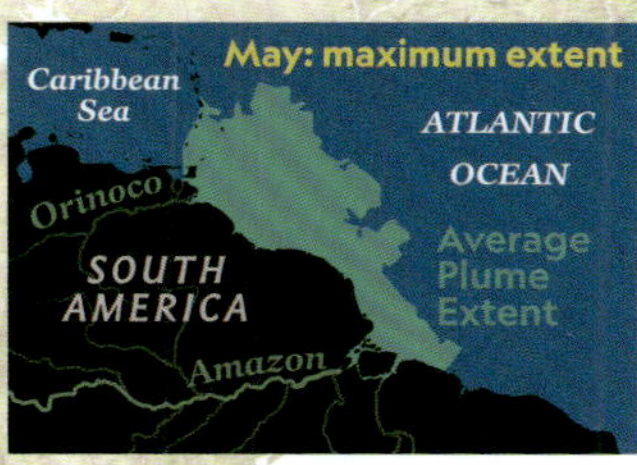

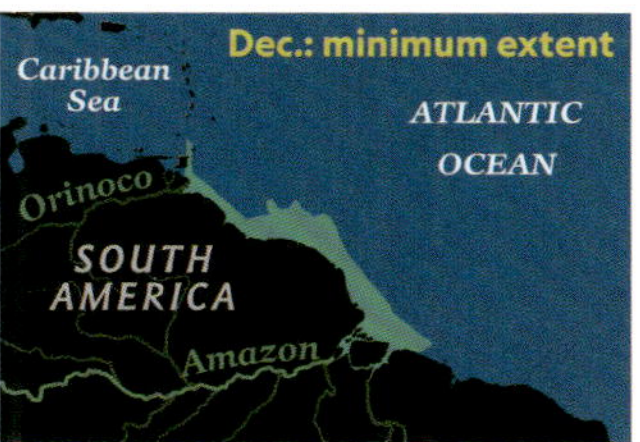

The Amazon River doesn't end when it meets the Atlantic Ocean. Instead, it becomes a massive plume of fresh water that fans out across the Atlantic for hundreds of miles. The plume's reach varies with winds and river discharge, flowing northwest toward the Caribbean before turning east. The deluge of fresh water creates a lower-salinity surface layer that interacts with underlying ocean currents. From high above, the plume appears jade green thanks to its composition of sediment, organic material, and chlorophyll a, the primary pigment in phytoplankton.

I was hooked. With the Amazon River and its tributaries in dire need of a spotlight, I stepped away from the sea and launched into an ambitious plan to shift the world's focus from the trees to the river and its aquatic underworlds.

THE AMAZON RIVER IS A WATERSHED that covers nine countries—and the truth is, you cannot take it on without a lot of preparation. During almost three years of planning and research, I read 406 books and 1,525 scientific papers and spoke to dozens of experts. Every day in the field is a precious gift, and the more I understand about geology, biology, hydrology, ecology, and animal behavior, the more effective I can be as a storyteller.

I assembled more than 1,200 pounds (540 kg) of equipment, from ice axes, mountaineering crampons, and mosquito nets to antibiotics, wet suits, and fins. To make photographs, I brought nine Nikon cameras, four underwater housings, 20 lenses, 10 lights, two drones, and more batteries and chargers than you can possibly imagine.

For 396 days, I followed the course of the Amazon River and myriads of tributaries from across South America, from the Andes in the west to the Atlantic in the east. Unlike many explorers who ventured here before me, I spent most of my time below the river's surface, revealing a rarely glimpsed underworld.

I began by exploring shallow meltwater streams on 19,000-foot (5,790 m) snow-capped volcanoes and eventually ended up diving on sponge reefs in the Atlantic Ocean, north of the river's mouth. I was on a mission to photograph Amazonian species—some so outlandish they could have been extras in a science fiction film. I encountered pink river dolphins that sonically navigate flooded forests, armored fish that weigh as much as silverback gorillas, and electric eels that can deliver 600-volt shocks—powerful enough to kill a human.

Some people might think that an ocean photographer has no business in the Amazon—and at the beginning of my journey, I would have agreed with them. Now I think that the opposite is true. It was a real advantage not having on-the-ground experience, because I went in with a beginner's mindset. Everything I photographed was new and exciting to me, which ushered in a refreshing approach to this type of storytelling. This book would have looked very different had I been a photographer with 30 years of experience in tropical rainforests instead of oceans.

At the same time, my familiarity with aquatic ecosystems and the underwater realm served me well. The moment I got onto the rivers and went underwater, my decades of ocean experience instinctively kicked in. In fact, there were many surprising similarities between the Amazon and the oceans. Apart from the dolphins, the flooded forests reminded me of marine ecosystems: manatees grazing on aquatic plants, stingrays hunting in leaf litter on submerged forest floors. Many of the fish species had remarkably similar counterparts in the ocean, like barracuda, needlefish, and butterfly fish.

In fact, tens of millions of years ago, parts of Brazil and Peru were a shallow ocean, inundated by water from the Caribbean Sea. Both the oceans and the Amazon River function as essential climate regulators, helping to stabilize temperature and maintain balance among Earth's ecosystems. The river regulates atmospheric moisture and the distribution of rainfall, creating a cyclical system of evaporation and precipitation. The oceans act as heat reservoirs, absorbing and distributing solar energy across the planet, transferring heat from the Equator to higher latitudes to regulate global temperatures. And both systems are crucial to the global water cycle, because the Amazon transports enormous amounts of fresh water from land to the sea, affecting ocean salinities and currents. The ocean serves as the source for much of the water vapor that forms clouds, precipitates over land, and runs into the Amazon River watershed.

I made 490,064 photographs during my 396 days following the river and its tributaries downstream across the Amazon Basin. My altitudinal gradient ranged from 19,685 feet (6,000 m) in the Peruvian Andes to 65 feet (20 m) below the surface of the Atlantic Ocean. I experienced temperature extremes from 5°F to 104°F (-15°C to 40°C), and most days this project was right at the edge of impossible. It certainly was the most ambitious and difficult thing I have ever done. But it was also the most worthwhile and rewarding.

The Amazon has changed me. When I started my journey, the rainforest and high Andes were scary, unfamiliar places. But by the end, my fears and insecurities were replaced by awe and wonder. I now care as much about the Amazon's hidden headwaters in Bolivia as I do about the Galápagos Marine Reserve; I am as passionate about pink dolphins as I am about sea turtles.

I hope that shining a light on this neglected aquatic realm will inspire others to realize what is at stake in the face of dams, climate change, and overfishing. My sojourn in the region has also rekindled my love for the ocean. Two years of not feeling the sweet embrace of salt water has made my heart grow fonder. And though I will soon return to the ocean realm to tell stories, my relationship with the Amazon is far from over. I know I'll be back. ■

PART ONE

ANDES

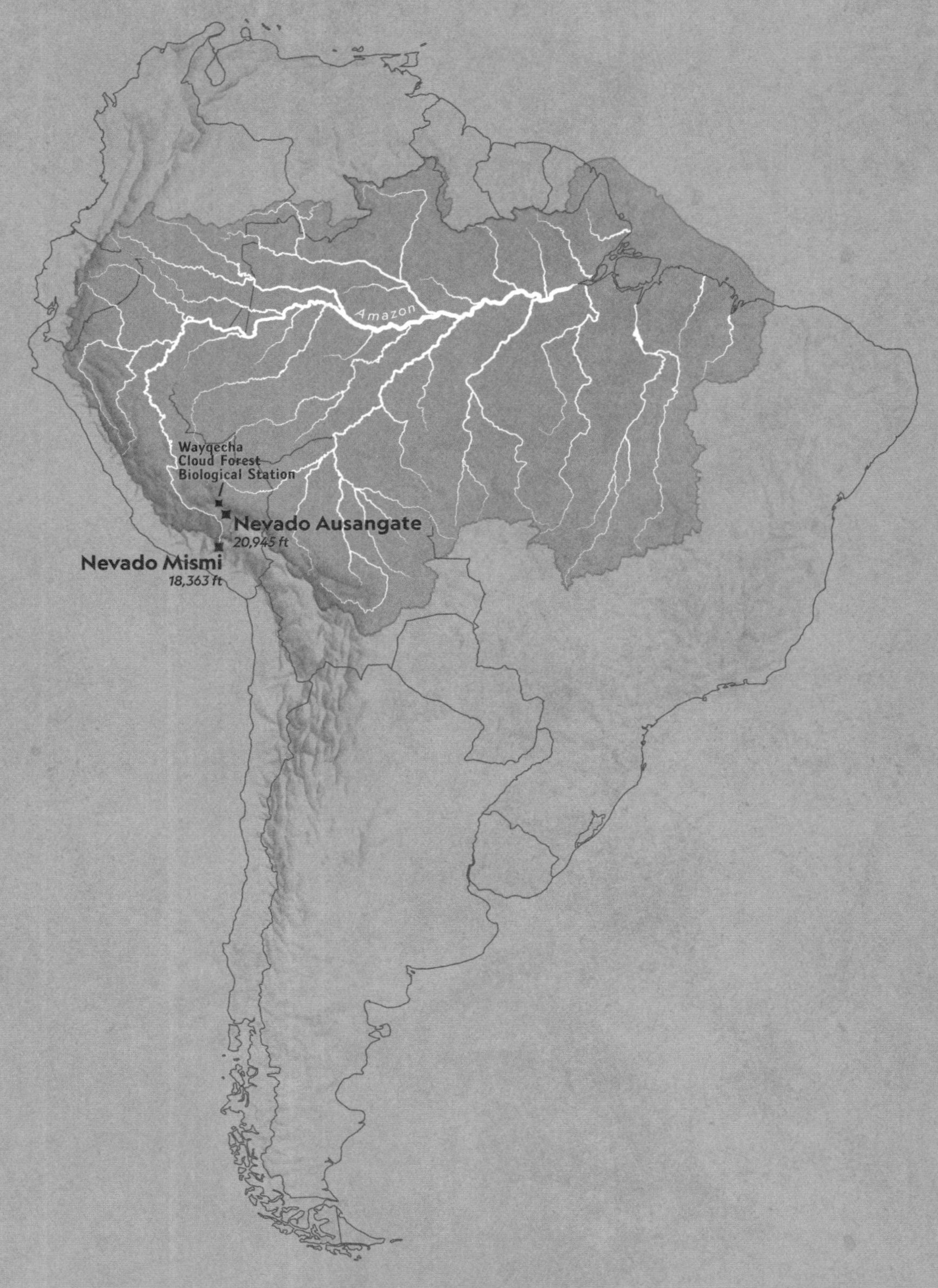
Amazon
Wayqecha
Cloud Forest
Biological Station
Nevado Ausangate
20,945 ft
Nevado Mismi
18,363 ft

RIVERS ARE LIKE STORIES; to understand them, one must start at the beginning and follow them to the end.

The Amazon River is a complex braid, and technically there isn't just a single point of origin. Instead, it has an almost infinite number of beginnings, scattered across the Andes and the ancient granite highlands of the Brazilian and Guiana Shields. Collectively, they give rise to more than 1,000 tributaries and tens of thousands of streams, eventually joining the main stem of the Amazon River in Brazil's lowland rainforests. (Only the Rio Negro, the Amazon's largest left-bank tributary and the most voluminous black-water river in the world, is not sourced in the mountainous terrain; it is birthed from more than 11 feet (3 m) of rain that falls every year in the lowland rainforests of Colombia's Puinawai Natural Reserve.)

My journey to photograph the birthplaces of the Amazon River begins in the Chila Mountains of western Peru. As I stand on the summit of 18,363-foot-high (5,597 m) Nevado Mismi, I straddle the South American continental divide. All meltwater from ice and snow on one side flows into the Pacific Ocean, while everything on the other side is Amazon River bound. From the ridge, water seeps into the porous jumbled rock and reemerges from a tall crack in the face of a cliff as a spring bursting with vigor.

Above me, Andean condors perch on well-worn ledges; during the night, the giant feathers they've left behind are entombed in a frozen mist. The escarpment is dotted with icicle-lined caves, resembling the gaping mouths of frozen dragons. When the sun's warming rays hit the mountain in late morning, the spring sputters back to life. The icicles begin to melt, and drop by drop, the water starts to flow forcefully downstream again, transforming an oxygen-starved desert into a lush and productive ecosystem.

Nobody lives closer to the Nevado Mismi source of the Amazon River than Feliciano. For more than 50 years, he has herded alpacas and llamas, depending on the life-giving alchemy of the *bofedales*—peat-forming wetlands—to provide grazing for his herds.

A treasure trove of firsthand local environmental history, Feliciano laments at length on how the weather and climate have changed. He remembers when the Nevado Mismi was covered in glaciers, its peak draped in snow even in summer. Now, the glaciers are long gone, and in summer the summit resembles a lifeless Martian landscape. Less water flows off the mountain, and the bofedales are in danger of drying up and transforming back into deserts. If this happens, Feliciano will have to round up his herds and pack up his homestead, since the landscape will no longer provide for him and his animals.

To learn more about how climate change is impacting the Andean source regions of the Amazon River, I team up with fellow National Geographic Explorers Baker Perry and Tom Matthews, along with a group of expert Peruvian and Bolivian mountaineers. Our goal is to install the highest weather station in the northern Andes on the summit of Nevado Ausangate, an imposing mountain that towers above Peru's Cusco region.

During the expedition, I reach the highest point of my journey: 19,685 feet (6,000 m). Making photographs at that altitude is extremely difficult, as the amount of available oxygen is less than half of that at sea level. In the tight embrace of oxygen-starved air, everything feels like hardcore exercise: unzipping the tent door, putting on shoes, even boiling water for tea. Pounding head and pounding heart become the norm. Despite needing more calories to stay alive up there, I have no appetite, and sleep is hard to come by. Every time I drift off, my oxygen levels drop, and I wake up gasping for air. The cycle repeats itself throughout the night, and during the few precious minutes of sleep I manage to get, I dream of warm tropical oceans and sharks.

The mountains that form the naissance of the Amazon Basin's rivers are important water towers that have provided for more than a thousand years across a cultural landscape occupied by civilizations. Andean peoples have close bonds with these peaks; the Apu deities are said to reside there alongside the water that gravity relinquishes. Complex rules and philosophies govern its use, especially in areas with chronic water shortage.

During the festival of Qoyllur Rit'i, thousands of pilgrims trek up the 15,000-foot-high (4,570 m) Sinakara Valley. They celebrate the stars, particularly the reappearance of the constellation Qullqa (Pleiades) at the winter solstice, indicating the upcoming harvest and a time of plenty.

Pilgrims hope that the mountain spirits will bestow blessings upon them. *Ukukus,* men clad in shaggy alpaca robes and woolen masks to resemble Andean bears, climb onto Colque Punku Glacier and spend the night battling cursed souls said to inhabit the snowfields. Before climate change caused the glacier to retreat dramatically, the ukukus harvested ice, believing it to hold medicinal and healing properties. Now they climb simply to pray at dawn—both to the Andean mountain deities and Catholic saints.

While the treeless slopes of the Andes birth many of the Amazon tributaries, the lower-elevation montane cloud forests spur their growth into truly formidable river systems. Cloud forests are some of the wettest biomes on Earth, and their forest canopy is almost permanently enshrouded in fog. The trees here literally harvest water by capturing moisture from clouds, water dripping along branches and trunks to the forest floor and eventually flowing downslope into rivers. This ecosystem functions as a de facto watershed despite not being permanently submerged by water, and is so humid that it can be classified as a wetland alongside salt marshes and coral reefs.

Cloud forests are also some of the most endangered habitats on Earth. Climate change and deforestation are the two biggest threats; if greenhouse gas emissions continue at the current rate, they will dry out and shrink forest distribution by 80 percent. In tandem, the harvest of firewood and land clearing for grazing and agriculture have had major negative impacts over the last three decades. However, what cloud forests remain are truly special and are home to two flagship species: Andean bears (aka spectacled bears) and torrent ducks.

Andean bears are secretive, mysterious, and rarely encountered, enveloped in mythology and folklore. They migrate seasonally along altitudinal gradients between lowlands and high-altitude puna grasslands, but cloud forests are their stronghold. Though these bears subsist mainly on a diet of plants such bromeliads, tantalizing evidence suggests they also hunt fish in cloud forest streams.

Torrent ducks, endemic to Andean headwater rivers, are white-water specialists. They can swim and dive in fast-flowing rivers and navigate powerful rapids with ease. Strikingly colored, these ducks nest in riverside caves and feed on the larvae of benthic invertebrates. Unlike me, they are well adapted to altitudes of up to 13,120 feet (4,000 m) and can thrive at such lofty heights because of high levels of hemoglobin, an oxygen-carrying protein in their red blood cells. Though not yet listed as endangered, their numbers are in decline due to competition for their aquatic invertebrate prey from introduced trout and the damming of rivers for hydroelectric schemes. Without the torrent duck's shrill calls echoing off the walls of deep canyons, carved out by eons of water flow, the Amazon Basin would be a much poorer place.

The source regions of the Amazon River are beautiful, harsh, complex, and vitally important to the many ecosystems that lie downstream. My explorations among the high peaks and deep valleys have sparked not only my curiosity but also my sense of adventure as I prepare to follow the water to lower elevations, where a completely different world awaits. ■

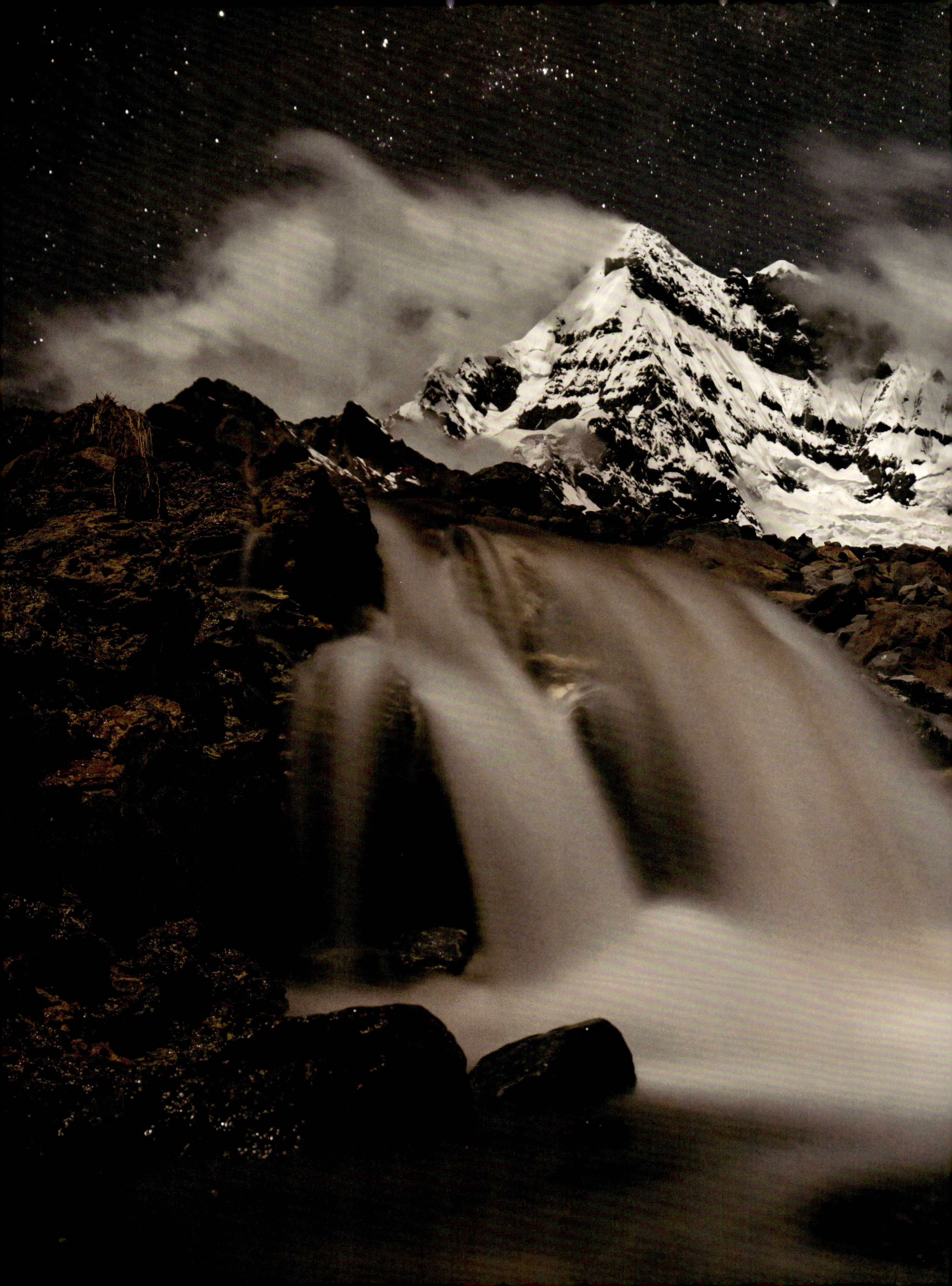

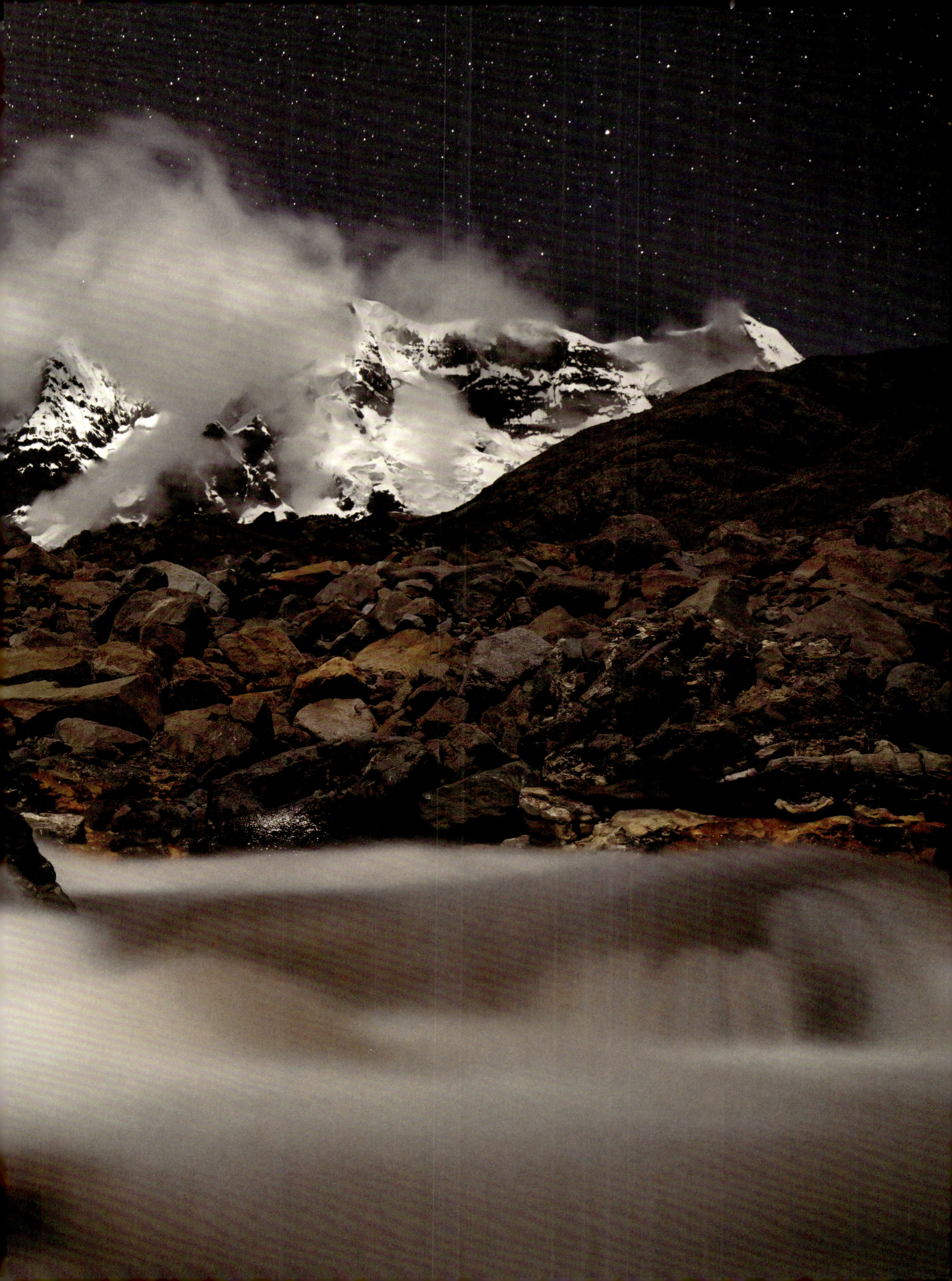

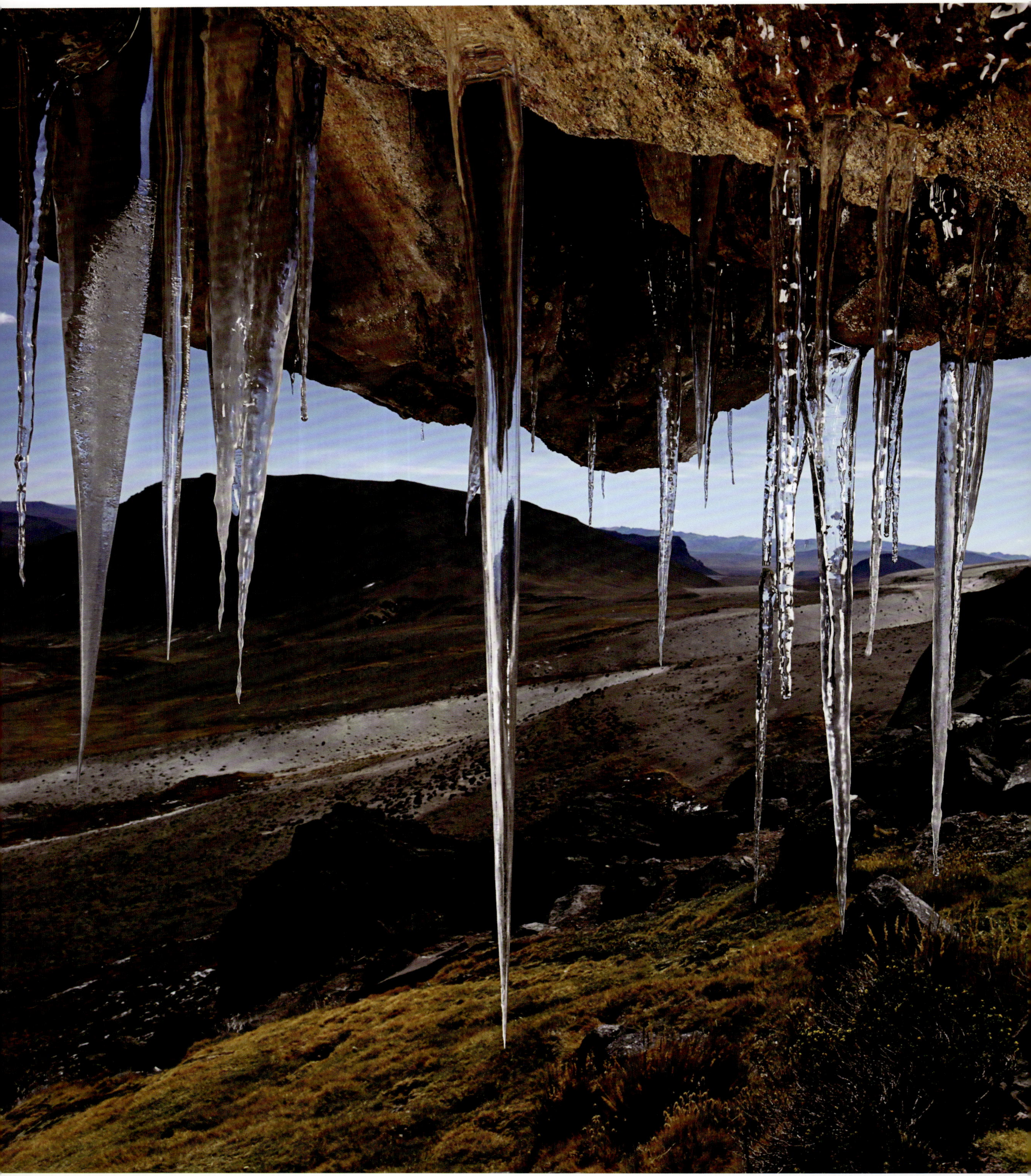

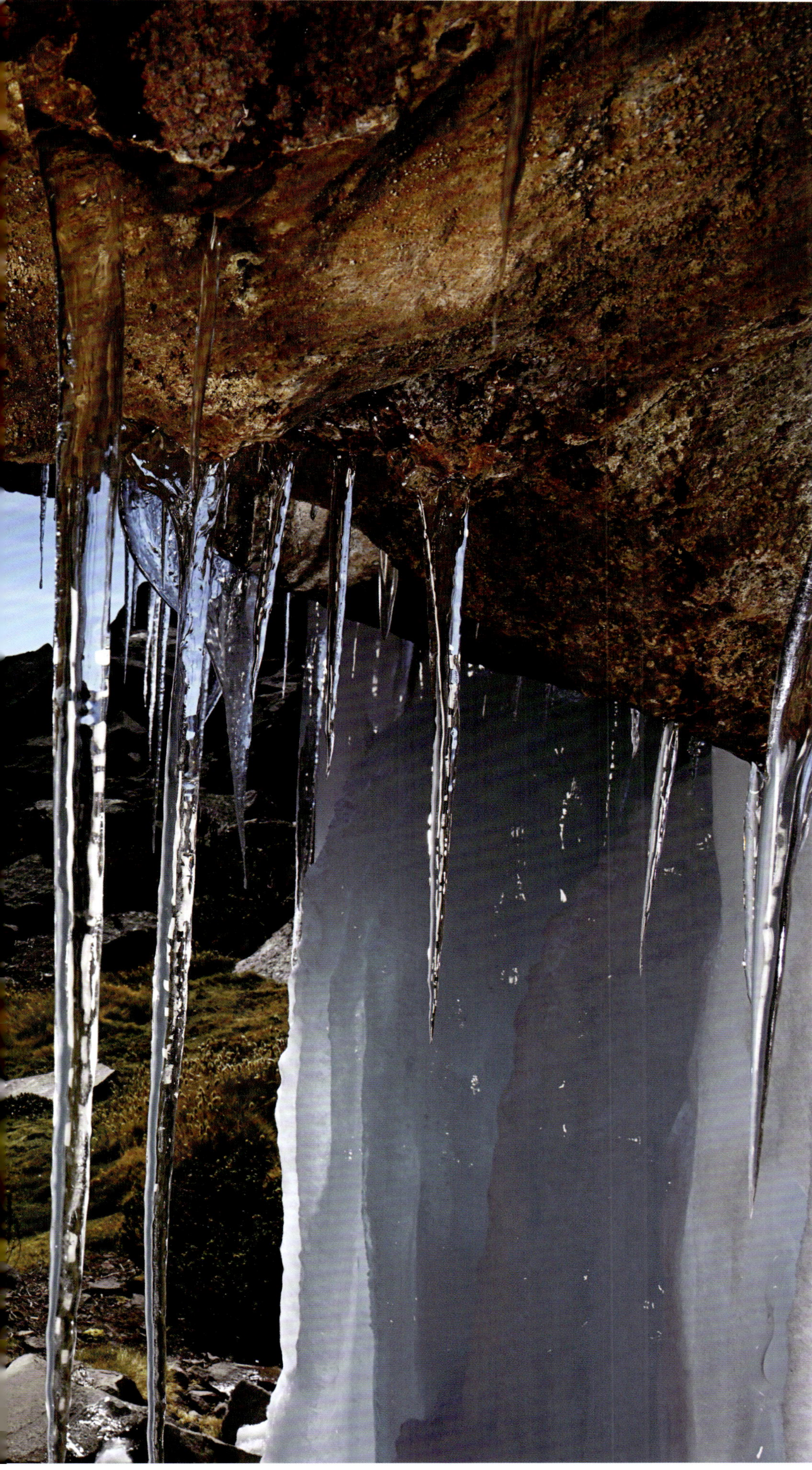

The escarpment below Nevado Mismi's summit is dotted with icicle-lined caves resembling the gaping mouths of frozen dragons. When the sun's warming rays hit in late morning, the icicles begin to melt, and drop by drop, water flows forcefully downstream.

PAGES 20–21: Fringed in clouds against the night sky, Nevado Ausangate, the highest mountain in the Andes of southern Peru, looms above a glacial melt waterfall. Communities and ecosystems hundreds of miles downstream rely on natural water towers like Ausangate as a primary freshwater source, especially during the dry season and times of drought.

PAGES 24–25: In the Peruvian Andes, icy condor feathers glisten in the mists of a cliffside spring on the slopes of Nevado Mismi. While streams and tributaries coalesce from many directions to become the Amazon River, this volcanic peak is the most distant source of uninterrupted flow from the river's mouth at the Atlantic Ocean.

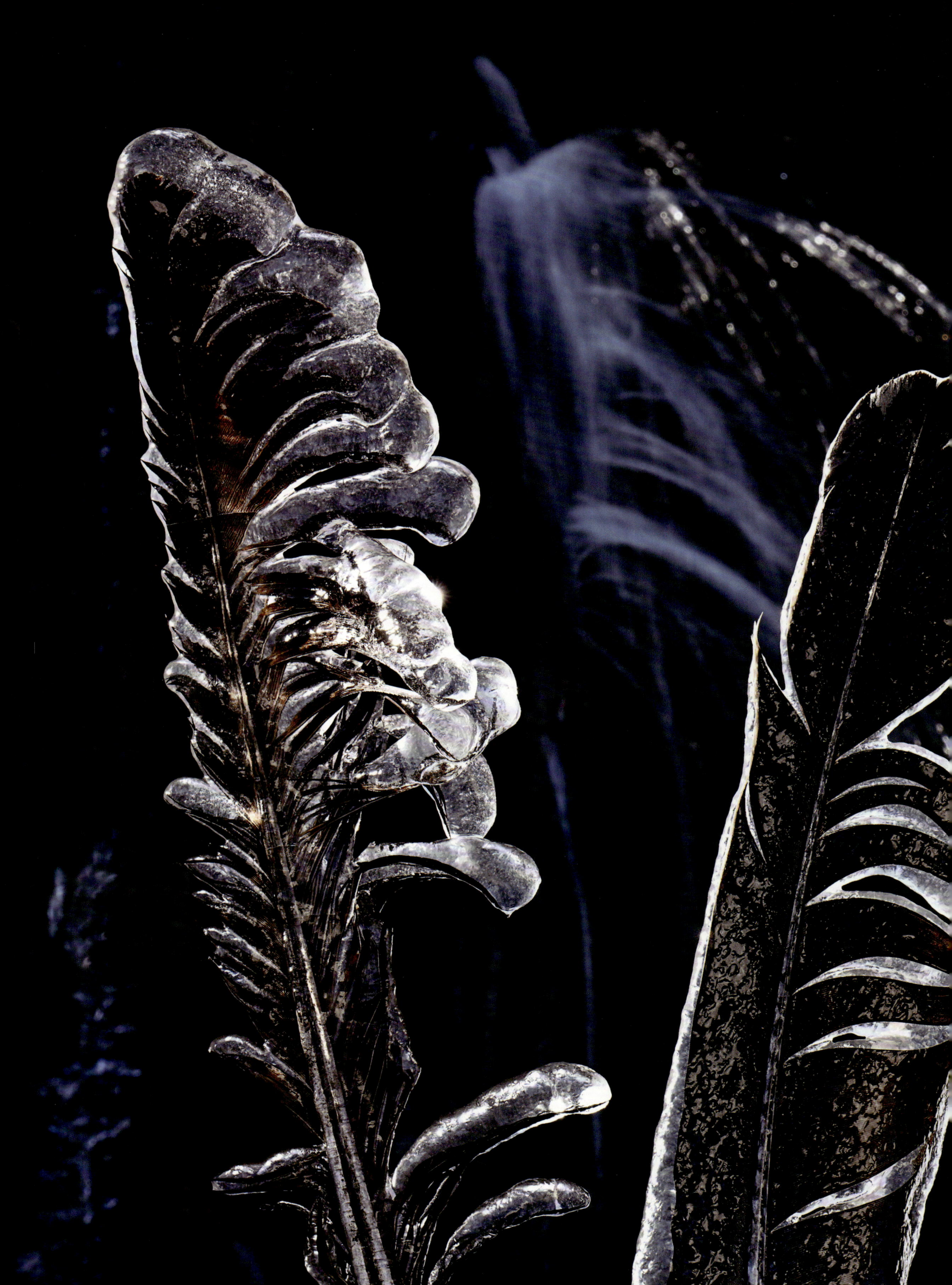

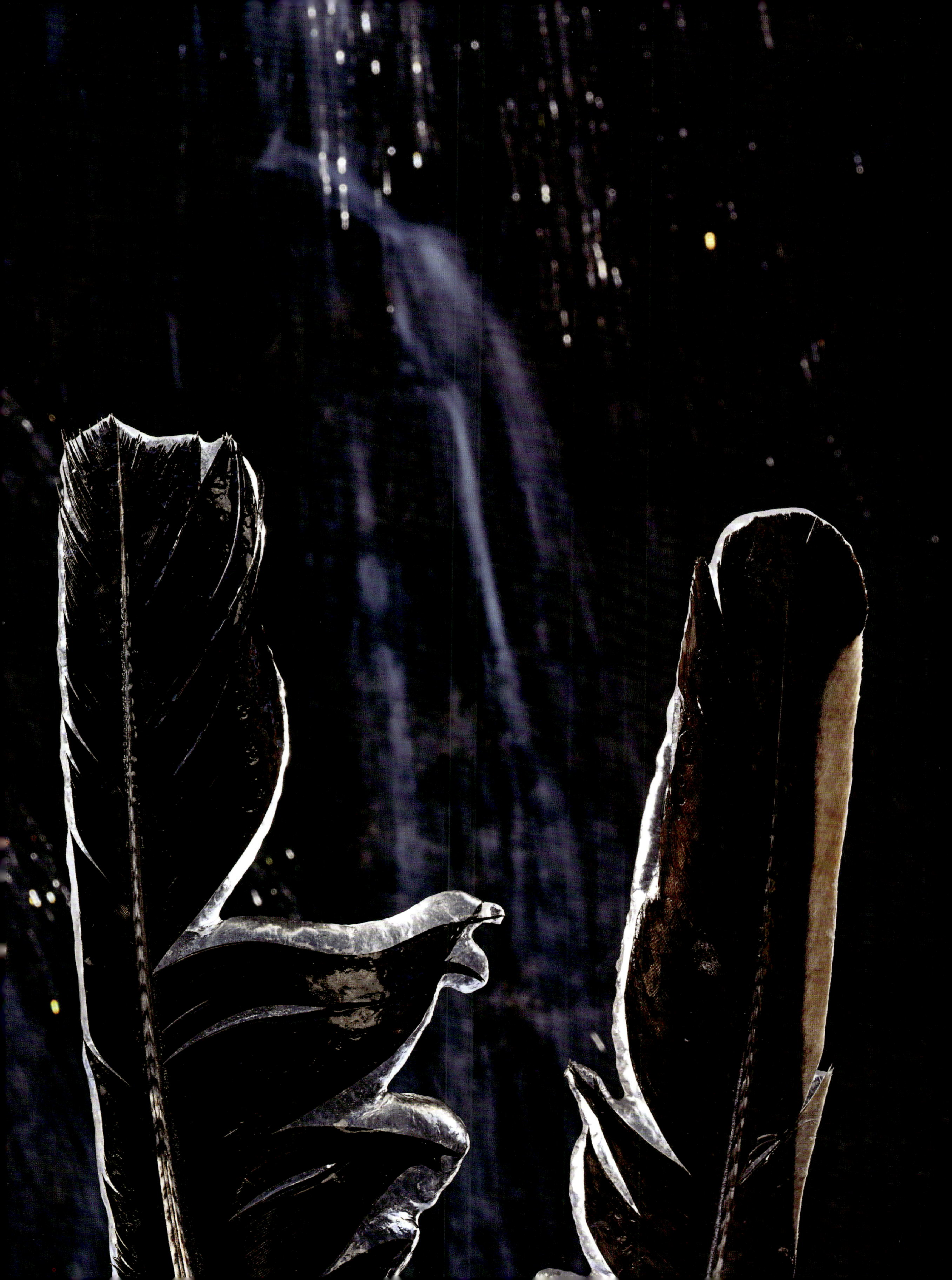

South America's continental divide runs right through the 18,362-foot-tall (5,597 m) summit ridge of Nevado Mismi. Meltwater from ice and snow on the west side flows into the Pacific Ocean, while everything on the east side is Amazon River bound. All the while, Sabancaya, an active stratovolcano, erupts 21 miles (34 km) to the southwest.

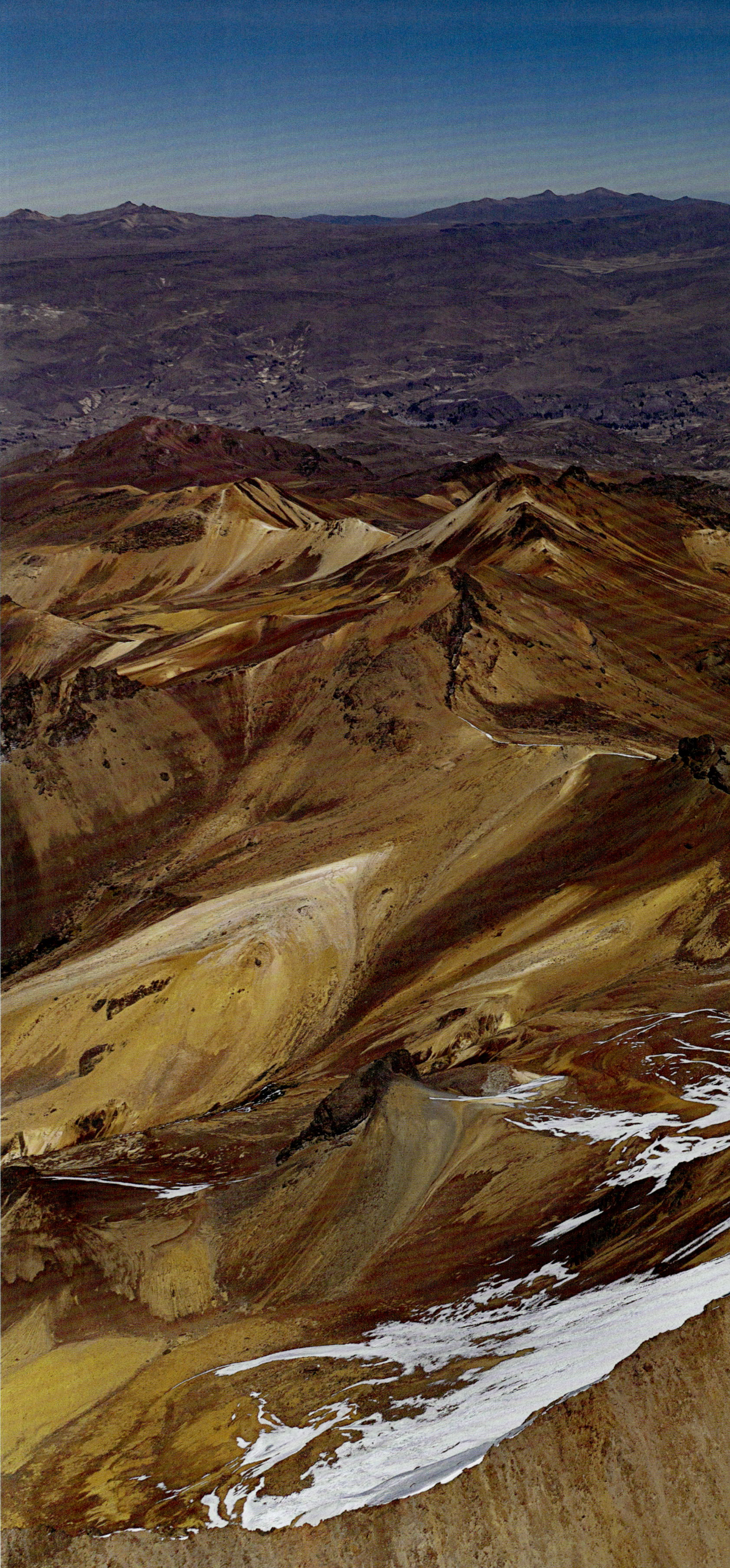

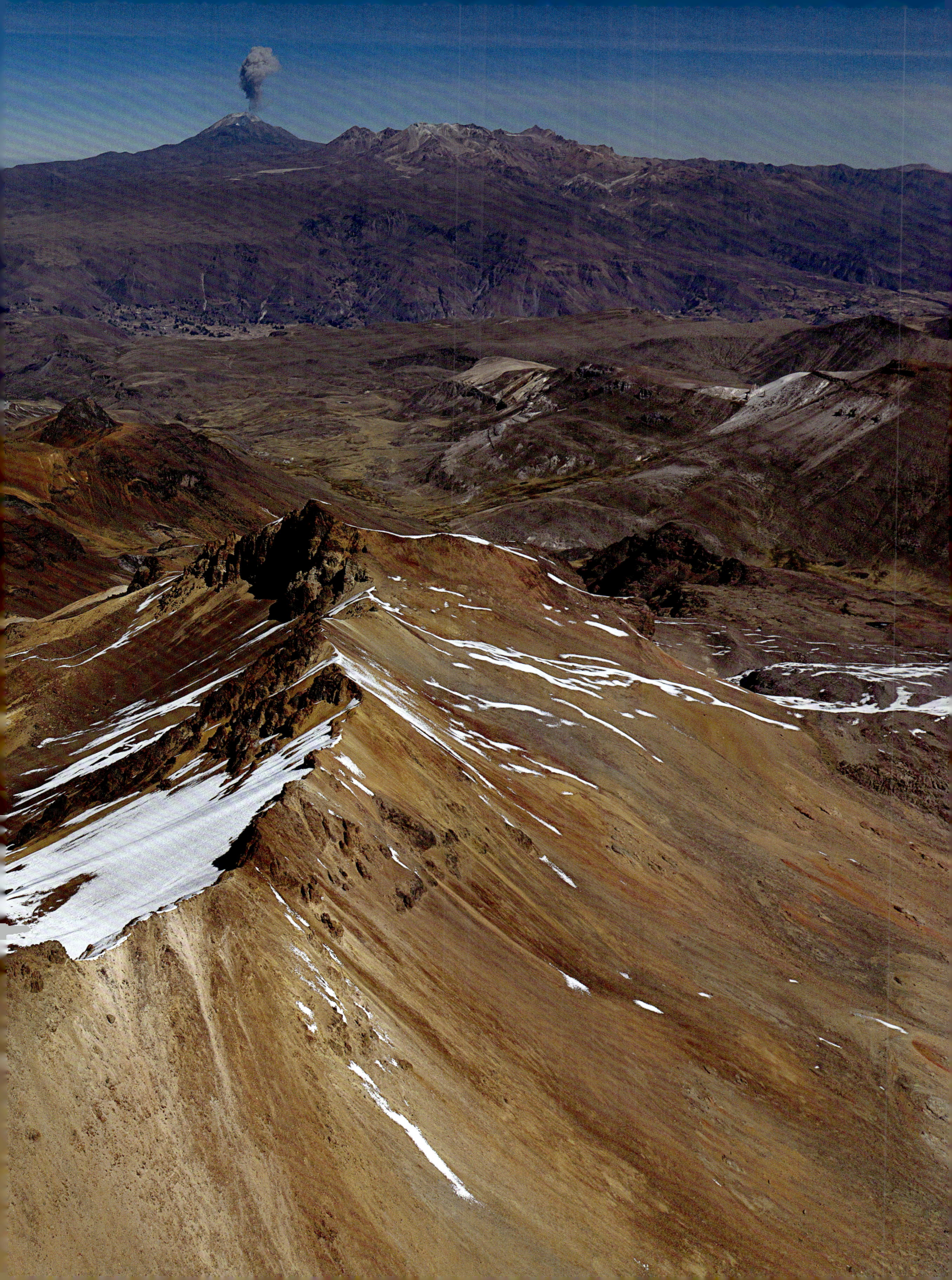

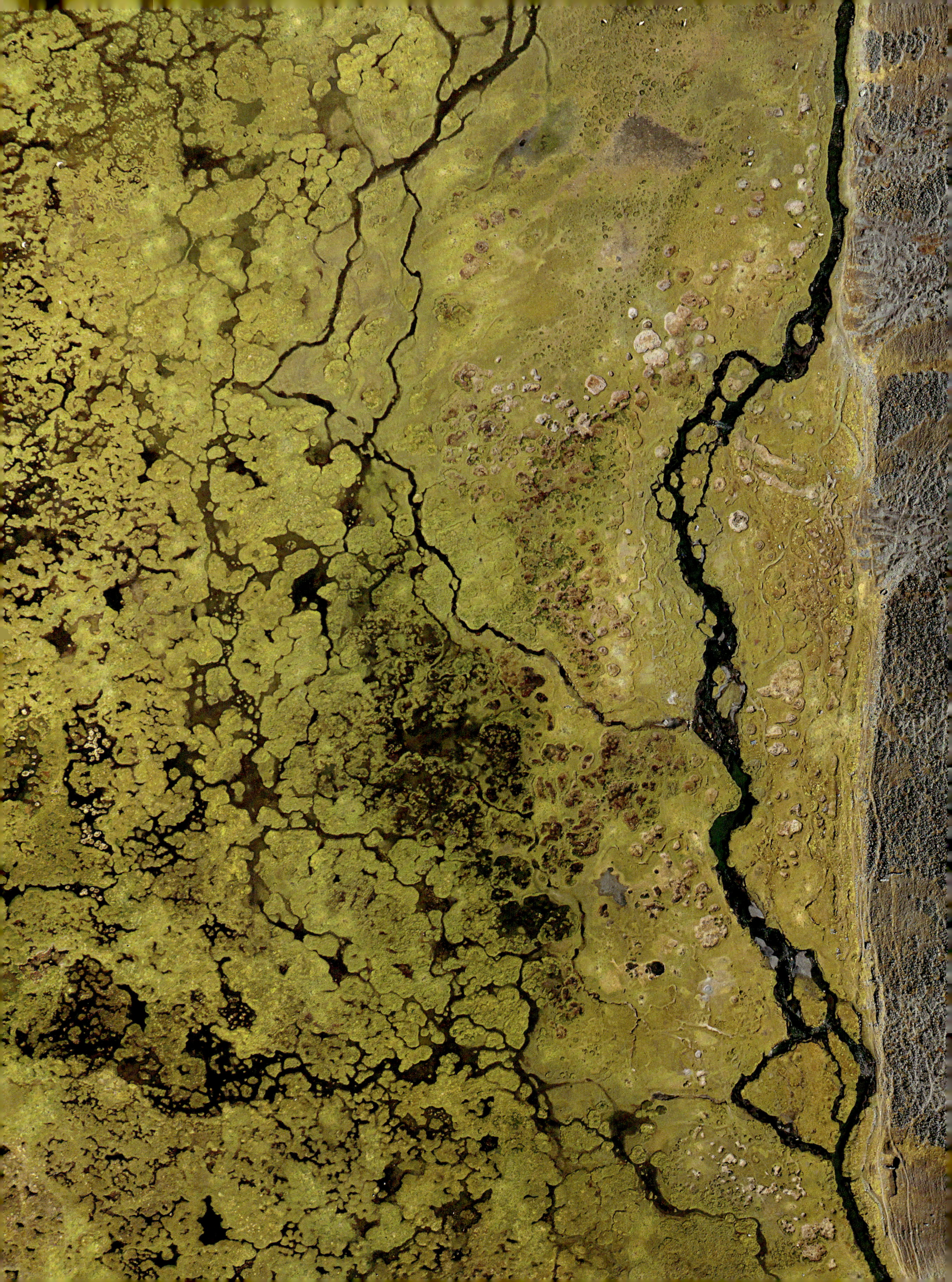

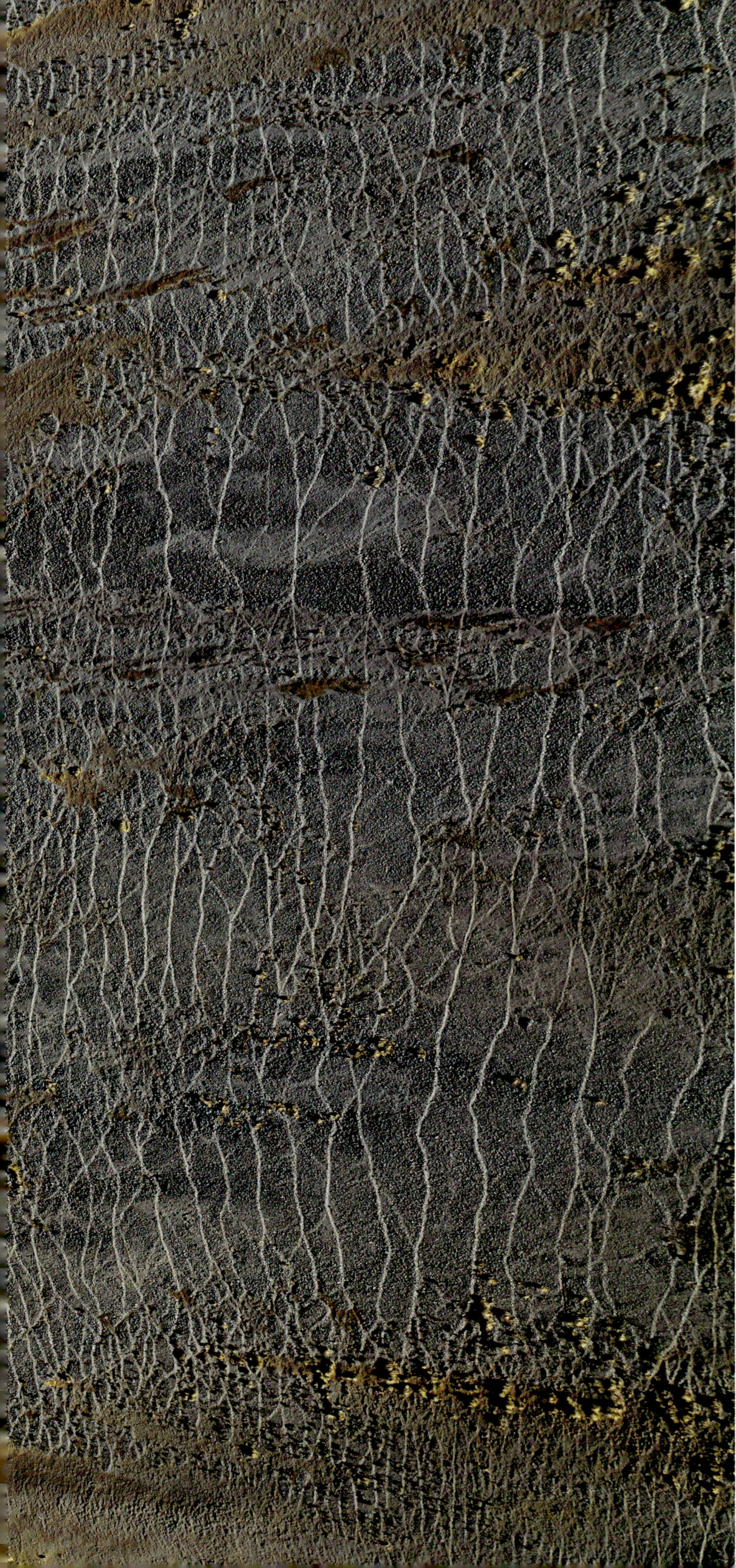

High above the Peruvian Andes, patterns are etched into a valley. On the left of the image, a web of watery veins courses through a mossy peat bog at the valley bottom. The lines to the right are trails that herds of alpacas, llamas, and vicuñas have scored into the hillside.

PAGES 30–31: Feliciano, a local alpaca farmer, relies on water from the nearby Carhuasanta, a river that forms part of the Amazon's headwaters and is fed by winter snows on Peru's Nevado Mismi. For more than 50 years of herding alpacas and llamas, he has depended on the alchemy of *bofedales* (peat-forming wetlands) to provide grazing for his herds.

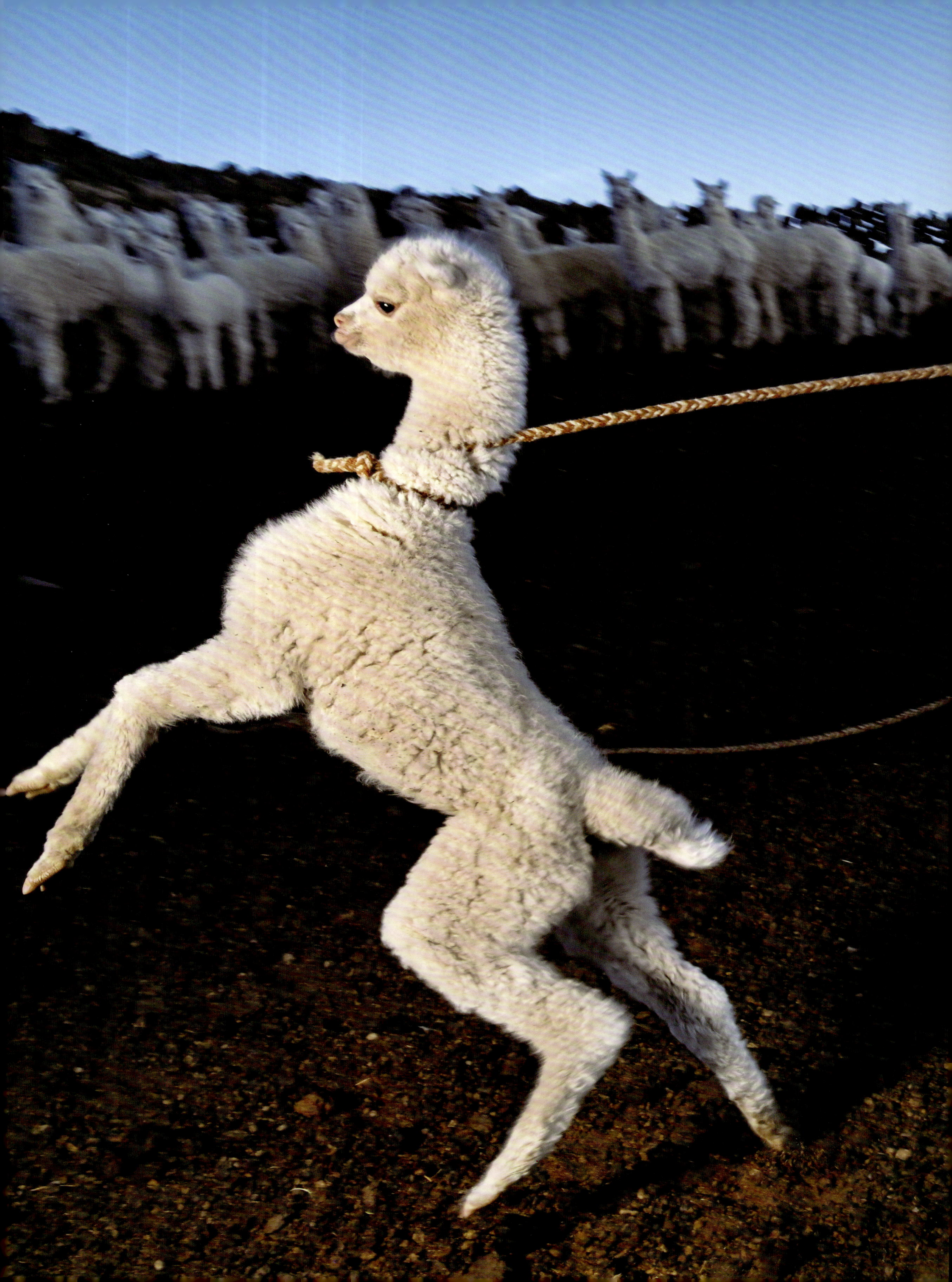

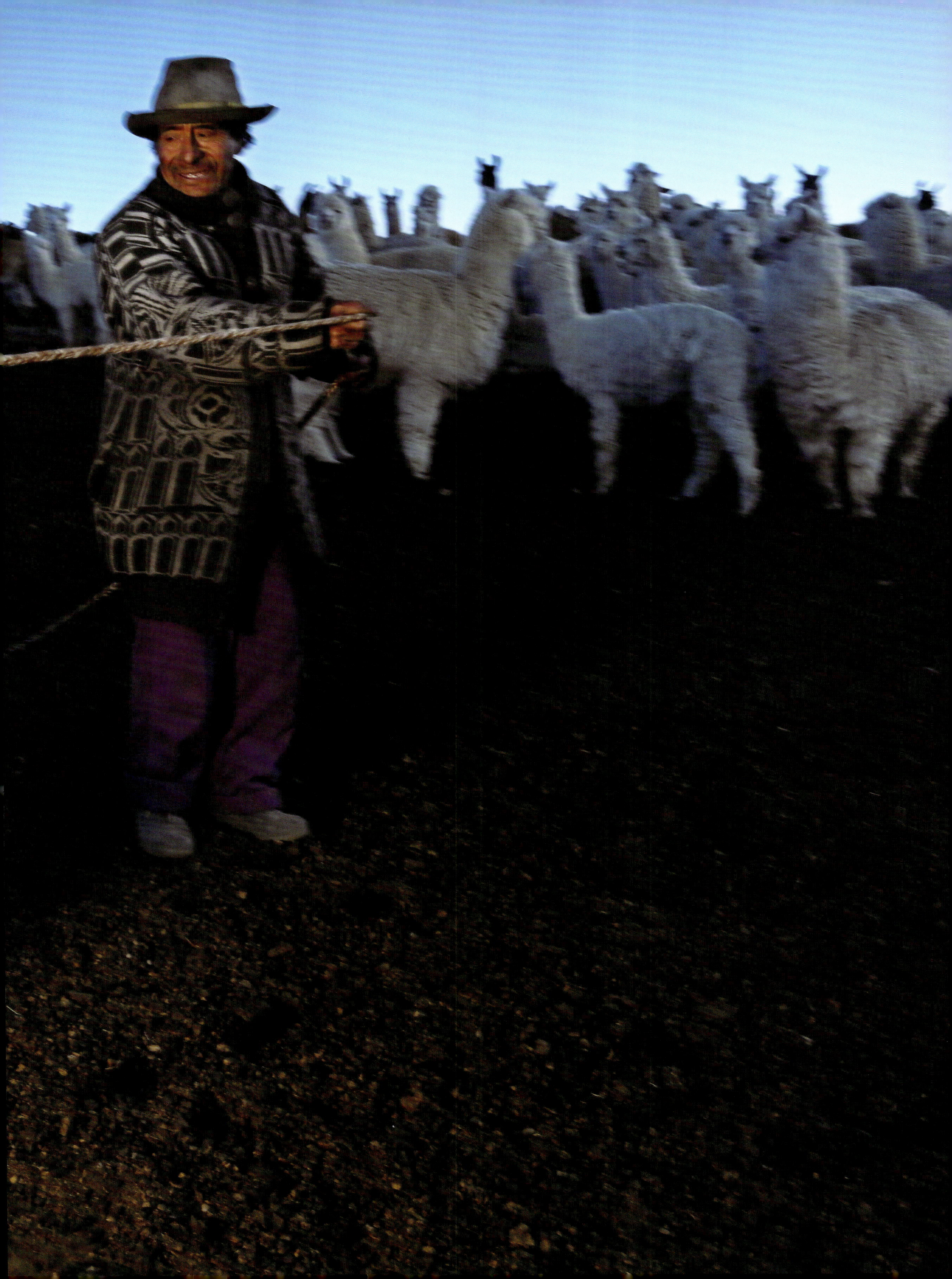

Nevado Ausangate's imposing and unclimbed west face towers above a glacial lake, tinted turquoise by dissolved minerals. Fed by a precariously perched hanging glacier, it often undergoes catastrophic break-off events, transferring vast volumes of ice and snow to the valley floor below.

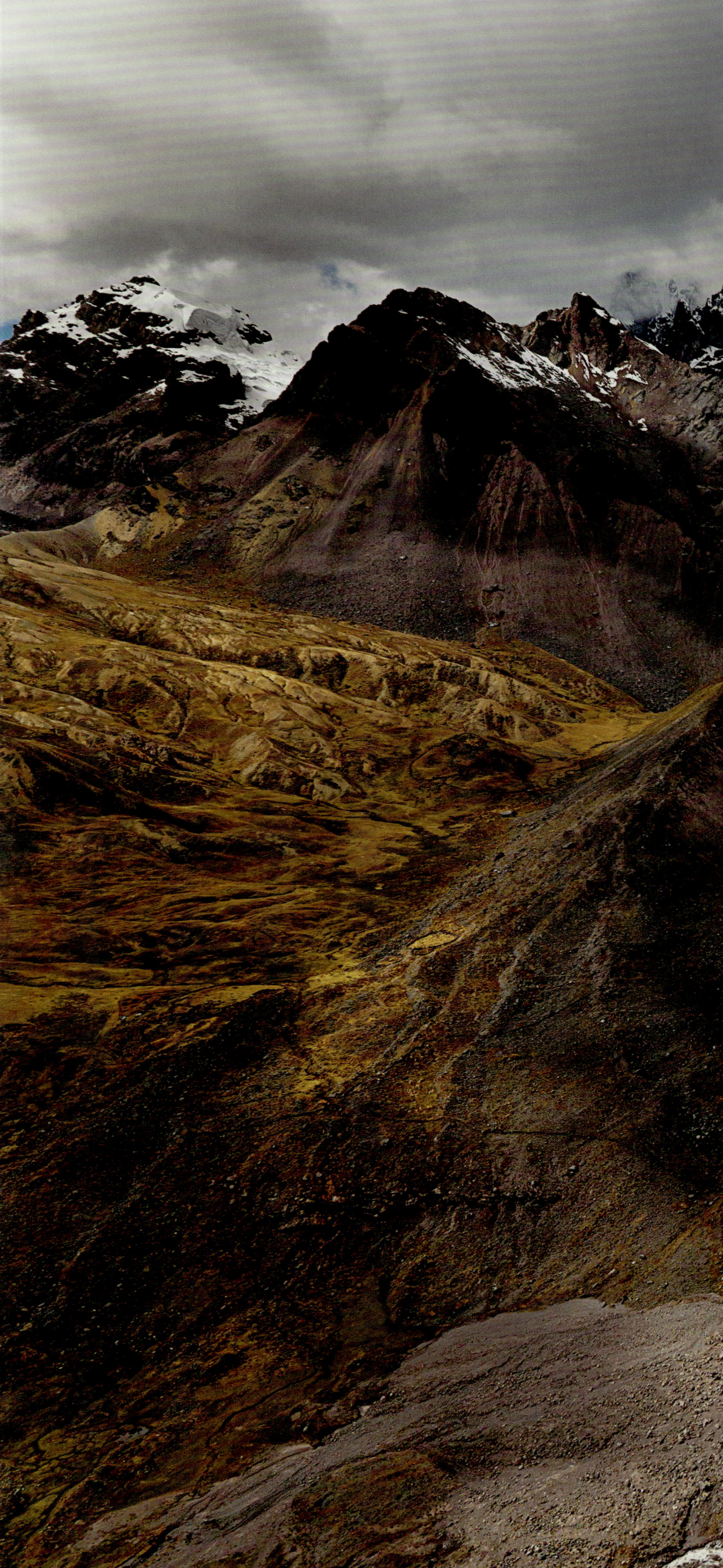

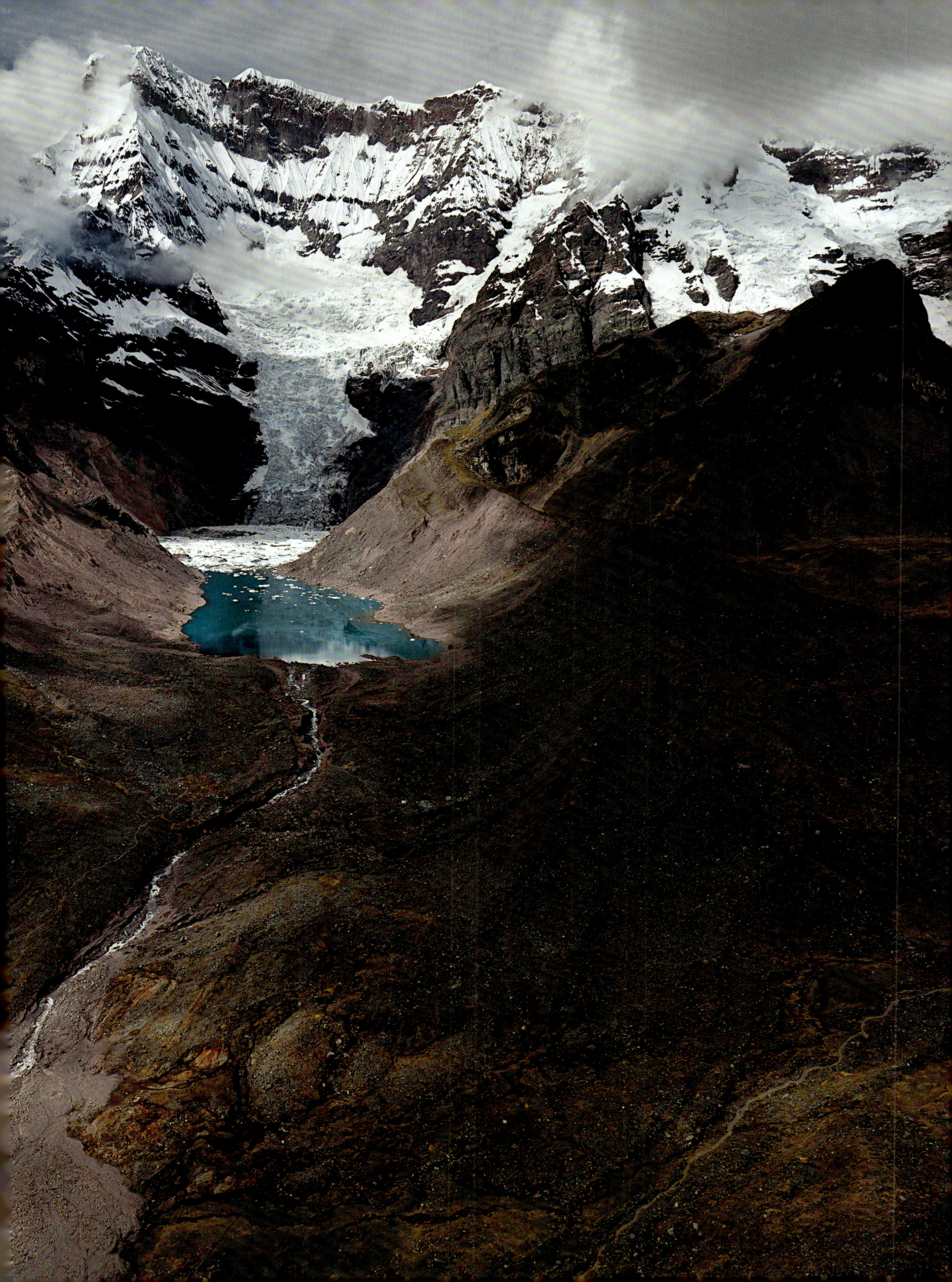

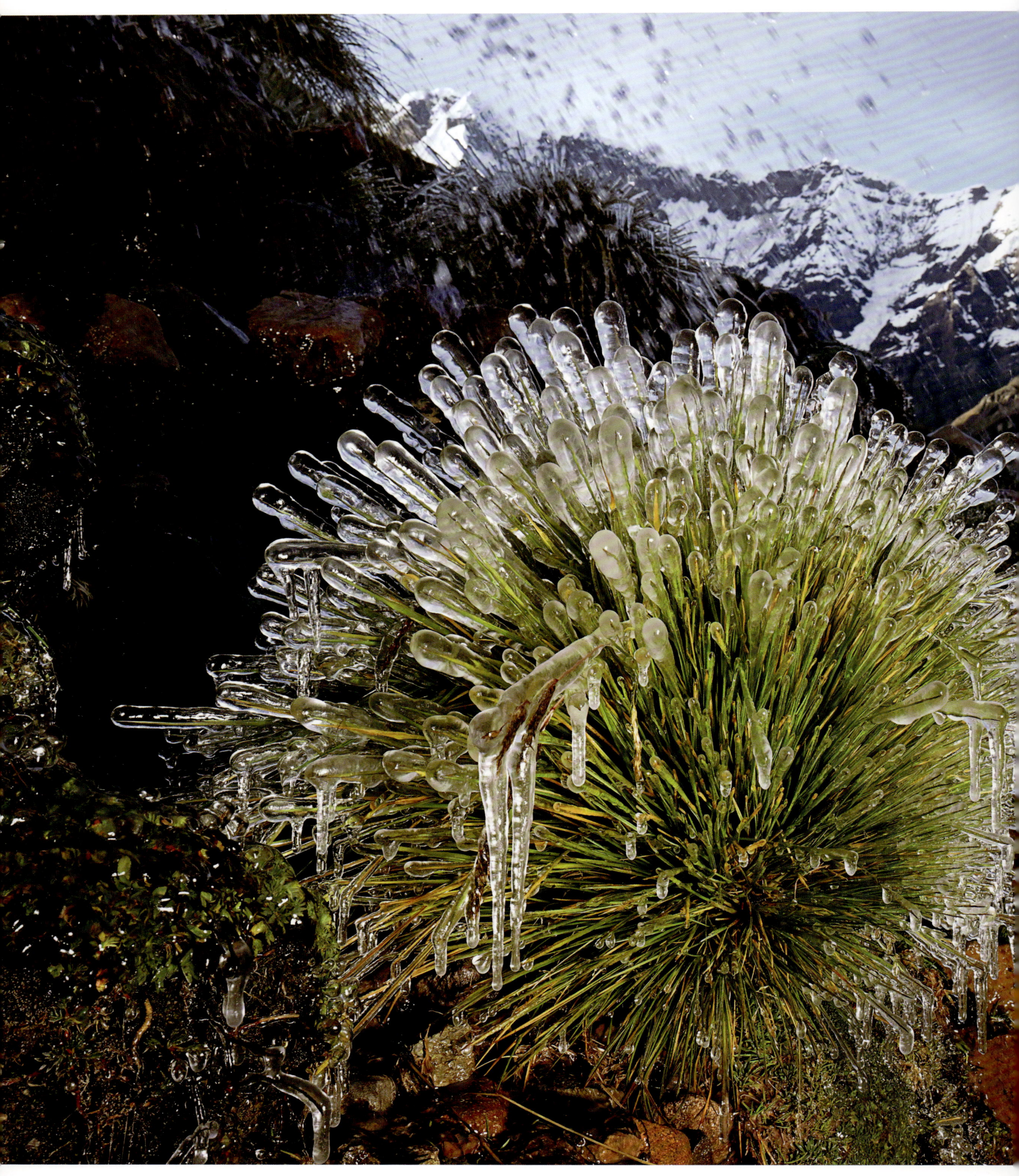

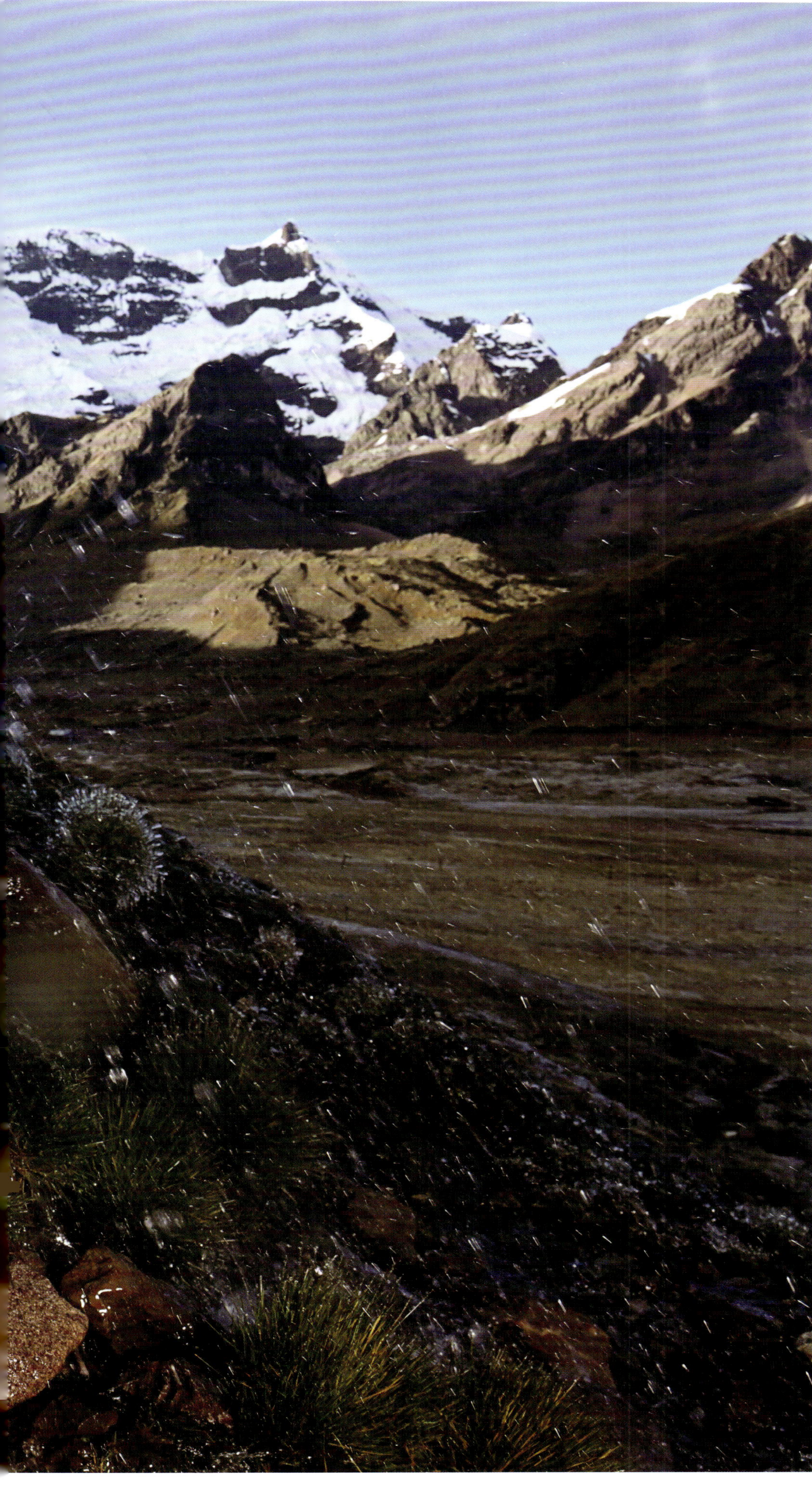

Only where springs exhale their life-giving elixir do native grasses grow in abundance. The tropical high Andes experience extreme daily temperature fluctuations; at night, water vapor freezes into ice crystals to form frost on grasses. The grasses exhibit a mechanism called freezing tolerance, in part by synthesizing antifreeze proteins that can inhibit the growth and recrystallization of ice in intercellular spaces.

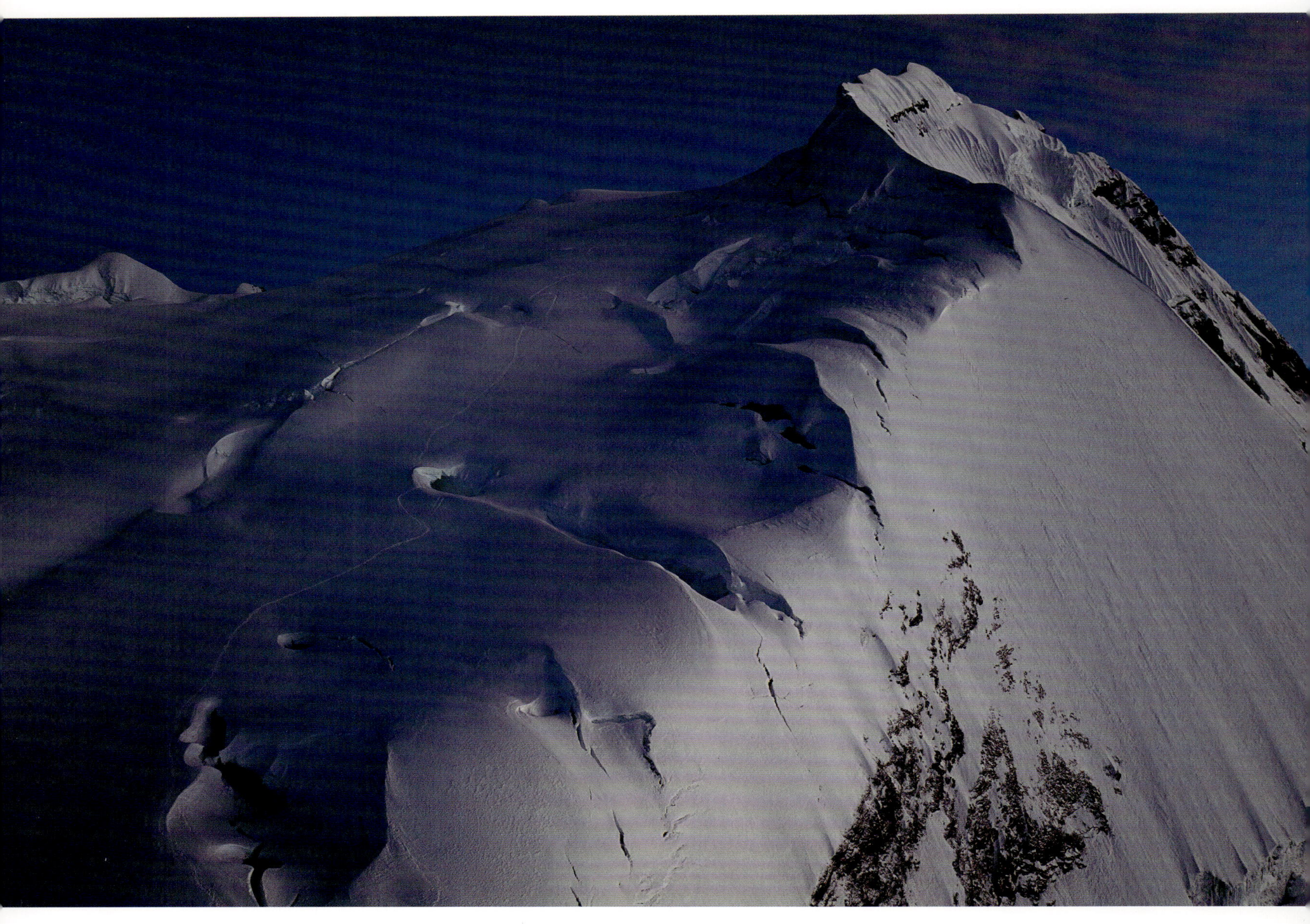

ABOVE: The snowy summit of Nevado Ausangate might appear pristine, but a recent National Geographic expedition found high concentrations of microplastics on the peak, transported by strong winds from far away. The expedition also discovered that the mountain is approaching the world record for highest average solar radiation; darkening from black carbon released by Amazon forest fires and deposited on snow and ice could hasten glacial retreat.

OPPOSITE: Climbers from the National Geographic Society and Rolex Perpetual Planet Amazon Expedition traverse a snow-covered ridge as they approach high camp at just under 19,685 feet (6,000 m) on Nevado Ausangate. They carry heavy loads that include a sophisticated weather station and equipment to dig and analyze snow pits.

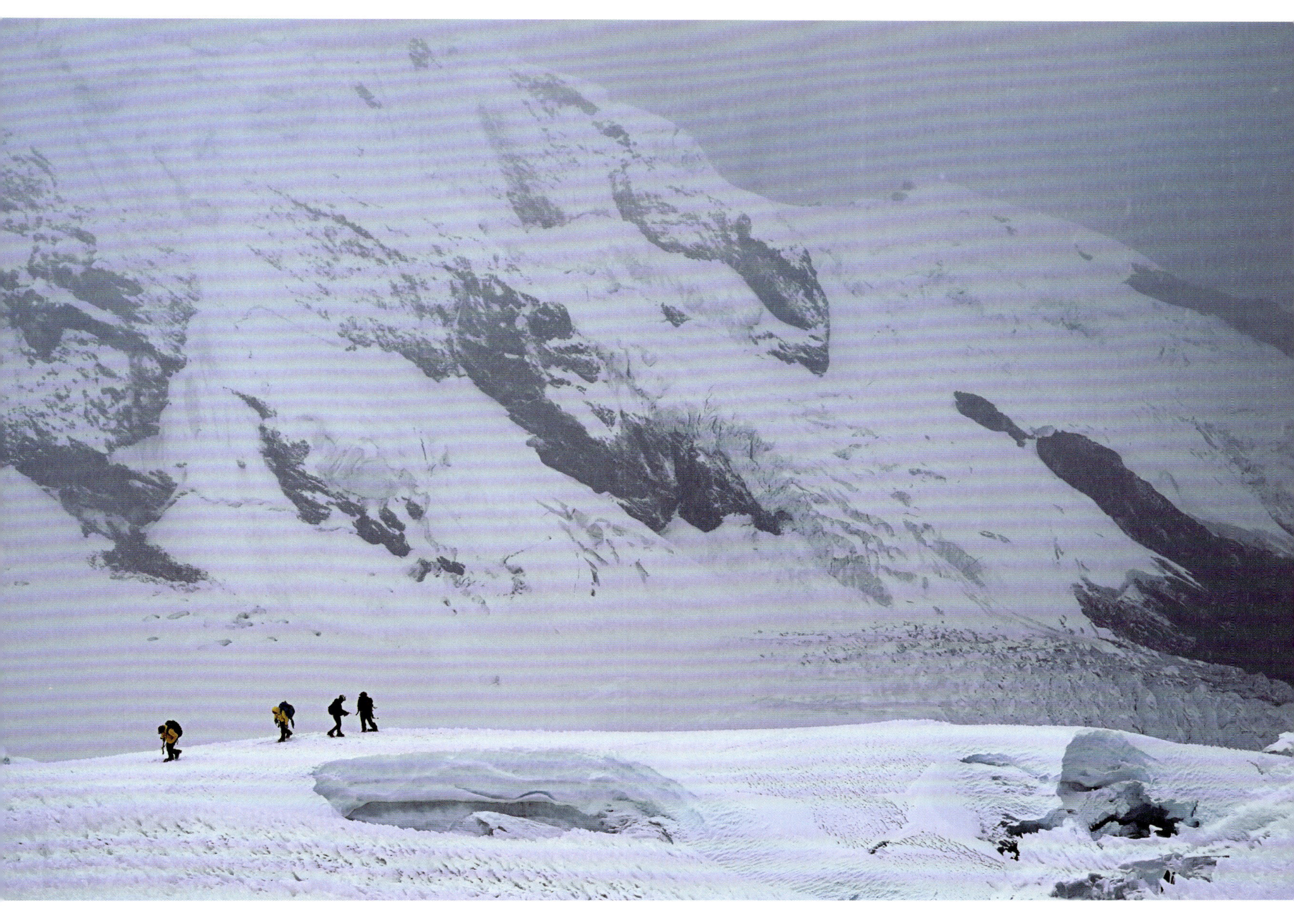

PAGES 38–39: National Geographic Explorers Tom Matthews, Baker Perry, and their team test a weather station near base camp before installing it on Peru's Nevado Ausangate. Its destination will be just below the summit at 20,830 feet (6,349 m), making it the highest weather station in the tropical Andes. It will collect near-real-time meteorological data, such as temperature, humidity, radiation, and snow depth, all of which will aid scientists in observing the impacts of climate change on critical water resources that affect local communities.

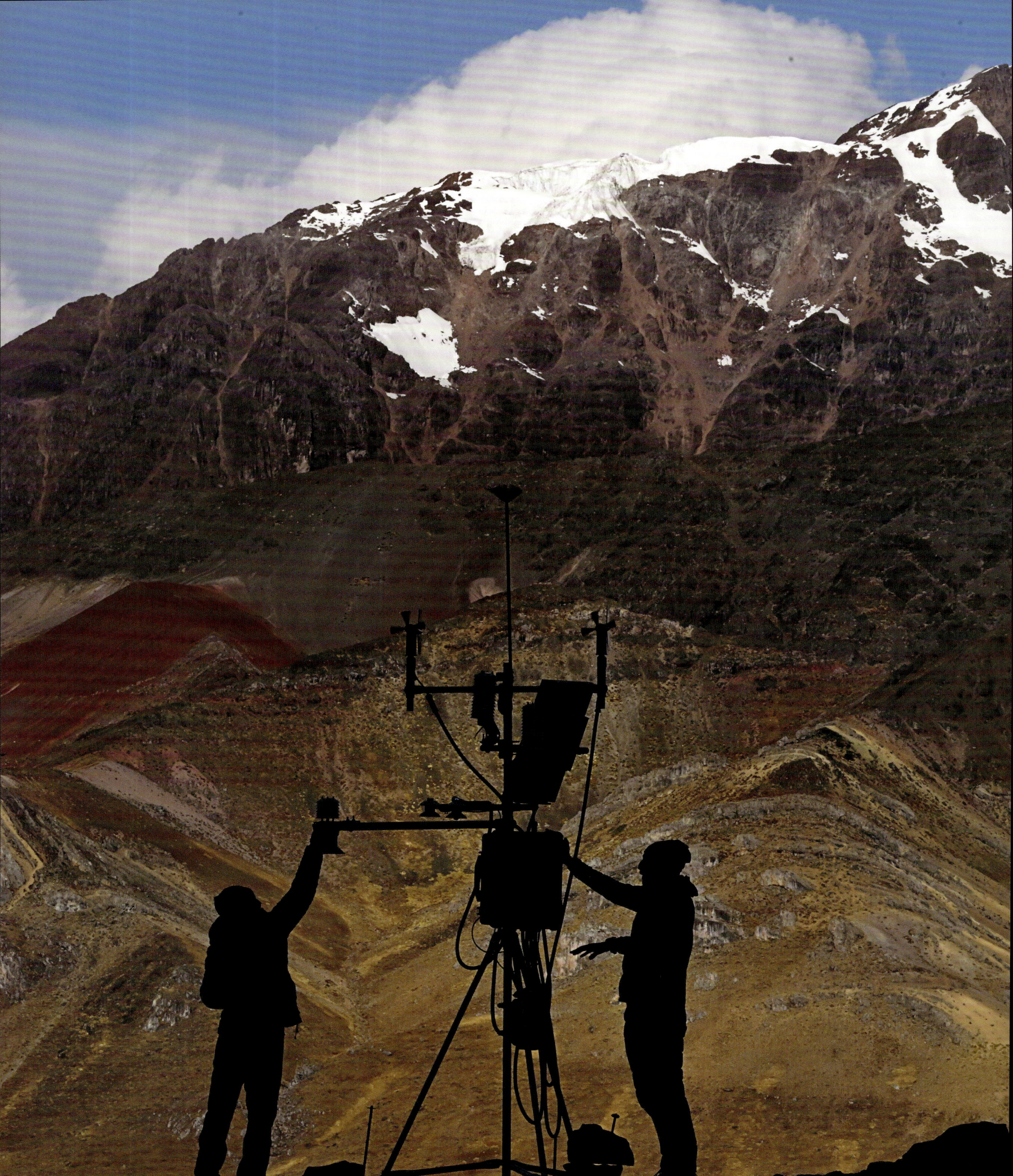

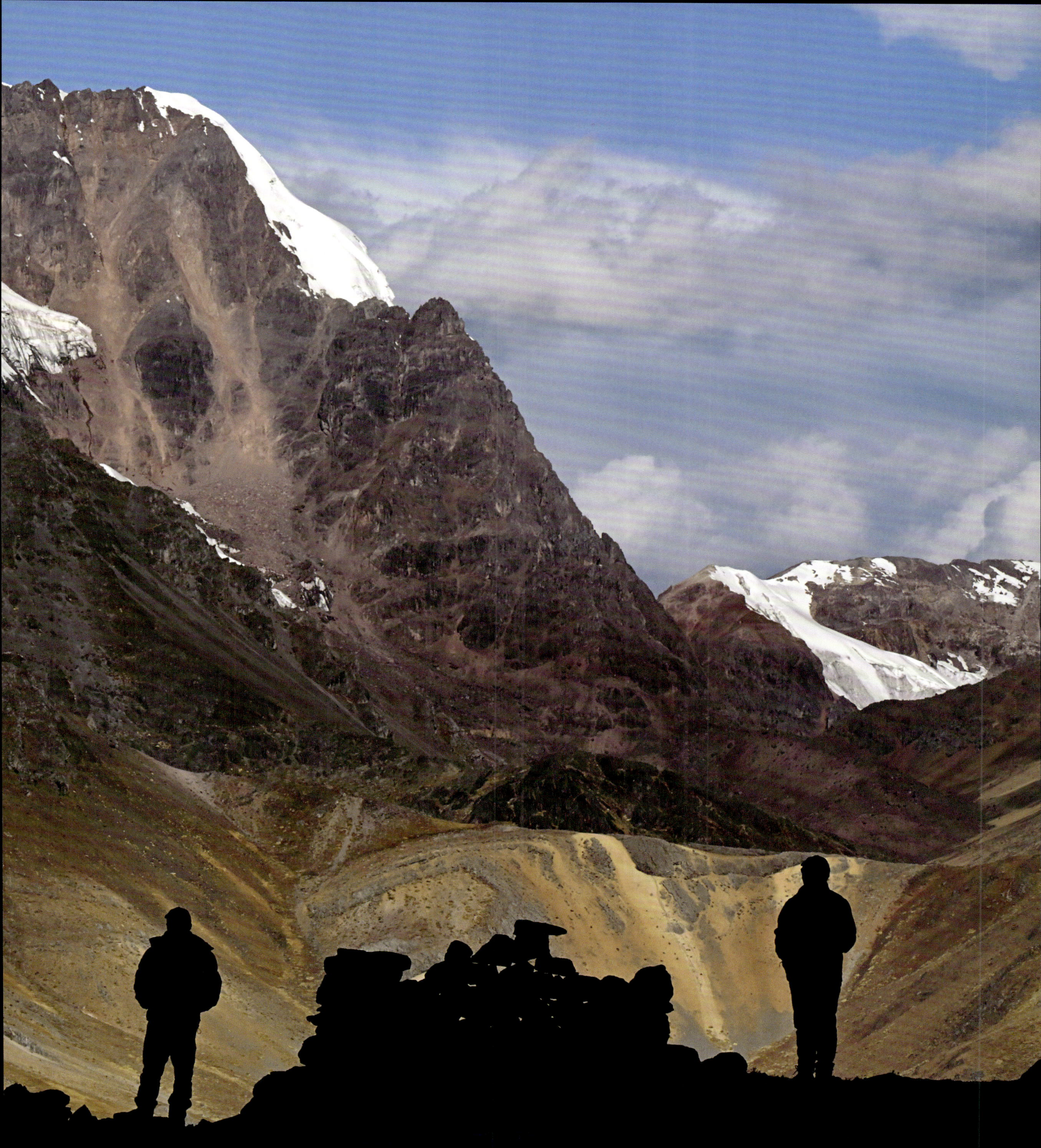

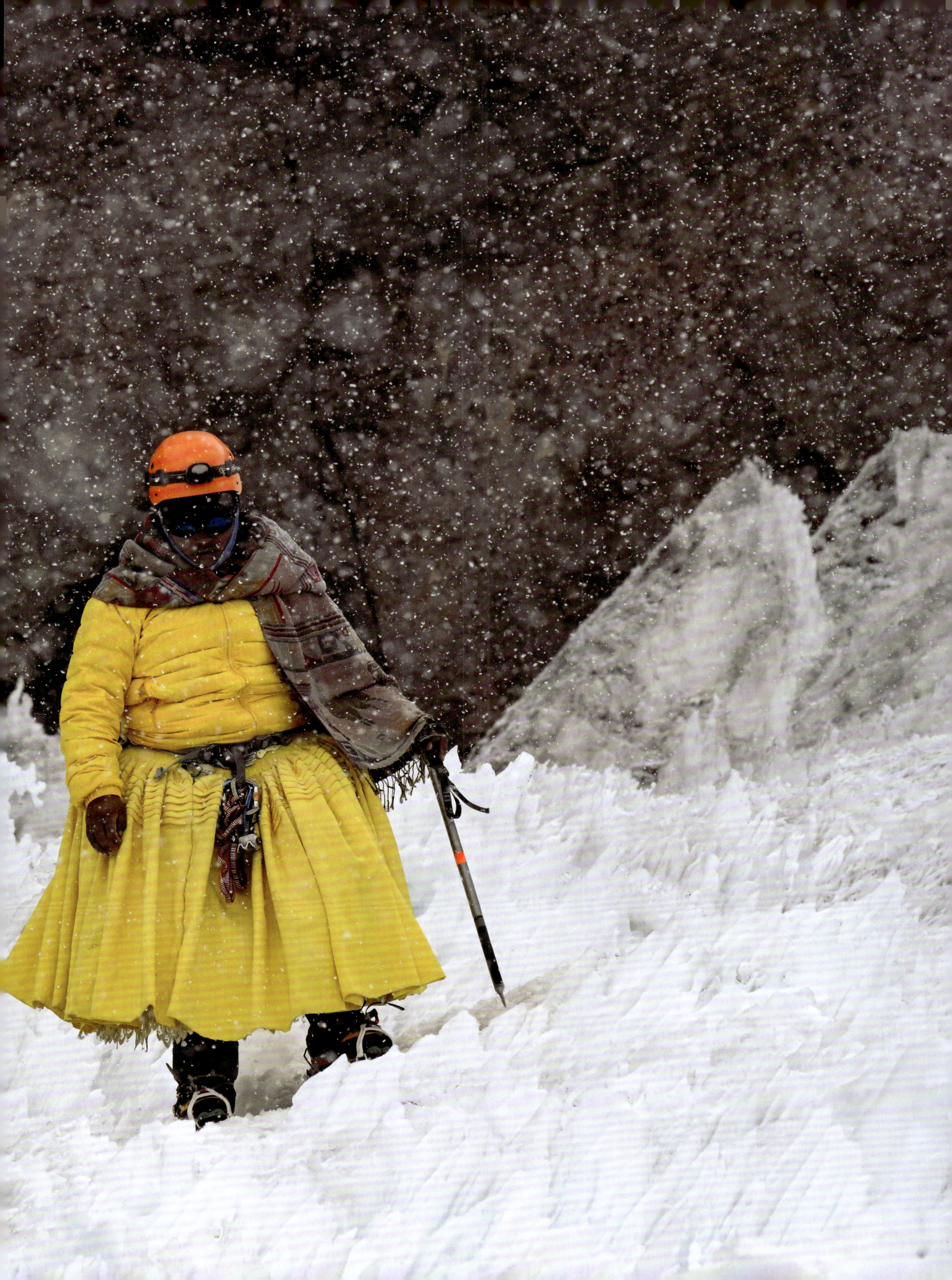

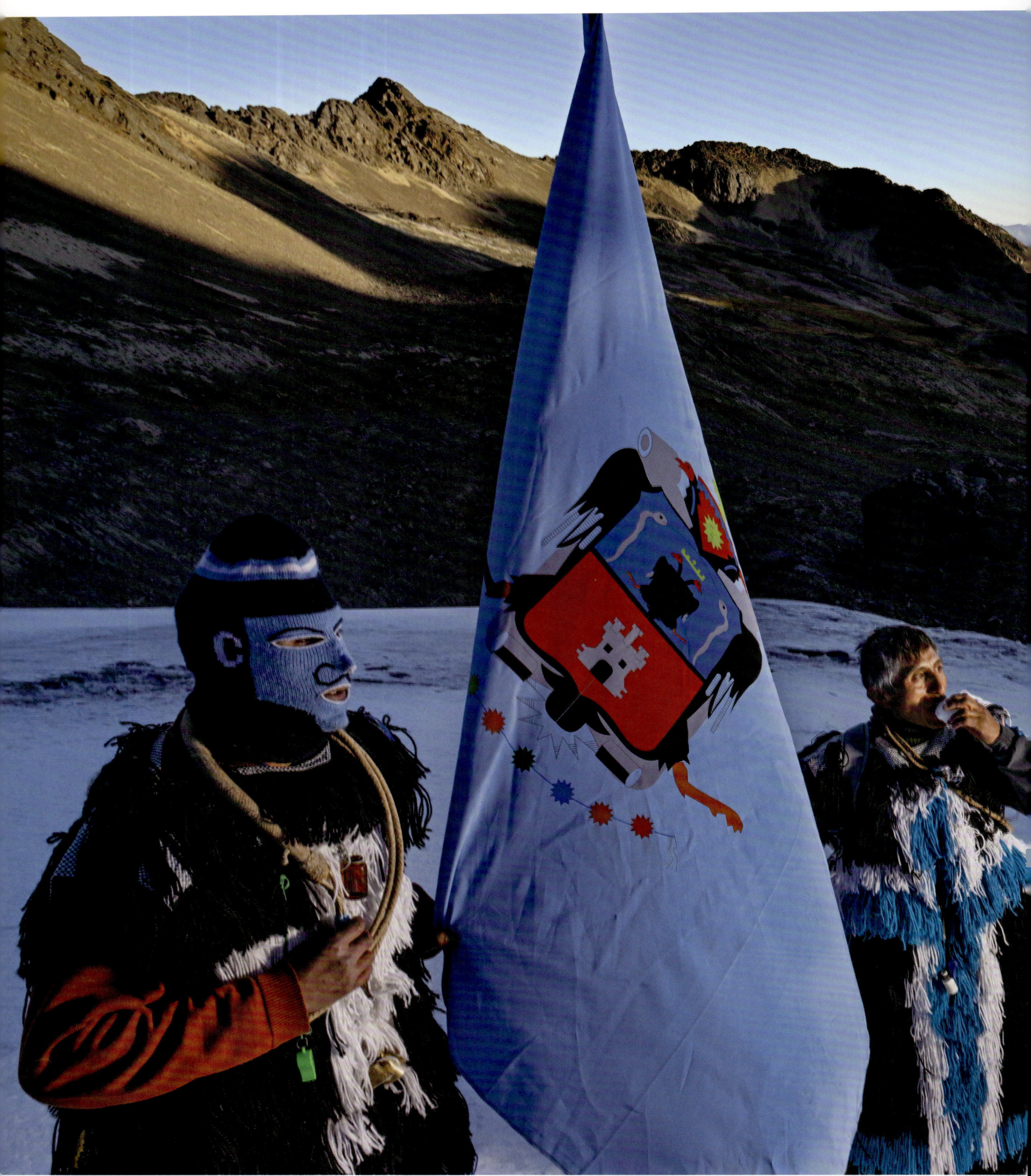

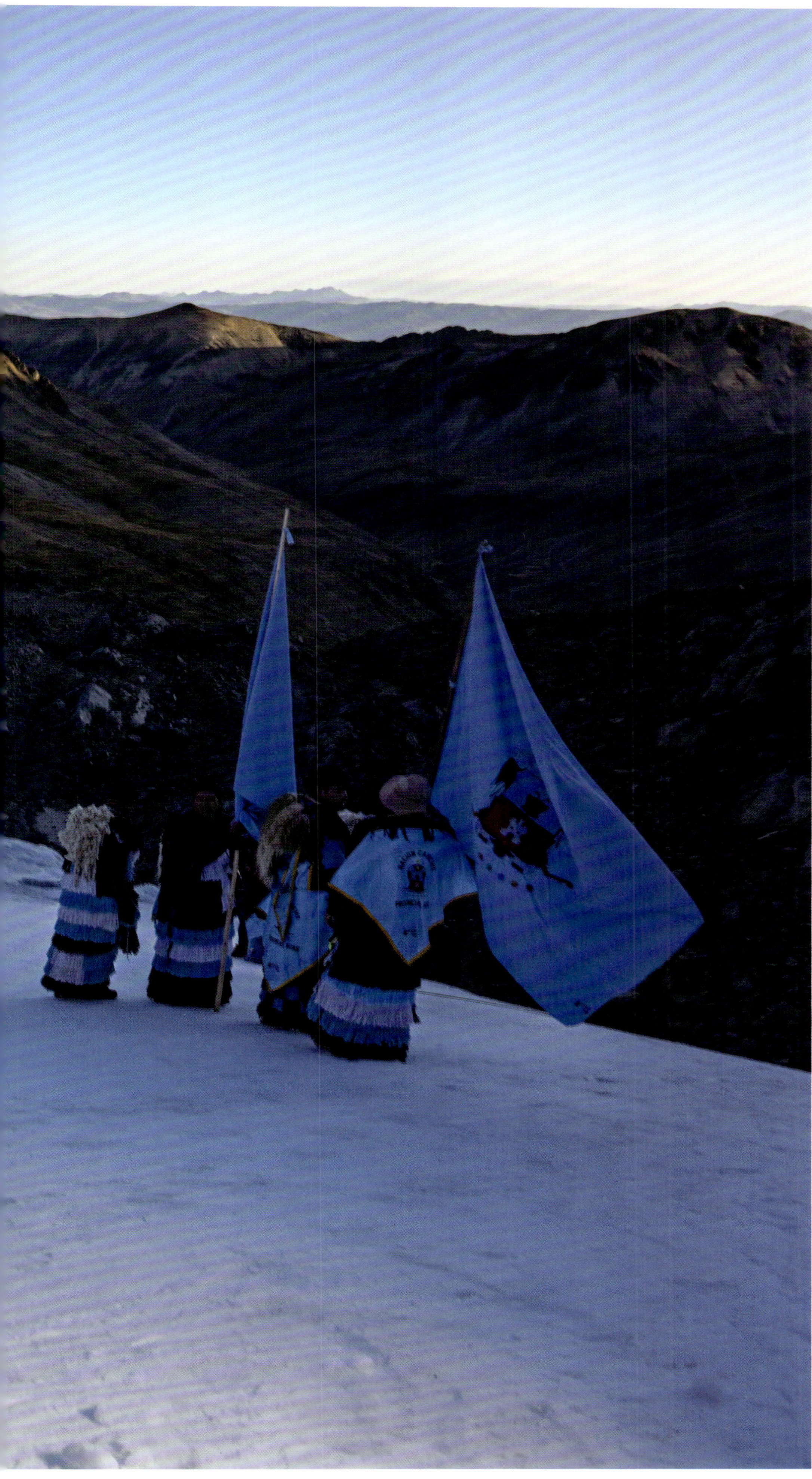

Pilgrims dressed up as *ukukus,* mythical bear-humans, climb glaciers above Peru's Sinakara Valley during the Qoyllur Rit'i festival. The once plentiful ice, considered sacred, is now receding due to climate change; in fact, 30 percent of Peru's glaciers have melted away since 2000. The ukukus used to cut large blocks of glacier ice and carry them on their backs down into the valley, where the melted water was believed to have medicinal properties. Today, the harvest of glacier ice is prohibited, and the closest the ukukus come to reliving the old days is occasionally eating small pieces of snow and ice.

PAGES 40–41: Combining a traditional skirt with alpine gear, Senobio Llusco, a member of Bolivia's Aymara people, accompanies a National Geographic team to install a weather station atop 20,945-foot-high (6,384 m) Nevado Ausangate in the Peruvian Andes. Among the station's tasks: recording moisture of the glaciers, whose high-altitude melt helps feed the Amazon River.

PAGES 44–45: Qoyllur Rit'i takes place every year in May or June, coinciding with the Feast of Corpus Christi, and combines elements of both Catholicism and ancient Andean beliefs. Each year, more than 100,000 devotees take part in the largest Indigenous festival on the continent. Some pilgrims carry heavy wooden crosses up the mountain slopes, across high passes, and onto glaciers at more than 16,400 feet (5,000 m) before descending back into the valley.

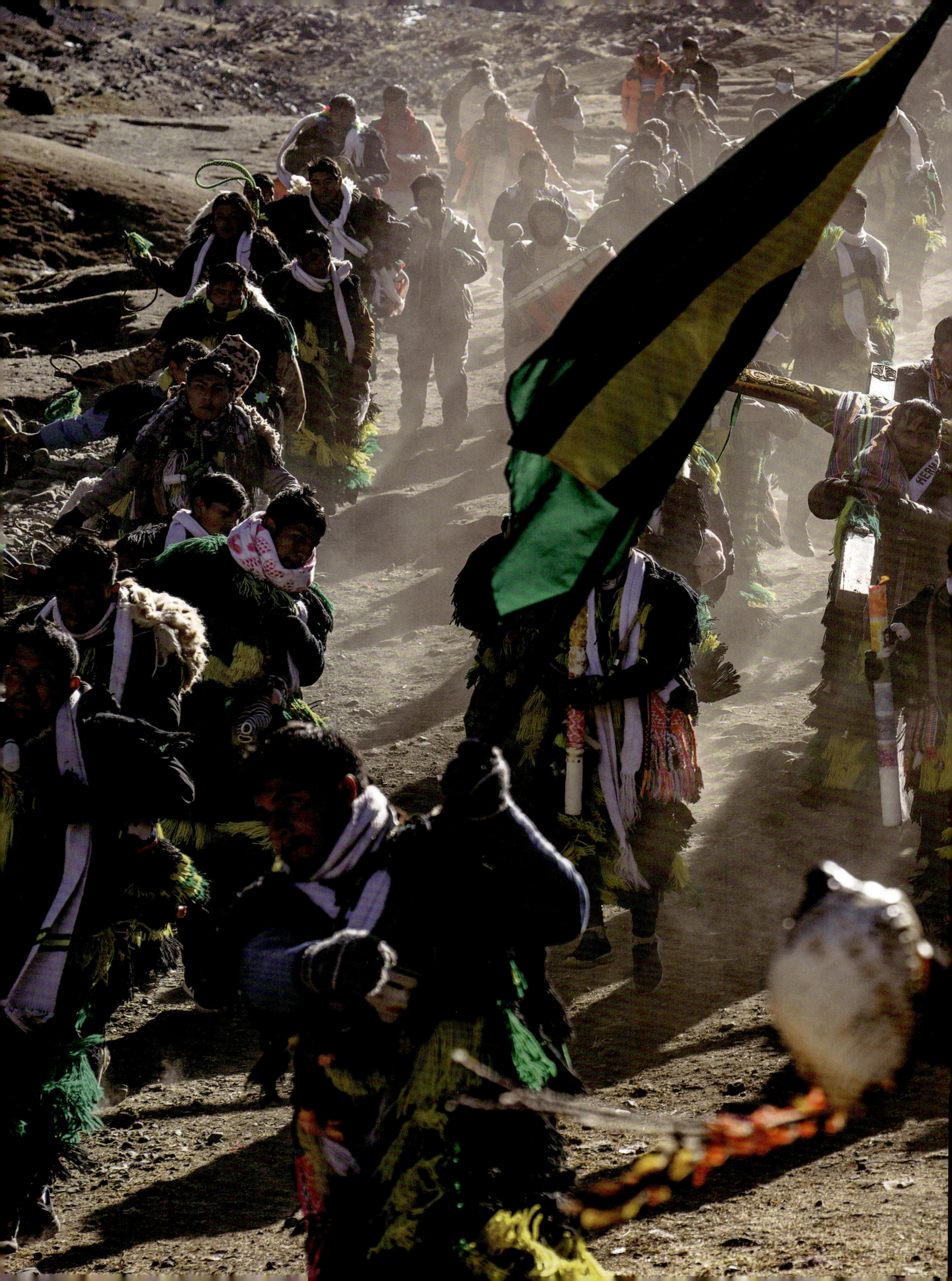

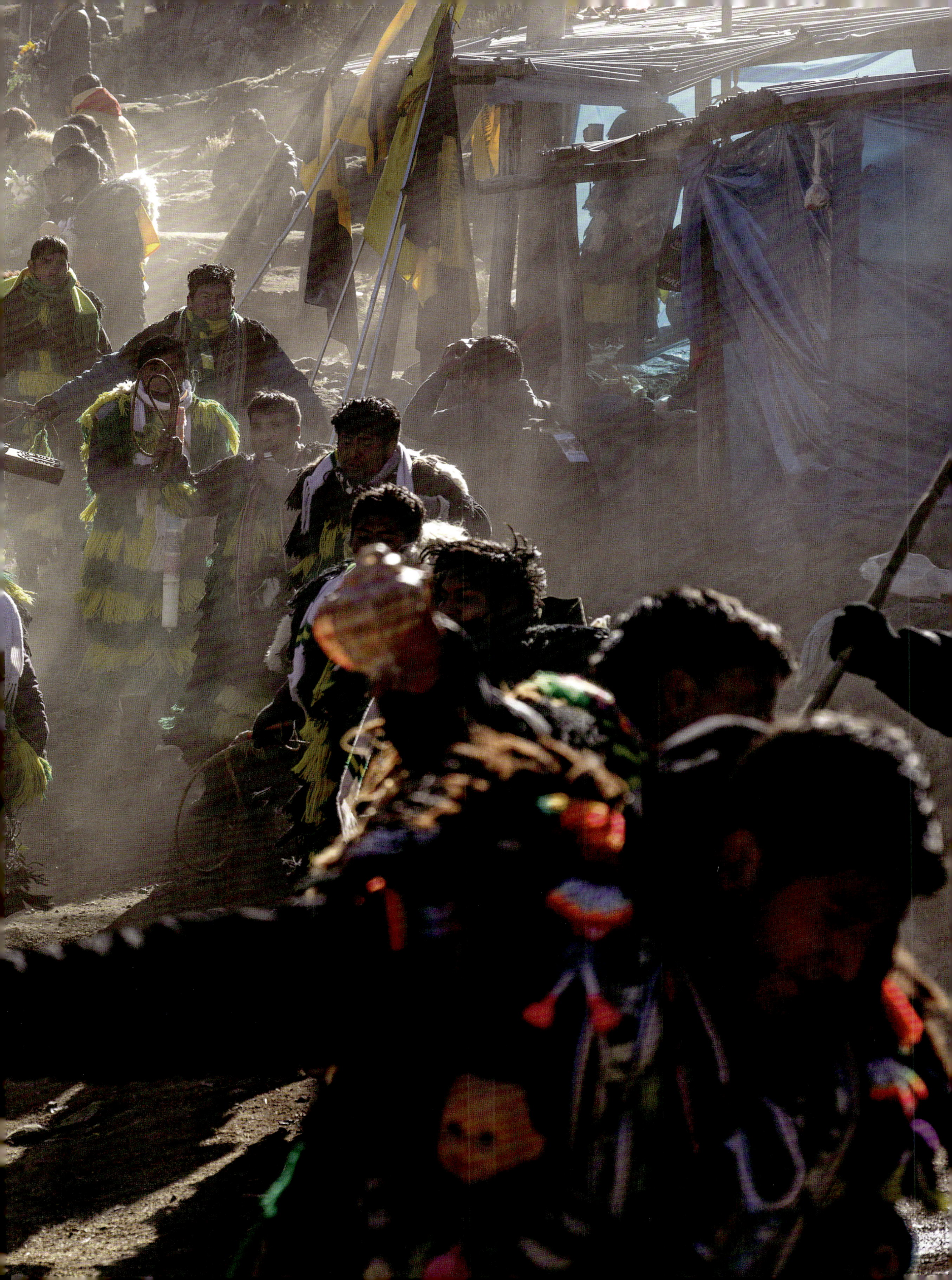

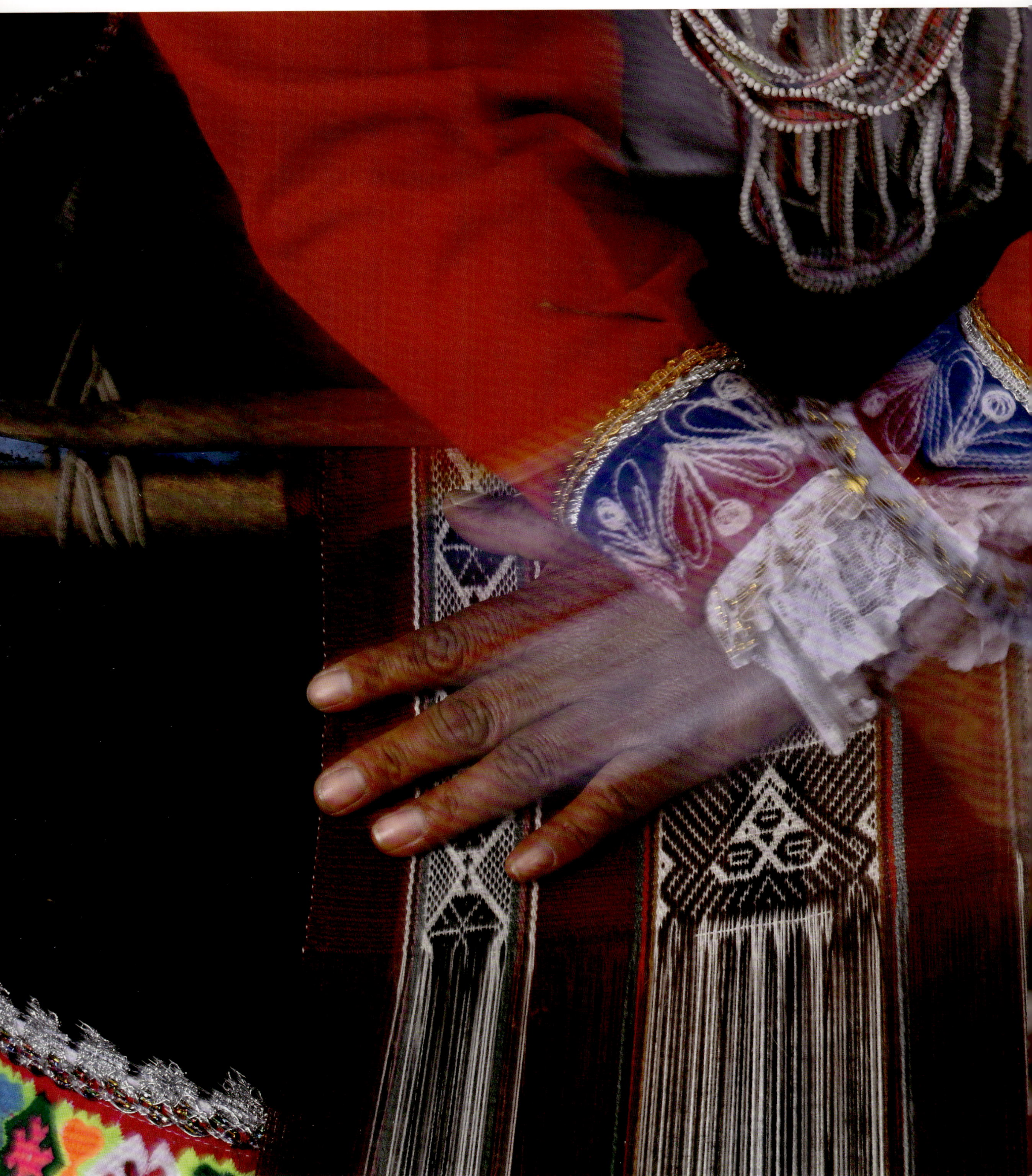

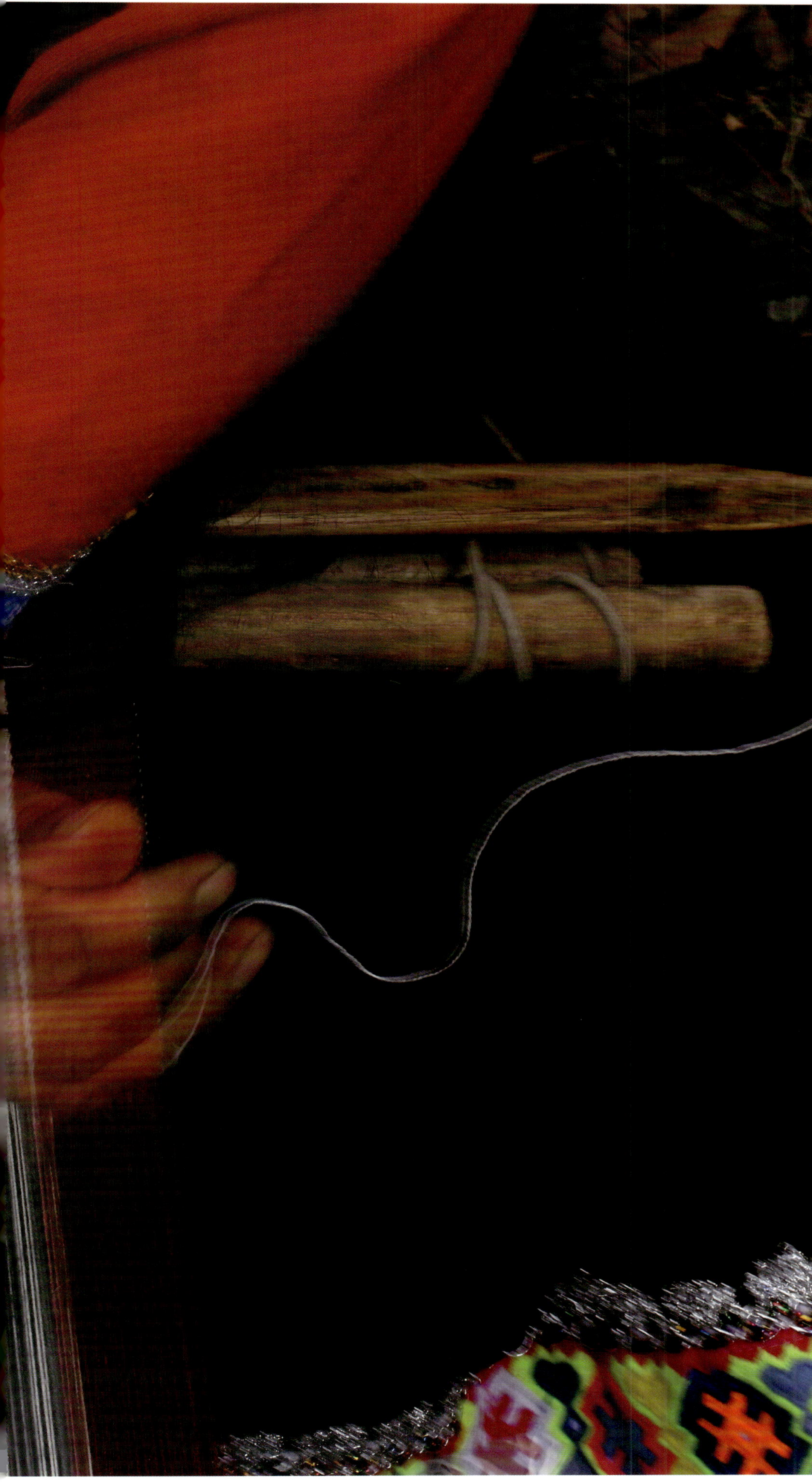

A Peruvian artisan weaves an image of an *ukuku,* the Andean bear *(Tremarctos ornatus)* venerated in Quechua stories and a vital part of Amazonia's Andean ecosystem. Accompanying geometric details are often symbols of daily Andean life, portraying rivers, stars, agricultural tools, or the sun. Weaving is a lifeblood of Andean culture passed down for generations, and each piece is a unique self-expression of the artisan and her community.

PAGES 48–49: From glacial trickles to mighty tributaries that empty into it from every direction, the Amazon River system carries more water than any other on Earth. Rainwater swells the Papallacta River as it roars around a pair of torrent ducks *(Merganetta armata)* perched on a boulder in Ecuador's Guango Cloud Forest Reserve. Endemic to South America's Andes, they hold territories on fast-flowing rivers at altitudes of up to 13,120 feet (4,000 m).

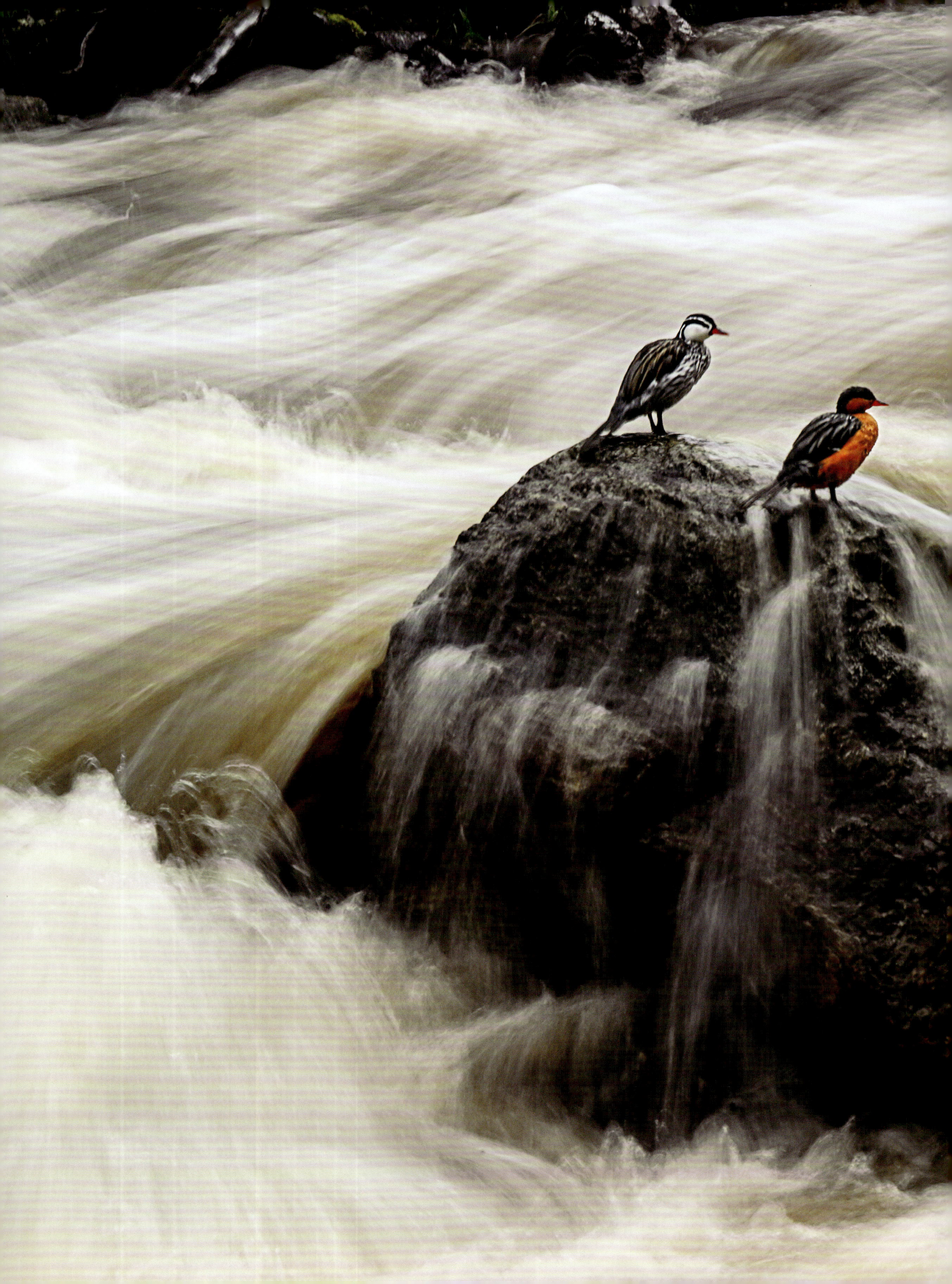

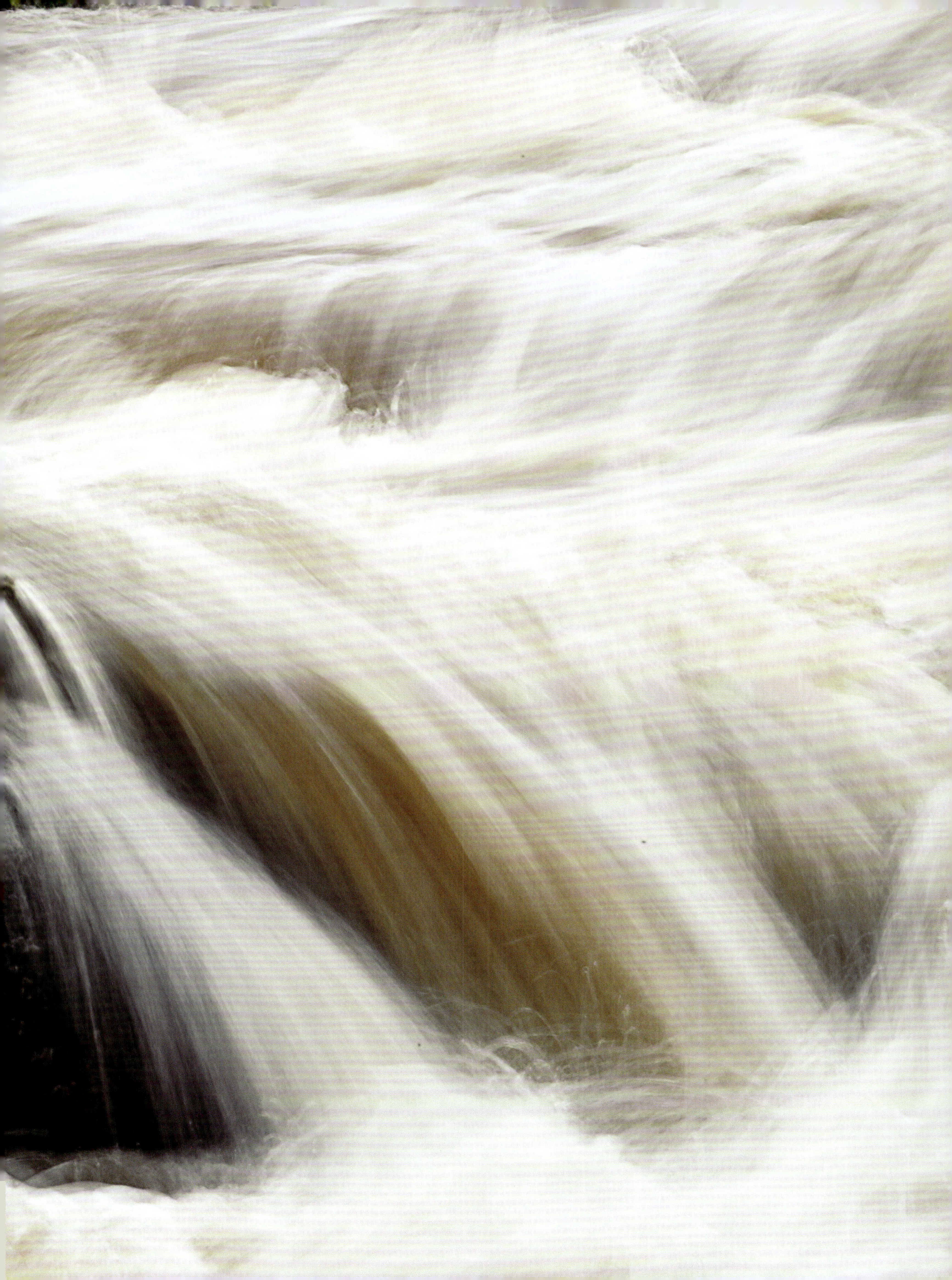

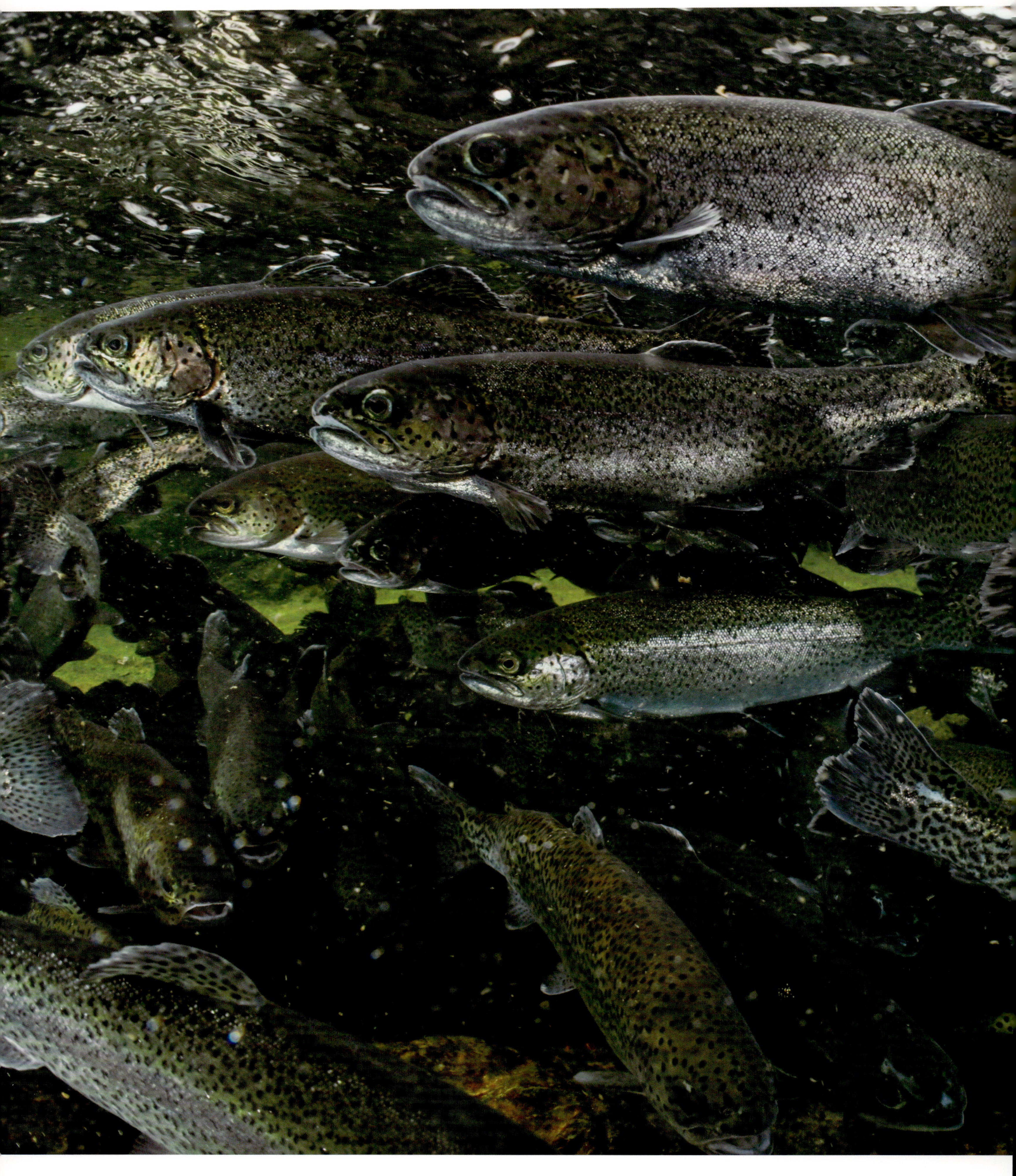

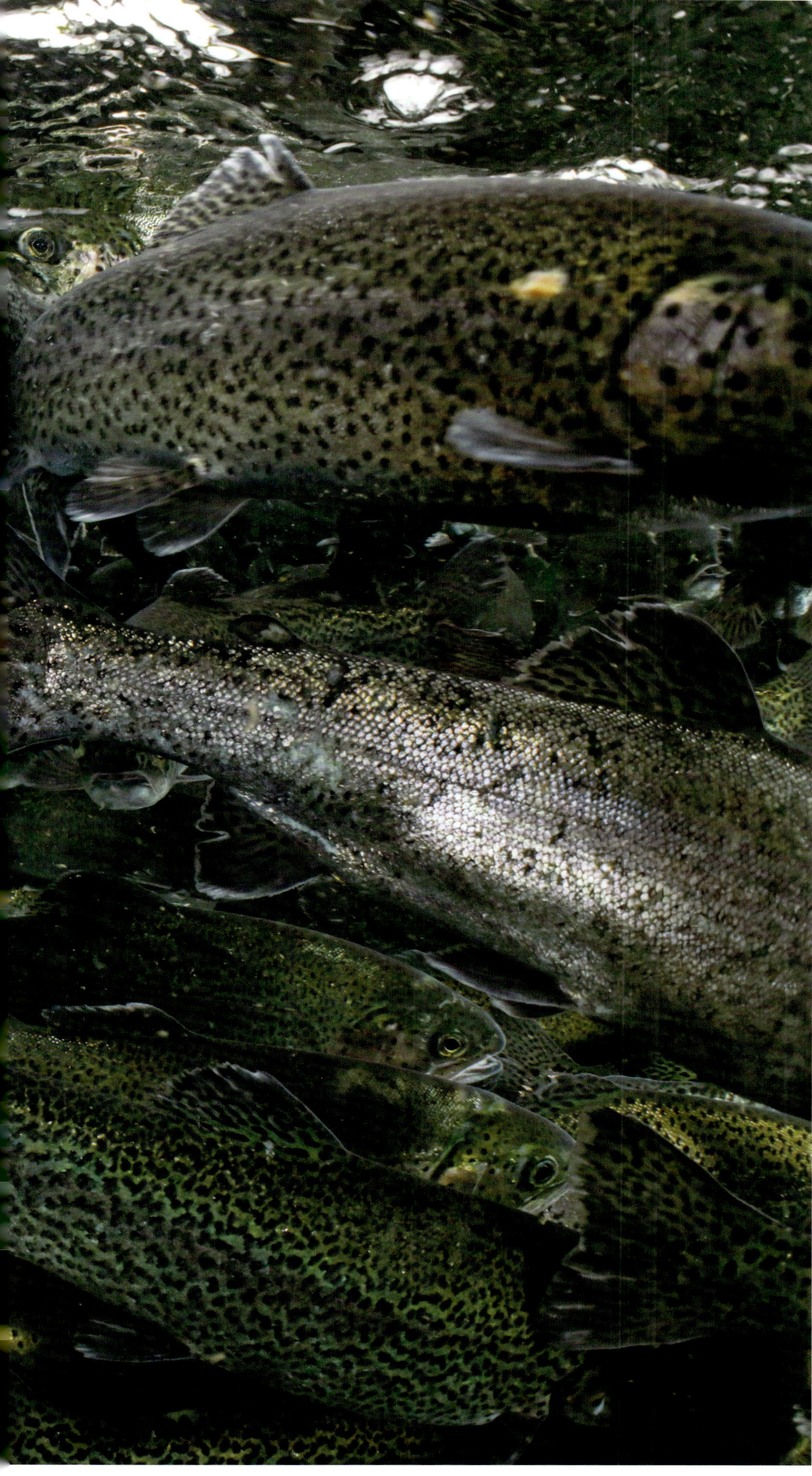

Rainbow trout *(Oncorhynchus mykiss)* were introduced into streams in the Ecuadorian Andes in the 1920s and, with the absence of indigenous predators to keep their populations in check, have dramatically impacted native biodiversity. They outcompete torrent ducks for their aquatic invertebrate prey and aggressively feed on the tadpoles of endemic Andean glass frogs and other threatened amphibians.

PAGES 52–53: Andean bears *(Tremarctos ornatus)* are omnivores, known to eat more than 300 different kinds of plants, but they are especially fond of bromeliads, palms, and fruits. Bear biologist Ruthmery Pillco Huarcaya believes these bears play an important structuring role in their ecosystem. By consuming seeds in the lowlands and defecating in the mountains, they're helping to preserve forests by dispersing tree seeds at cooler, higher altitudes as the climate warms.

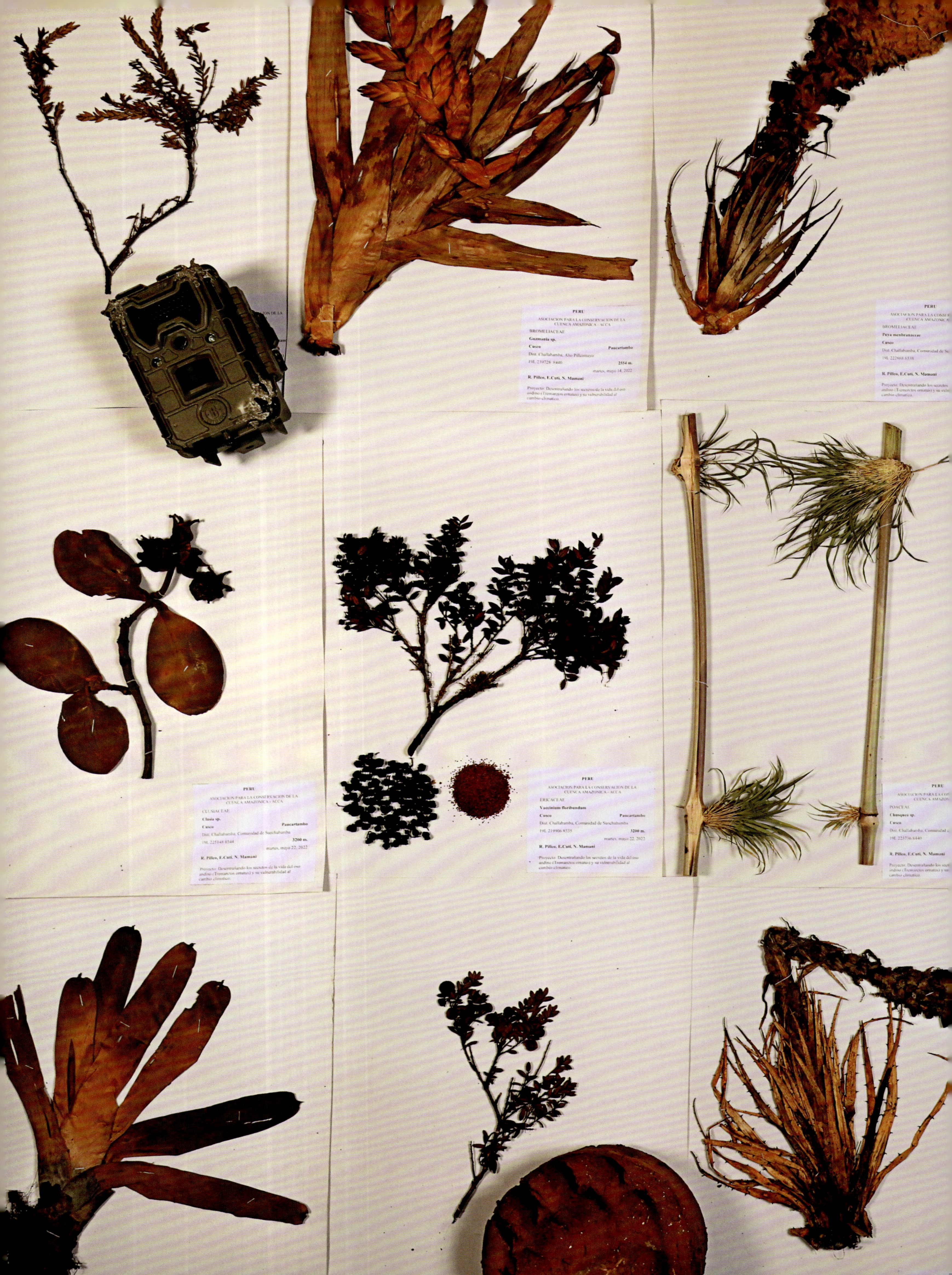
PERU
ASOCIACION PARA LA CONSERVACION DE LA CUENCA AMAZONICA - ACCA
BROMELIACEAE
Guzmania sp.
Cusco
Paucartambo
Dist. Challabamba, Alto Pillcomayo
19L 239728 8440
2554 m.
martes, mayo 14, 2022
R. Pillco, E.Cuti, N. Mamani
Proyecto: Desentrañando los secretos de la vida del oso andino (Tremarctos ornatus) y su vulnerabilidad al cambio climatico.
PERU
ASOCIACION PARA LA CONSERVACION DE LA CUENCA AMAZONICA - ACCA
CLUSIACEAE
Clusia sp.
Paucartambo
Cusco
3200 m.
martes, mayo 22, 2022
R. Pillco, E.Cuti, N. Mamani
PERU
ASOCIACION PARA LA CONSERVACION DE LA CUENCA AMAZONICA - ACCA
ERICACEAE
Vaccinium floribundum
Cusco
Paucartambo
Dist. Challabamba, Comunidad de Sunchubamba
19L 219906 8535
3200 m.
martes, mayo 22, 2022
R. Pillco, E.Cuti, N. Mamani
Proyecto: Desentrañando los secretos de la vida del oso andino (Tremarctos ornatus) y su vulnerabilidad al cambio climatico.

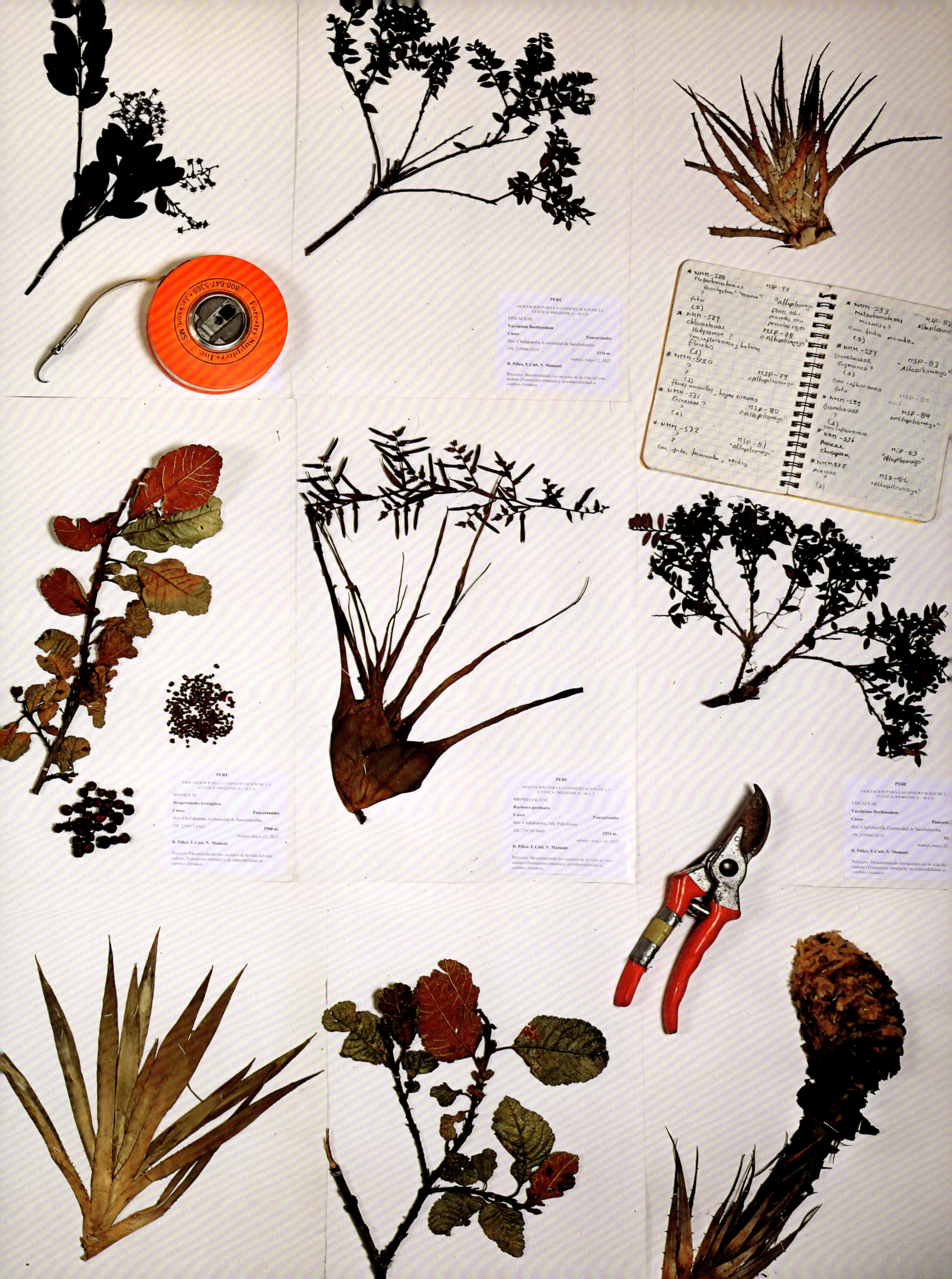
Forestry Suppliers Inc.
800-647-5368
Jackson MS
PERU
ERICACEAE
Vaccinium floribundum
Cusco
Paucartambo
3334 m.
martes, mayo 22, 2022
R. Pillco, E.Cuti, N. Mamani
PERU
ROSACEAE
Hesperomeles ferruginea
Cusco
Paucartambo
Dist. Challabamba, Comunidad de Sunchubamba
2960 m.
martes, mayo 22, 2022
R. Pillco, E.Cuti, N. Mamani
PERU
ASOCIACION PARA LA CONSERVACION DE LA CUENCA AMAZONICA - ACCA
BROMELIACEAE
Racinaea pectinata
Cusco
Paucartambo
Dist. Challabamba, Alto Pillcomayo
2554 m.
sabado, mayo 14, 2022
R. Pillco, E.Cuti, N. Mamani
Proyecto: Desentrañando los secretos de la vida del oso andino (Tremarctos ornatus) y su vulnerabilidad al cambio climatico.
PERU
ERICACEAE
Vaccinium floribundum
Cusco
R. Pillco, E.Cuti, N. Mamani

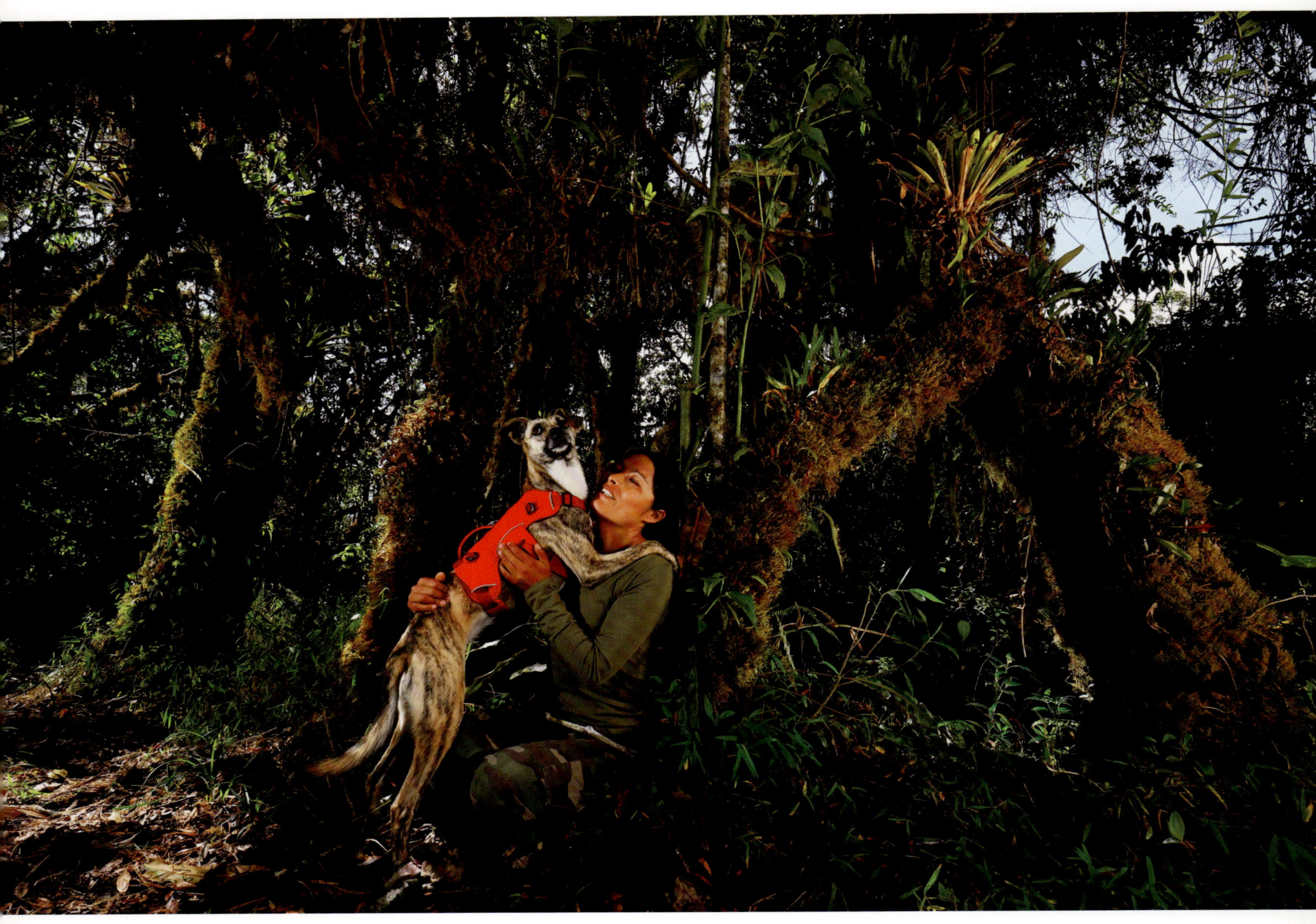

ABOVE: To carry out her research, biologist Ruthmery Pillco Huarcaya treks deep into the wilderness that surrounds Peru's Wayqecha Cloud Forest Biological Station. Her companion tracker dog, Ukuku, whose name is a word for "bear" in the local Quechua language, joins her on the trails to help her team follow and study the elusive, fast-moving Andean bear.

OPPOSITE: After a thorough medical checkup by wildlife veterinarian Diego Rolim, a tranquilized Andean bear named Ruru is fitted with a lightweight collar. Before detaching after a set period, the collar will geolocate the bear's exact location, while a tiny video camera will give the researchers a unique point of view. In less than two years, they have watched collared bears cross rivers, sleep high in tree canopies, munch on bromeliads, and even eat a monkey.

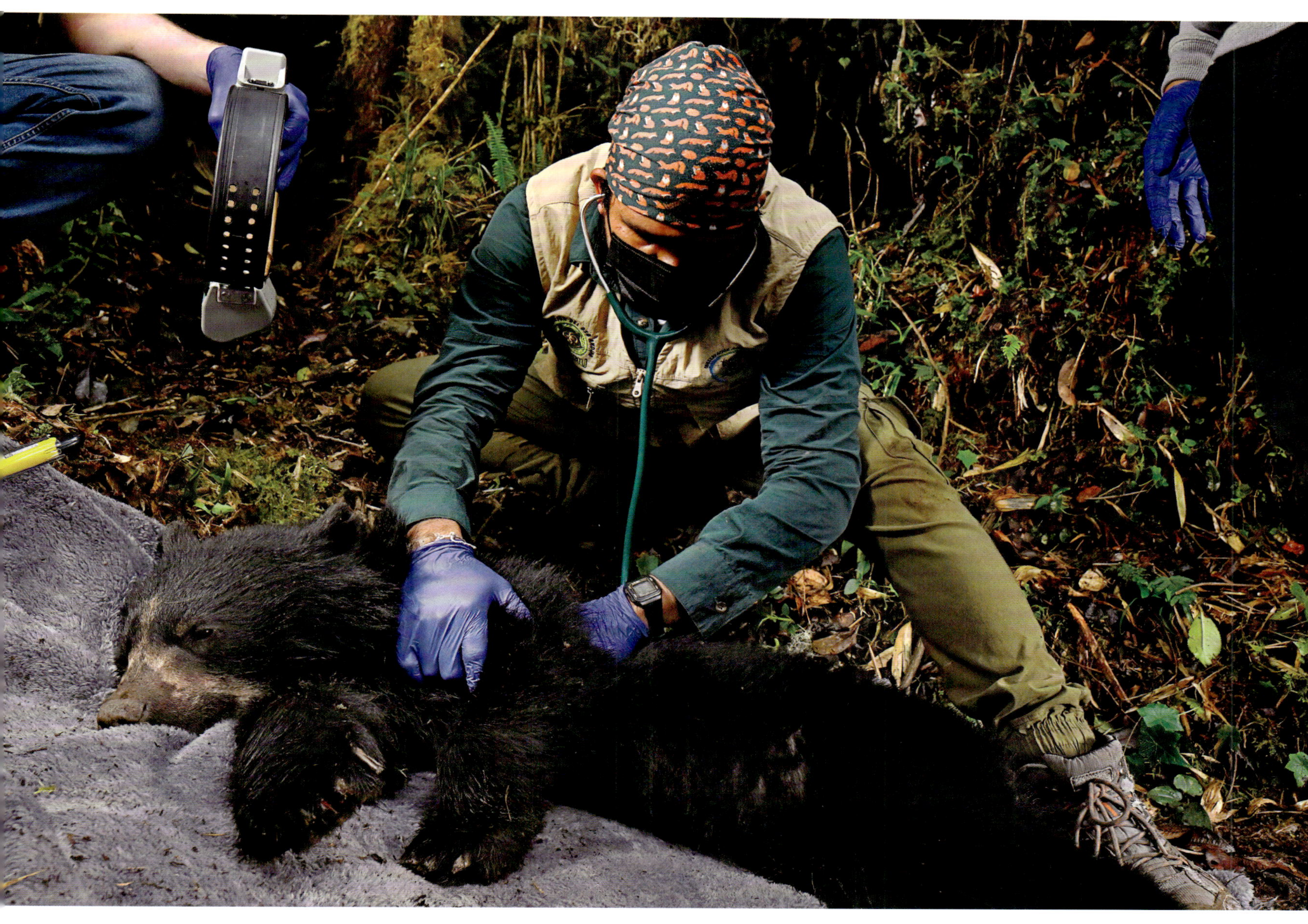

PAGES 56–57: The only bear species in South America, the Andean, or spectacled, bear was made famous by the Paddington children's books and films. Expert tree climbers with curved claws, they are perfectly adapted to cloud forests but also seasonally migrate to feed on bromeliads in puna grasslands at elevations up to 14,760 feet (4,500 m).

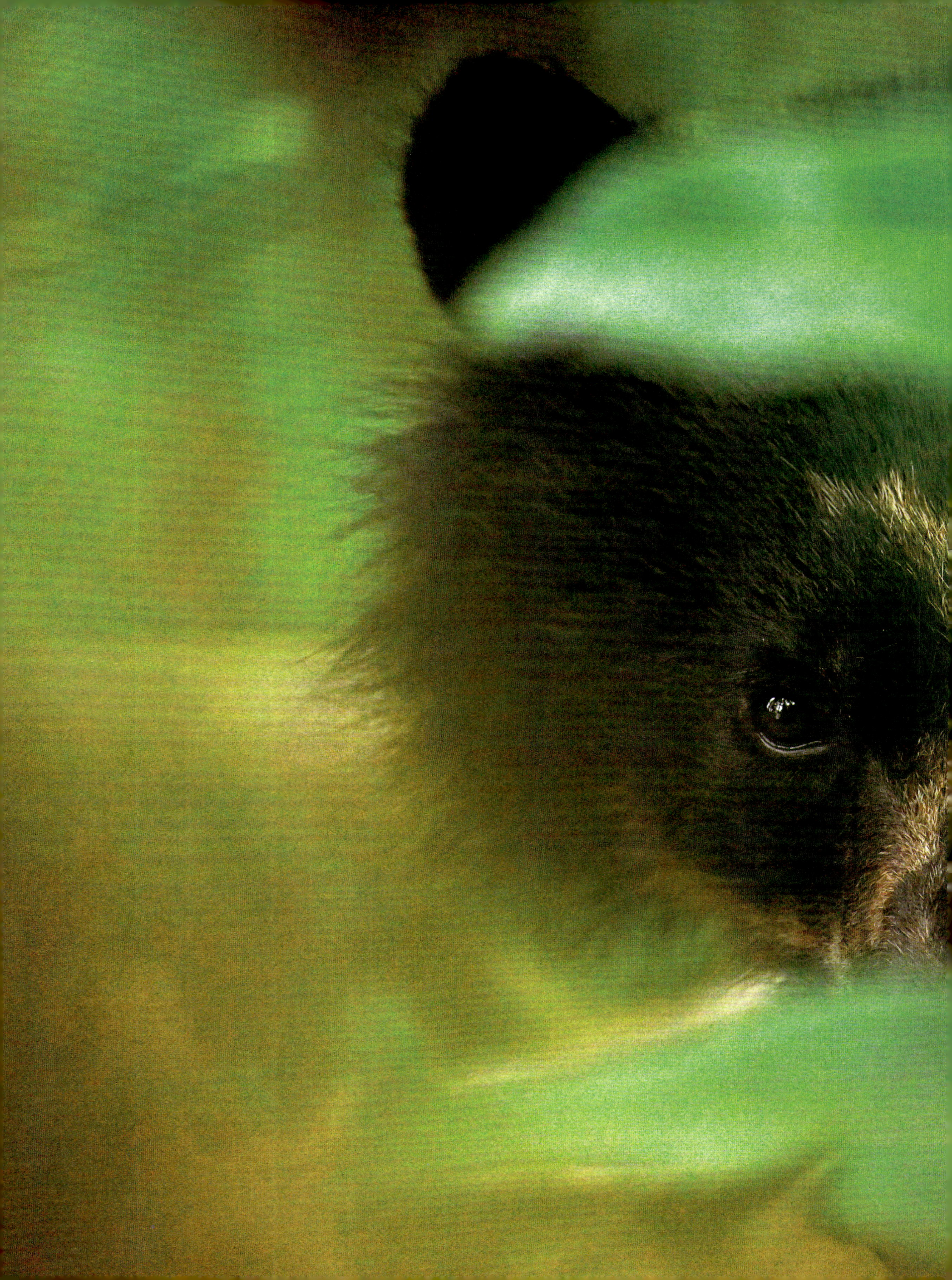

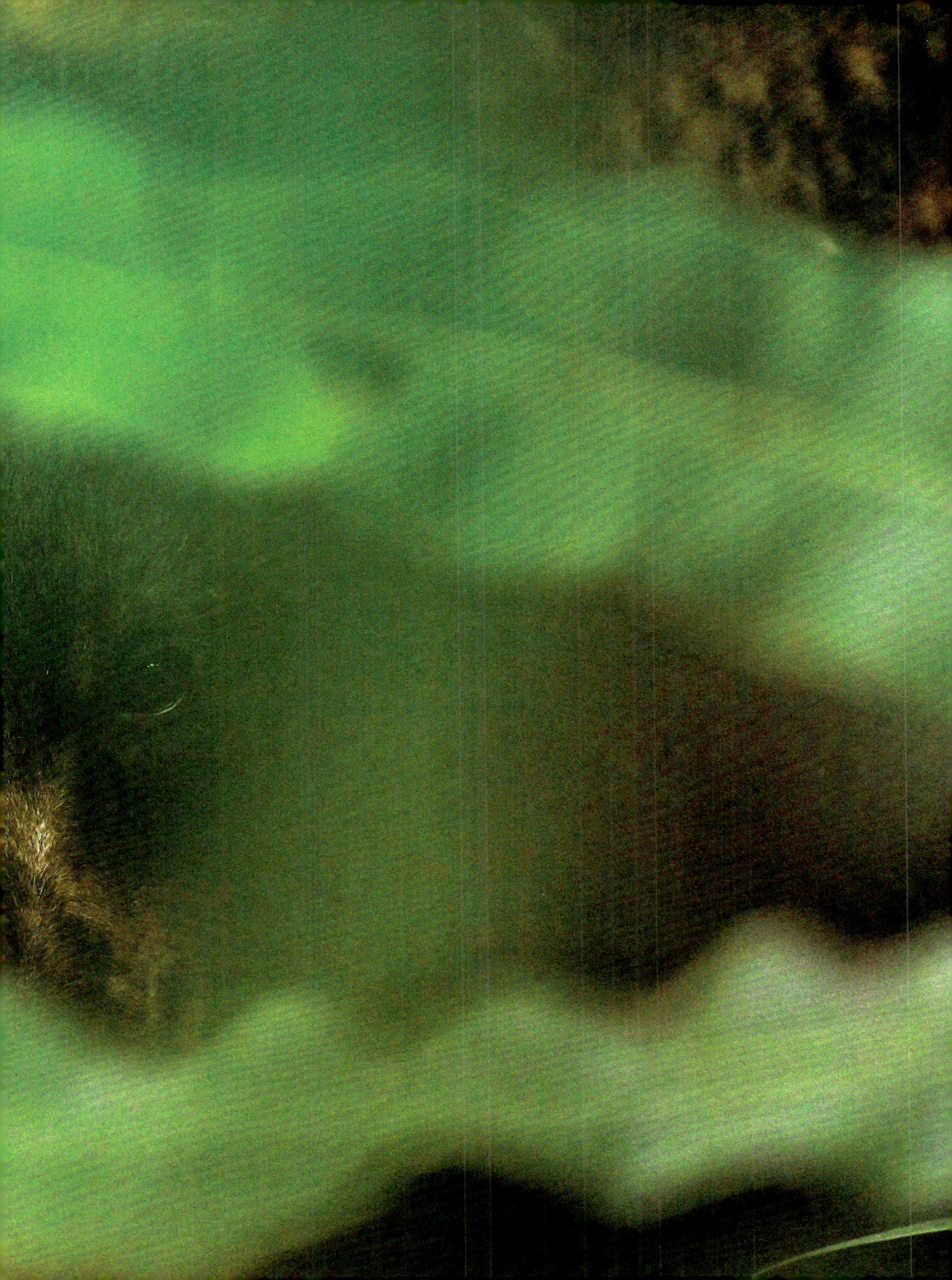

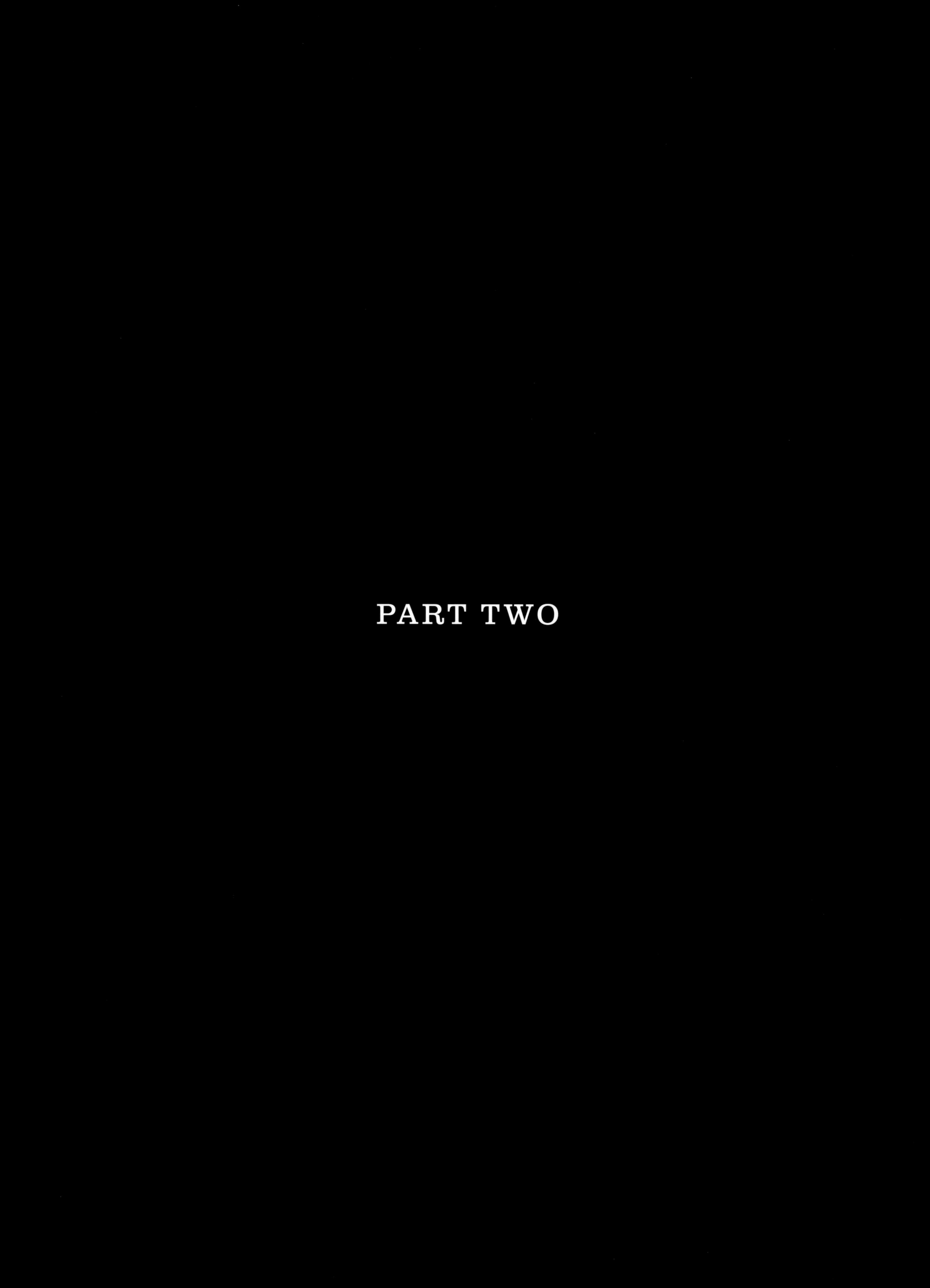

PART TWO

HIDDEN HEADWATERS

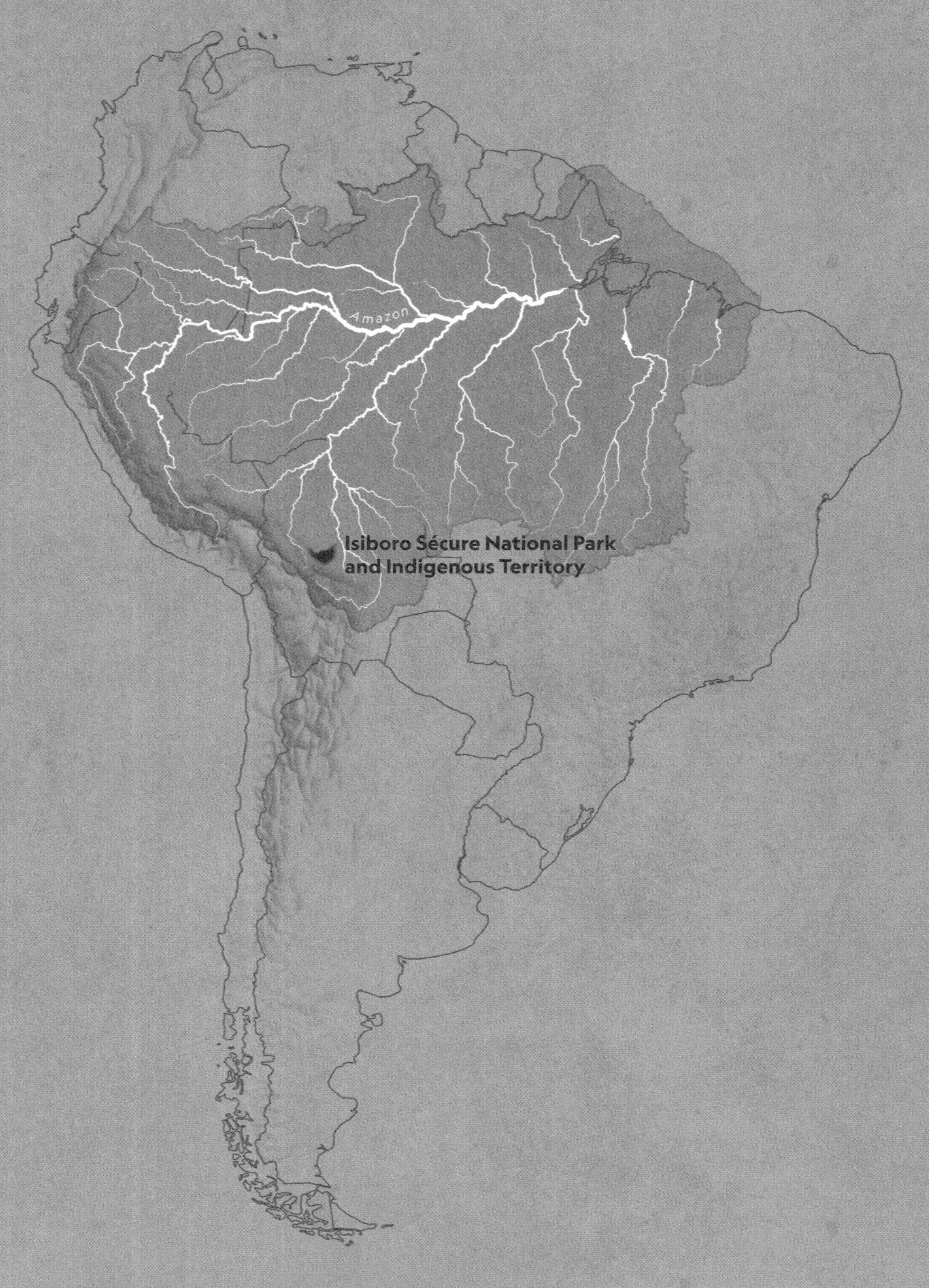
Amazon
Isiboro Sécure National Park
and Indigenous Territory

BOLIVIA'S ISIBORO SÉCURE National Park and Indigenous Territory is the traditional land of the Tsimané and Yuracaré people, who have hunted and fished here for millennia. In the wet season, they stalk terrestrial animals, like tapirs and monkeys; in the dry season, the bulk of their protein comes from fish, much of it caught ingeniously with bows and arrows. The Indigenous owners of this territory are not only skilled hunters, but also effective stewards of the landscape who keep the lowland rivers and forests healthy and ecologically intact. But it is by no means untouched or pristine.

Fortunately, the headwaters of the Sécure and Pluma Rivers, located in the adjacent Eva Eva Mountains, are. Everybody I spoke to in the local communities says that nobody in living memory has traveled into or hunted or fished there. My friend Roycer Herbi from the village of Oromomo tells me that nobody knows this place and that "the jungle here defends itself with thunder, lightning, and dangerous, fast-flowing water." Felix, the chief of La Asunta, adds, "Our ancestors never went there because they feared the many dangerous animals that live there."

I am hooked, but these hidden headwaters are nearly impossible to reach on foot or by boat. Fortunately, my friend Marcelo Pérez, an Argentine conservationist living in Bolivia, is quick to assist. He has been running fly-fishing trips along the lower reaches of the rivers in partnership with the local communities for more than a decade; in 2022, he took to the air to explore these remote mountains for the first time. A year later we join forces and, using a small helicopter and toting hundreds of pounds of underwater photographic gear, we fly above the headwaters with the goal of exploring the underwater worlds of these remote Amazonian rivers for the very first time.

Already from the air, I can see that the waters are clear and full of large fish. We land on a gravel riverbank next to a deep pool, near a small waterfall just upstream. I am so excited I can't get into my wet suit fast enough. Using scuba tanks is not an option in this remote part of the Amazon, so I have to free dive, accomplishing everything I need while holding my breath.

In the shallows I am quickly enveloped by a large school of sábalos. Millions of these silvery blue fish migrate from the lowlands into the headwaters to spawn every year; they nourish predators like caiman, otters, pumas, and jaguars. During these migrations, the river turns from liquid to nearly solid with fish.

Suddenly I'm distracted by flashes of shimmering light at the edge of my visibility. A school of five-foot-long (1.5 m) golden dorados—a fish the Indigenous people call the river jaguar—pass by. These are the undisputed apex predators of

These headwaters are unlike anywhere else on Earth. The rivers teem with fish, and the forest abounds with wildlife so diverse it defies belief.

the Amazon. They have a fierce-looking armored head and are covered in golden scales.

I swim out into deeper water, the shadows of giants below me. The *maturo,* or gilded catfish, can grow to the size and girth of a refrigerator; both Indigenous and river people in the Amazon tell stories of these giants swallowing children whole. They are intimidating and easily dwarf my five-foot-six (168 cm) frame. So before my first dive, I call out to my assistant that if one of them should grab me by the head, he should dive down and poke it in the eyes and gills. Of course, my uneasiness is misplaced, and they turn out to be surprisingly gentle and curious.

My mind is blown after a month of exploring these miraculous headwaters. One day, when I think things couldn't get any better, I notice a giant cowbird perched on what I think is a rock in the middle of the river. Suddenly the rock surfaces and transforms into one of the Amazon's most elusive animals: a lowland tapir. Like a ferry passenger, the bird rides around on its back as more cowbirds swoop in to catch biting flies that plague tapirs during the end of the hot dry season.

With the tapir distracted by the birds, I submerge and ride the current. After less than a minute of drifting, I make out that she is female; swimming around her are schools of expectant jatorana. The fish are eager for her to defecate, so they can pick out the undigested seeds. I get to within three feet (0.9 m) of the tapir and still no reaction; this is probably the first time she has ever encountered a human. Only when I exhale through my snorkel and she smells my foreign scent up close does she stick her head underwater for a closer inspection. With eyes wide open, she takes a good look at me, sinks to the bottom, and walks on the riverbed like a hippo toward the shallows. Emerging from the river, she slowly disappears into the thick jungle lining the riverbanks.

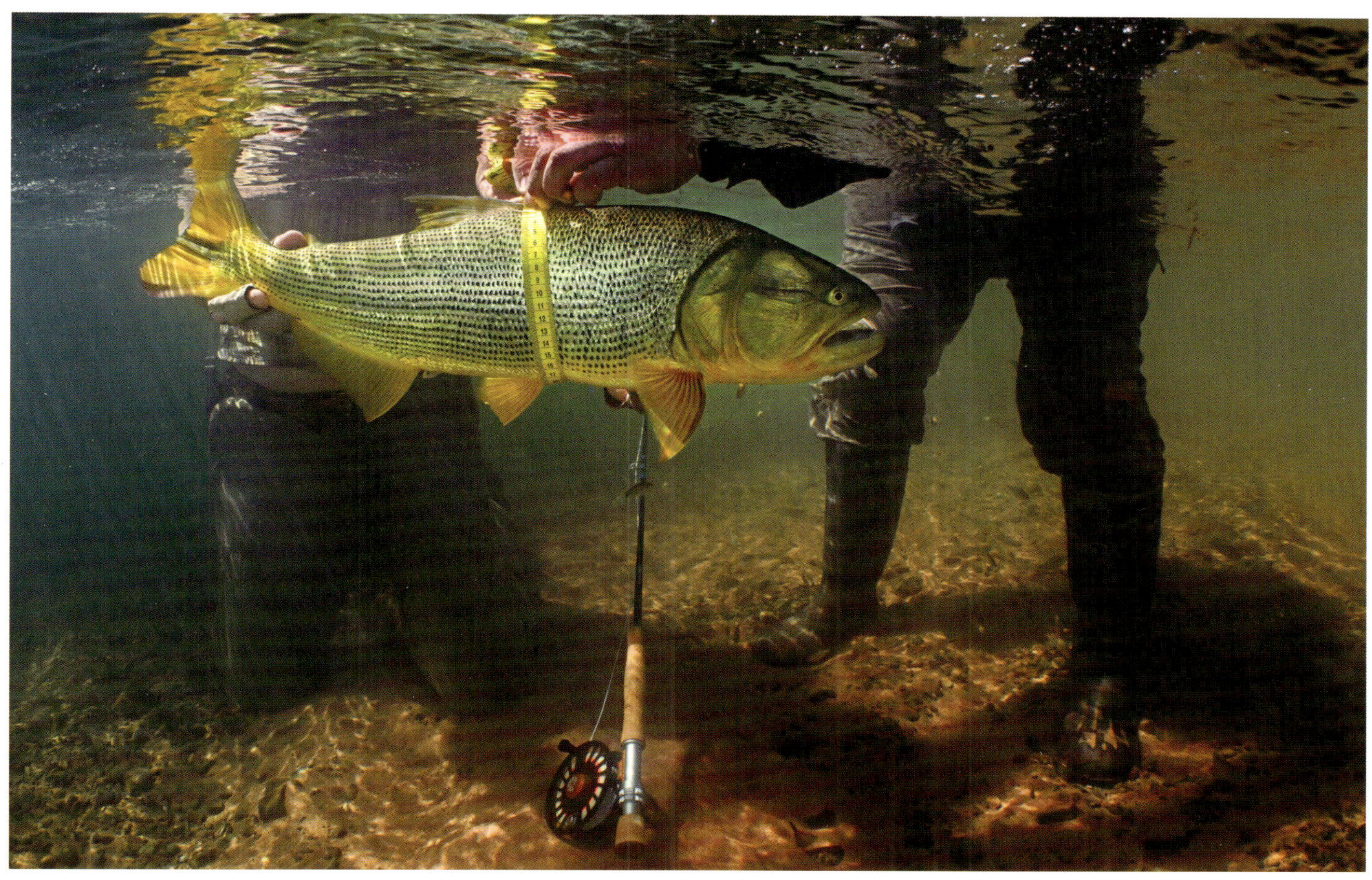

A golden dorado caught on a fly rod is measured, and small pieces of its fins are clipped for DNA analysis. Recent genetic research suggests this golden dorado could in fact be a new species, isolated and distinctly different from other populations farther south and east.

These headwaters are unlike anywhere else on Earth. The rivers teem with fish, and the forest abounds with wildlife so diverse and abundant it defies belief. The Indigenous people that live adjacent to these mountains are proud to be the guardians of this prehistoric landscape, and they believe that it should be kept exactly how it is.

I couldn't agree more. But current threats like agriculture, logging, and road construction loom just outside Isiboro Sécure's boundaries. To date, only its remoteness and a novel partnership with Indigenous communities around catch-and-release fly-fishing have kept these threats at bay. Community leaders, Bolivian scientists, Indigenous storytellers, and fly-fishermen need to come together to safeguard this one-of-a-kind aquatic wilderness park from all future exploitation. A pioneering merger of science and storytelling is required to protect what I believe to be the last pristine clear headwater rivers in the Amazon Basin. ■

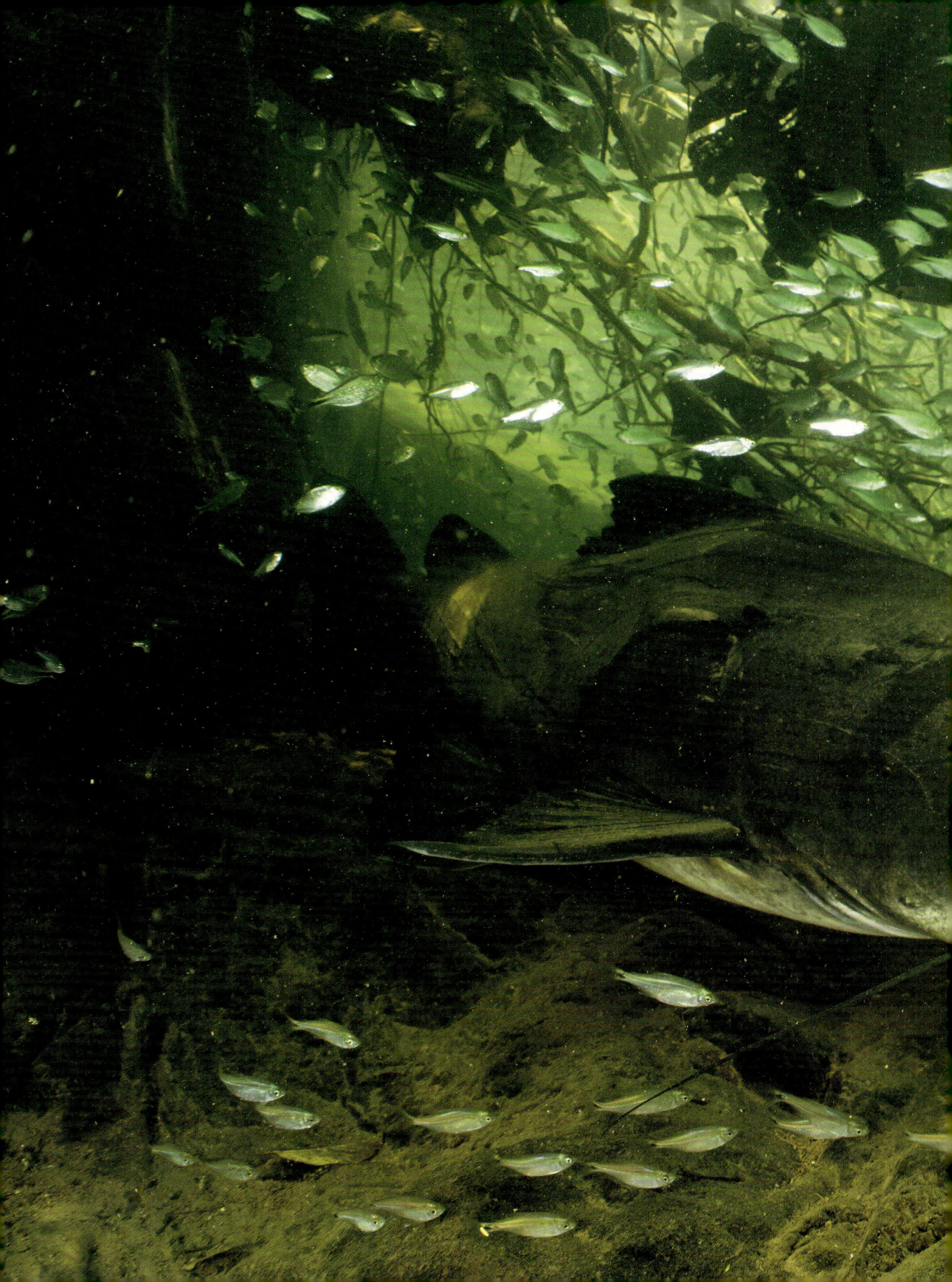

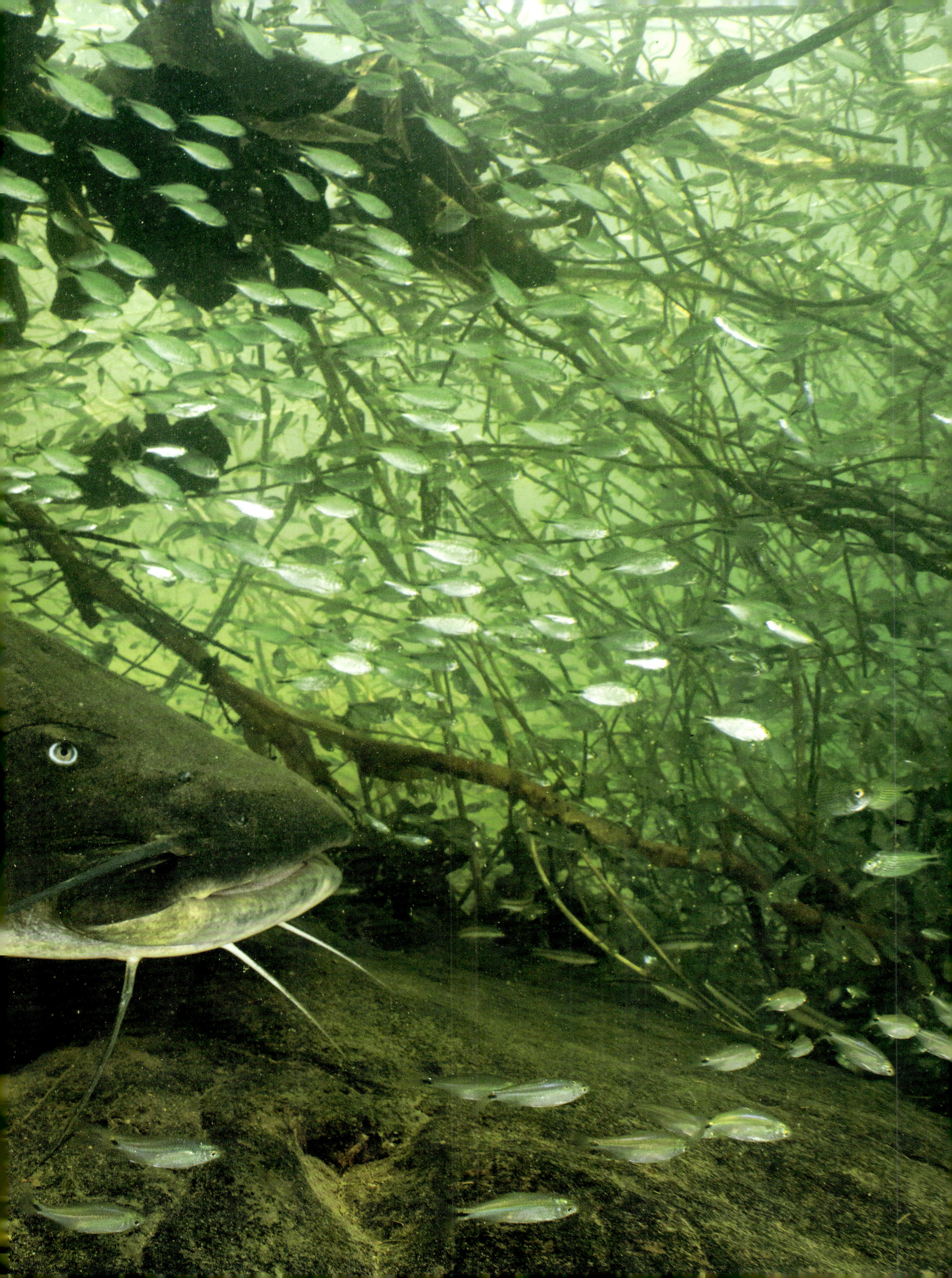

Hidden away in a remote, rarely visited corner of Bolivia lies a landscape of rainforested mountains with wild valleys and clear, fast-flowing rivers. The Eva Eva Mountains are nearly impossible to reach by foot or by boat, and even members of the Indigenous communities that live nearby believe that their ancestors have never hunted or fished there.

PAGES 64–65: Encircled by baitfish, a *maturo,* or gilded catfish *(Zungaro zungaro),* rests in its daytime hiding spot beneath an overhang of rock and tree branches. This fish can reach the dimensions of a refrigerator, growing almost seven feet (2 m) in length and weighing more than 150 pounds (70 kg).

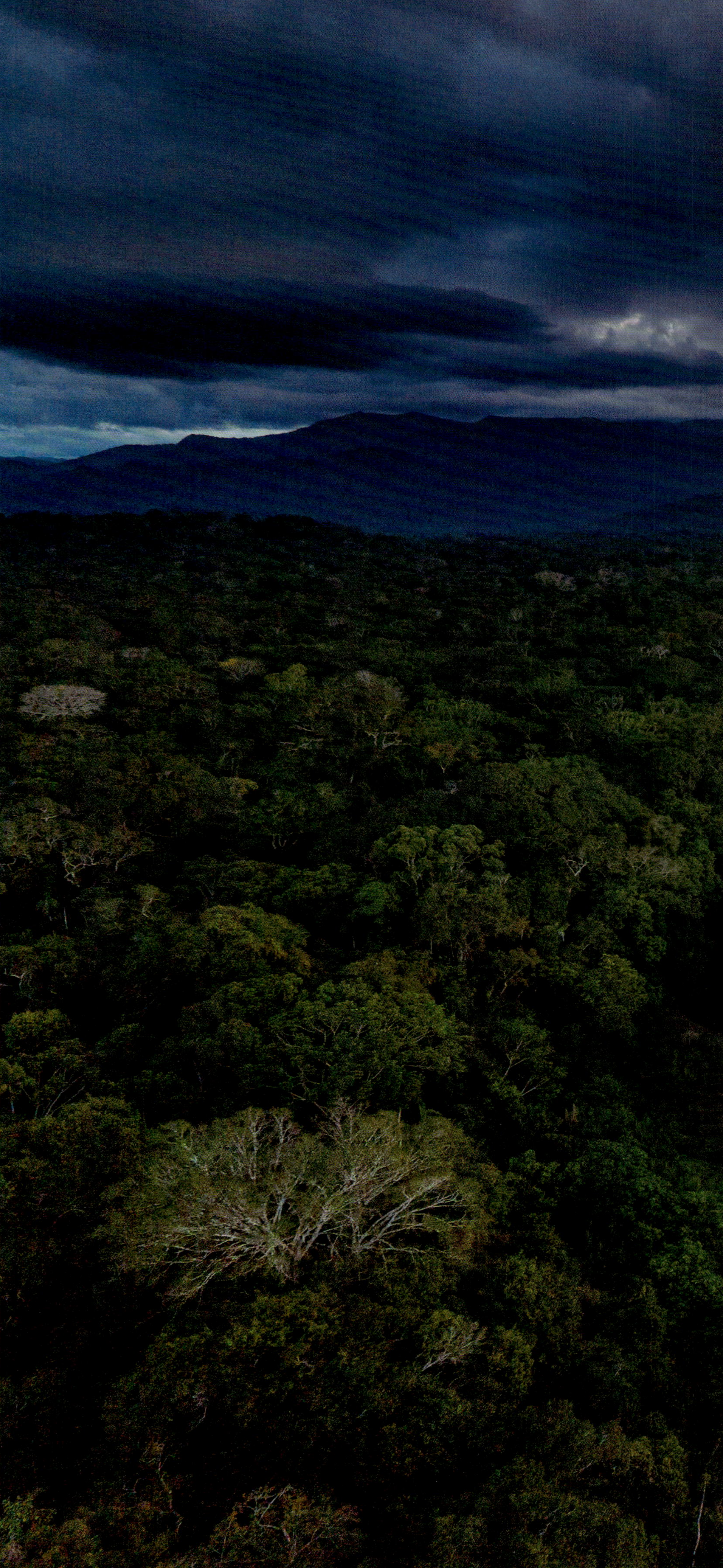

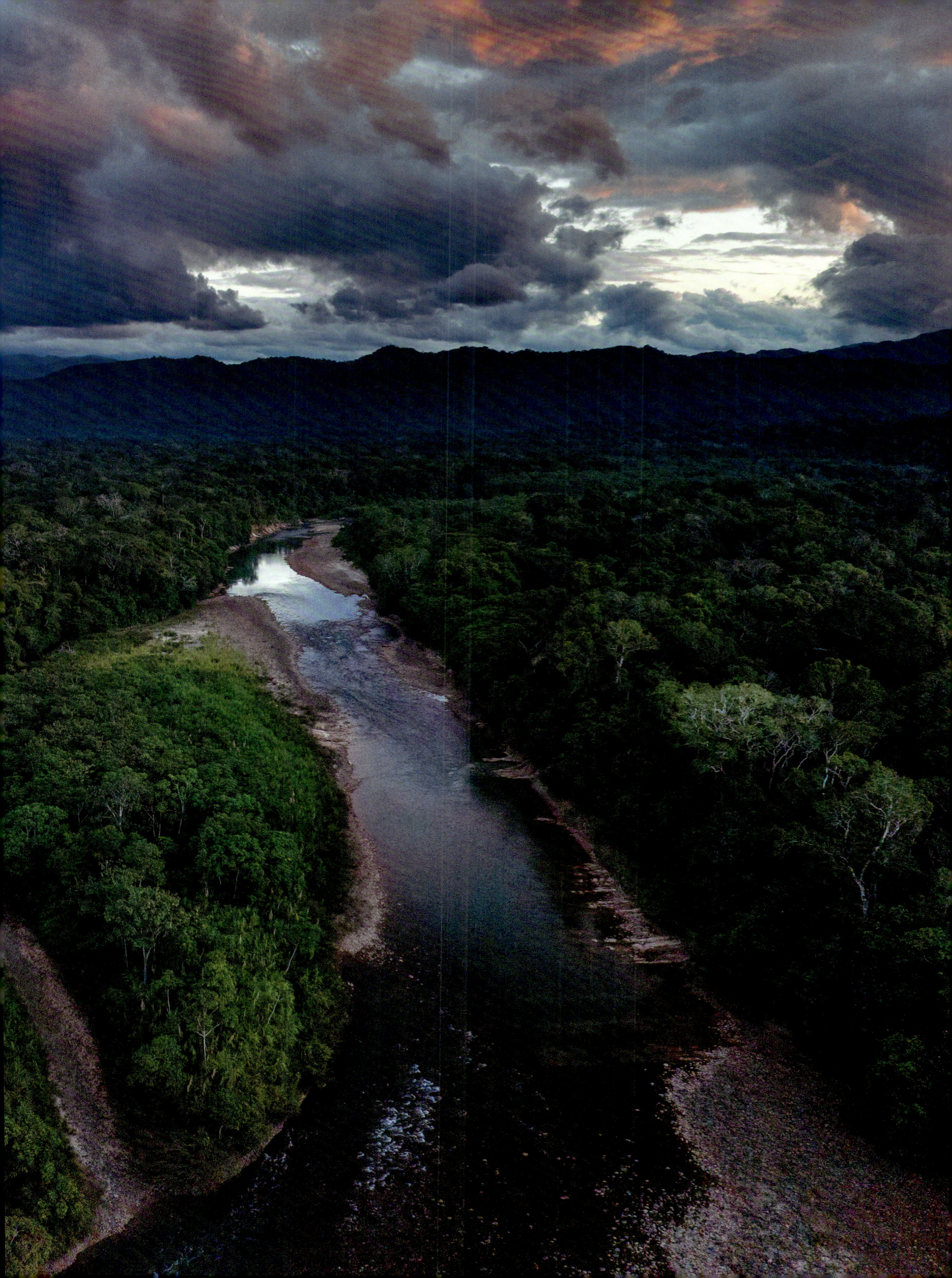

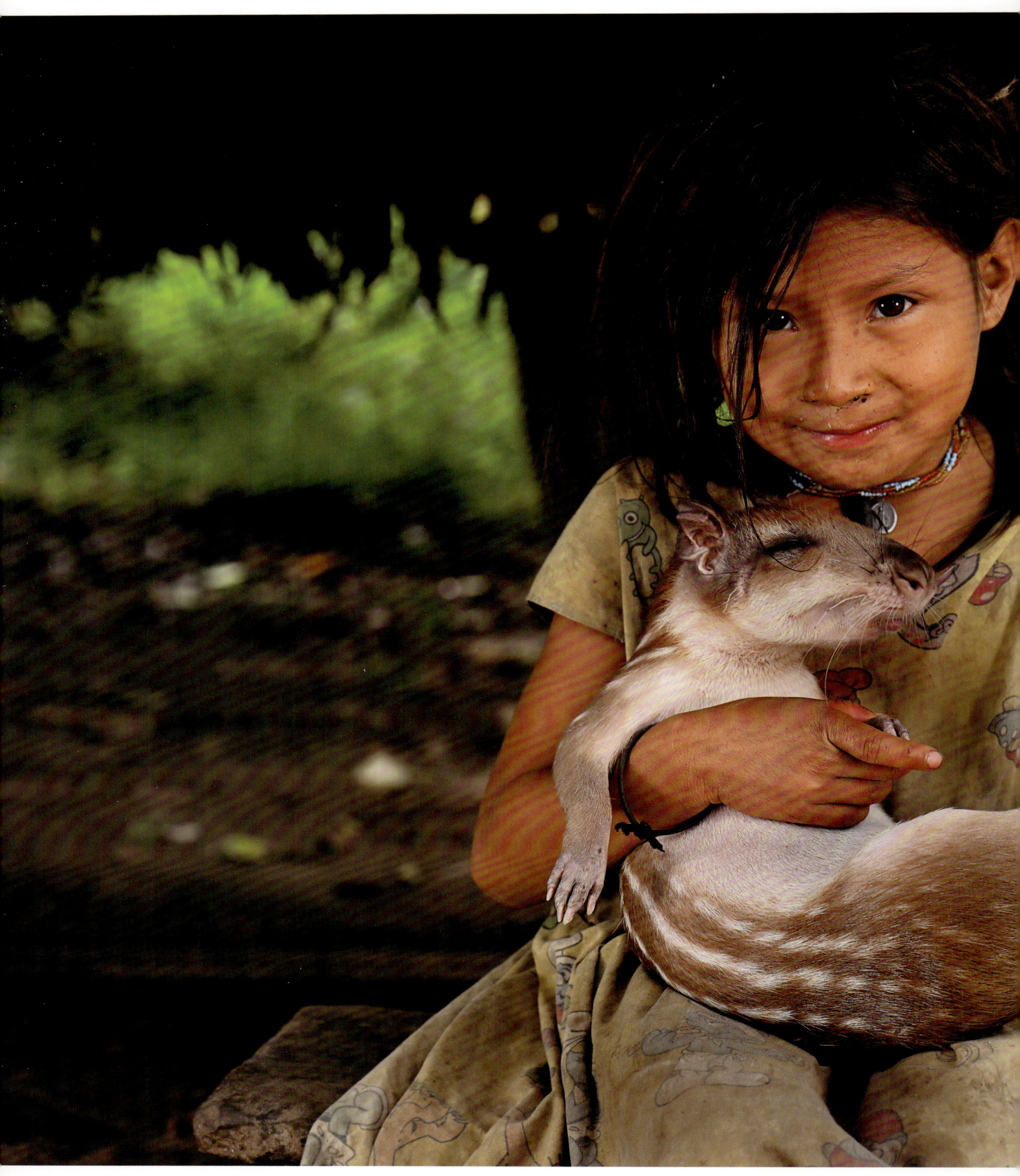

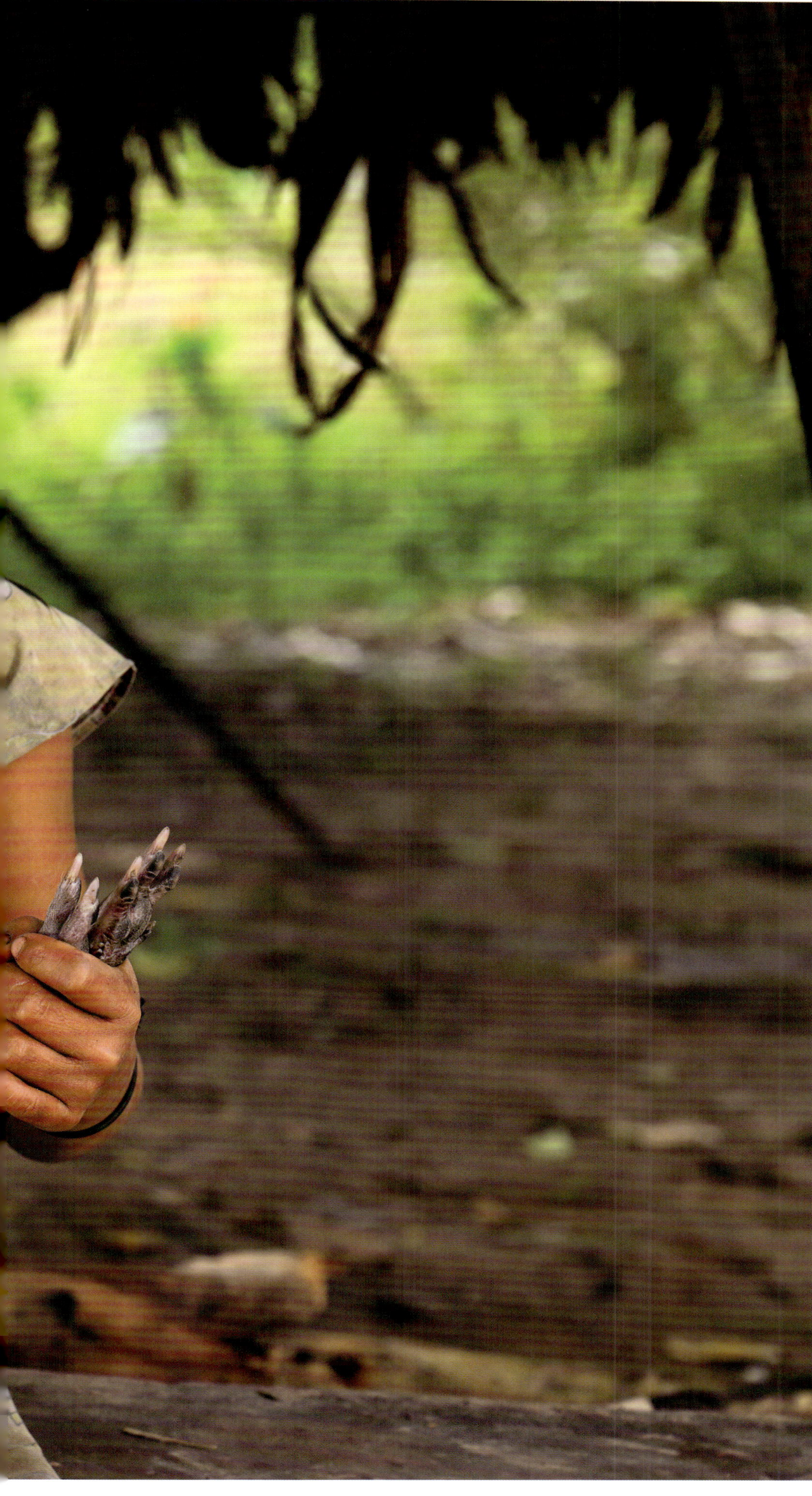

A girl holds her pet paca in the village of La Asunta, located deep in the heart of Bolivia's Isiboro Sécure National Park and Indigenous Territory (TIPNIS), now home to more than 12,000 people from three Indigenous groups (the Tsimané, Yuracaré, and Mojeño-Trinitario). They have lived here for thousands of years.

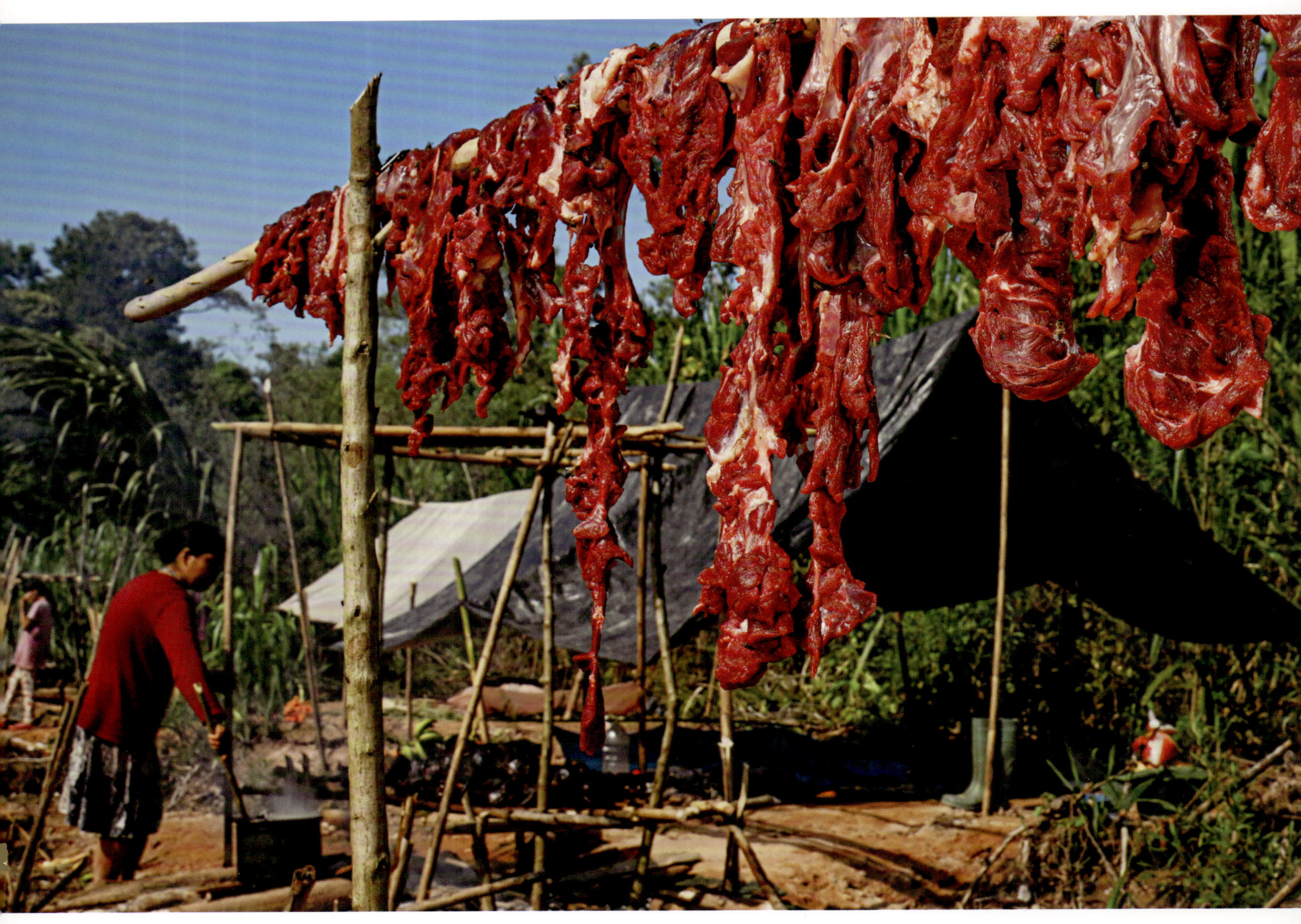

ABOVE: Tapir meat dries in the sun at a remote hunting camp located a few days' travel by canoe from the village of Oromomo. During the wet season, tapirs and monkeys are sought after, while fish becomes the dominant protein staple during dry conditions.

OPPOSITE: The nearest supermarket is weeks away by canoe, and subsistence hunting is the only way for Indigenous people to consistently and affordably access protein. Bows are the most common hunting tool, and different types of arrows target different species.

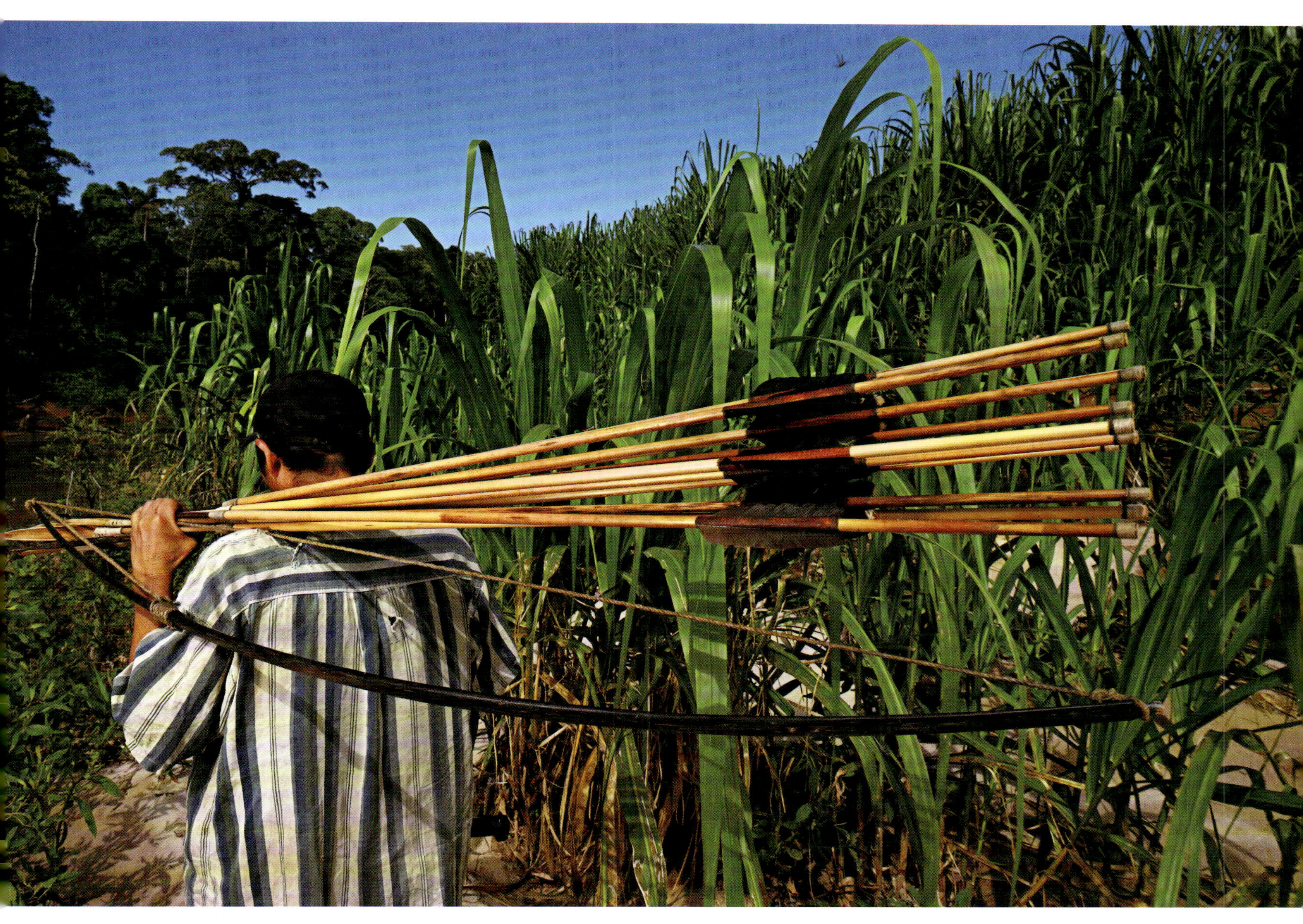

PAGES 72–73: A pair of pale-winged trumpeters *(Psophia leucoptera)* inspect a pile of feathers from which Demecio will choose just the right ones to give his arrows stability and greater accuracy in flight. Local people frequently keep and tame these birds because they are thought to kill snakes and for their ability to spot predators and give loud alarm calls.

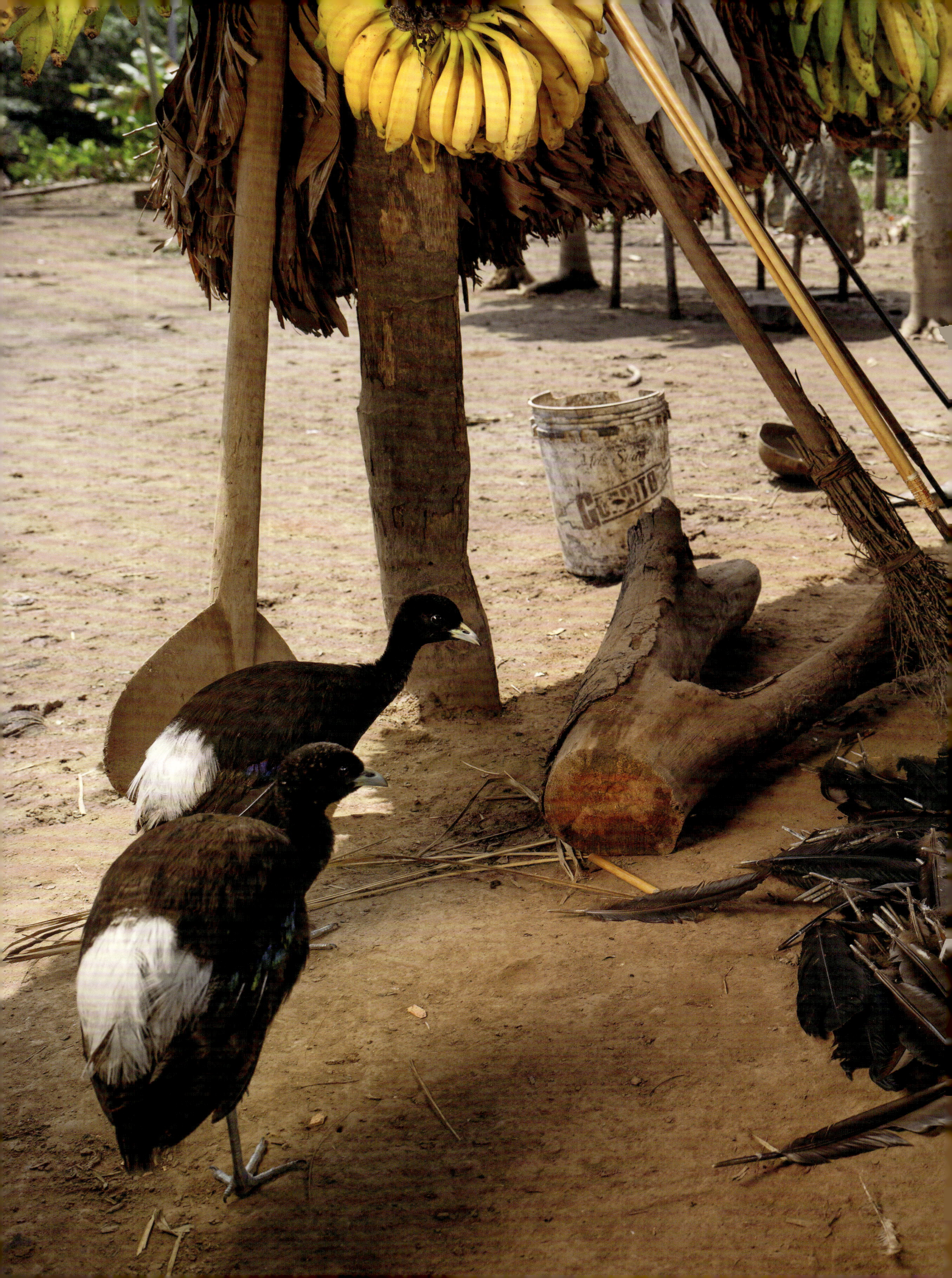

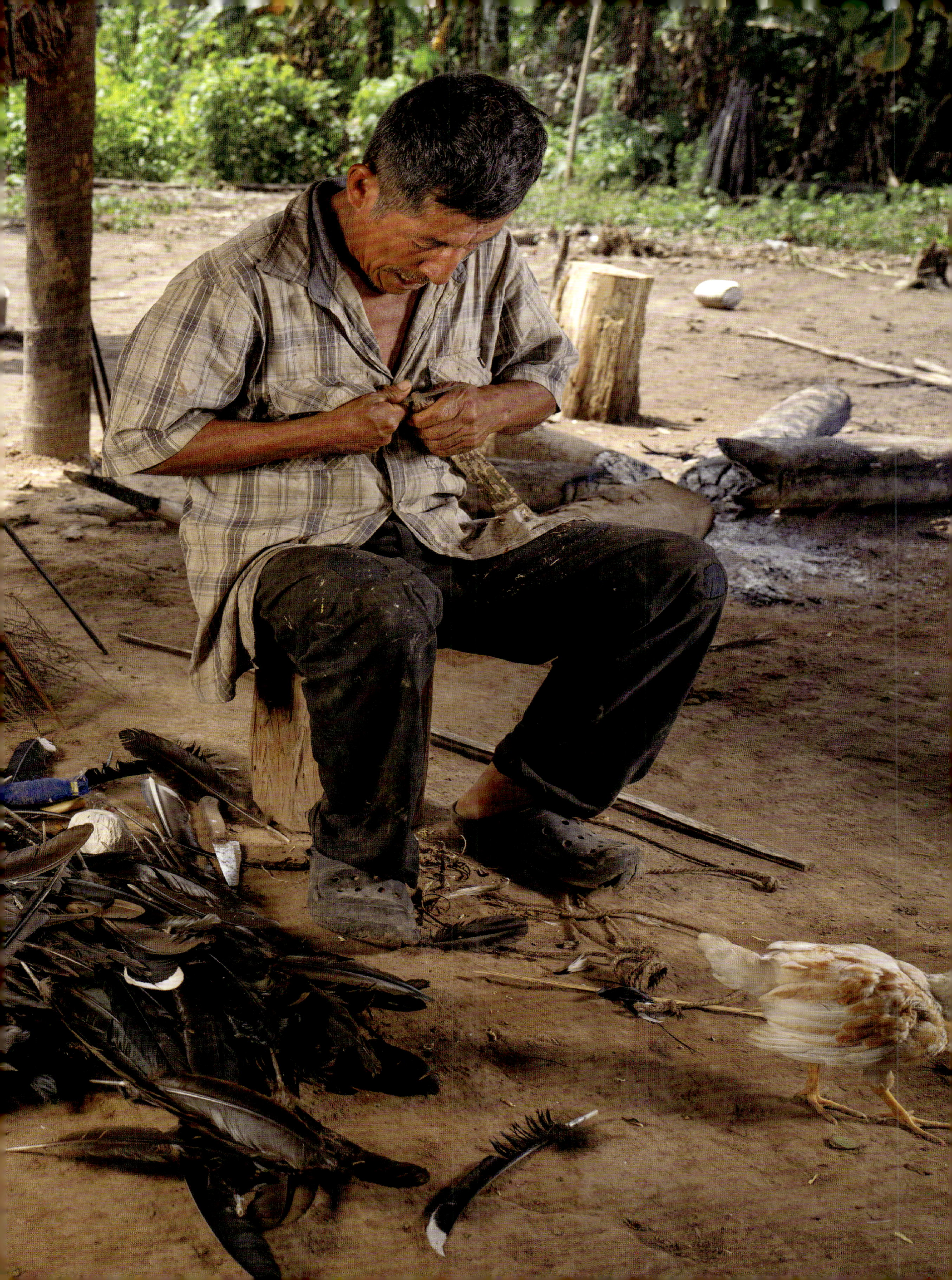

Trini Cari hunts for sábalos *(Prochilodus lineatus)*, which migrate in the millions upriver to the headwaters to spawn every year. They provide an important food source for predatory fish, terrestrial animals, and people. Despite the river almost turning solid with fish during this migration, it takes great skill to hunt them with bow and arrow.

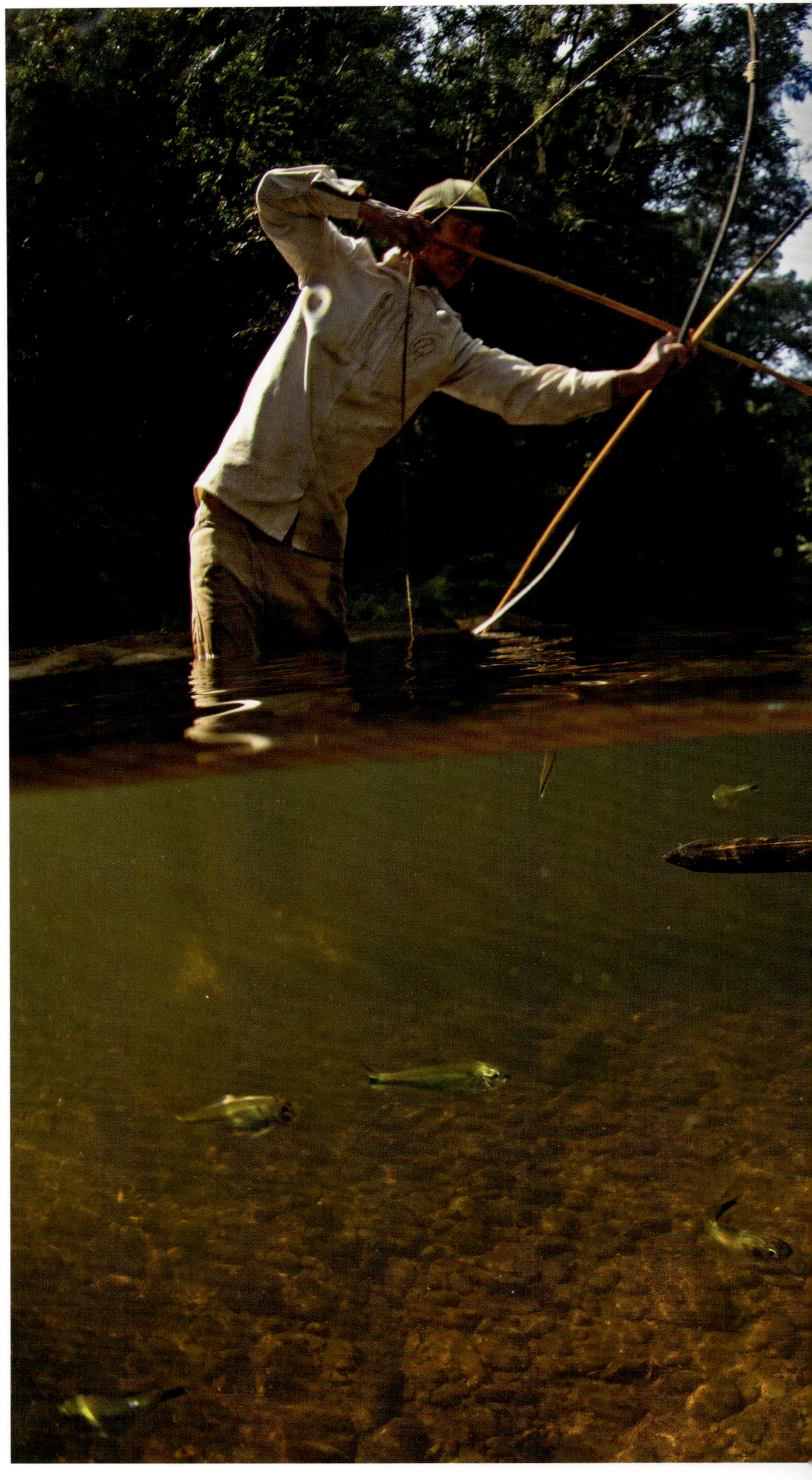

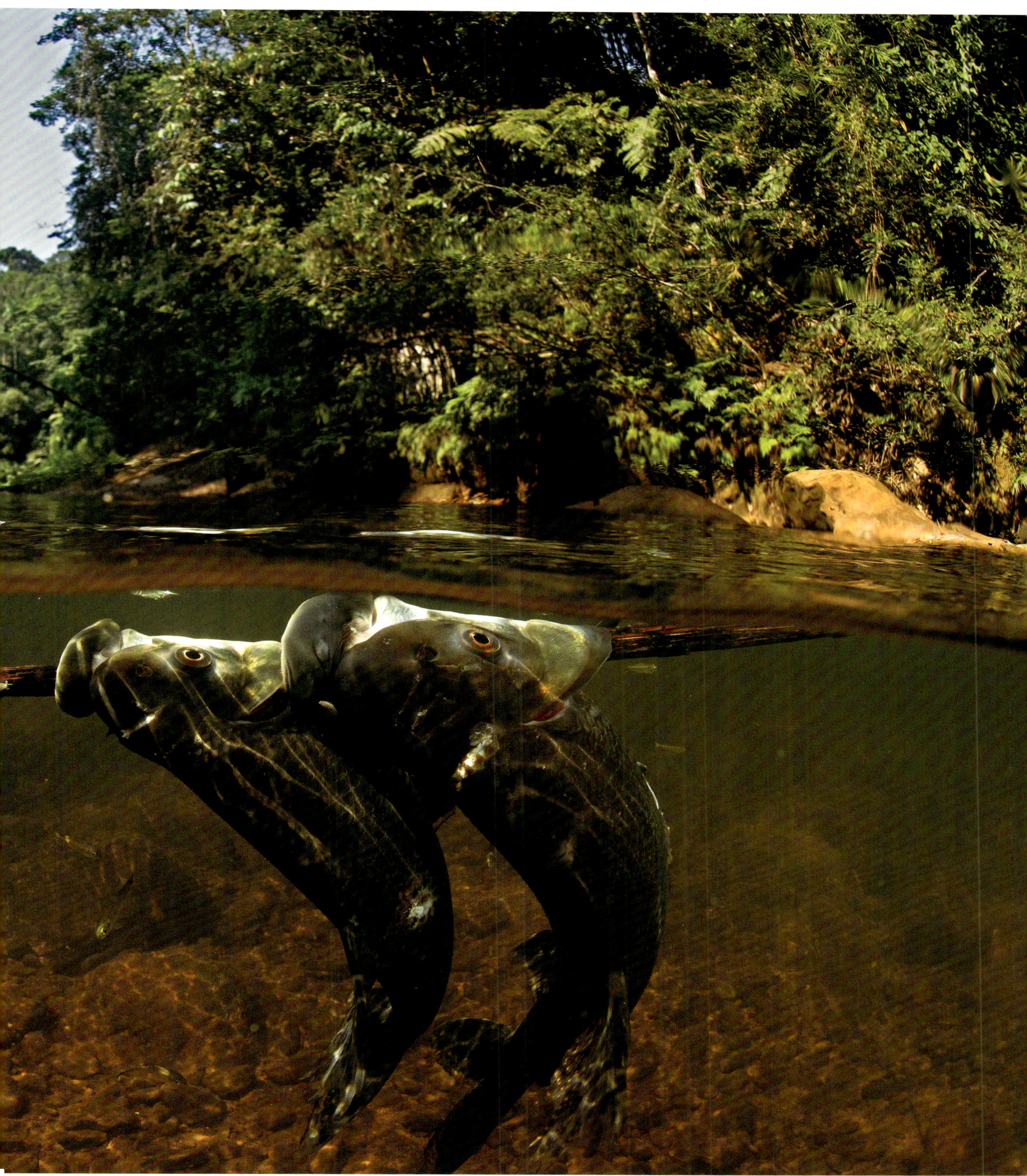

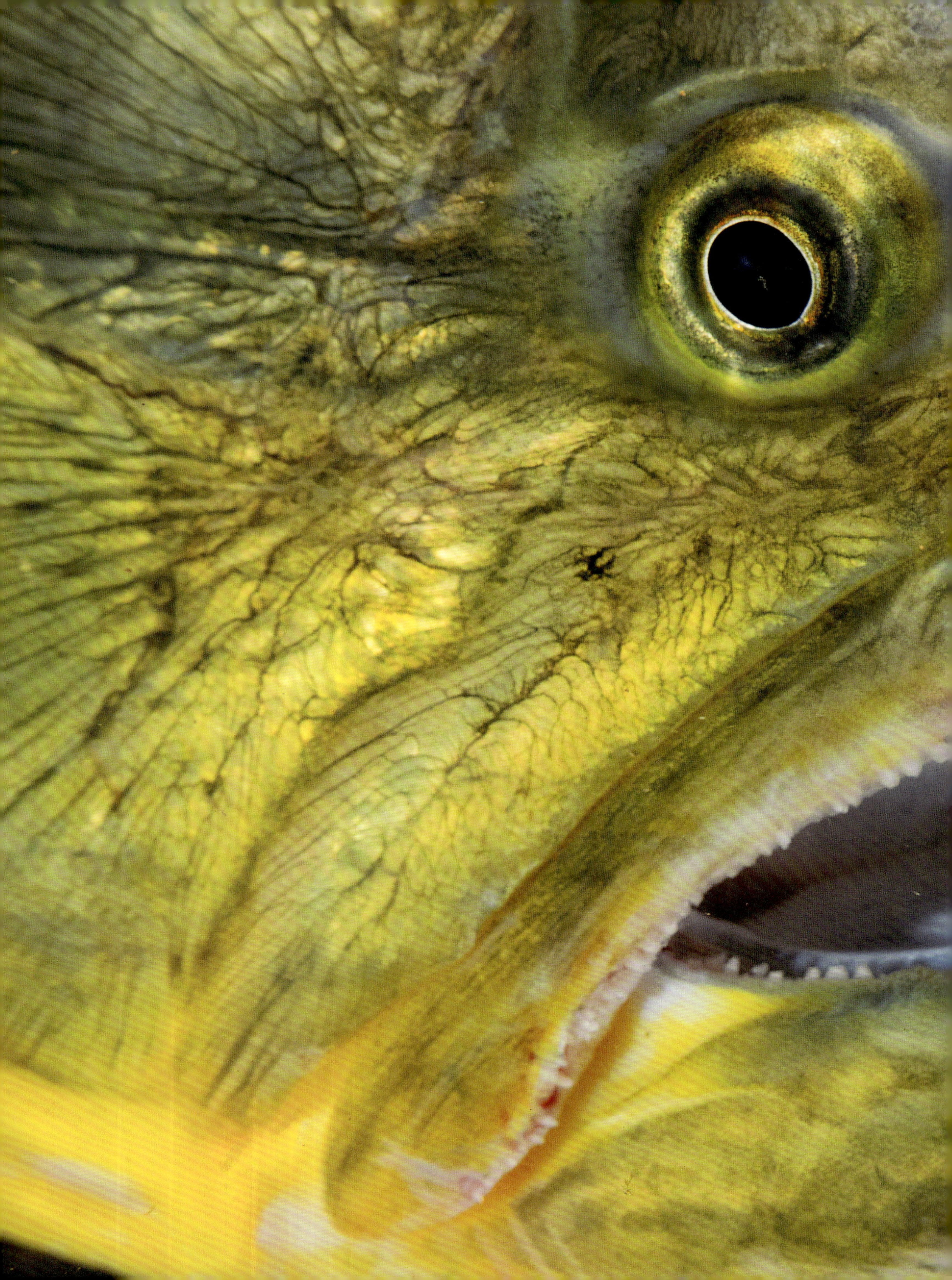

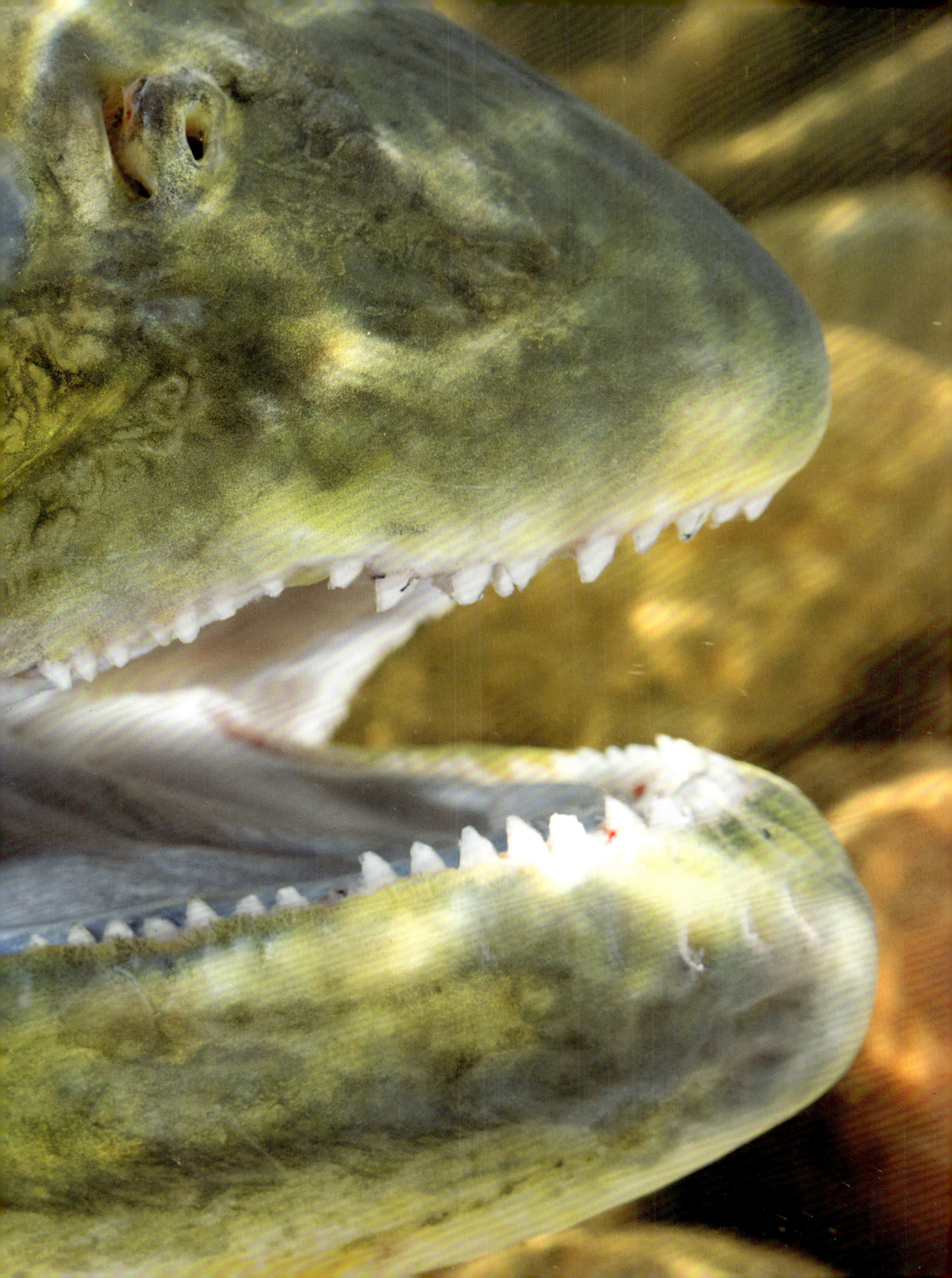

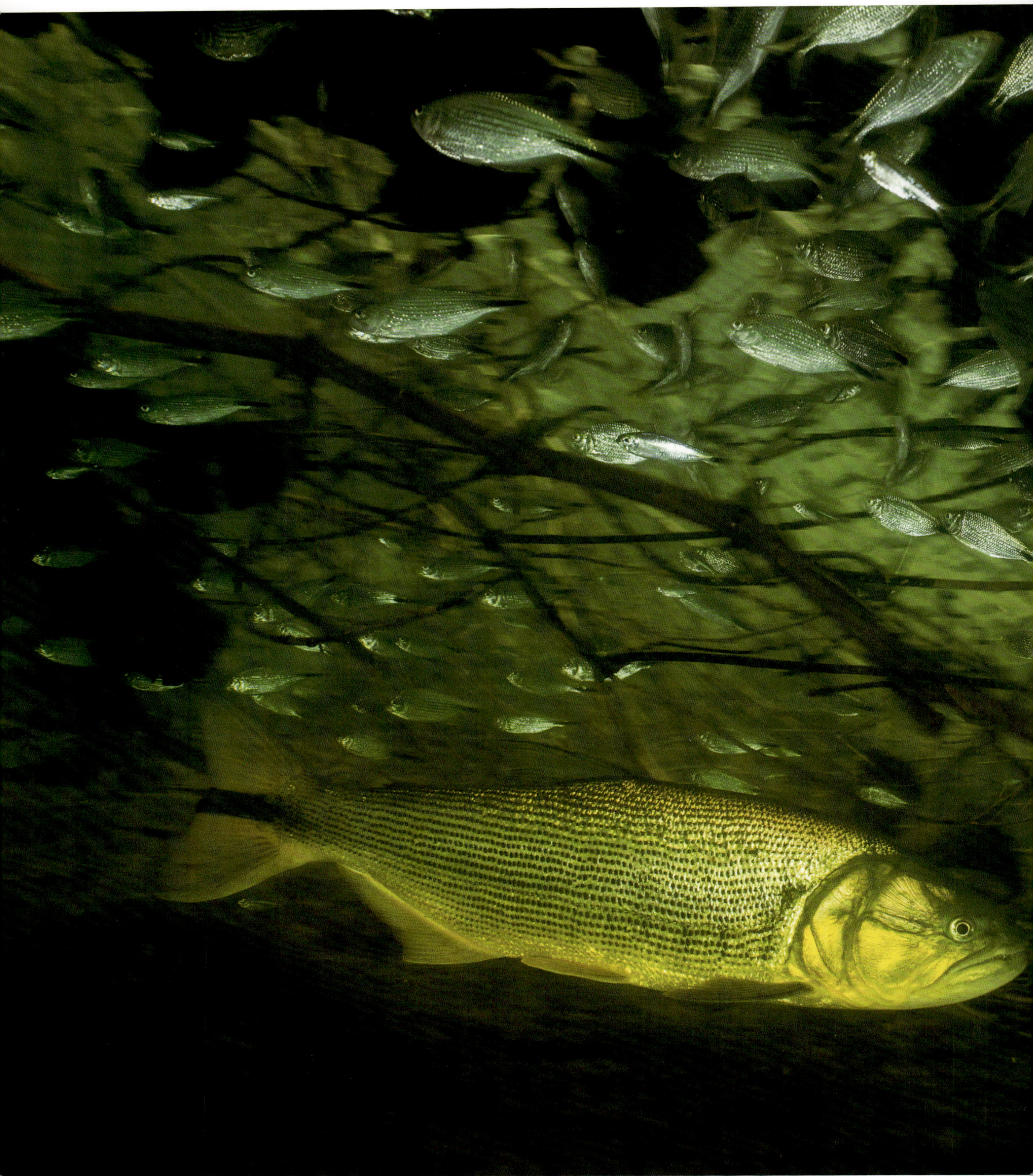

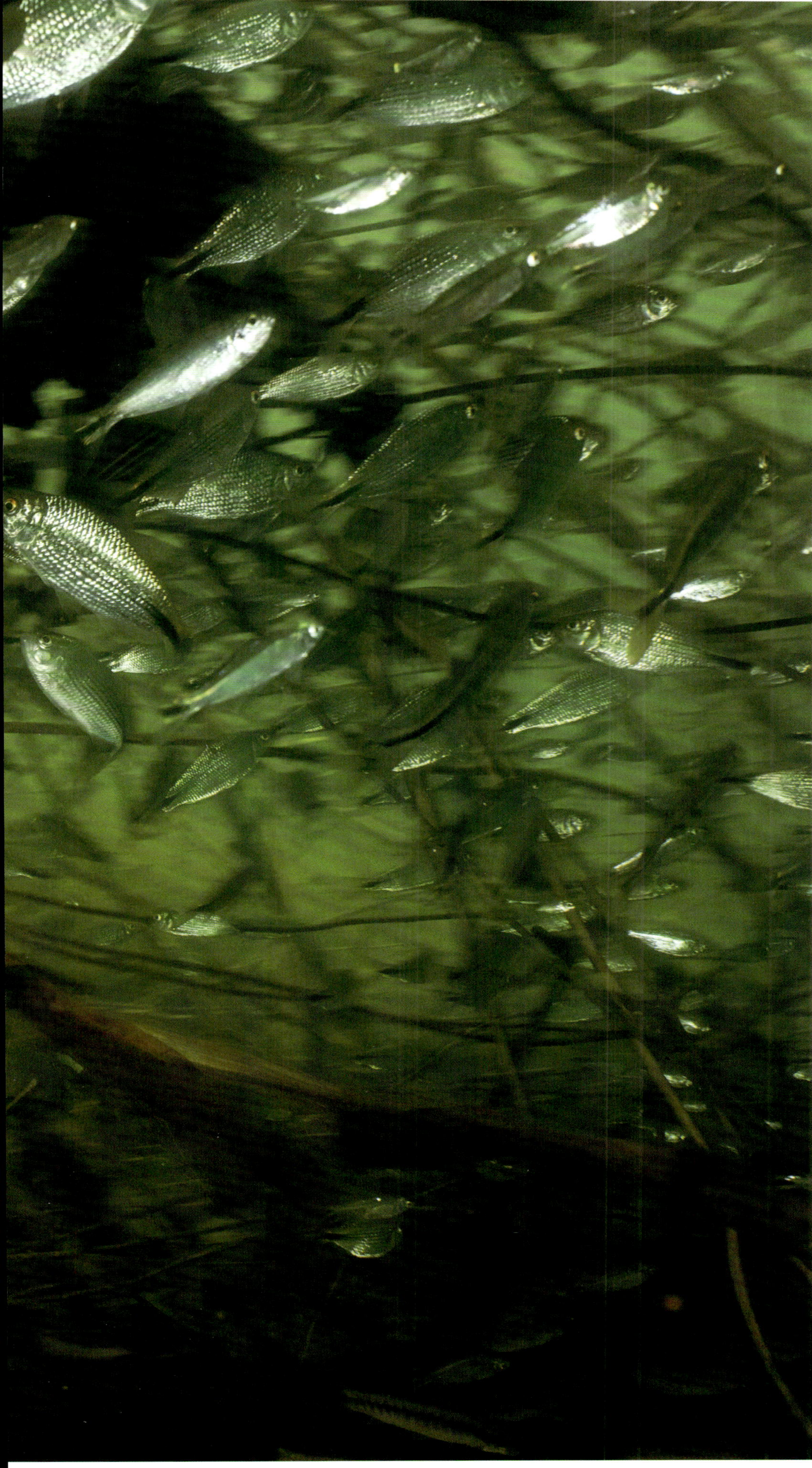

A golden dorado *(Salminus brasiliensis),* also known as a river tiger, attacks a school of small baitfish sheltering among the branches of submerged trees. While primarily a piscivore, golden dorados have also been recorded feeding on small vertebrates such as rodents, lizards, and birds. Because of their large size and prodigious strength, their only predators are jaguars and large caimans. In the Amazon watershed, the species is restricted to the Mamoré River Basin, which includes the headwaters of the Sécure and Pluma Rivers in Bolivia.

PAGES 76–77: The golden dorado is a four-foot-long (1 m), 75-pound (34 kg) predatory fish. These fish sit atop the aquatic food chain and can attain the ripe old age of 15. Every year they migrate upstream into the headwaters of the Eva Eva Mountains to spawn. The Tsimané people credit dorados with helping them hunt by herding shoals of sábalos into the shallows where they are easier to target.

The level of pristineness in these Bolivian headwaters is likely unparalleled in the Amazon Basin. My guide, Roycer Herbi, from the village of Oromomo, says that the jungle defends itself with thunder, lightning, and dangerous, fast-flowing water. Felix, chief of the village of La Asunta, adds that their ancestors never ascended into the headwaters because they feared the many dangerous animals that live there.

PAGES 82–83: A sábalo grazes algae and detritus from the riverbed, leaving in its wake a distinct trail of markings in the form of so-called "sábalo kisses." Despite its lowly status on the food web, the sábalo is without doubt the most important fish in the Bolivian headwaters of the Amazon River, nourishing river and rainforest predators and Indigenous people in equal measure.

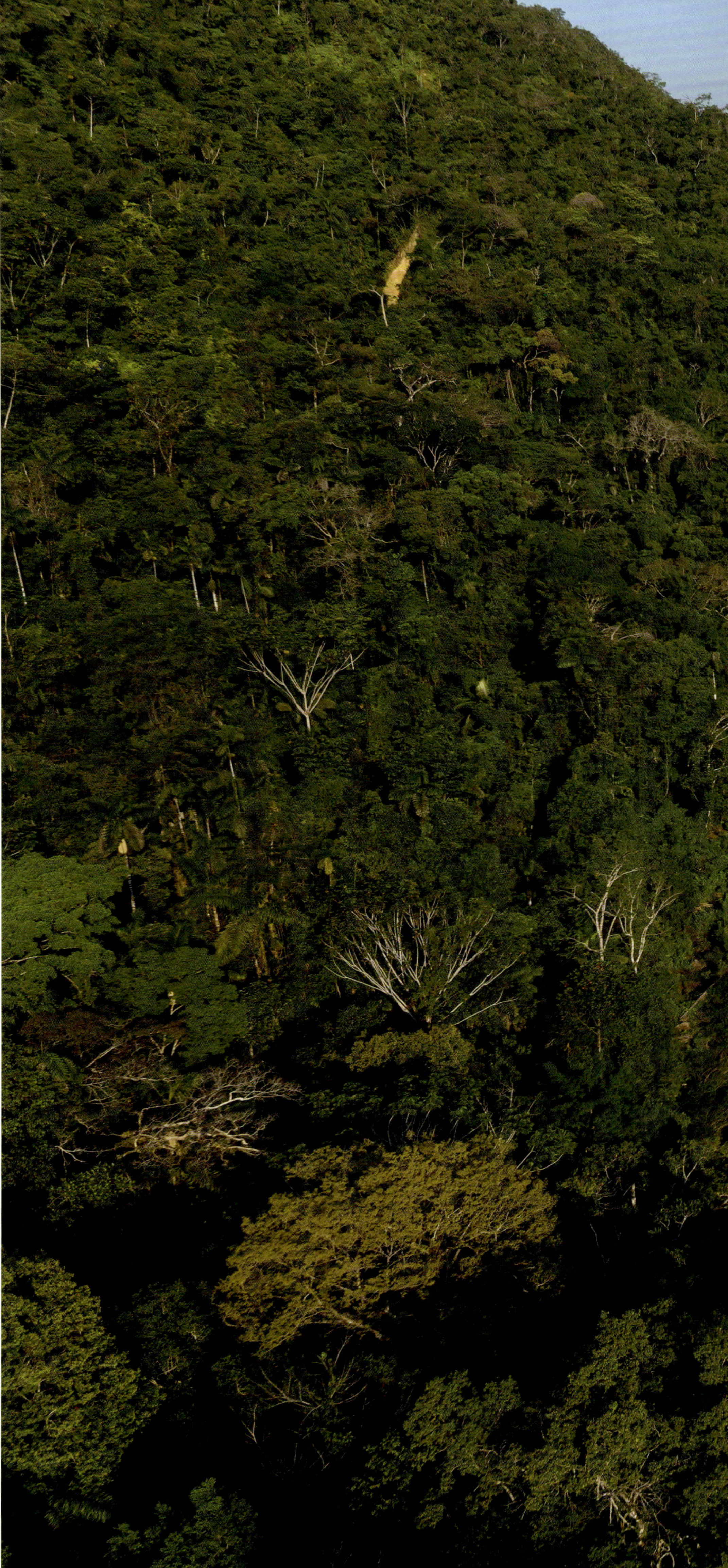

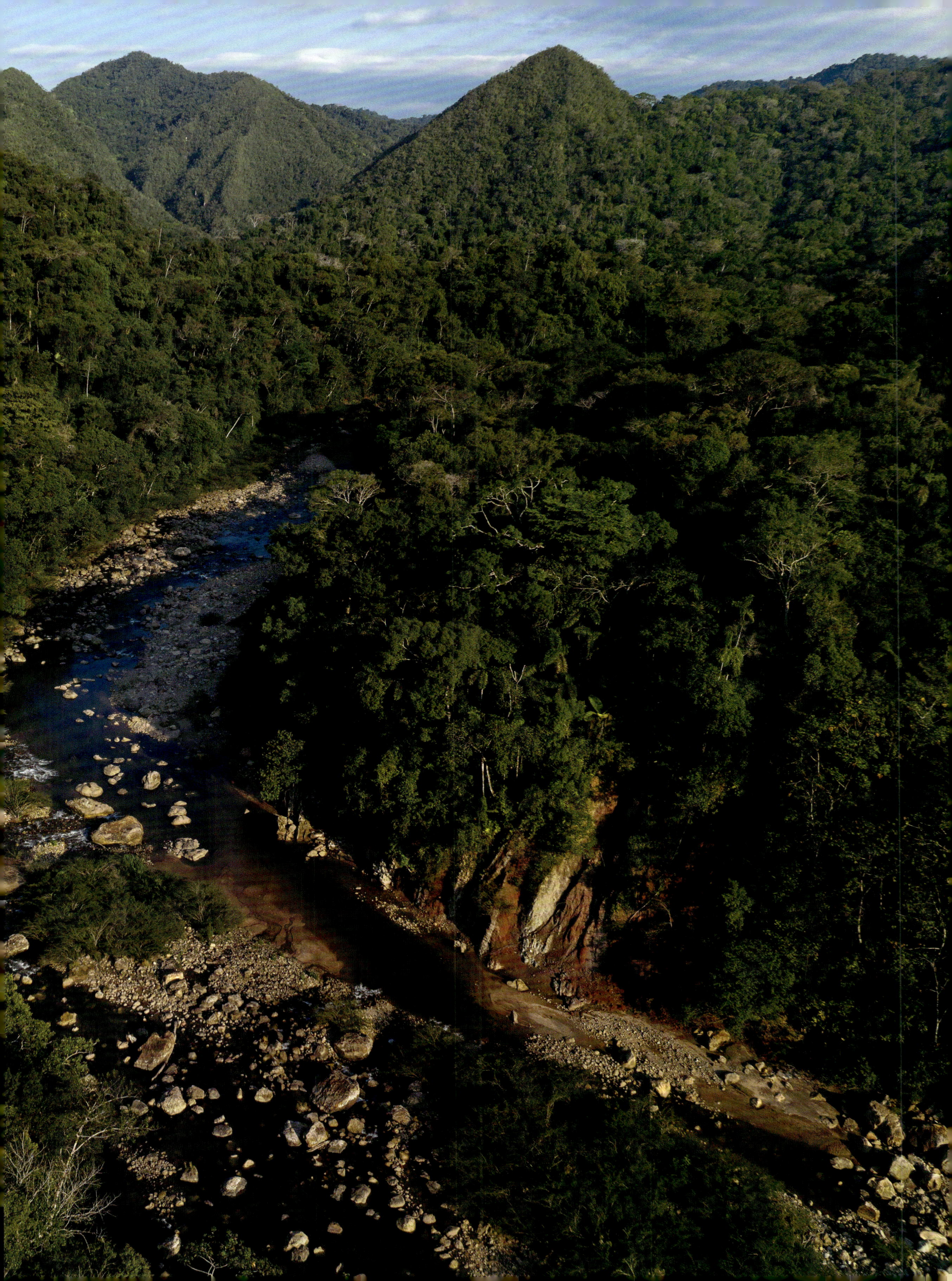

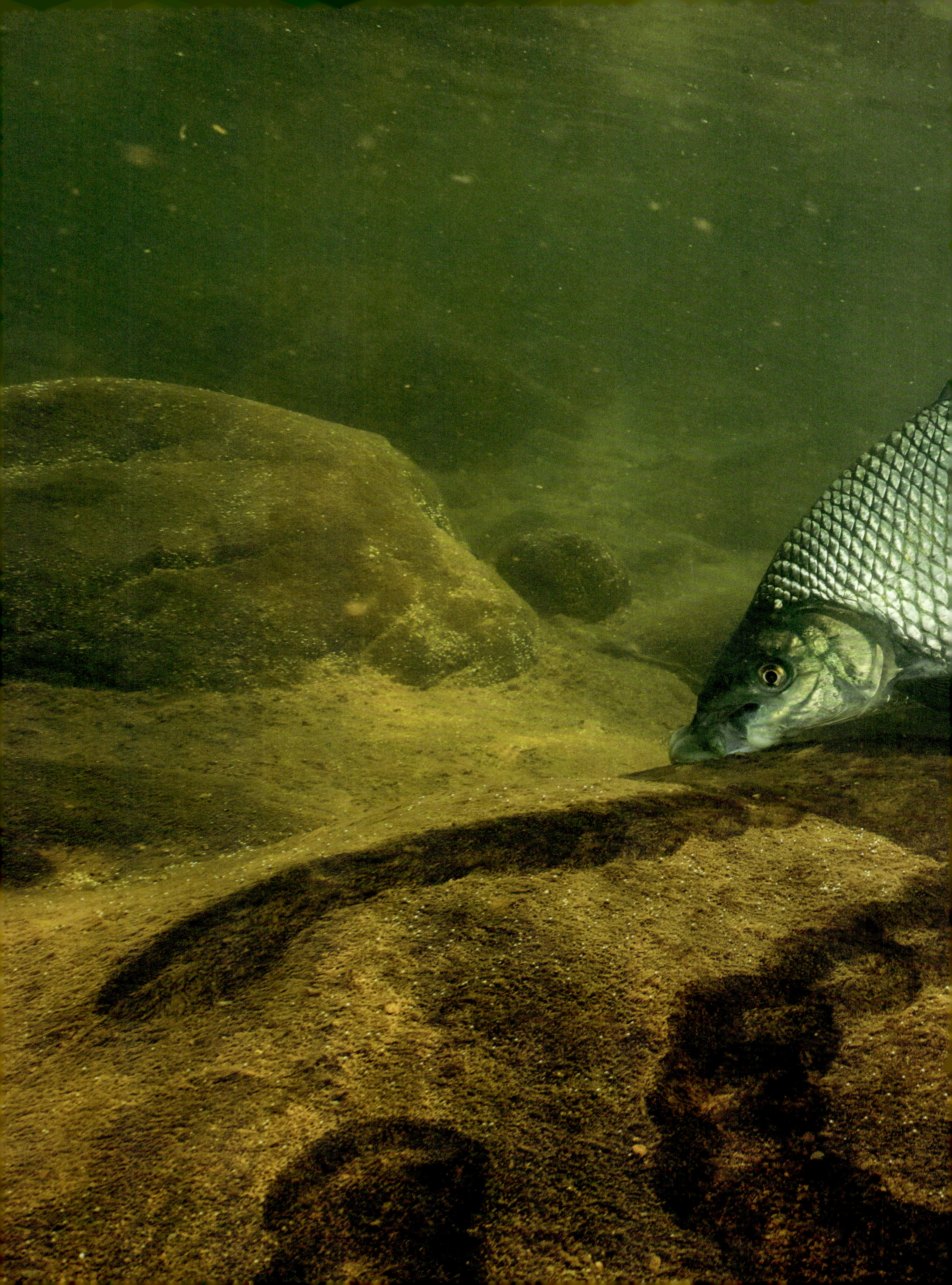

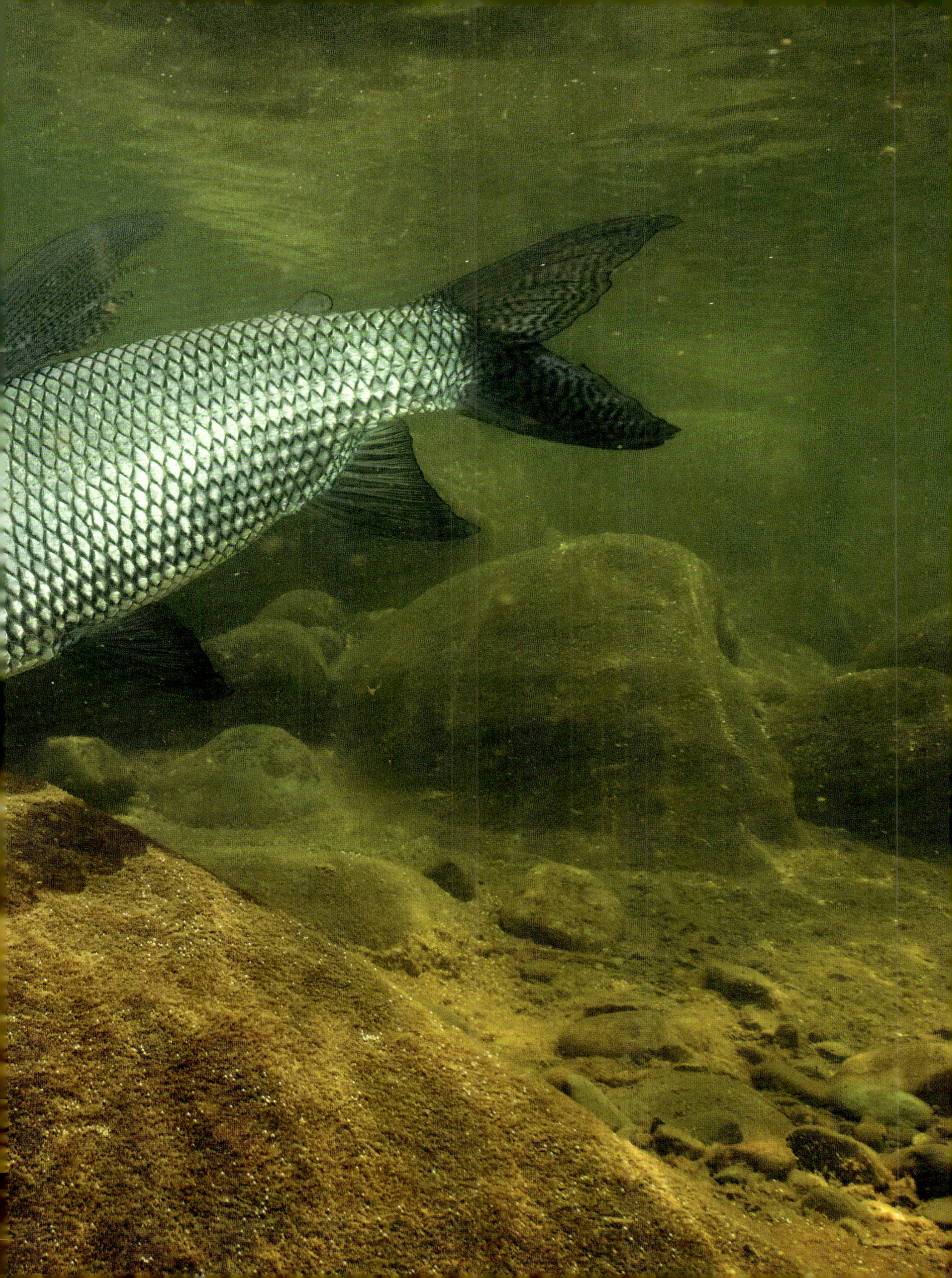

A school of pirapitingas *(Piaractus brachypomus)*, a large species of pacu related to piranhas, swims in a headwater stream. Known also as red-bellied pacu because of juveniles' colored underbellies, pirapitingas have two rows of sharp, flat teeth and can reach up to three feet (0.9 m) and weigh as much as 55 pounds (25 kg) as adults. In some deep pools, the schools of pacus can be so dense that they block out the sun.

PAGES 86–87: Marcelo Pérez and Untamed Angling have been running catch-and-release fly-fishing trips along the lower reaches of the rivers in partnership with the local Indigenous communities for more than a decade. He recently introduced helicopter fly-fishing expeditions into the most remote reaches of the headwaters. Fly-fishers from around the world are attracted to this remote wilderness for the chance to catch and release a golden dorado, bringing in half a million dollars in total yearly revenue for the local Indigenous communities, funding ranger stations to guard against illegal activities, and creating jobs outside extractive industries like logging.

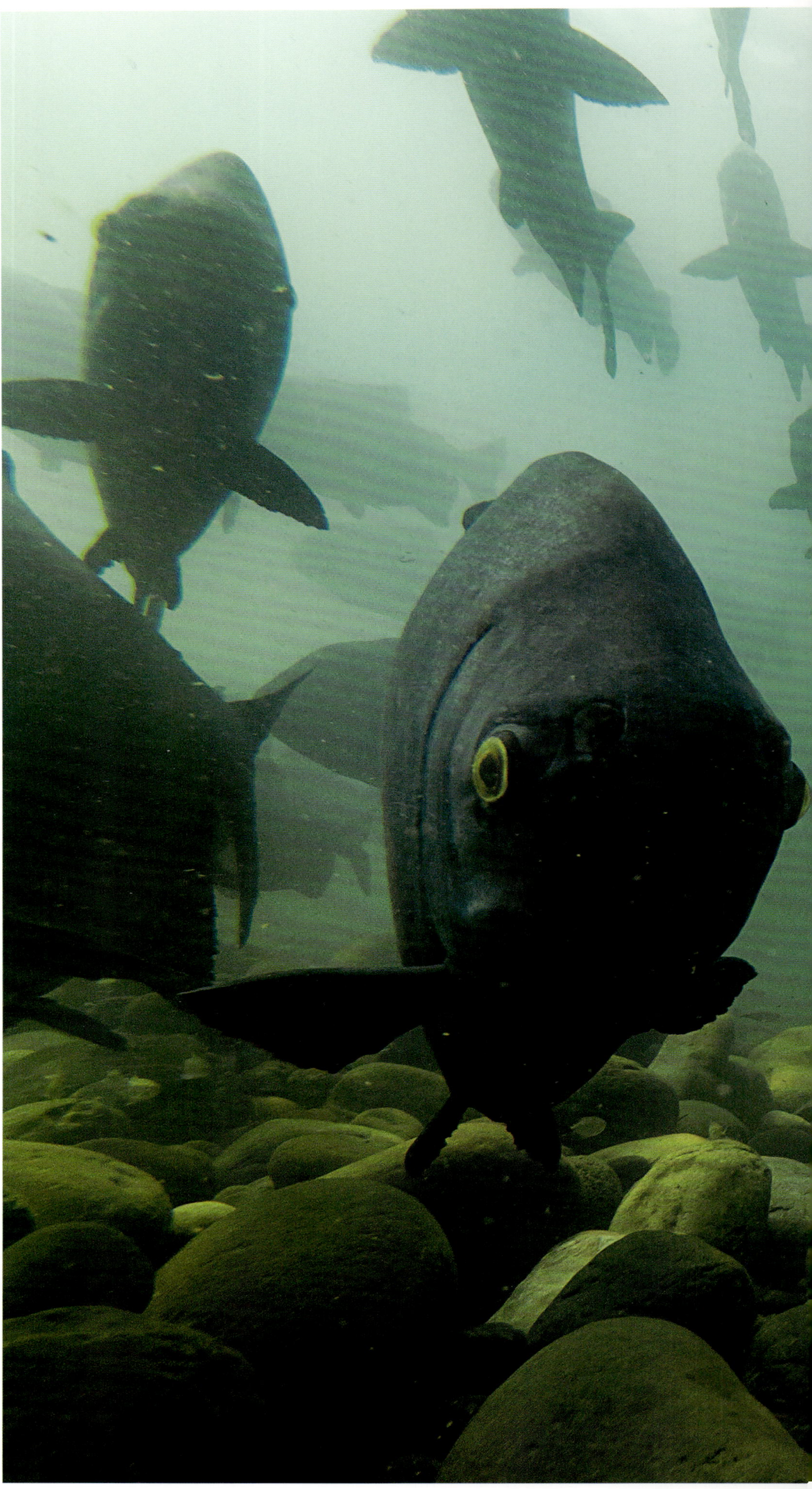

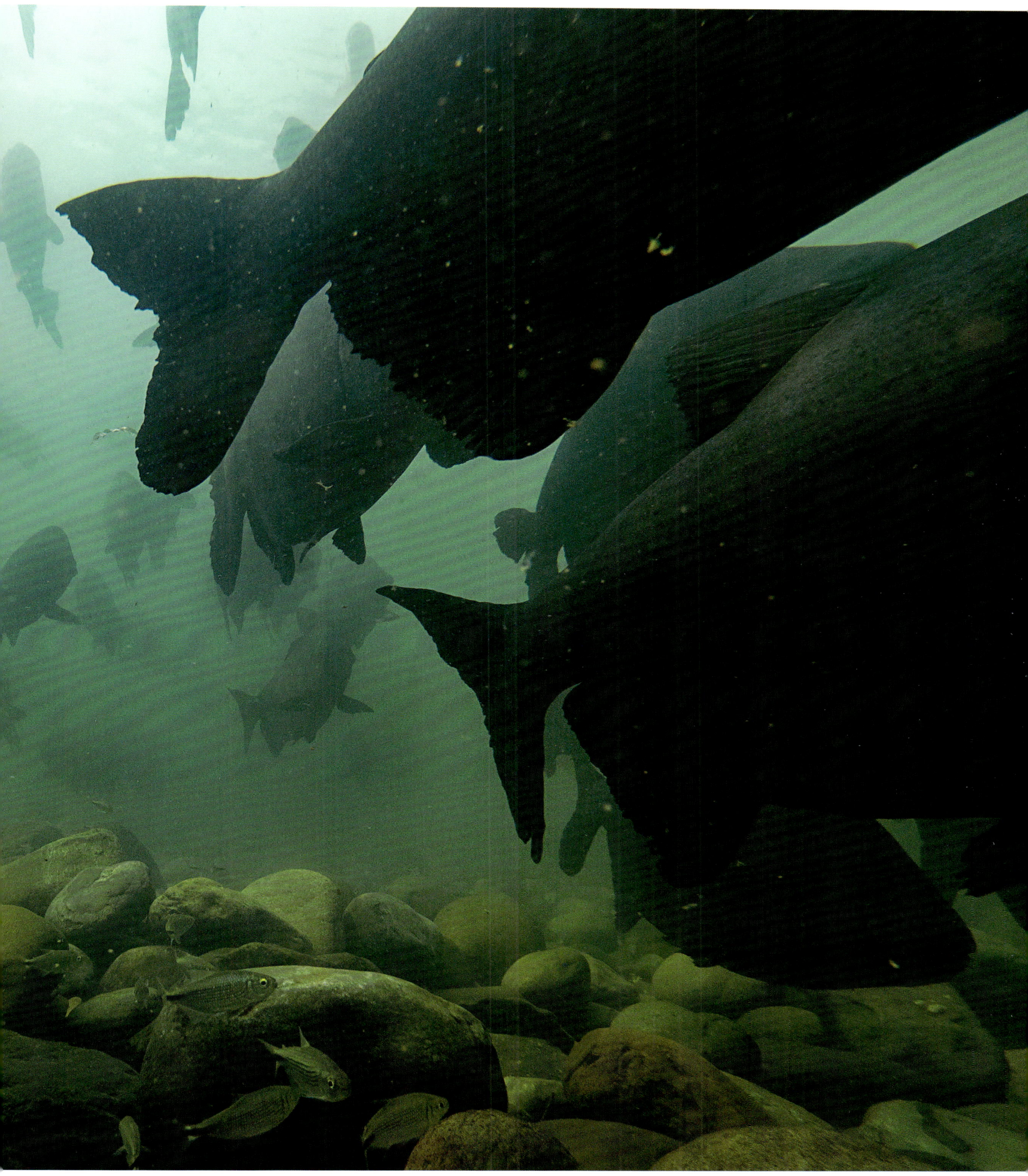

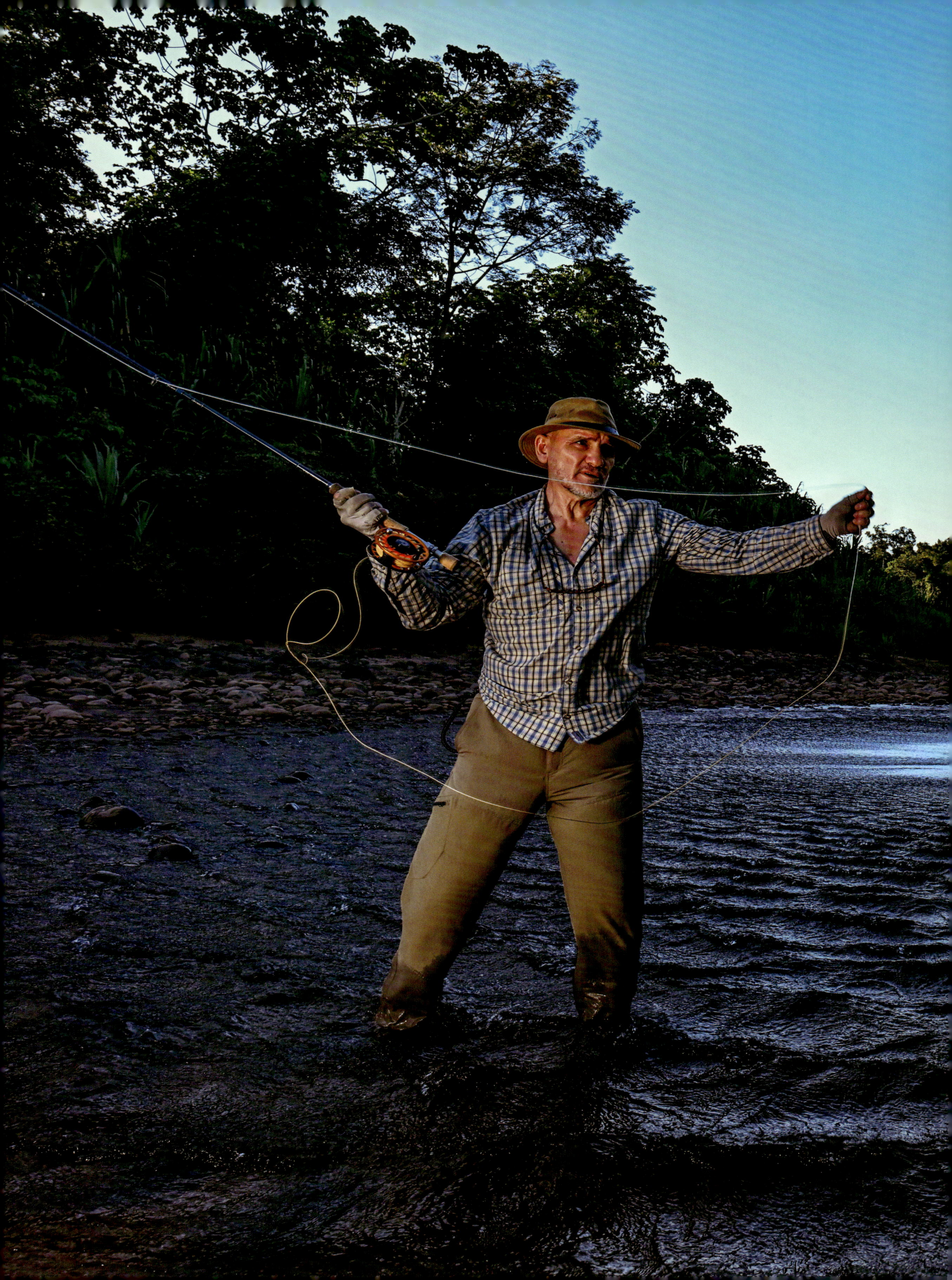

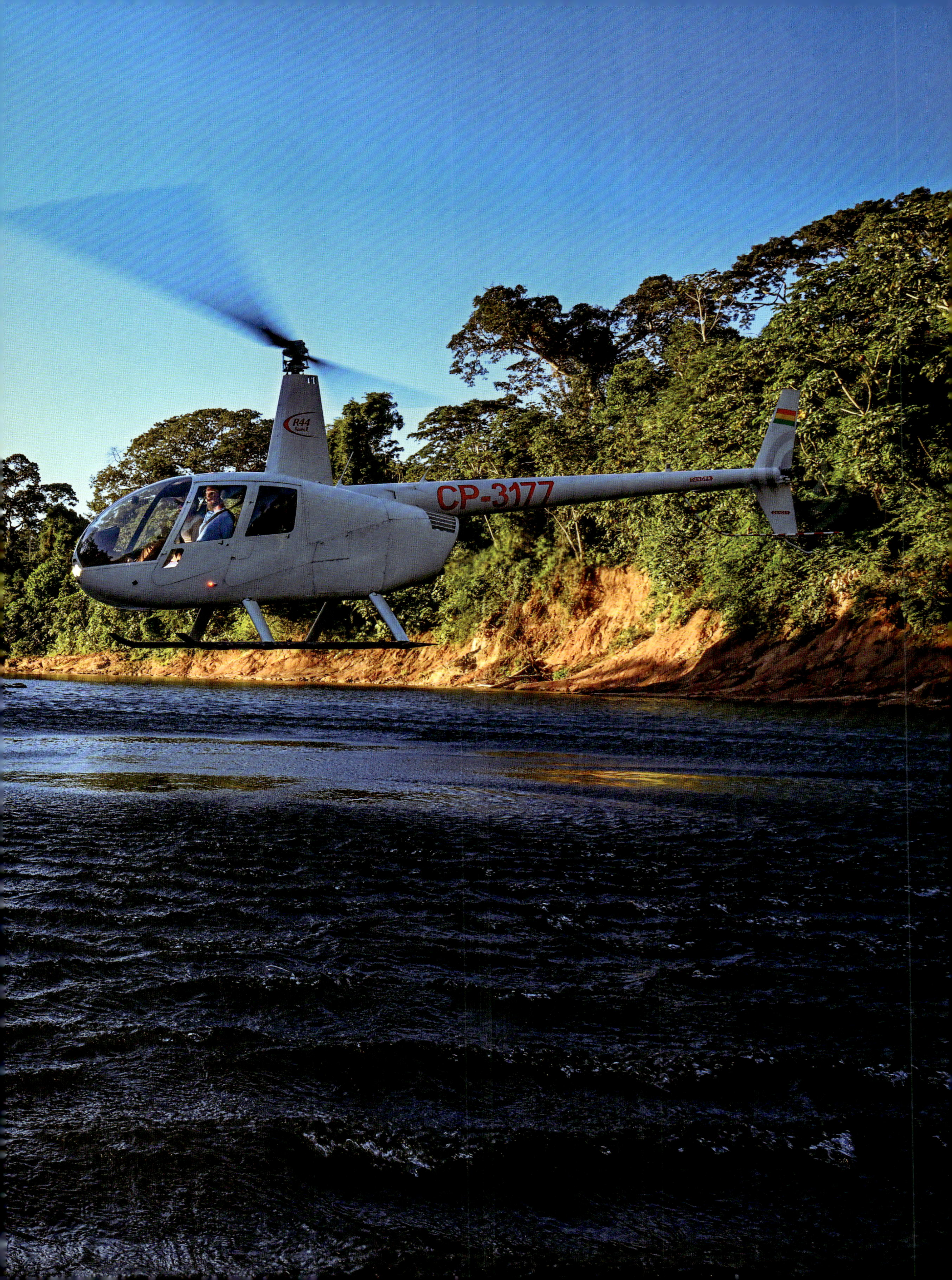
R44
CP-3177

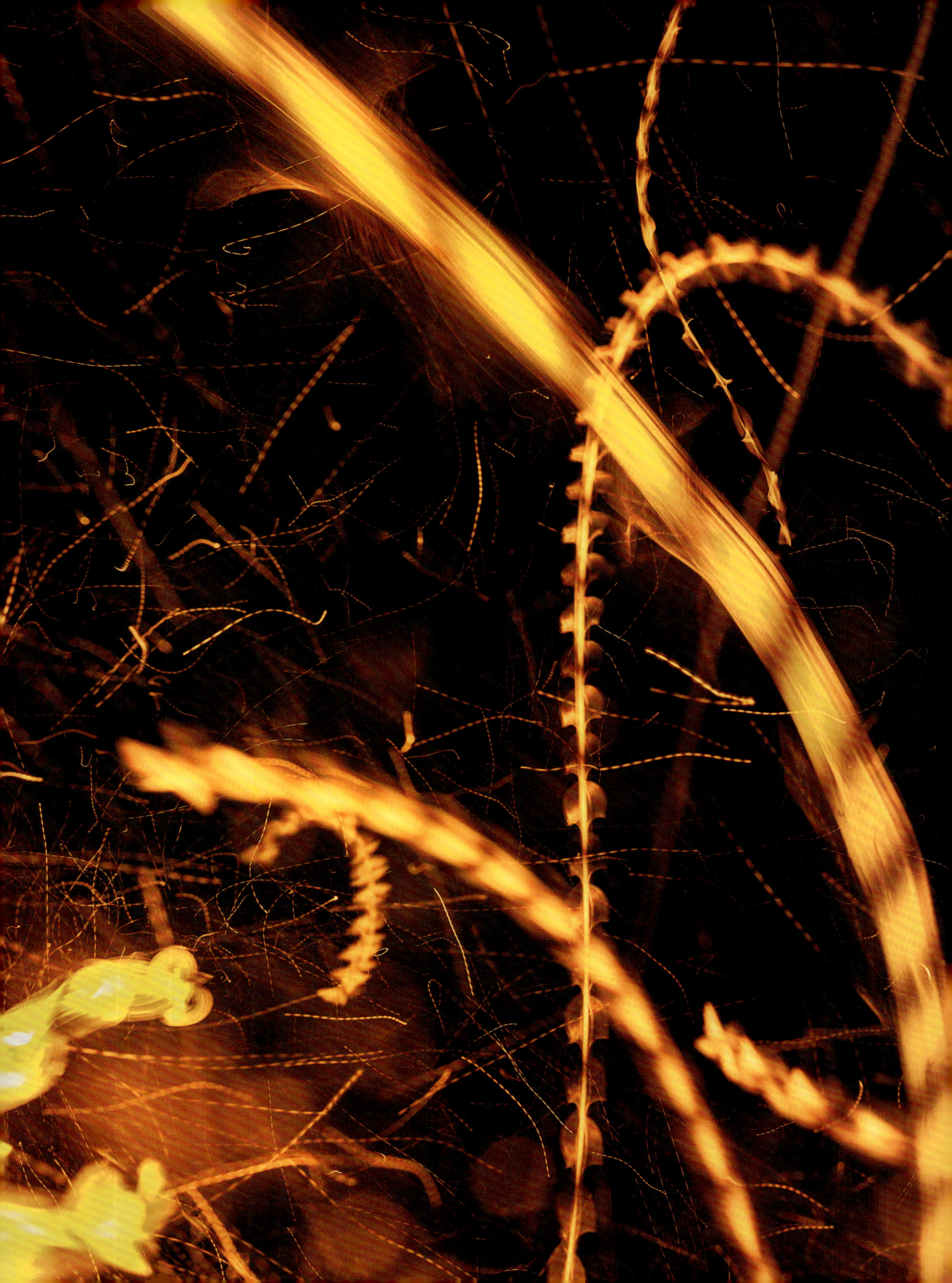

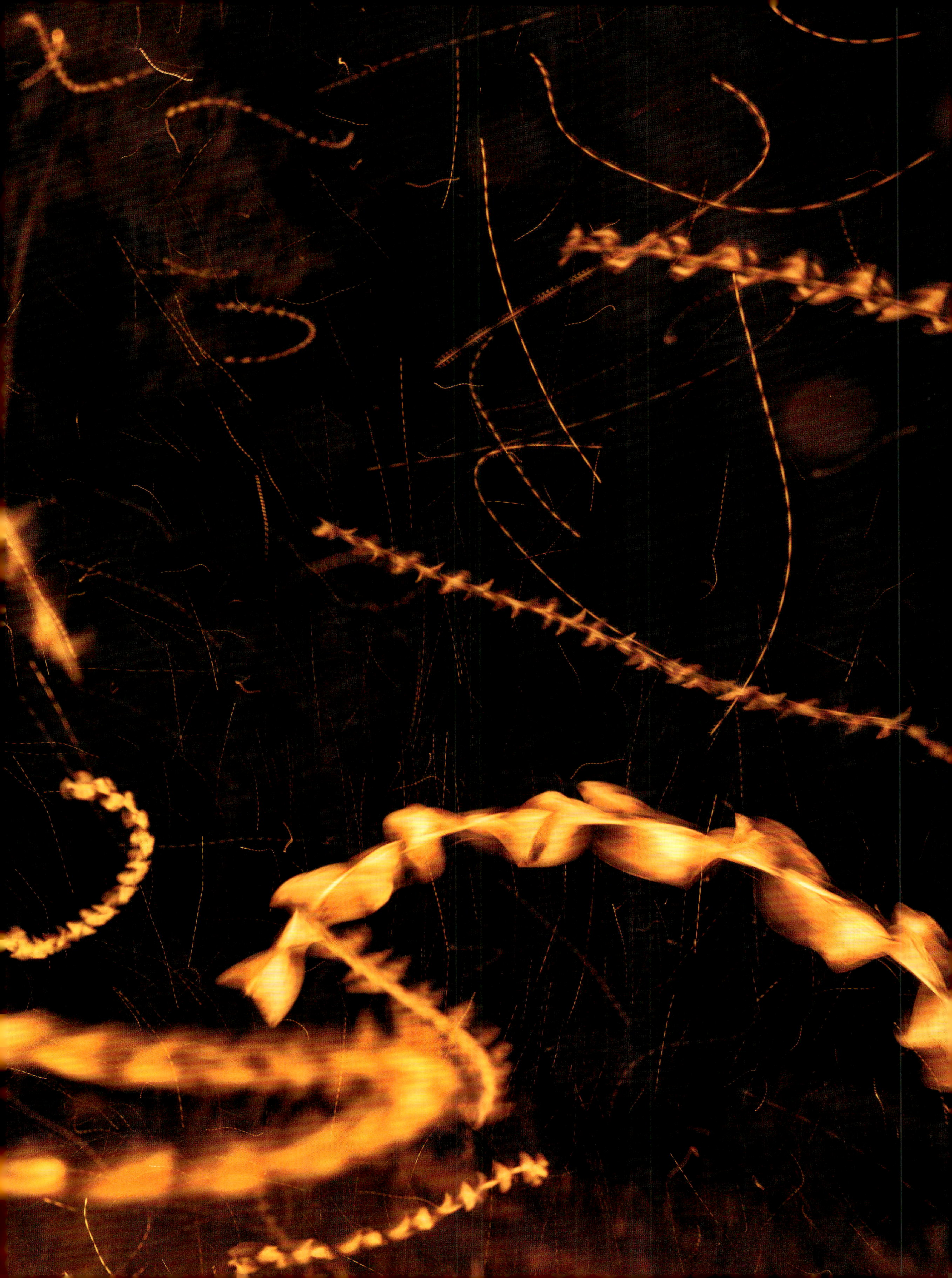

Cuvier's dwarf caiman *(Paleosuchus palpebrosus)*—first described by French zoologist Georges Cuvier in 1807—is to this day the smallest of all crocodilians in the Americas. What it lacks in size, it makes up for in body armor, with thick, bony bases on its dermal scales providing some protection against predators like jaguars and large anacondas.

PAGES 88–89: A long-exposure frame captures the glowing flight trails of cicadas, moths, and mayflies emerging at night in Bolivia's Isiboro Sécure National Park and Indigenous Territory (TIPNIS). Little is known about the insects of this part of the Amazon, but scientists are hopeful that biodiversity surveys will soon begin to collect data on bugs and other fauna and flora.

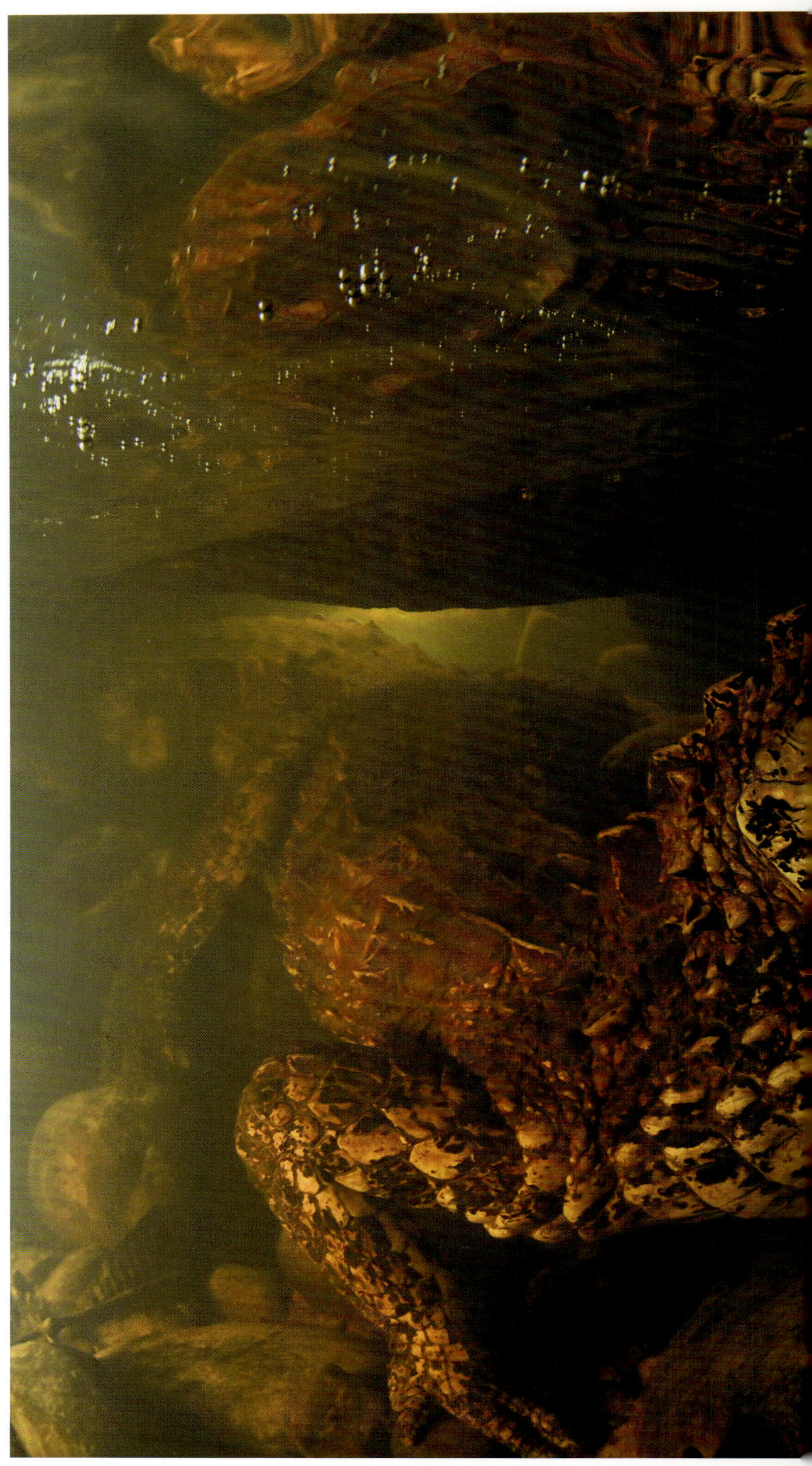

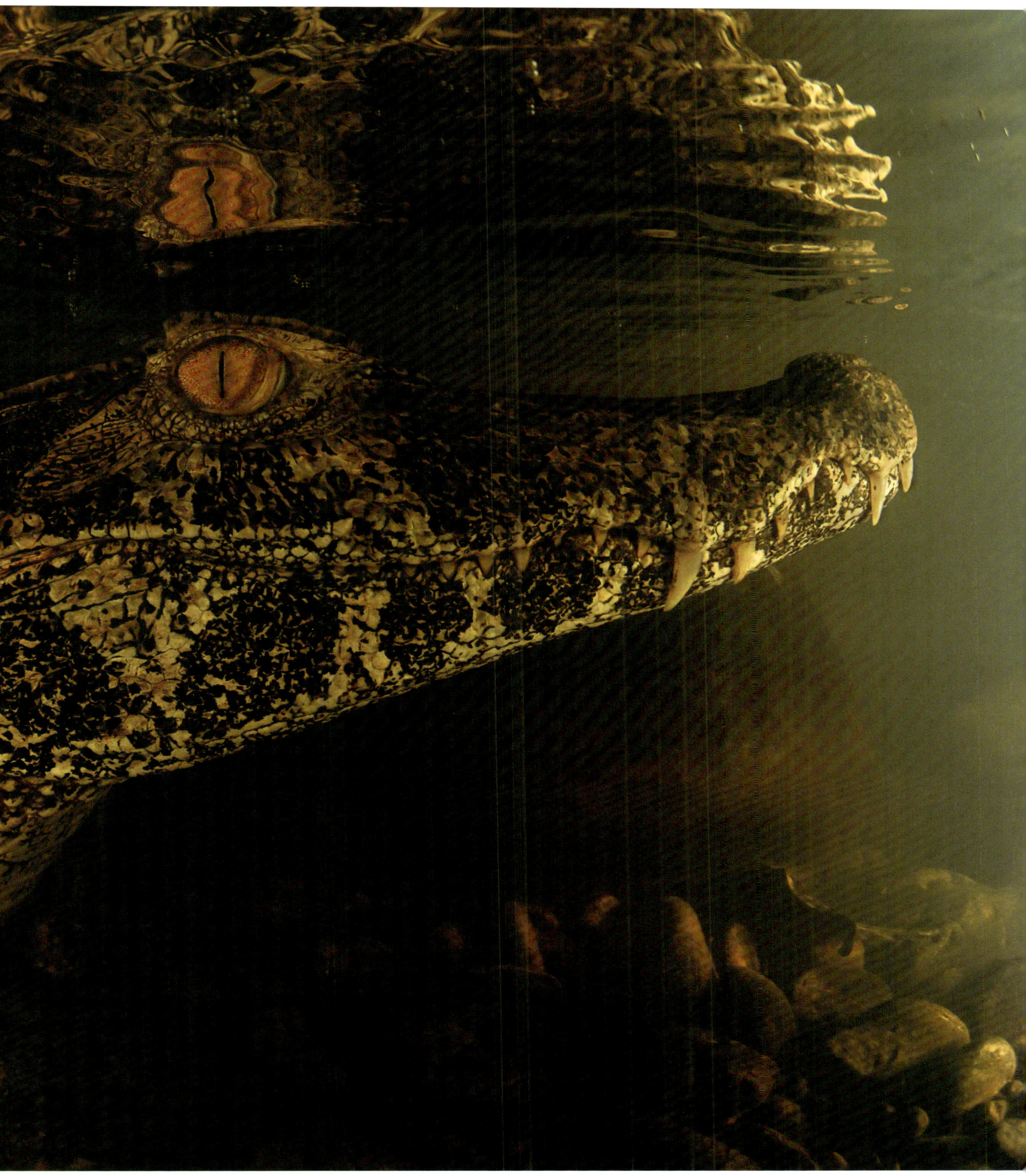

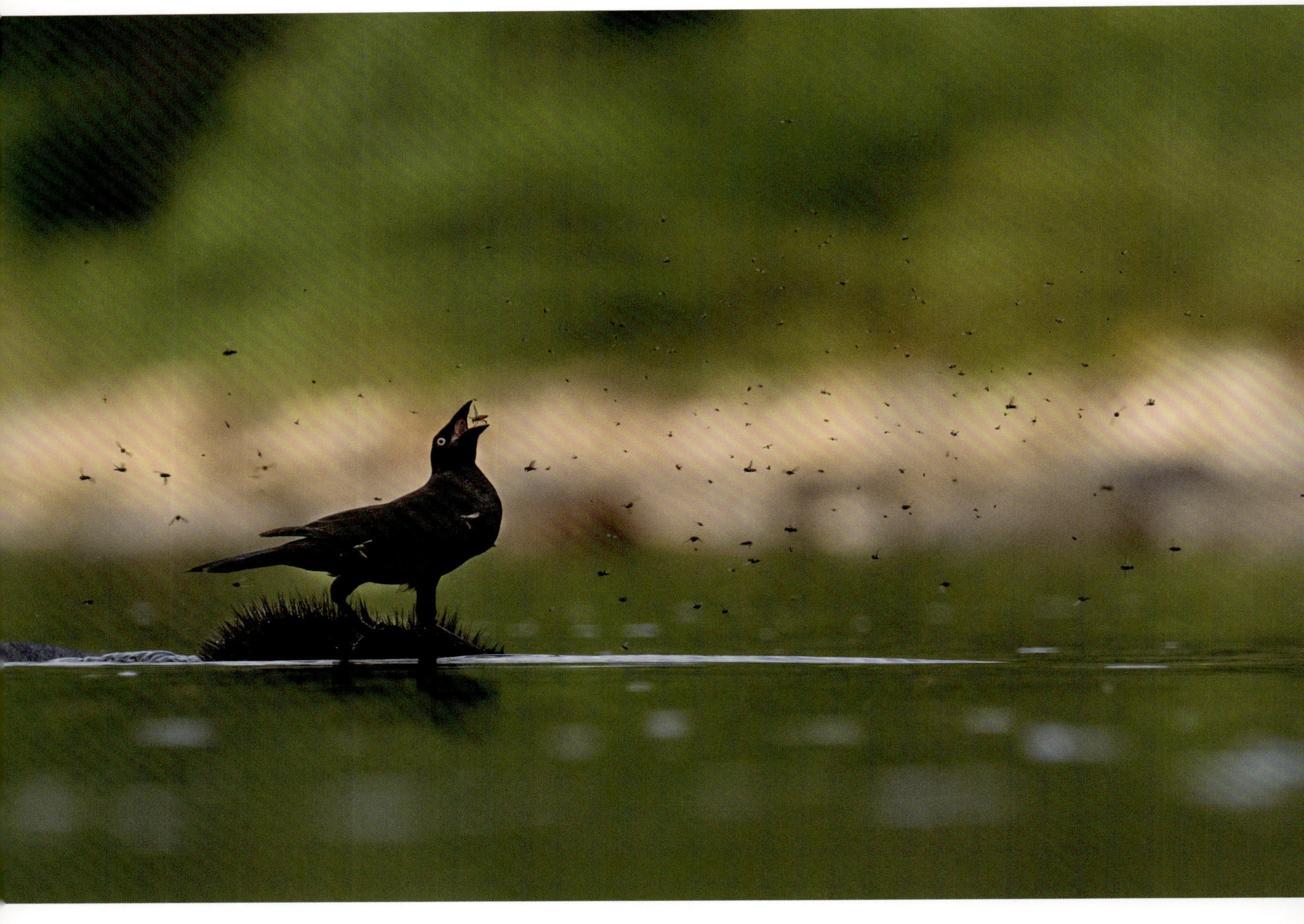

ABOVE: I was in between dives when I noticed a giant cowbird *(Molothrus oryzivorus)* perched on what I thought was a rock in the river. Suddenly the rock turned into one of the Amazon's most elusive animals: a lowland tapir *(Tapirus terrestris)*.

OPPOSITE: A tapir swims across a deep pool in a tributary stream with a giant cowbird on its back. Due to the geographic isolation and lack of human activity at the headwaters, animals like the notoriously shy tapir are naive and still uncharacteristically curious about people.

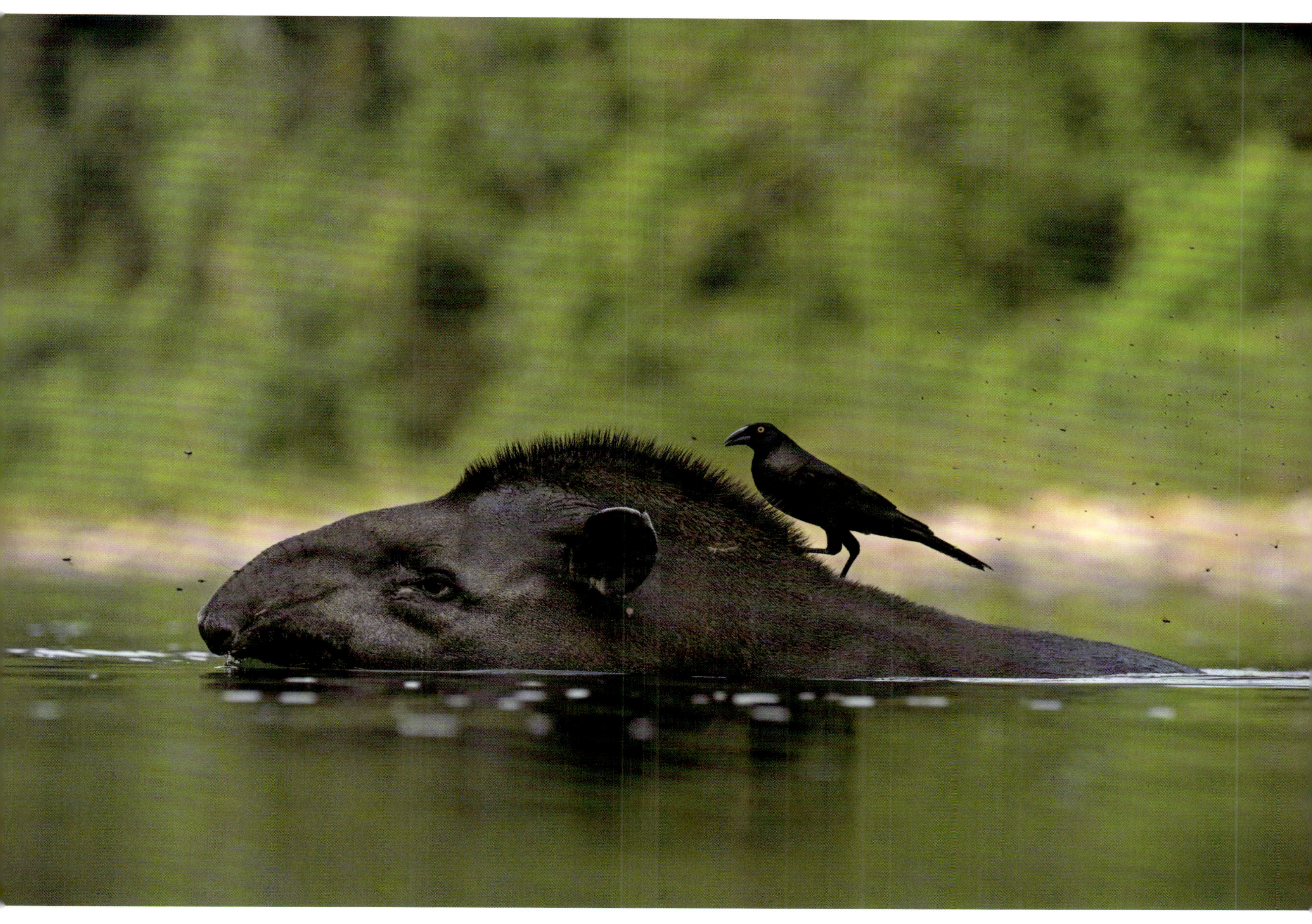

PAGES 94–95: A giant cowbird swoops over a lowland tapir to hunt biting horseflies that feed on mammalian blood. During the hot dry season in the Bolivian Amazon, tapirs are besieged by biting flies and seek refuge in streams and rivers every afternoon.

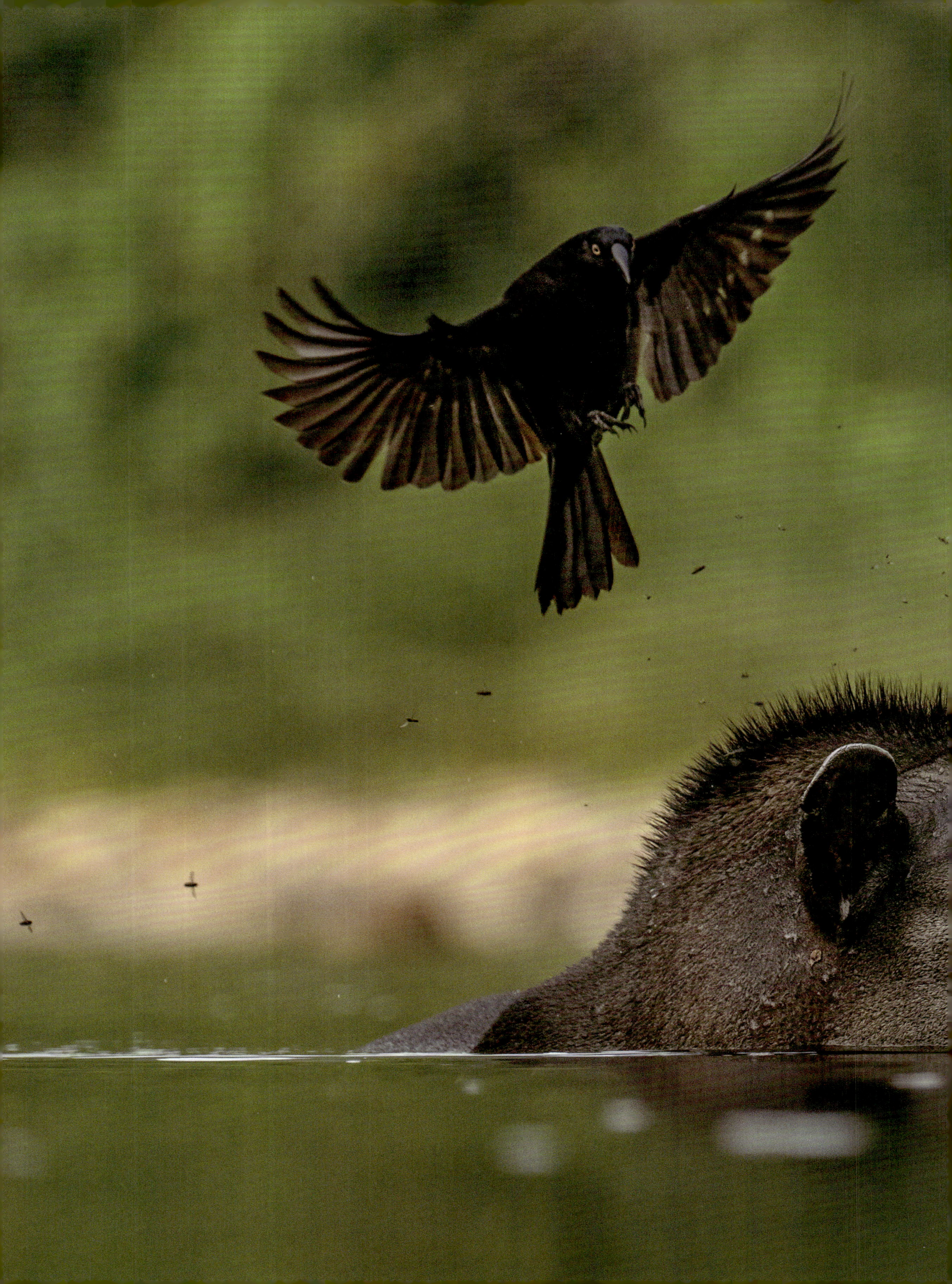

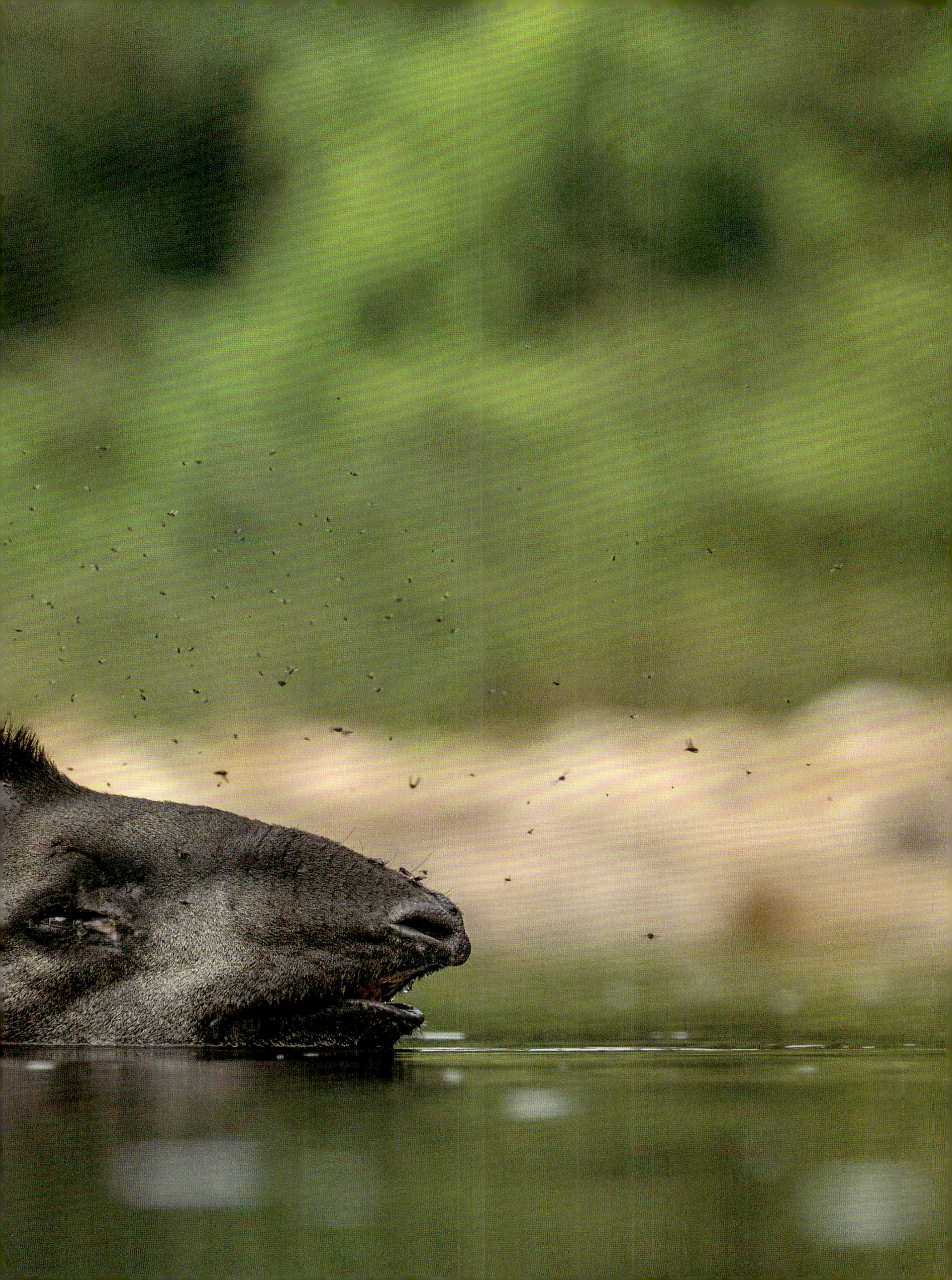

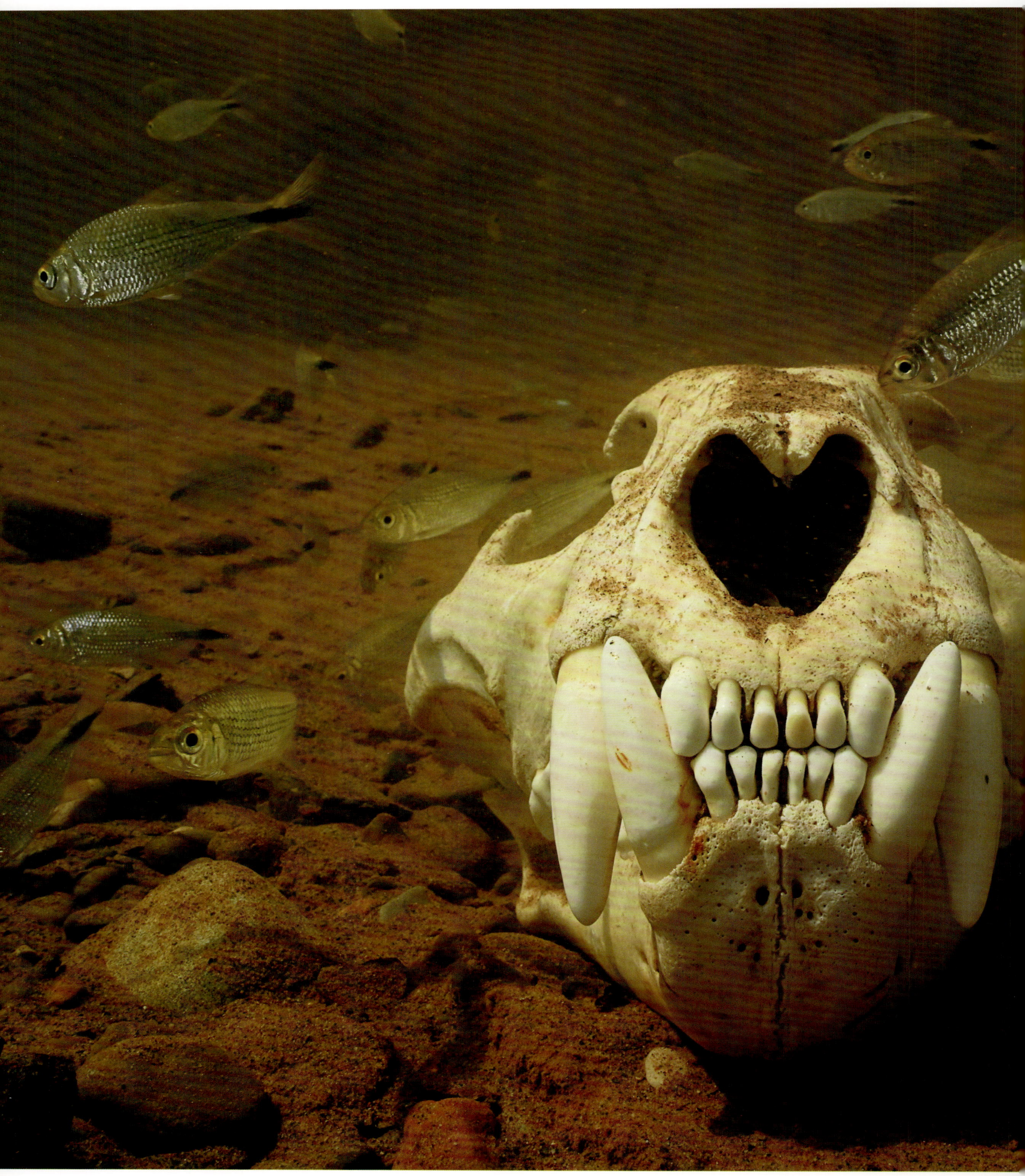

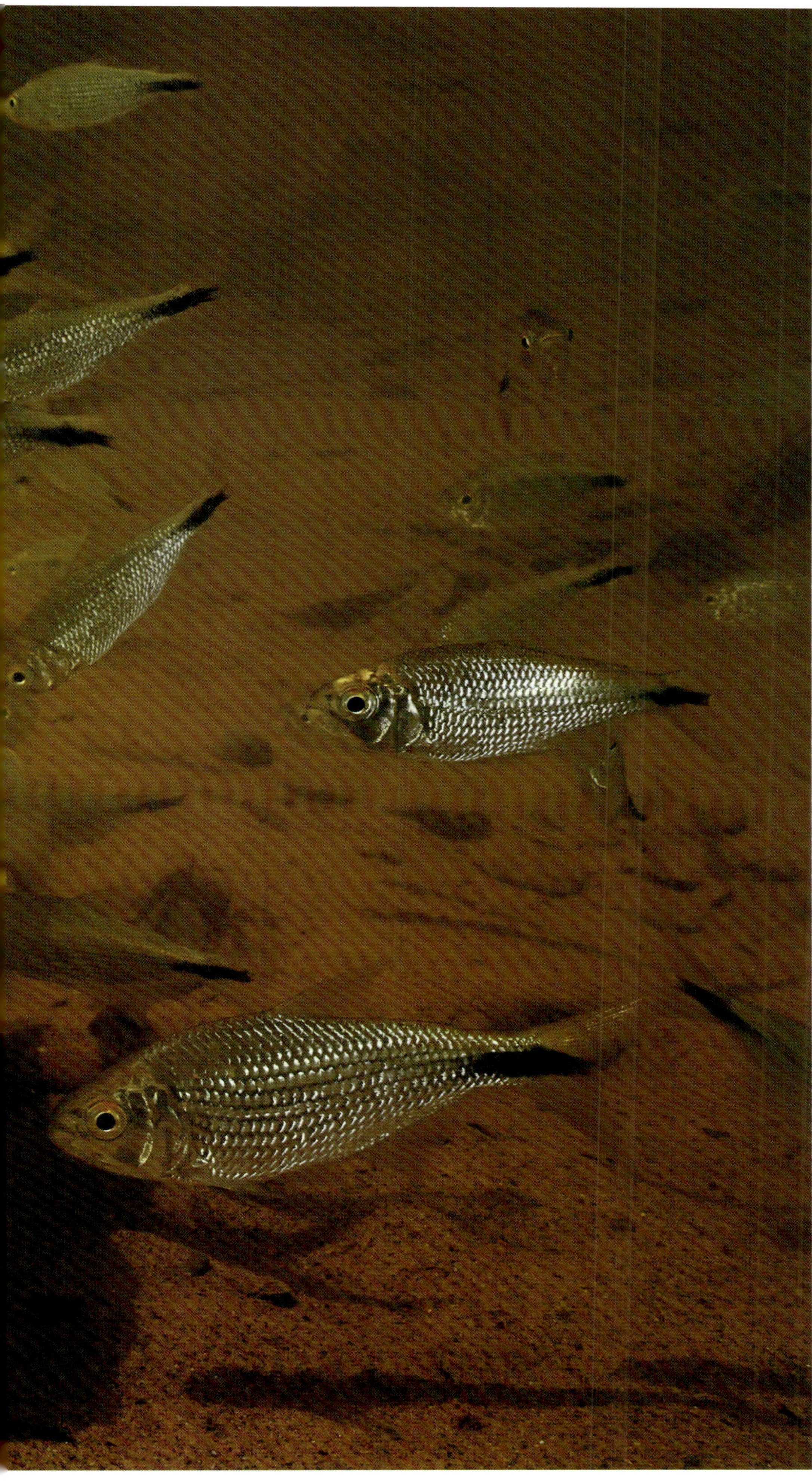

A submerged jaguar skull becomes a focal point for a school of *sardenas* in a headwater tributary of the Pluma River. Most reserves in the Amazon were created with terrestrial biodiversity, like jaguars, in mind, making the protection of aquatic habitats often an incidental afterthought. Freshwater-centric protected areas are very rare, and with some downstream expansions, Isiboro Sécure National Park and Indigenous Territory in Bolivia could become one of the few examples where aquatic keystone species like the golden dorado are protected across their complete range.

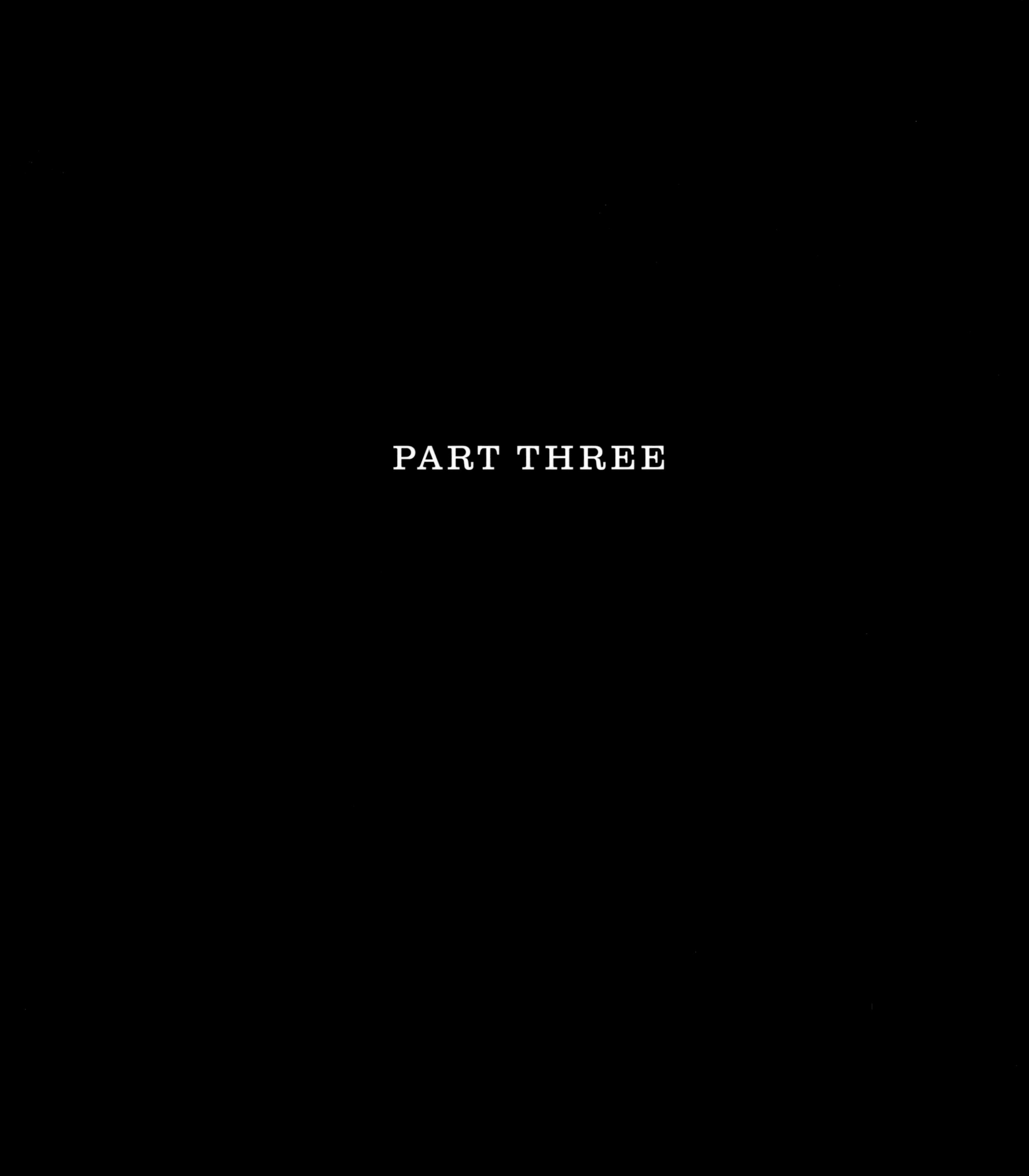

PART THREE

CHIRIBIQUETE

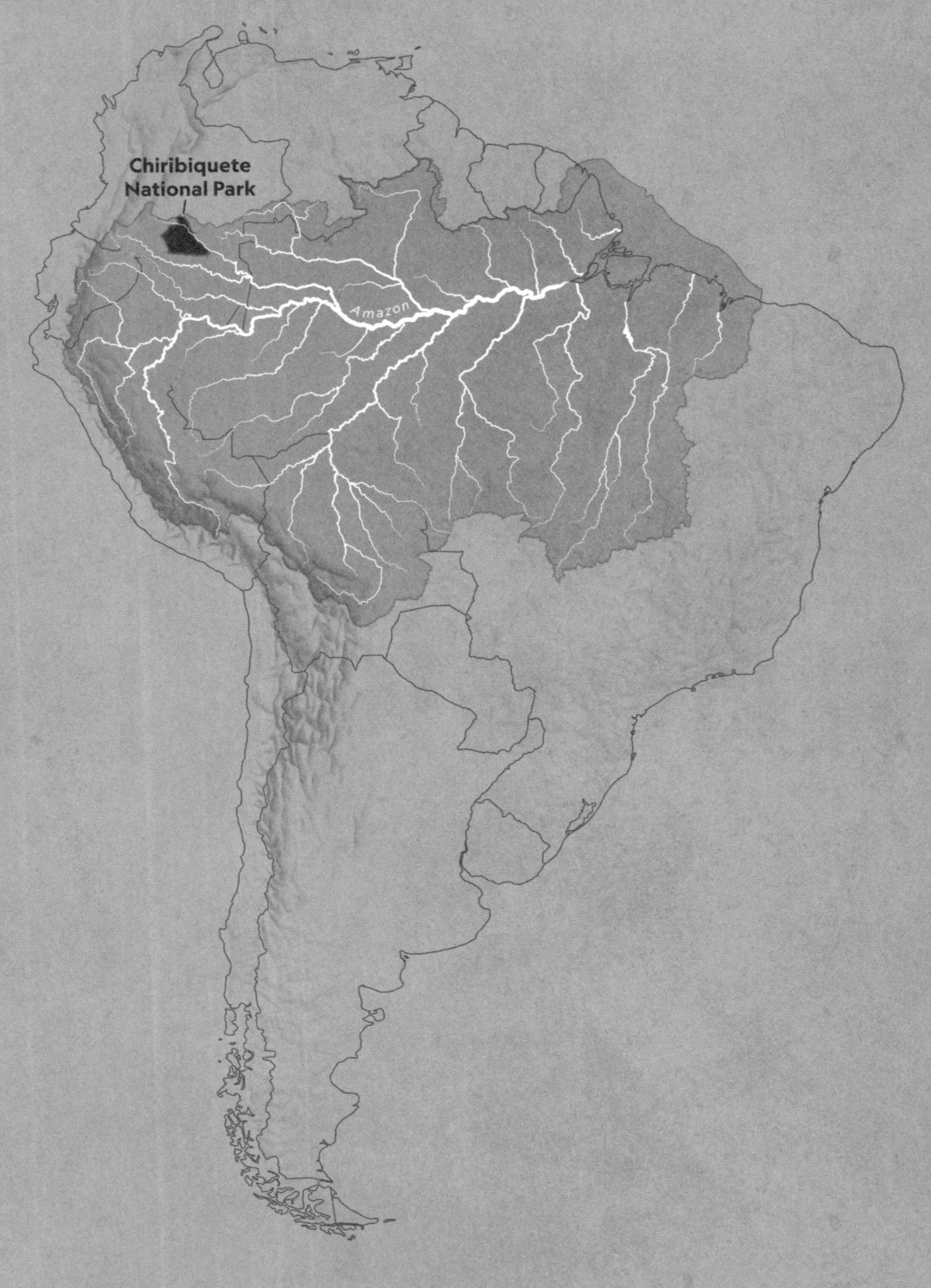

Chiribiquete
National Park
Amazon

Two jaguars leap into the river, lunging at pacas. These oversize rodents, with blotched and striped coats, are agile swimmers. Piranhas, attracted by the commotion, hover nearby.

I'm witnessing this riveting scene, but not underwater, as I usually am when I'm on assignment for National Geographic. Instead of diving to photograph this aquatic life, I've climbed to a rocky ledge far above the rainforest. The jaguars, pacas, and piranhas are not flesh and blood; they are prehistoric artworks painted with hematite, a bloodred iron oxide, in exquisite detail.

These pictographs are tens of thousands of years old and evidence of humankind's long relationship with the world's greatest freshwater ecosystem. Here, the Amazon's first inhabitants painted the most ancient visual stories ever told about the great river. More than 70,000 paintings—the oldest in the Americas—have been discovered in 58 cave shelters, cementing the park as this hemisphere's Louvre of rock art. I am in awe, as if seeing the ceiling of the Sistine Chapel for the first time. Far from Rome, we are in the largest tropical rainforest national park on the planet.

We are only the ninth expedition on record to be granted permission to explore Colombia's largest national park. Chiribiquete protects a spectacularly dense rainforest peppered with dramatic tabletop mountains called *tepuis*. We land on a tepui atop a tiny patch of uneven rock. The helicopter barely fits. The location appears idyllic, but it feels like we've set up camp on a furnace. As the rock absorbs sunlight, it heats the air in our tents to more than 100°F (38°C). I try to fall asleep, desperate for a breeze. My sweat forms mini-wetlands on my mattress. I feel like a rotisserie chicken.

We wake to the sound of thousands of tiny helicopters: The sweat bees are here. Soon the entire camp—camera cases, boots, clothing, plates, cutlery, anything left outside—is covered in creatures. I make the mistake of leaving my tent zipper slightly cracked and soon end up with dozens of roommates. The bees overwhelm us; resistance is futile. I let them quench their thirst from the sweat lake in my belly button. They crawl in between our fingers, behind our ears, into our noses; one even slips beneath my eyelid. A head net becomes more important than underwear.

In the lowlands, near rivers that flow through the park, there are hardly any sweat bees, but I was advised not to stay there. The remnants of Revolutionary Armed Forces of Colombia (FARC) rebel forces are said to still use these tributaries when the water is high enough. I prefer bees to AK-47s.

This place was only discovered as one of the world's foremost and extensive rock-art repositories in the 1980s, when a storm pushed Colombian archaeologist

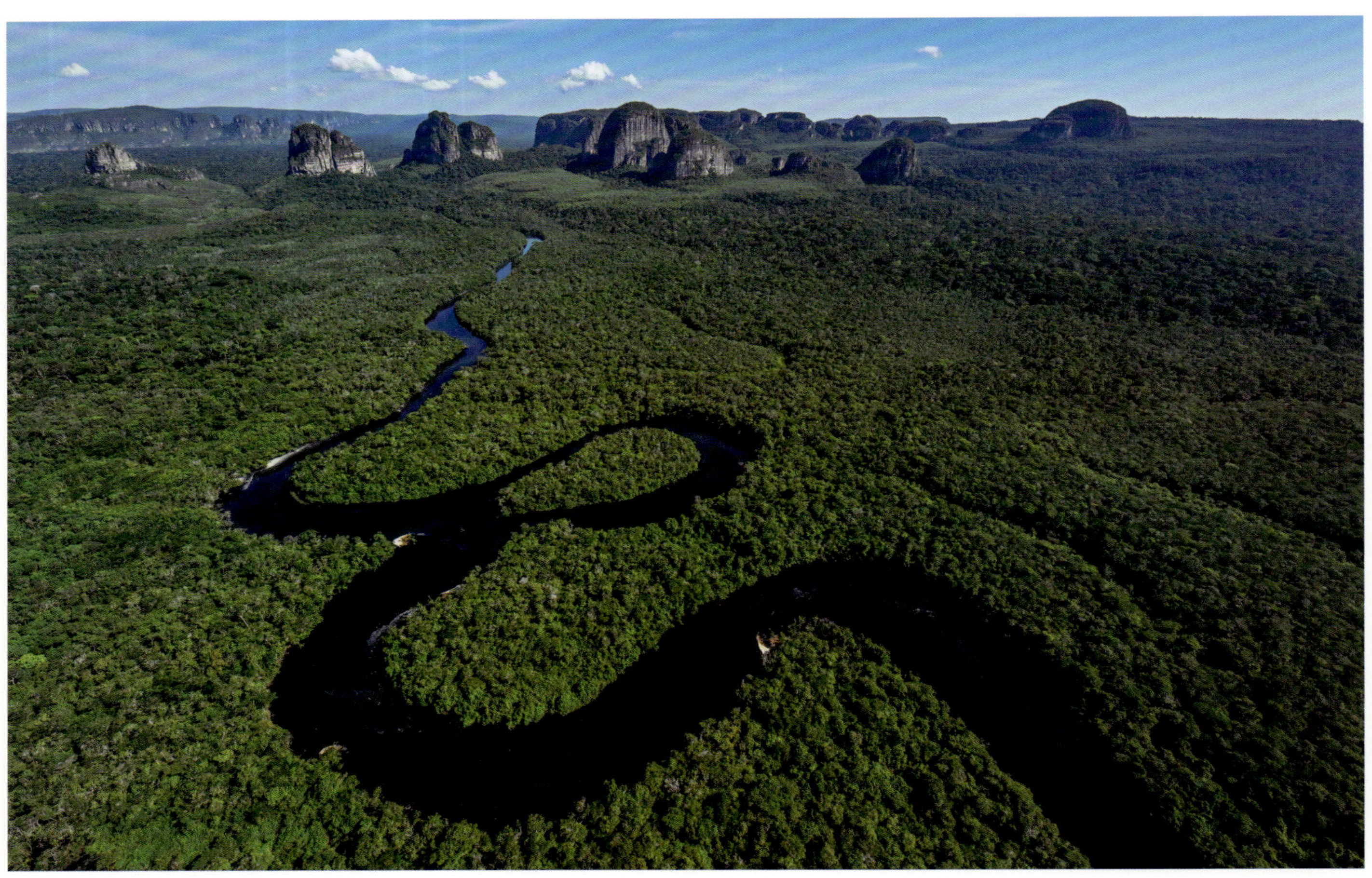

Chiribiquete is the largest national park in Colombia and the largest tropical rainforest protected area in the world. Declared a UNESCO World Heritage site in 2018, the park presently occupies 16,600 square miles (43,000 km^2) of granite *tepuis,* tropical forests, savannas, and rivers. Biogeographically, Chiribiquete is situated in the Guyana Province, home to at least 1,801 plant species, 57 amphibians, 238 fish, and 410 different types of birds. It also hosts 30 percent of the Colombian Amazon's bat diversity and 10 percent of the country's butterflies.

Carlos Castaño-Uribe's Cessna off course and he spotted a mountain range that wasn't on any of his maps. He returned to explore, surveyed the pictographs, and has since devoted his life to documenting Chiribiquete.

The oldest paintings here have been radiocarbon-dated to 20,000 years ago. But the youngest are from the 1970s, and compelling evidence shows that some are even more recent. Castaño-Uribe found a small hearth with animal bones and pigments arranged beneath some paintings, indicating the art continues to be important in Indigenous cosmology and ceremonial activities. Indigenous Karijona, Murio, or Urumi people—uncontacted or living in isolation since violent encounters with rubber tappers in the 1800s—inhabit the headwaters of the park's most important rivers. More than 50 miles (80 km) of difficult terrain separate them from our campsite, but every night before falling asleep I listen intently for the rustle of leaves or the crack of a twig.

Every morning, I set out by helicopter and then on foot, climbing steep and densely forested slopes, hacking through thick foliage, rappelling cliffs, and hauling ladders to traverse dark and damp canyons. In Chiribiquete, I see hundreds of pictographs. The panel called "Hojarasca" ("Fallen Leaves"), with its depiction of jaguars hunting pacas among piranhas, speaks to me the most deeply. The way they are painted on an overhang gives the sense of being underwater and looking up as the scene plays out above.

Castaño-Uribe thinks these paintings—which may have been part of religious rituals—were likely made by shamans who traveled from across the northwest Amazon Basin to Chiribiquete. Certain animals play important roles in Indigenous cosmology: Jaguars can be protectors and sources of power. Through the ingestion of sacred plants such as yagé, Baniwa shamans are said to transform into jaguars to communicate with spirits. Anacondas are often considered the creators of the universe; according to a Desano legend, a giant snake ascended the Amazon River, traveling like a submarine and carrying the ancestors of all mankind on its back.

After we hack through dense foliage for hours, a dark canyon spits us out onto a narrow ledge next to a vertical cliff. We arrive at a rock-art site named "Los Gemelos" ("The Twins"). Depicting stingrays, otters, and human-turtle hybrids, the paintings are magnificent and fiercely protected by bees—not the stingless sweat bees that had tormented us at camp, but the more virulent honeybees that had constructed their hive above the paintings. In less than a half hour, the team collectively endures more than a hundred stings.

As we pack up our base camp and wait for the helicopter, I walk a short distance from the group to reflect on what I've seen. Although our mediums may differ—ancient sandstone versus paper and digital screens—I realize that my ancient counterparts and I are telling surprisingly similar stories about the Amazon River. The shamans painted to communicate with supernatural beings to ensure balance between humans and nature; I photograph and tell stories because the natural world is under siege and our relationship with biodiversity urgently needs recalibration. The Amazon's aquatic world is threatened by dams, mining, overfishing, pollution, logging, and climate change; the rivers especially are in dire need of a spotlight, and it is now my turn to carry that torch. Gazing at these vivid and timeless pictures, I feel deeply connected to the Amazon's first storytellers. And I hope that my images will stand the test of time even a fraction as well as theirs. ■

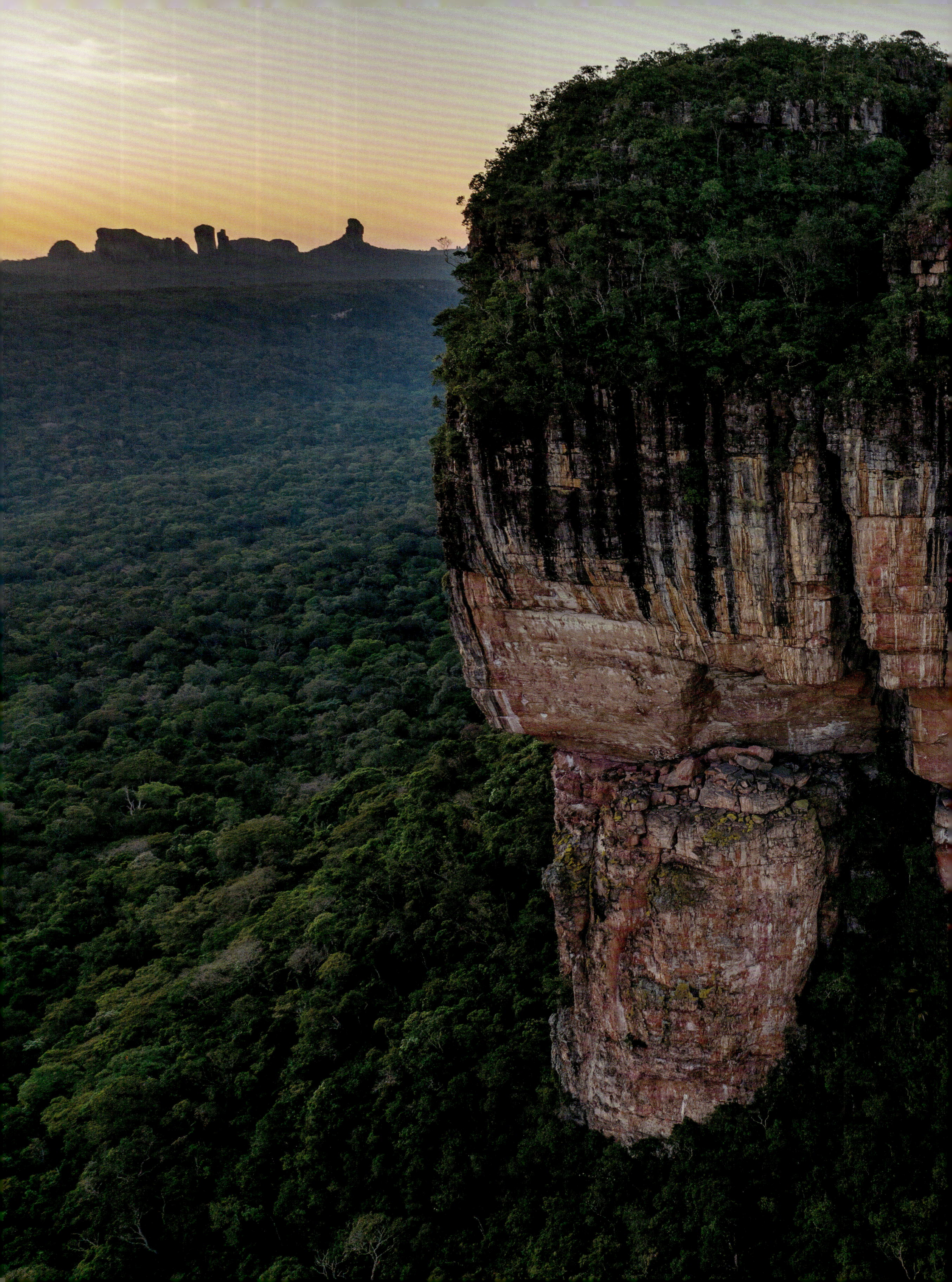

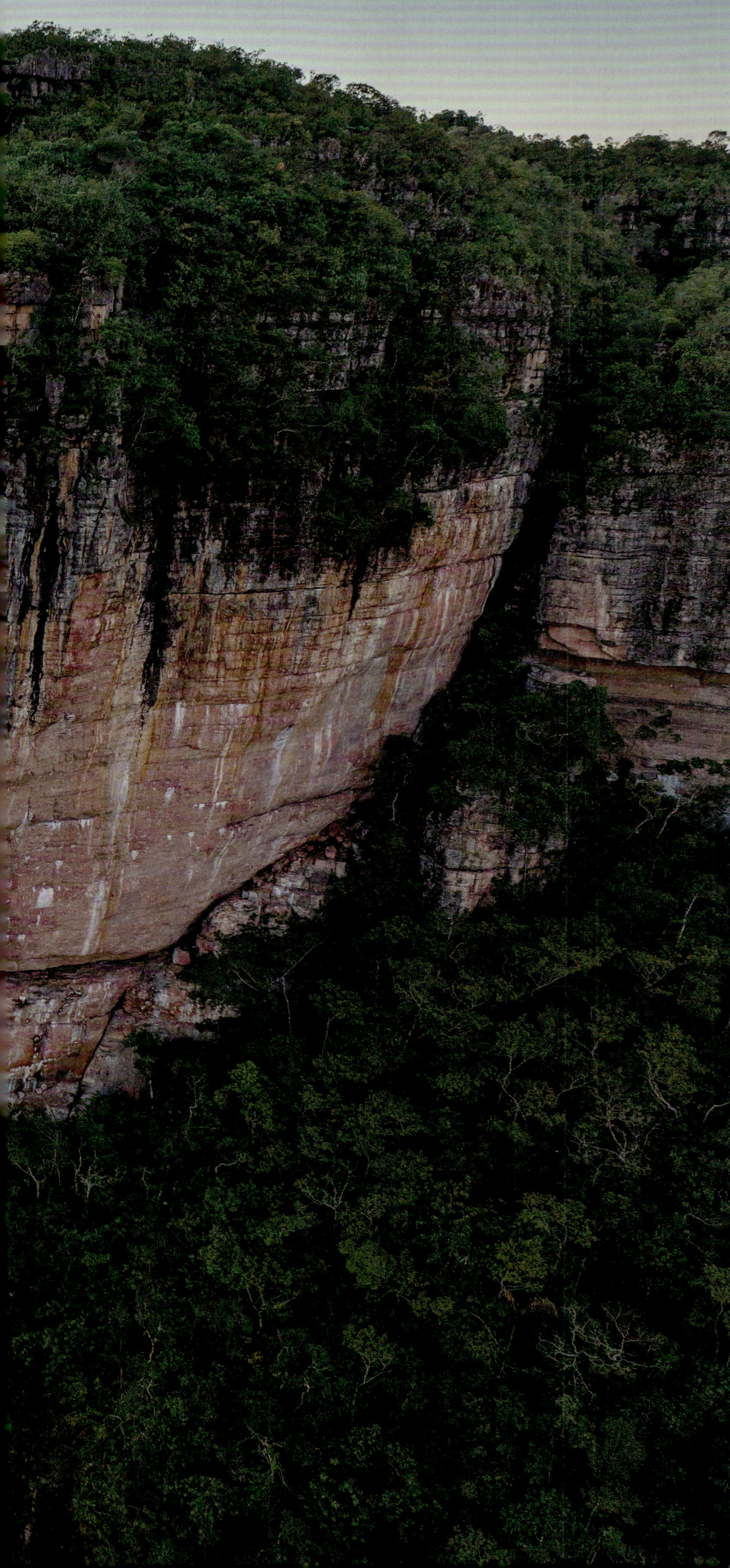

The ancient shaman artists chose the most inaccessible and spectacular locations to create their pictographs. The "Hojarasca" ("Fallen Leaves") panel—with its jaguars hunting pacas among piranhas—is located on the pillar to the left. Ours was only the ninth expedition to be granted permission to explore vast Chiribiquete National Park, and future endeavors are likely to discover new rock-art sites for years to come.

PAGES 106–107: The park's highest mountains are more than 3,280 feet (1,000 m) tall and rise abruptly from the rainforest floor, creating complex microclimates. Some of the 177 inches (450 cm) of rain that fall on the park are created in situ. Water vapor rising from the forest feeds moisture-rich clouds, accelerating the formation of rain. In general, more than half the precipitation of the Amazon rainforests is returned to the atmosphere through evapotranspiration, where moisture is drawn up from the roots, gathers on leaves, and is returned into the air, safeguarding a fifth of the world's freshwater.

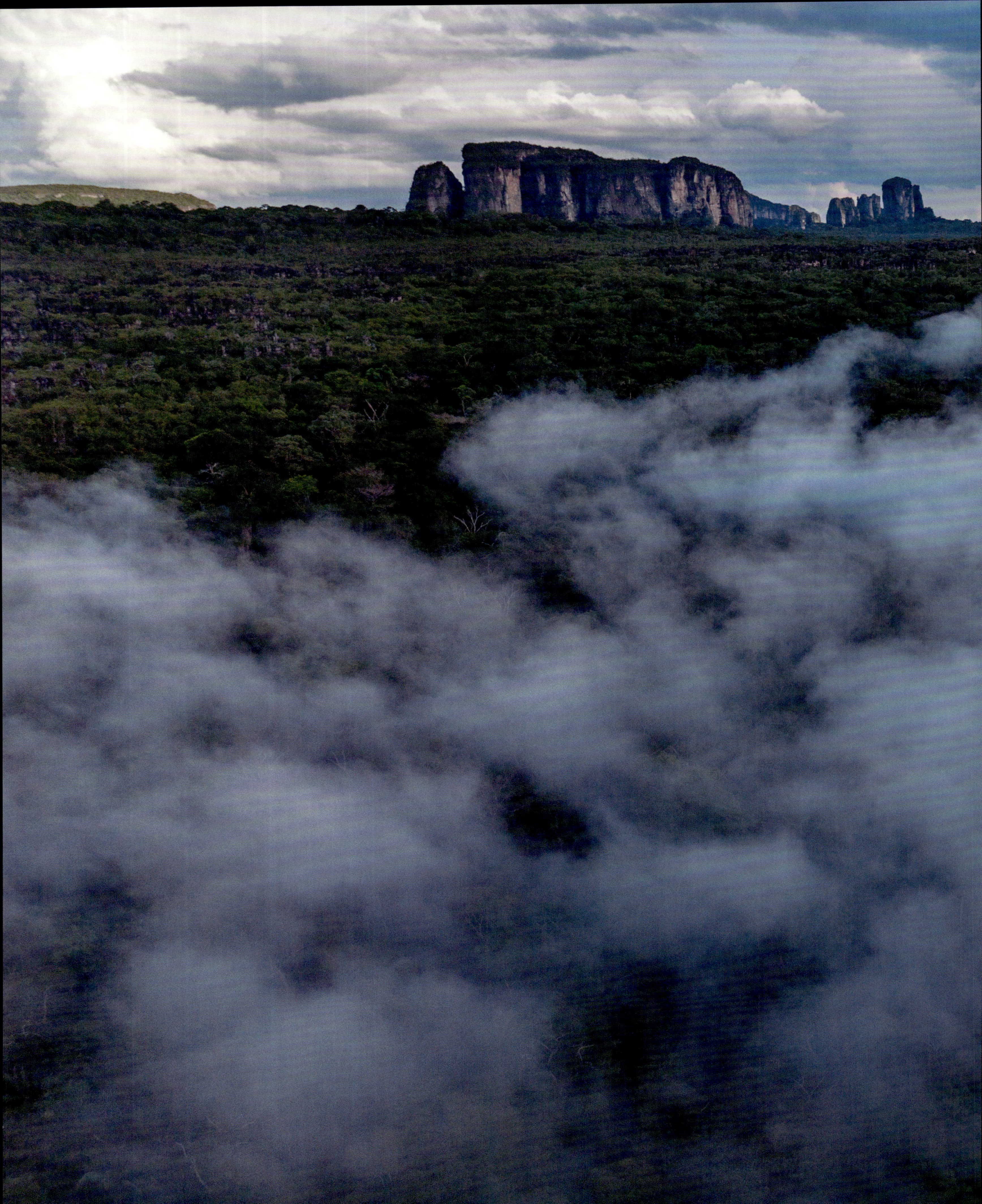

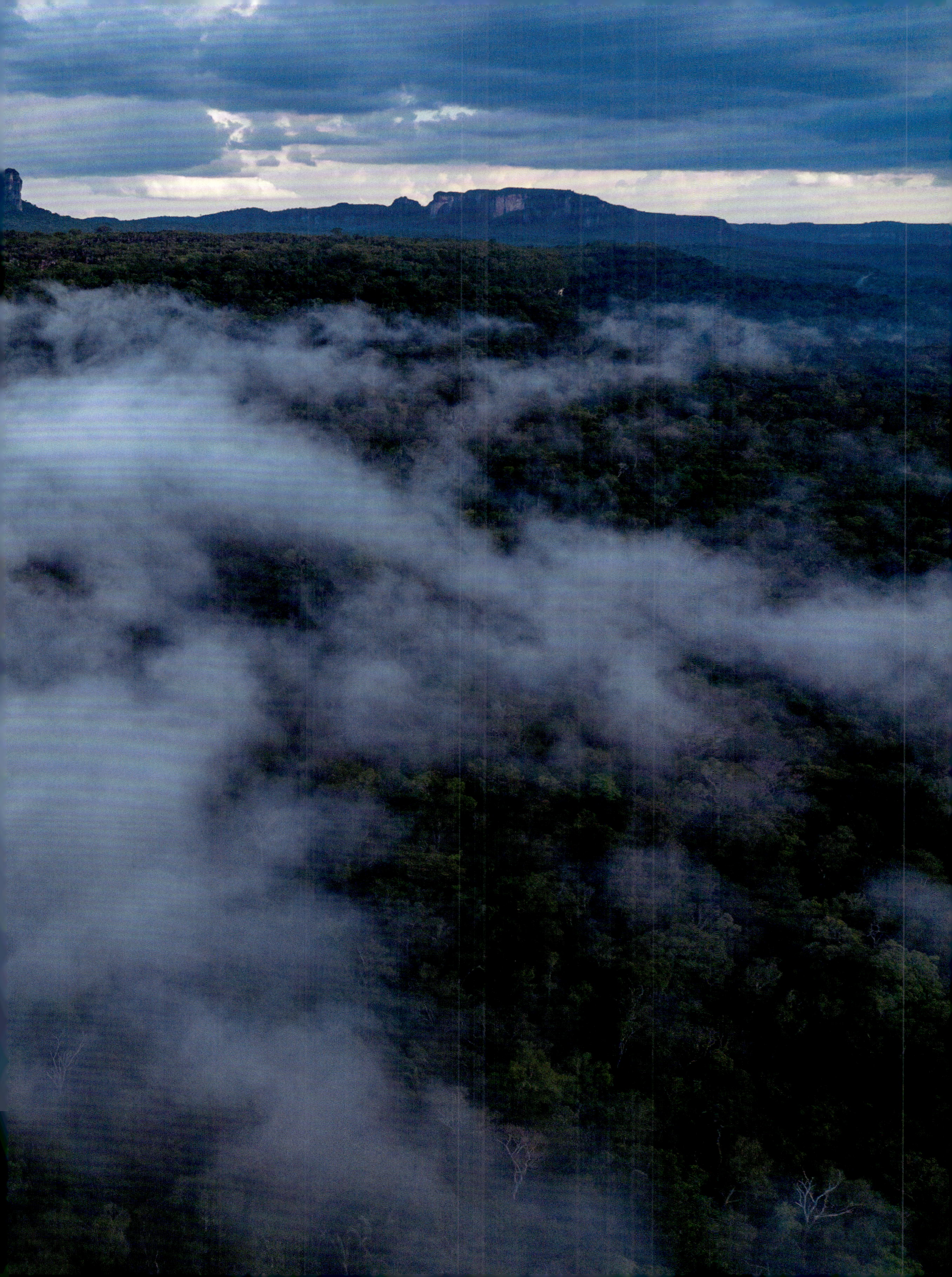

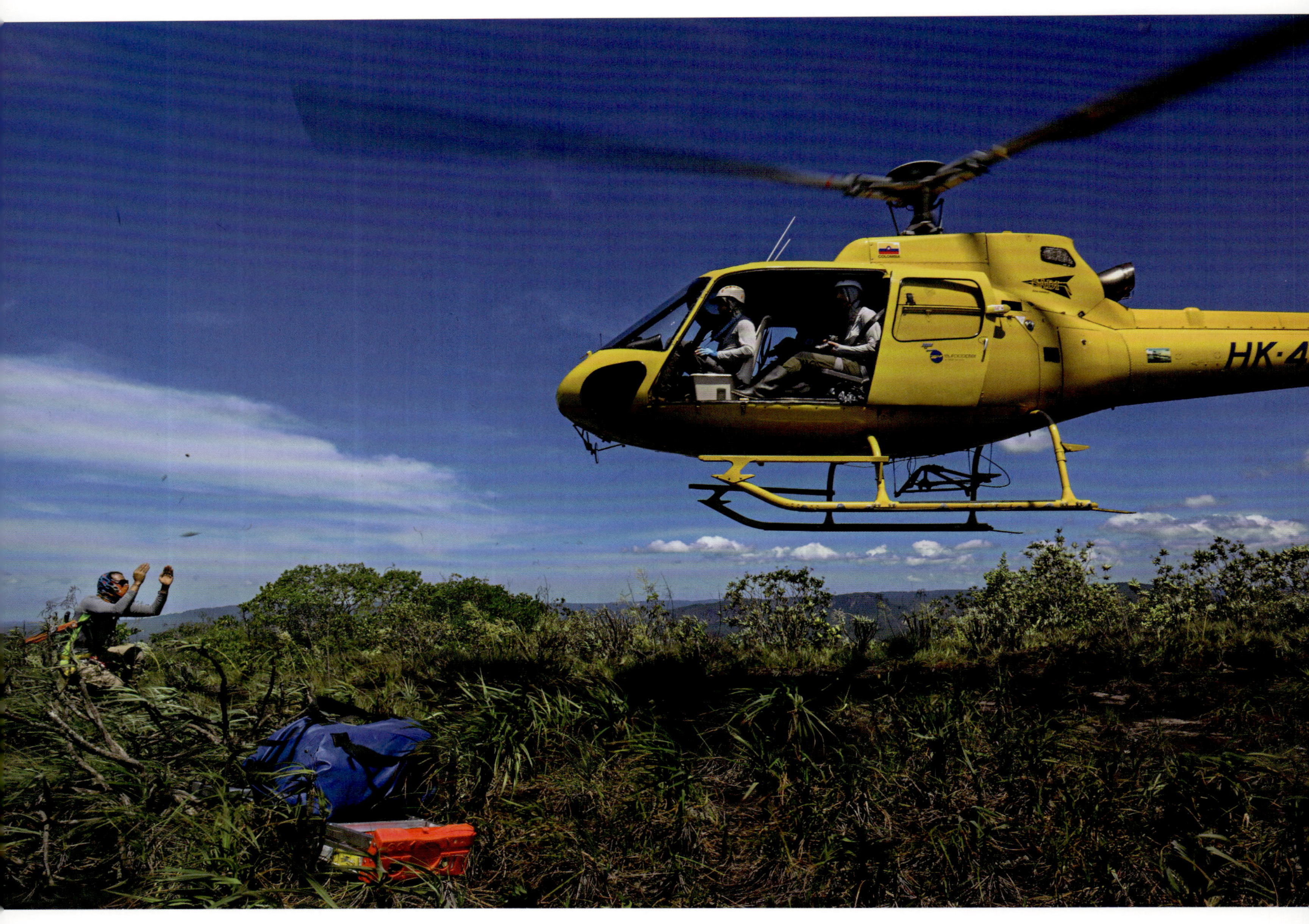

ABOVE: A helicopter was key for getting to and around Chiribiquete as the terrain is almost impossible to traverse on foot. To access the rock art, the team landed on the summits of *tepuis,* descended on foot through slot canyons, and rappelled to access pictographs painted in some of the most inaccessible places.

OPPOSITE: Bees are synonymous with Chiribiquete, both the stinging and sweat-drinking kind. At least 11 species of sweat bees abound on the *tepuis,* and they quickly overwhelmed expedition leader Jota Arango. Within minutes, hundreds arrived to lap up the nutrients and proteins in his sweat. On this expedition, a head net became mandatory every time we left the sweltering sanctuary of our tents.

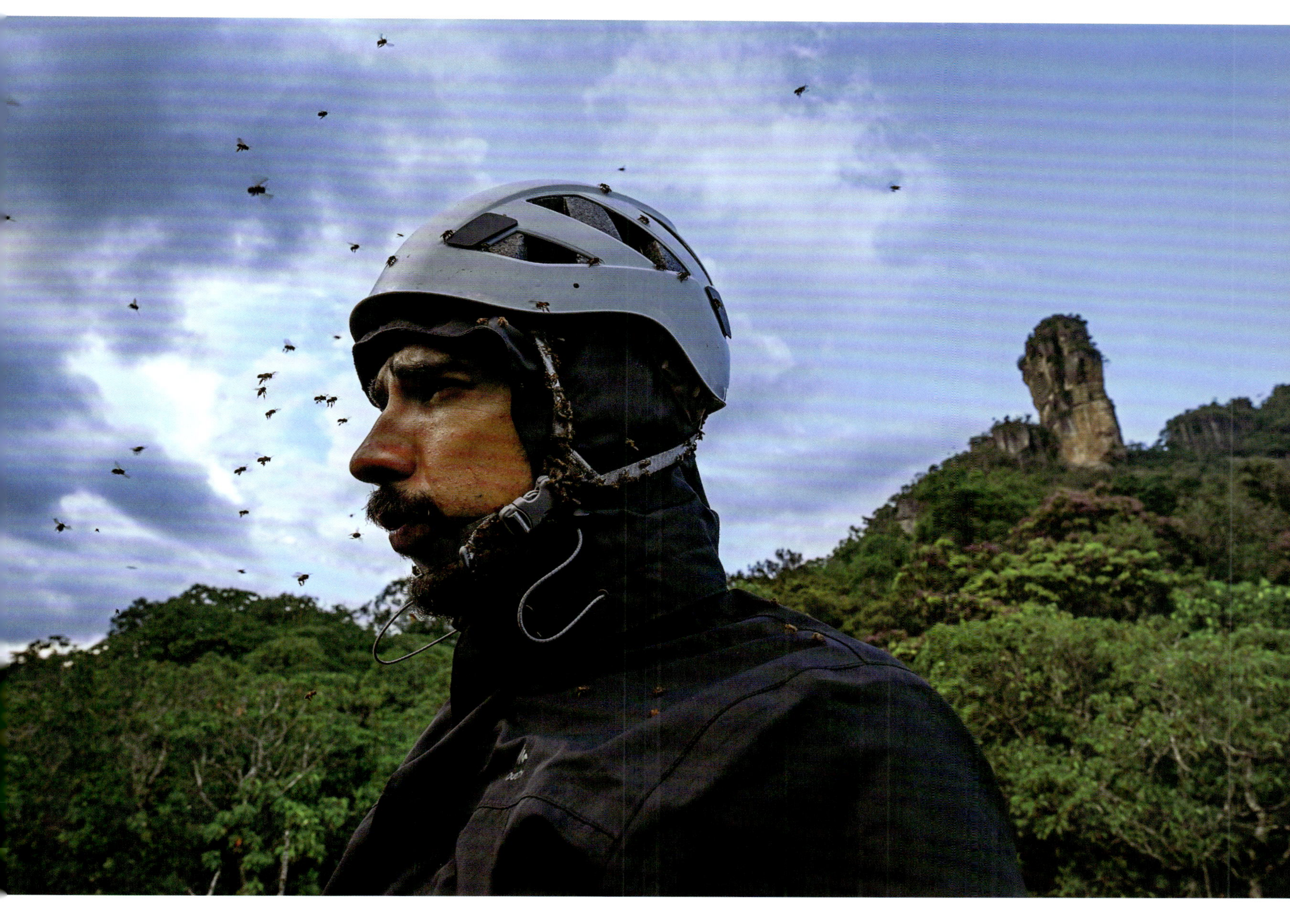

Archaeologist Carlos Castaño-Uribe is dwarfed by a rock-art panel named "Los Gemelos" ("The Twins"). The pictographs depicting jaguars, otters, stingrays, and human-turtle hybrids are breathtaking—and fiercely protected by honeybees. After enduring more than 100 stings, the expedition team had to abandon this location in a hurry.

PAGES 112–113: Jaguars leap at pacas while piranhas swim on a panel known as "Hojarasca" ("Fallen Leaves"). More than 75,000 paintings have been discovered in Colombia's Chiribiquete National Park. Some are 20,000 years old, making them the oldest known rock art in the Americas. The pictographs show fauna and flora, people, and geometric patterns. Large jaguars and aquatic life are common motifs.

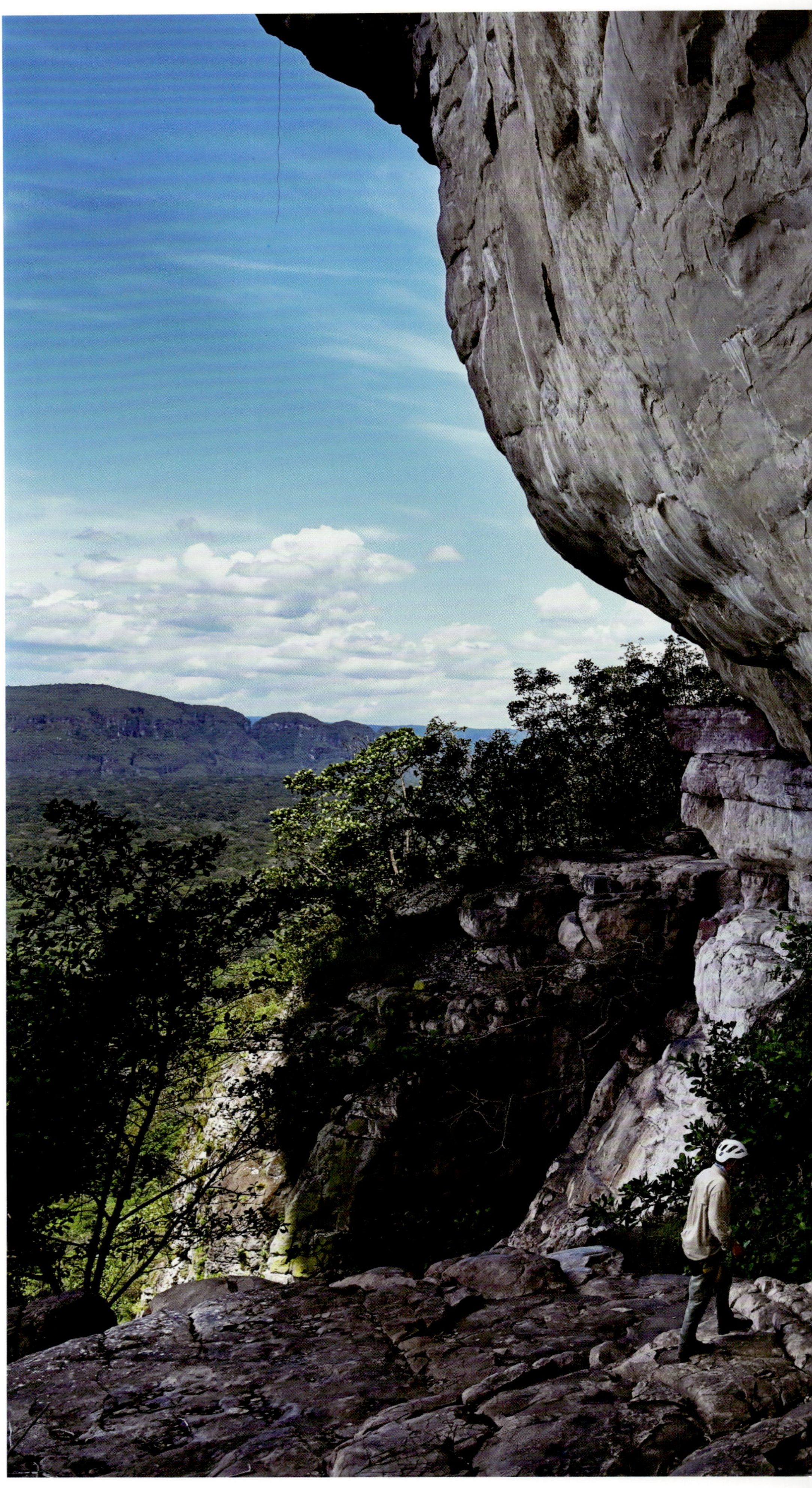

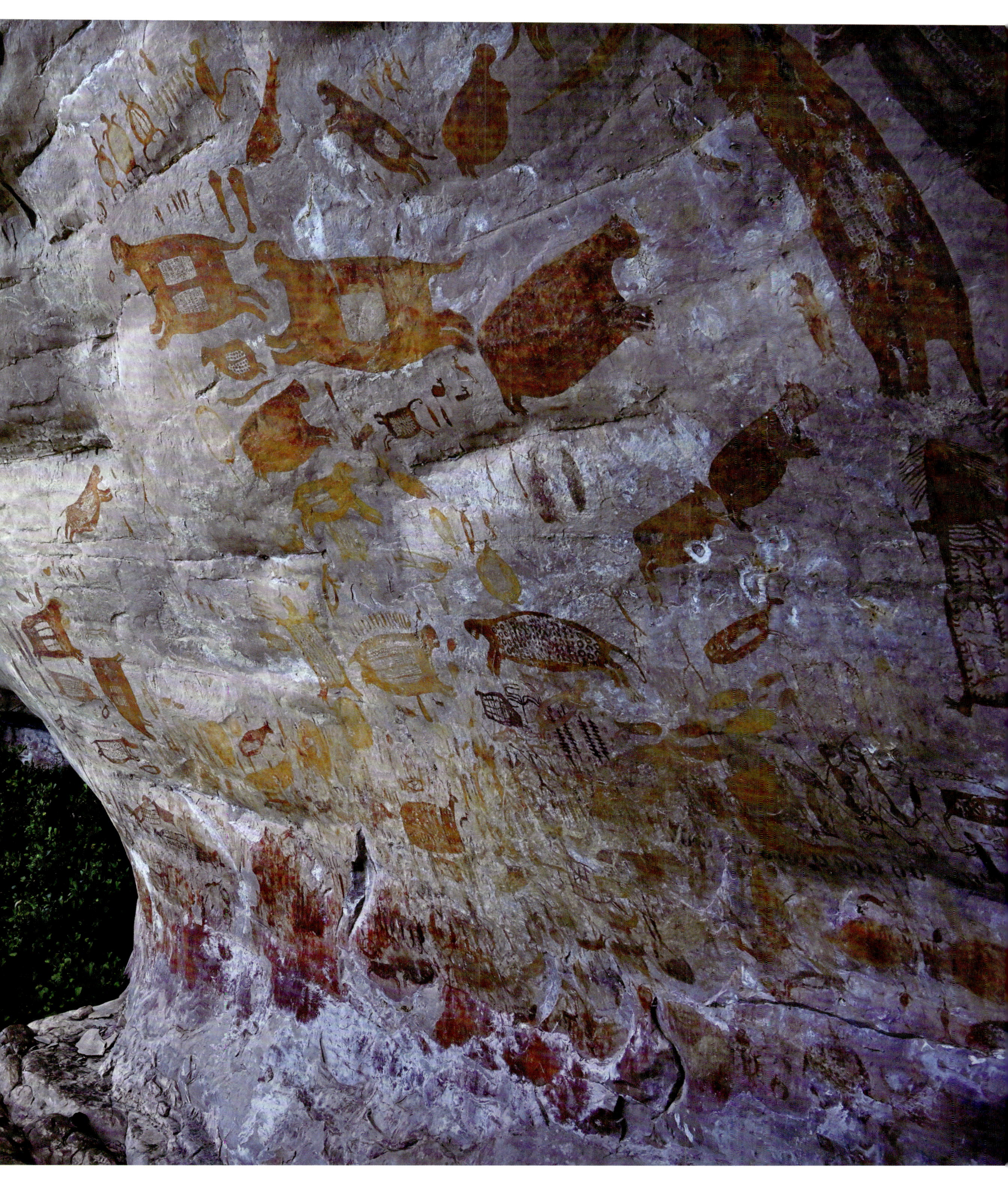

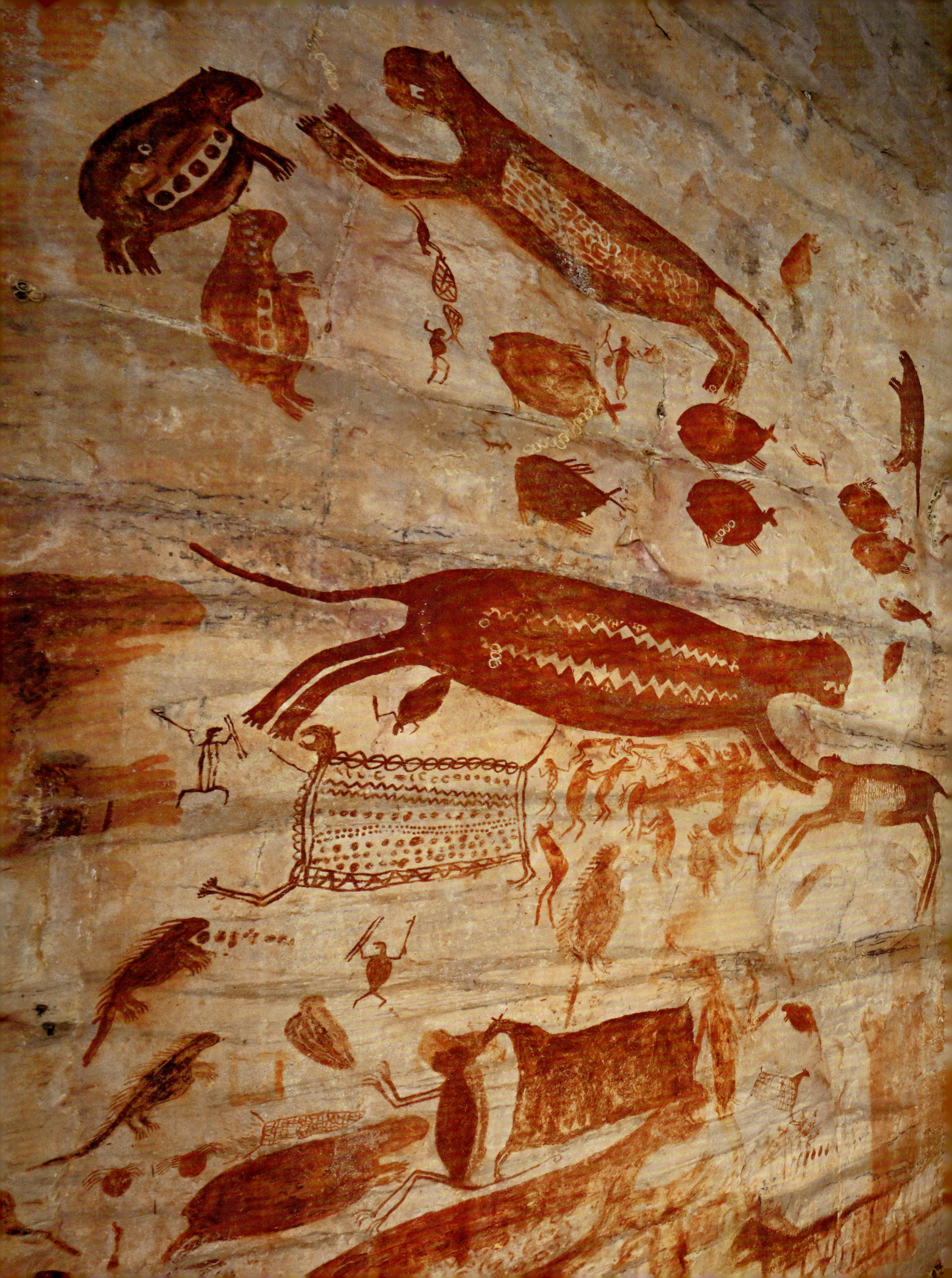

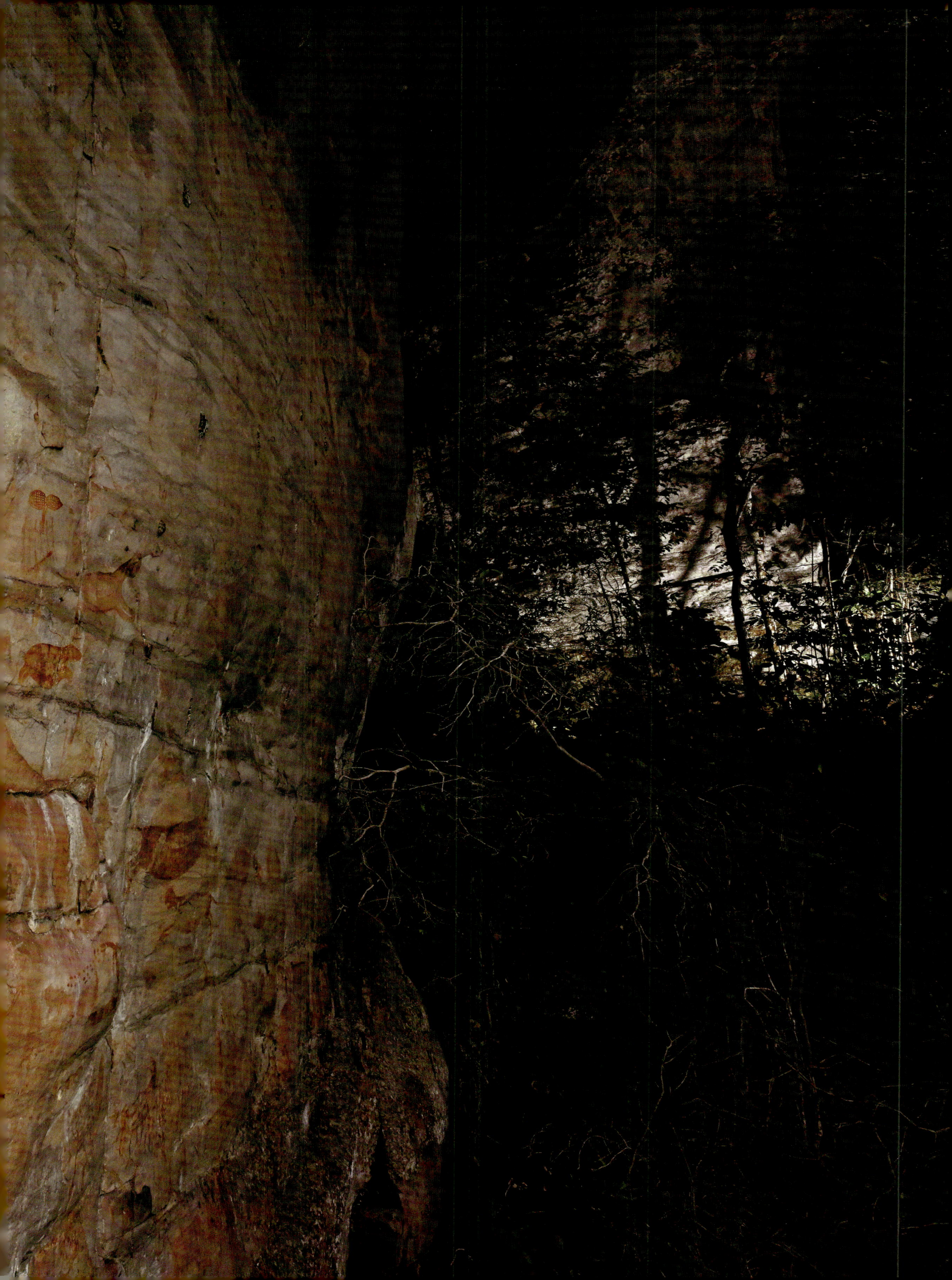

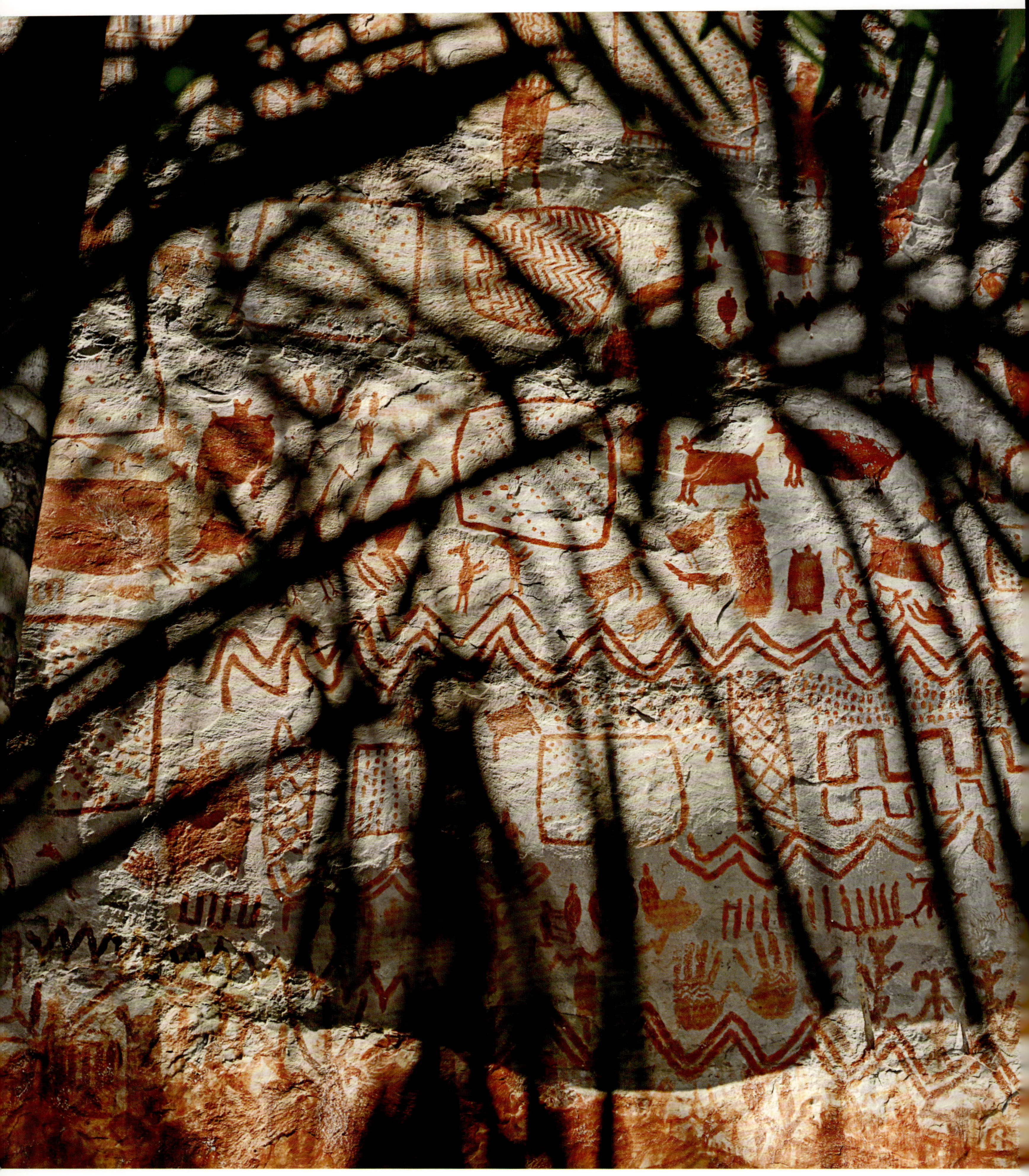

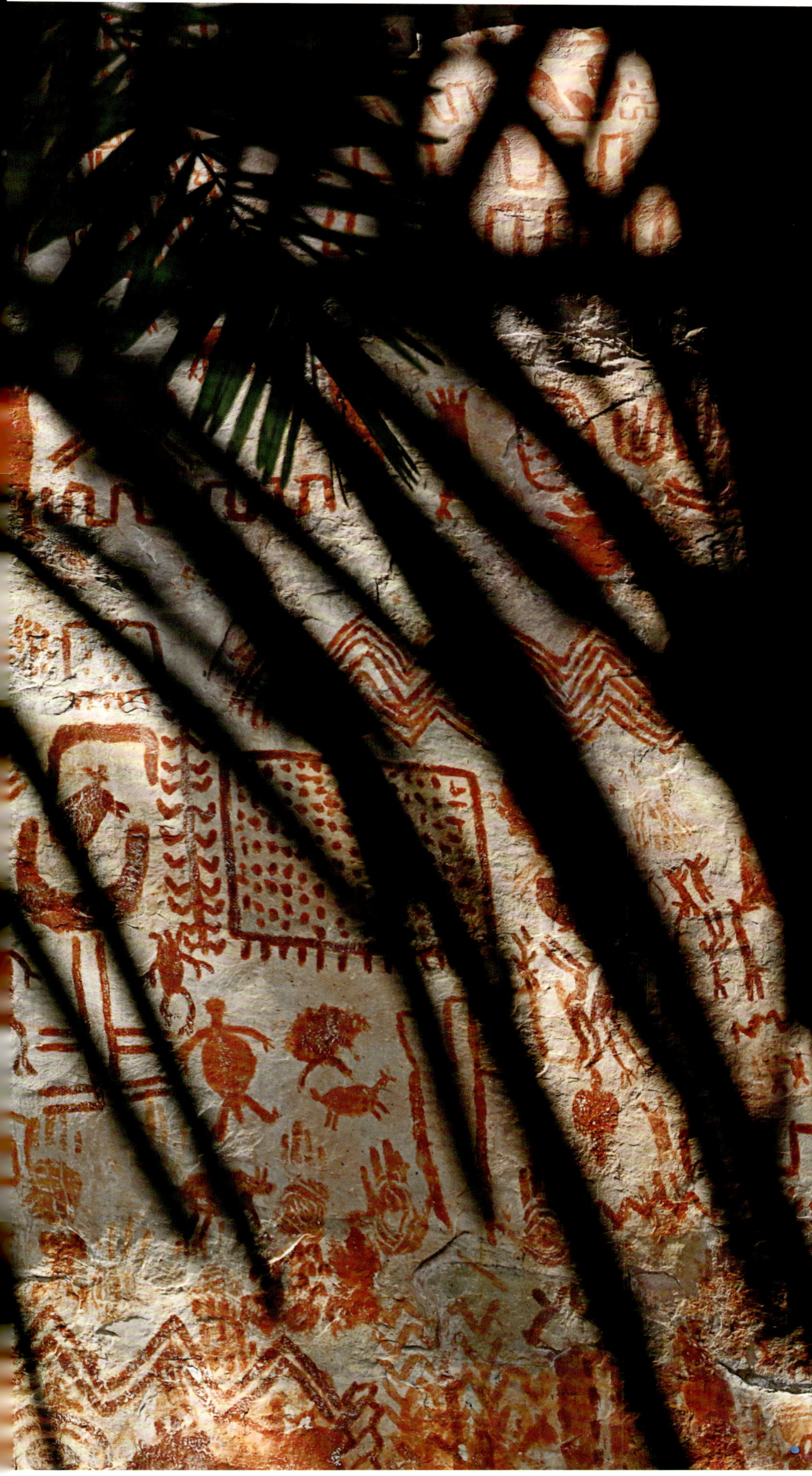

Some of Colombia's other mountain ranges also harbor extensive troves of rock art. In the Serranía de la Lindosa to the north, pictographs—believed to depict now extinct South American megafauna such as ground sloths and horses—are younger than those in Chiribiquete.

PAGES 116–117: The Serranía de la Macarena mountain range, like Chiribiquete, is one of the westernmost outliers of the Guiana Shield, and its quartzite rocks are 1.2 billion years old. Flowing through it is the Caño Juntos, which drains into the Orinoco Basin and is studded with rapids and waterfalls. Some of its most unique features are circular pits, known as giant's kettles, which are sculpted by hard pebbles in small cavities that the current persistently rotates. The tiny rocks gradually carve away at the cavity walls, millimeter by millimeter, creating almost perfectly round pits in the riverbed.

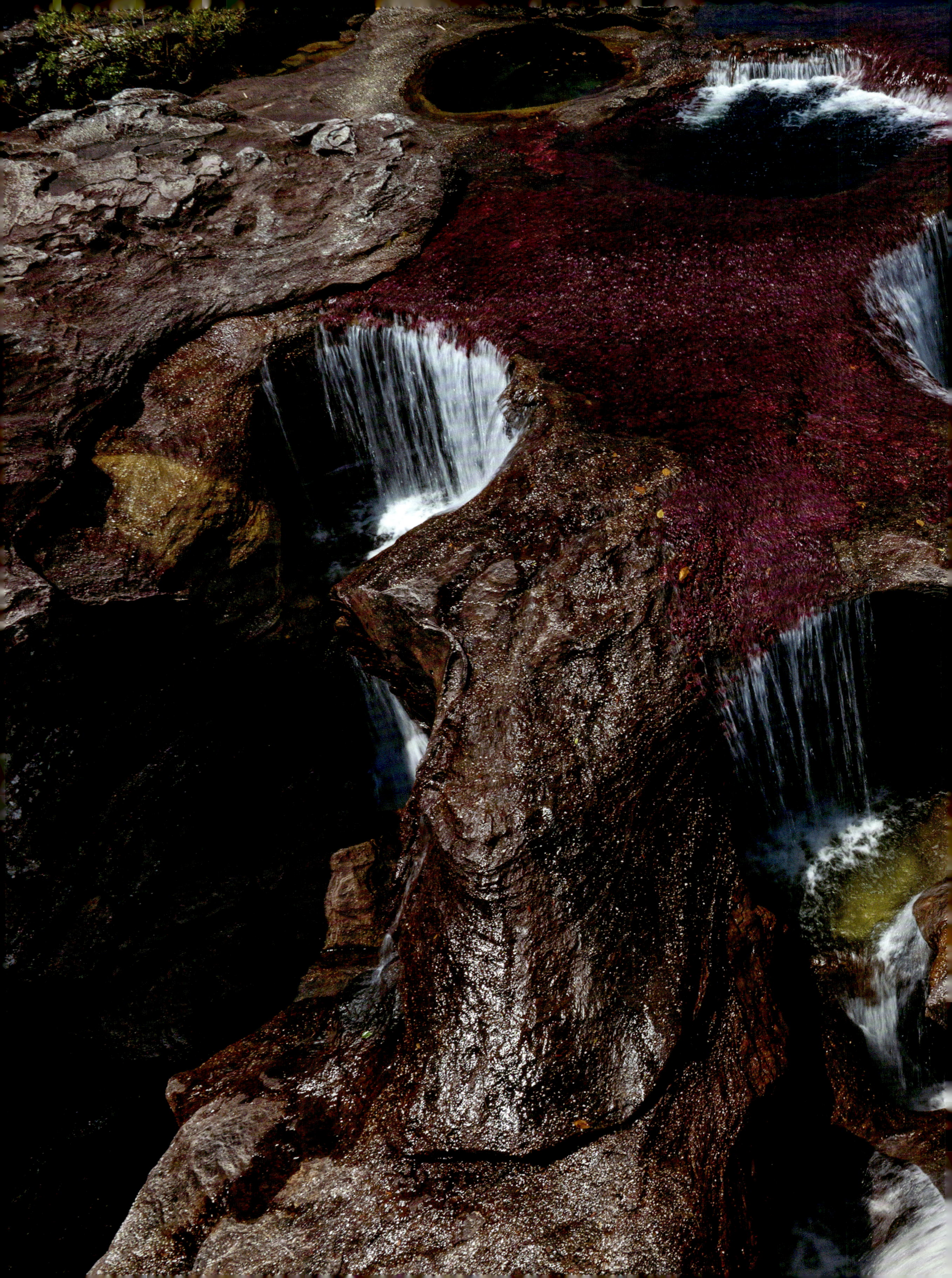

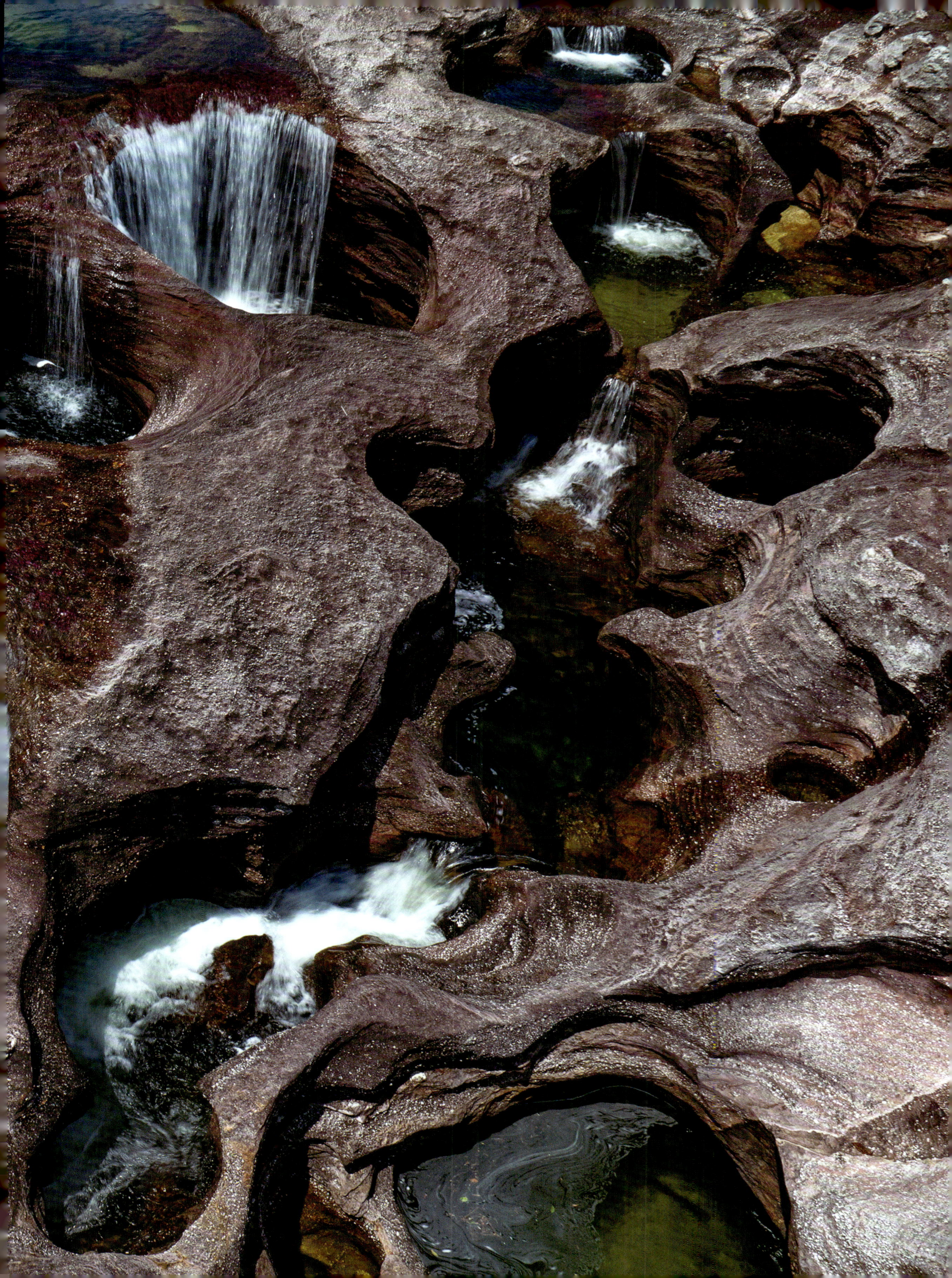

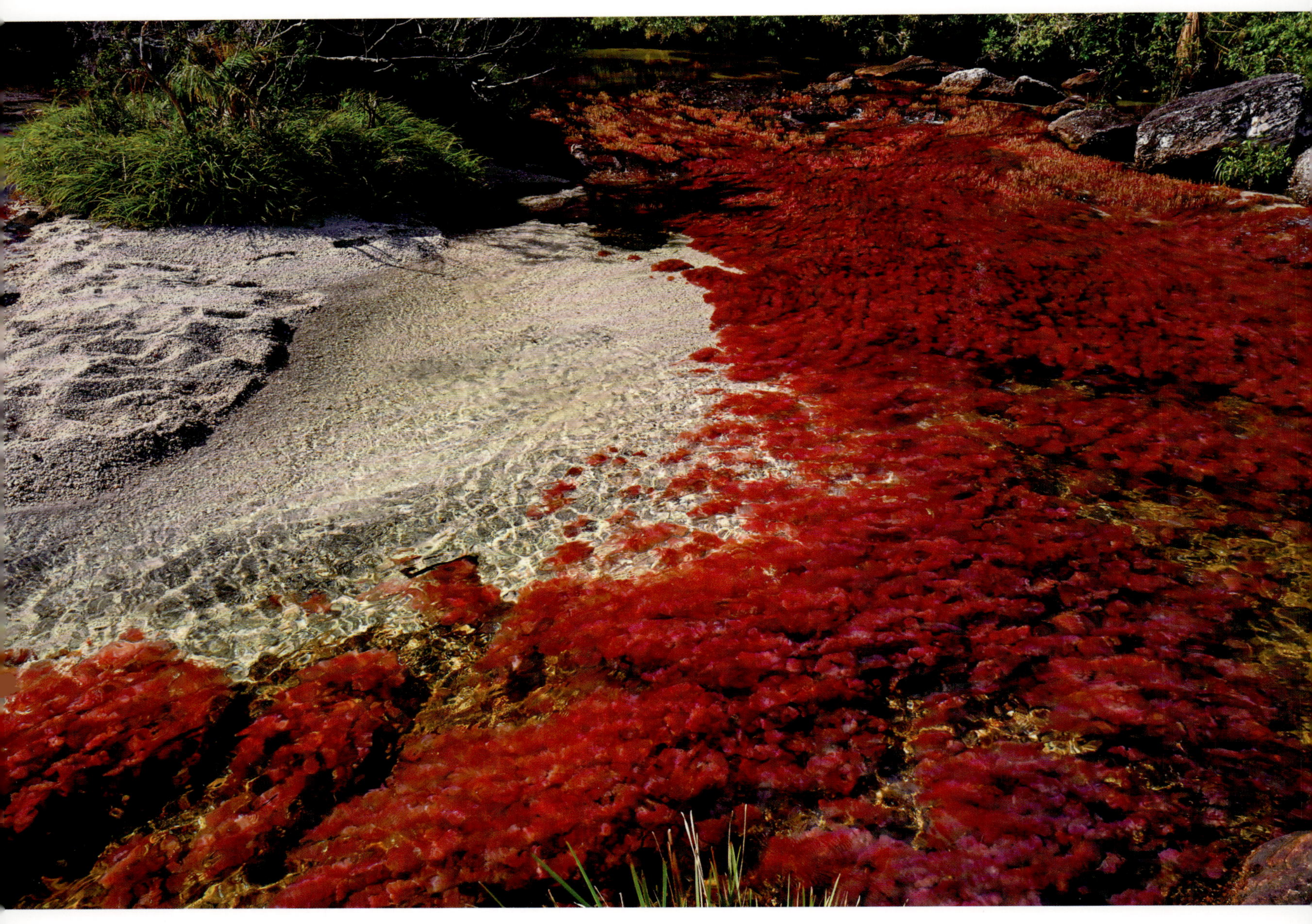

ABOVE AND OPPOSITE: The streams and small rivers birthed on rocky plateaus 105 miles (170 km) north of Chiribiquete are clear and home to unique aquatic fauna and flora. They are biological marvels that for most of the year look like any other stream, draped in hues of greens and browns. But for a short period between the wet and dry seasons, the rivers explode with color, as the endemic aquatic plant *Macarenia clavígera* bursts to life and turns a vivid red.

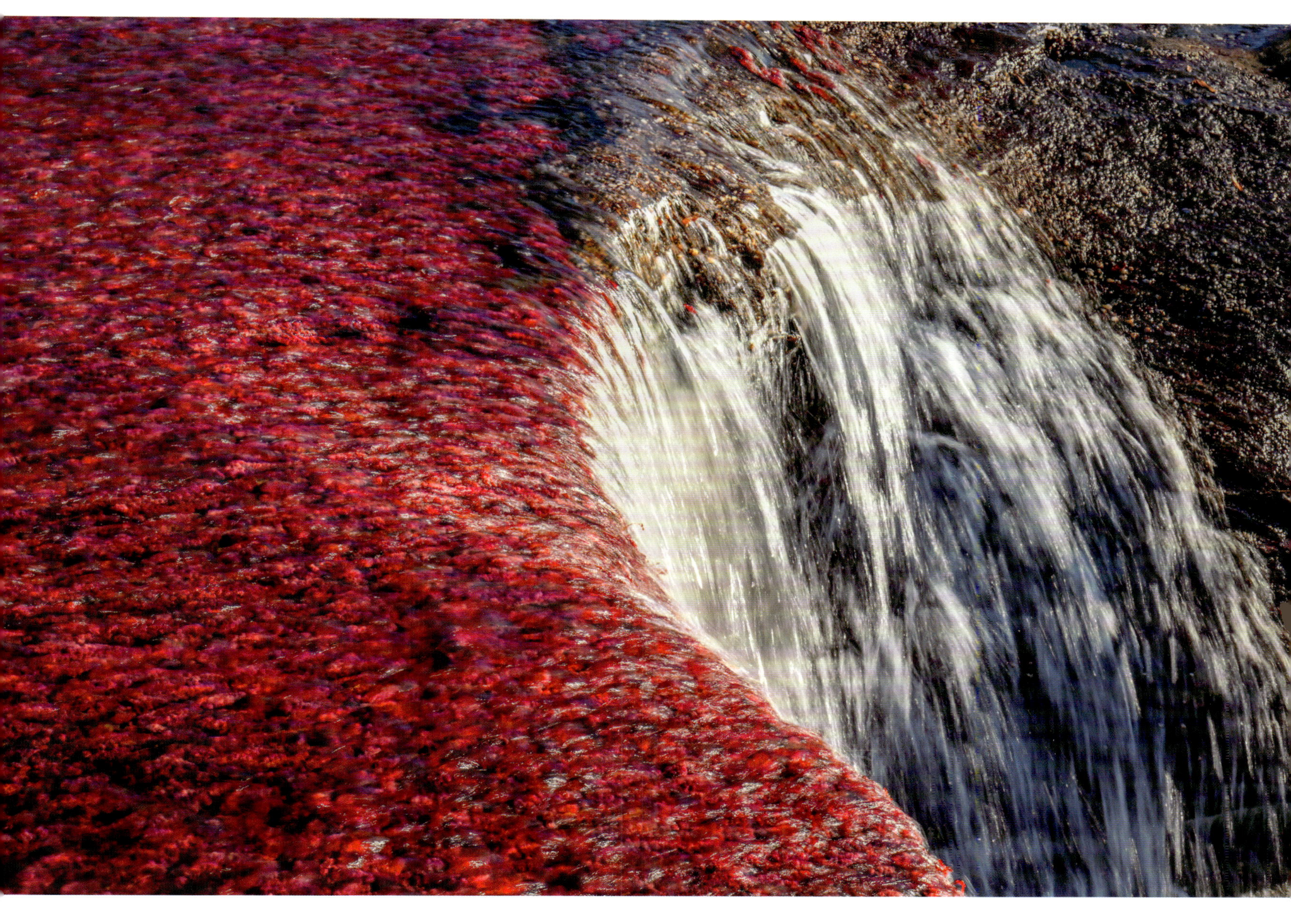

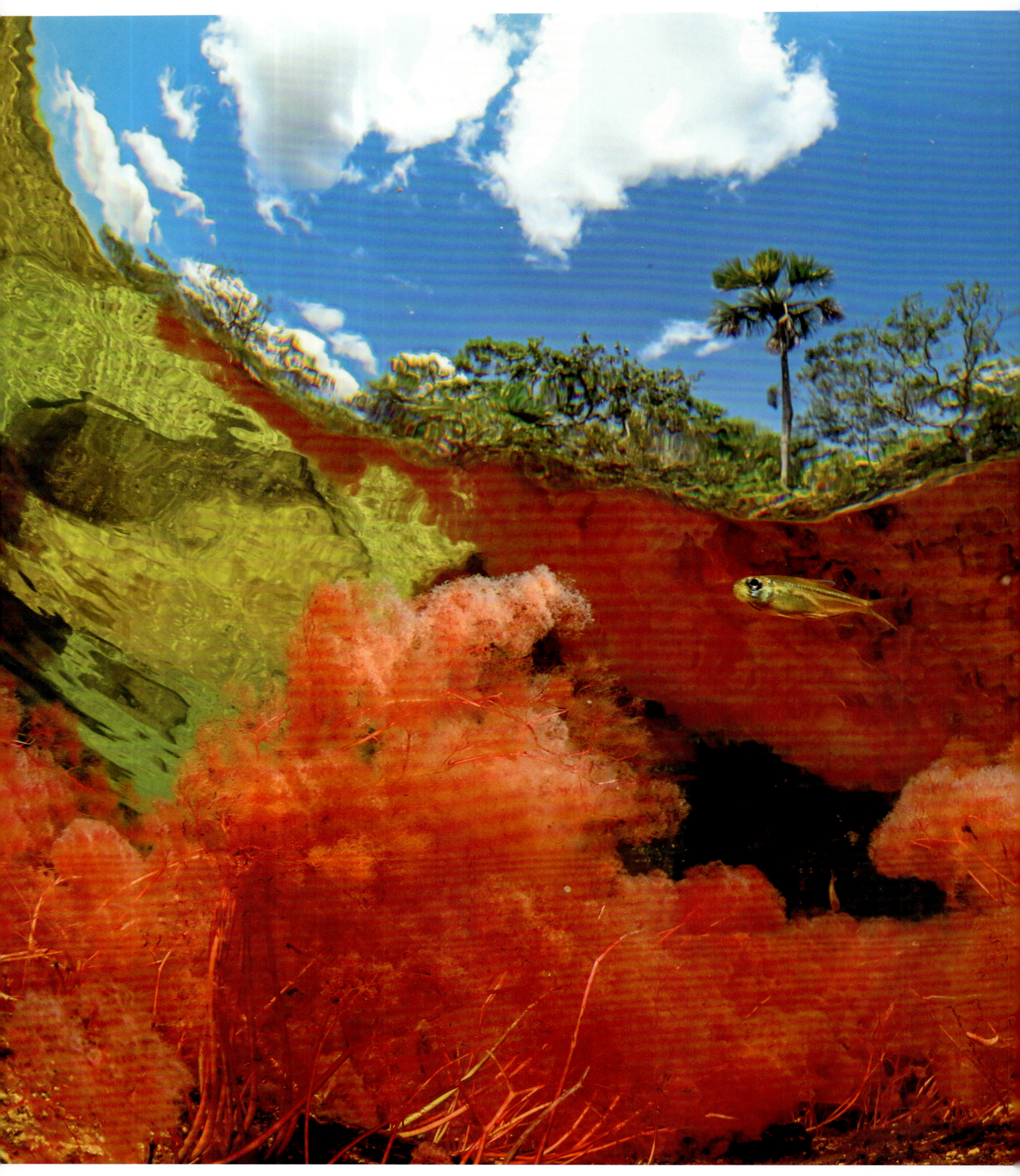

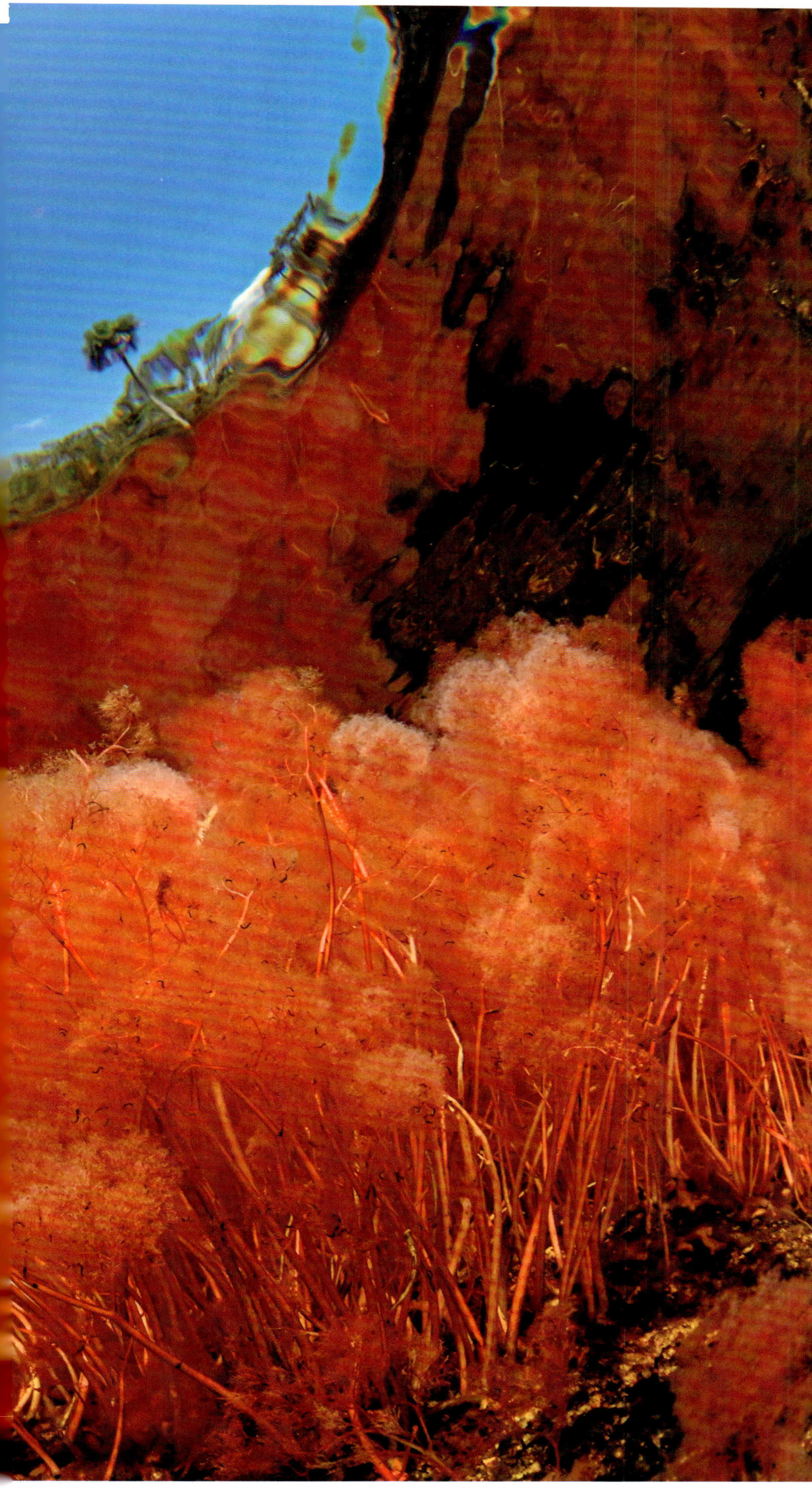

The Caño Juntos is a unique aquatic realm at the convergence of three large ecosystems: the Andes, the Llanos, and the Amazon rainforest. While diving Juntos, I frequently come across riverscapes that remind me of being on soft coral–studded reefs in the Indian and Pacific Oceans. The scenes are so breathtaking and colorful that often all I have to do is wait for one of the river's 80 species of fish to swim into the frame.

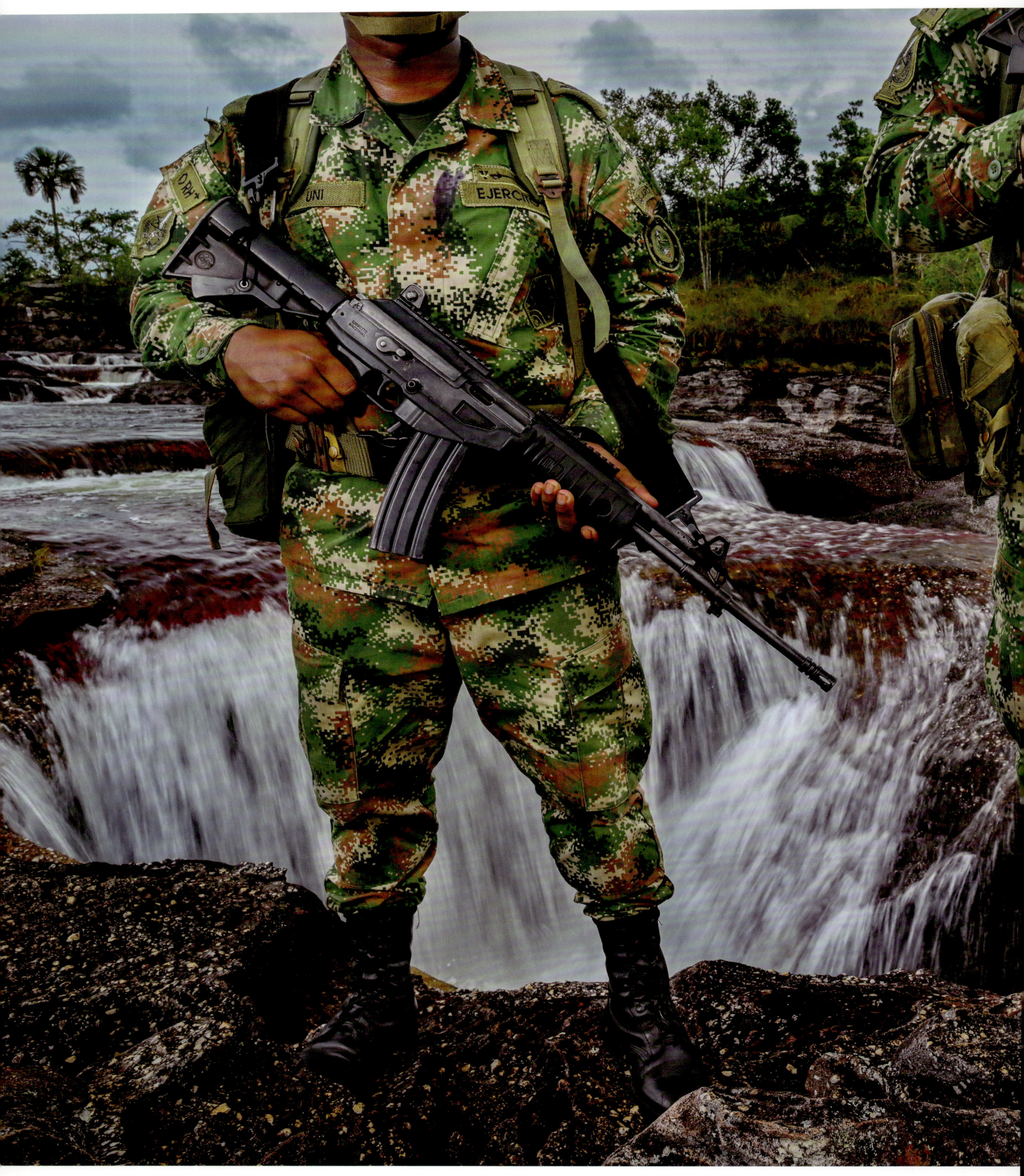

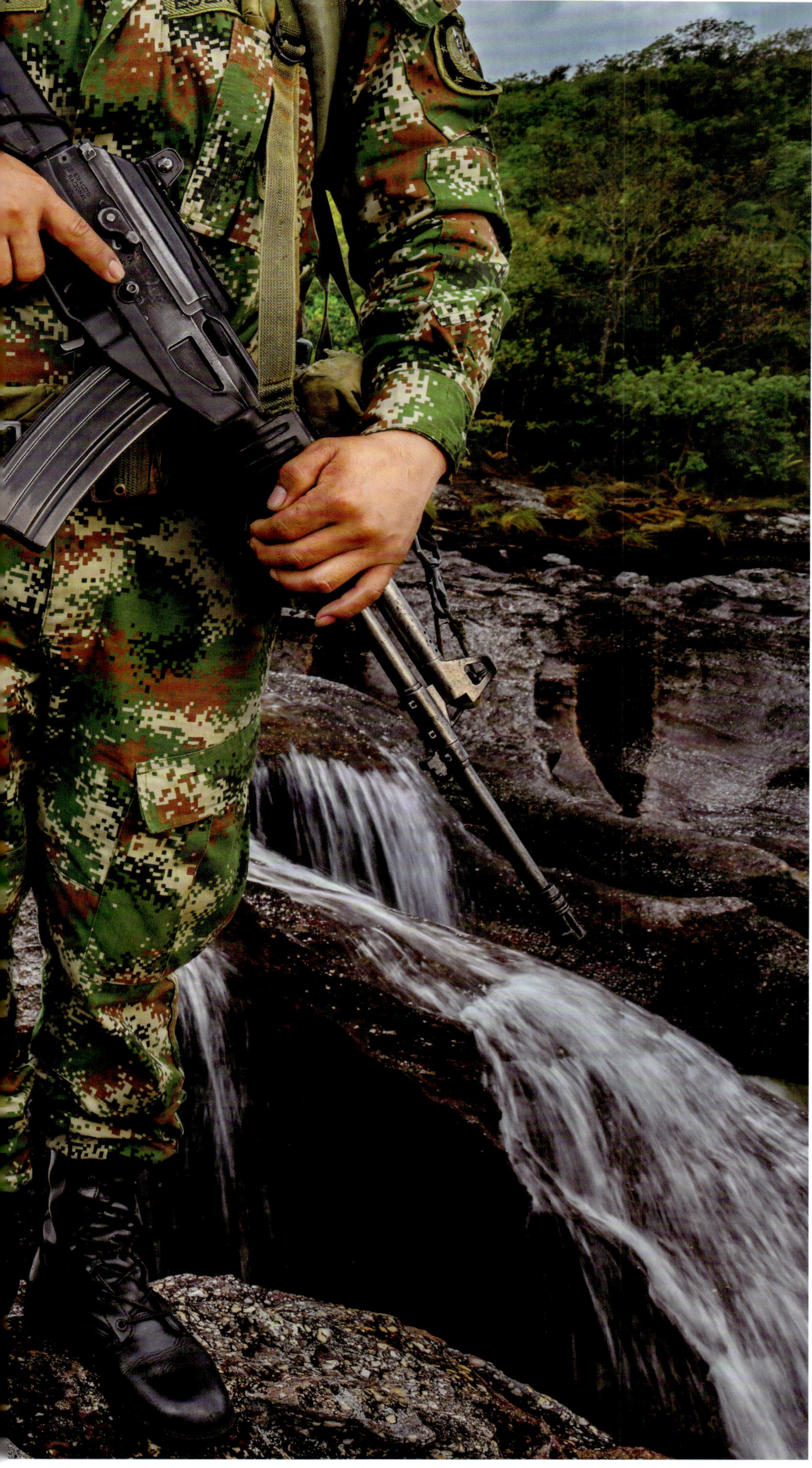

The wild landscape around the mountains of Chiribiquete, Lindosa, and La Macarena was once the epicenter of the FARC guerrilla movement, and some holdouts that did not sign the 2016 peace accord still move through the area. The Colombian military is therefore omnipresent and frequently patrols to enforce security.

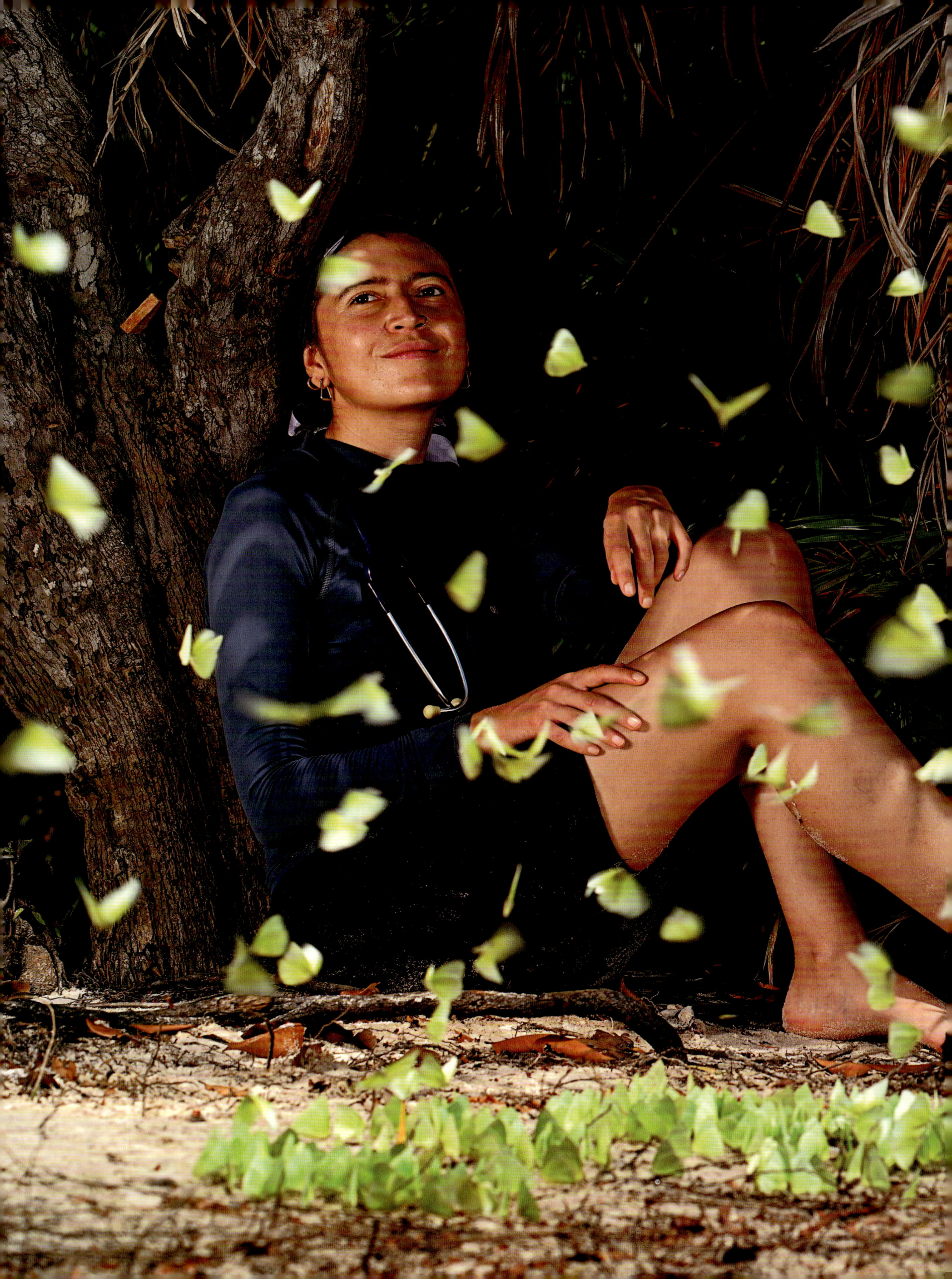

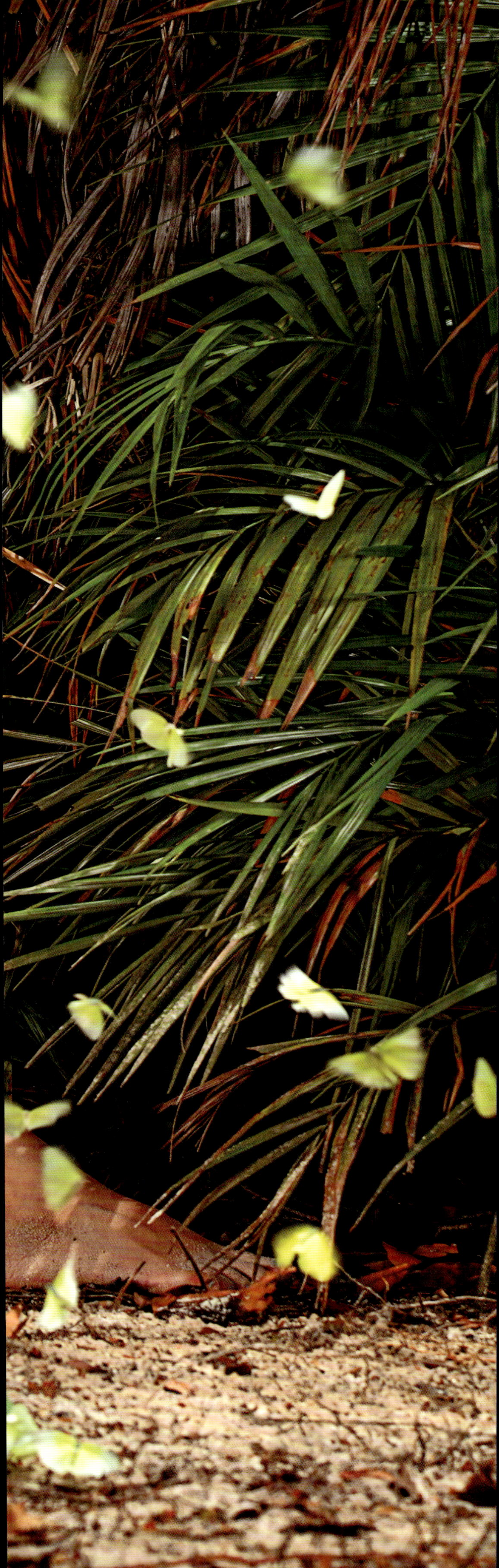

THE EXPLORERS

During my 396 days photographing and traveling across the Amazon River watershed, I cross paths, join forces, and collaborate with gifted scientists and conservationists, many of whom are fellow National Geographic Explorers. They study river dolphins, ancient rock art, the impacts of gold mining, Andean bears, and so much more.

Together, we scale high mountains, descend into deep canyons, canoe remote rivers, and explore vast forests. Our adventures give me a much deeper understanding of the inner workings of the Amazon watershed than I could ever have achieved on my own.

Archaeologist Carlos Castaño-Uribe

Colombian archaeologist Carlos Castaño-Uribe was the first to publish scientific descriptions of Chiribiquete rock art and was instrumental in the park's proclamation as a UNESCO World Heritage site in 2018. On one of his many expeditions, he found animal bones and feathers arranged next to fresh footprints beneath some paintings, indicating that the art continues to be important in Indigenous cosmology and the ceremonial activities of some of the nomadic groups who still live in voluntary isolation within the park today.

PAGES 124–125

Wildlife Veterinarian María Jimena Valderrama Avella

Colombian wildlife veterinarian María Jimena Valderrama Avella has dedicated her life to safeguarding the health of river dolphins and manatees across the Amazon and Orinoco River Basins. At Fundación Omacha, she leads the charge on pink dolphin health assessments and has organized six expeditions that ranged across the entire Amazon Basin.

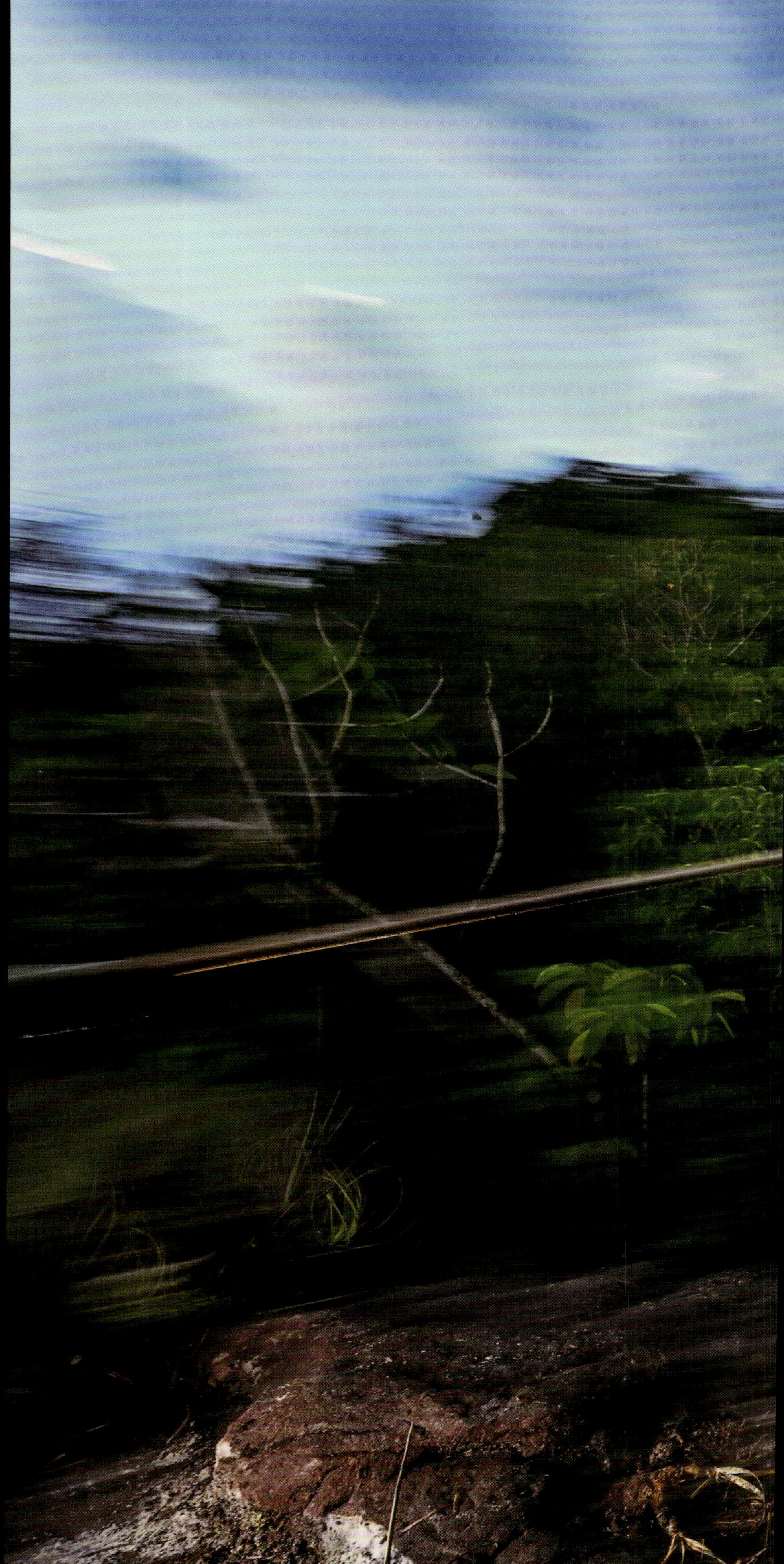

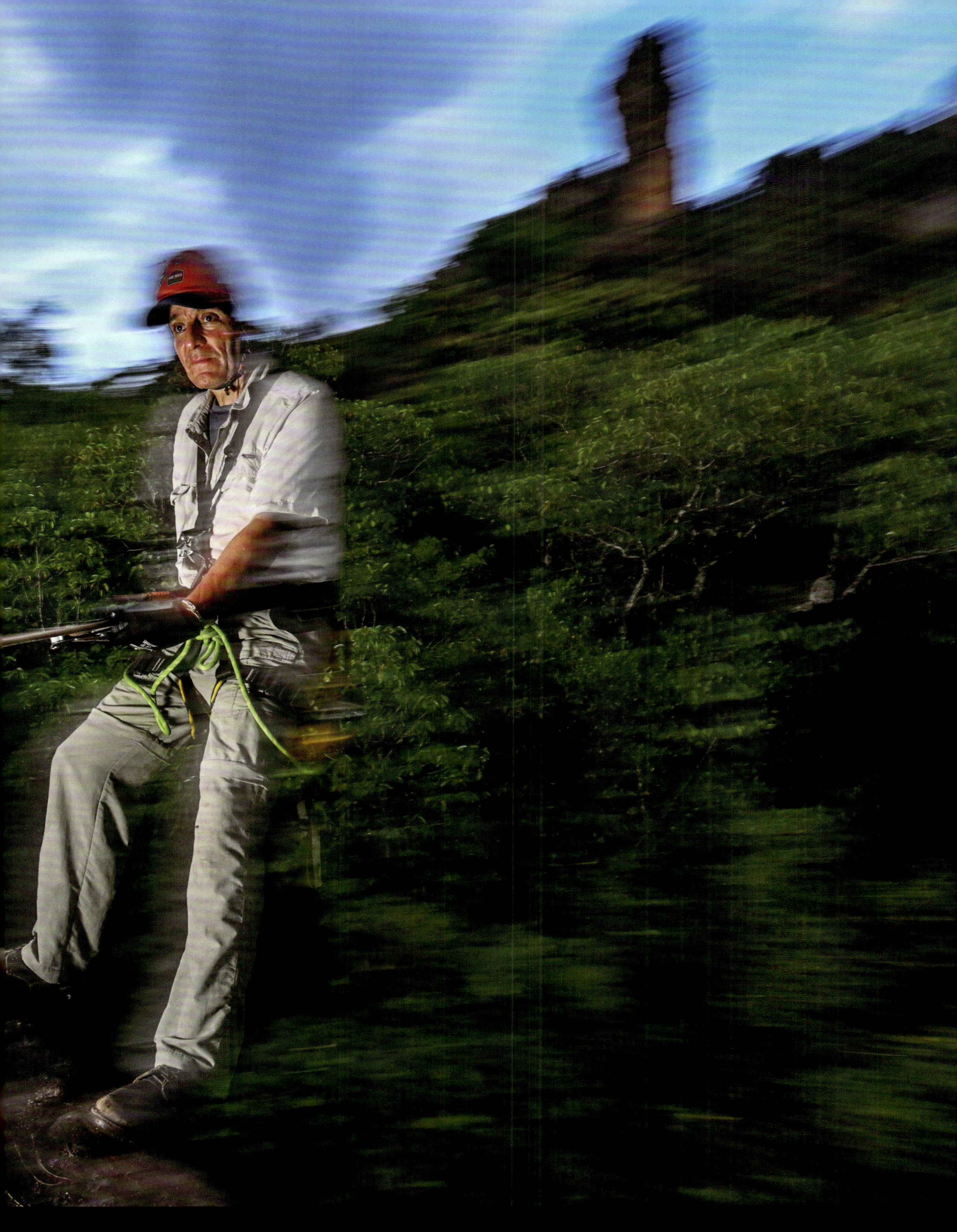

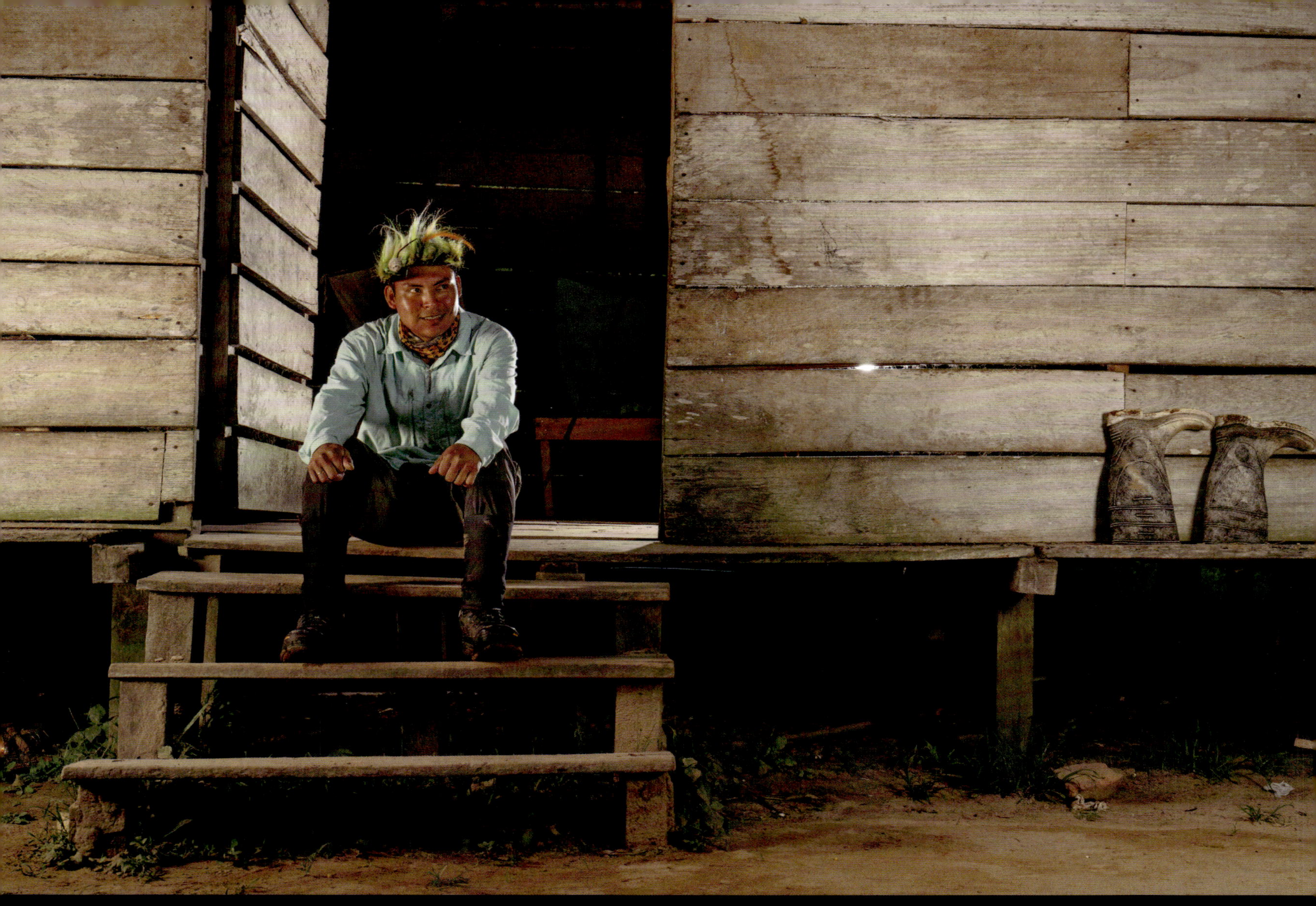

Fly-Fishing Guide and Photographer
Roycer Herbi

Roycer Herbi, an Indigenous Yuracaré fly-fishing guide, chaperones international fishers throughout Bolivia's Isiboro Sécure National Park and Indigenous Territory. He is also a talented and enthusiastic photographer and is currently working on visually documenting the largely unknown biodiversity of his tribe's territory. Having grown up among the forests and rivers, his naturalist expertise and instincts allow him to get closer to animals than any other photographer

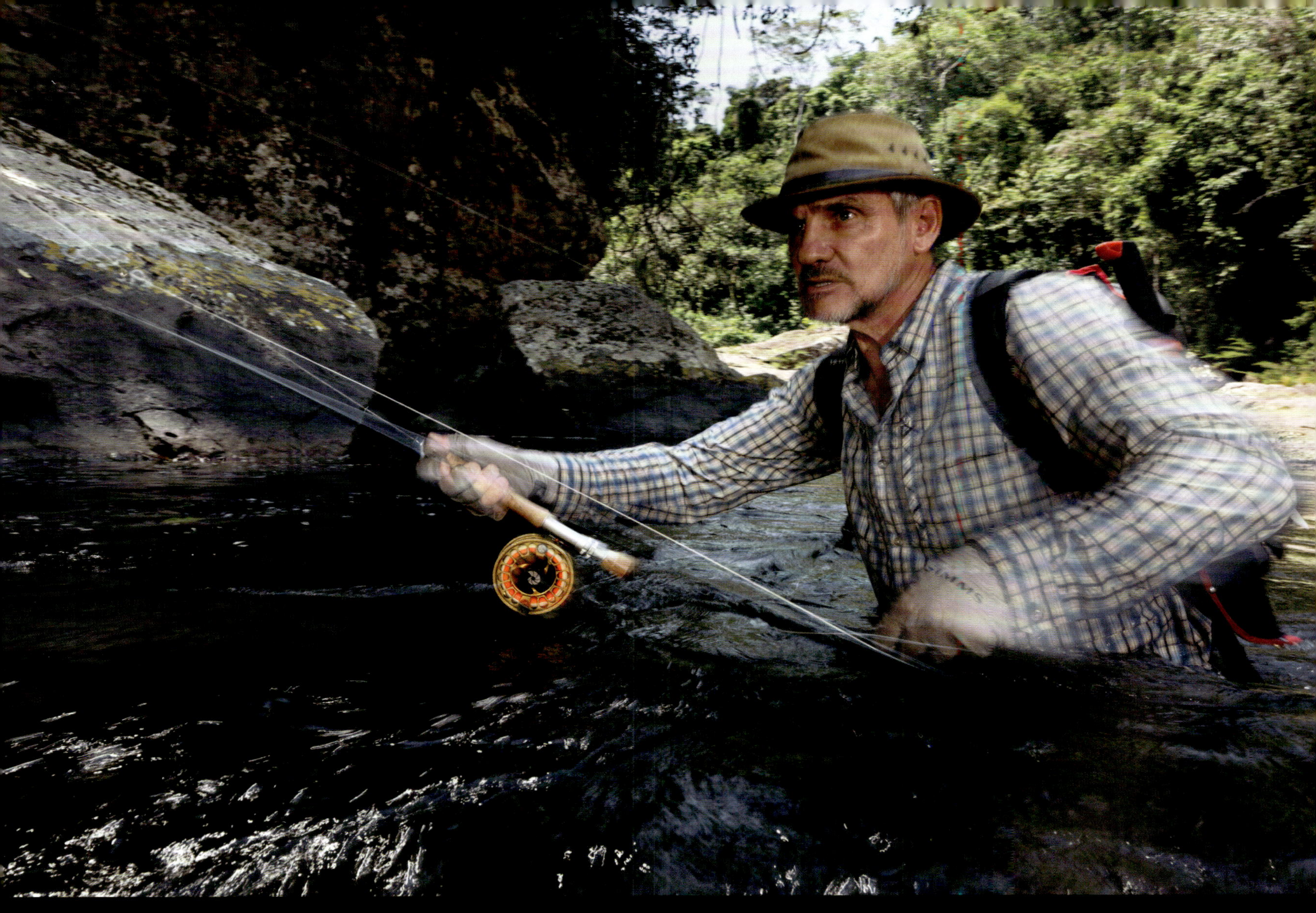

Fly-Fisherman and Conservationist
Marcelo Pérez

Marcelo Pérez, the founder and CEO of Untamed Angling, pioneered an innovative partnership between Indigenous groups and catch-and-release fly-fishing guides across the Amazon Basin, creating not only new revenue streams but also significantly improved education, medical services, and professional opportunities, especially for young people. His conservation priority is studying and protecting the pristine headwaters of the Sécure and Pluma Rivers in Isiboro Sécure National Park and Indigenous Territory in Bolivia.

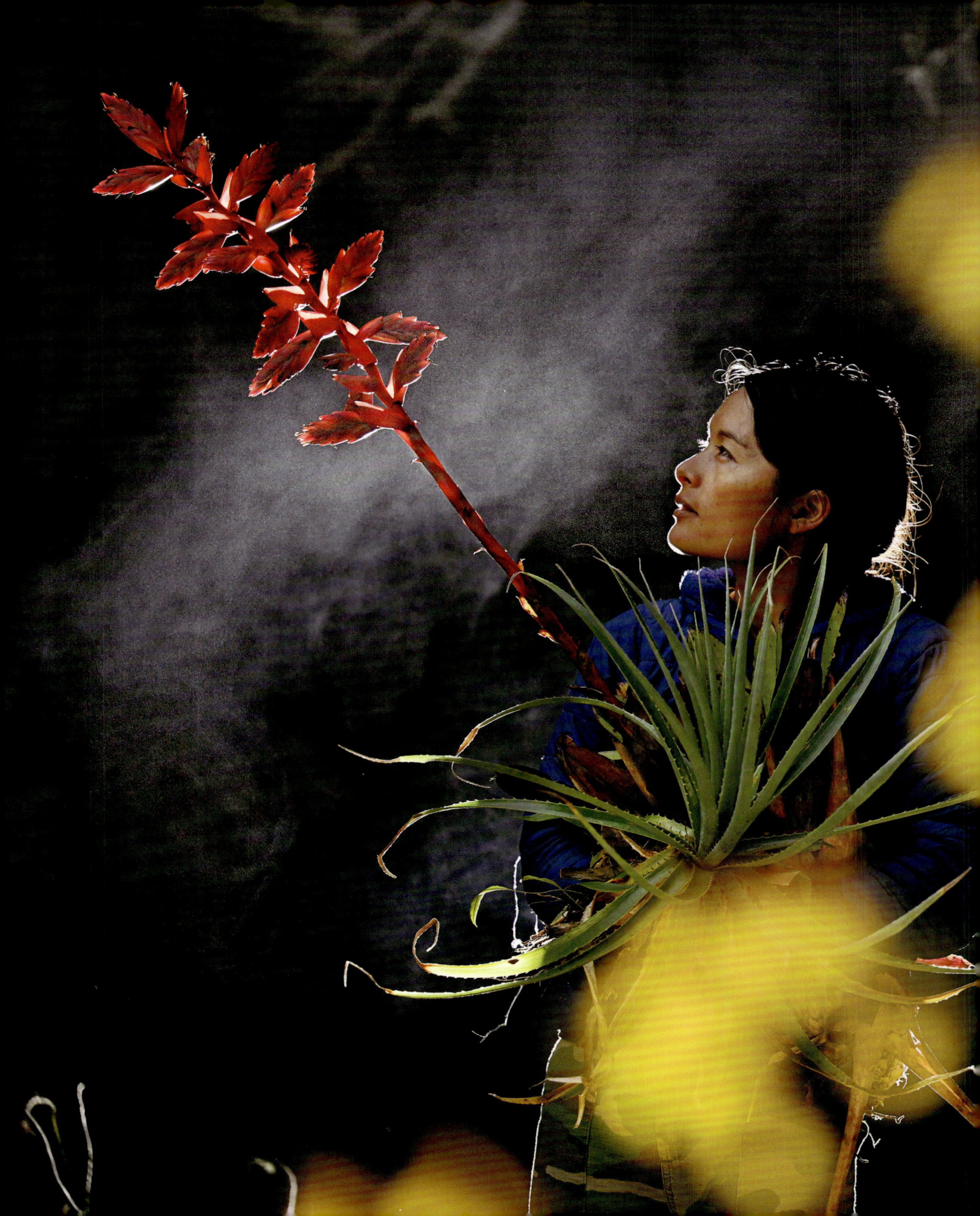

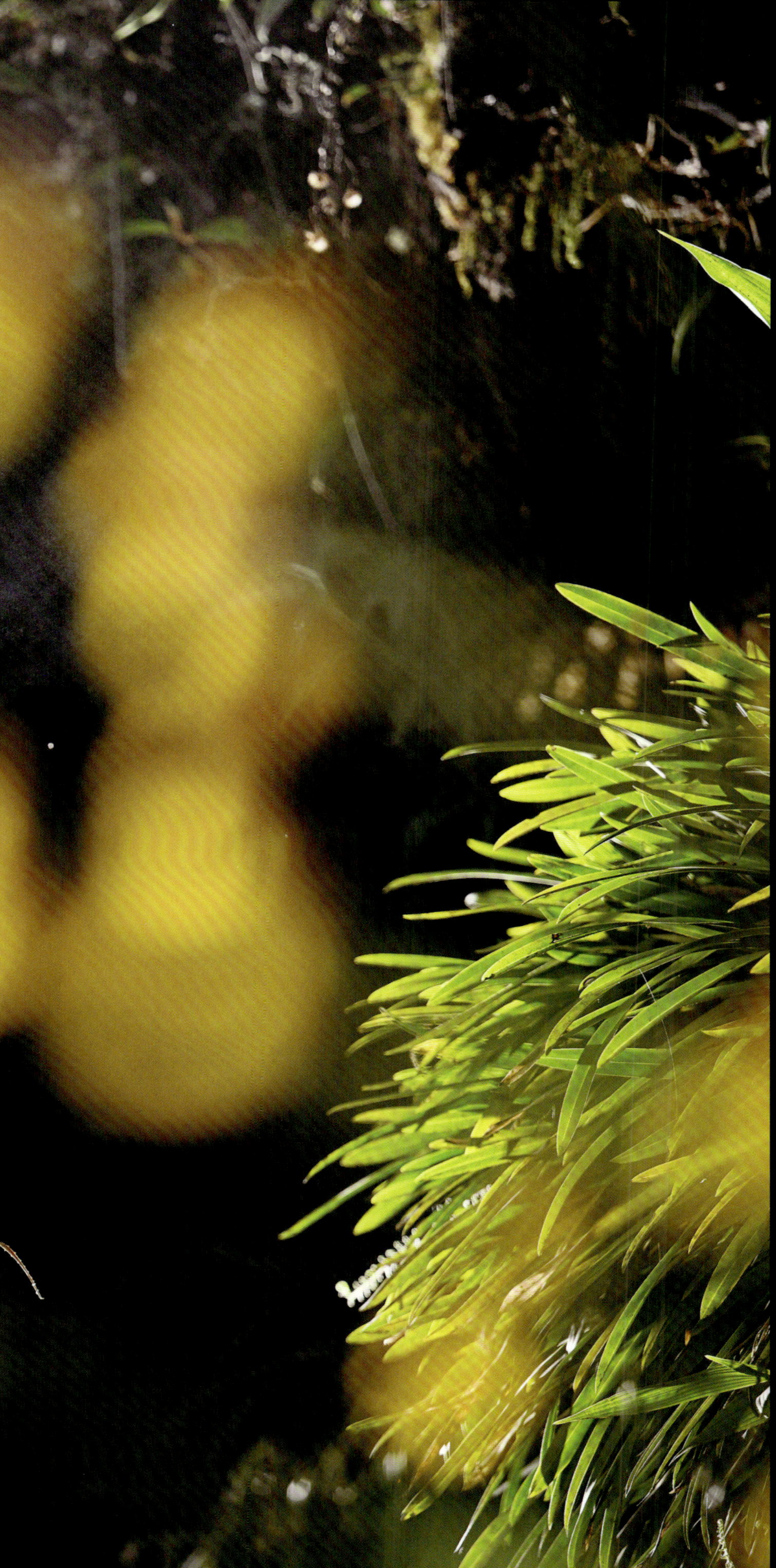

Andean Bear Researcher Ruthmery Pi Huarcaya

Ruthmery Pillco Huarcaya v raised in a Quechua village from the Wayqecha Cloud Biological Station, which is current home, 9,840 feet (3 above sea level. The area i to a flowering bromeliad, a food of the Andean bear. H and her team spend weeks difficult conditions explorin forests and grasslands to a the health of the Andean b population and study its rol maintaining the rain-genera cloud forests of the Andes.

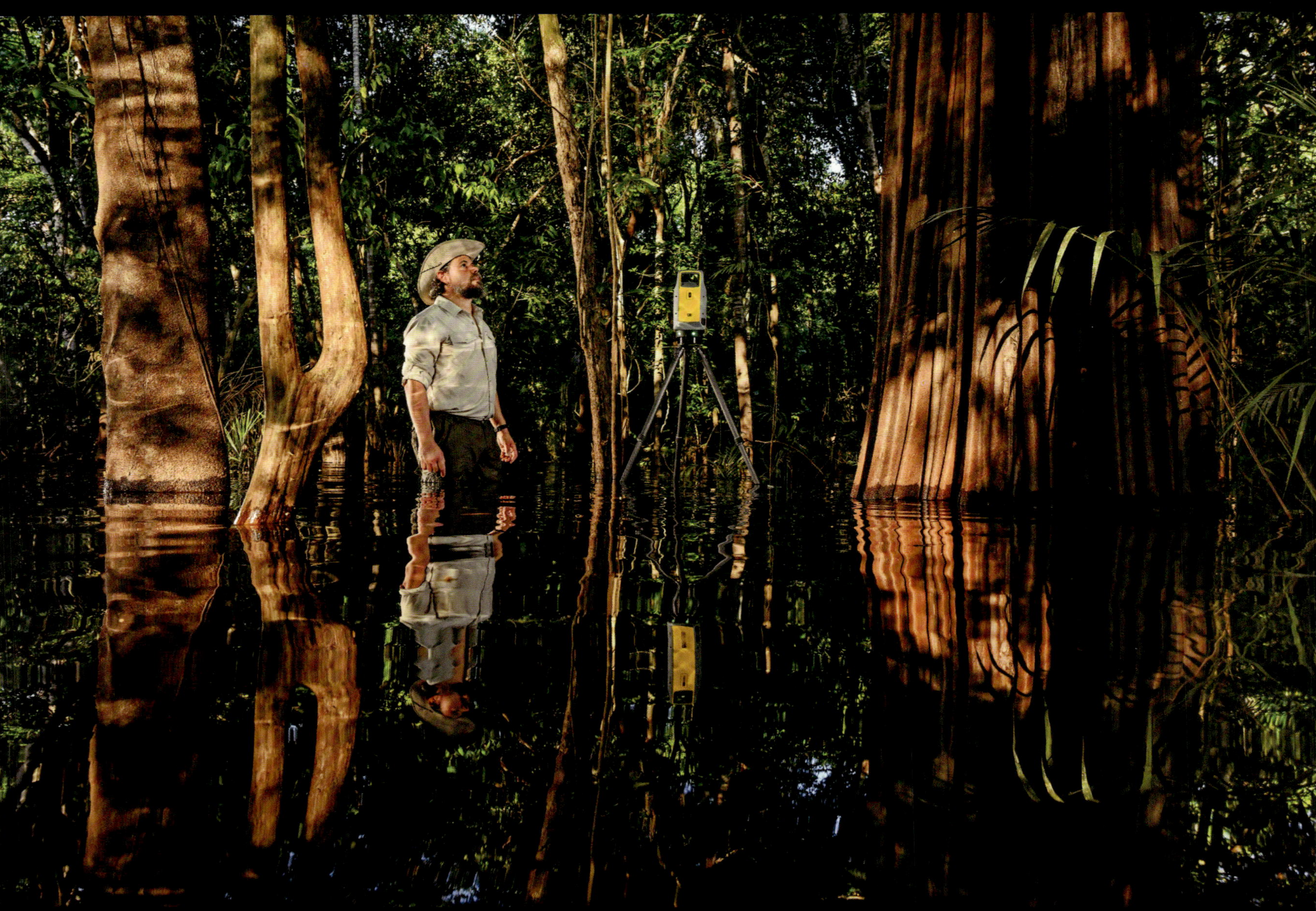

Digital Ecologist
Thiago Sanna Freire Silva

Brazilian scientist Thiago Silva calls himself a digital ecologist and uniquely fuses expedition field research with technology to answer some of the Amazon Basin's most pressing research questions. He uses lidar (light detection and ranging) to scan vast swaths of flooded forest and to build interactive virtual models that are detailed down to individual leaves. Silva and his scientific collaborator Julia Tavares are in a race to protect these forests from increasing environmental extremes triggered by climate change and hydroelectric dams.

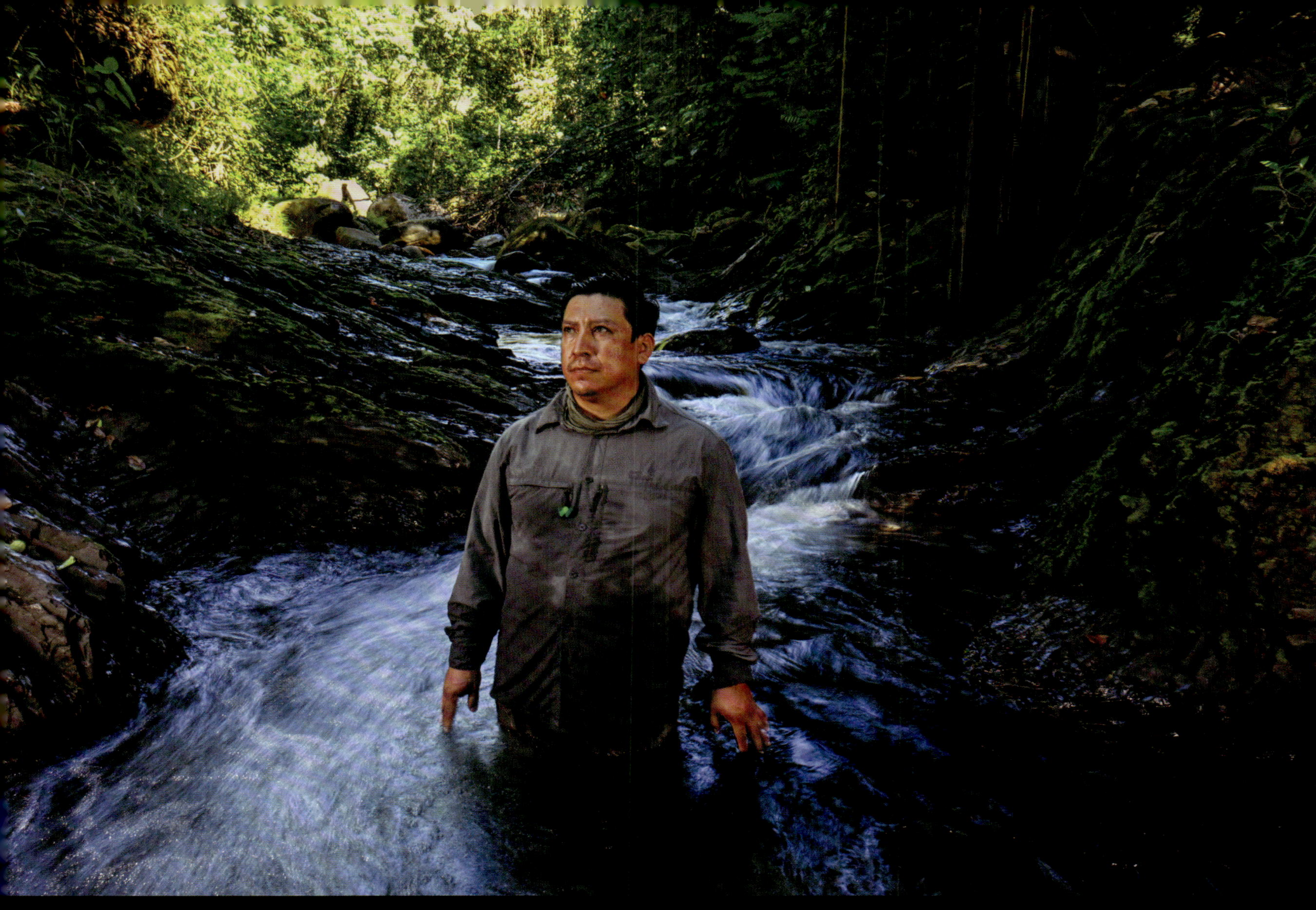

Freshwater Fish Biologist
Guido Miranda

Guido Miranda is one of Bolivia's foremost experts on Amazonian freshwater fish and works as a biologist for the Wildlife Conservation Society. He recently explored the pristine headwaters of the Sécure and Pluma Rivers in Isiboro Sécure National Park and Indigenous Territory. "You get a sense that you're in a place unlike anywhere else. Very few humans have ever set foot here."

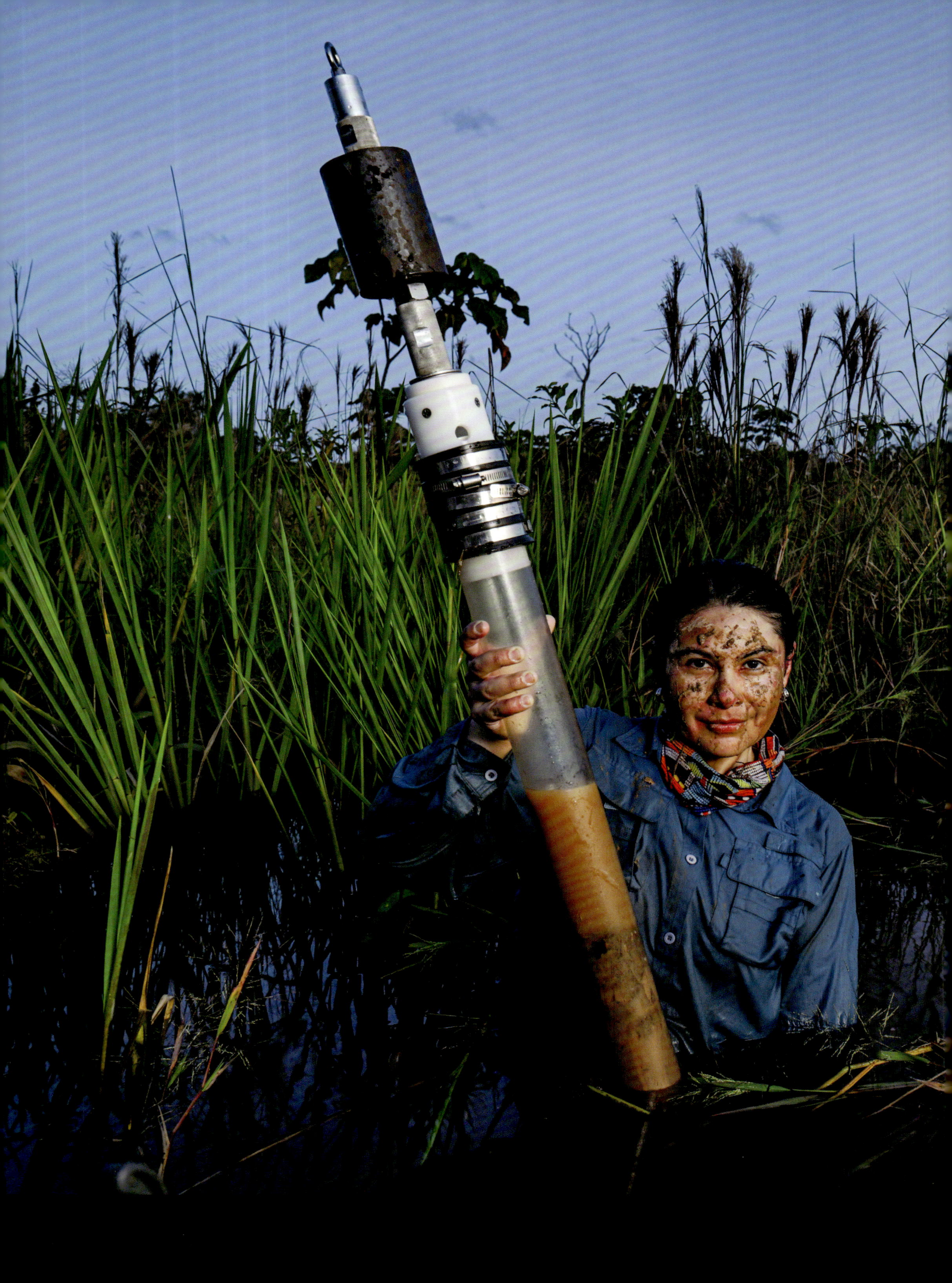

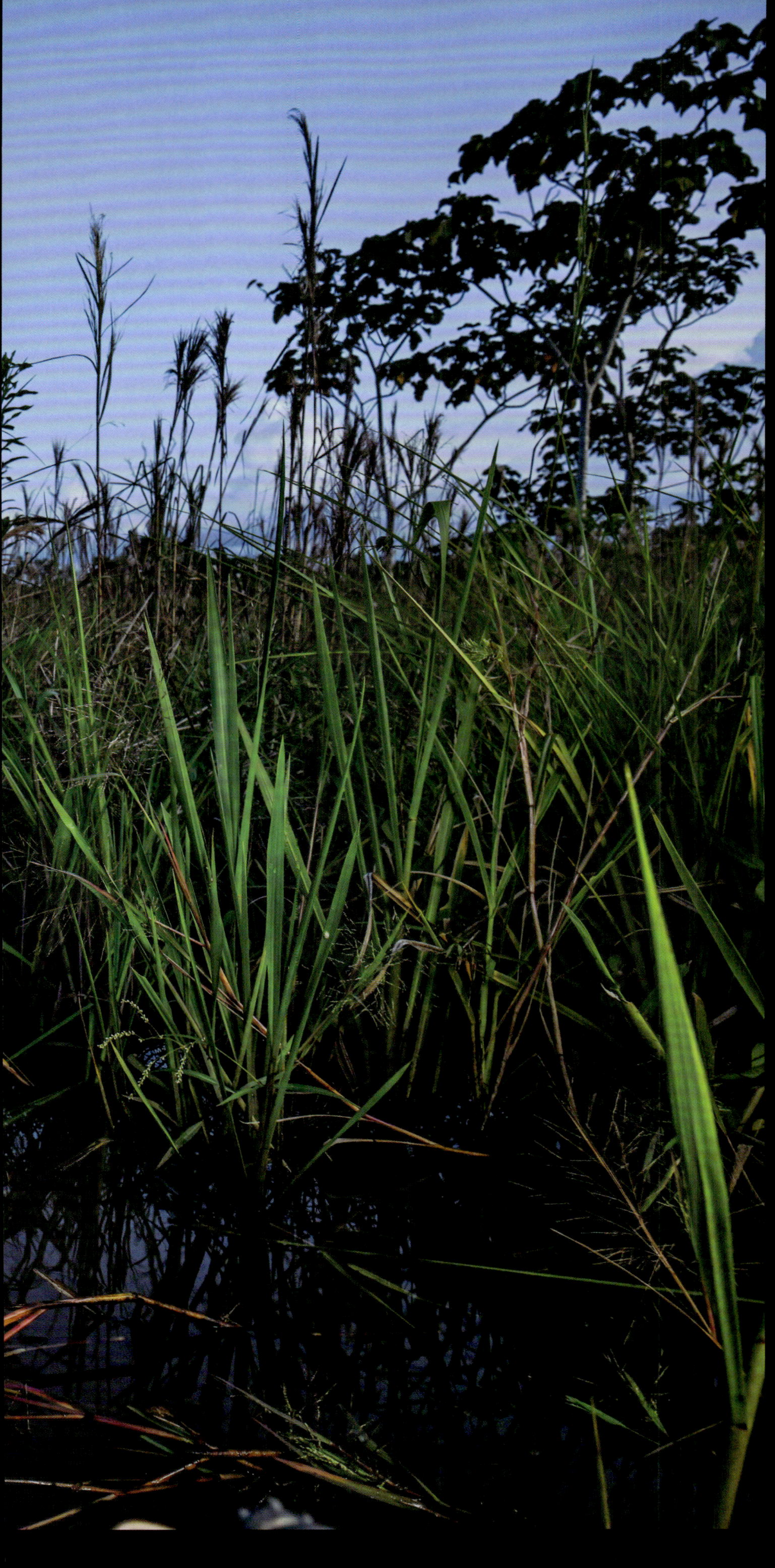

Geologist Jennifer Angel-Amaya

Colombian geologist Jennifer Angel-Amaya conducts research on the impacts of gold mining and the presence of mercury in the Amazon Basin. Her Ph.D. investigates how mercury, used to concentrate gold during the mining process, is distributed downstream. She is also developing methods capable of detecting mercury from gold mining operations in the field, which will allow local communities to monitor the health of their own environments.

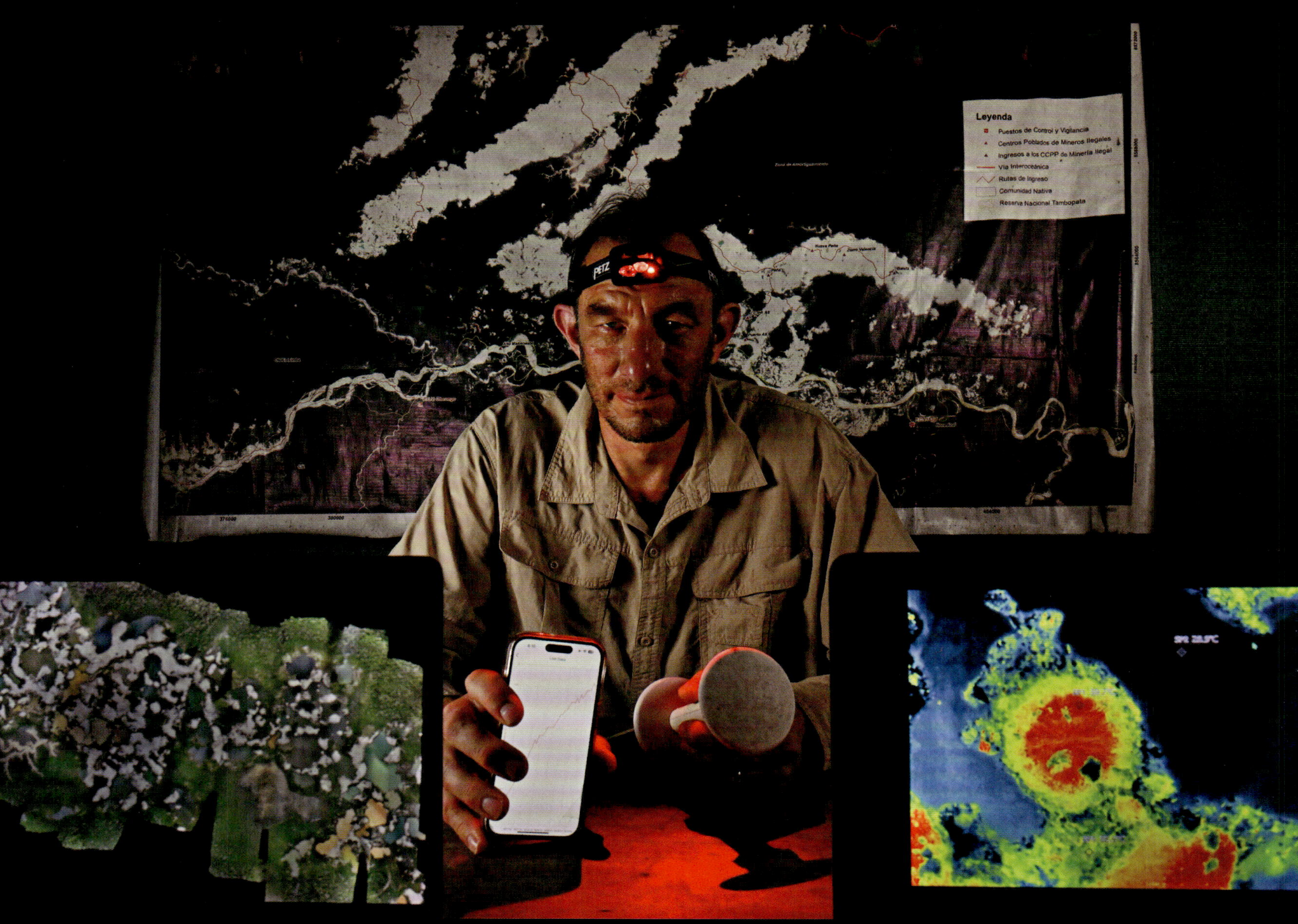

Hydrologist
Josh West

At the Azul ranger station in Peru's Tambopata National Reserve, Josh West, a hydrologist at the University of Southern California, sits surrounded by maps and screens showing areas of forest cleared and mined for gold. He holds tools used to log and track soil moisture, which varies dramatically between intact forests and recently mined areas.

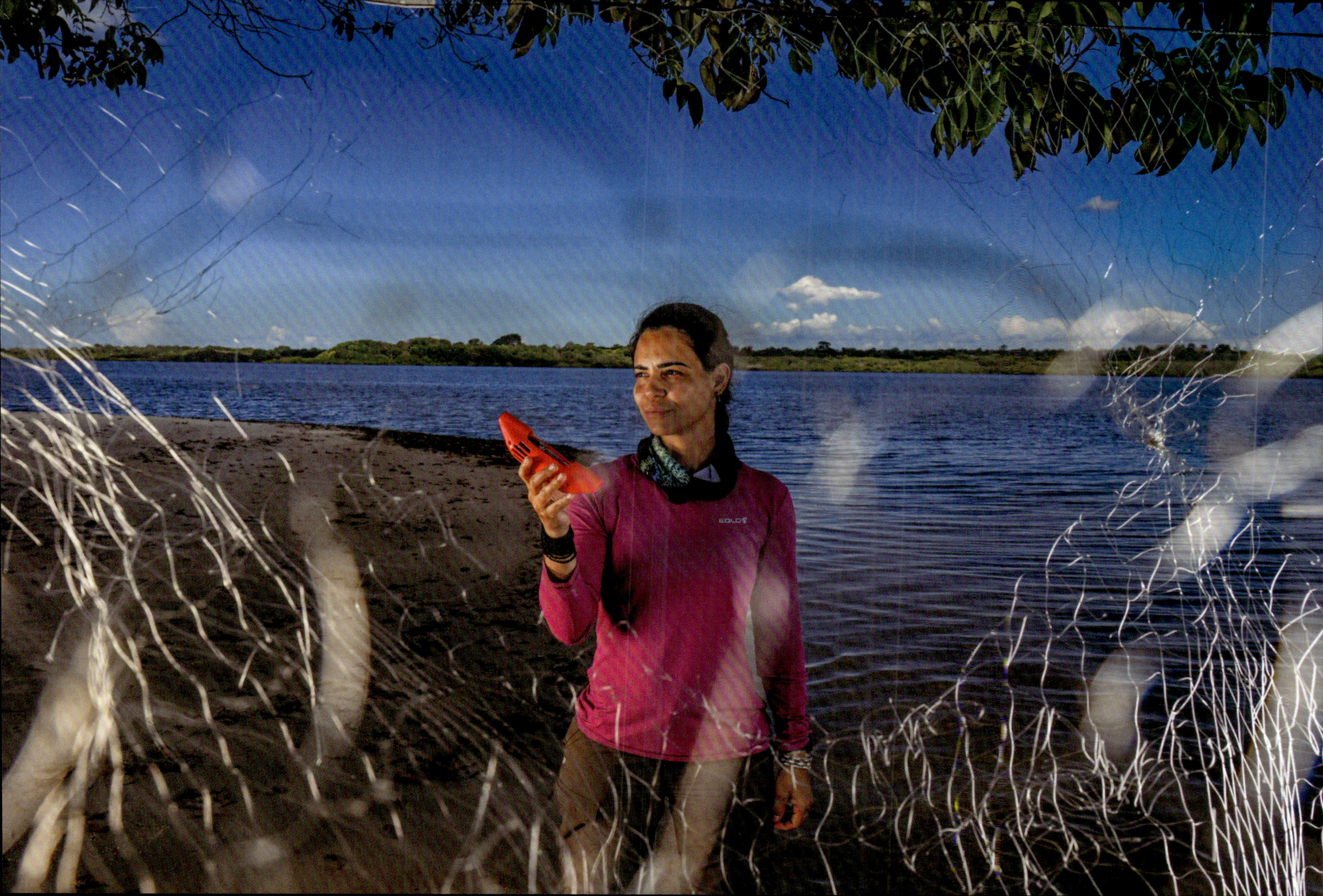

Conservation Biologist
Mariana Paschoalini Frias

Brazilian dolphin researcher Mariana Paschoalini Frias spends much of her time trying to keep the peace between pink dolphins and fishermen. She is currently trialing an underwater acoustic device: a pinger that emits sounds the same frequency at which these dolphins communicate. She hopes the sounds will keep the dolphins away from nets and prevent them from stealing fish, making them targets of fishermen's ire.

Microbial Ecologist
Hinsby Cadillo-Quiroz

Hinsby Cadillo-Quiroz, a Peruvian microbial ecologist at Arizona State University, uses a drone to investigate the recolonization of artificial ponds created by gold mining activities in the Amazon rainforest. He has seen an unexpected amount of wildlife returning to the devastated landscapes and found some promising solutions for their regeneration. Cadillo-Quiroz also studies the variation of methane and carbon storage across mining regions and how this impacts climate change.

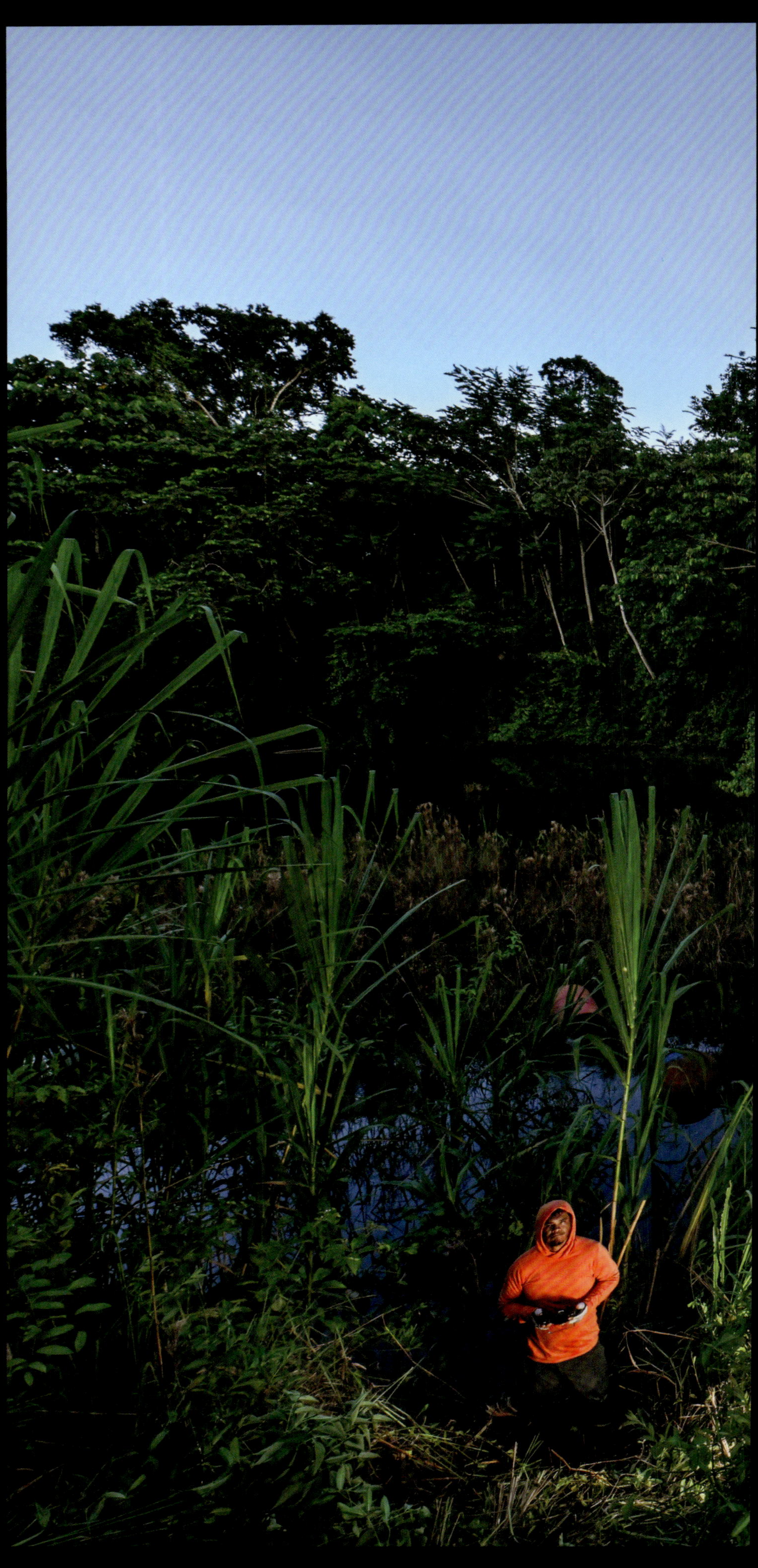

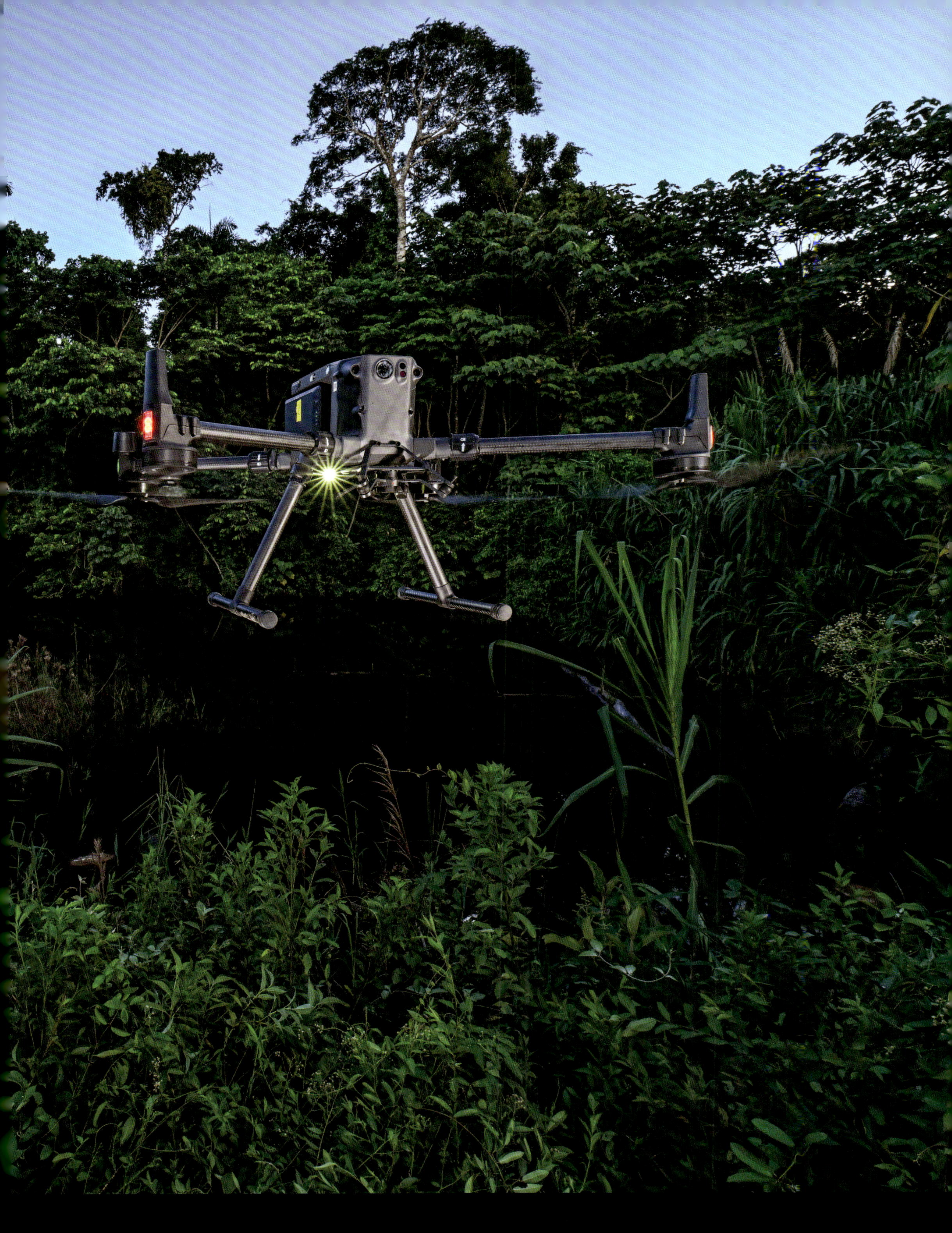

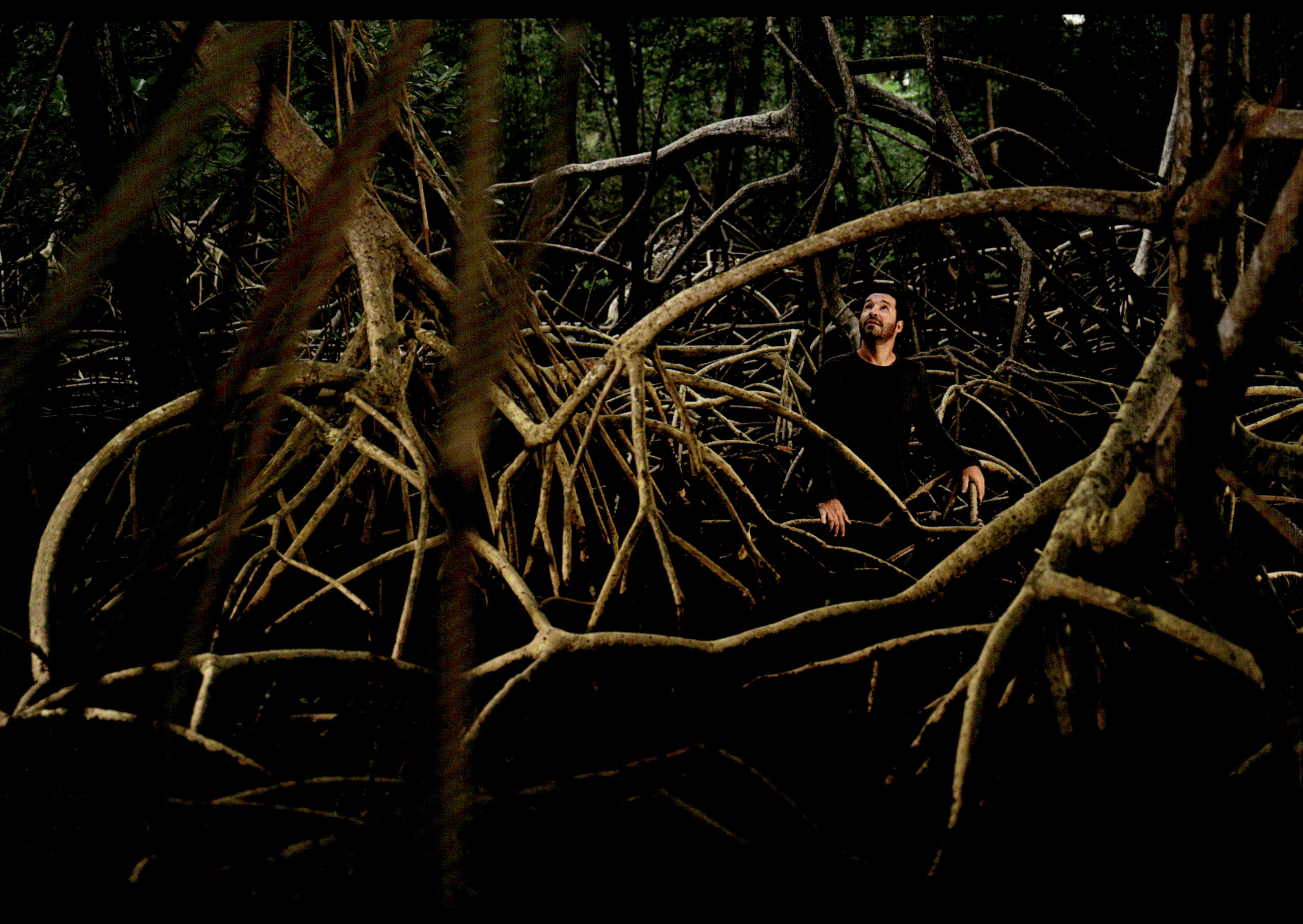

Marine Ecologist
Angelo Bernardino

On an island at the Amazon's mouth, marine ecologist Angelo Bernardino takes a break on a tangled maze of mangrove roots. Together with Margaret Awuor Owuor, they survey mangroves, engage with local people about the forests' importance to community life, and educate on how the forests store vast amounts of carbon and combat climate change.

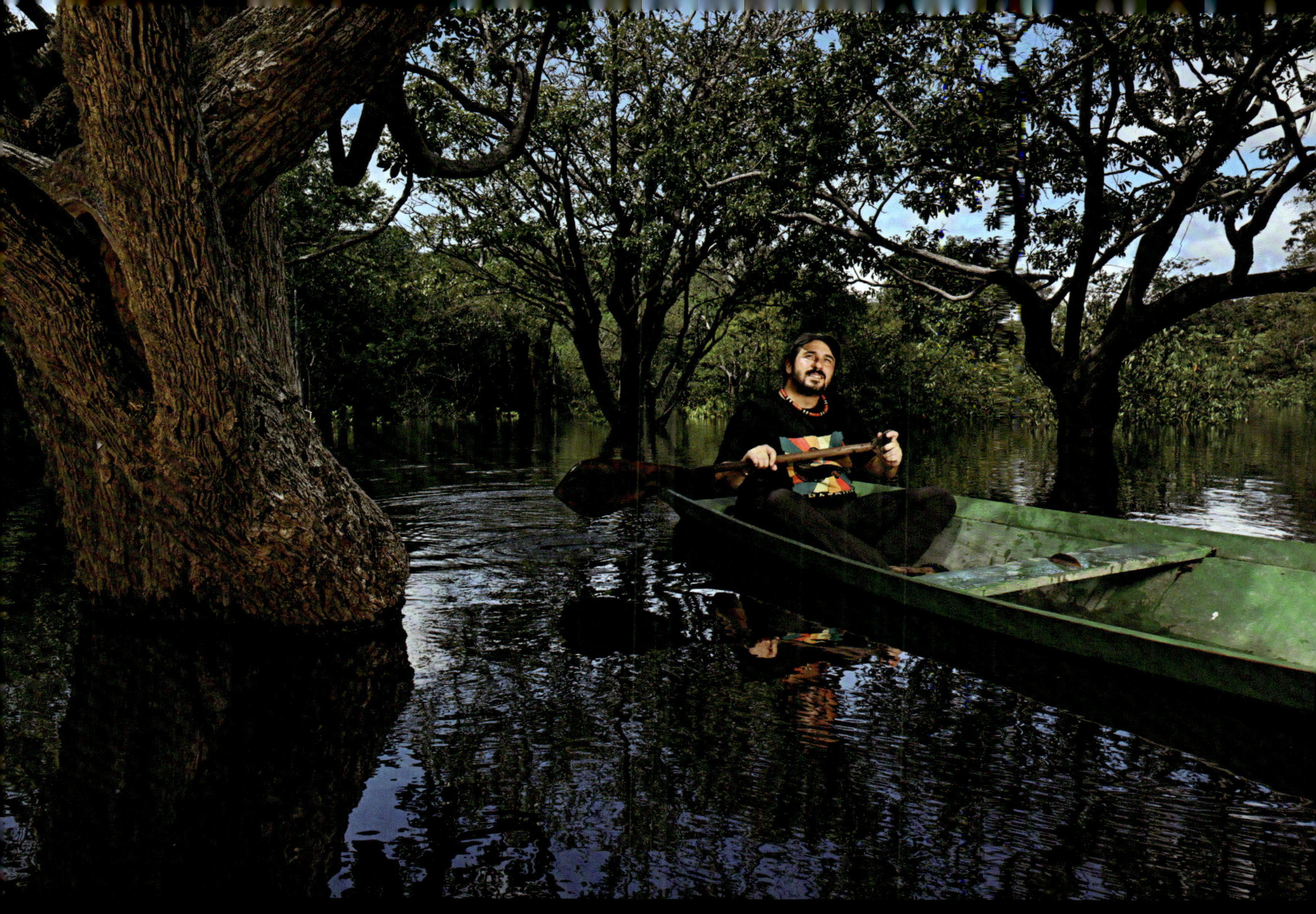

Ecologist
João Campos-Silva

João Campos-Silva, Andressa Scabin, and their colleagues collaborate with local communities along the Juruá River to study and protect six of the Amazon's key riverine megafauna. They recently became the first people in the world to attach a GPS tag to an arapaima, the world's largest scaled freshwater fish, and through local protection helped increase its population by 600 percent.

Aquatic Biologist Fernando Trujillo

Fernando Trujillo, one of the world's foremost experts on pink dolphins, maintains a scientific skull collection at his research station in the southeast of the Colombian Amazon. During a conversation with Trujillo outside the field station, he tells me that once the rains begin, the entire landscape will be submerged by at least 16 feet (5 m) of water. He says dolphins will then literally swim among the trees around us, which is what inspired this photograph. I secure the skulls at heights in the tree that will be submerged by the next flood period, and after carefully placing five studio lights across the scene, I am able to create this environmental portrait.

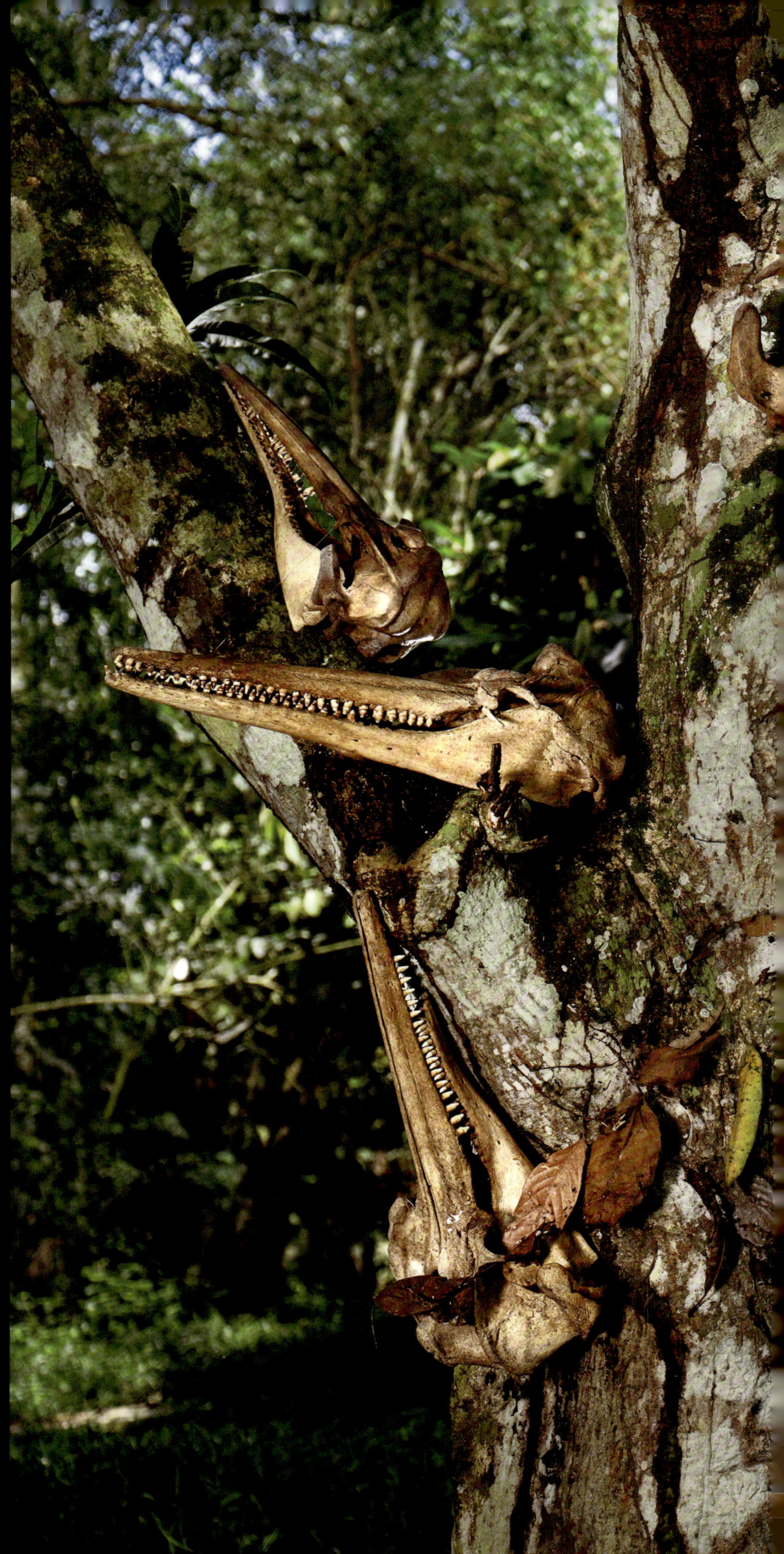

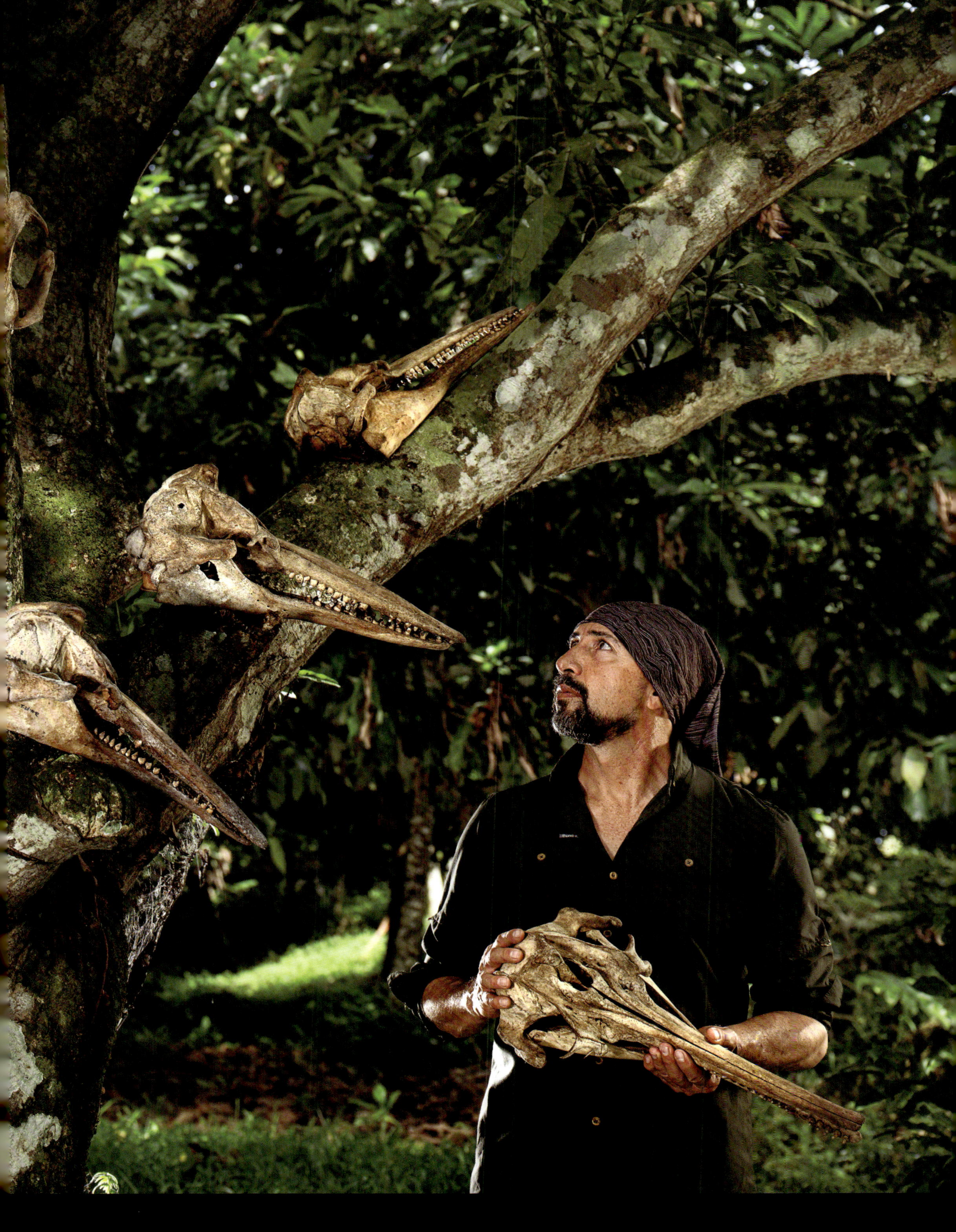

PART FOUR

LOWLANDS

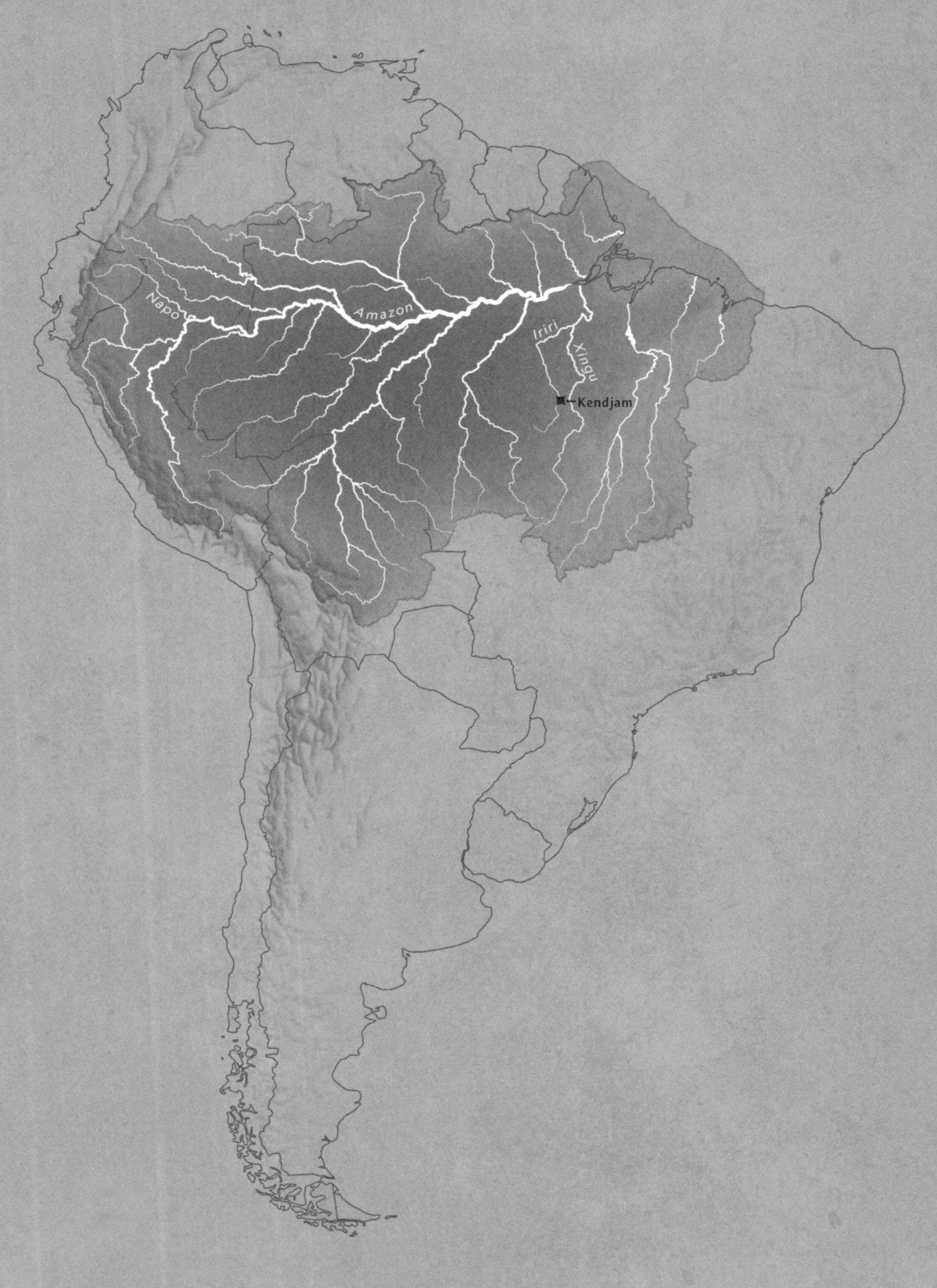
Napo
Amazon
Iriri
Xingu
Kendjam

FREE DIVING AMONG the flooded rainforests of the Rio Negro, I anticipate wild encounters with beasts covered in scales or scutes behind every submerged tree. My weight belt cinched tight around my waist and a snorkel's mouthpiece firmly between my lips, I am ready for almost anything. My first contact, however, is with a totally unexpected creature with long arms, a stubby tail, and green-tinged, algae-stained fur. My first thought is, *Shouldn't you be up a tree, safely browsing in the canopy, away from hungry caimans?*

I learn firsthand that despite being one of the slowest-moving land mammals, crawling along at just 6.5 feet (2 m) a minute, sloths can move surprisingly fast in water. Even with my long fins, I struggle to keep up with the creature dog-paddling ahead of me. I must be extra vigilant as one leads me through the flooded forest; the tips of palm leaves break the surface every few feet, the dark water expertly hiding trunks covered with giant five-inch (12.5 cm) knitting needle–like spines. Getting impaled would be grounds for a medevac and swiftly put an end to my adventure.

Sloths brave water to access areas they cannot reach by climbing from tree to tree to locate a new food source or potential mate. Three extra vertebrae in their skeleton allow them to keep their heads above water as they swim and navigate the maze of flooded trees with ease. Sloths are also exceptionally buoyant, thanks to the large amounts of methane gas trapped in their stomachs—a by-product of their diet, consisting mainly of hard-to-digest leaves. And, to put it indelicately, sloths can't fart. Fossil evidence shows that marine sloths lived alongside whales 2.5 to 5 million years ago; in a surprising throwback, their modern-day relatives can still hold their breath up to 40 minutes. To my surprise, sloths in the Amazon appear to be every bit as aquatic as they are arboreal.

During the dry season, the Rio Negro's floodplain forests resemble normal woodlands, inhabited by terrestrial species from anteaters to armadillos and peccaries to pumas. However, as the rains fall in the distant headwaters and rivers burst their banks, the forest begins to flood. Wildlife that reigned here during dry times must now retreat to higher ground or climb into the canopy to survive. In some areas, jaguars spend the entire wet season living and hunting in trees. The river may rise as much as 45 feet (14 m), birthing an aquatic ecosystem with fish swimming in places where birds once nested. Stingrays root for tasty morsels hidden in leaf litter on the submerged forest floor, and hollow tree trunks that sheltered arboreal porcupines now make cozy refuges for outlandish-looking catfish.

> **The ebb and flow of seasonal flooding make up the engine that drives the ecologies and life cycles of the Amazon River and its biodiversity.**

The floodwaters also provide for Indigenous people, like the Kayapó who live along the banks of Brazil's Iriri and Xingu Rivers, clear-water tributaries that flow over granite bedrock. Yellow-spotted river turtles are an important source of protein here, and in addition to collecting their eggs from exposed sandbanks during the dry season, many Kayapó communities also hunt these reptiles underwater.

Standing on the prow of a canoe, Djokro Kayapó from the village of Kendjam scans the waters ahead for the slightest disturbance that might indicate the presence of a turtle below. When he spots one, he leaps with reckless abandon headfirst into the water. Miraculously, he manages to catch one by its shell underwater, and a few seconds later surfaces with the turtle securely in his hands. Although many Indigenous groups in the Amazon harvest freshwater resources, very few immerse themselves so completely. But the Kayapó are uniquely comfortable holding their breath underwater—so much so that they can move large rocks while crawling along the submerged riverbed to open up navigable passages for their canoes to travel through shallow rapids.

The Kayapó revere and respect the payara, or vampire fish, above all other species, and it plays a central role in their culture and cosmology. Payaras can grow to 3.5 feet (1 m) long, weigh up to 40 pounds (18 kg), and possess saber-like teeth, evolved to stab and slash prey. Their large eyes allow them to hunt in the darkness of the river's deepest reaches and ambush their favorite prey—piranhas—from below. In villages along the Xingu River, elders and shamans use the payara's long fangs to cut longitudinal scars into their arms; this scarification ritual is a rite of passage into manhood, transforming boys and young men into warriors. The process pays respect to the river and allows the spirit of the payara to enter and live on in the body of the warrior. The scars represent power and harness the payara's life force, turning its wearers into better hunters and fishermen. This ritual is repeated during different stages of a life, and men can have multiple sets of overlapping scars. The more fish they catch and scars they earn, the greater their stature in the community.

Due to their fierceness and size, payaras have few predators, with giant otters likely being notable exceptions. The world's largest otters—up to 6.5 feet (2 m) long and 75 pounds (34 kg)—can tackle almost any aquatic prey as they roam the flooded forest in packs of up to 10 individuals. Reminiscent of the wolves of North American woodlands, they hunt in groups and sometimes coordinate their efforts, allowing them to catch up to nine pounds (4 kg) of fish every day.

Giant otters make use of a complex repertoire of communication consisting of 22 distinct vocalizations: everything from barks and explosive snorts to low growls and piercing screams. In fact, different otter families have their own unique audio signatures. One of my fondest memories is of being serenaded by a symphony of otter hums, whistles, squeaks, whines, and wails as I paddled through the waterways and flooded forests of Ecuador's Napo River.

The ebb and flow of seasonal flooding make up the engine that drives the ecologies and life cycles of the Amazon River and its biodiversity. Nowhere is this more apparent than along the floodplain, where 96,525 square miles (250,000 km²) of forest are covered seasonally by water. Despite making up just 3 to 4 percent of the Amazon Basin, floodplains are among the most productive and species-rich aquatic ecosystems. Unfortunately, floodplain forests are one of the most threatened biomes in the Amazon. Due to intensive logging, forest clearing for ranching, and oil extraction, deforestation occurs at an alarming rate. In addition, the construction of dams alters the ancient seasonal rhythms of rising and falling water by disrupting the critical flow of nutrients and sediments to the detriment of both biodiversity and the communities that live along the water's edge.

With seasons in flux and floodwaters ebbing, the annual migration out of floodplain forests is about to begin. Aquatic wildlife of all guises and sizes will travel to river channels that are deep enough to hold abundant water throughout the dry season. I, too, will make this journey, alongside the most charismatic of all the Amazon creatures: the boto, or pink dolphin. ■

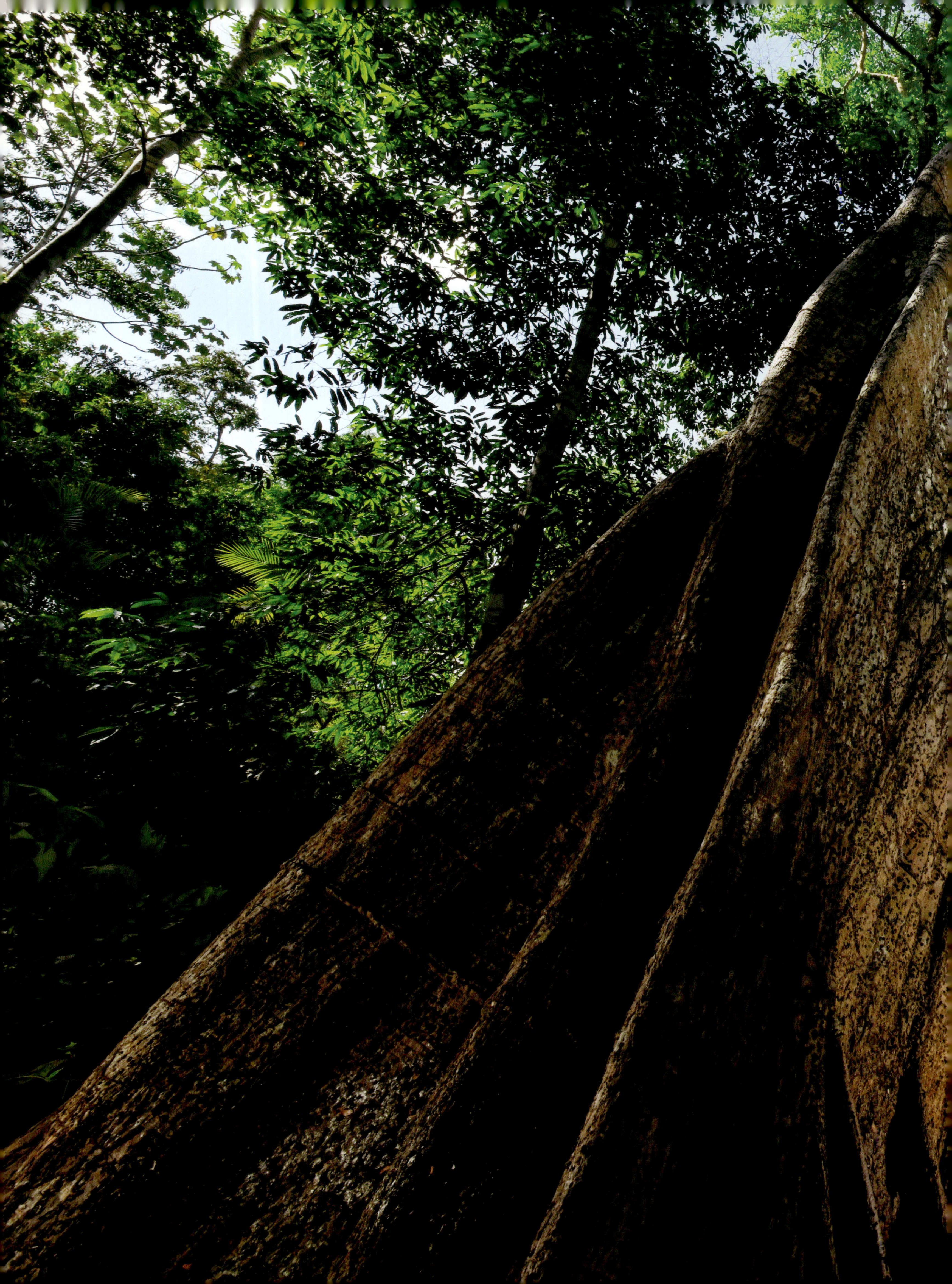

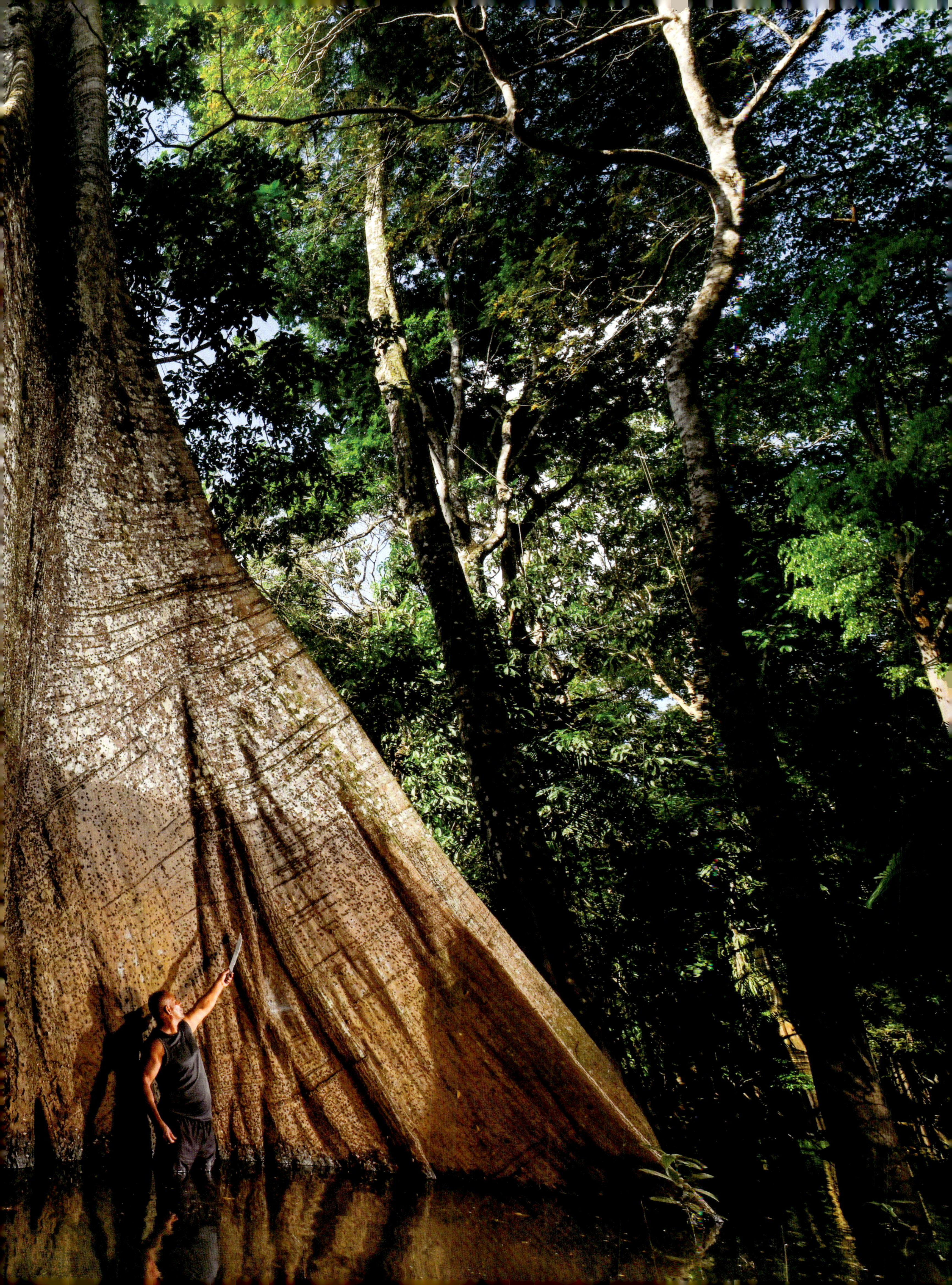

Across the Amazon lowlands, the waters' seasonal dramatic rise and fall drown and then expose forested terrain along the Rio Negro, one of the major tributaries feeding the Amazon River. The world's longest black-water river, it flows across the 400 islands that make up the Anavilhanas archipelago, protected within a park since 1981.

PAGES 150–151: In a flooded forest along Brazil's Rio Negro, jungle guide Roberto Abdias Gomes da Silva points toward the high waterline on the massive buttress roots of a kapok tree, a species that can grow more than 200 feet (60 m) tall. Its trunk acts like a water tank, storing moisture during seasonal floods to sustain it through dry periods.

PAGES 154–155: A freshwater ocellate river stingray *(Potamotrygon motoro)* skims through a shallow stream in Colombia's Bojonawi Nature Reserve. The Orinoco, Bojonawi's main river, flows north of the Amazon, but floods reshape geography and seasonally connect the two great basins.

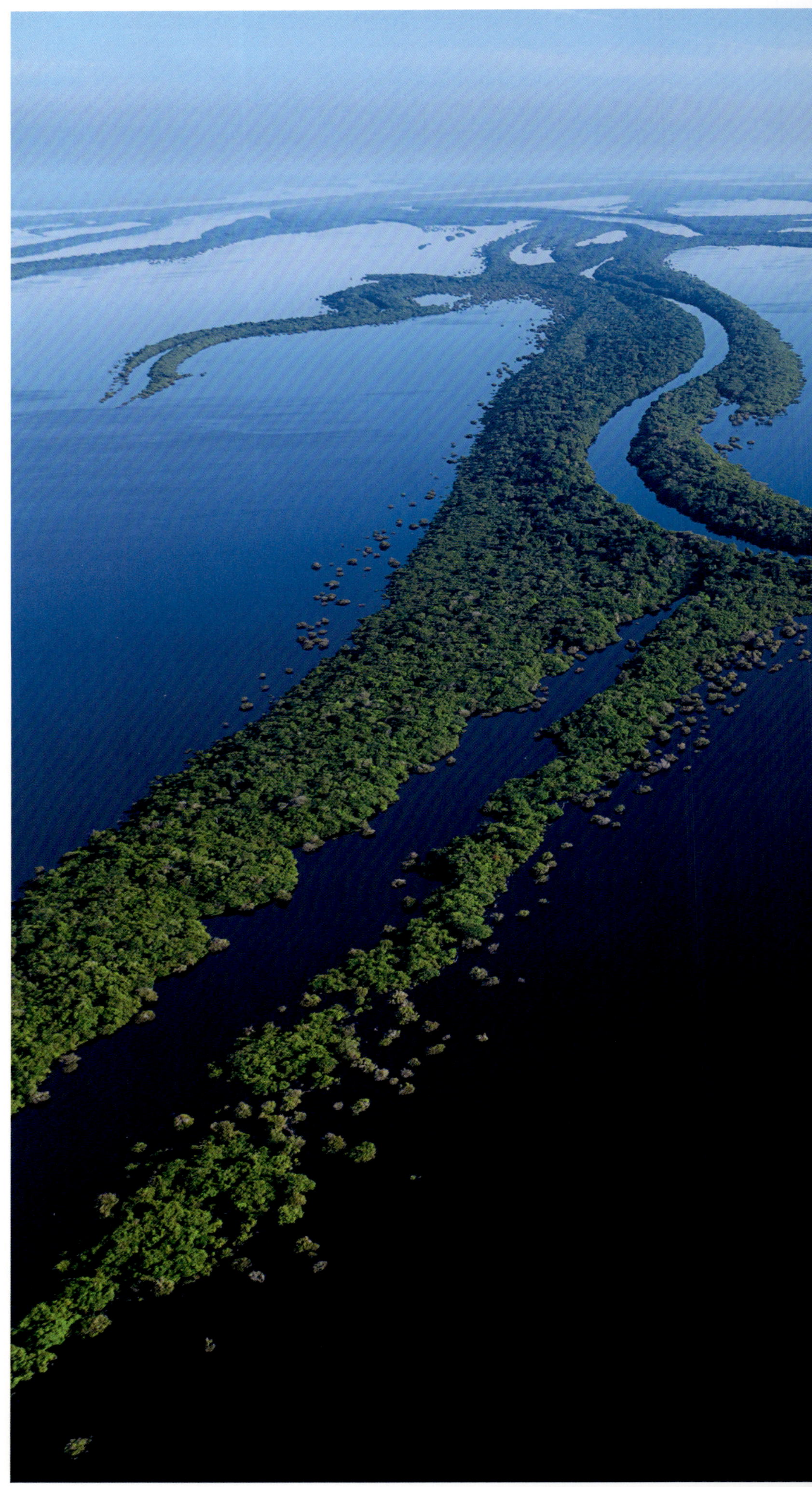

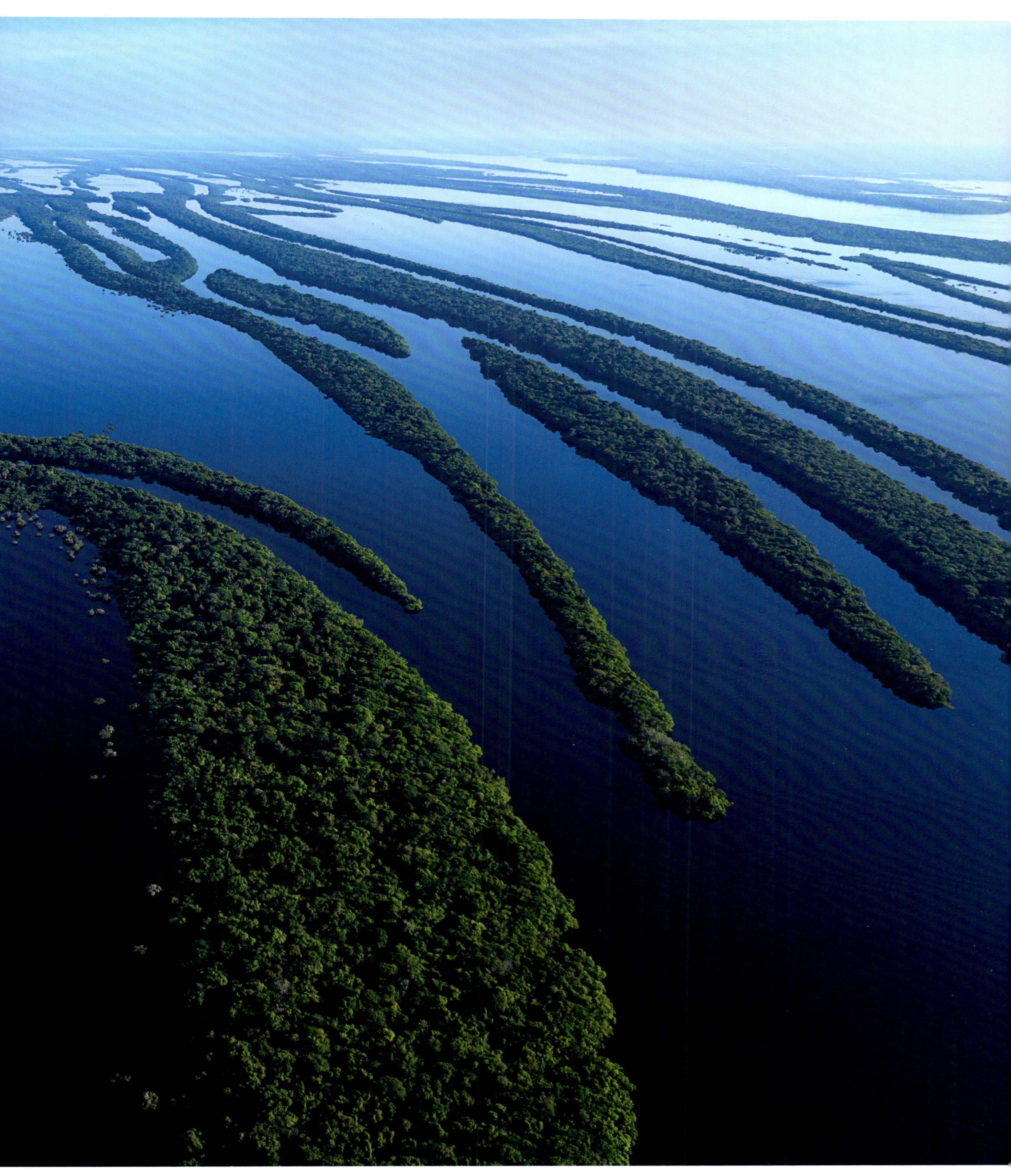

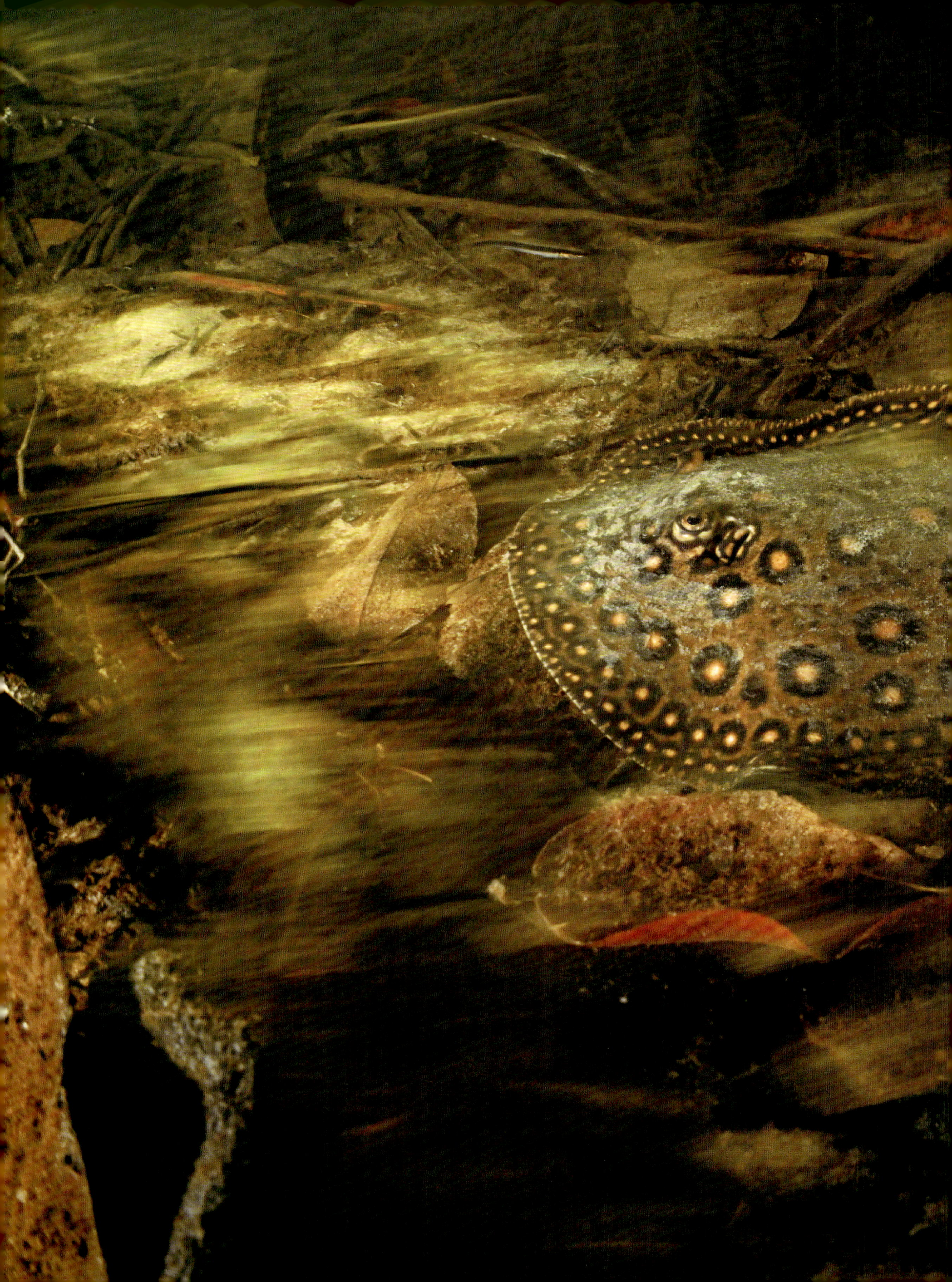

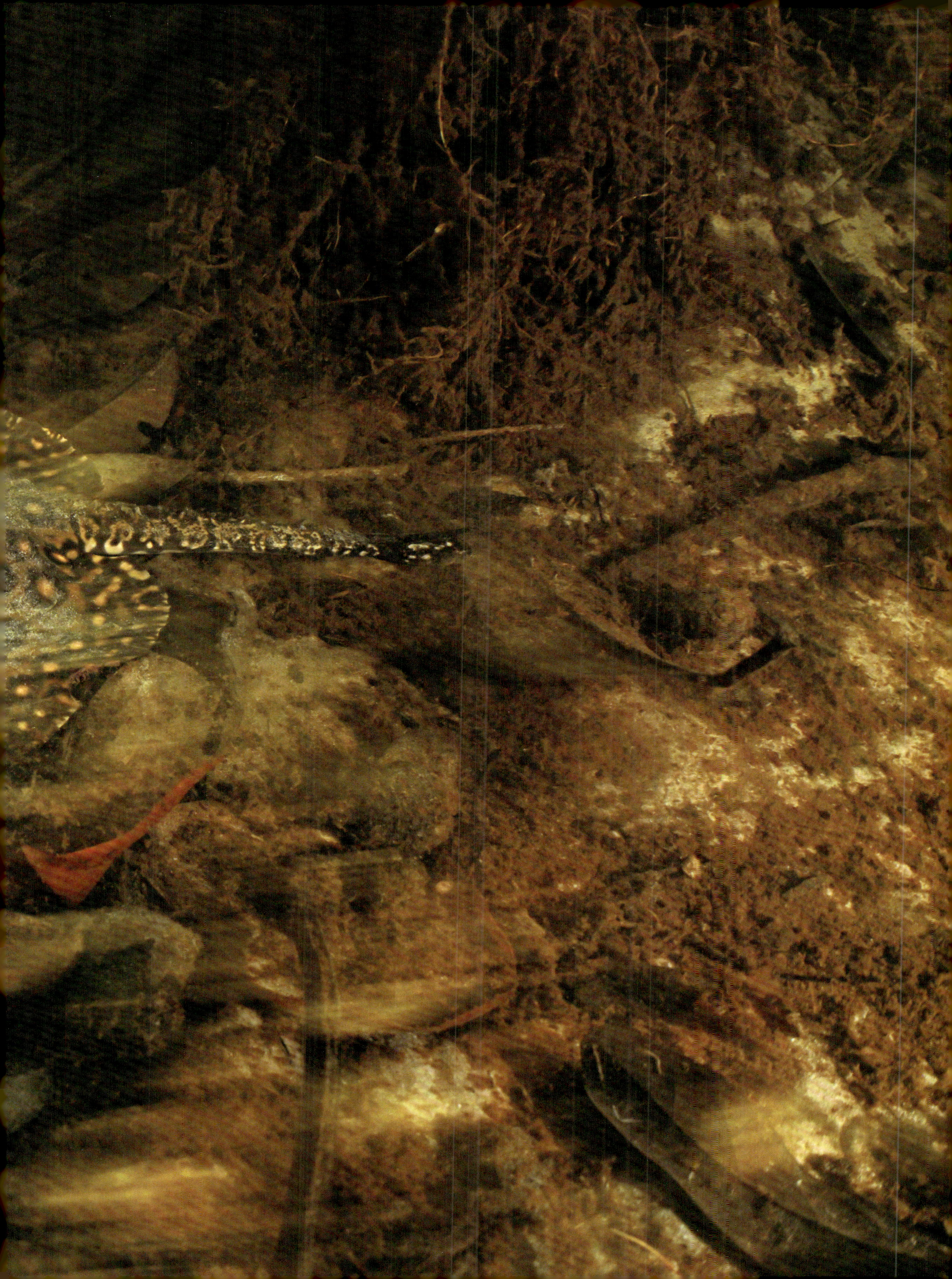

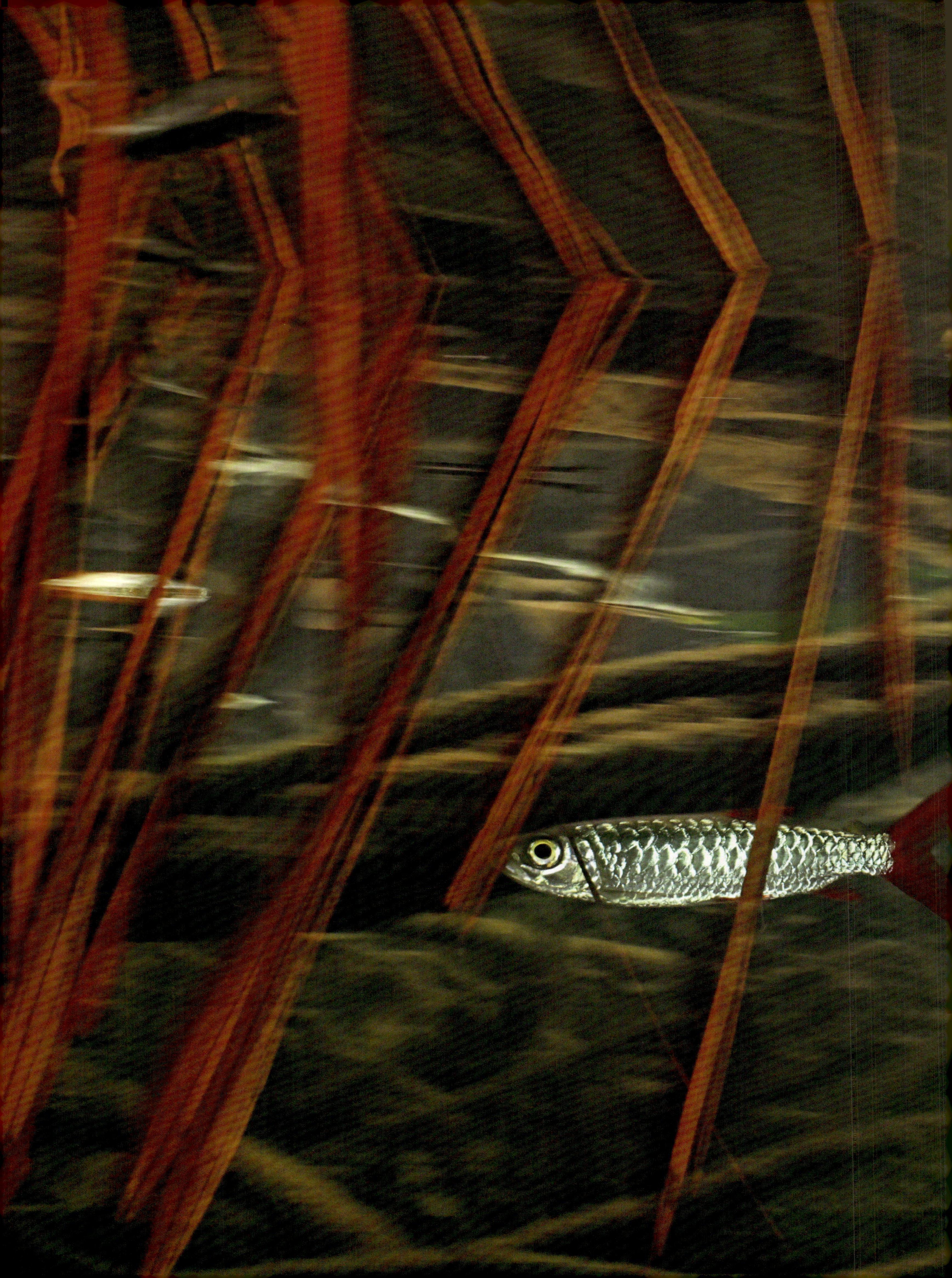

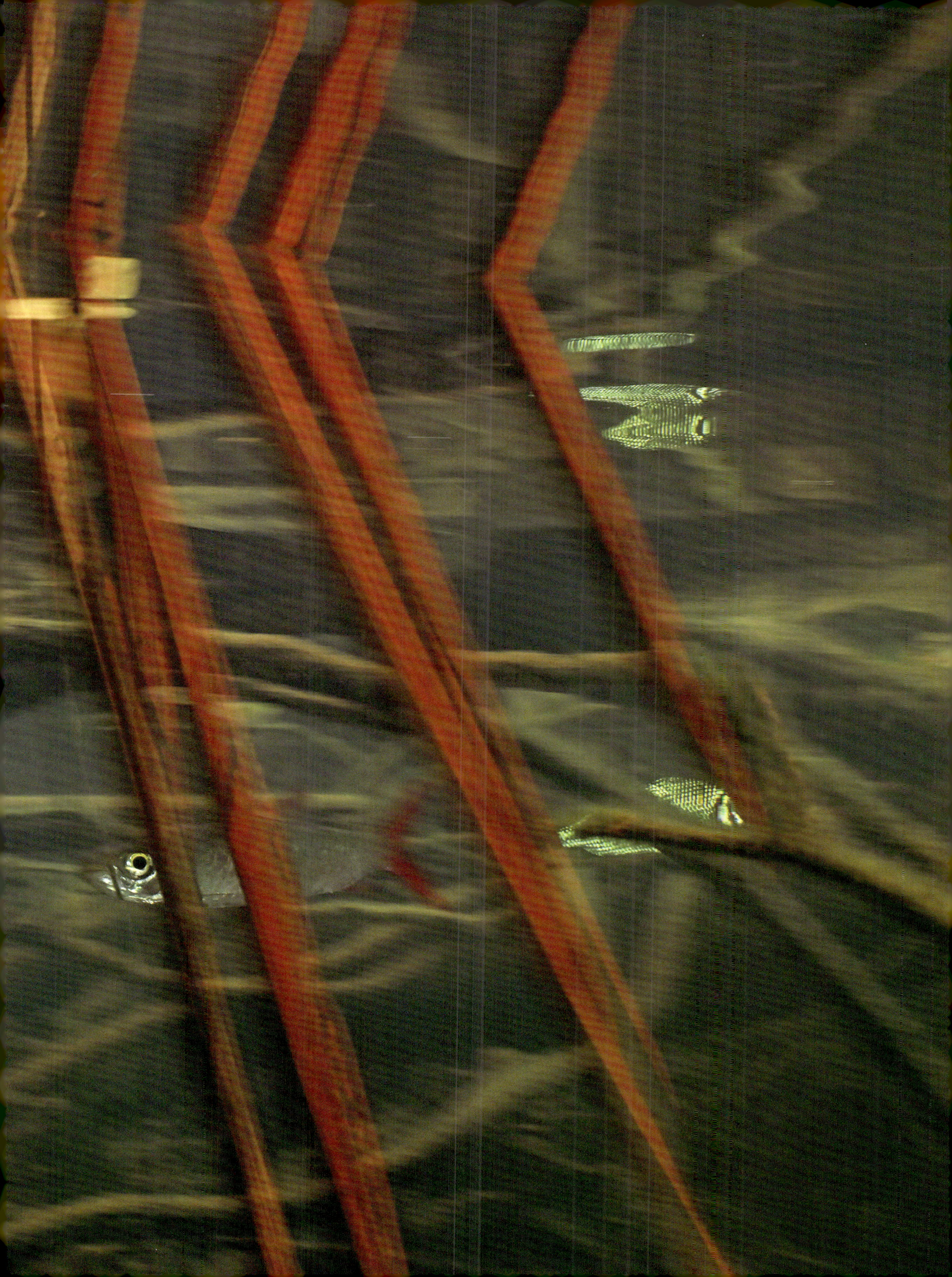

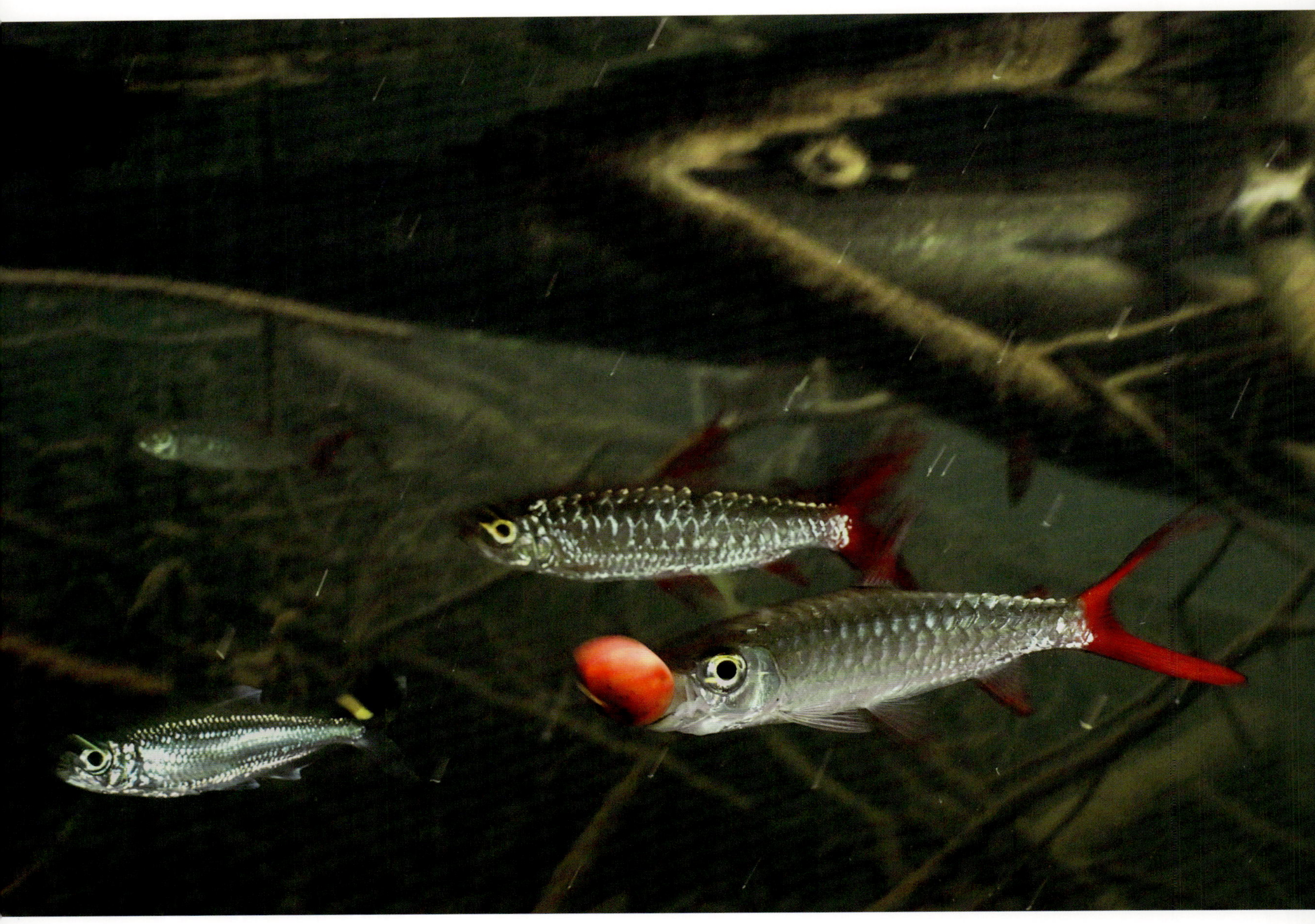

ABOVE: Pink-tailed chalceuses *(Chalceus macrolepidotus)* are very active fish that prefer well-oxygenated surface waters, where they feed predominantly on aquatic invertebrates. During parts of the year, they also readily consume seeds and fruits, and they have been known to leap from the water to target insects above the surface.

OPPOSITE: Flag cichlids *(Mesonauta egregius)* are endemic to the Meta and Vichada River Basins, both tributaries of the Orinoco River, which connects to the Rio Negro in the Amazon Basin via the Casiquiare River. Small groups with well-established hierarchies appear to defend these territories on the river bed or around fallen trees, especially during breeding season.

PAGES 156–157: Pink-tailed chalceuses are small freshwater fish with large, noticeable scales and a tail that is usually dark red to pink. In the Amazon biogeographic province, they are restricted to the Rio Negro and Orinoco River Basins, as well as coastal rivers in Guyana, Suriname, and French Guiana.

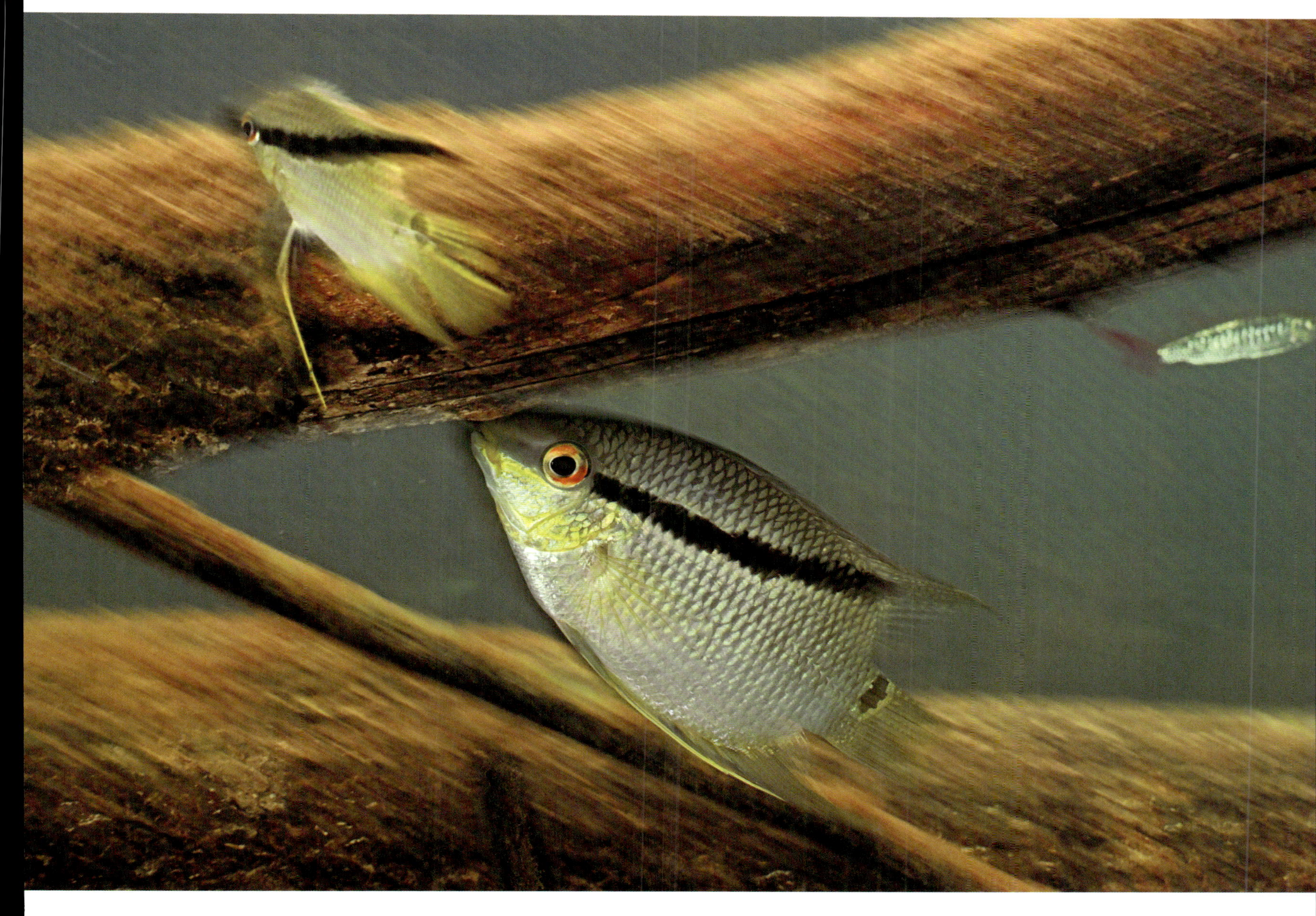

At depths of 50 feet (15 m) or more, rainy season lowland floods can temporarily submerge some of Amazonia's grandest trees, like this *Swartzia polyphylla,* known locally as an *arabá*. When dry season comes, previously submerged limbs that were once fish hangouts become sturdy platforms for monkeys and nesting birds.

PAGES 162–163: A blue-eye catfish *(Platydoras hancockii)* seeks shelter in a hollowed-out tree trunk in a stream flowing through the Colombian Amazon. In these small rivers, there is a distinct shift in biodiversity from day to night. Much like owls, catfish emerge from their hiding places and become active as darkness sets in.

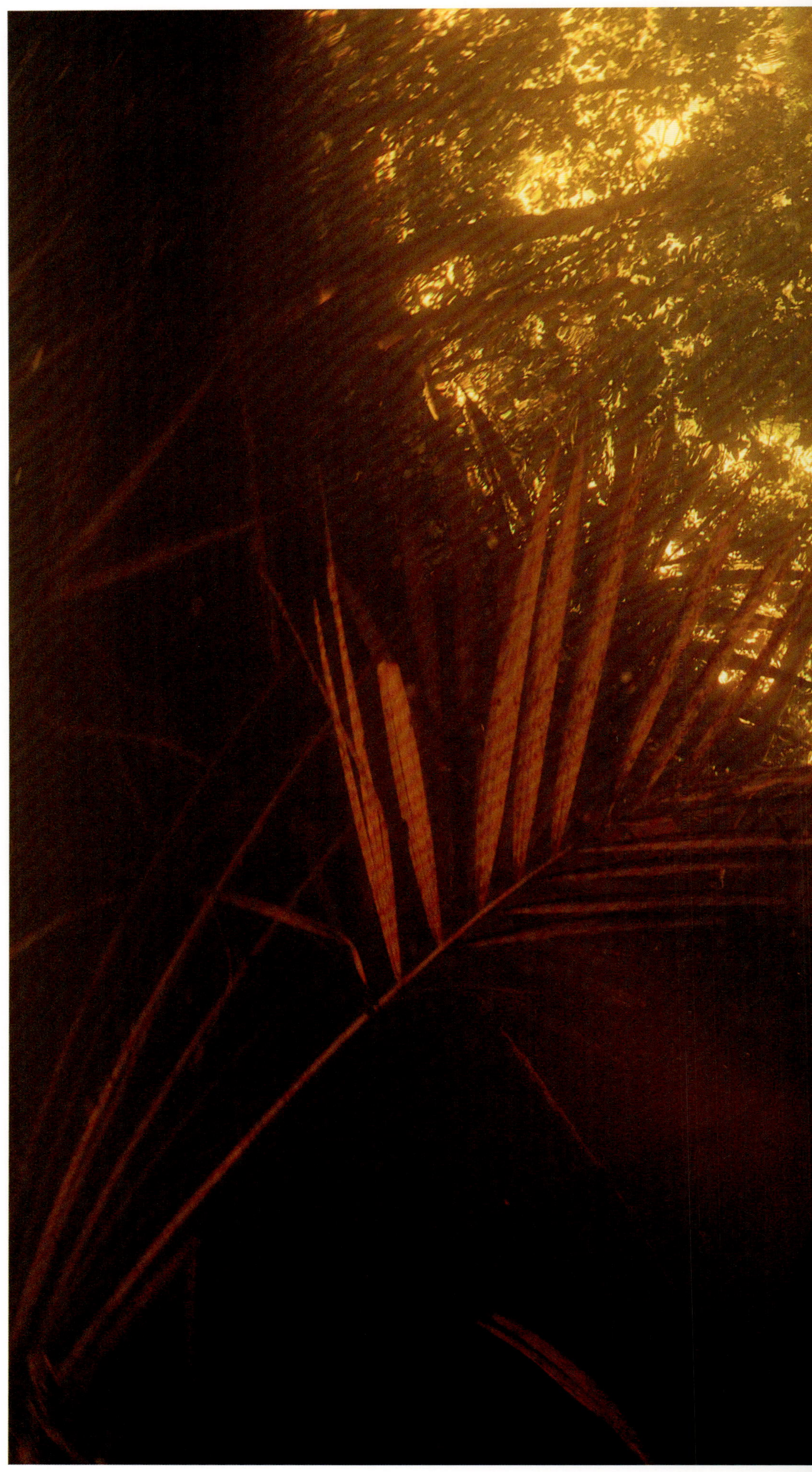

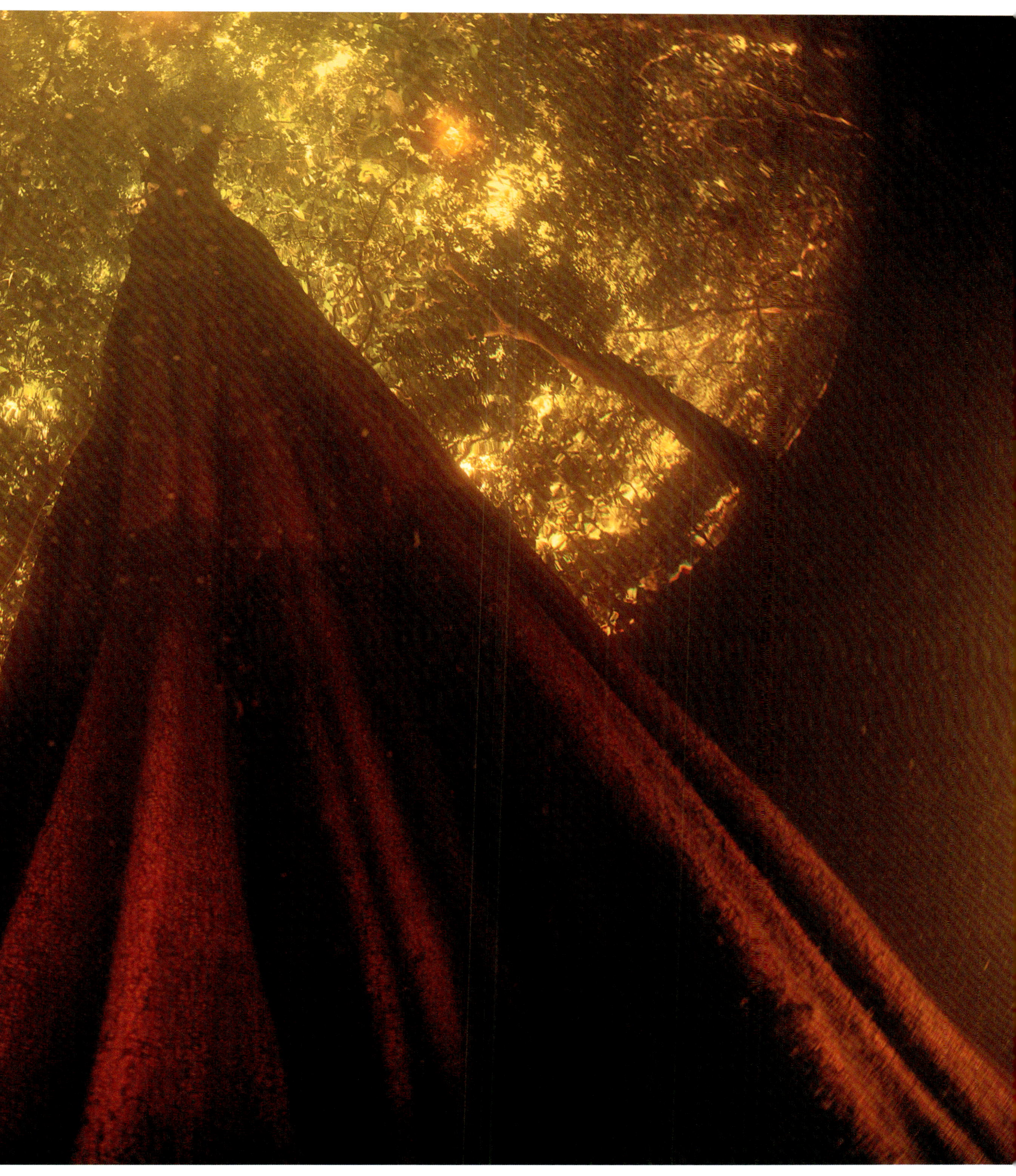

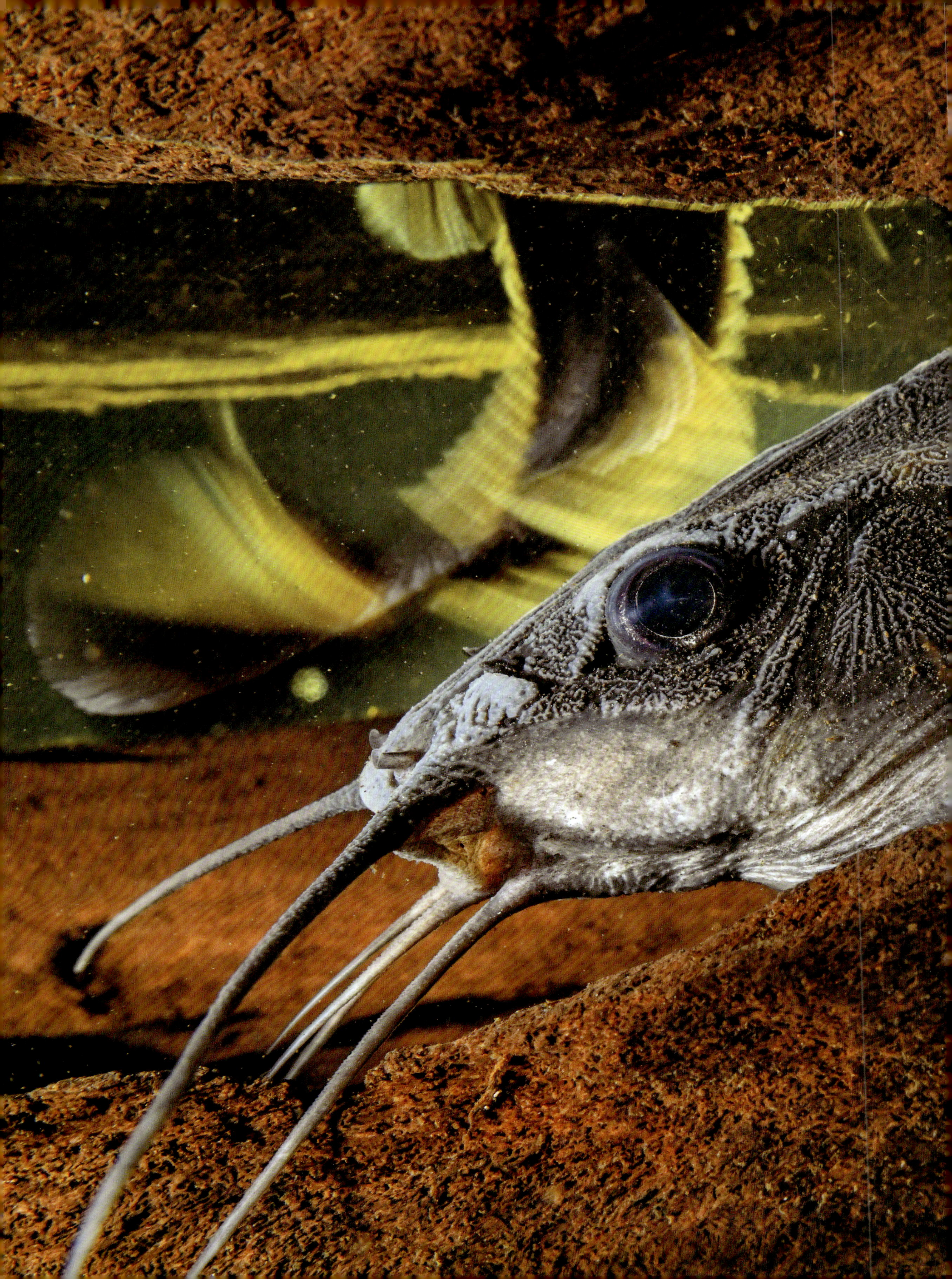

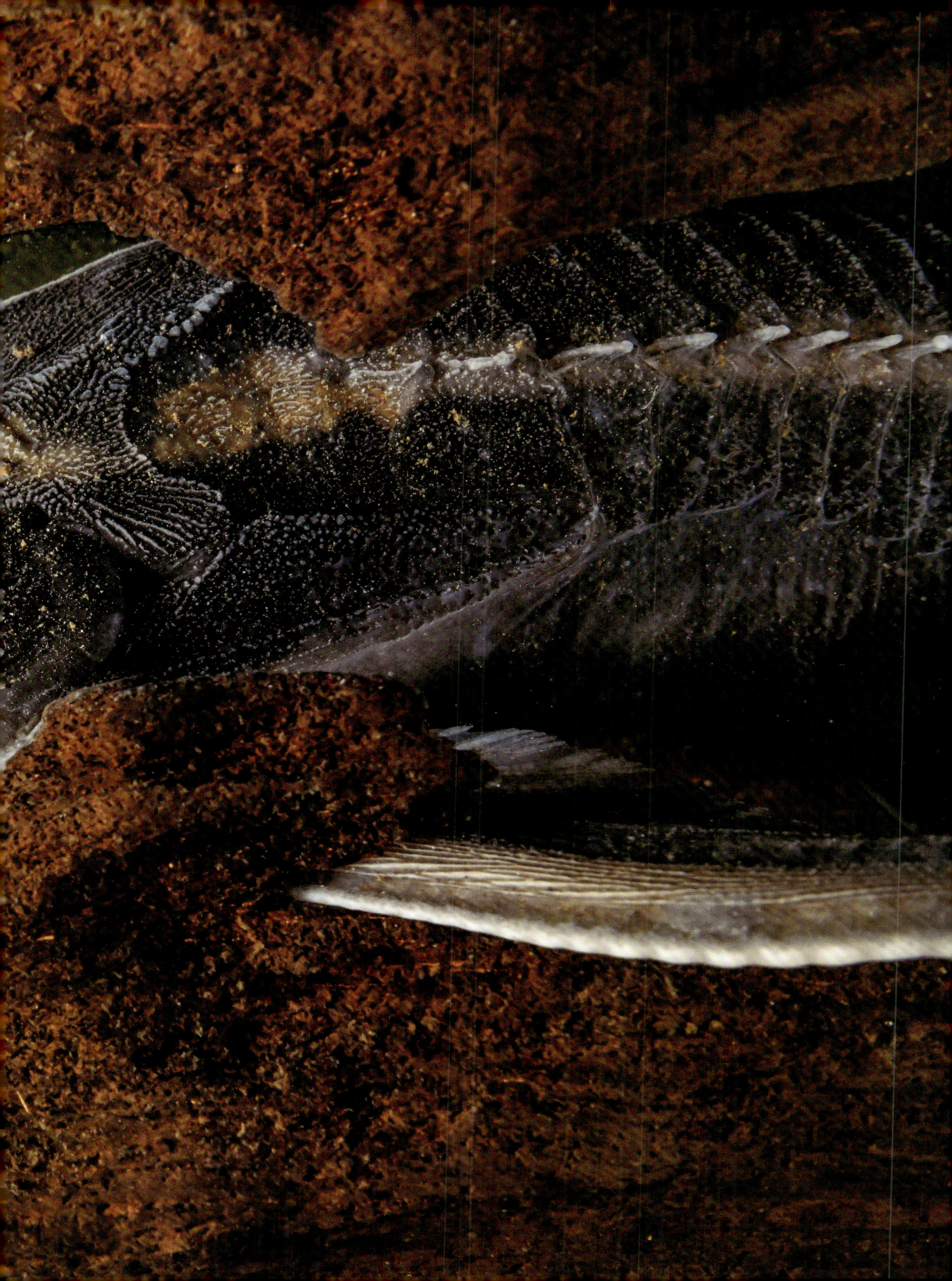

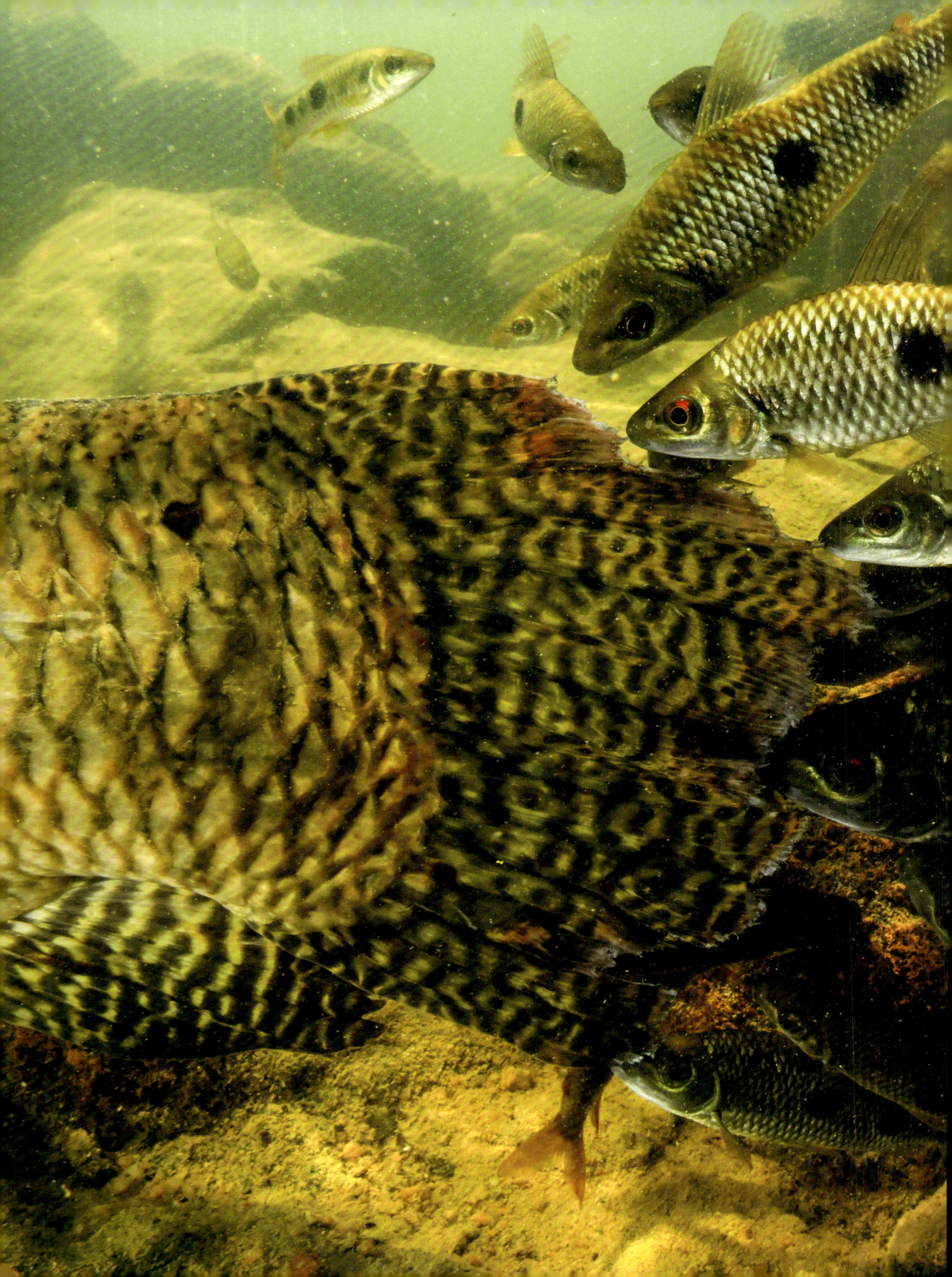

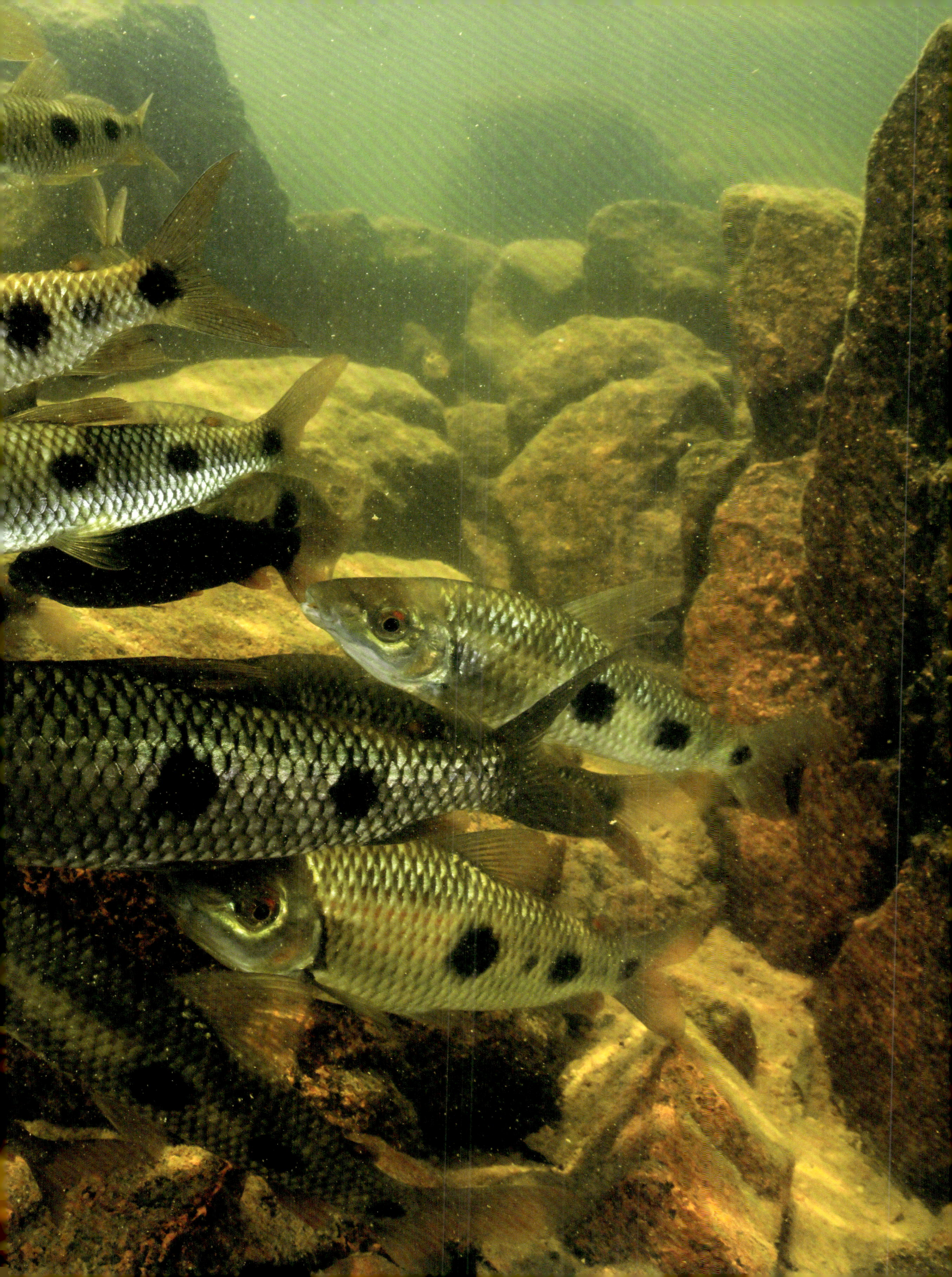

A brown-throated sloth *(Bradypus variegatus)* emerges from the water after swimming through a flooded forest. Sloths might be slow climbers, but they are surprisingly strong and fast swimmers. Using their long arms as paddles, they can cover 33 feet (10 m) in less than a minute. By lowering their heart rate, they can hold their breath underwater for up to 40 minutes.

PAGES 164–165: The threespot leporinus *(Leporinus friderici)* uses its strong teeth to crush seeds, termites, and fruit. However, in an unusual scenario encountered in Brazil's Iriri River, a large group was found biting away at the trailing caudal fin of a dying wolffish *(Hoplias lacerdae)*, locally known as a *trairão*.

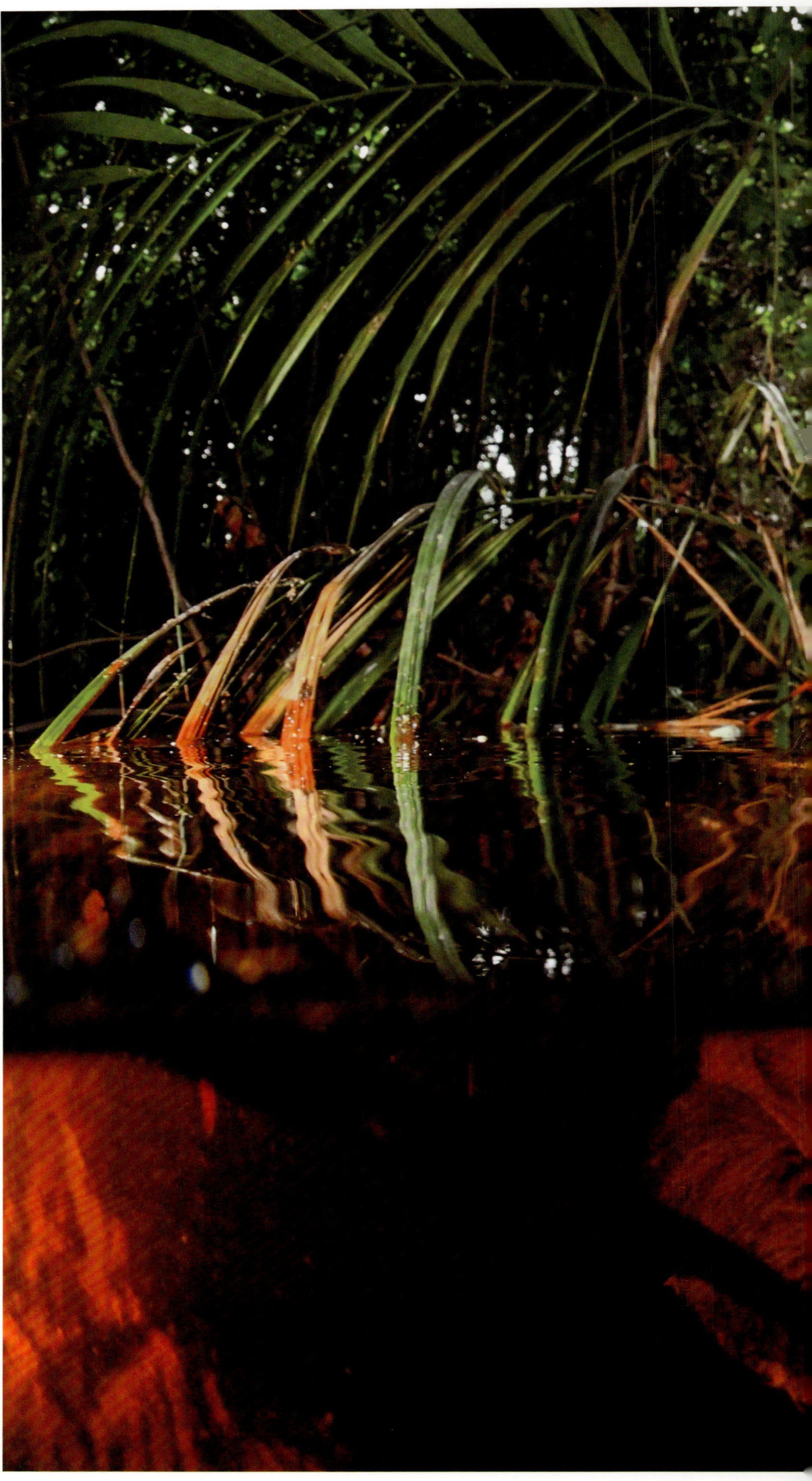

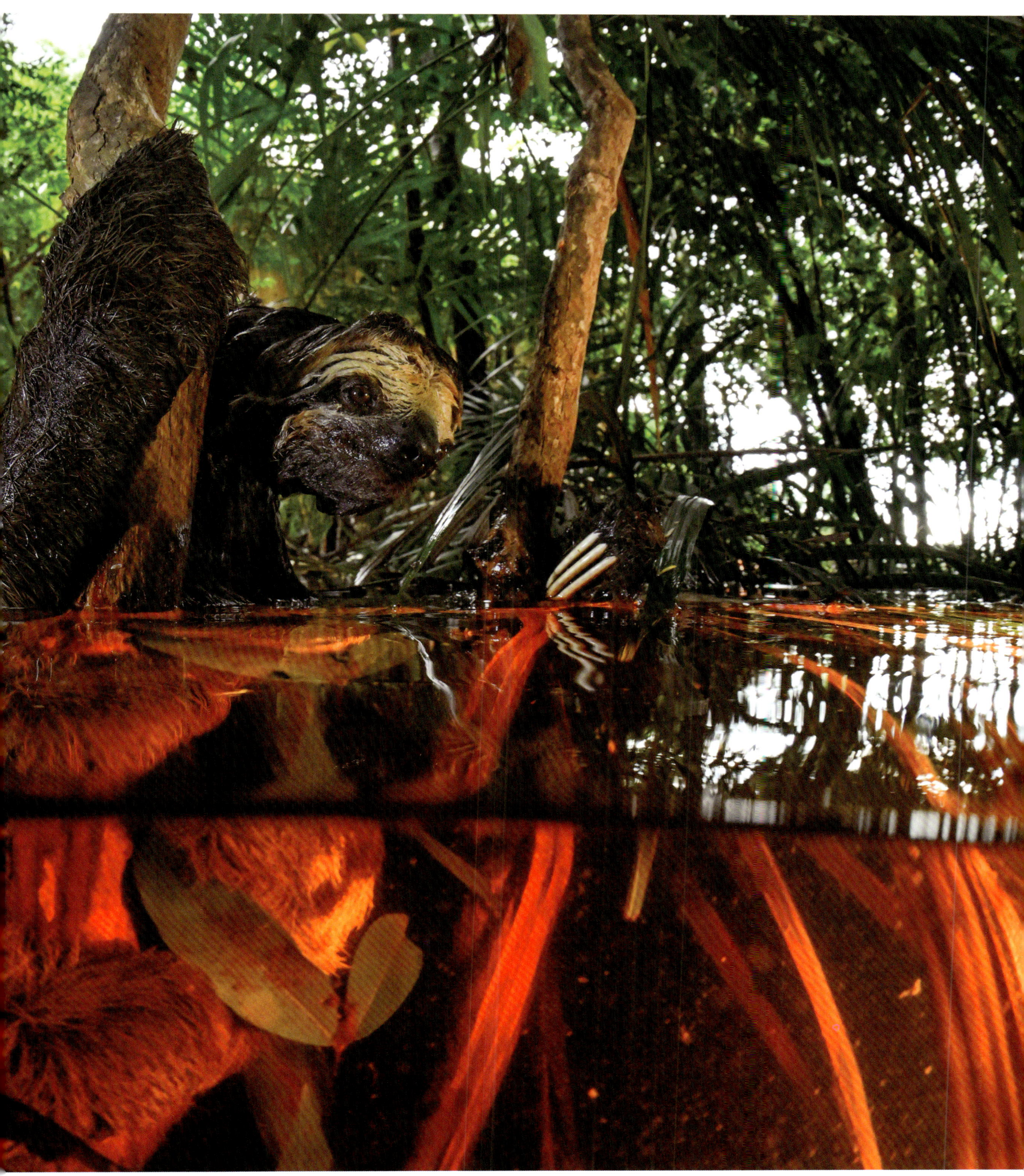

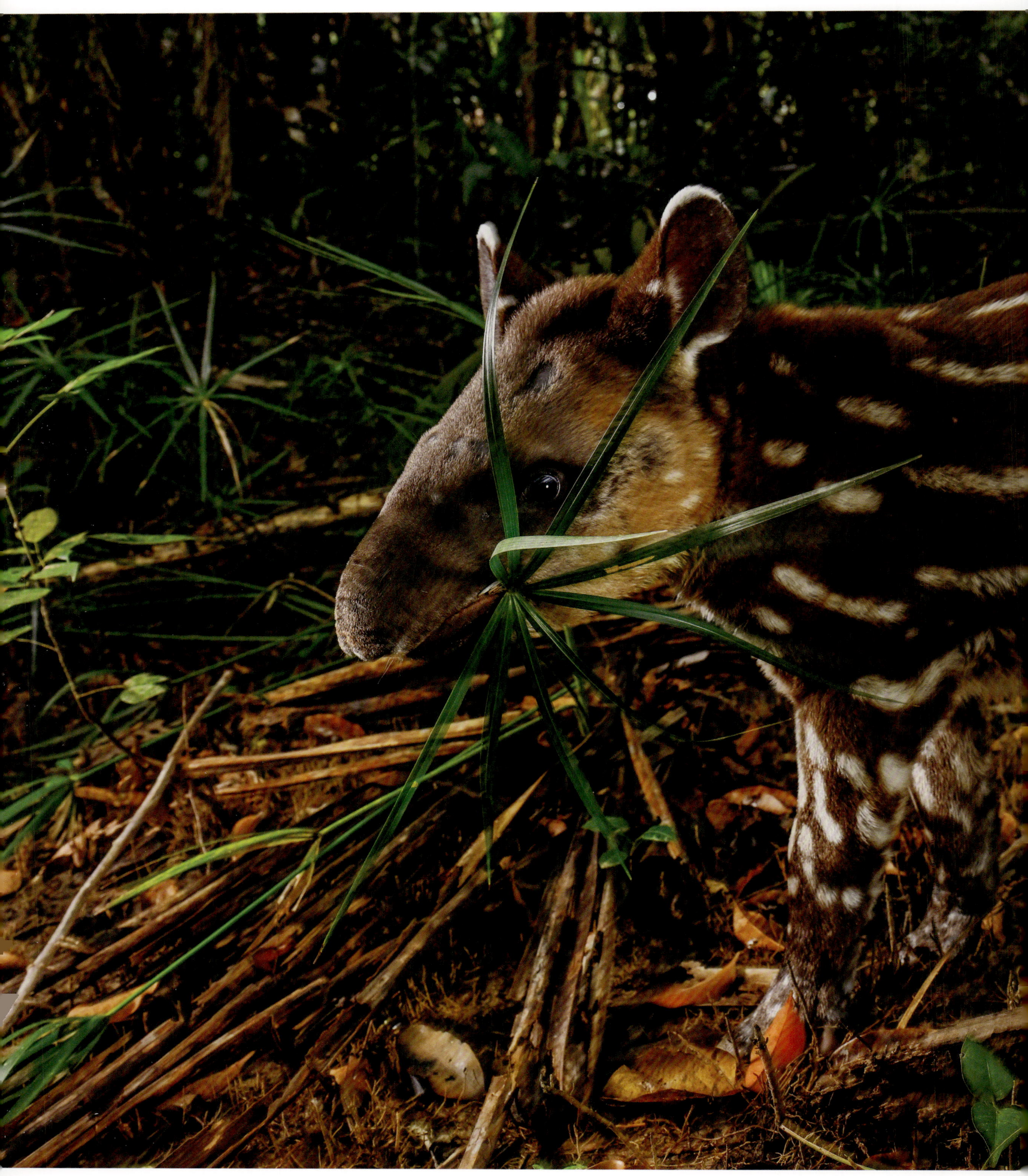

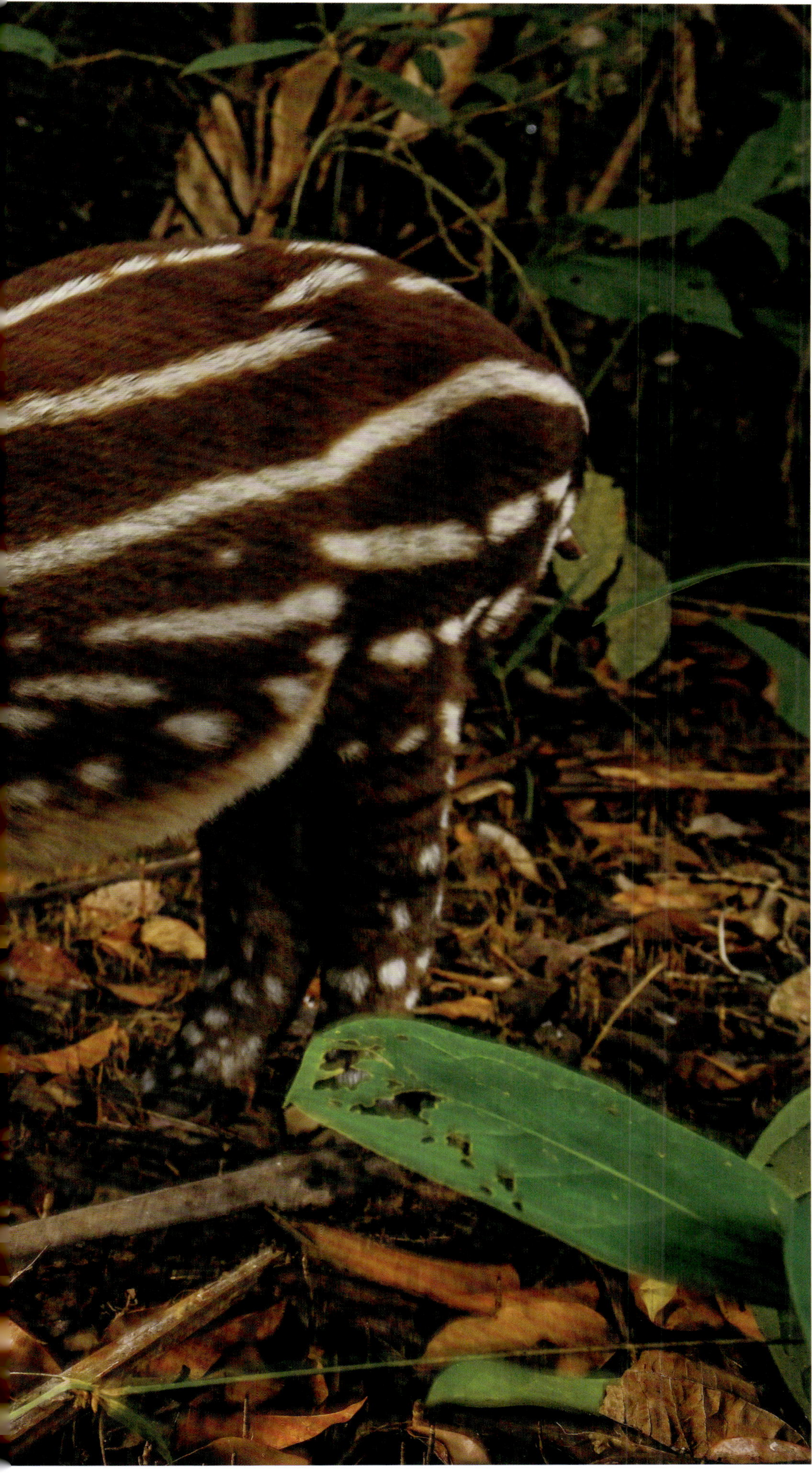

Adult lowland tapirs are by and large uniformly brown, but their young are born decked out in white stripes and spots that serve as camouflage against predators. The closest living relatives to tapirs are rhinos, having shared a common ancestor 50 million years ago. The tapirs' large teeth are designed to grind up plants and seeds, while their prehensile snout is used to access leaves and fruits.

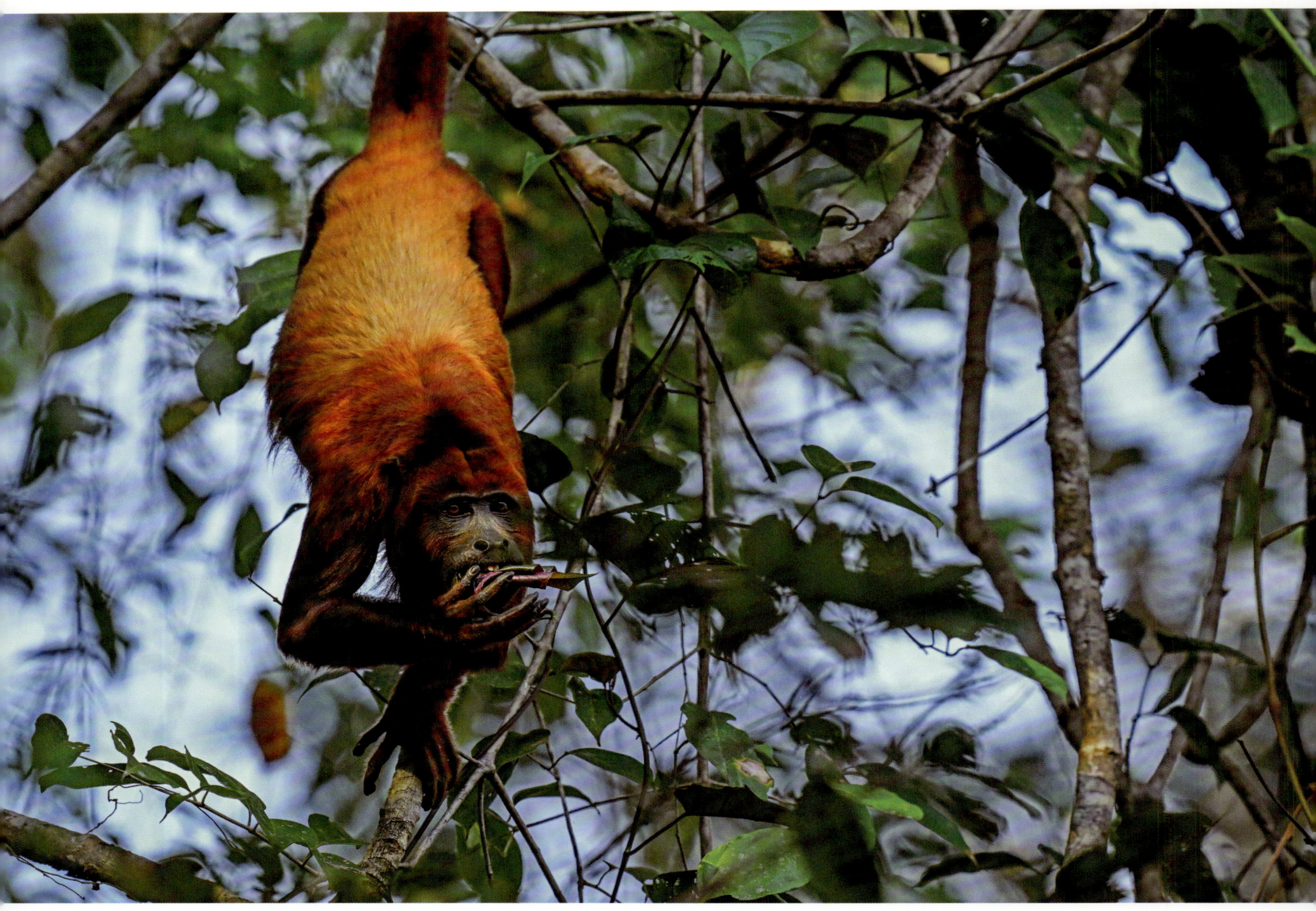

ABOVE: Colombian red howler monkeys *(Alouatta seniculus)* have high dietary standards. They try to select only the best leaves and fruits, and this leads them to healthy rivers and streams—trees near clean water sources reliably produce fresh, nutrient-rich leaves. It's impossible to ignore the monkeys' presence in the Amazon; their territorial, guttural vocalizations penetrate the soundscape and travel for miles.

OPPOSITE: A giant river otter *(Pteronura brasiliensis)* chews on a fish caught in a flooded forest in Ecuador's Napo River Basin. These endangered mammals are the largest otters in the world, reaching up to six feet (1.8 m) in length, and are one of the main predators in the Amazon. They sleep in holes and caves on the land but spend most of their days hunting in the river.

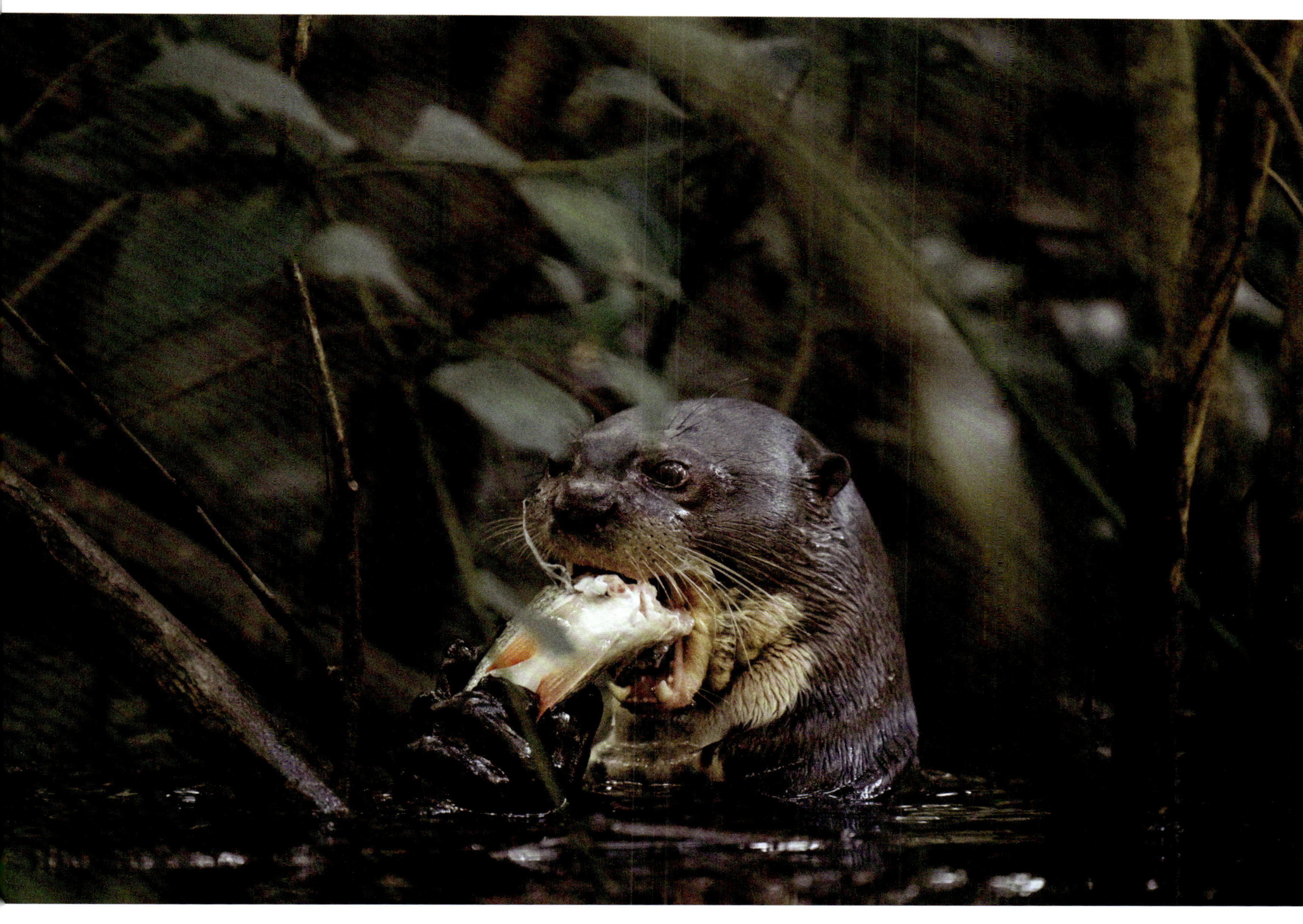

PAGES 172–173: A trio of hoatzins *(Opisthocomus hoazin)* perch over a stream by the Napo River. These birds are closely tied to water. They build their nests above rivers and lakes as a protective measure. If predators try to raid their nests, the young chicks leap into the water and swim below the surface to escape. Once it's safe, they use their claws to climb back to their nests.

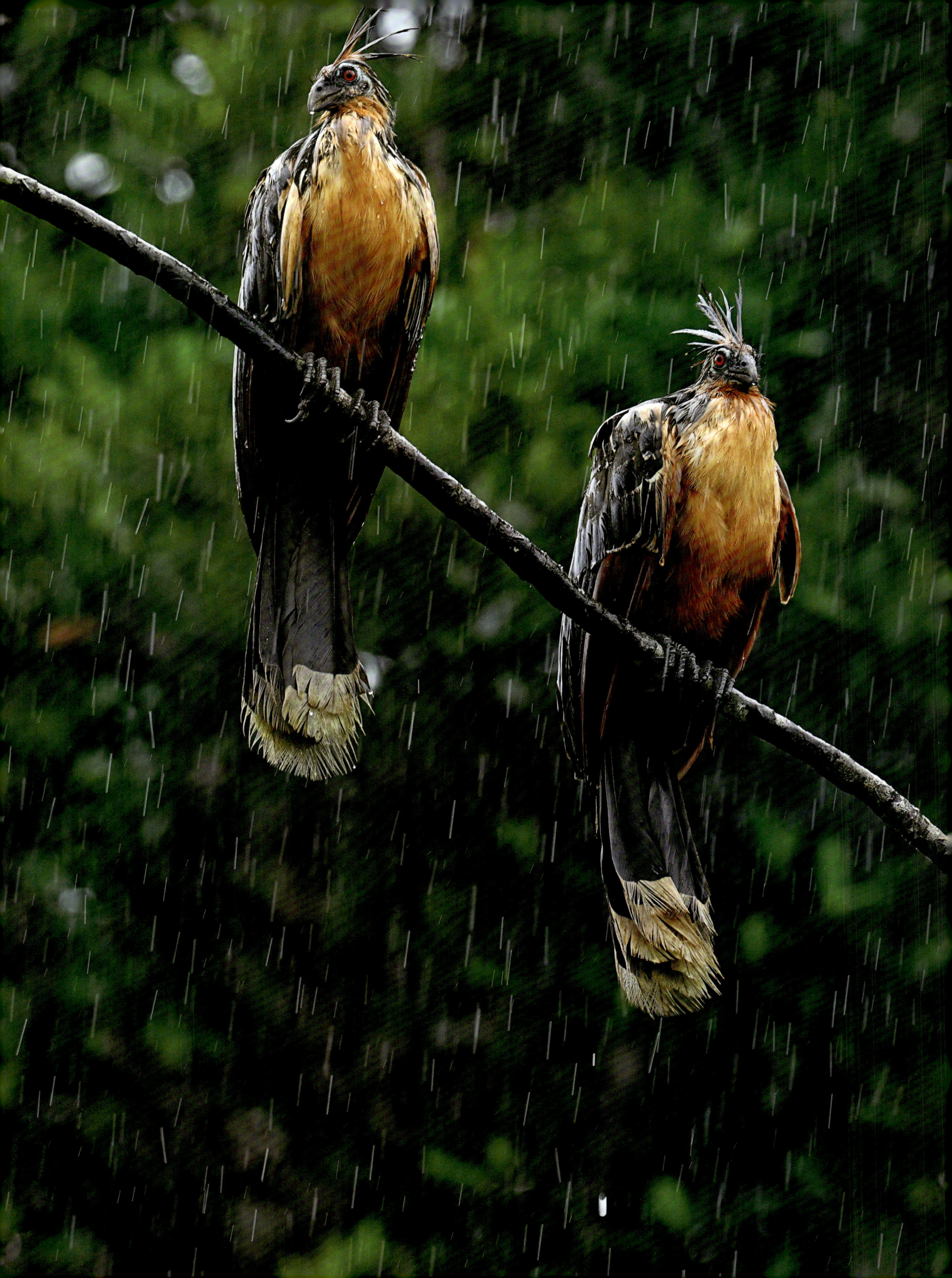

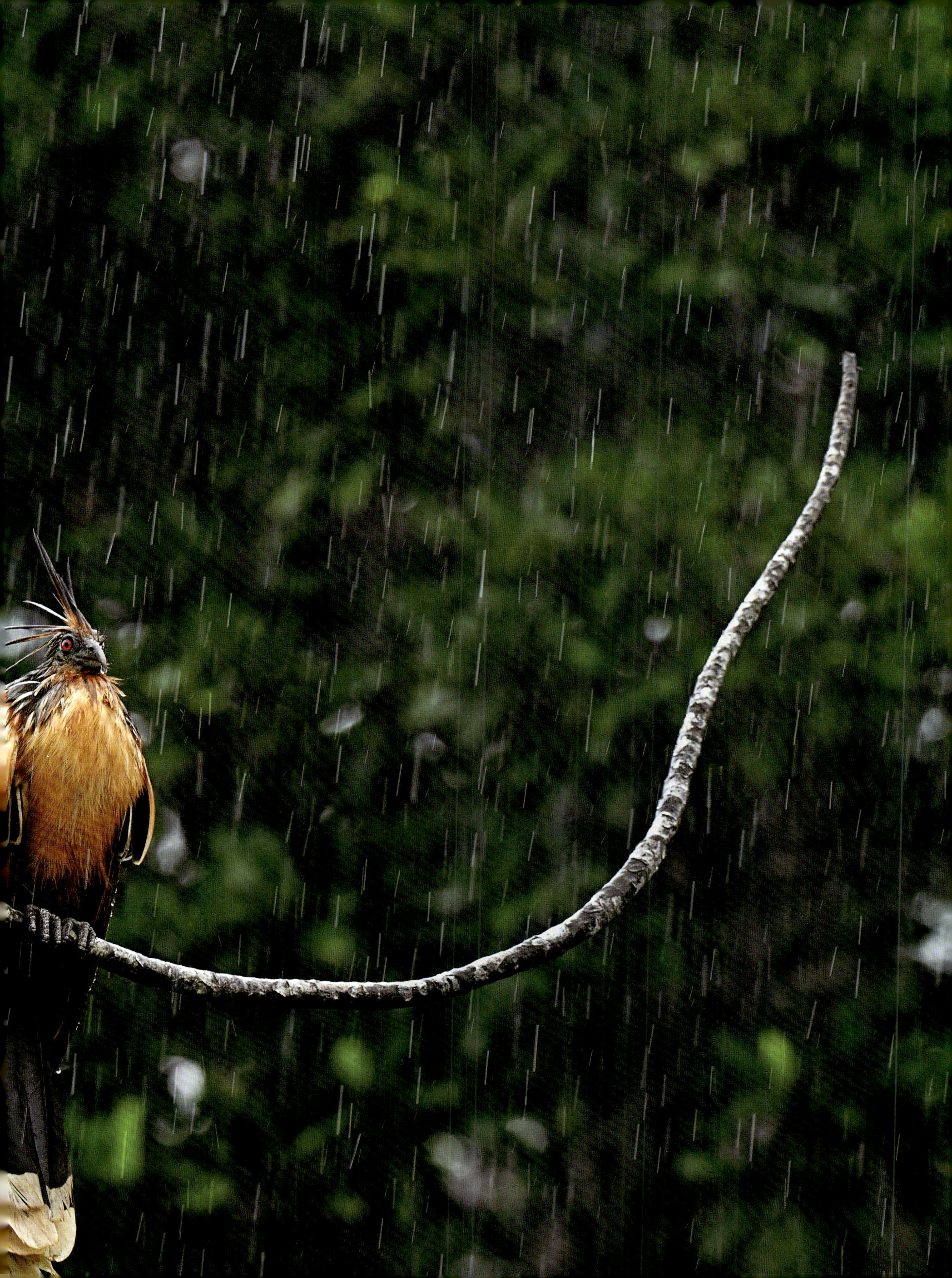

When the floodwaters recede, uncovering mineral-rich soils, butterflies are often the first to arrive on the scene. They gather en masse and eagerly drink waters rich in sodium, magnesium, and other nutrients that can otherwise be scarce in a rainforest. This behavior is known as mud-puddling.

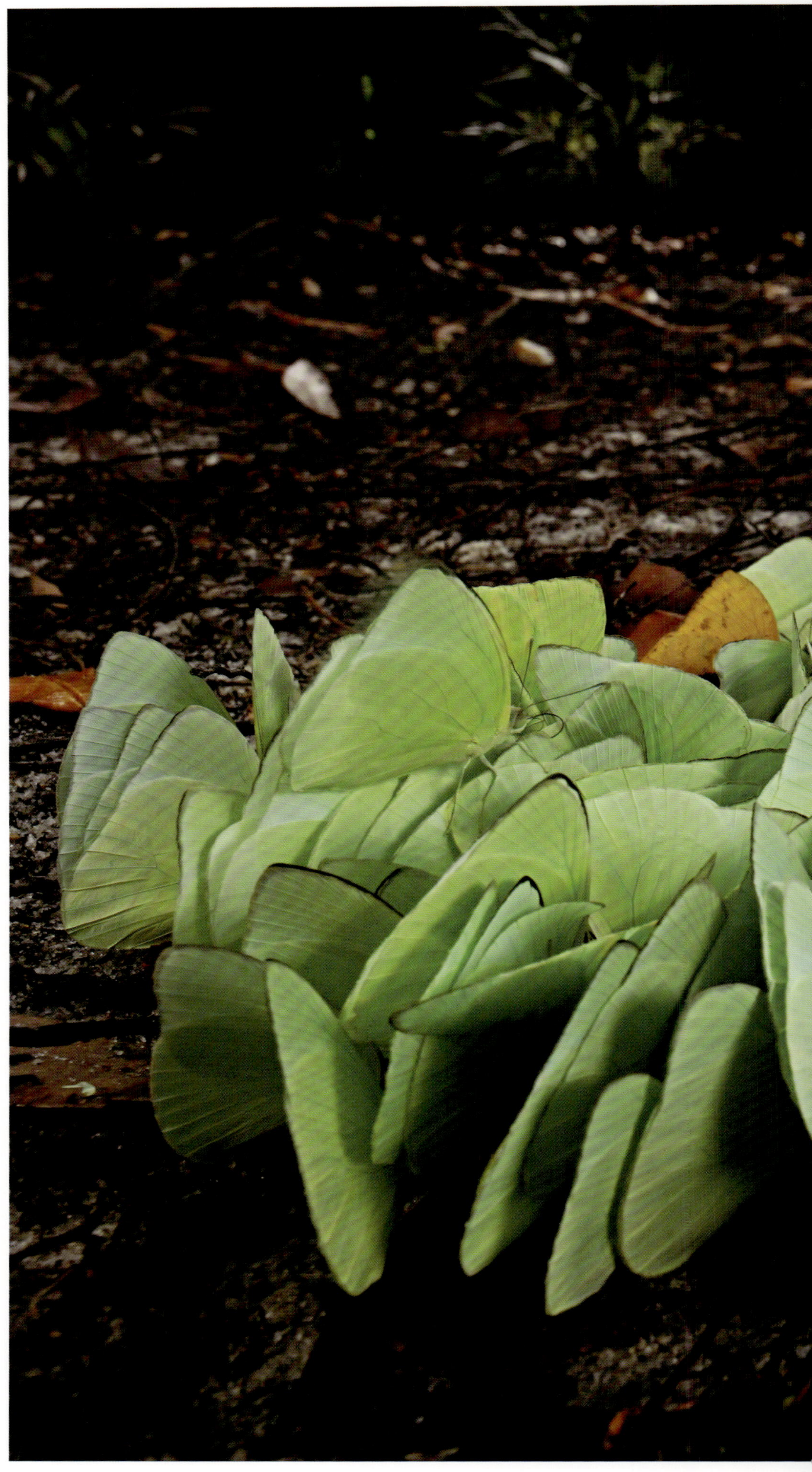

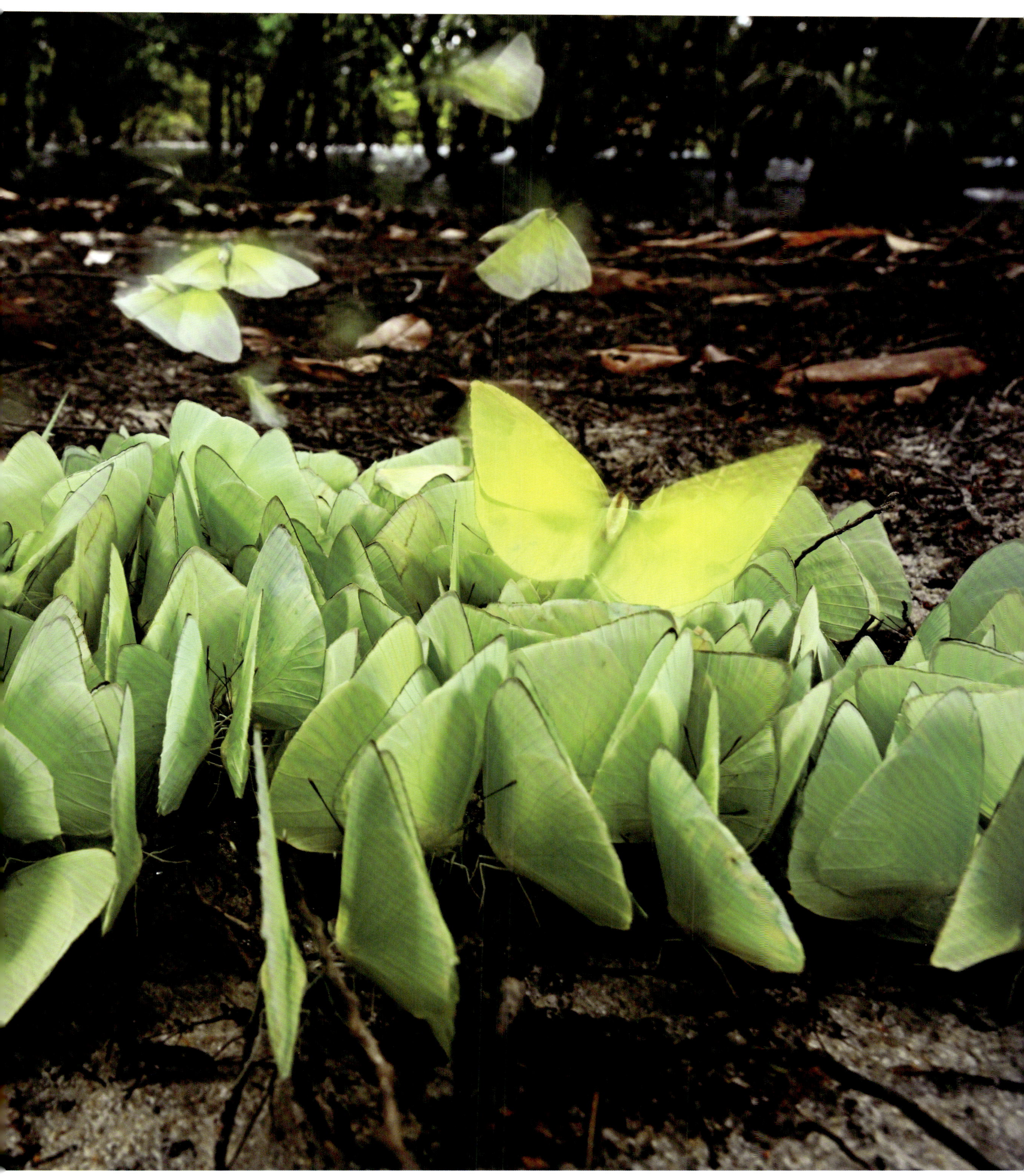

A butterfly perches on the shell of a yellow-spotted river turtle *(Podocnemis unifilis)* to drink the turtle's tears. The butterfly's proboscis, equipped with spines and barbs, acts like a suction, allowing the insect to obtain essential minerals and proteins, especially sodium, directly from the liquid in the turtle's eye.

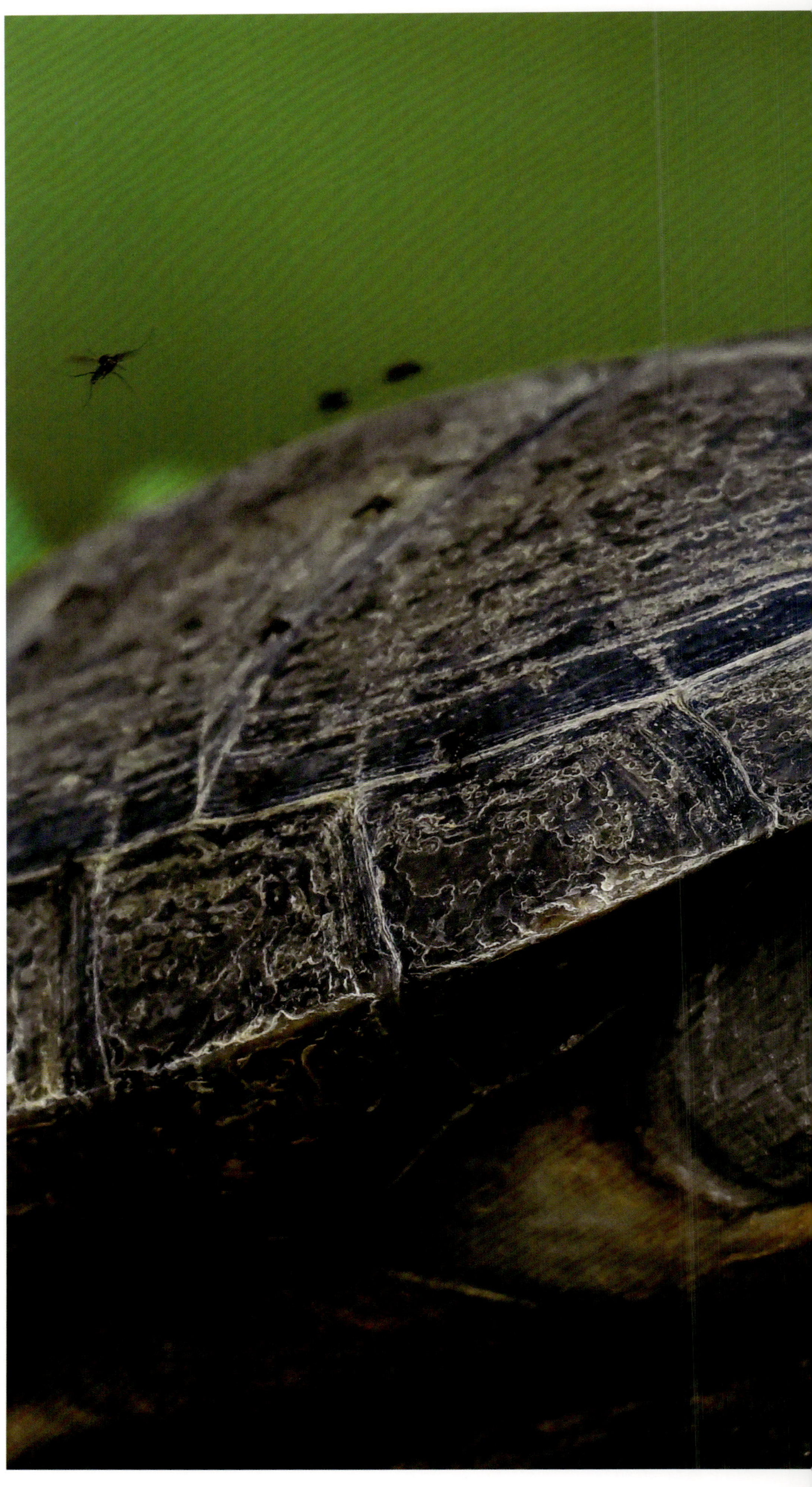

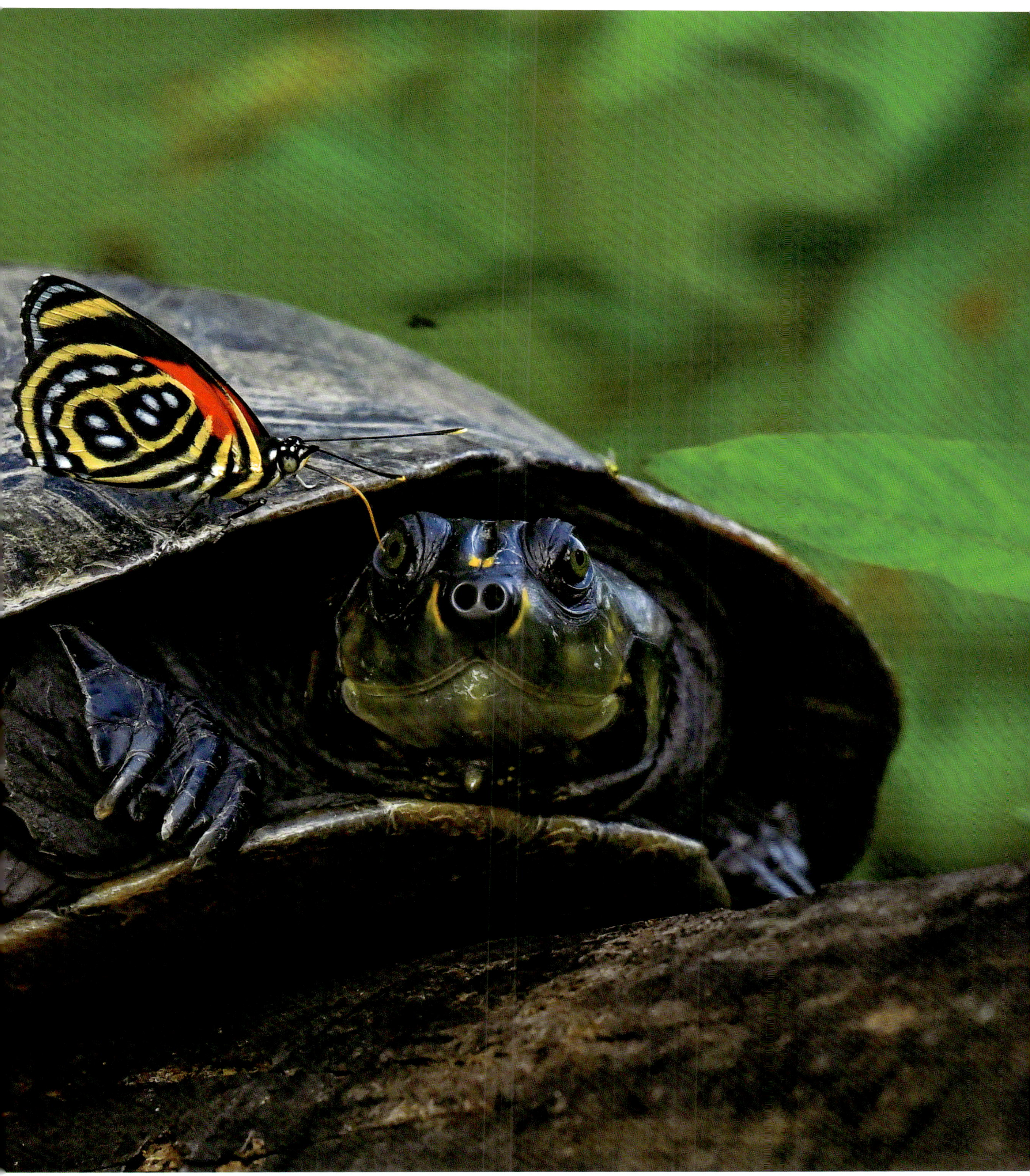

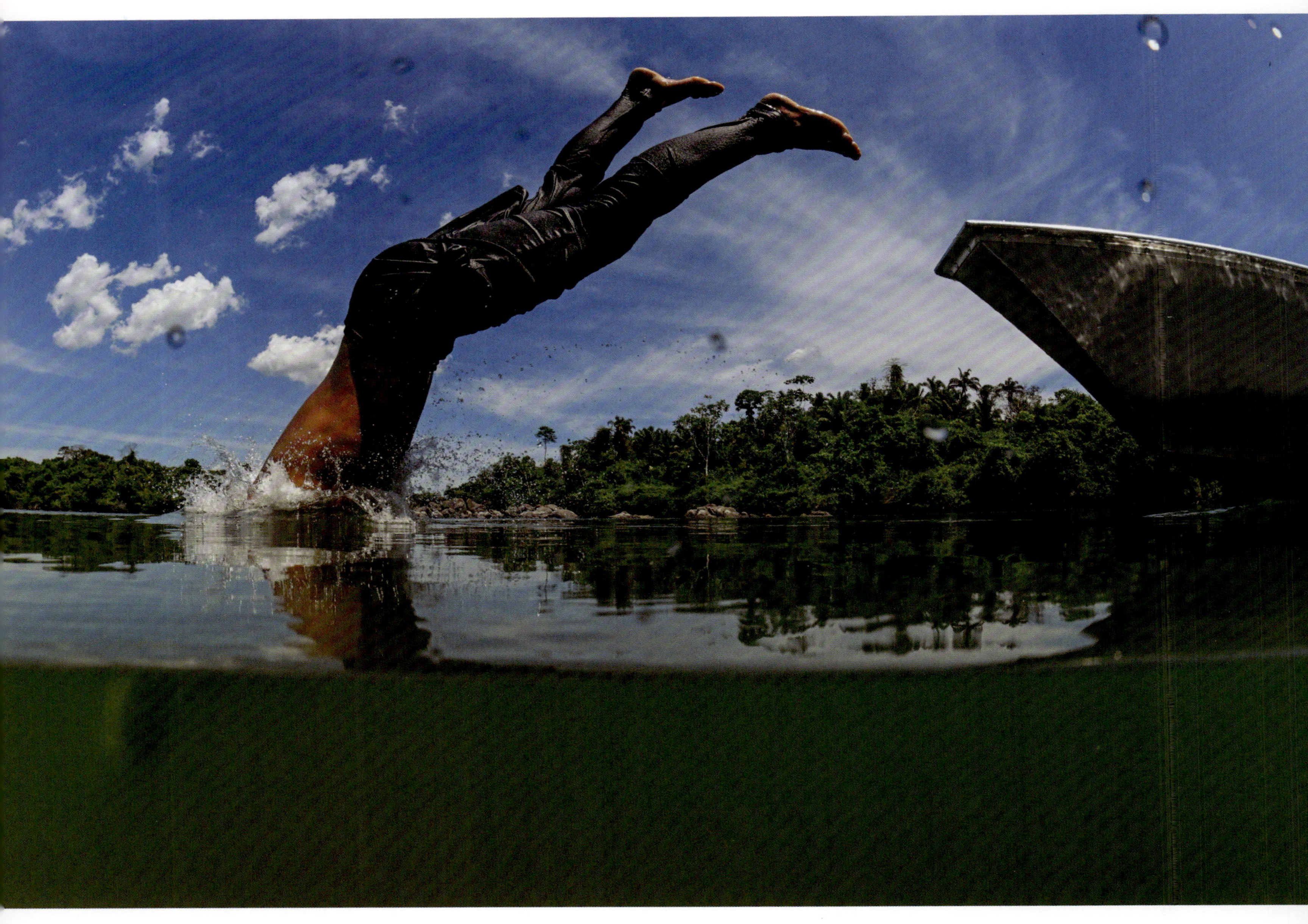

ABOVE: Jumping headfirst from the bow of a canoe is the most common—and effective—way the Kayapó target and capture yellow-spotted river turtles in Brazil's Iriri River. These turtles are an important and readily available protein source for people of the Kendjam village.

OPPOSITE: Bepgogore Kayapó harvests turtle eggs from a nest dug into an exposed sandbank during the dry season. Community programs and anti-poaching laws now protect turtles and their eggs in many parts of Amazonia, but subsistence hunting and egg collecting is still permitted on many Indigenous lands.

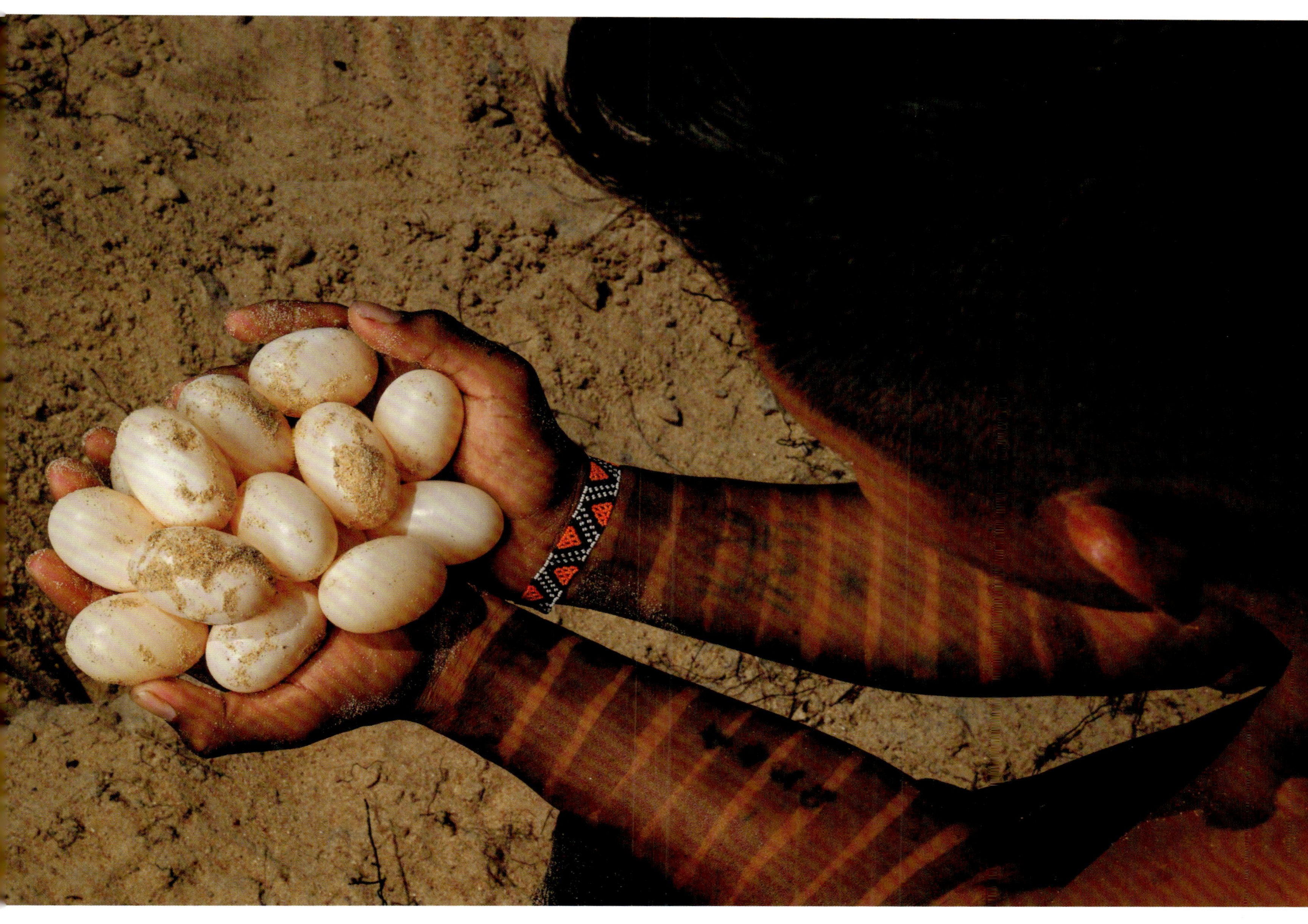

PAGES 180–181: Guide Djokro Kayapó, his reflection eerily clear in the smooth waters of Brazil's Iriri River, grasps a yellow-spotted river turtle. The water was so calm that it reflected the intricate Kayapó body paint on Djokro's arms and the turtle on the underside of the river's surface.

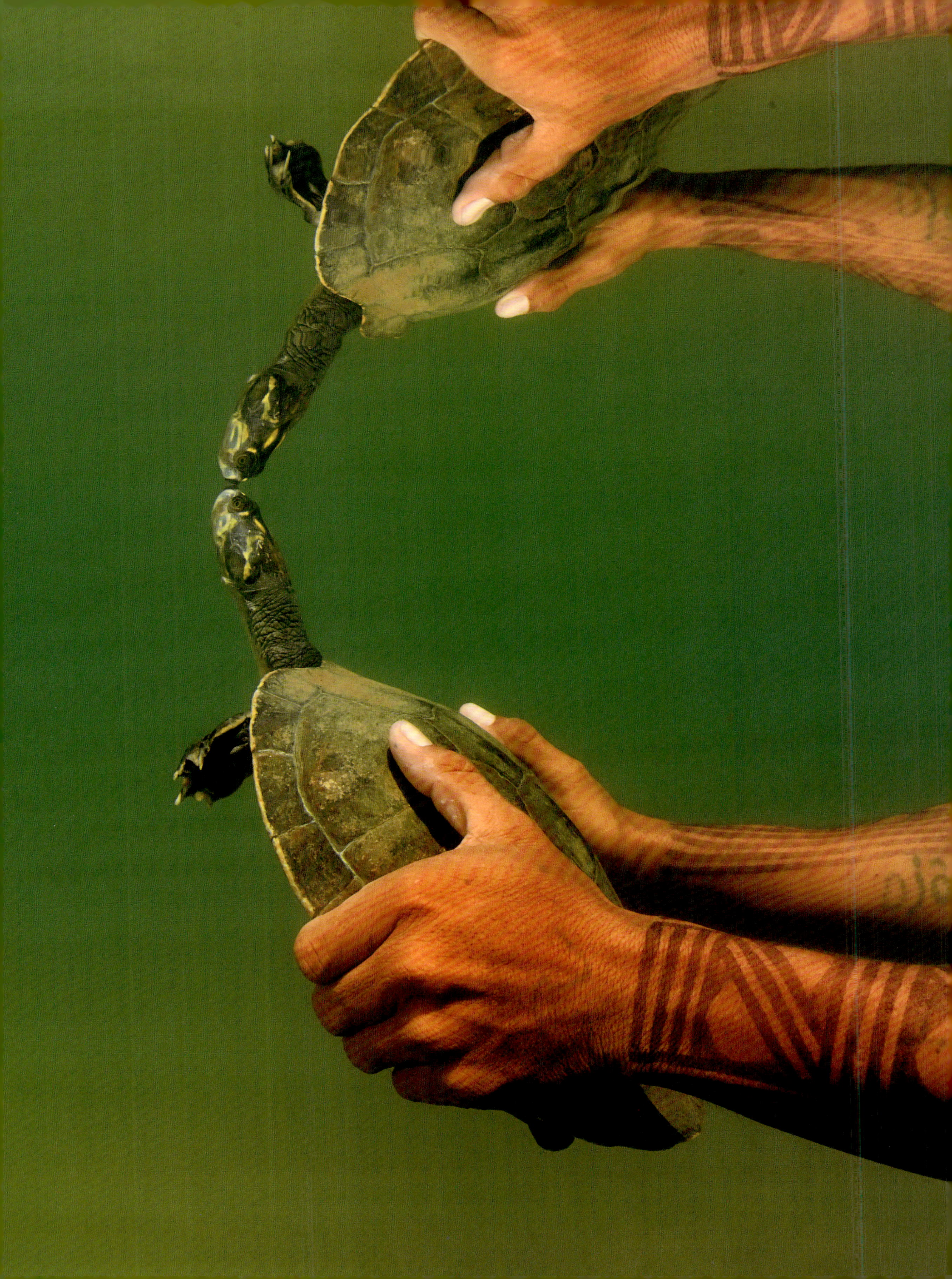

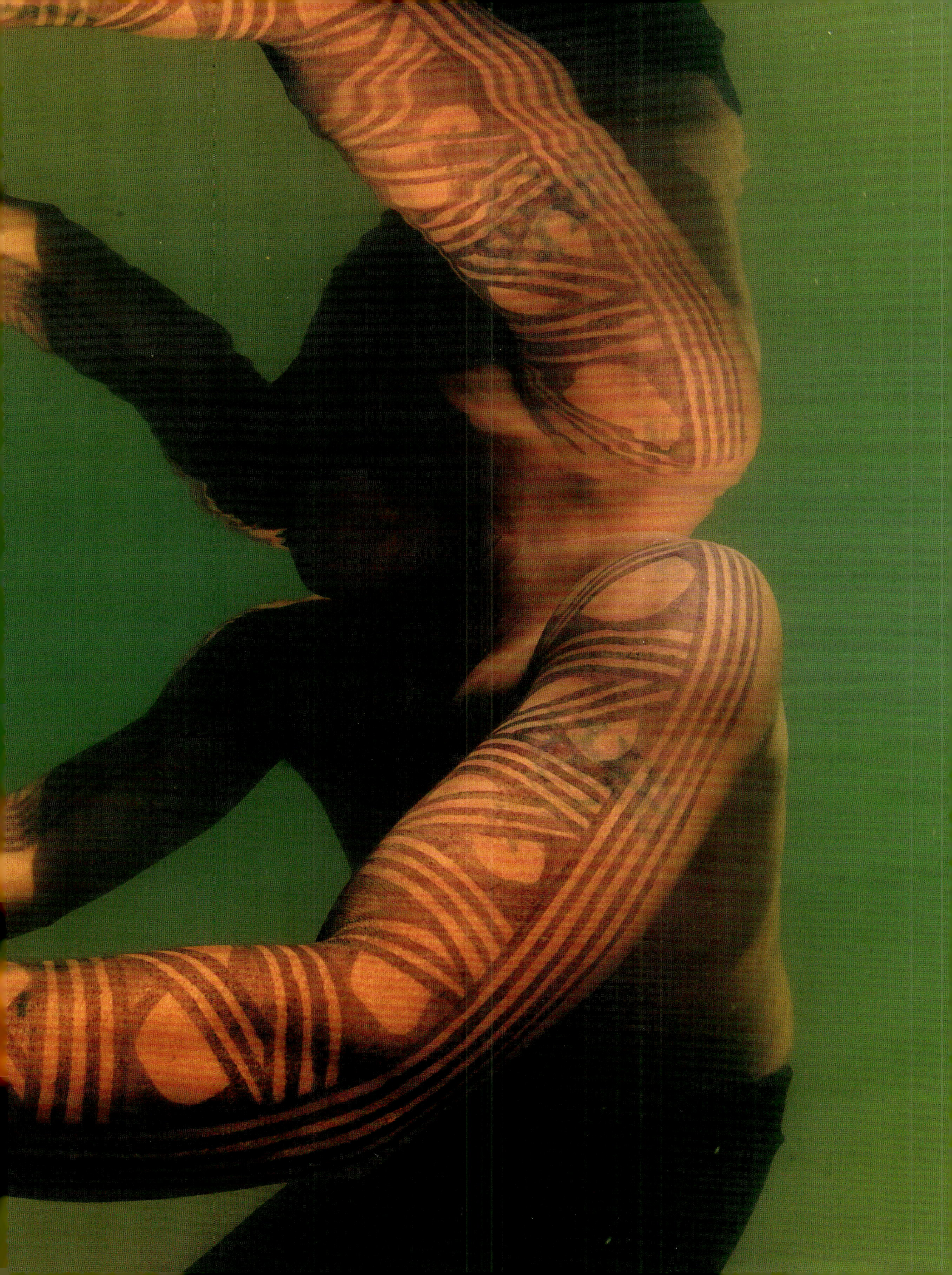

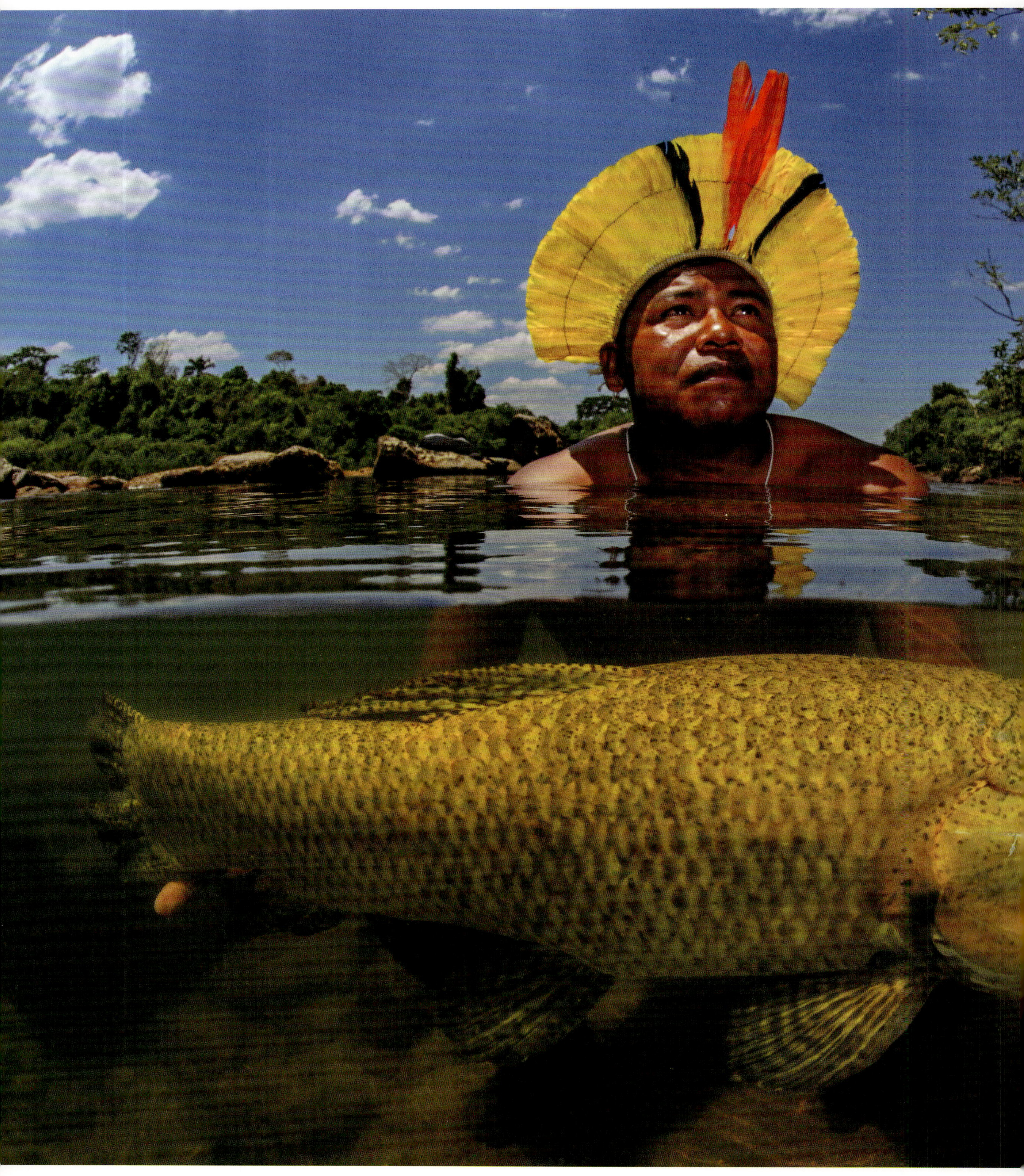

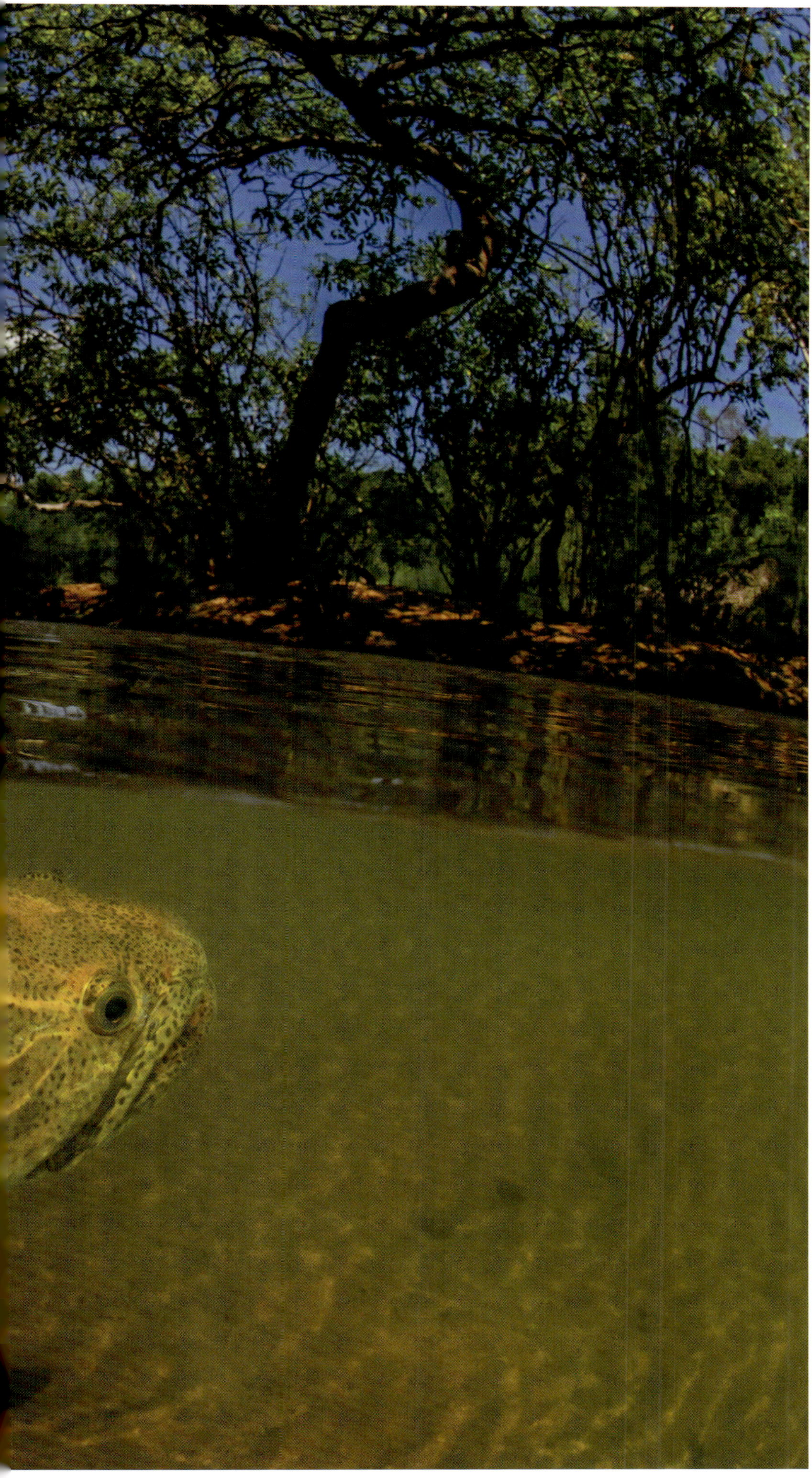

Ydjare Kayapó—who, like other male members of his tribe, wears a ceremonial headdress while working as a guide—crests Brazil's Iriri River. In front of him is a freshwater wolffish, a tropical predator with prominent, canine-like teeth. This fish is prized for the quality of its flesh, and the village of Kendjam was built at its current location in part because a nearby creek once held an abundance of wolffish.

PART FIVE

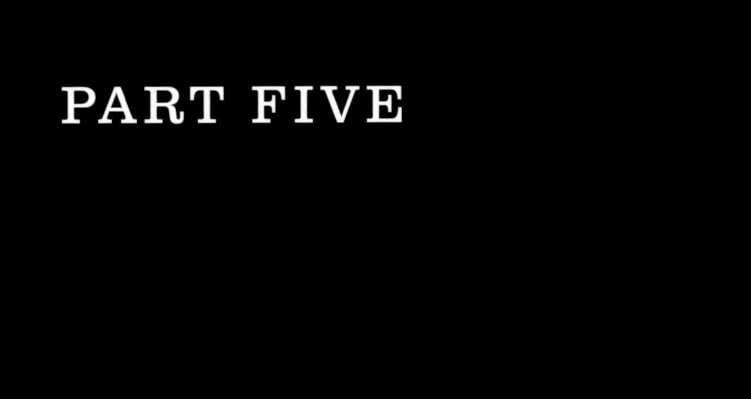

RIO NEGRO

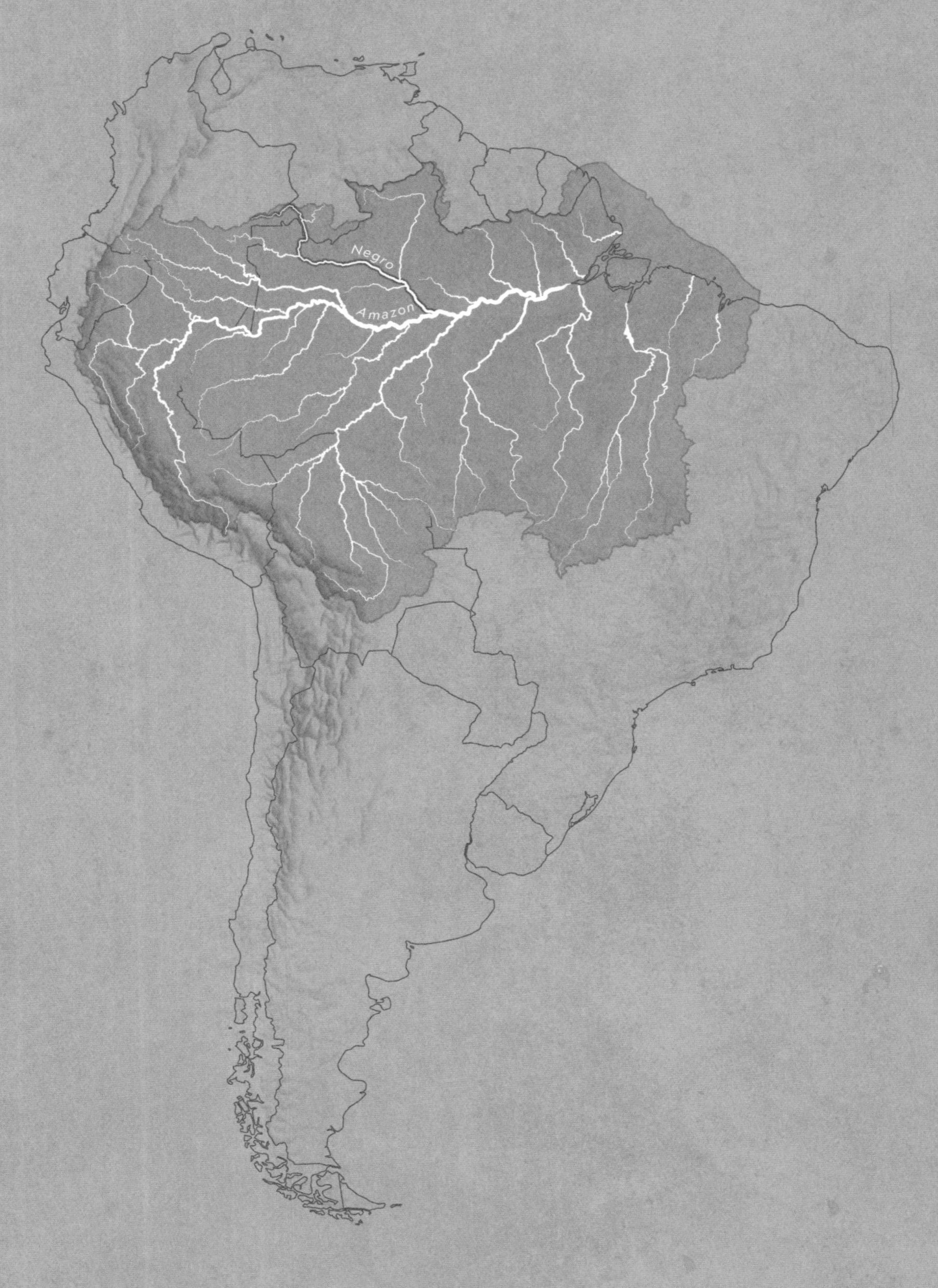

Negro
Amazon

THE WATER IS CLEAR but dyed red by tannins; it voraciously swallows light like a black hole. Free diving just a few meters down, my world goes dark. I can't see them, but they can "see" me. Their sonar emits a rapid series of clicking noises—30 to 80 per second—allowing them to navigate in pitch-black conditions. After a minute of holding my breath, I slowly ascend to the surface. I still can't see a thing, but I know they're following me.

Finally in the shallows, with sunlight bouncing off the sandy river bottom, I get my first good look at a boto, or pink river dolphin. Its long jaw is studded with 25 to 28 pairs of teeth on top and bottom: some designed for grabbing, others for crushing prey. It has a huge bulbous melon as a forehead and tiny eyes, giving it the look of a monster in a horror film. These dolphins are to the flooded forest what lions are to the African savanna or polar bears to the Arctic tundra. But despite their fearsome-looking jaws, they can be surprisingly gentle and curious.

Their stubby, paddle-shaped pectoral fins have perfectly evolved to navigate across topographically complex habitats at high speeds, deftly swimming just inches away from submerged trees. They allow a huge dolphin—an almost nine-foot-long (2.7 m) weathered male—to hover just inches from me, gently probing my head with its rostrum. He opens wide and fully extends his formidable jaw, his teeth almost touching my mask. The unique unfused vertebrae in his neck allow him to turn his head 180 degrees from side to side, and, much to my amazement, he effortlessly takes my snorkel in his mouth, tasting it for a few seconds before spitting it out. He swims around me a few more times, then loses interest and disappears again into the dark depths of the Amazon River.

The boto has a complicated and often contentious relationship with the people of the Amazon Basin. This charismatic animal is a keystone species in the daily lives and cultural traditions of riverine people across the region. But how botos are perceived and treated varies across communities. The Tikuna people—indigenous to southeastern Colombia—deem pink dolphins to be guardians of the underwater realm and mischievous spirits. They are said to seduce young women at the river's edge and to steal them away to an enchanted world of ancestral longhouses in underwater cities. In ritual dances, Tikuna elders don dolphin masks and pink robes made from the bark of the *yanchama* tree to enact the botos' role in their cosmology through song and dance.

On the other hand, the fishermen of Brazil's Rio Negro, who target the vast schools of fish that migrate in and out of flooded forests, have a very different point of view. Botos are highly intelligent and have learned to associate the sounds of

> Pink dolphins are a true flagship species that can protect entire river catchments across the Amazon. But they're currently listed as endangered due to fisheries, habitat loss, dam construction, and climate change.

boats and nets with an easy meal. The moment a fish is caught, they rush in and rip it from the net, leaving behind gaping holes. Because fish are currency and nets are a considerable financial investment, these botos are lambasted as thieves and viewed as a threat to food security. But the stakes are equally high for the dolphins, and an unknown number become entangled and drown every year.

In stark contrast, the many wildlife enthusiasts and nature tourists who visit the Amazon are enamored with pink dolphins, and riverine communities are cashing in on this interest. To ensure reliable close encounters, locals regularly provision dolphins with fish. This habituates them to people, leading to satisfied visitors but also hotly contested conservation complications. In some areas, many botos now display signs of obesity; some juveniles likely never learn to hunt, almost exclusively begging for food from people.

Pink dolphins are a true flagship species that can protect entire river catchments across the Amazon. But they're currently listed as endangered due to fisheries, habitat loss, dam construction, and climate change. Exact numbers are unknown, but as many as an estimated 4,000 botos might be killed every year in Brazil alone. Apart from becoming entangled in fishing nets, botos are also being targeted, their flesh used as bait to fish for piracatinga, a scavenger catfish. Despite the prohibition of commercial fishing for piracatinga in Brazil and Colombia, there is evidence that the trade persists, and the practice of using botos as bait has expanded to Venezuela, Peru, and Bolivia. Because of the important part pink dolphins play in the culture and legends of the Amazon, dolphin body parts—especially

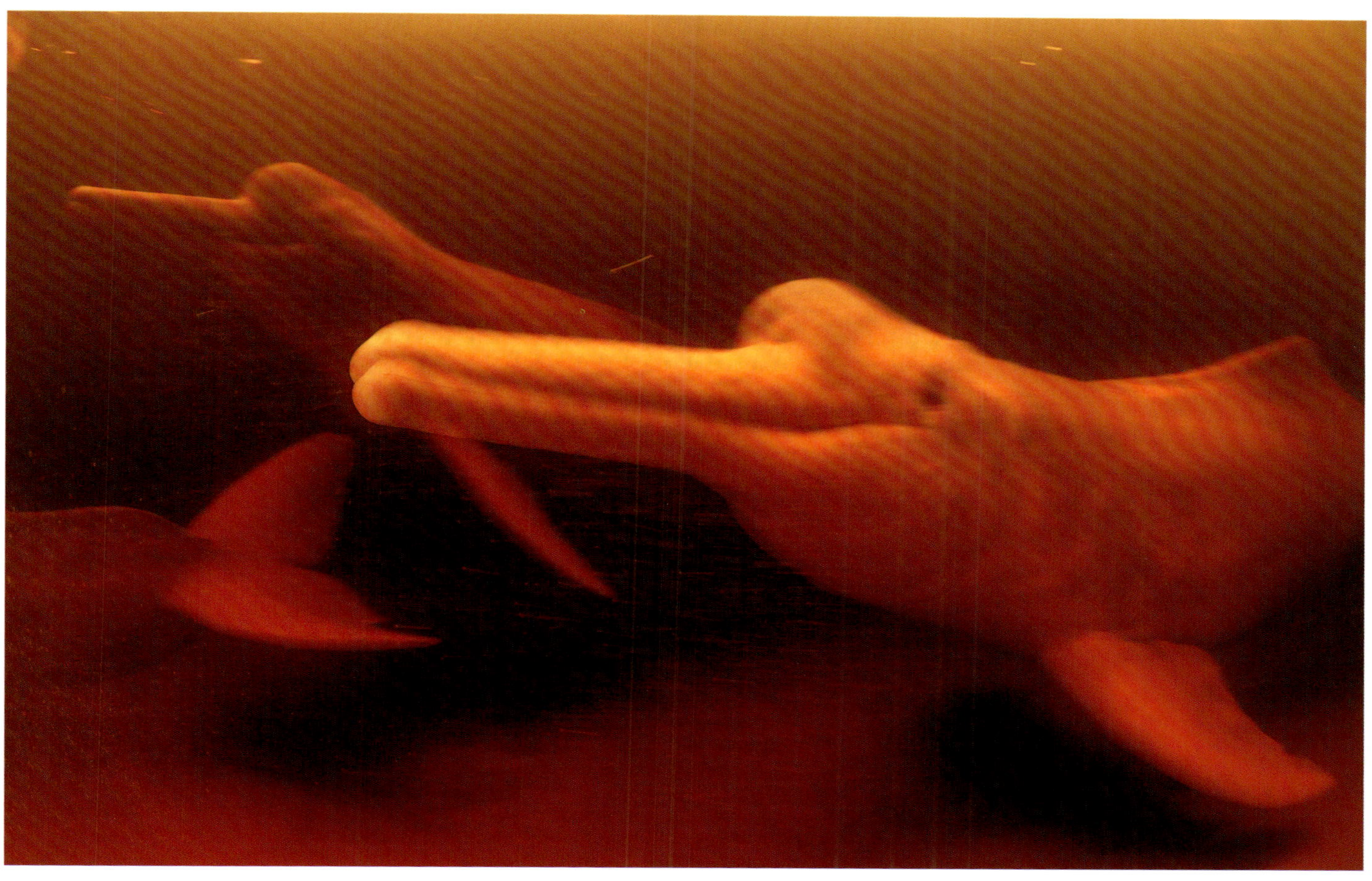

A pink river dolphin, or boto *(Inia geoffrensis),* hovers across a shallow sandbank inside a flooded forest. When the annual 50-foot-high (15 m) floodwaters peak in the Amazon Basin, these dolphins penetrate deep among the trees to catch migrating fish. High up in the tree canopy where birds and monkeys foraged in the dry season, dolphins now reign supreme.

the gonads, eyes, and teeth—are sold and used as love charms and amulets and are readily available in most large riverine cities.

In recent years, climate change and a historic drought have also wreaked havoc on pink dolphin populations. In 2024, the Amazon experienced its worst drought since records began—more than 140 consecutive days without precipitation. High daytime temperatures in tandem with low water levels resulted in water temperatures of rivers and lakes rising, killing more than 200 dolphins in Lake Tefé in Brazil.

If pink dolphins are going to survive in this world despite us, they will need our help. Only with the cooperation of people who live alongside the Amazon River, whose lives are most closely intertwined with these compelling creatures, can there be any meaningful conservation outcome. ■

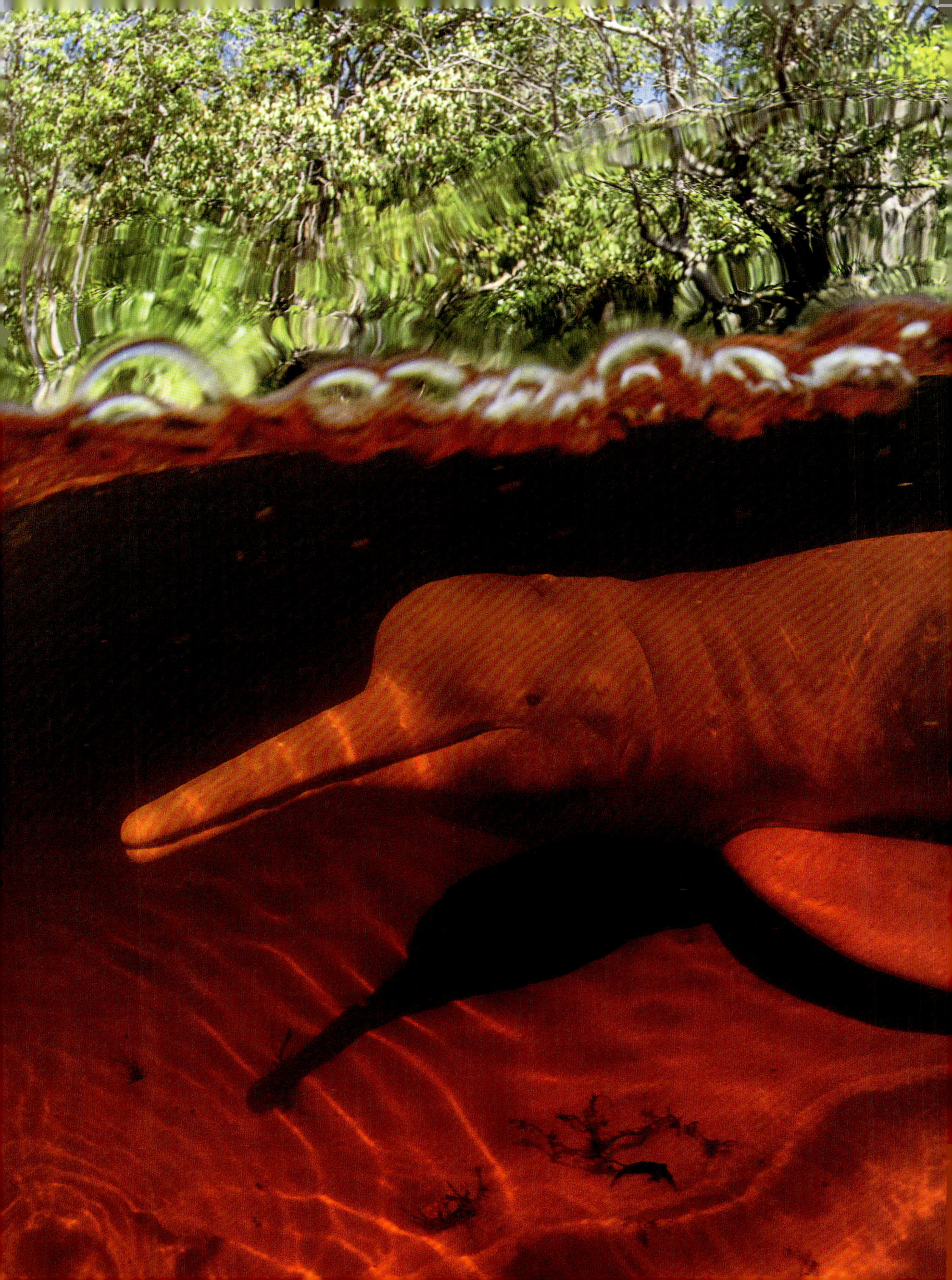

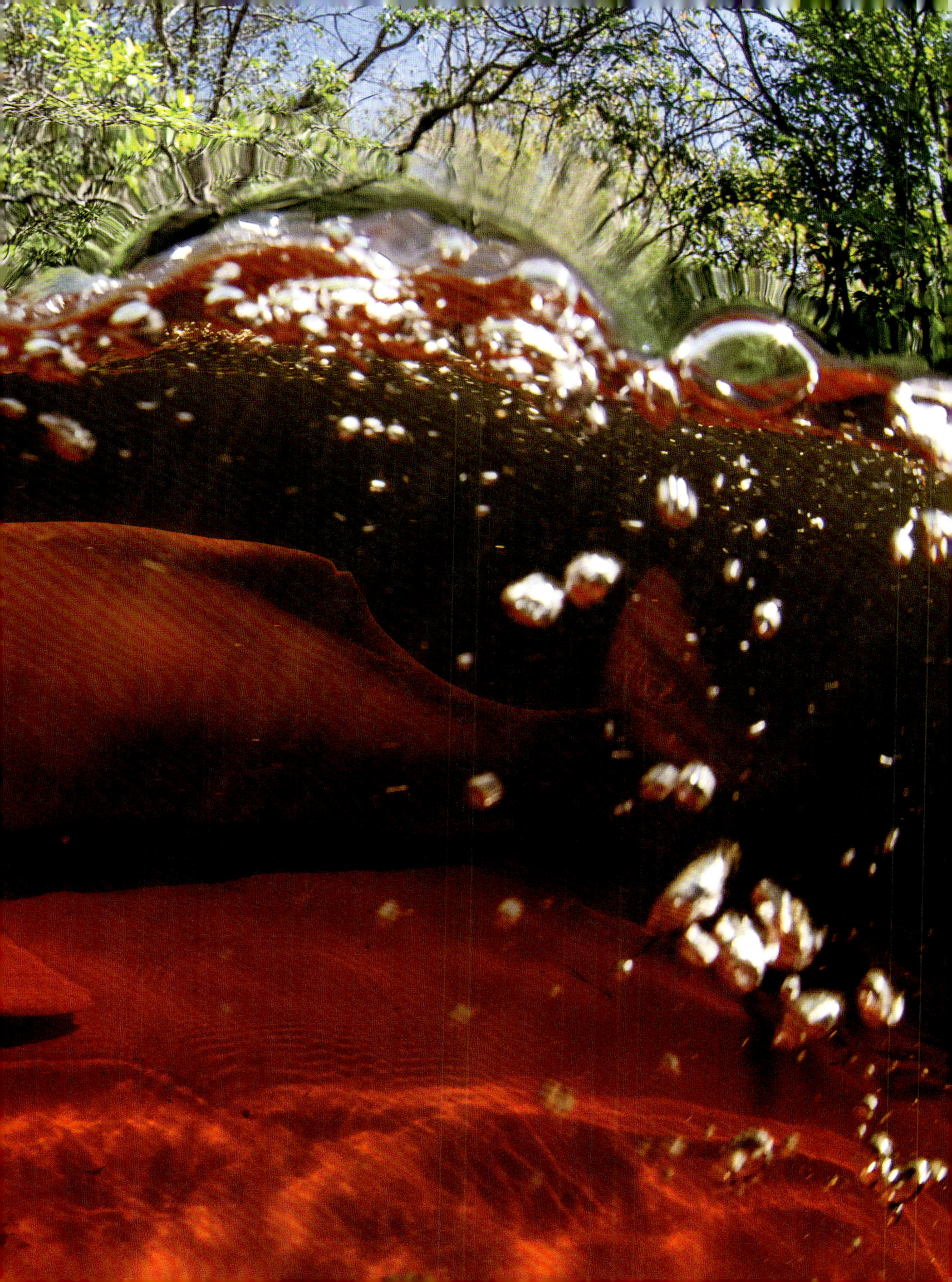

Sunlight illuminates a pink river dolphin swimming across a flooded clearing in the Brazilian Amazon. Exquisite shadows of leaves and branches are only thrown onto the submerged forest floor when the water's surface is calm enough and the sunlight penetrates through a gap in the forest canopy.

PAGES 190–191: A pink dolphin uses its sonar to navigate a path between tree trunks in a flooded forest. Dolphins emit a series of clicks—30 to 80 per second—that bounce off obstacles and potential prey. These dolphins also have small hairs growing on their snouts that help them find their way at closer range, especially in murkier waters.

PAGES 194–195: Dolphins have been the subject of folklore and mythology in Indigenous communities across the Amazon for generations. At Puerto Nariño in Colombia, elders don pink dolphin masks and dance around the fire inside the maloca or longhouse while singing songs that enact the pink dolphins' role in their cosmology.

PAGES 196–197: In southwest Colombia, Tikuna elders Nuria Pinto and Pastora Guerrero construct pink dolphin masks and robes made from the bark of the *yanchama* tree. The designs are painted with vegetable dyes and symbolize the original cosmic connection between the people and the environment.

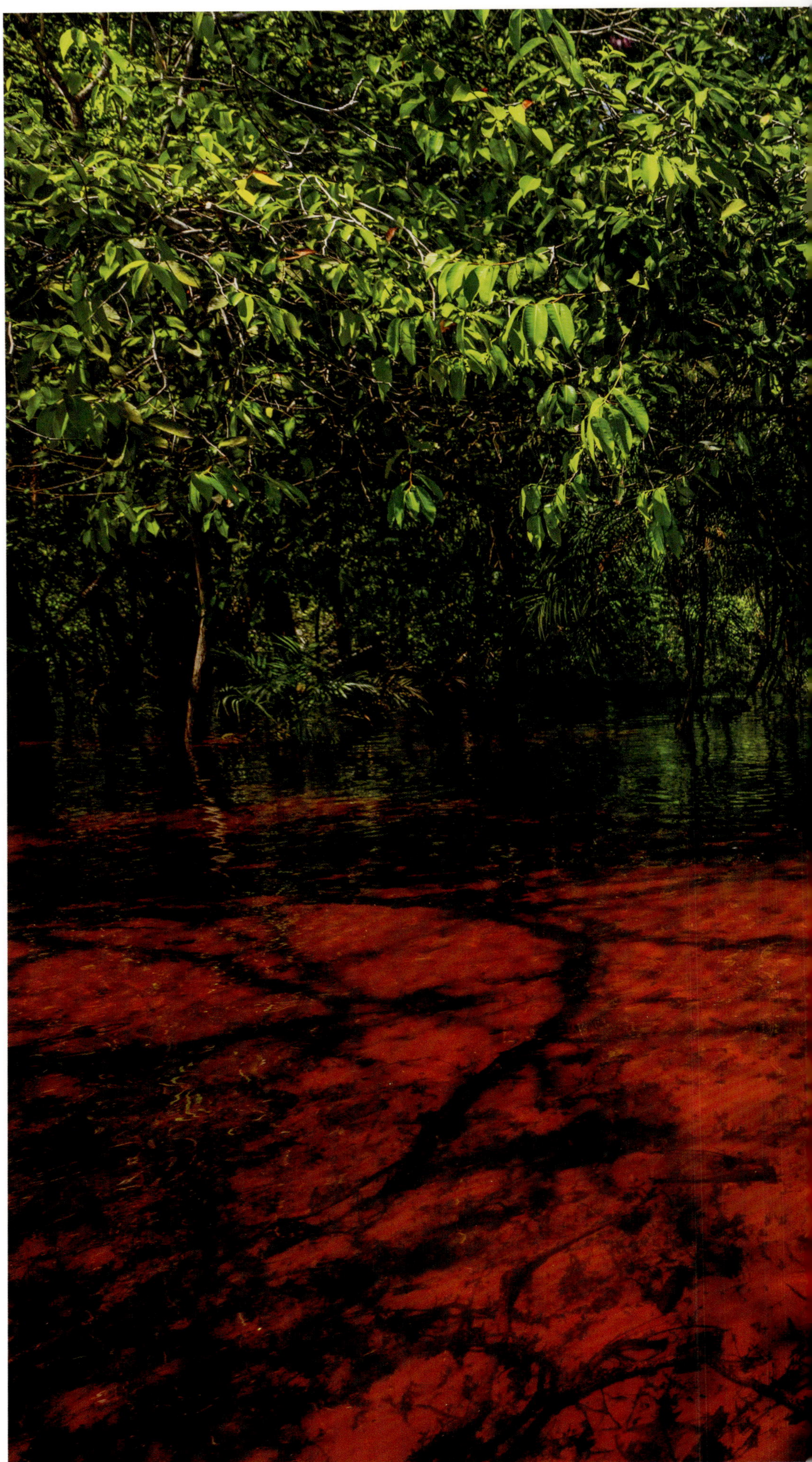

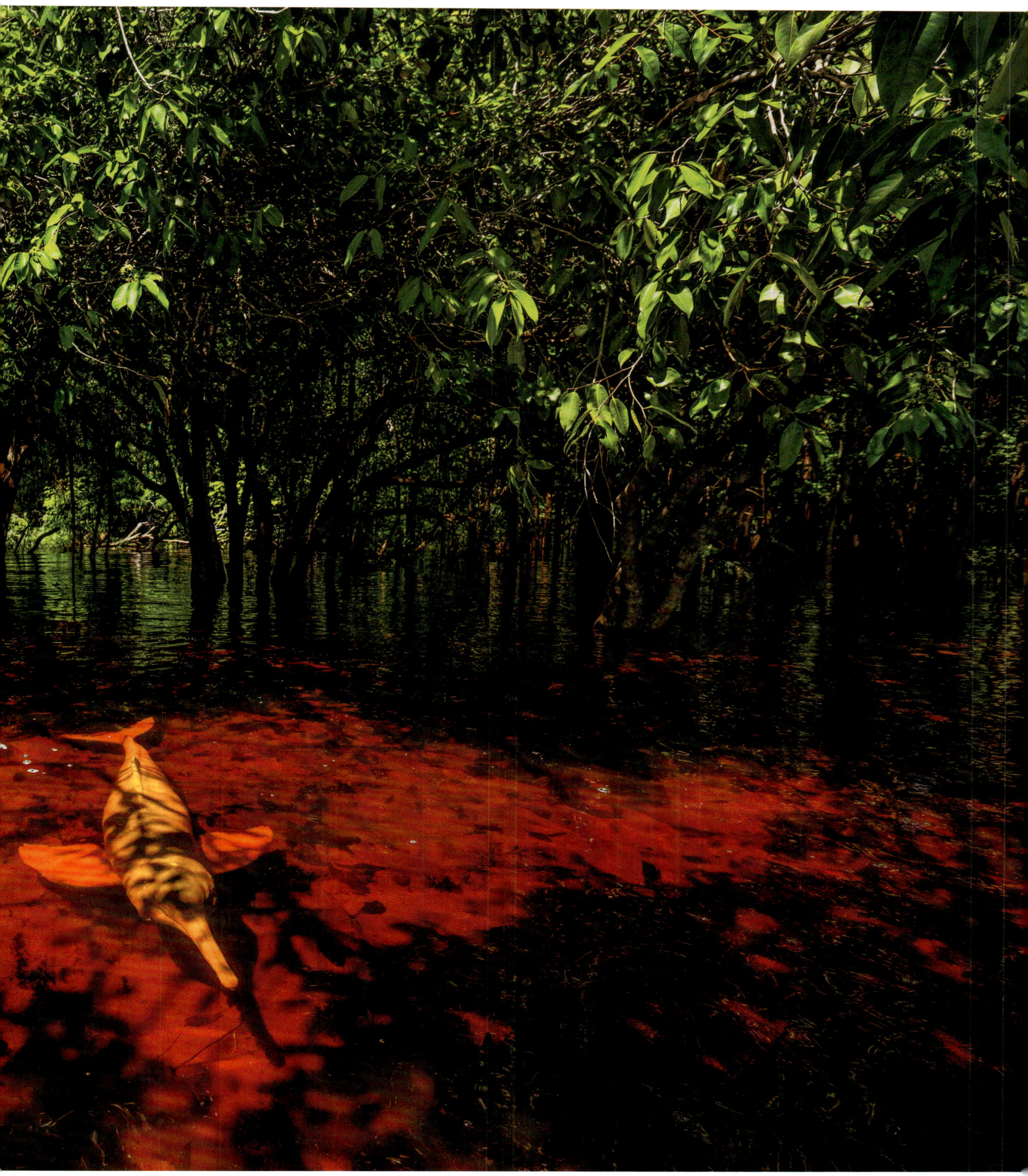

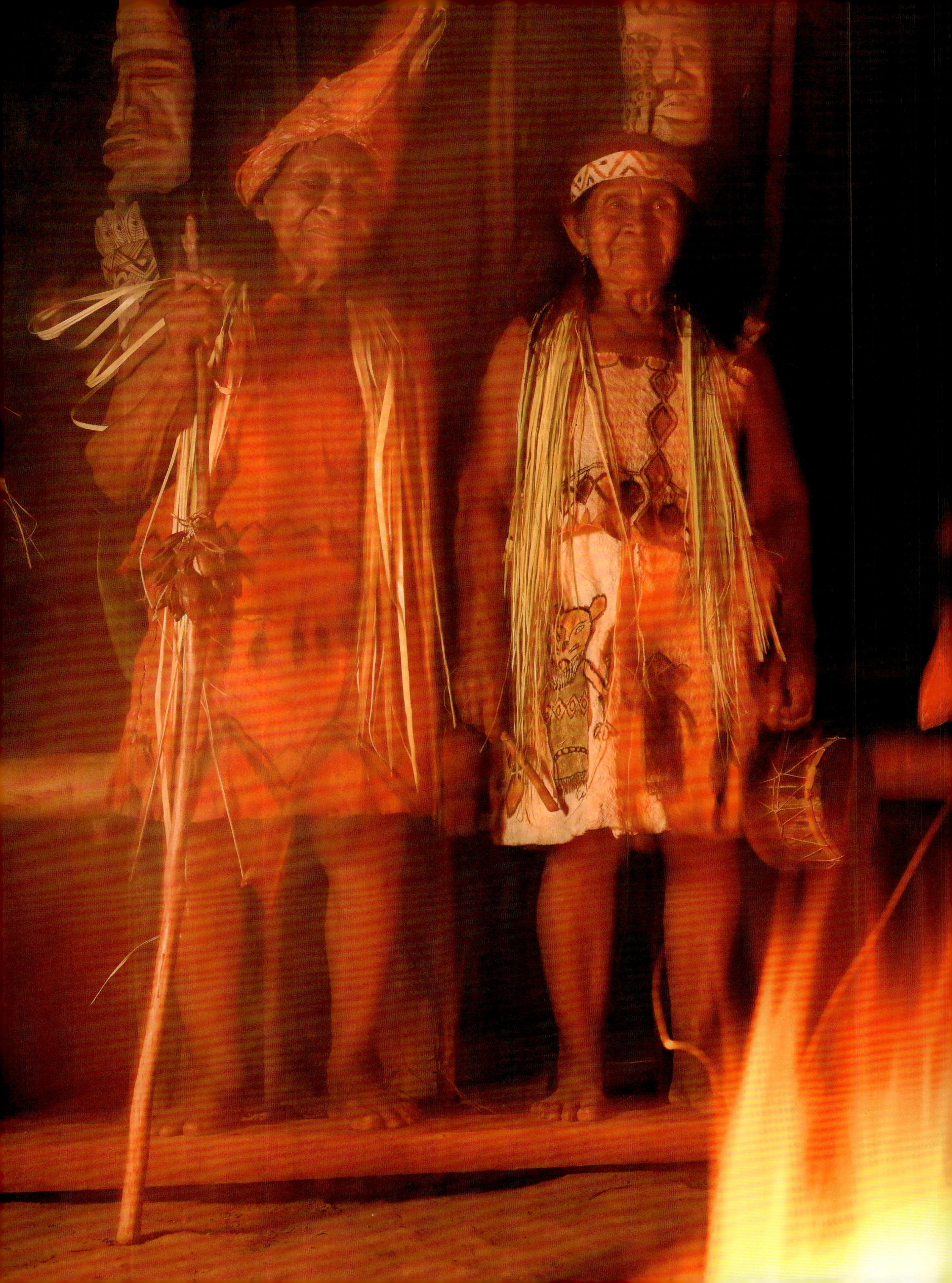

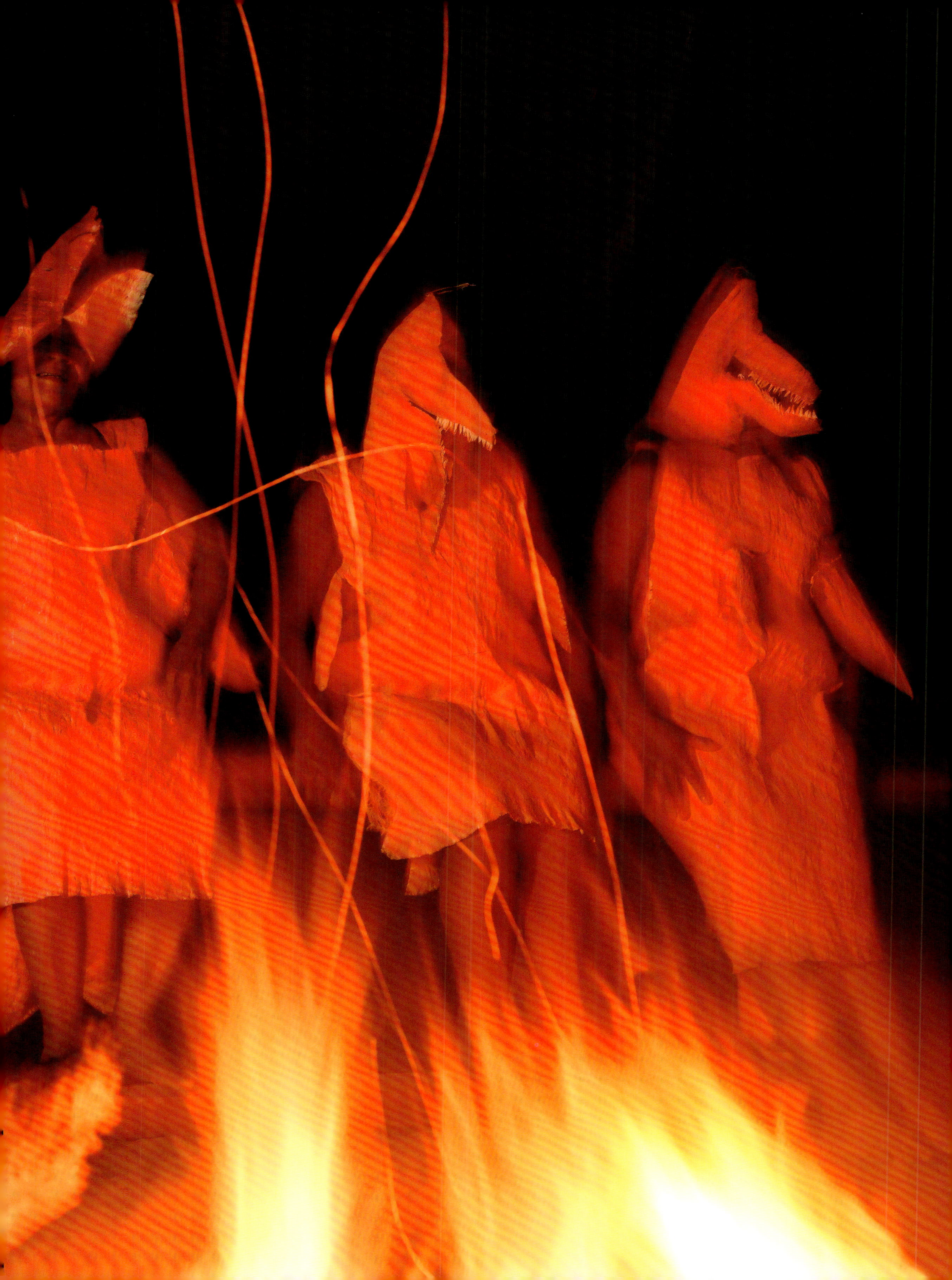

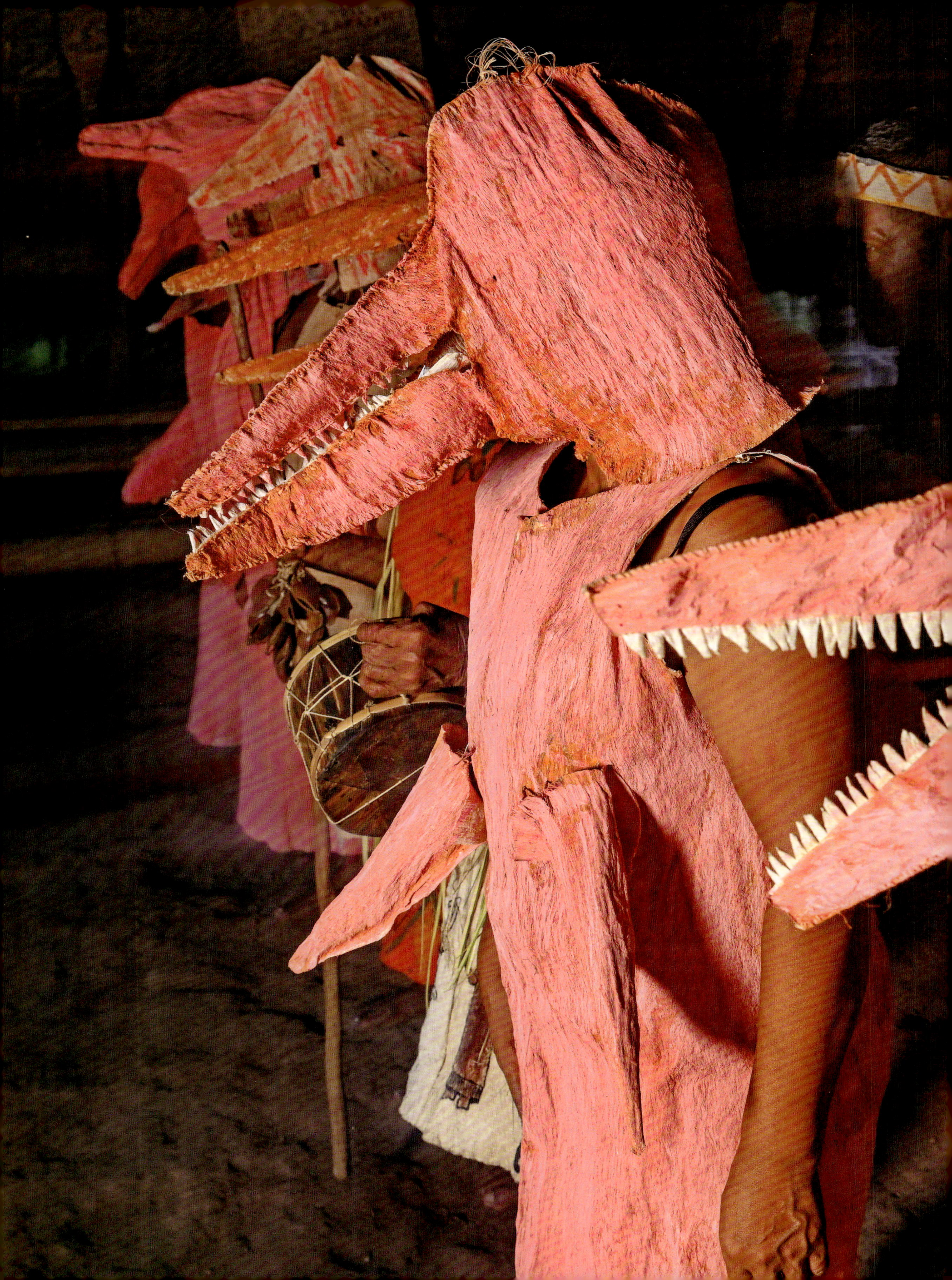

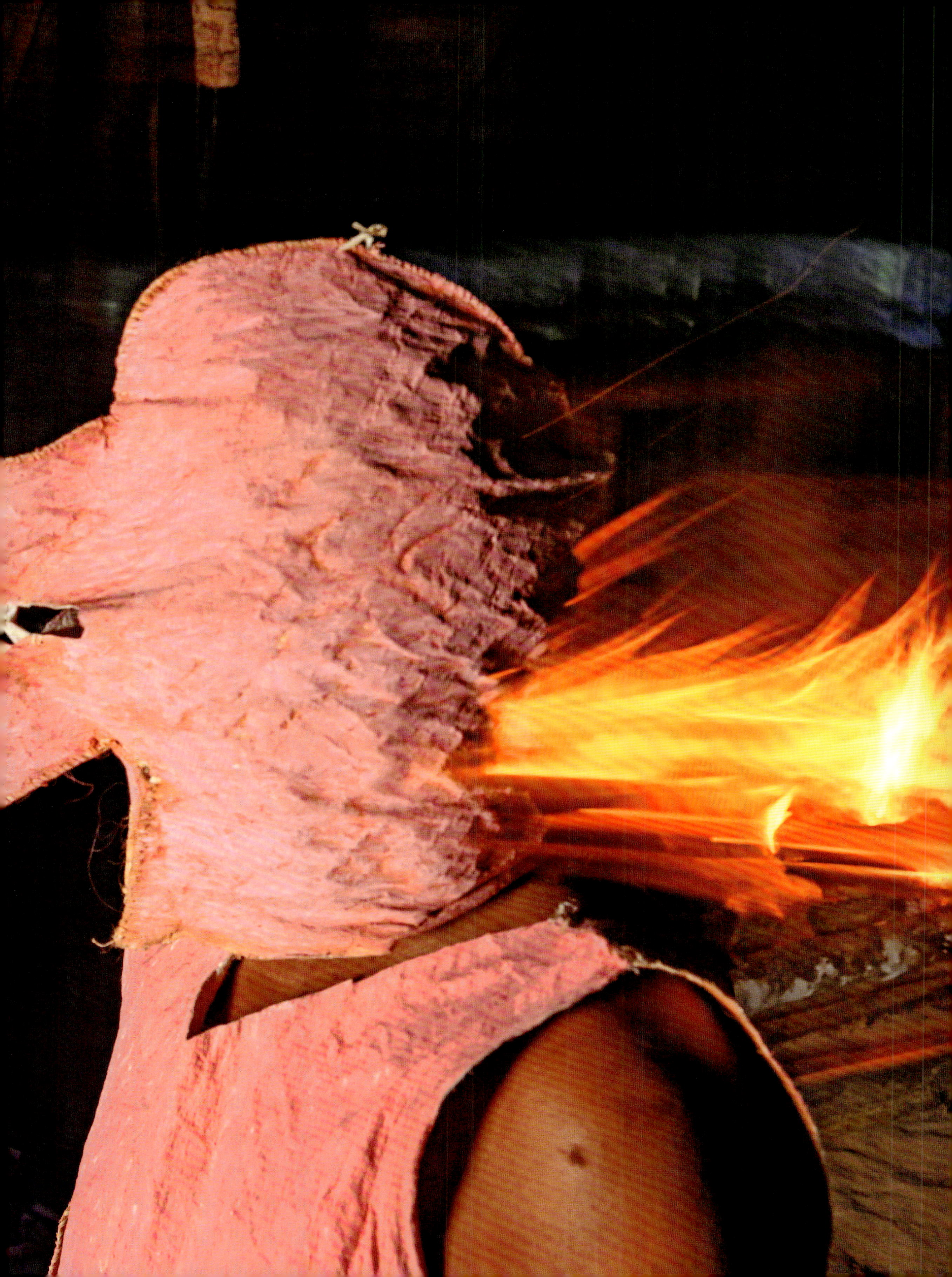

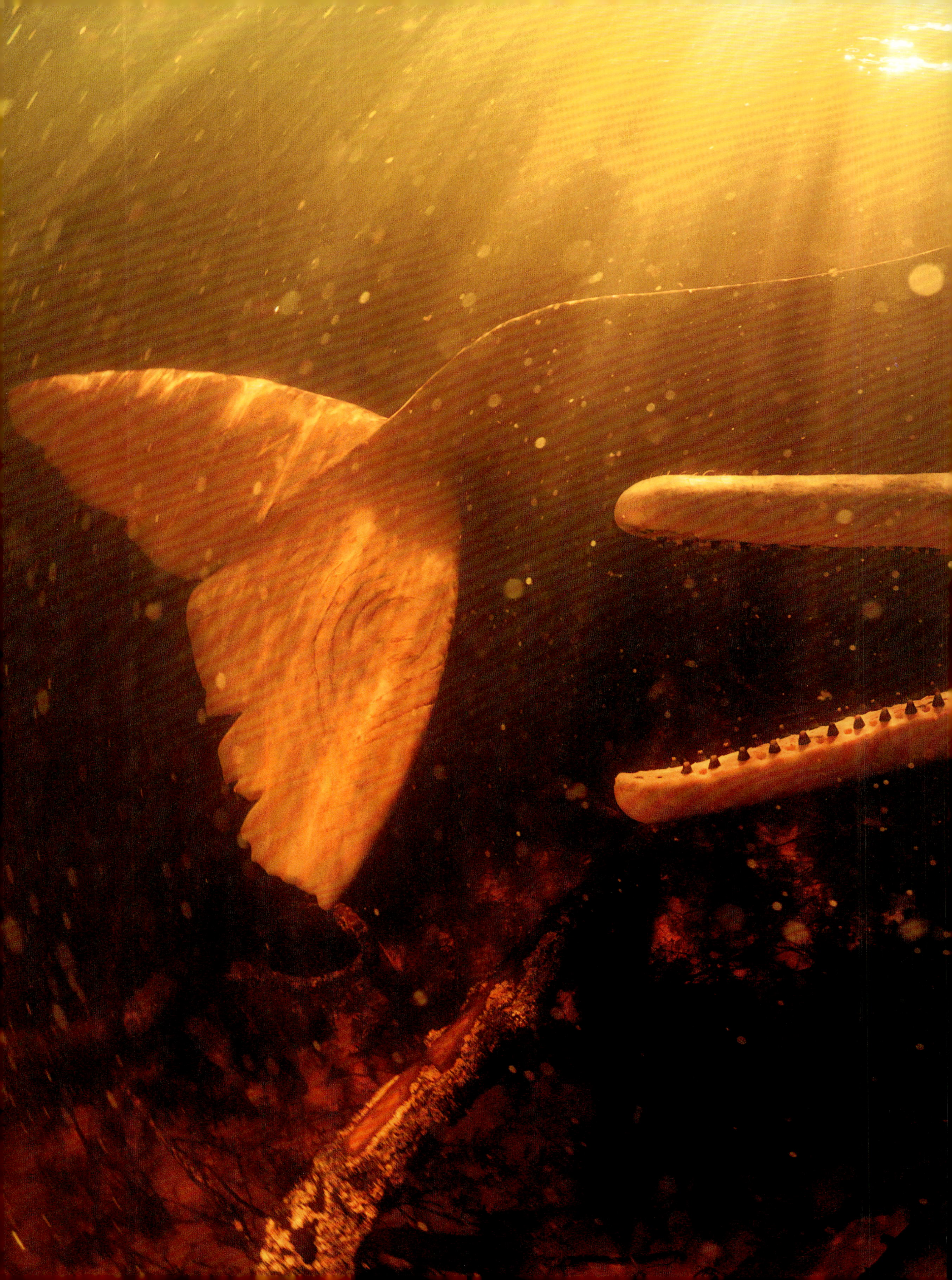

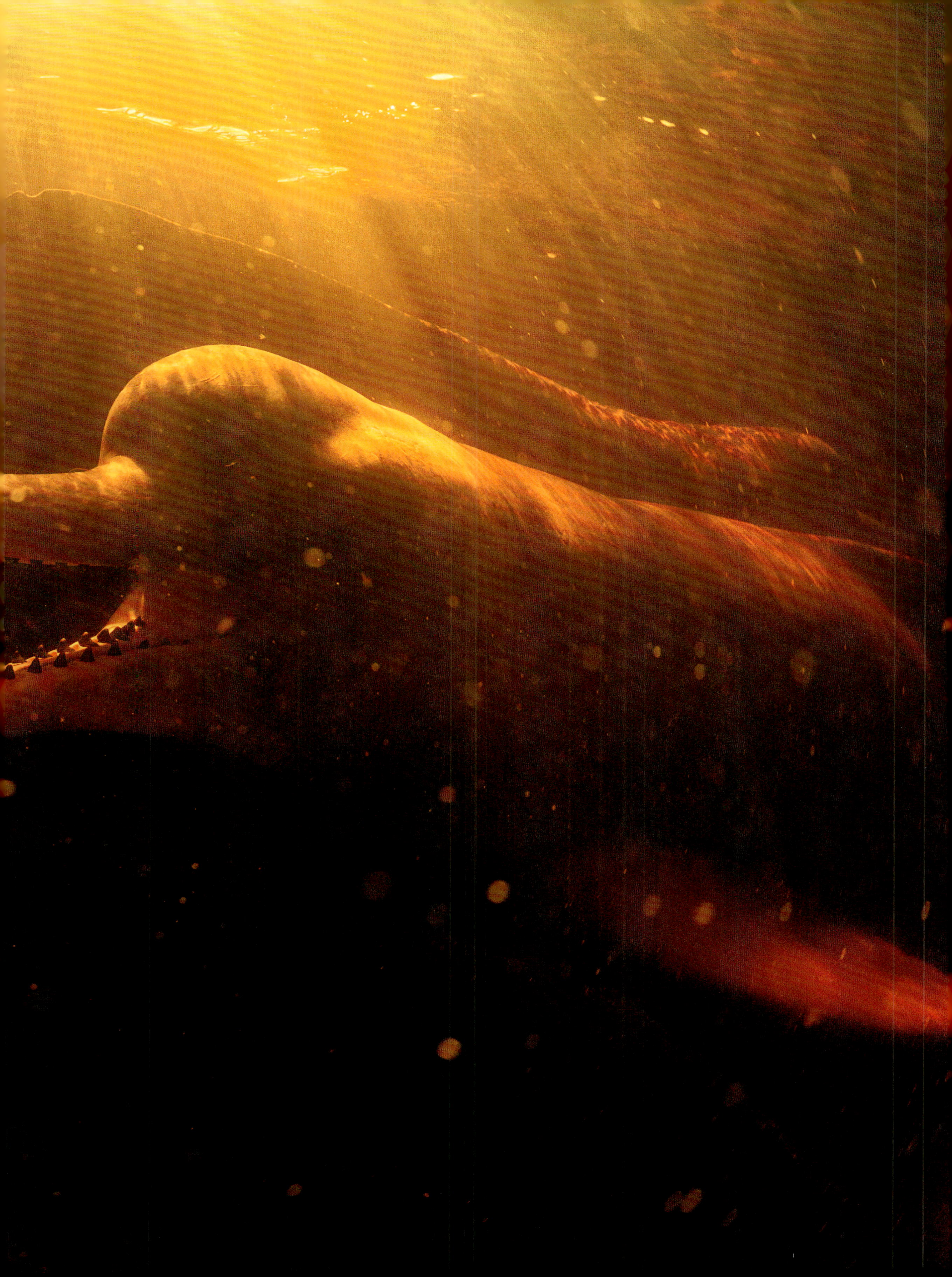

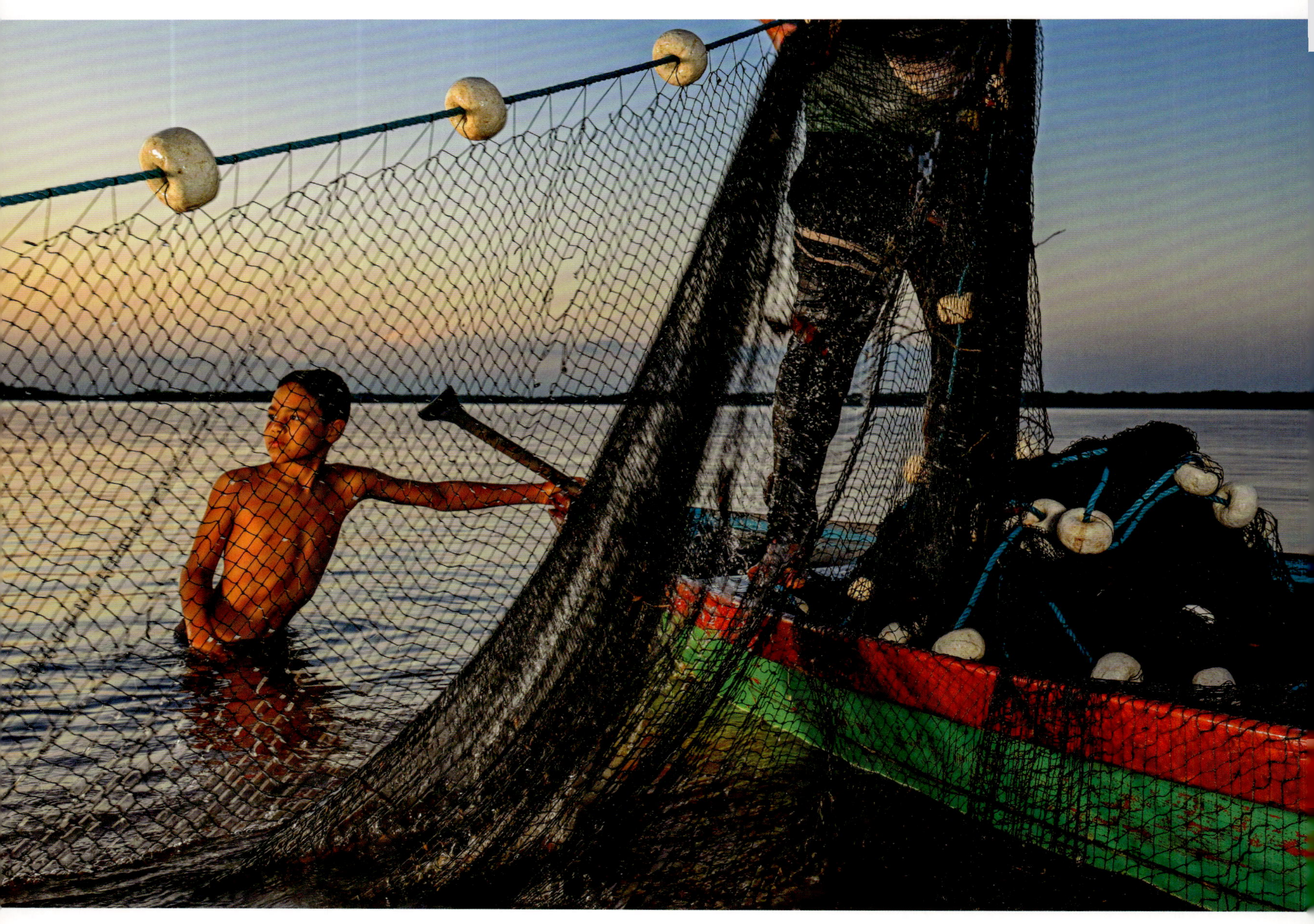

ABOVE: Communities that live alongside Amazonian rivers have some of the highest rates of fish consumption in the world, about 110 pounds (50 kg) per person annually. A recent large-scale watershed-wide survey revealed that overfishing is threatening the ecosystem's ability to continue to feed people.

OPPOSITE: Botos are highly intelligent, the smartest of all river dolphins, and have learned to associate the sounds of fishermen's boats with sustenance. The dolphins appear the moment a net is set and don't leave until they have secured an easy meal.

PAGES 198–199: A pink dolphin boldly displays its teeth, 25 to 28 pairs on both the upper and lower jaws. The teeth differ in shape and length, some designed for grabbing and others for crushing prey. In most instances, pink dolphins have an enchanted and almost comical look, detracting from their role as a formidable apex predator.

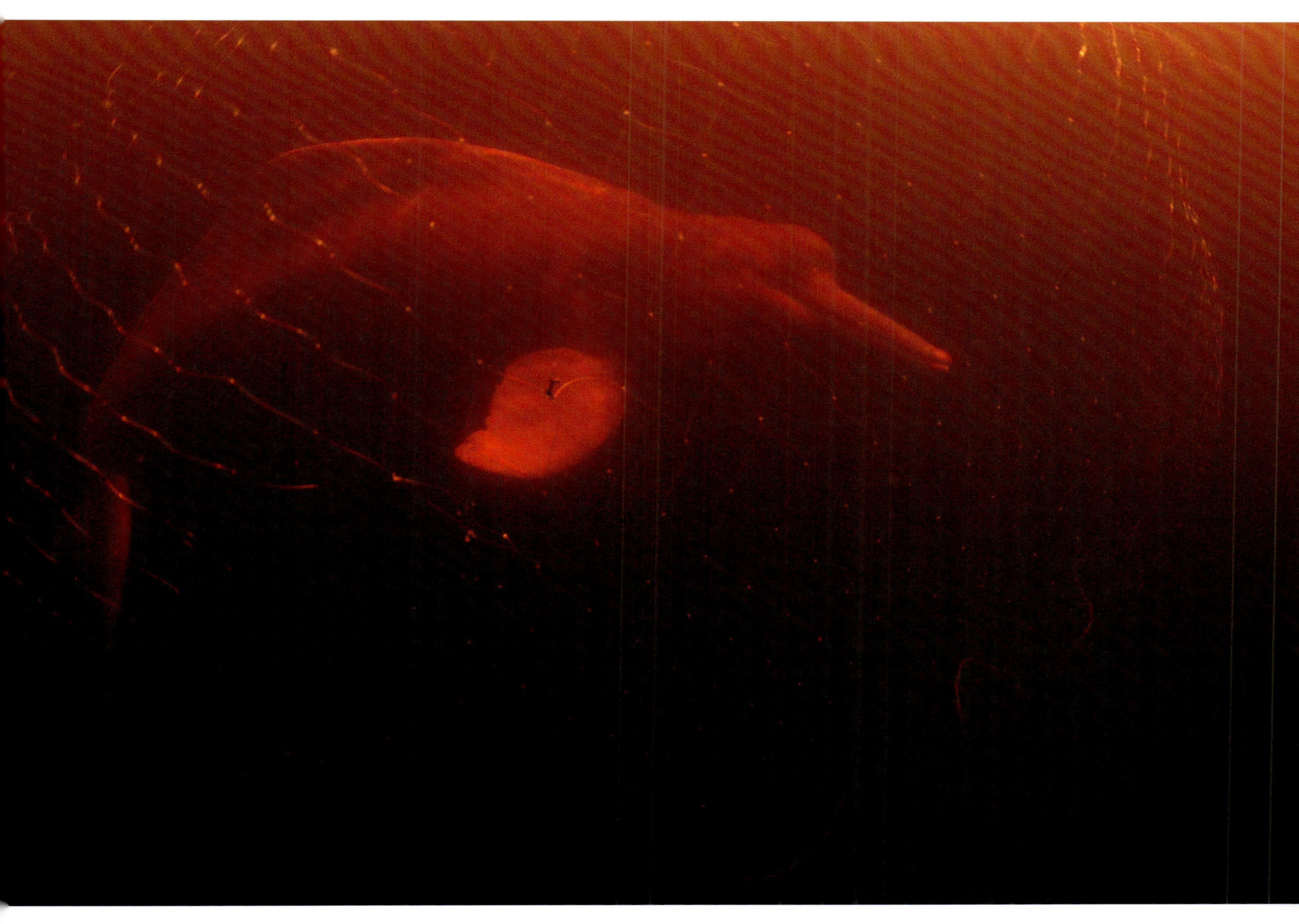

PAGES 202–203: The fishermen of Brazil's Rio Negro specialize in targeting the vast schools of fish that migrate in and out of flooded forests as water levels drop. Migratory fish contribute about 93 percent of fish caught in the Amazon Basin and earn $436 million annually.

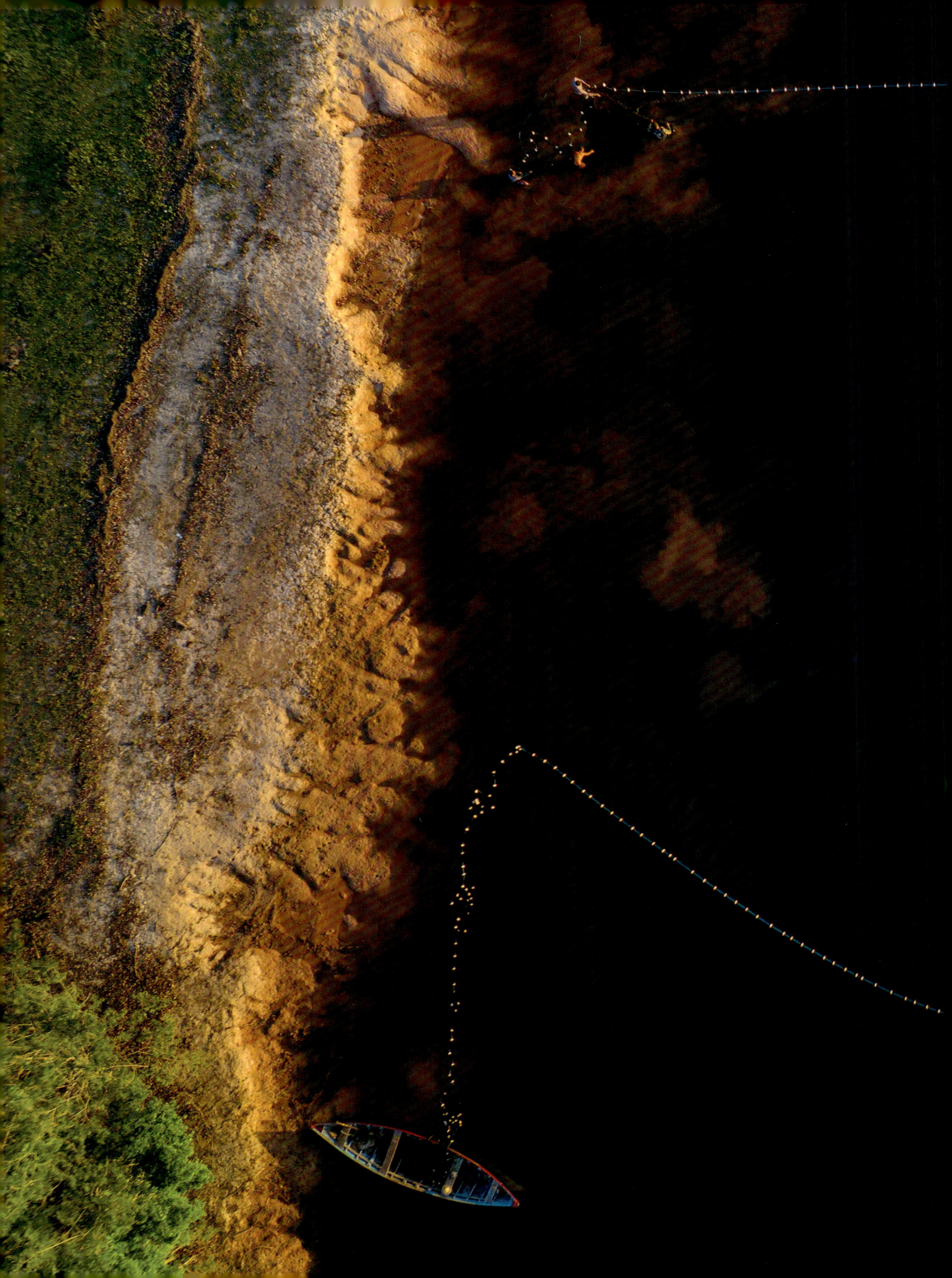

An agile pink dolphin rushes in and rips a fish from a net, damaging the net in the process. Because fish are currency and nets are a considerable financial investment, botos are often viewed as a threat to food security. This type of depredation can also be dangerous to the dolphins, as an unknown number are entangled and drown every year.

PAGES 206–207: Fernando Trujillo (far left) and his team carry out a health assessment on a large boto. Data collected on blood parameters, reproductive health, genetics, and mercury contamination provide actionable information not only about dolphin populations but also on the health of the entire river system. To minimize the dolphin's stress, all work is completed in less than 15 minutes before the animal is released back into the river.

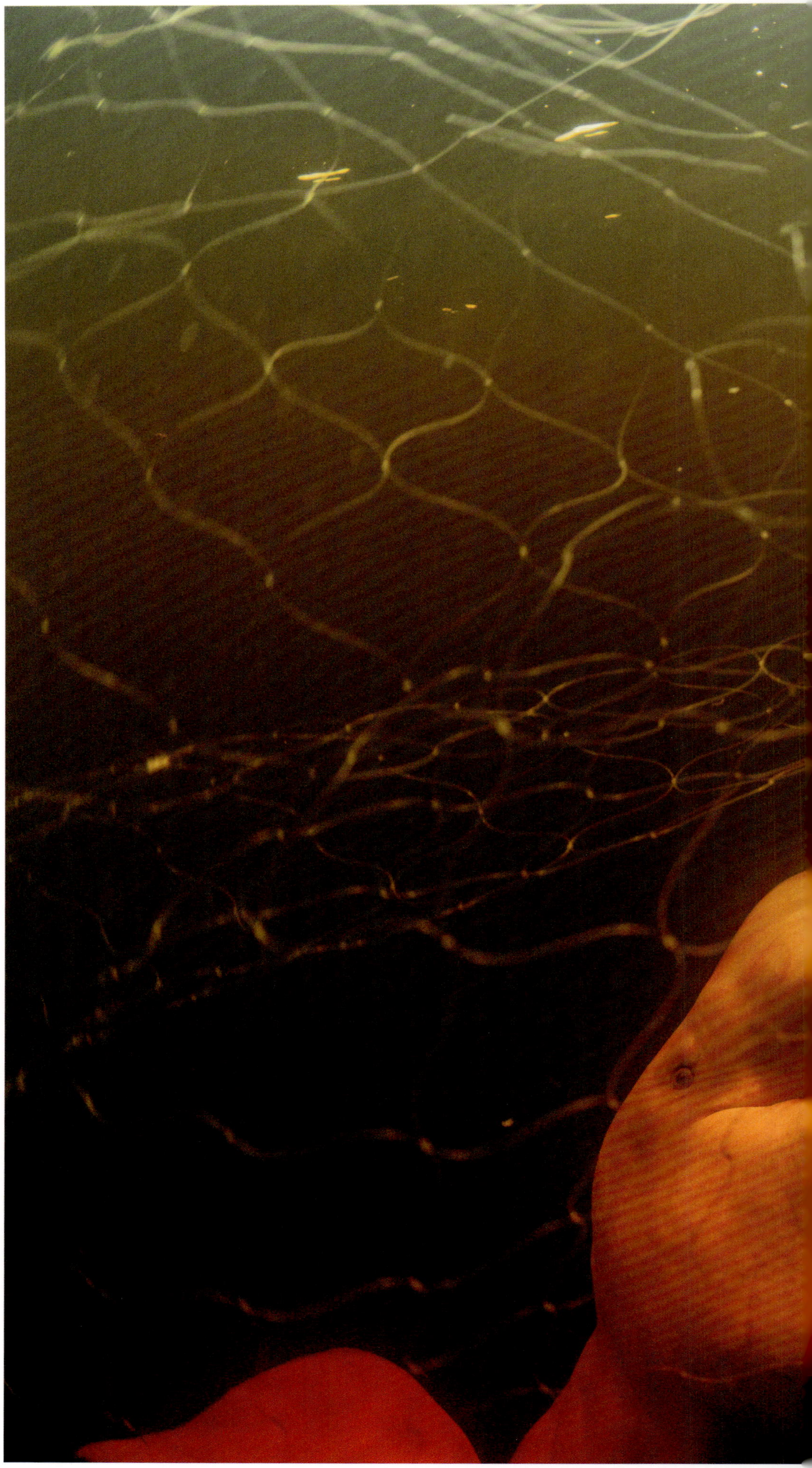

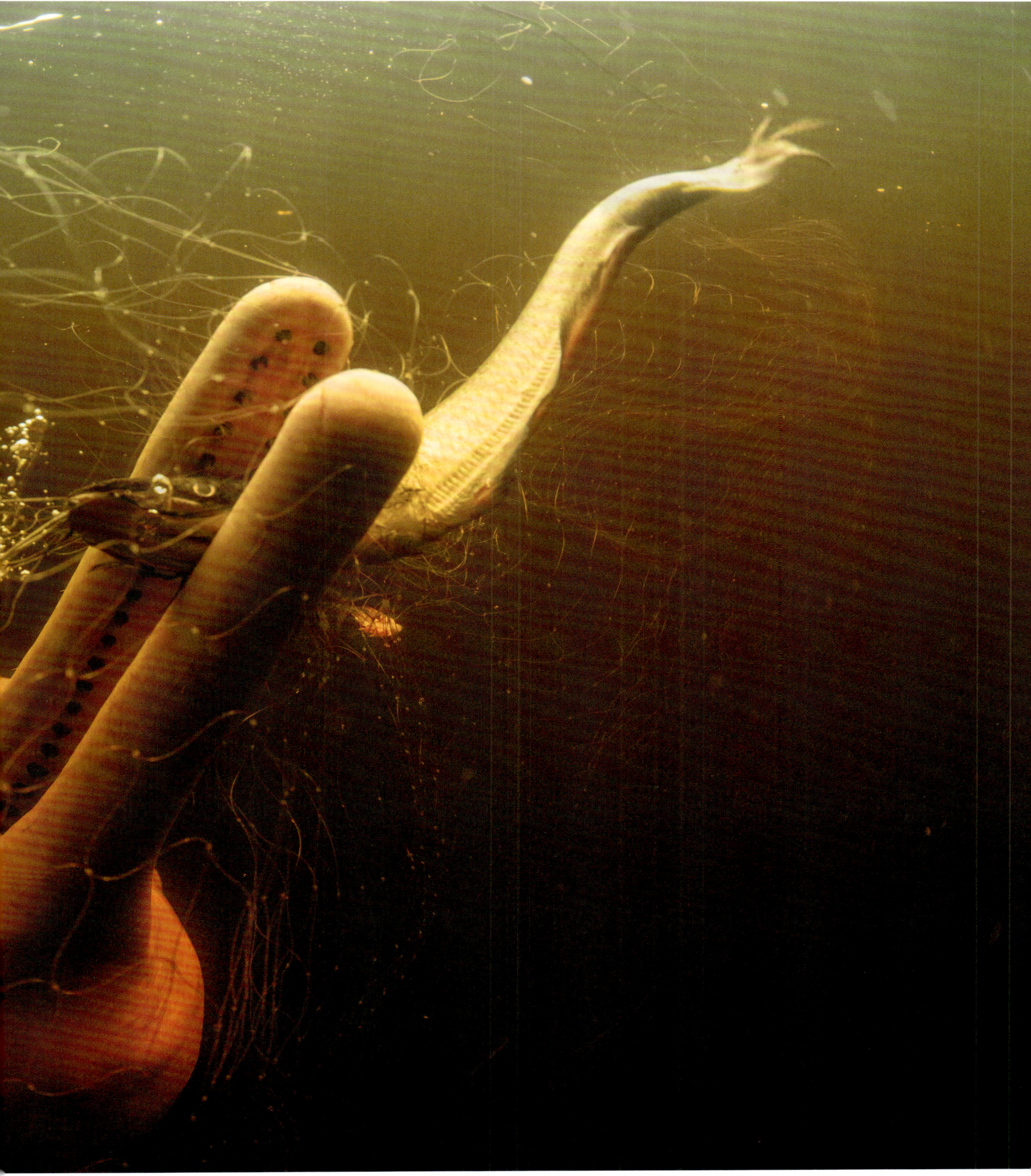

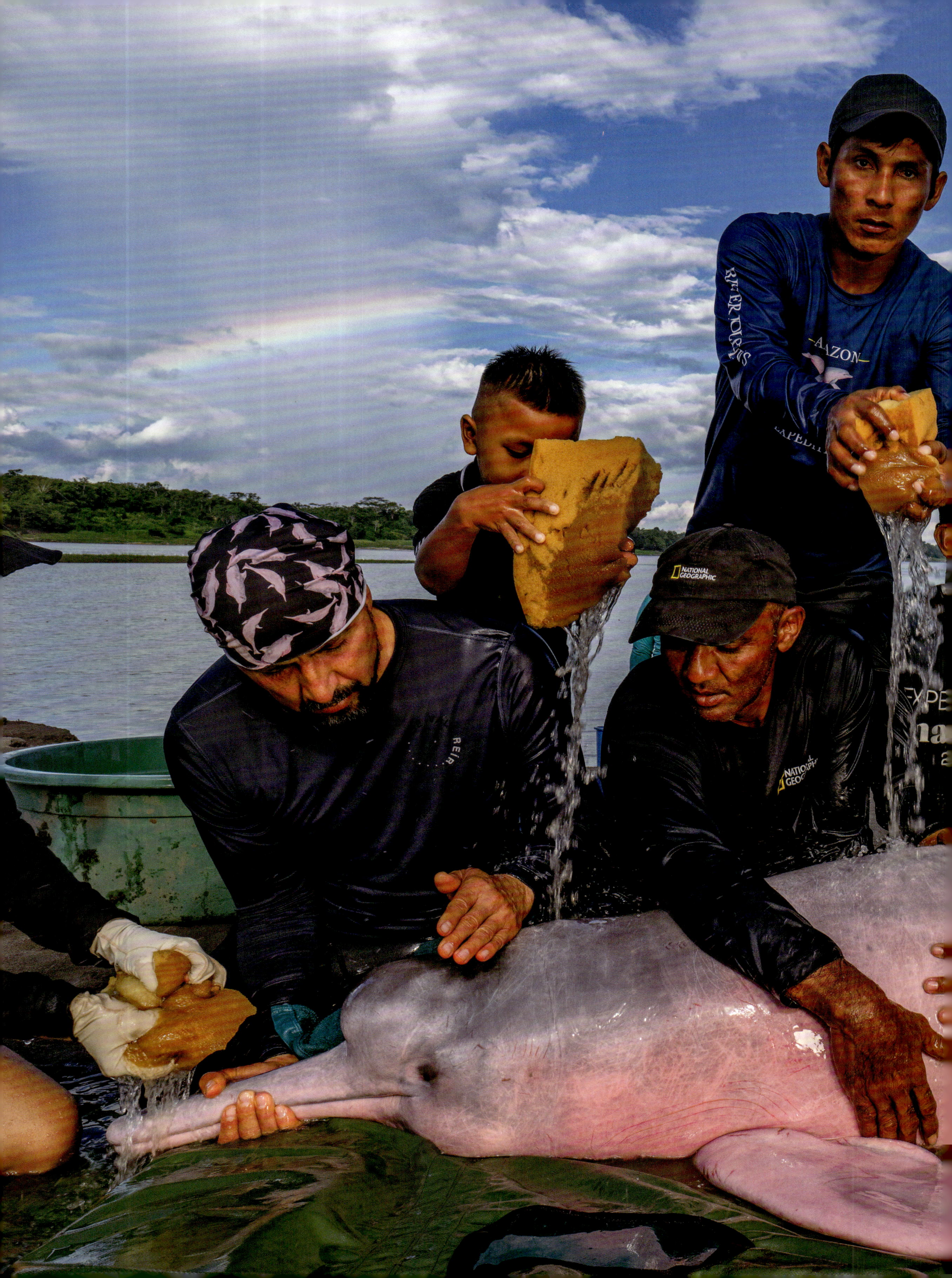
NATIONAL GEOGRAPHIC

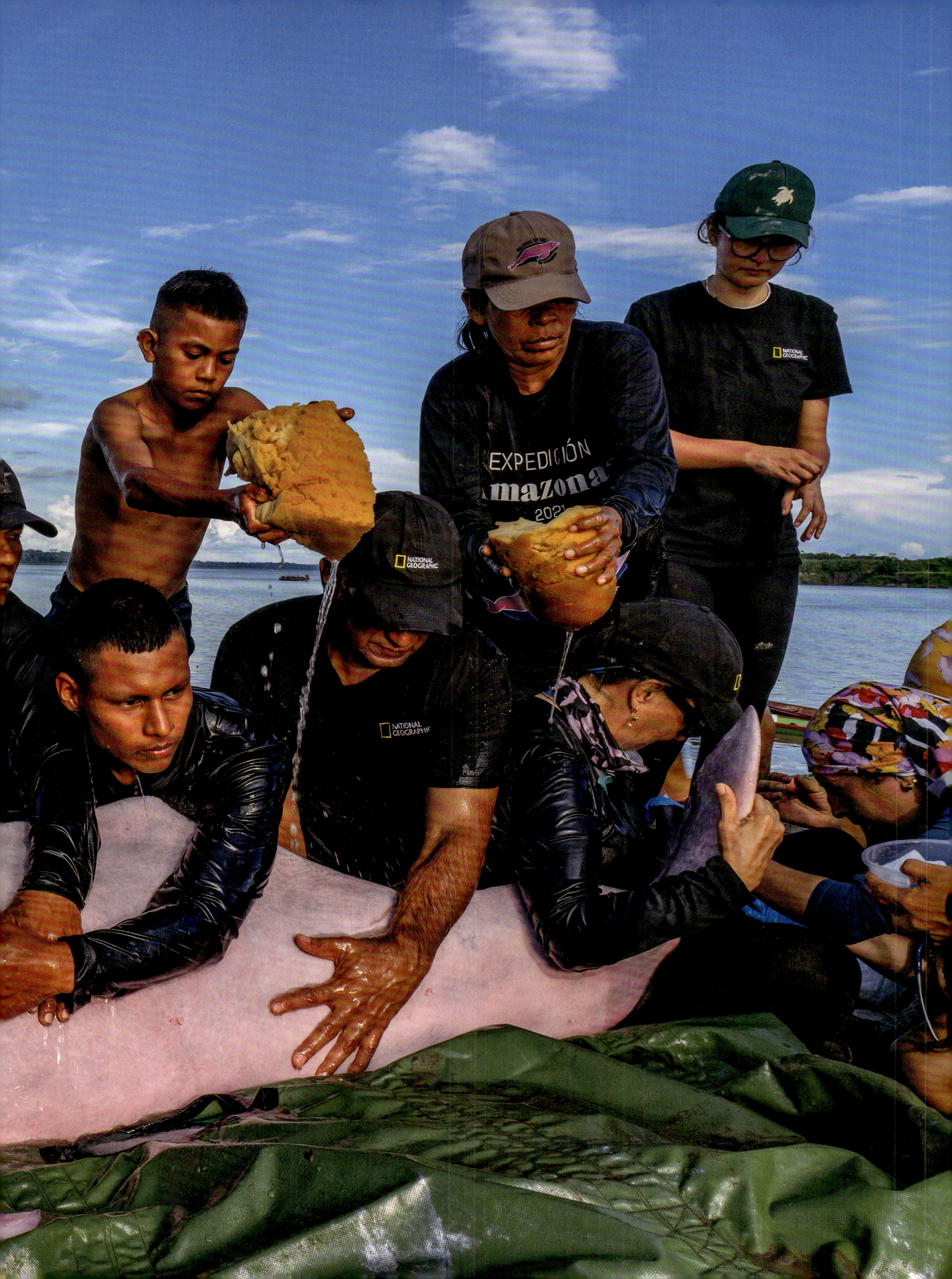

NATIONAL GEOGRAPHIC
EXPEDICIÓN
NATIONAL GEOGRAPHIC
NATIONAL GEOGRAPHIC

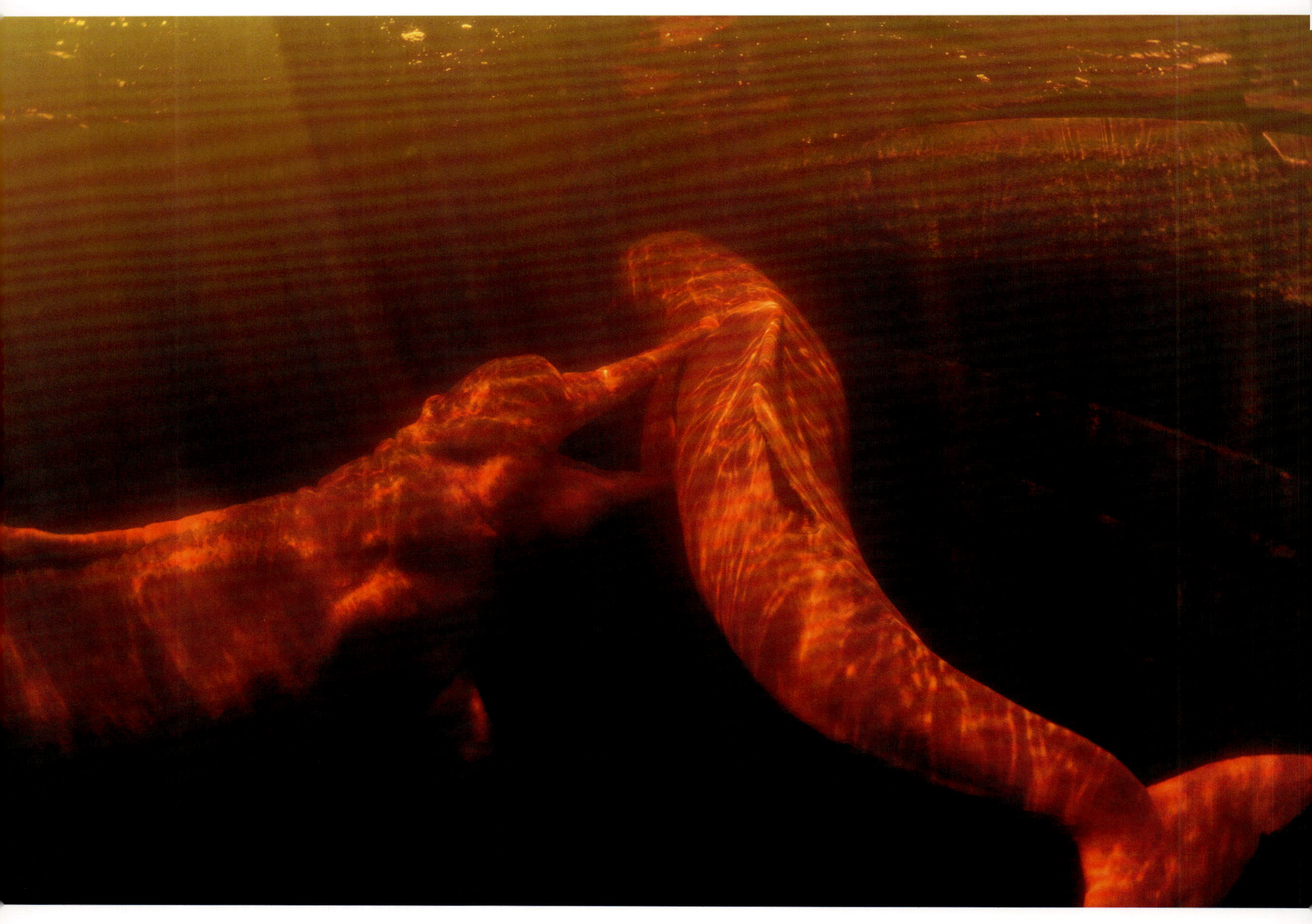

ABOVE: Pink dolphins are to the flooded forest what lions are to the African savanna or polar bears to the Arctic tundra. Males are more aggressive and often bite or strike each other with their heads or tails. Because of this behavior, scars accumulate all over the dolphins' bodies as they age, and some scientists believe that this is what makes older male dolphins appear pinker.

OPPOSITE: Pink dolphins' stubby, paddle-shaped pectoral fins have perfectly evolved to navigate across topographically complex habitats at high speeds, deftly swimming just inches away from submerged trees.

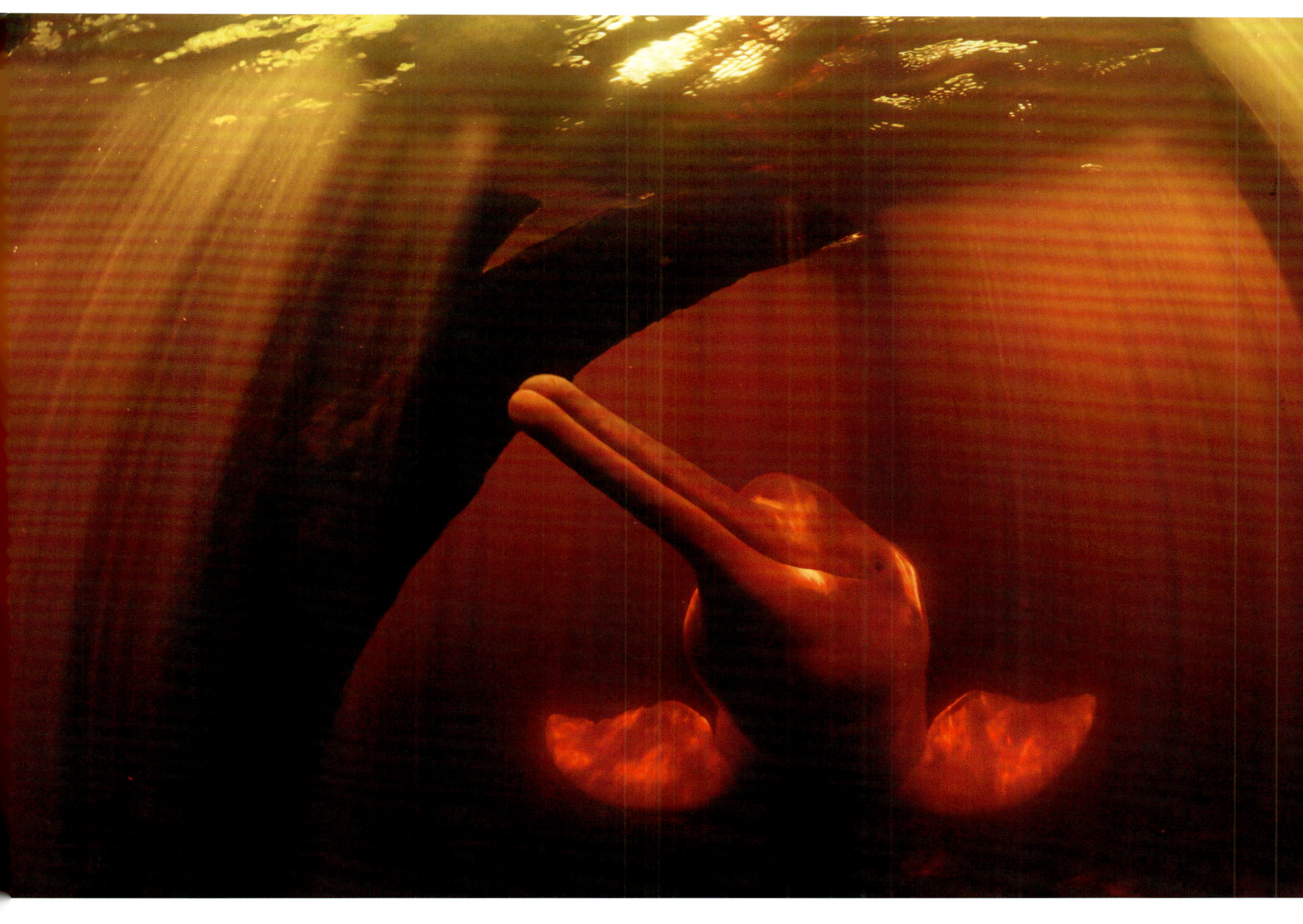

PAGES 210–211: Tourists come to the Amazon Basin every year to see pink dolphins, and riverine communities are cashing in on this popularity. Across Brazil, Colombia, Peru, and Bolivia, dolphin tours are creating jobs and bringing economic and social benefits to local people.

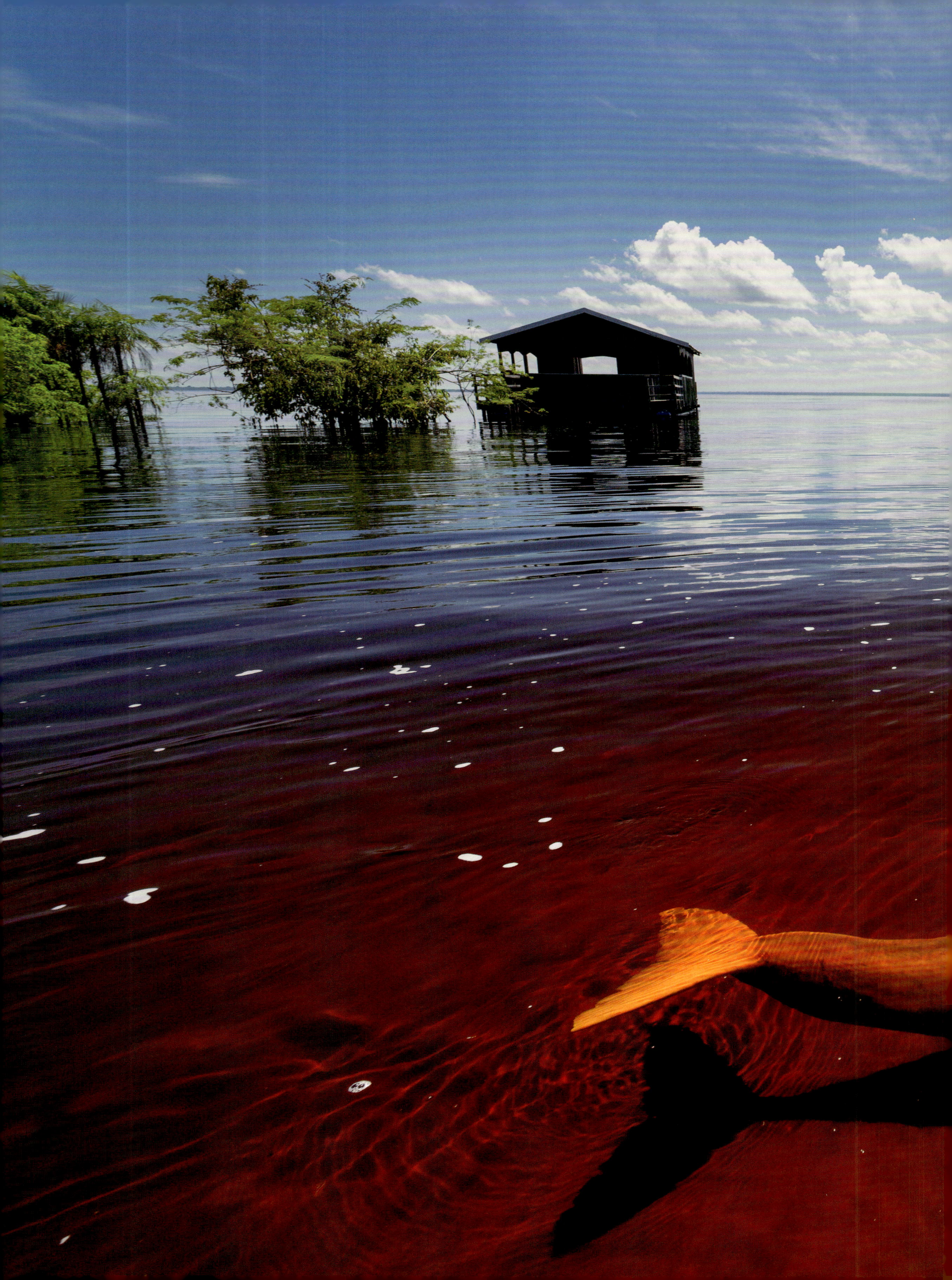

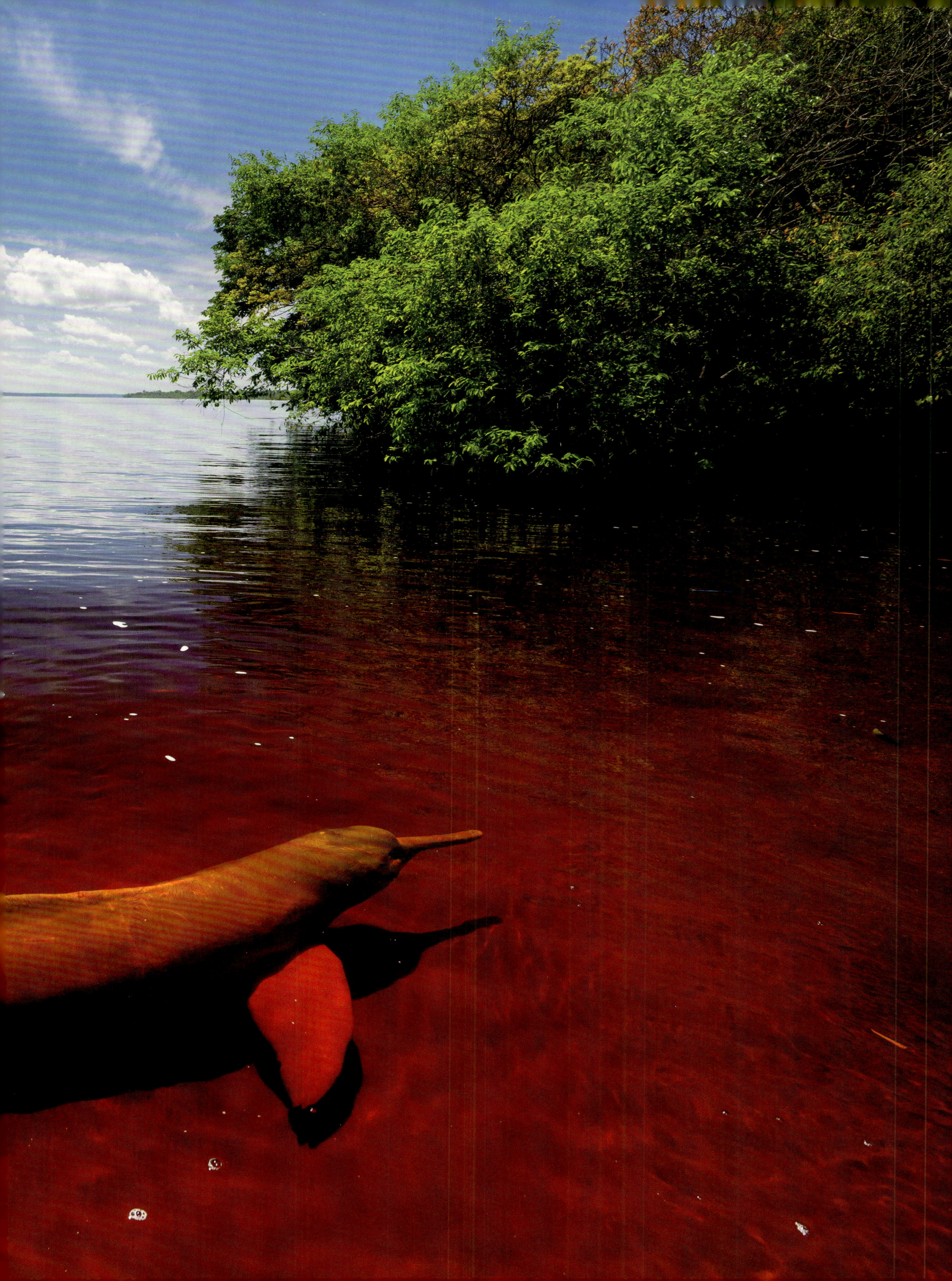

A boto perches upright in the water column waiting to receive a fish handout from a local dolphin tourism operator. To ensure reliable close encounters, locals regularly feed fish to dolphins, creating a negative feedback loop. Many resident botos are displaying signs of obesity, and some juveniles will likely never learn how to hunt, reconciling themselves to almost exclusively begging people for food.

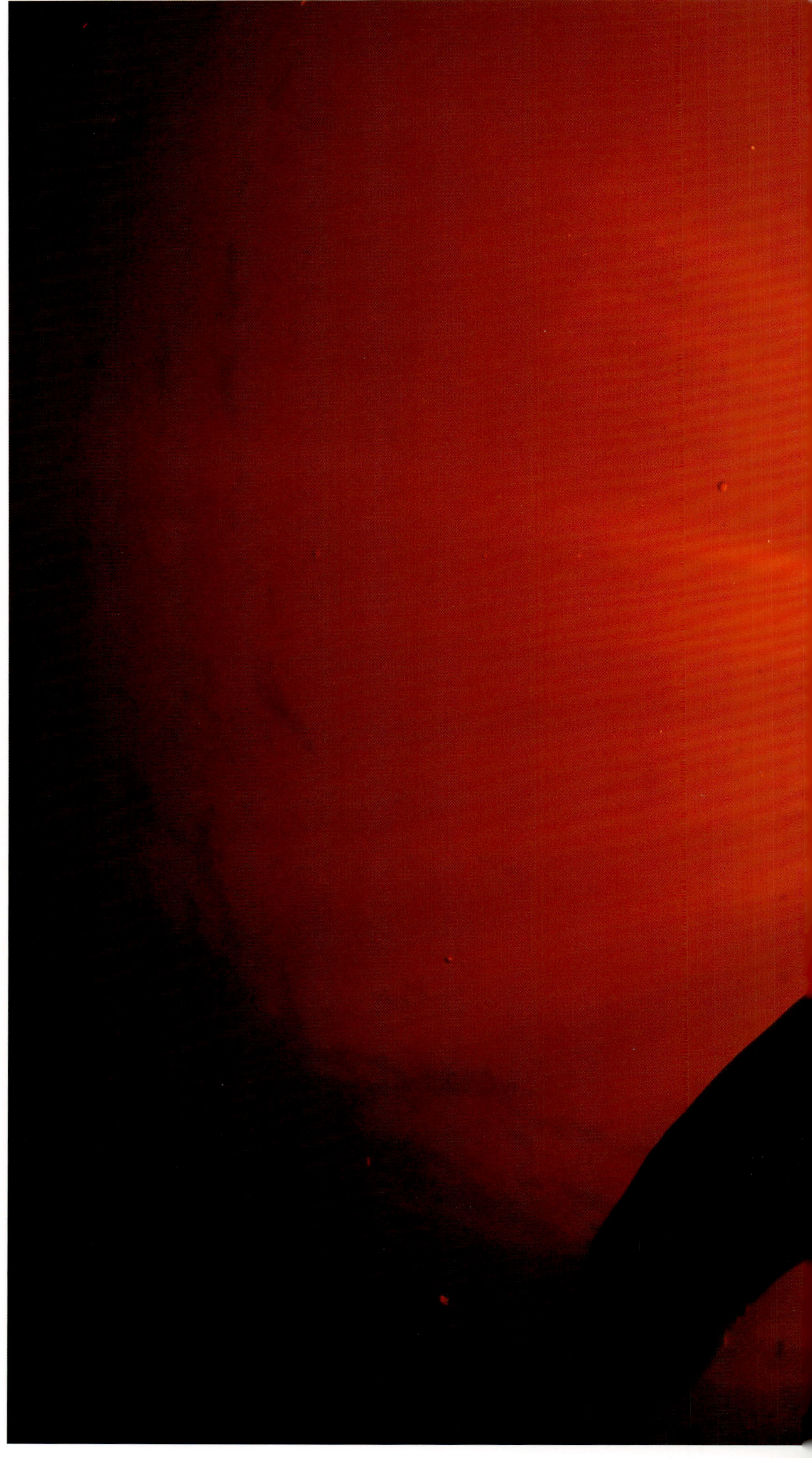

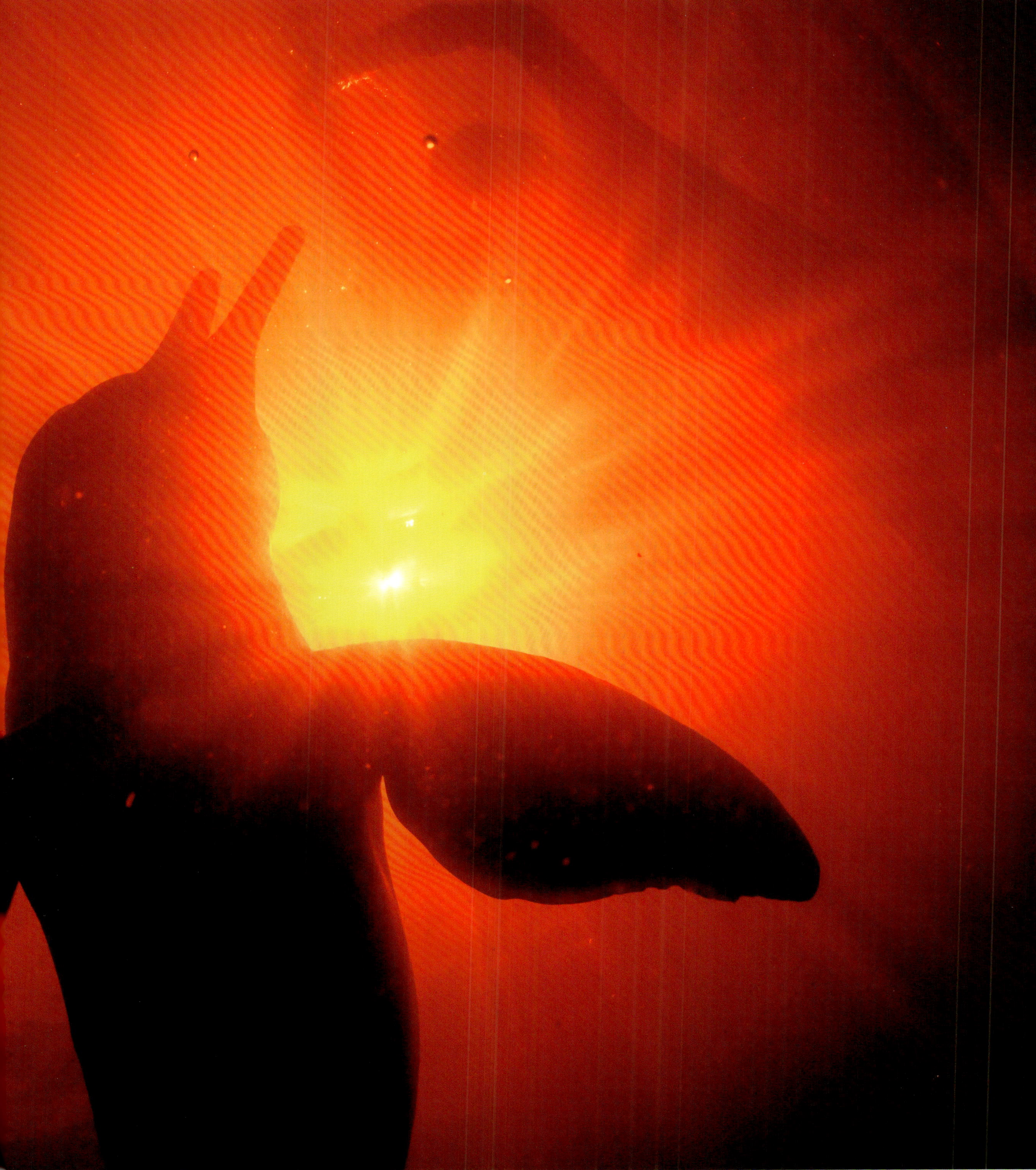

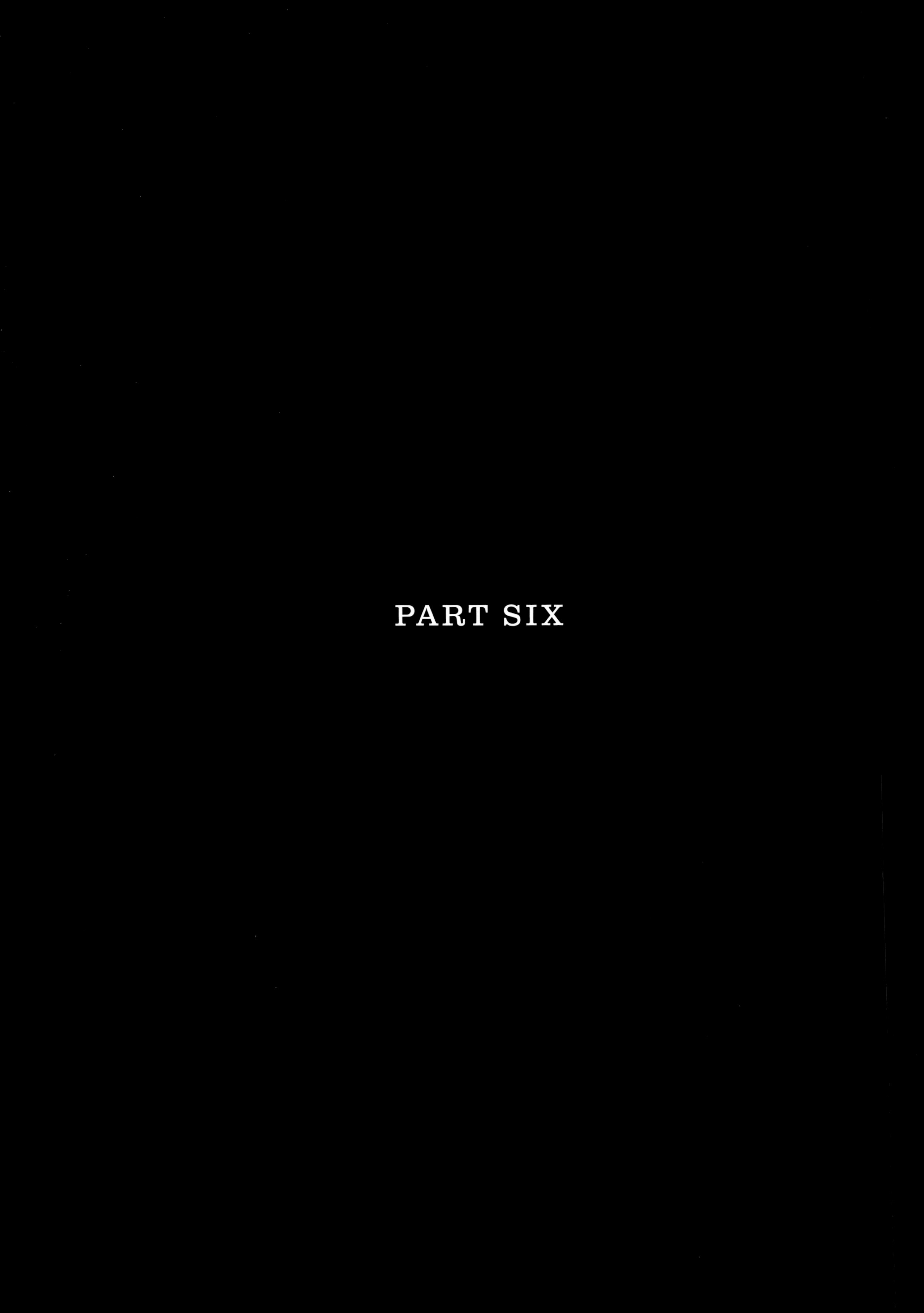

PART SIX

ATLANTIC

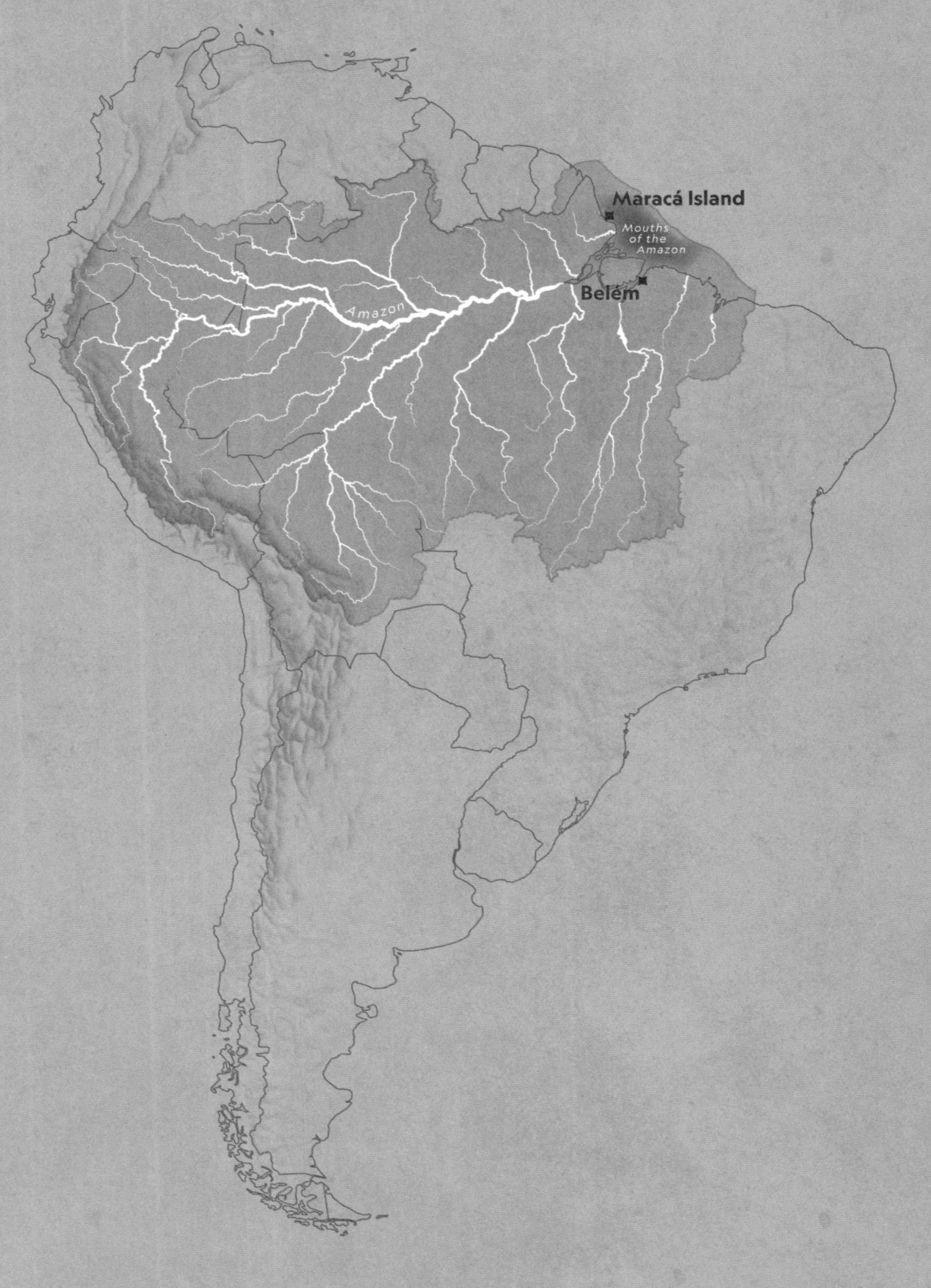
Maracá Island
Mouths of the Amazon
Belém
Amazon

A jaguar moves his 200-pound (90 kg) frame with feline perfection, gliding effortlessly across the mud. Exquisitely camouflaged among a maze of mangrove roots, he is one of approximately 40 jaguars holding territory on Maracá Island. The cats survive by scavenging the island's muddy beaches; stranded tucuxi dolphins are a favorite. They also catch fish trapped by falling tides in the island's narrow channels.

Despite sitting 10 miles (16 km) offshore from the Brazilian mainland, Maracá is home to one of the highest-density jaguar populations in South America. Over eons, the cats here have become experts at thriving amid the battleground between the Atlantic Ocean and the world's mightiest river.

I finally arrive at the mouth of the Amazon, more than 3,725 miles (6,000 km) downstream from its most distant source of uninterrupted flow in Peru, where I began my journey. More than a year ago, I photographed icicled streams and mountain torrents in the Andes, and I can't believe this is the same river. Here, the river is a staggering 235 miles (378 km) wide. The tropical lowland rainforests that have lined its banks give way to one of the largest mangrove forests on our planet. Sequestering twice as much carbon per hectare as the Amazon rainforest, mangroves play a critical role in storing carbon dioxide, the main gas responsible for global warming. Unfortunately, logging these mangroves for shrimp farming and other types of agriculture is dramatically reducing their ability to help mitigate climate change.

The mangroves are not, however, where the Amazon River ends. Vast quantities of fresh water and sediment are discharged thousands of miles into the Atlantic Ocean, expanding the scope of what has traditionally been defined as the river's sphere of influence.

Near the coast, the river plume is nearly 100 feet (30 m) deep and 125 miles (200 km) wide. At the surface, high chlorophyll concentrations and astronomical primary productivity make it a nutrient-rich oasis that draws large predators including seabirds, whales, dolphins, and sharks. And these riches trickle down: Parallel to the mouth, the Great Amazon Reef System, discovered only 40 years ago, is made up of sponges, algae, and corals. It covers more than 600 miles (965 km) on the outer continental shelf at depths of nearly 330 to 660 feet (100 to 200 m).

As the plume runs northward along the coast of South America, it deposits sediments that create mudflats off the coasts of French Guiana and Suriname. With tides of up to 30 feet (9 m), these seas are some of the most turbid and biologically productive in the world. And the resulting intertidal flats make up the single most important wintering grounds for migrating birds from North America.

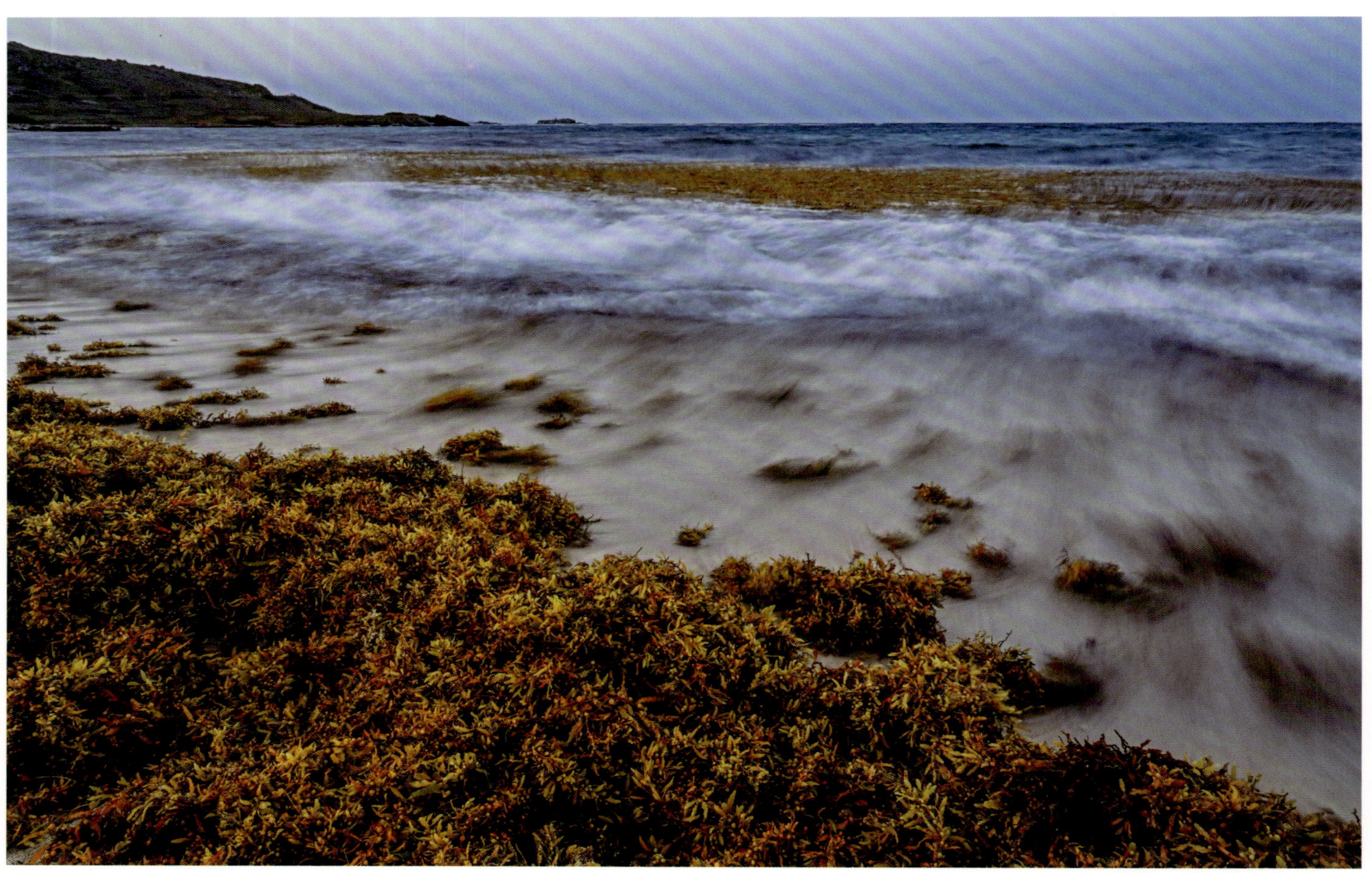

The Amazon River and its plume partly contribute to the sargassum algae blooms that clog shallow water habitats and beaches across the Caribbean.

For other marine creatures, however, the Amazon River plume is an impenetrable wall of fresh water and sediment. A biogeographical barrier that has existed for more than 10 million years, it spurred the development of two distinctly different biogeographic eco-regions: The so-called Brazilian Province sits to the south of the river mouth, while the Caribbean Province lies to the north. Through evolutionary isolation and large-scale oceanographic processes like freshwater nutrient pulses, the Amazon River has over millions of years shaped the Caribbean into the most biodiverse marine region of the Atlantic Ocean.

In fact, Amazon River water can be detected far and wide across the Caribbean, influencing oceanography and ecology as far north as Puerto Rico. Its presence leads to seasonal shifts in the fisheries of the Lesser Antilles, slows the growth rates of reef fish larvae off Barbados, and influences the reproductive success of commercially important species like the flying fish.

But the Amazon's influence can also be much more dramatic and destructive. The warm freshwater plume that sits on top of the saltier and colder ocean water can

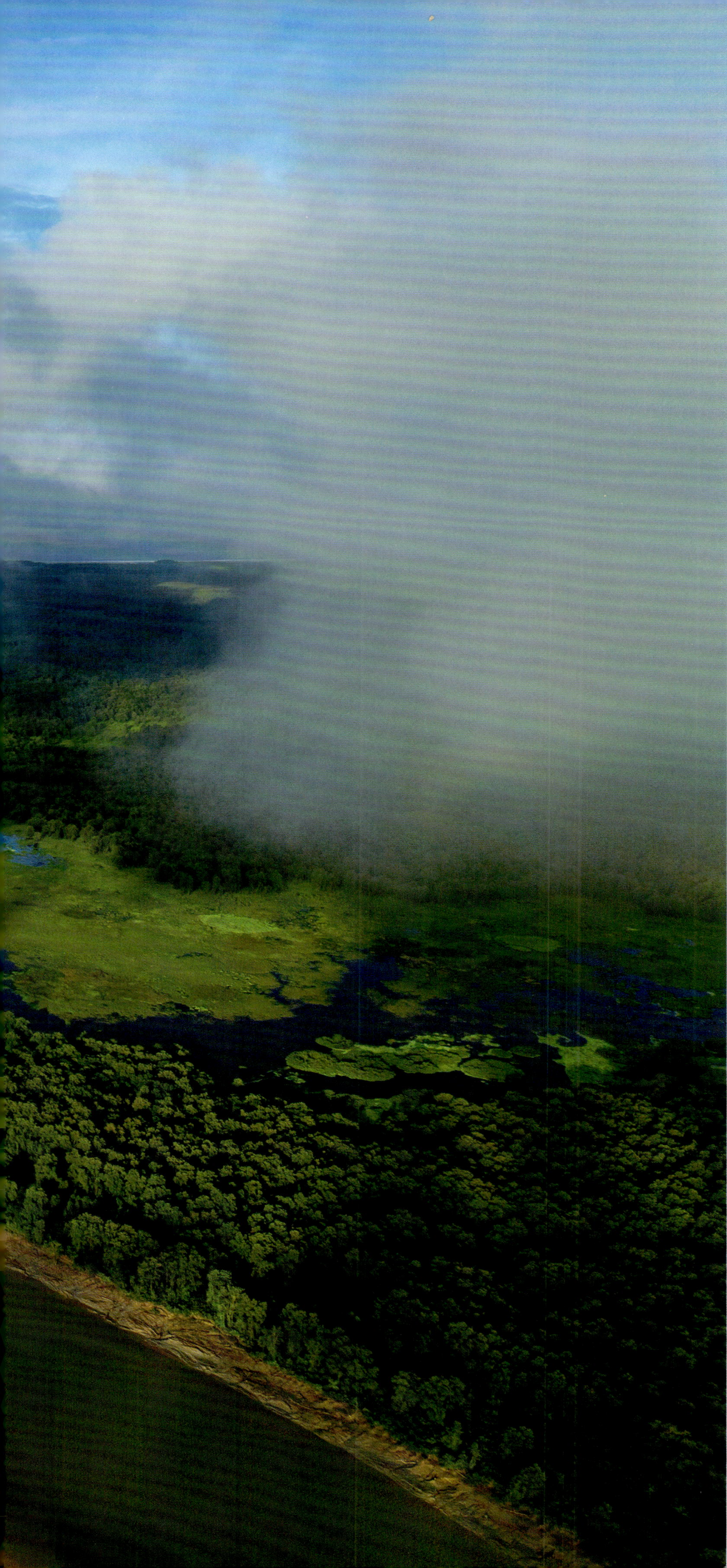

Where the Amazon River meets the Atlantic Ocean, tidal changes are sometimes ferocious. This zigzagging channel through Brazil's Maracá Island, which sits 10 miles (16 km) offshore, can rise 30 feet (9 m) in 30 seconds when the tide rushes in, forming powerful waves inside the channel. Its local name is Igarapé do Inferno (Hell Creek).

PAGES 222–223: An alert jaguar *(Panthera onca)* on Maracá Island sits quietly behind a mass of mangrove roots. Despite being a considerable distance from the mainland, Maracá hosts one of the highest densities of jaguars in South America. These cats are experts at surviving in mangroves and on beaches, catching their own fish and scavenging washed-up tucuxi dolphins *(Sotalia fluviatilis)*.

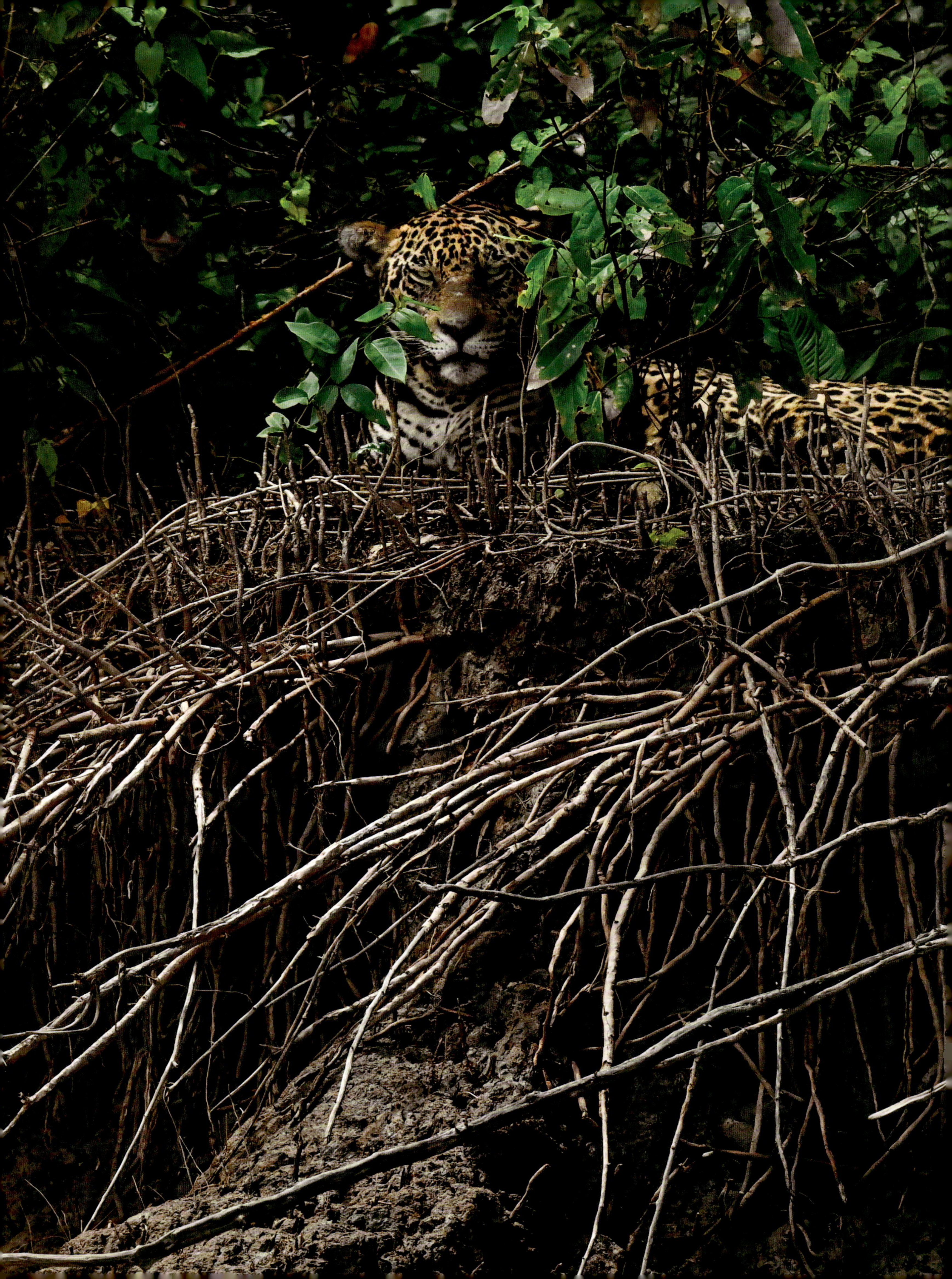

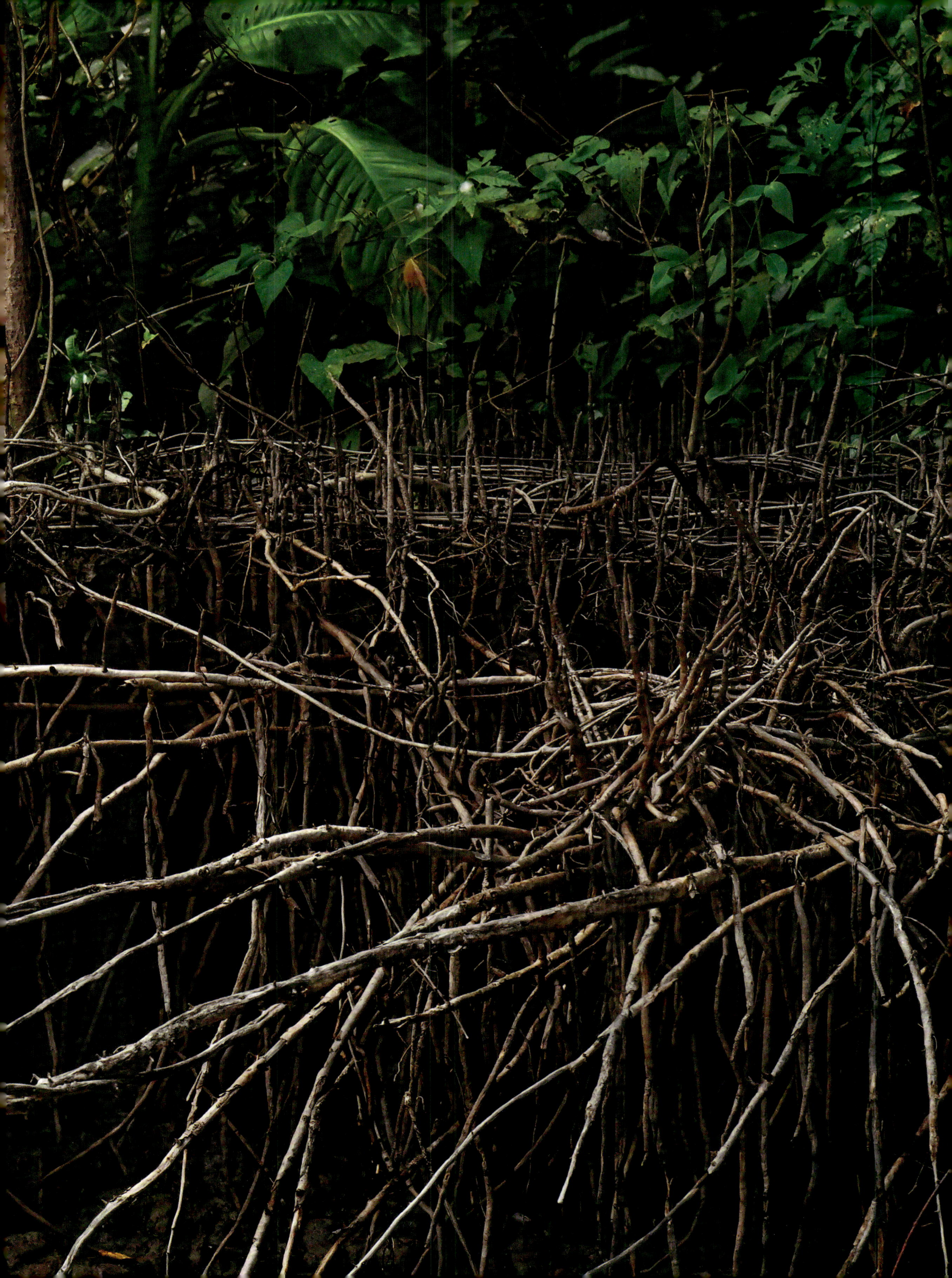

Maracá Island is ringed by vast and invertebrate-rich mudflats that are a critical foraging habitat for many species of birds, such as this scarlet ibis *(Eudocimus ruber)*. Its distinctive long, thin, curved bill is ideal for probing mud in search of red shrimp, which when consumed in large numbers are responsible for the bird's intense color.

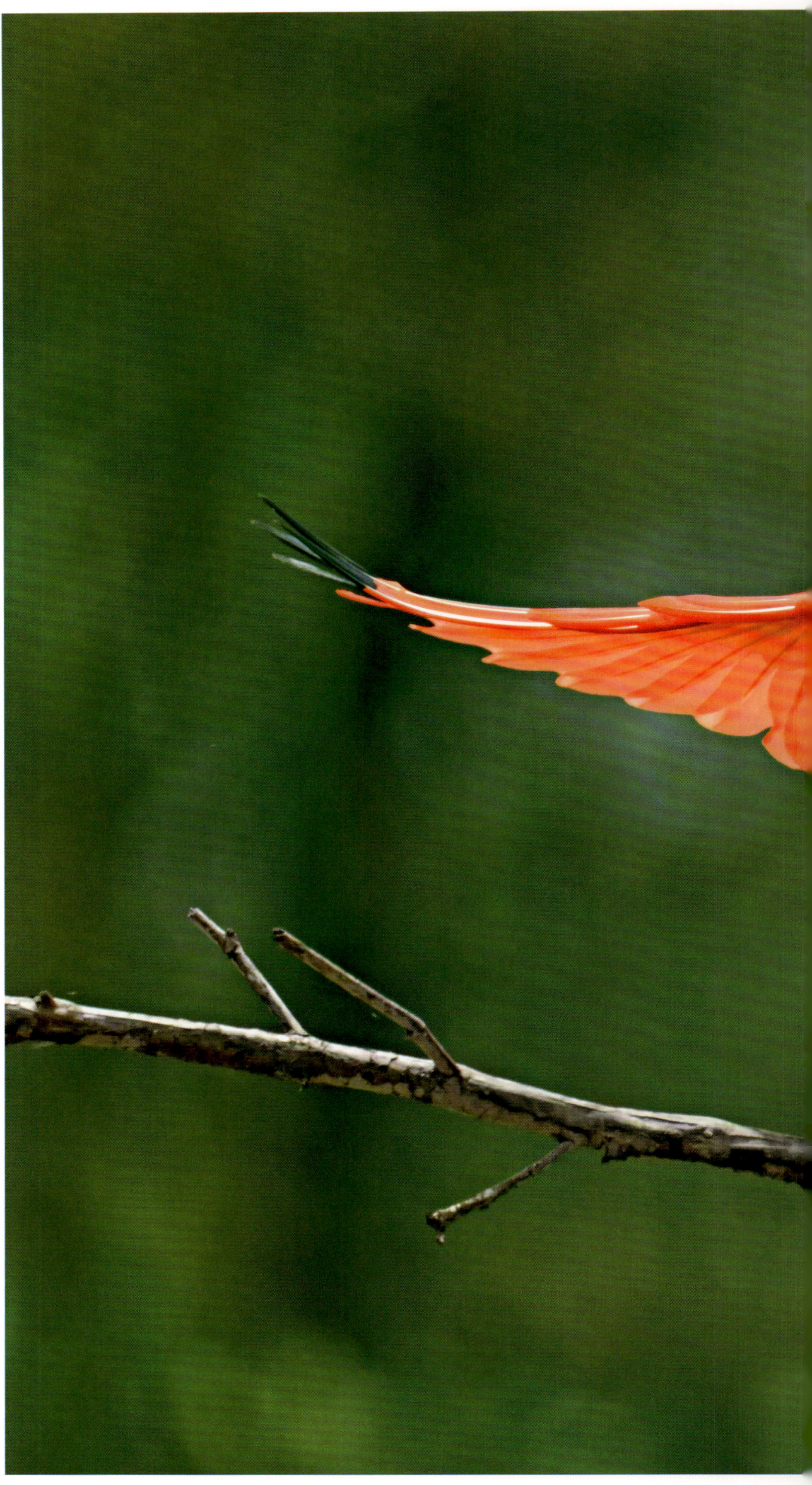

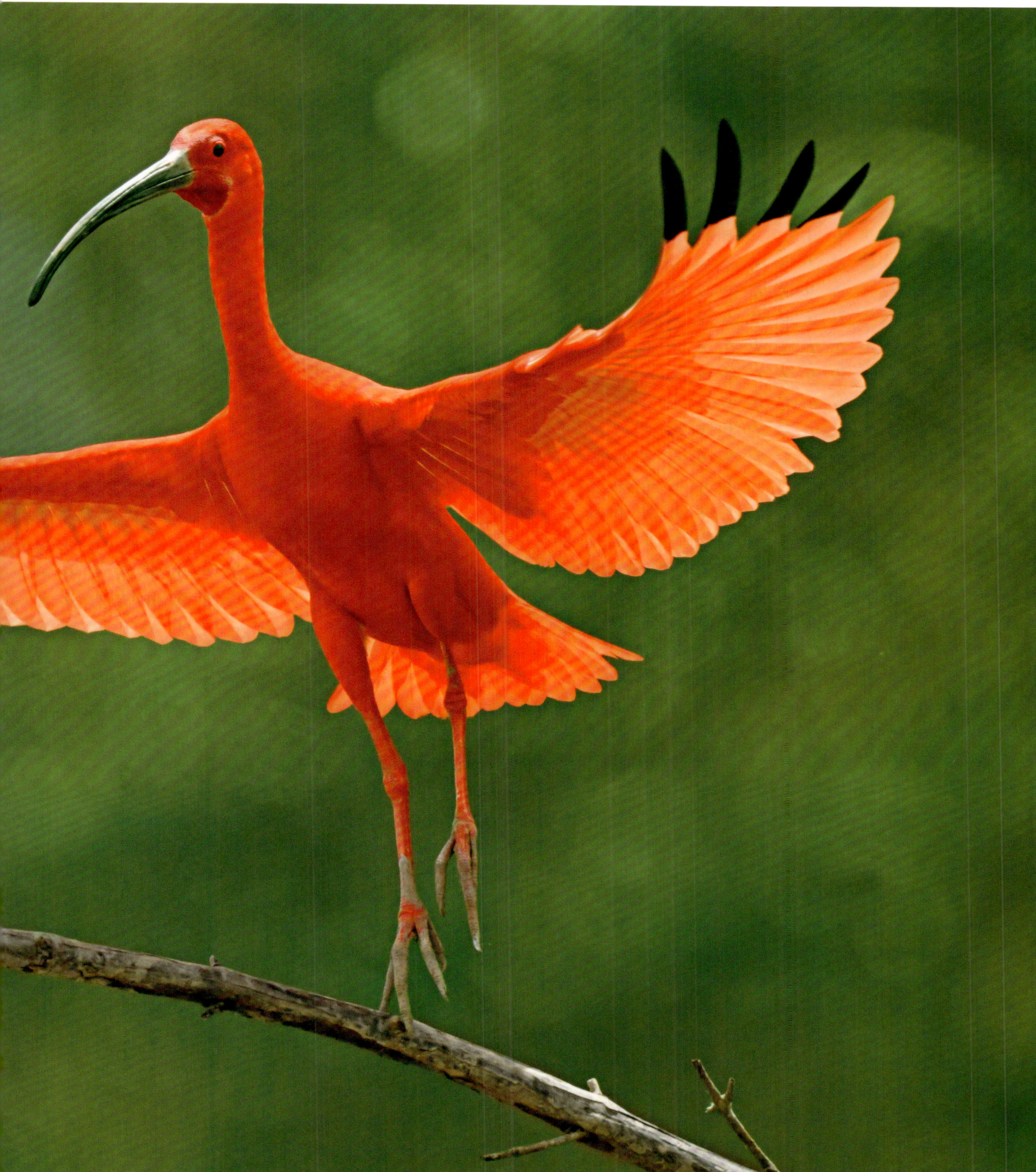

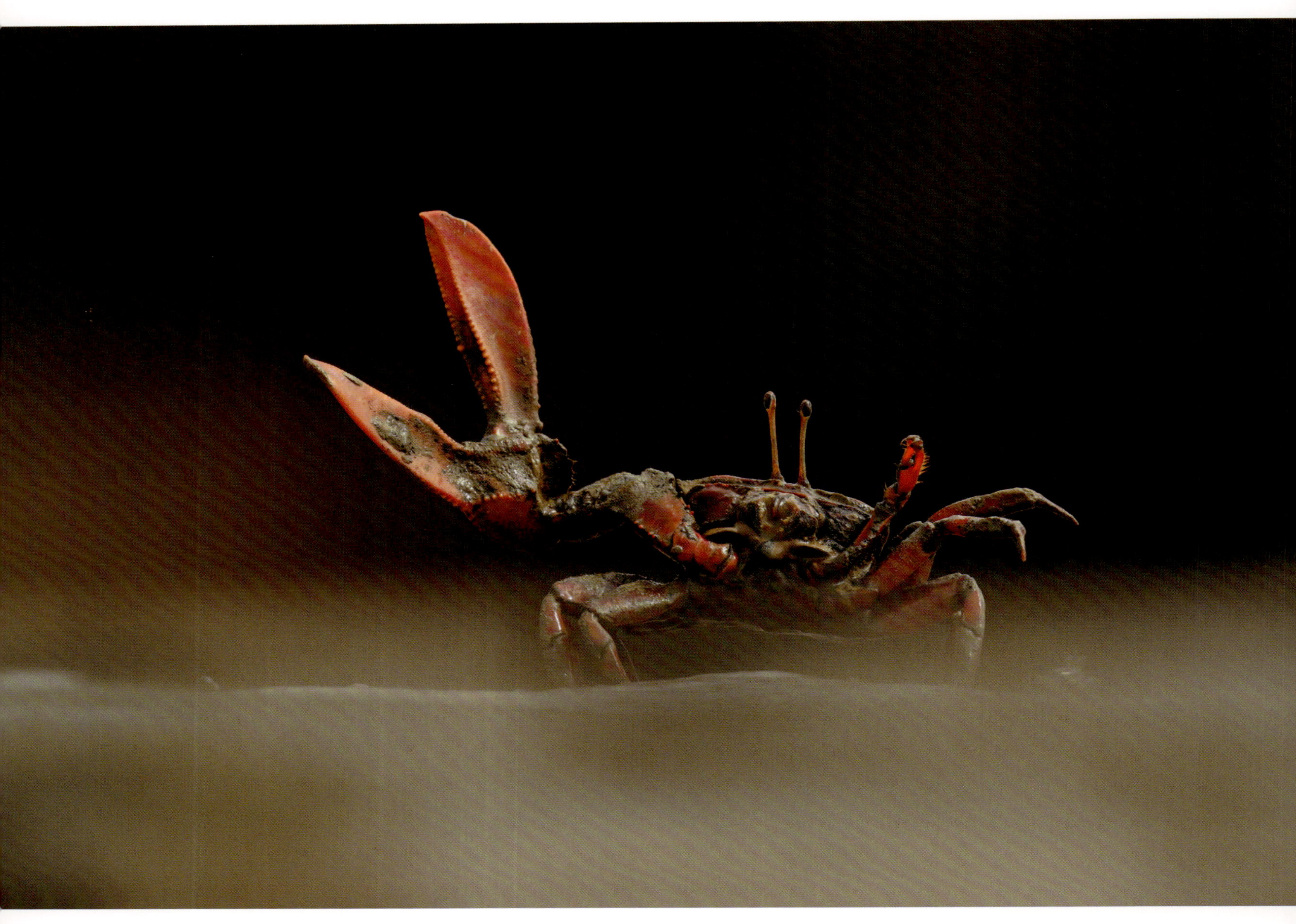

ABOVE: Brazilian fiddler crabs *(Uca maracoani)* are well known for their notable sexual dimorphism, where males have one claw that is significantly larger than the other. To win over females, male crabs must perform. The waving display consists of raising the major claw upward and then dropping it down in what we think of as a "come hither" motion. The female crab chooses whether she's interested based on claw size and the quality of the waving.

OPPOSITE: The rufous crab hawk *(Buteogallus aequinoctialis)* primarily inhabits the mangroves along the mouth of the Amazon River, and its diet consists almost entirely of crabs. Sitting on a low perch, scanning the mudflats, it will pounce with a short, energetic dive on any crab spotted. On the ground, the hawk quickly dispatches its prey to avoid being nipped by powerful pincers.

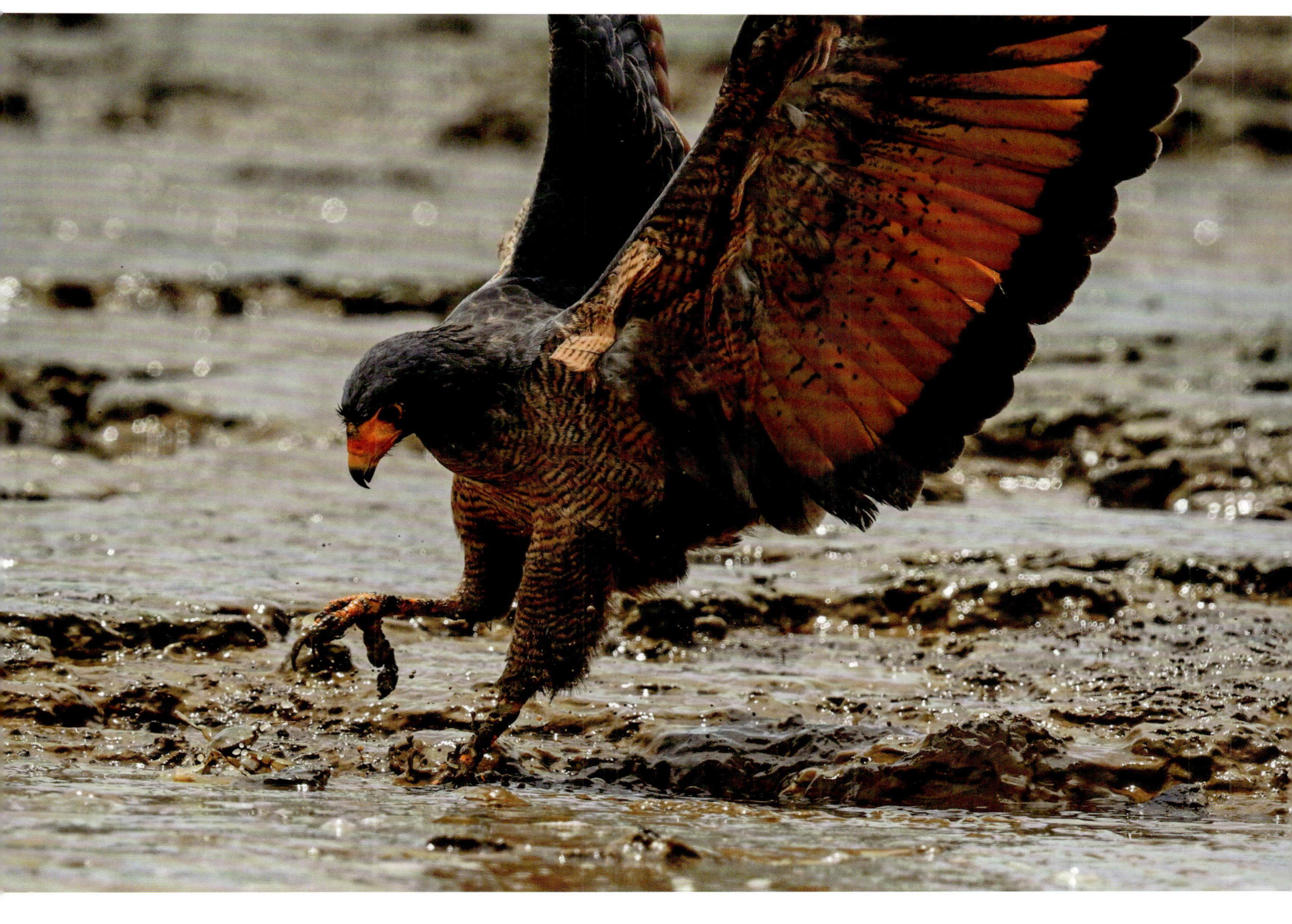

The fishing boats of Belém, the Brazilian port city near the Amazon's mouth, are popular perches for egrets, who have learned to scavenge fish discards. Most of Amazonia's inhabitants now live in rapidly growing cities like Belém, which has a population of 2.5 million.

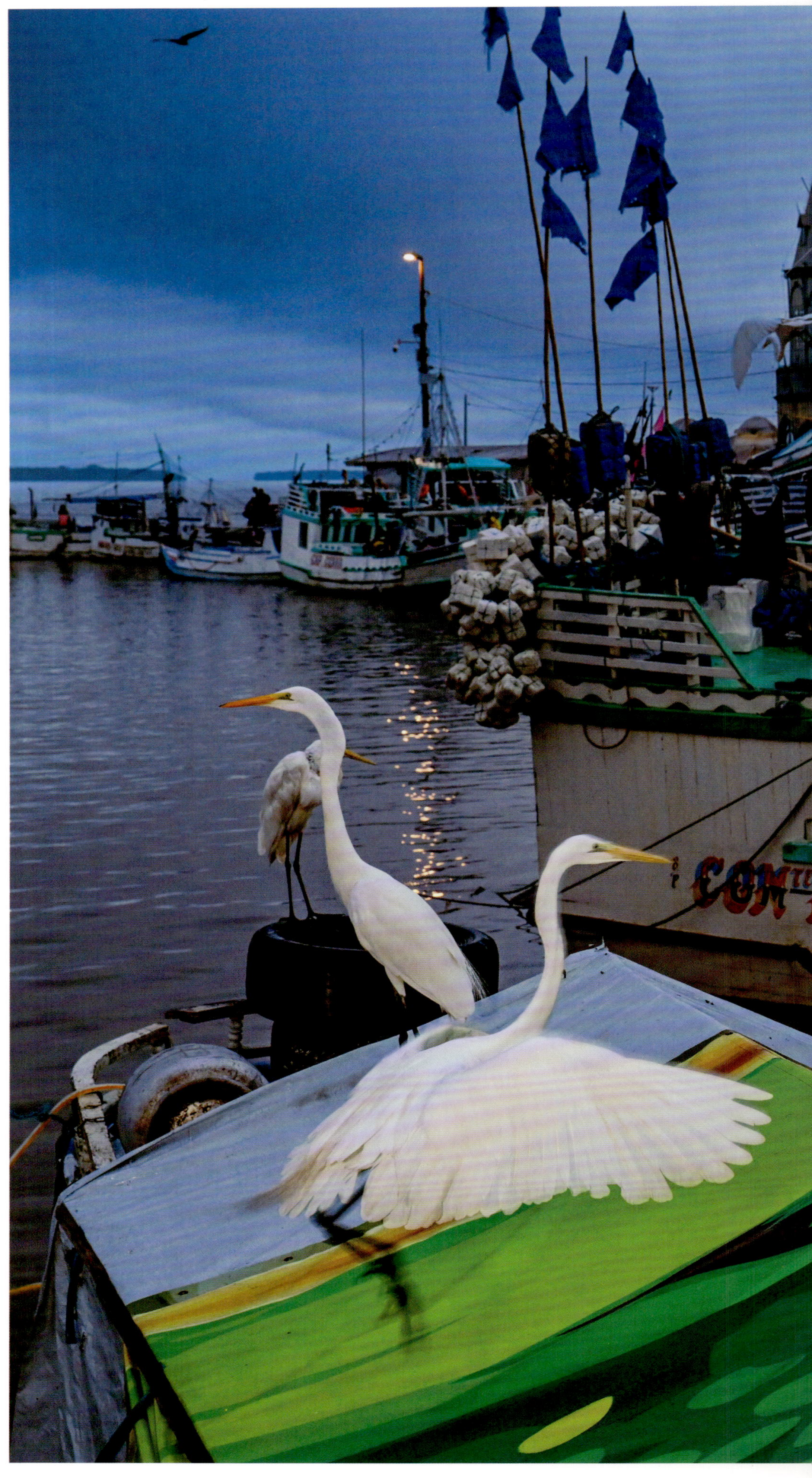

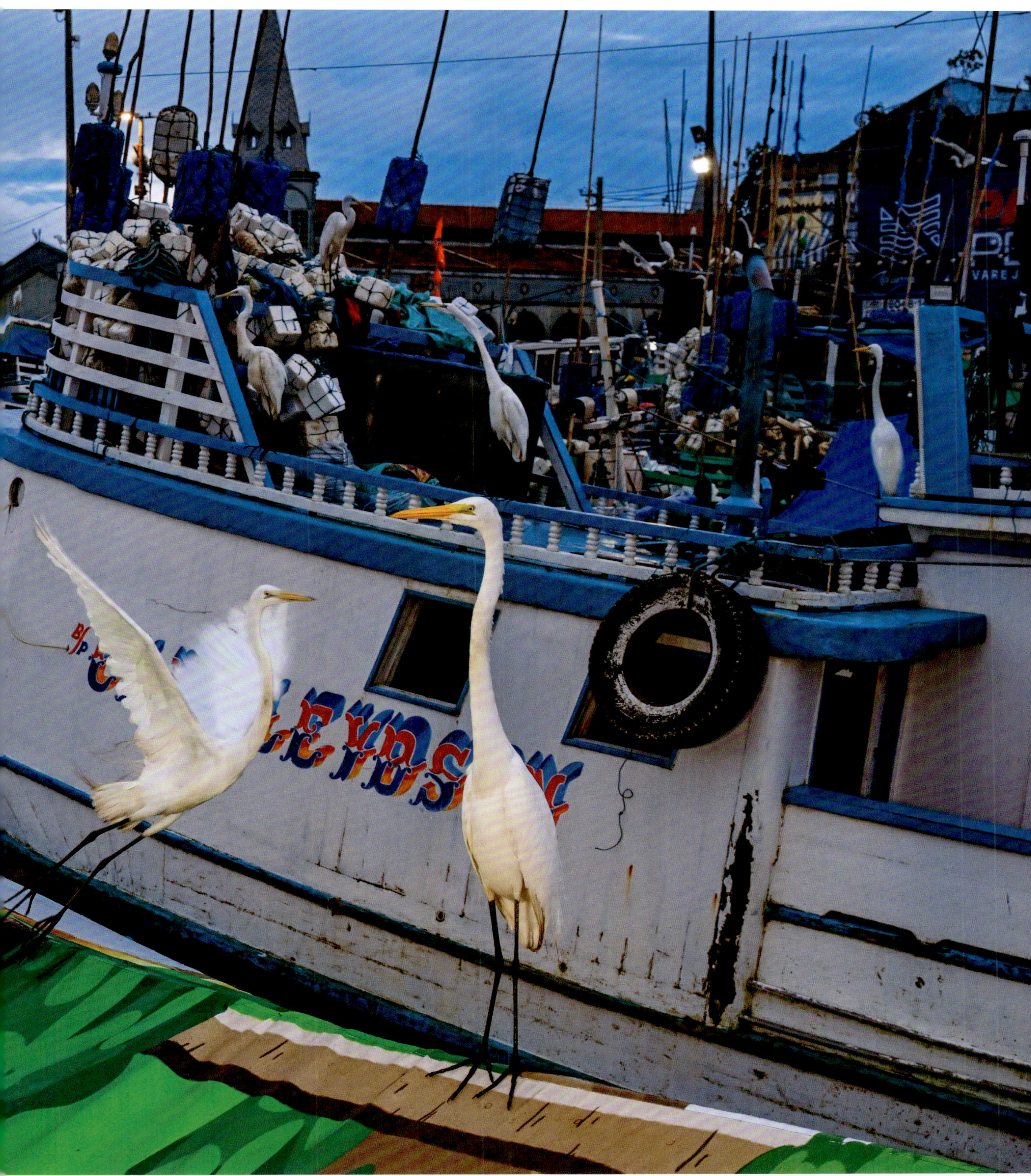

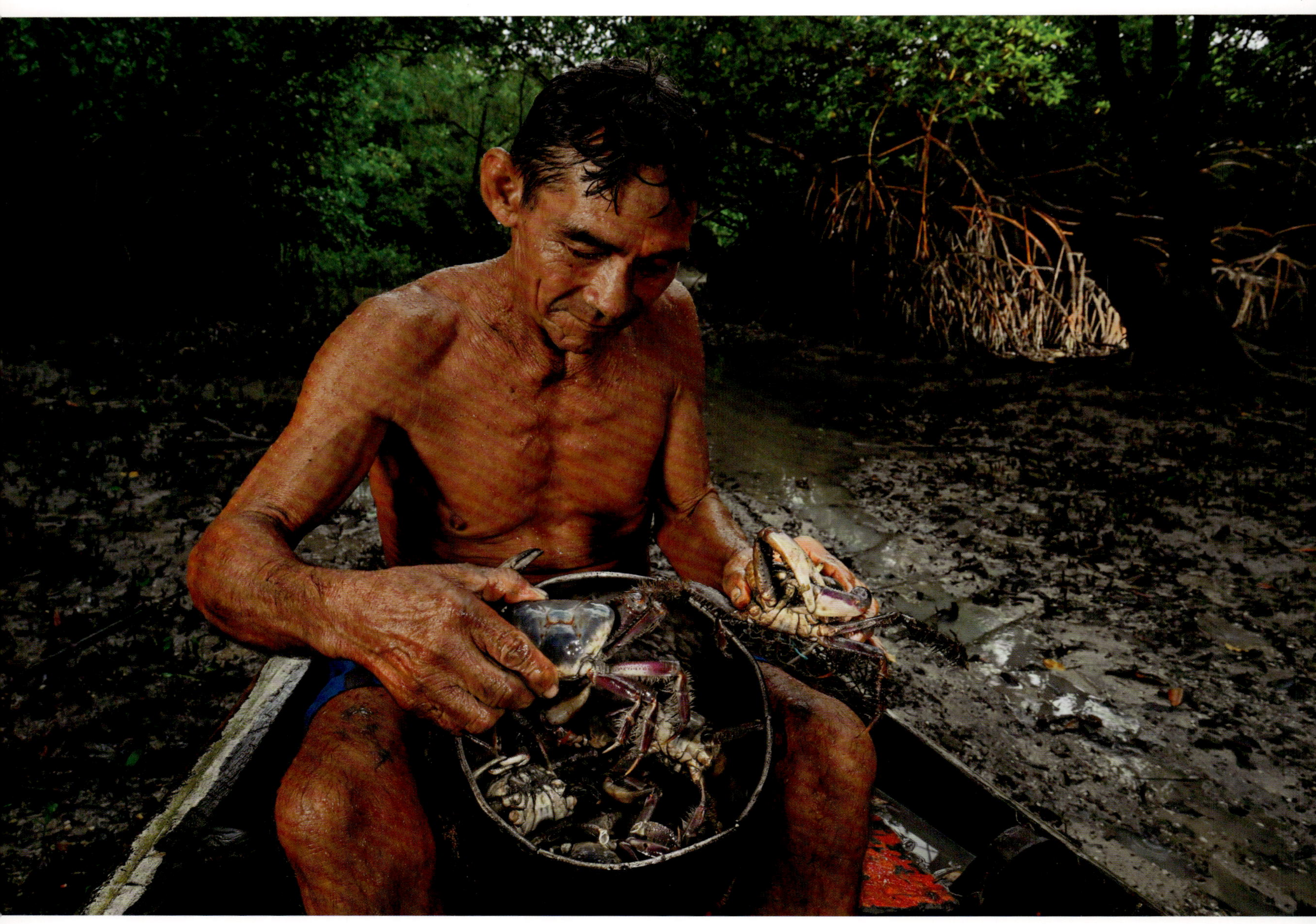

ABOVE: At the mouth of the river, mangrove branches and roots make protective hatcheries for marine life. On most days, subsistence crabber Simao Pinheiro da Costa ventures into these aquatic forests at low tide to dig out large mangrove crabs from their burrows.

OPPOSITE: Along the southern shores of the Amazon River's mouth, local families build fish fences, made from wooden poles they harvest in mangrove forests. The fence forms a barrier, and as the low tide recedes, it forces the fish to swim into a round, trap-like structure from which they can't escape.

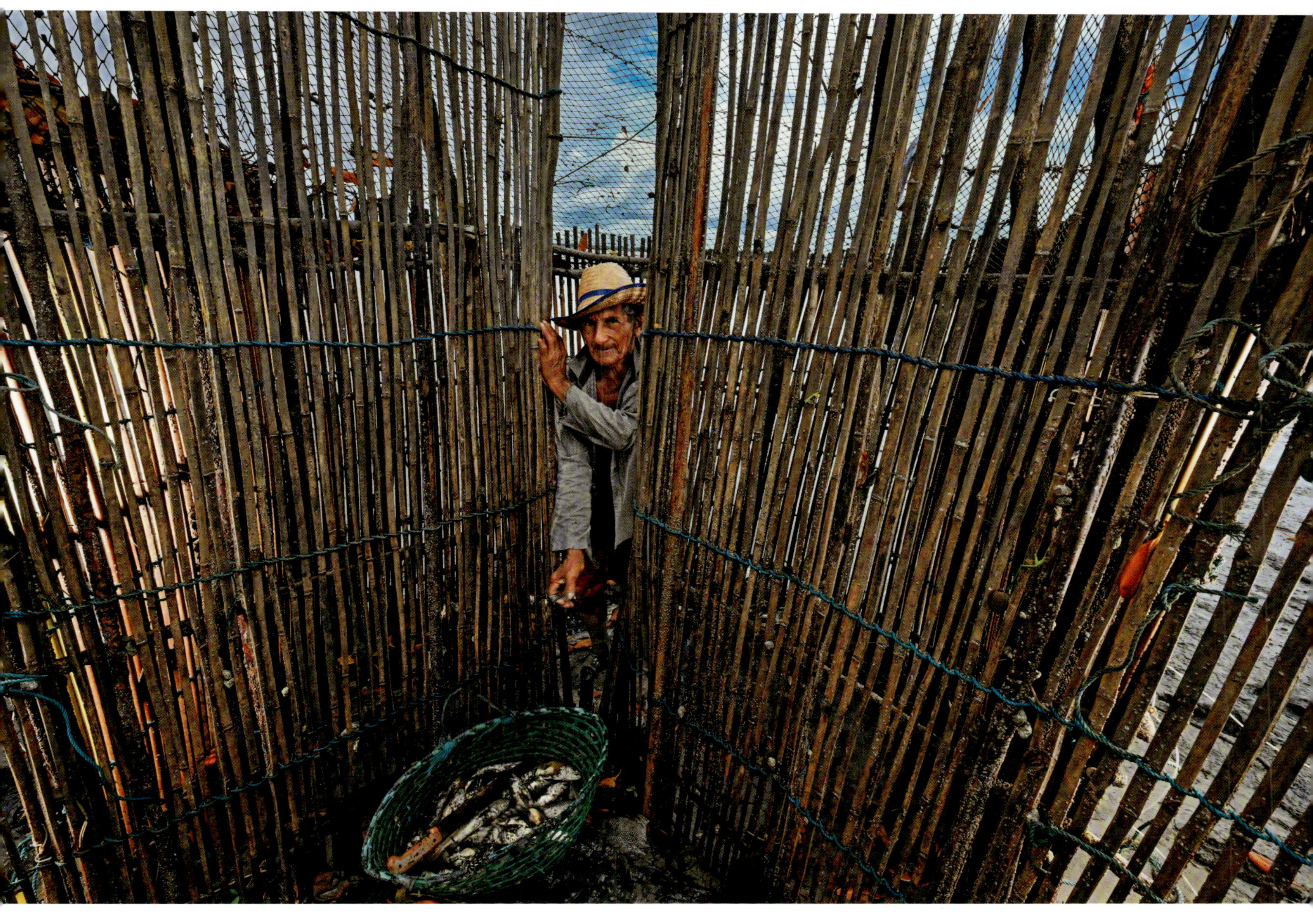

PAGES 232–233: Soaring like a pterodactyl toward the St. Giles Islands, the aptly named magnificent frigate bird *(Fregata magnificens)* makes long foraging trips far over the Atlantic Ocean, sometimes feeding in the productive maelstrom of the Amazon River plume.

PAGES 234–235: Studies have connected mercury from gold mining deep in the rainforest that washed into the ocean via the plume with weakened frigate bird immune systems, leading to infectious disease outbreaks in these tropical seabirds.

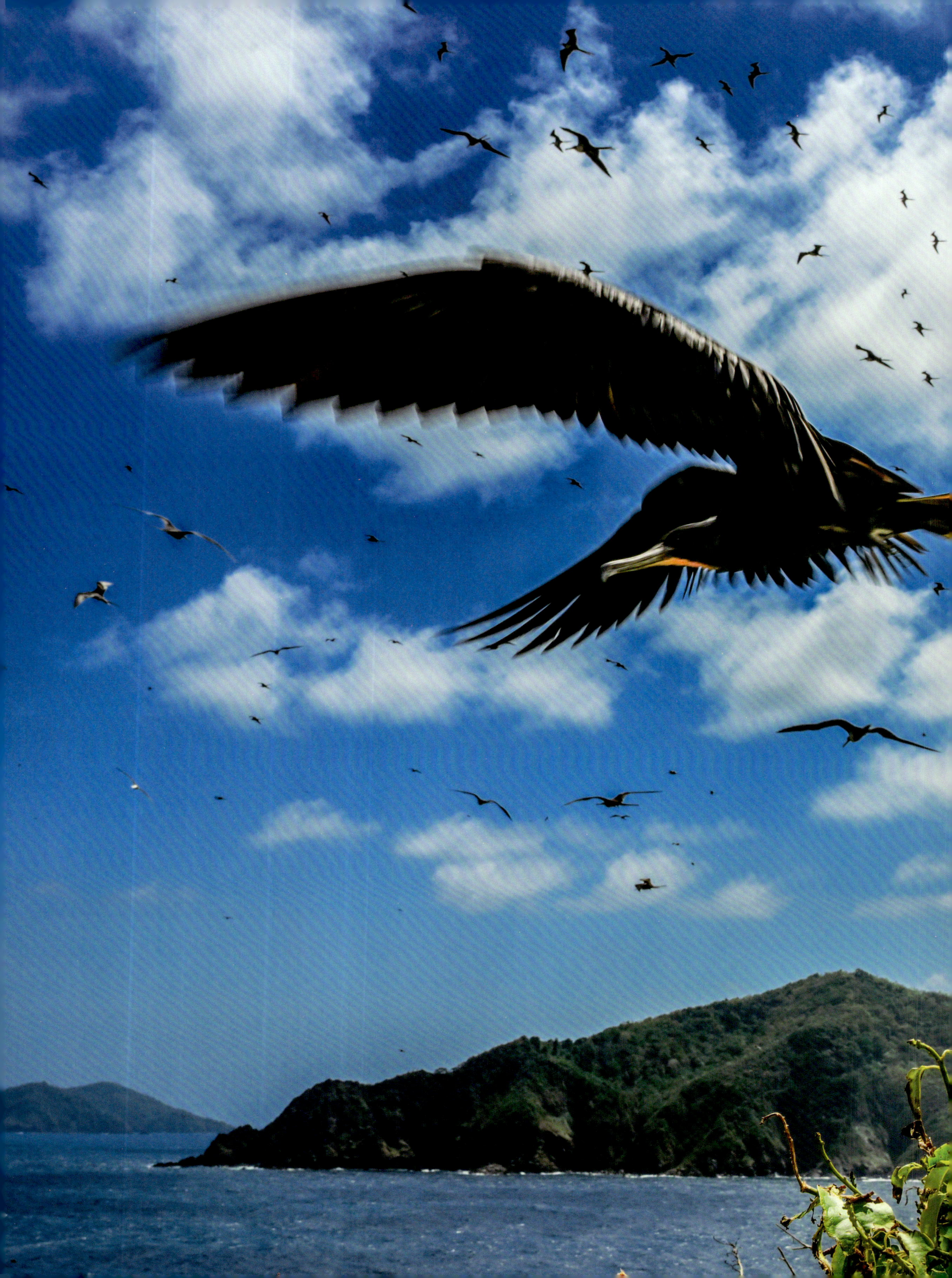

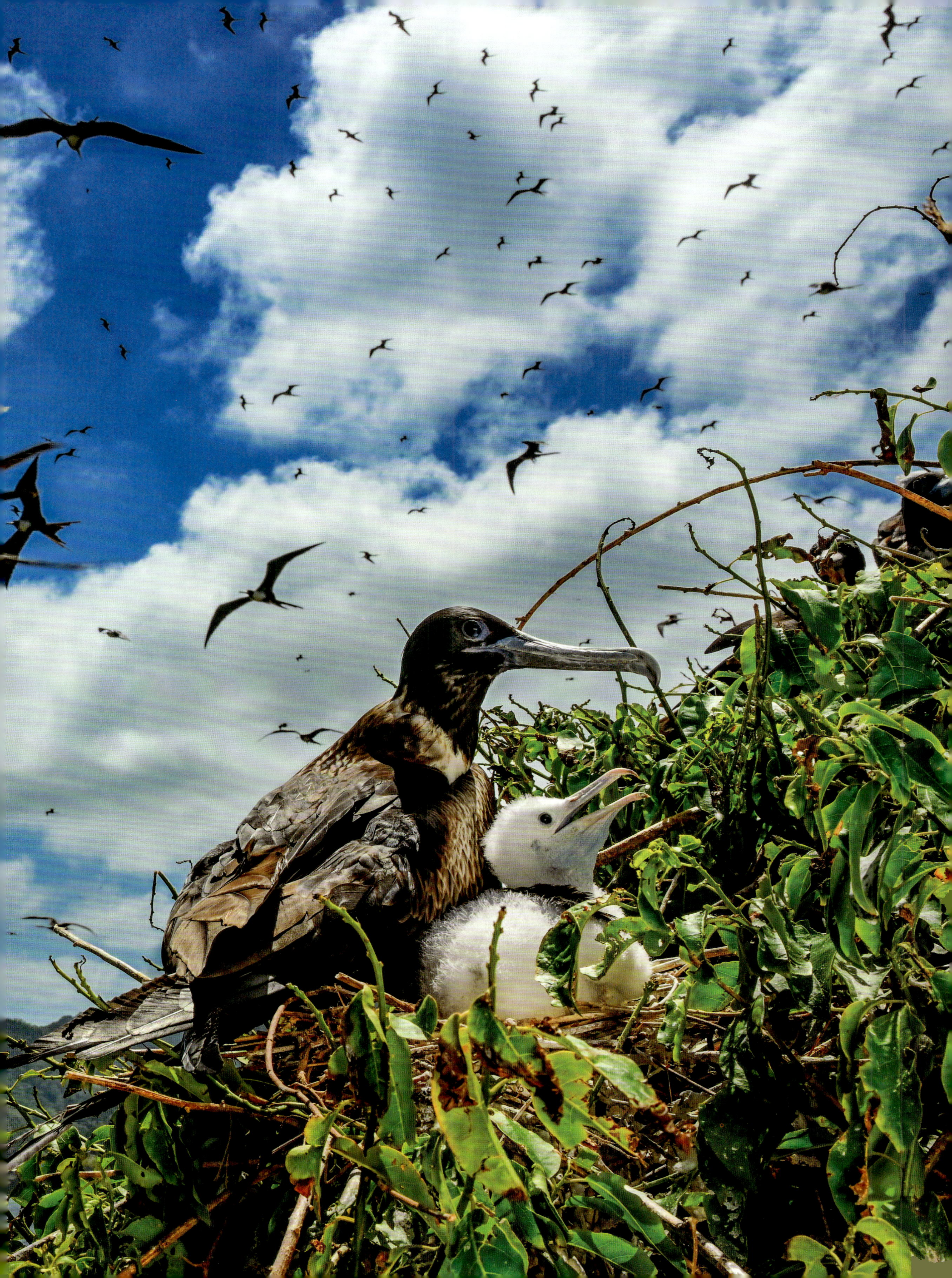

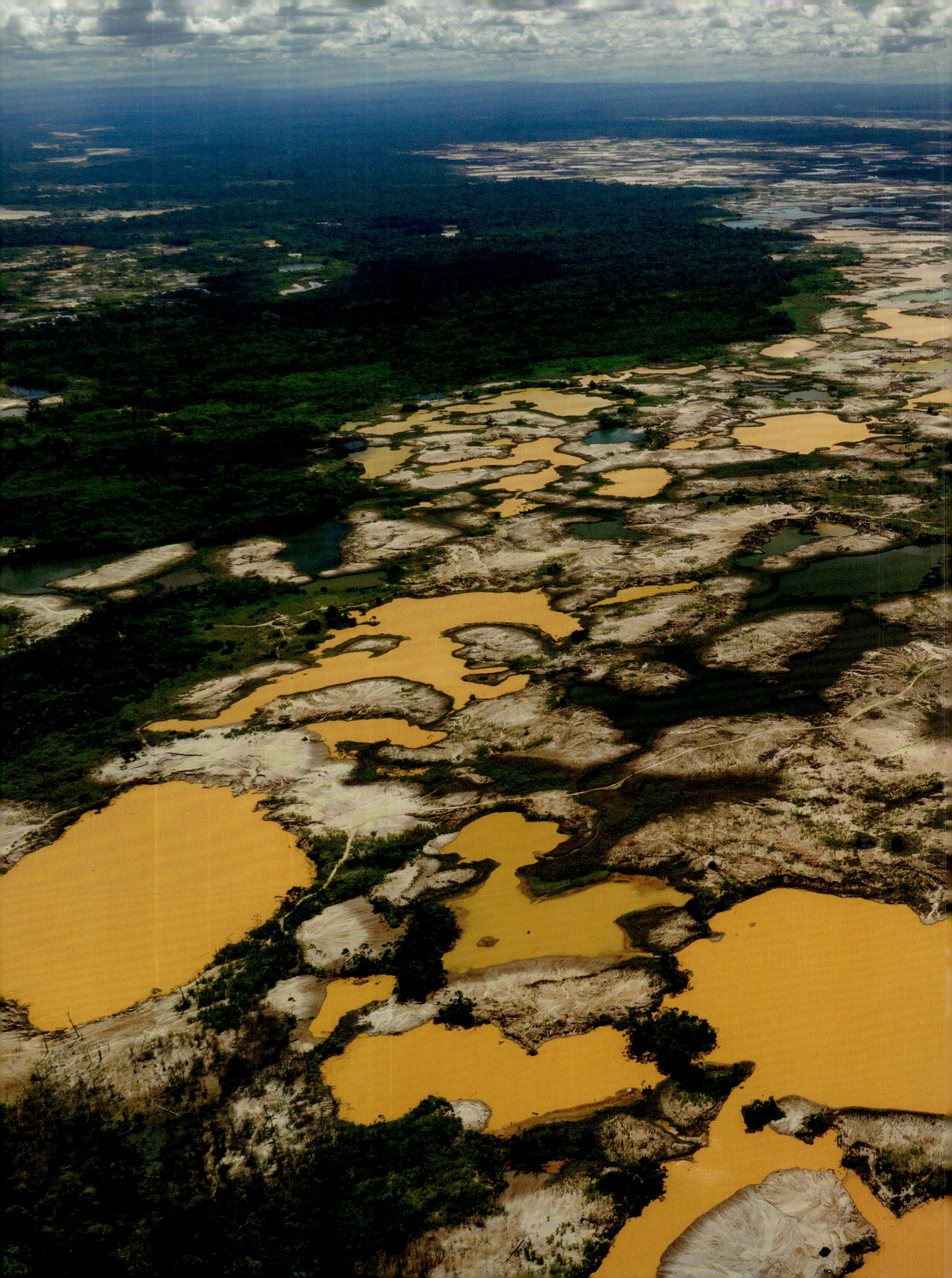

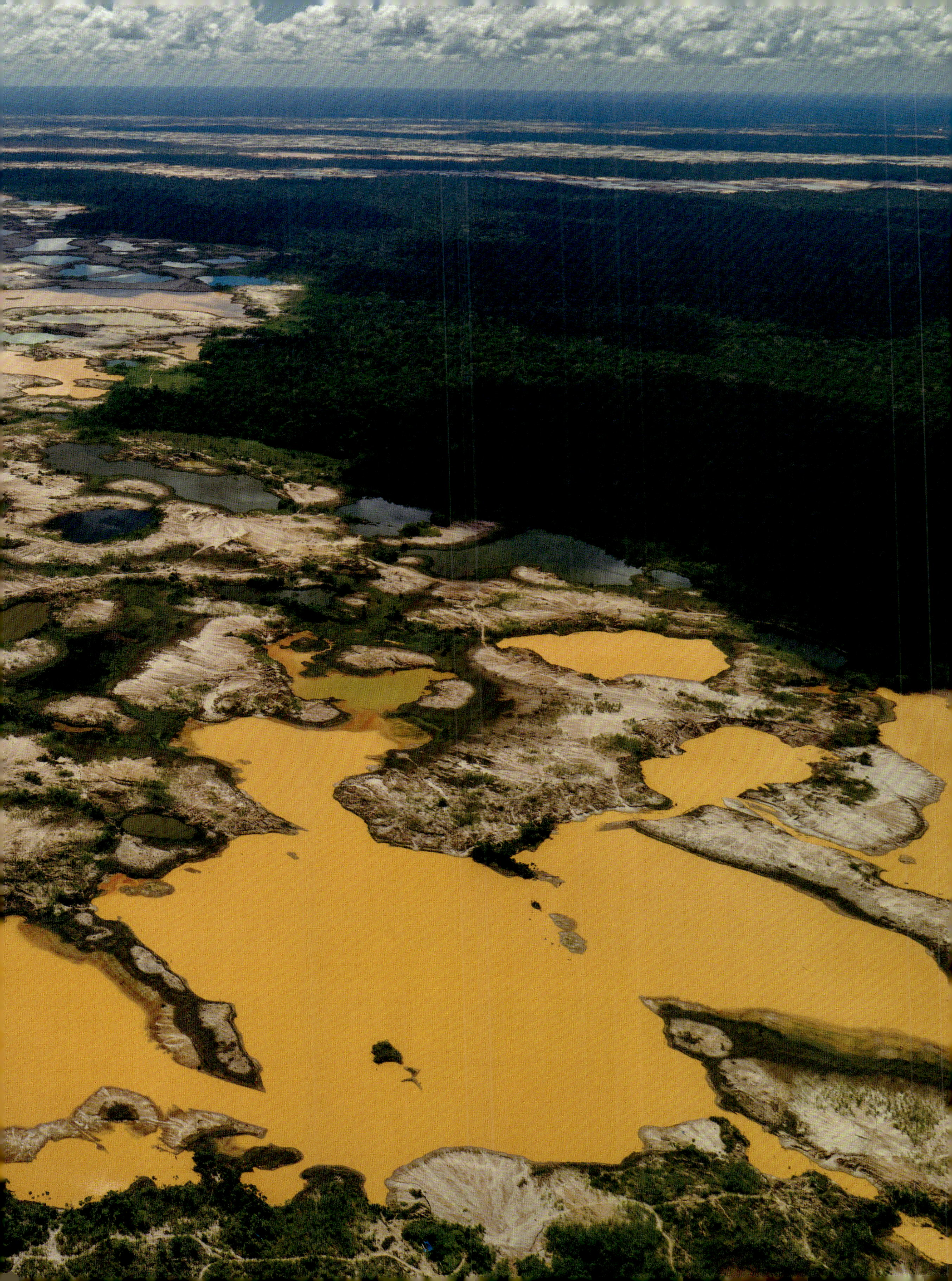

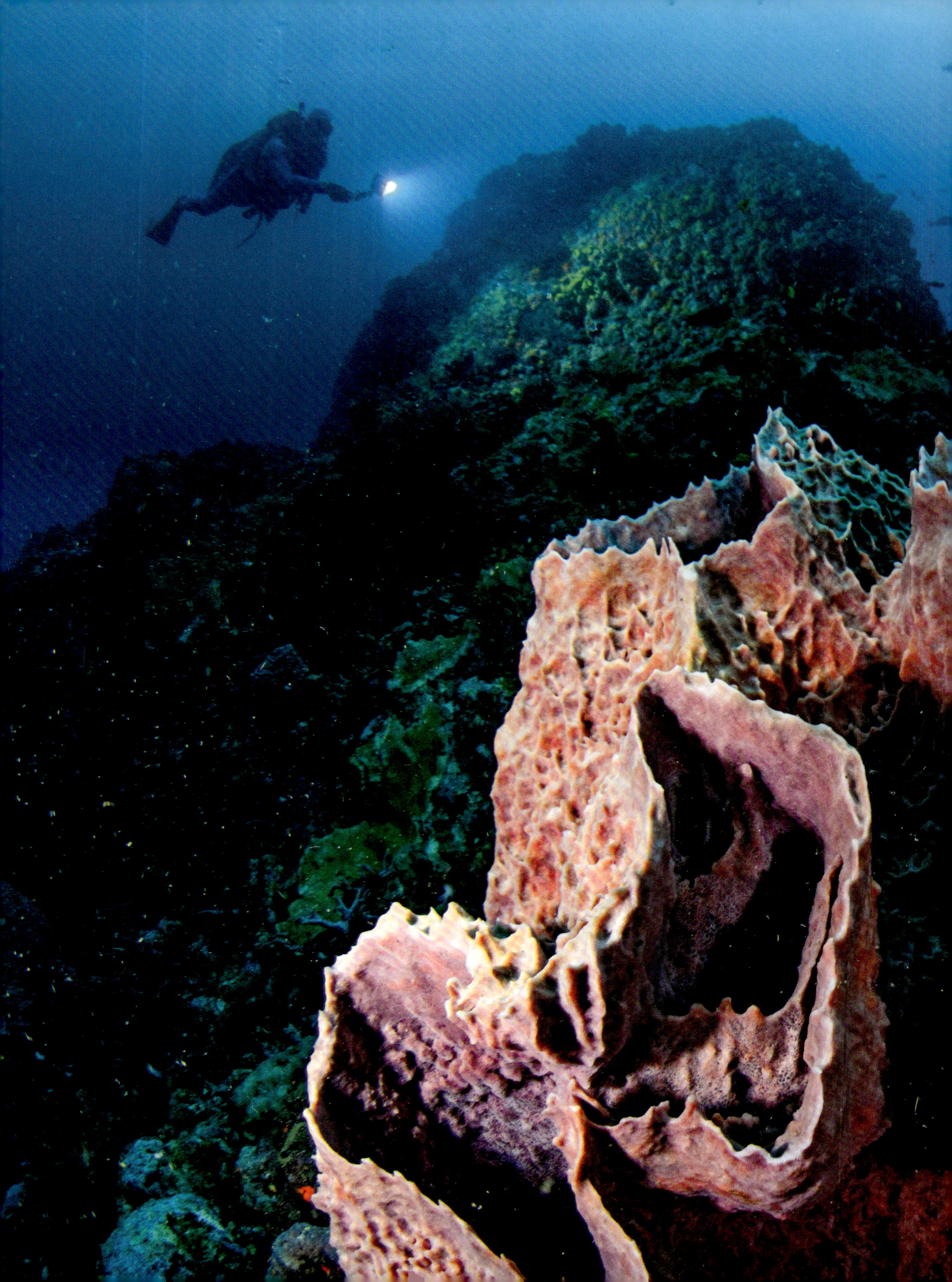

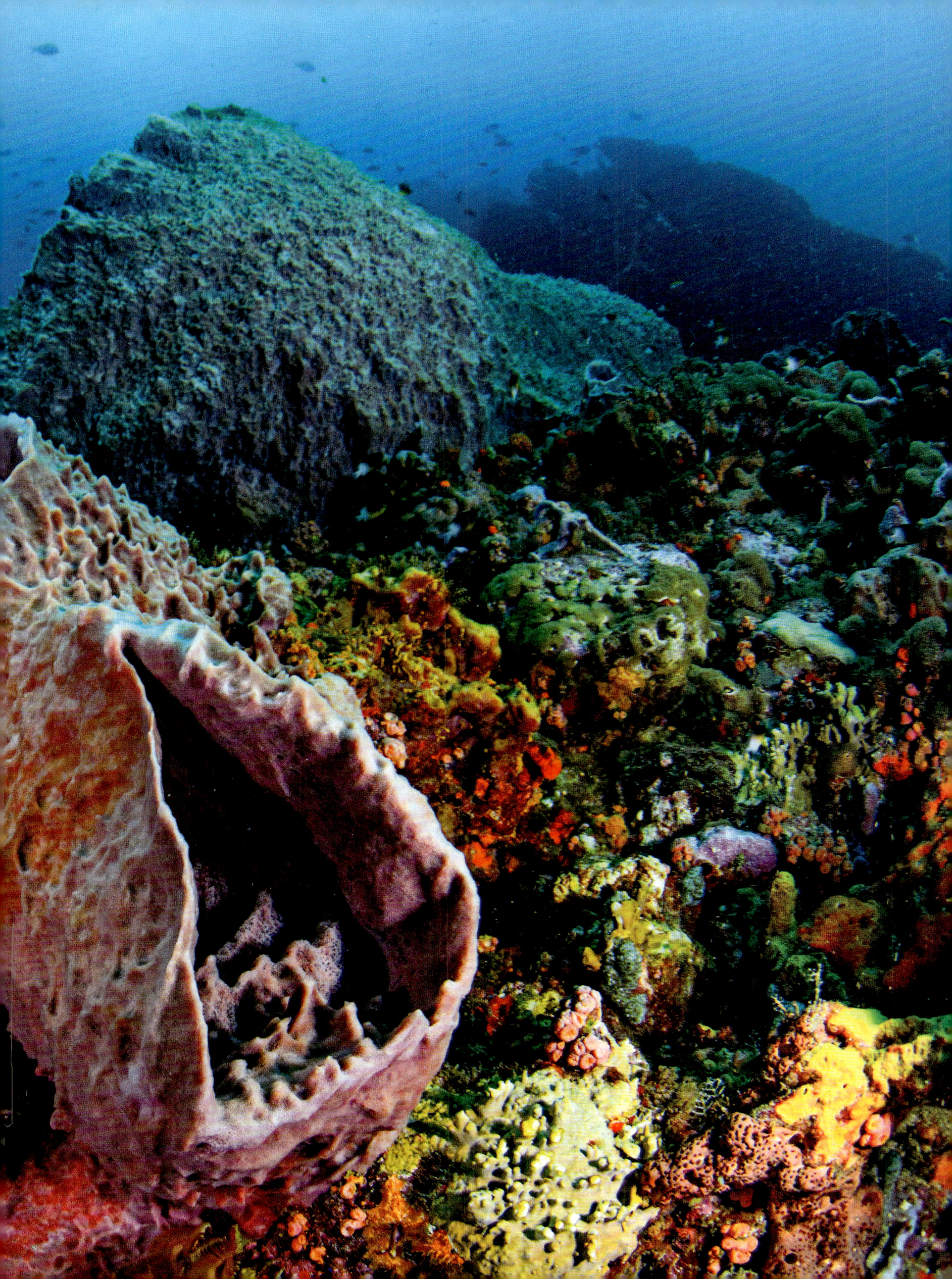

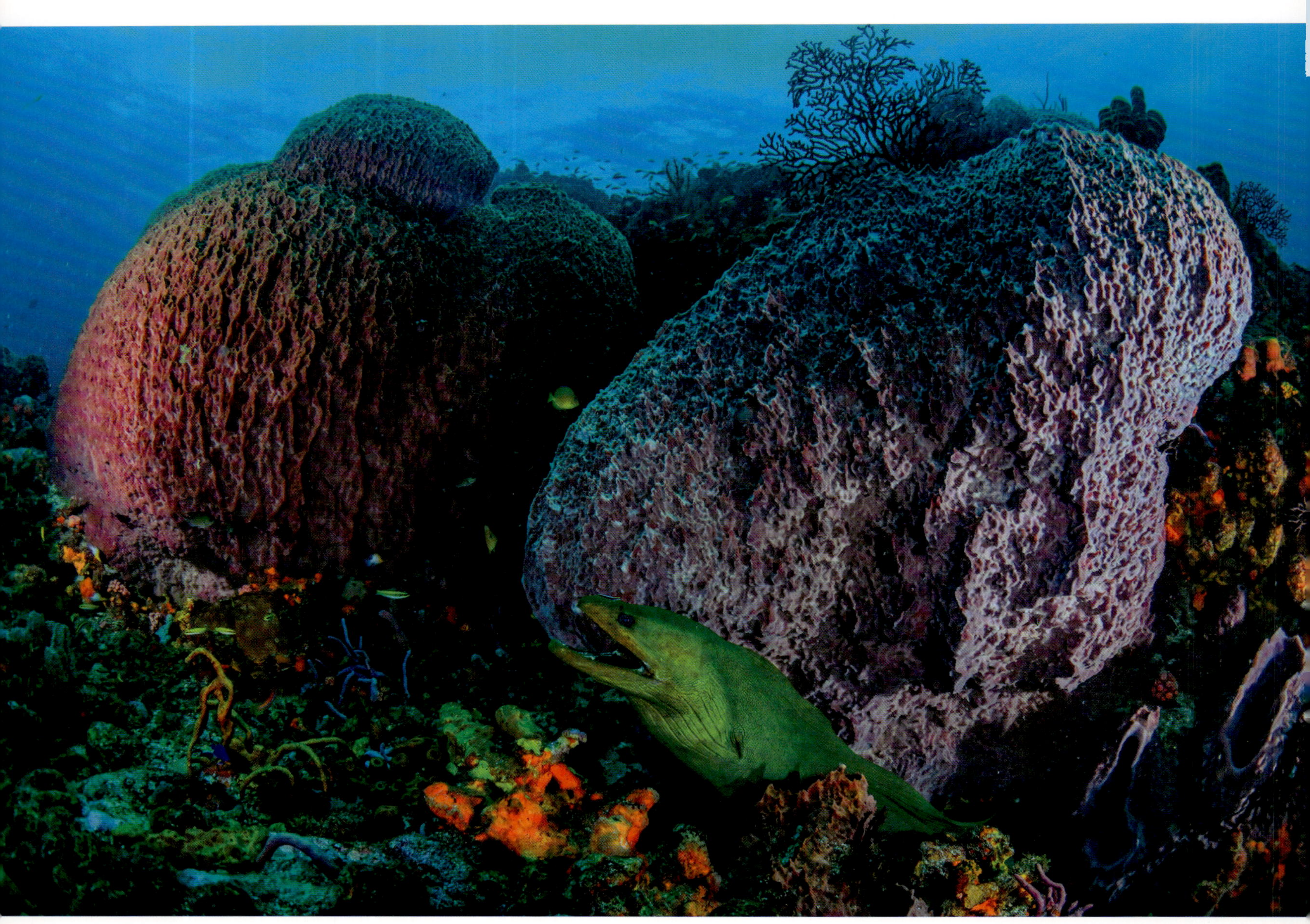

ABOVE: Giant barrel sponges can grow up to six feet (1.8 m) in diameter. The largest specimens may be more than 1,000 years old, placing them among the longest-lived of all animals. These "redwoods of the ocean" dominate the seabed along the northeast coast of Tobago, where, due to higher nutrient levels and greater water turbidity, hard corals tend to be sparse.

OPPOSITE: For many marine creatures, the Amazon River plume is an impenetrable barrier of fresh water and sediment, but not for invasive red lionfish *(Pterois volitans)*. Mistakenly introduced from their native Indo-Pacific into the Atlantic in the 1980s, they rapidly spread across the Caribbean and recently crossed the plume barrier, with specimens appearing on reefs south of the Amazon River mouth in Brazil.

PAGES 236–237: The Amazon pushes so powerfully into the Atlantic that it keeps on going—a sediment-rich freshwater river in the sea—more than a thousand miles (1,600 km) offshore. This sponge reef off the island of Tobago is seasonally fed by nutrients carried deep into the Caribbean by the Amazon and its smaller—but still mighty—neighboring river, the Orinoco.

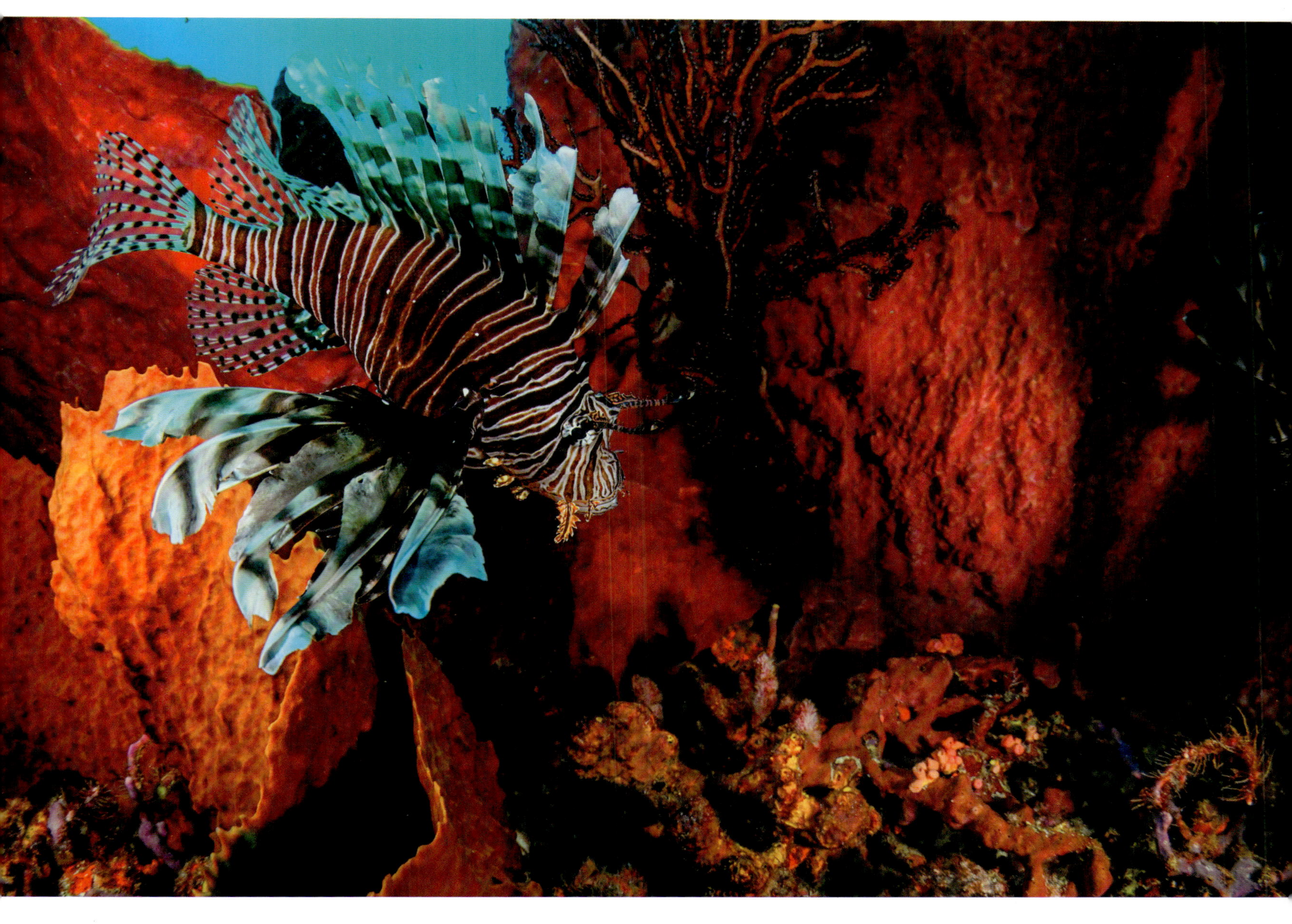

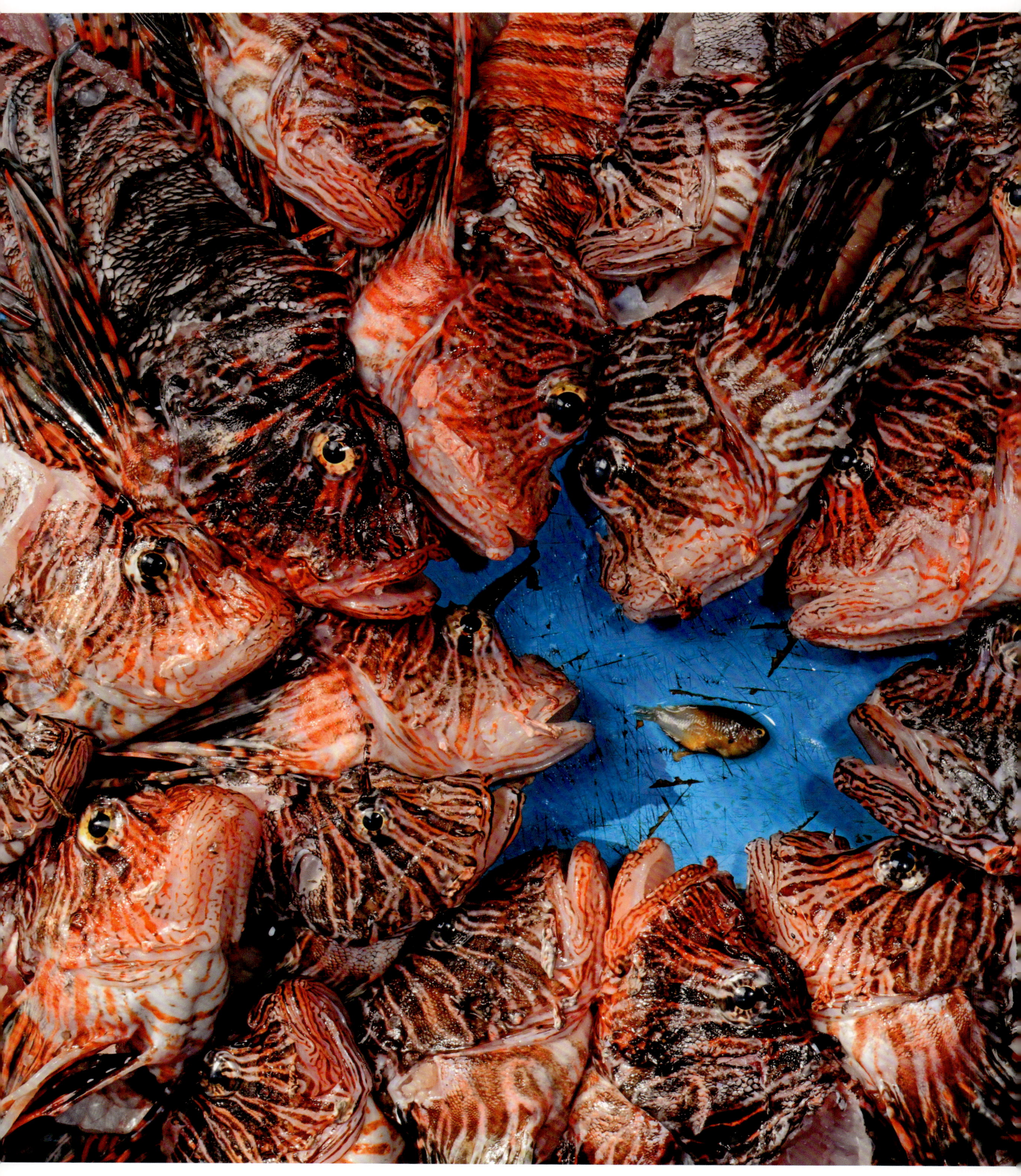

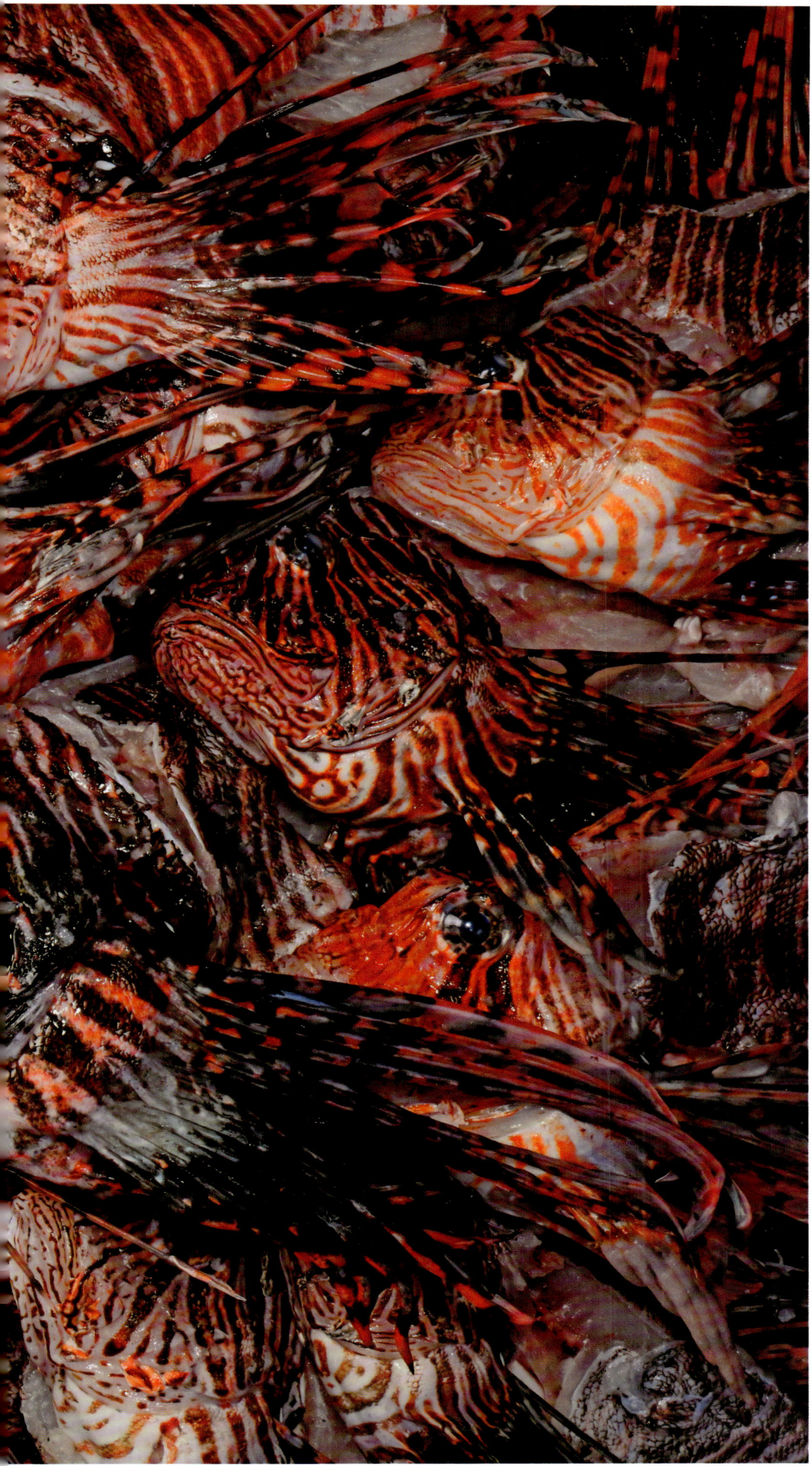

Invasive red lionfish *(Pterois volitans)* are a significant ecological threat to the coral reef ecosystems of the Caribbean and Atlantic Oceans. They consume native prey and displace potential competitors. Researchers have recently discovered that a single lionfish can reduce the recruitment and, in turn, population growth of native coral reef fish by almost 80 percent.

PAGES 242–243: A portion of the Amazon River plume north of the mouth runs along the so-called Amazon coast as far north as the island of Trinidad. Along the way, the sediments from the Amazon and other rivers form the beaches on which hundreds of endangered leatherback sea turtles *(Dermochelys coriacea)* lay their eggs every night during the nesting season.

PAGES 244–245: Leatherback turtle hatchlings scramble for the sea across a sandy beach covered in sargassum. The Amazon River, via its giant freshwater plume, has an outsize influence on the oceanography, biodiversity, and ecology of the Atlantic Ocean and the Caribbean Sea. Its impact can be felt as far as Puerto Rico, thousands of miles north of the river mouth.

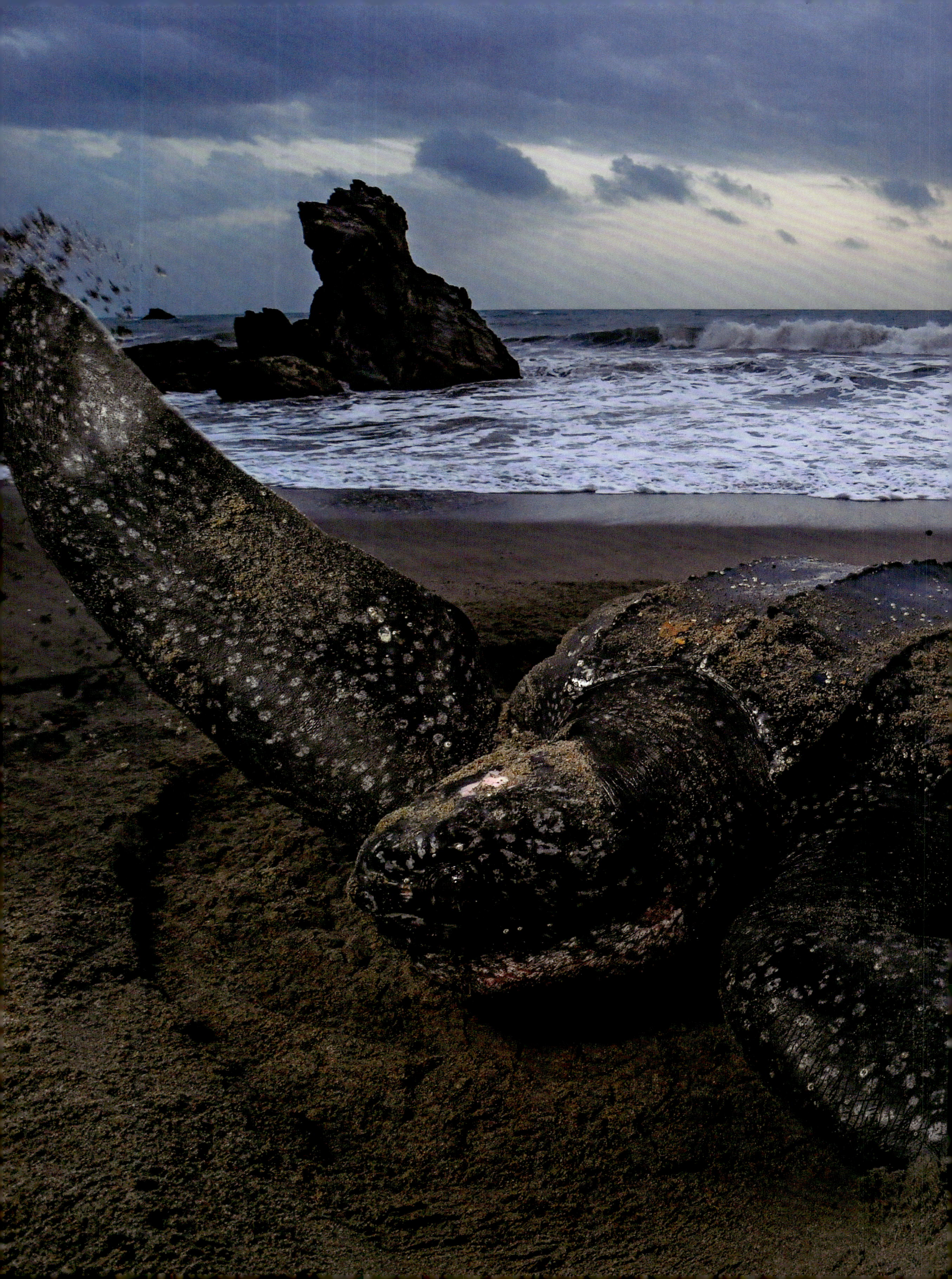

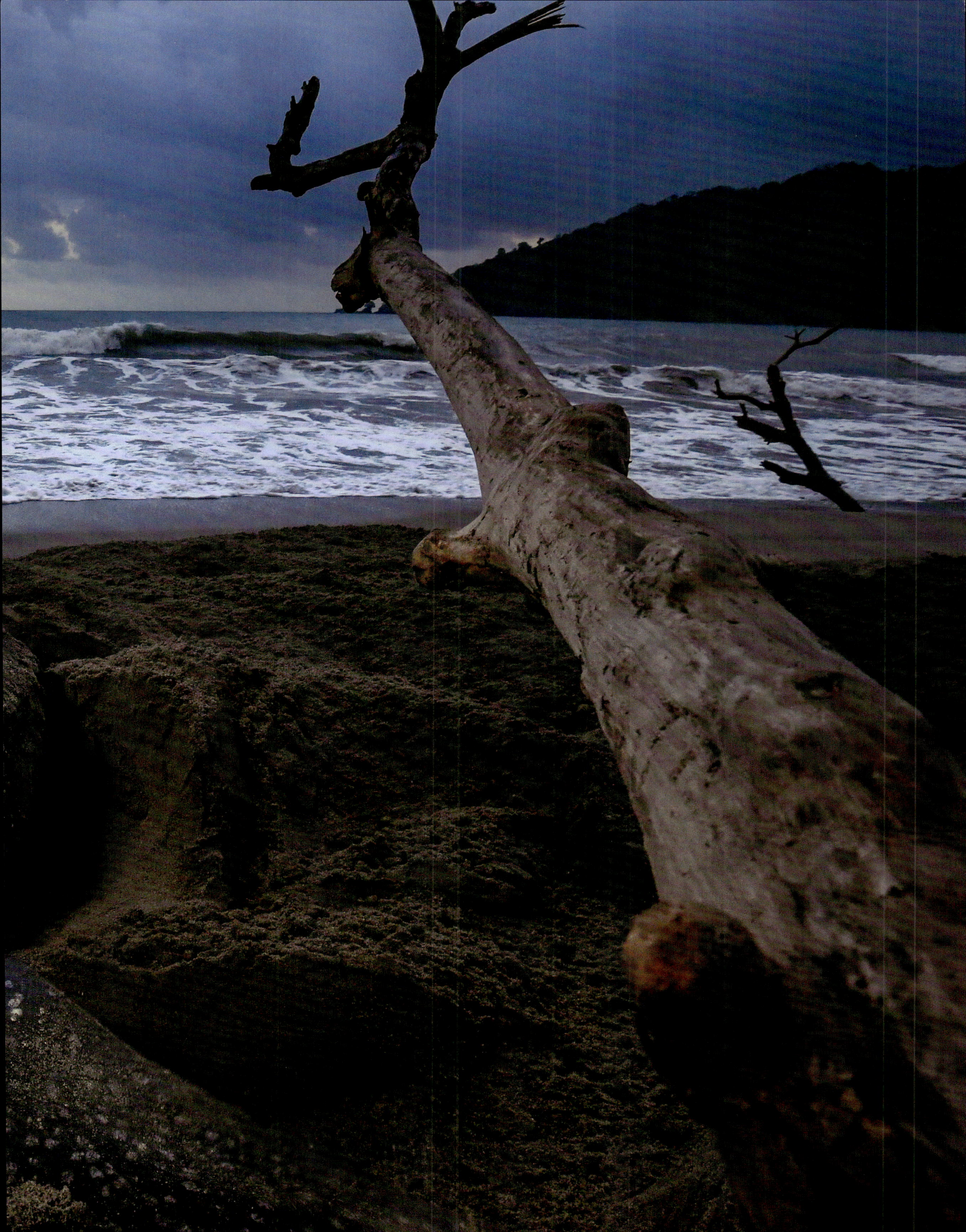

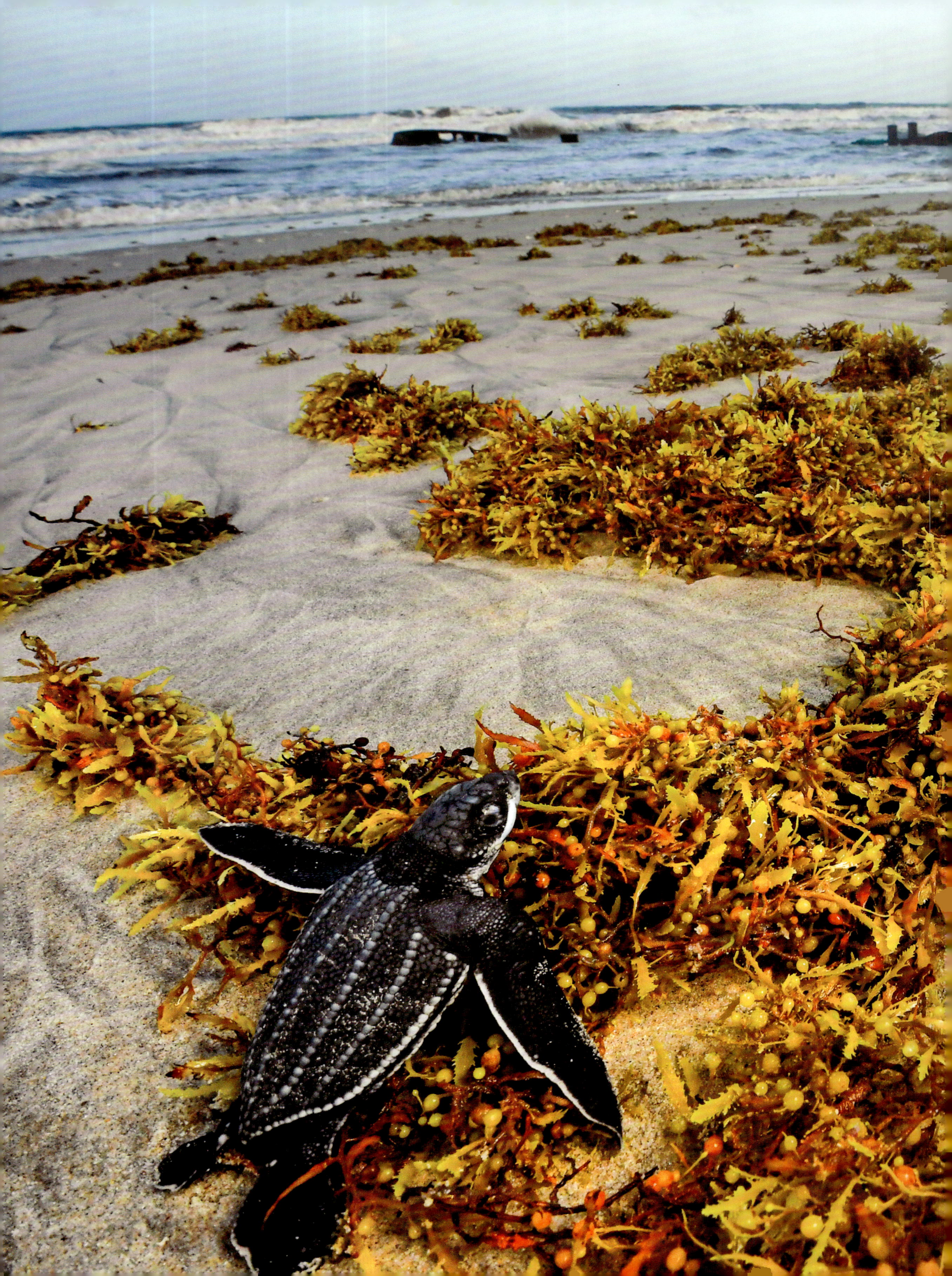

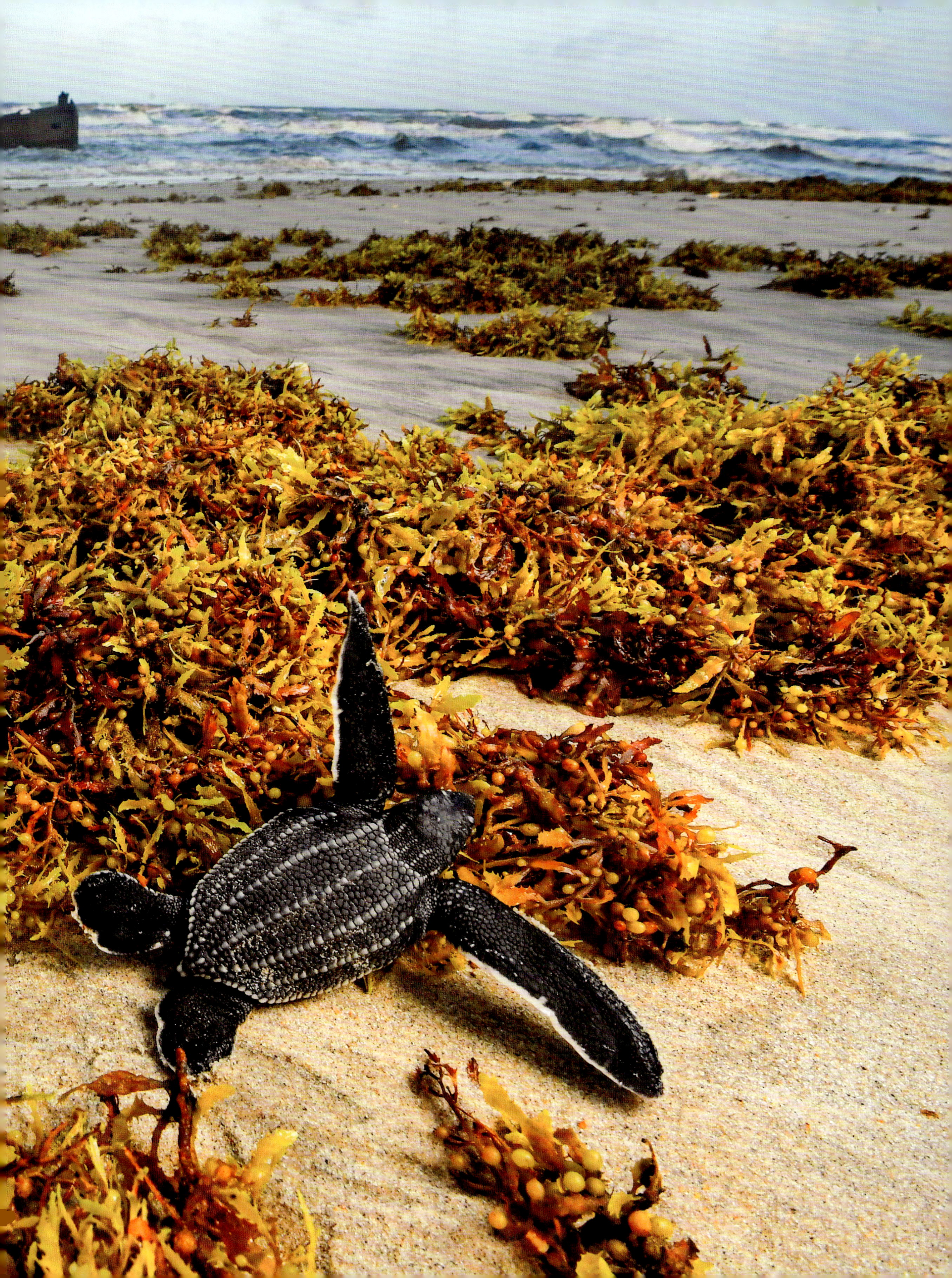

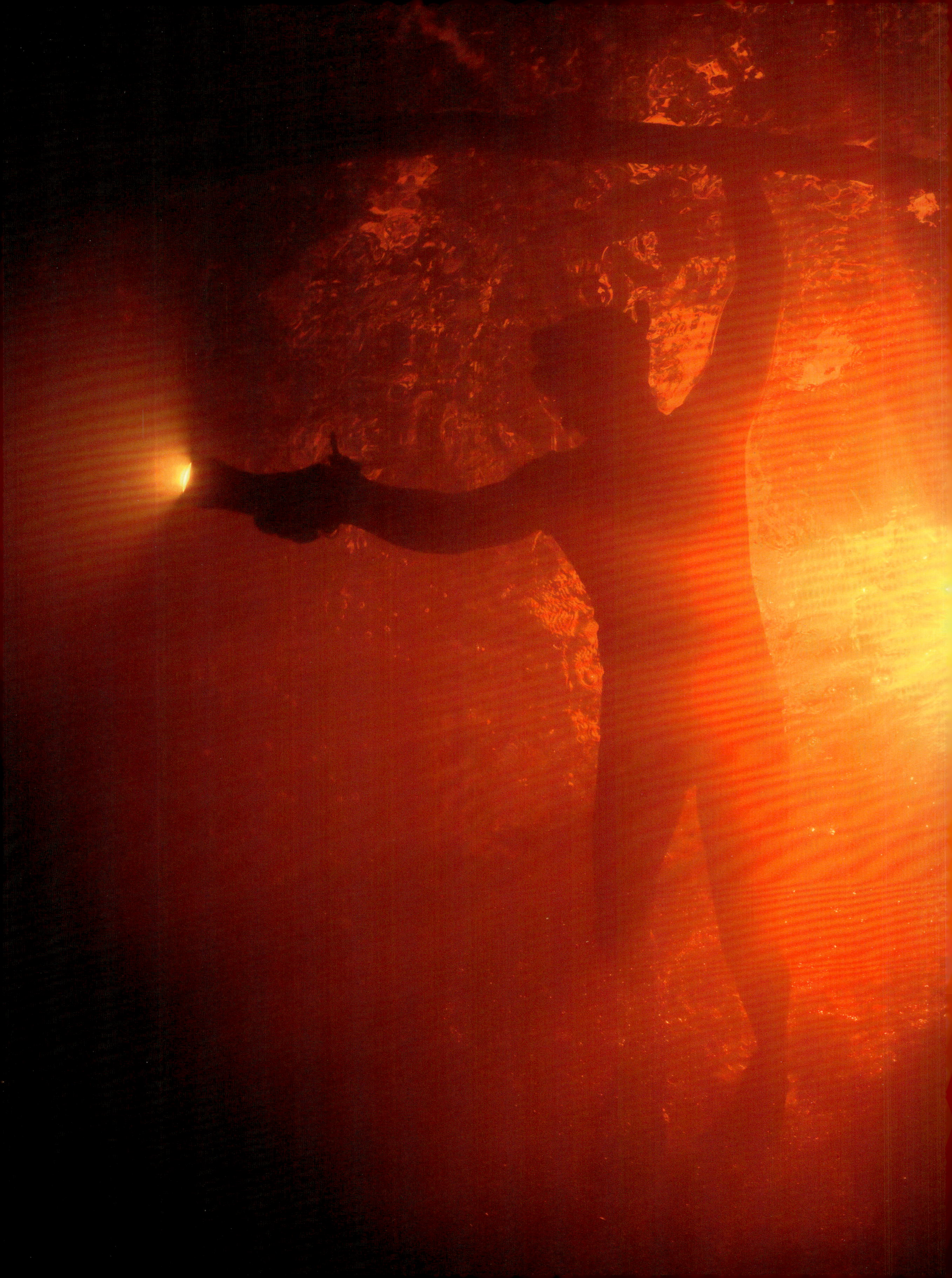

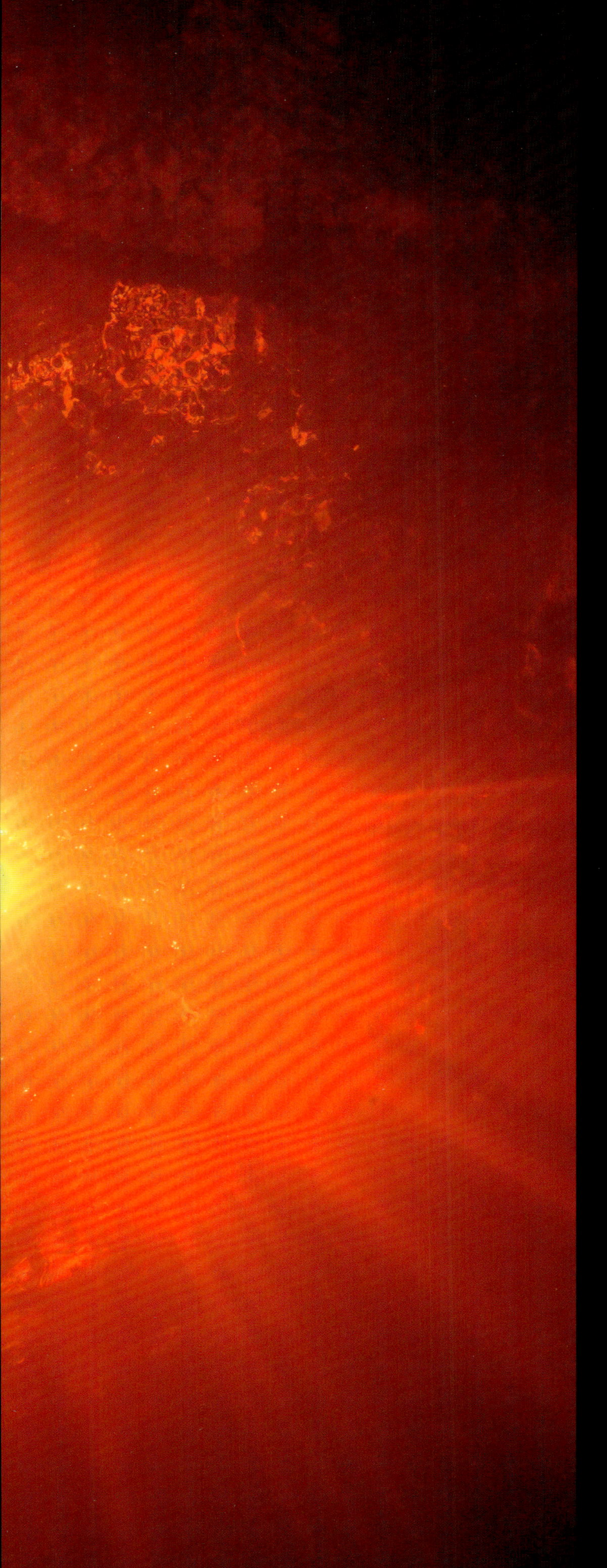

INTO THE FIELD

For 396 days, I roughly follow the course of the Amazon River and explore and dive its tributaries from west to east across South America, from the Andes to the Atlantic, embedding for months at a time in dozens of extraordinary locations across seven countries.

I begin on 19,000-foot (5,790 m) snowcapped volcanoes in Peru and eventually end alongside sponge reefs in the Atlantic Ocean thousands of miles north of the Amazon River mouth. All are challenging expeditions right at the edge of the impossible.

The behind-the-scenes vignettes that follow reveal the inner workings of my time in the field, as I try to capture the rarely glimpsed aquatic underworlds of Amazonia.

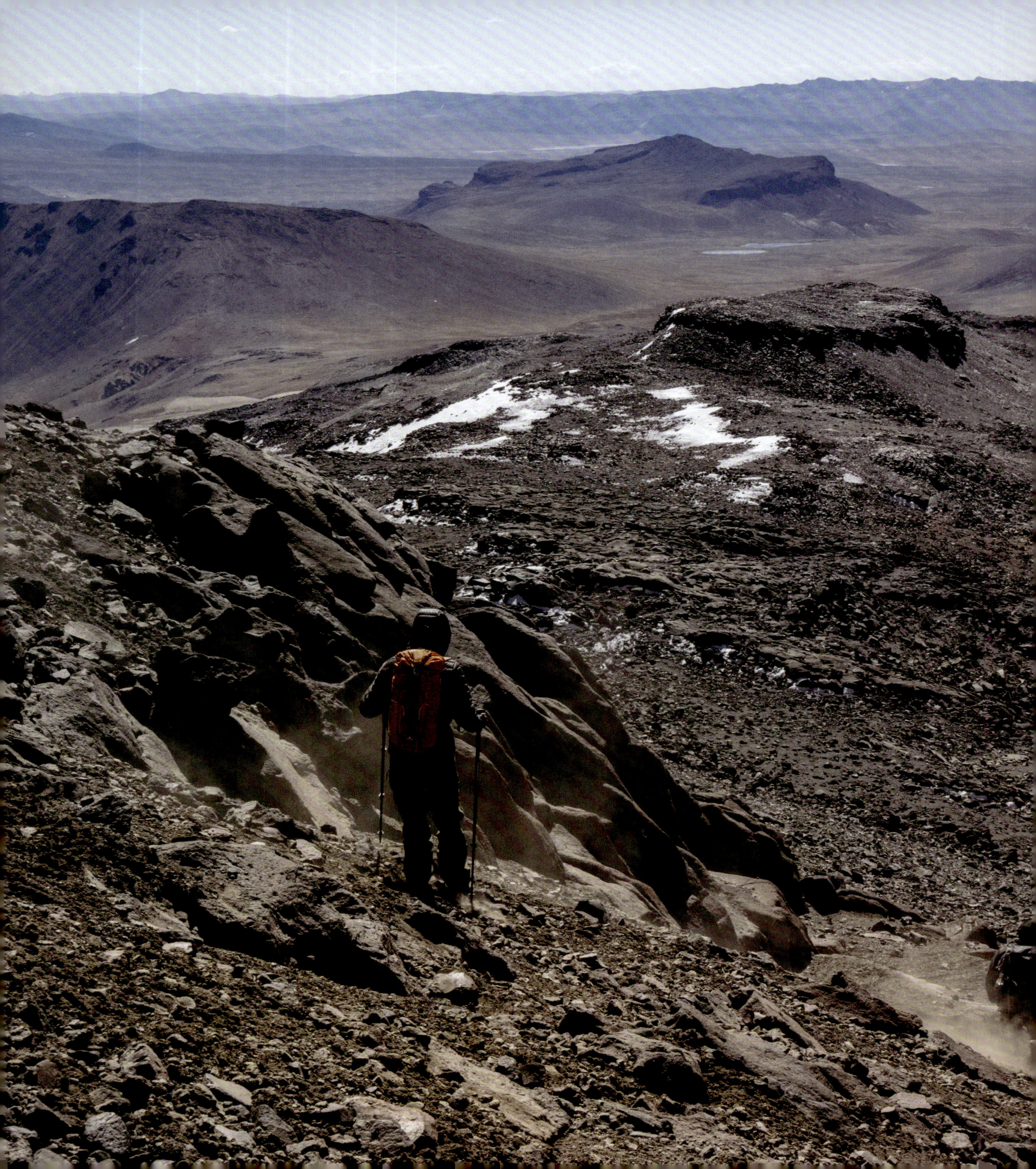

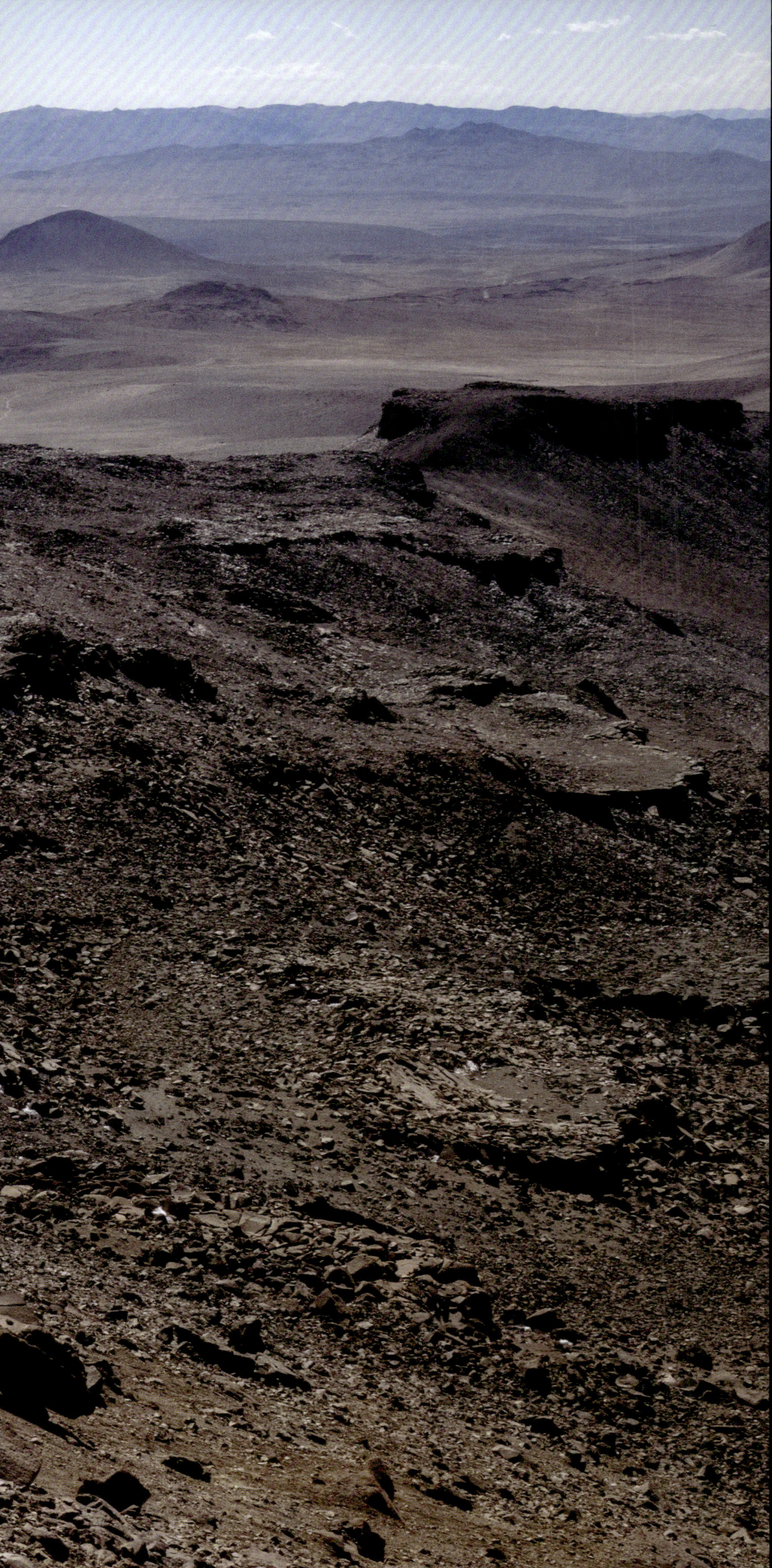

The Source

Few people would associate this high-altitude desert in the Andes with the birth of the world's most iconic rainforest river. But here in Peru's Chila Mountains, much closer to the Pacific Ocean than the lush tropical jungles of the Amazon, I tackle treacherous scree slopes to summit 18,363-foot-tall (5,597 m) Nevado Mismi. The meltwaters from its peak are considered the most distant year-round flowing source of the mighty Amazon River.

PAGES 246–247: Exploring Brazil's Rio Negro is like diving into a cup of strong black tea. Beneath the surface, it is as if someone has quickly dimmed the lights into total darkness. The dark red color is a result of tannins from the decay of plant detritus at the river's origins in the dense jungles of Colombia.

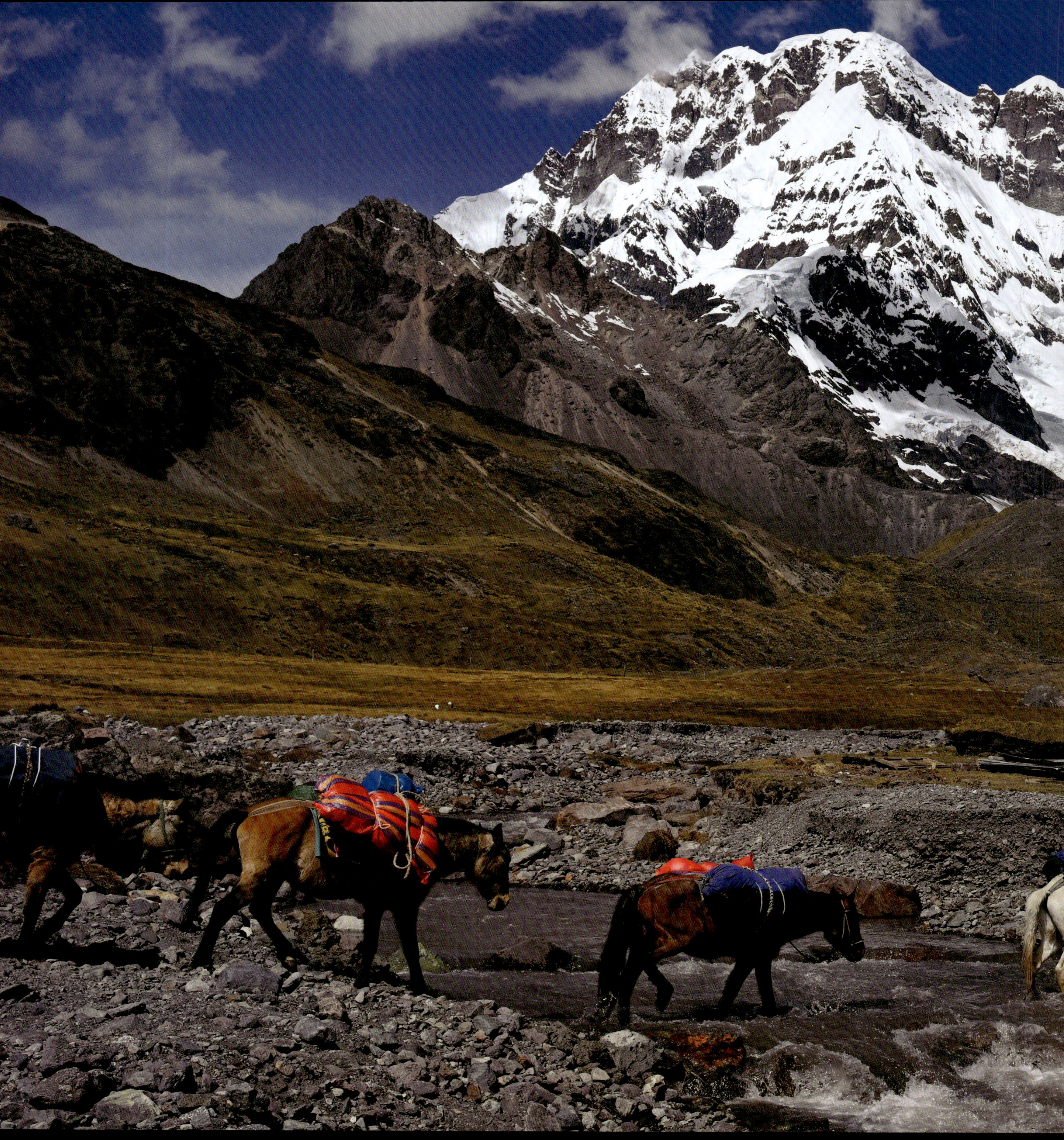

Nevado Ausangate

The approximate weight of all my expedition equipment is 1,200 pounds (540 kg), and we transport a good part of it around the base of 20,945-foot-tall (6,384 m) Nevado Ausangate on the back of a caravan of sturdy, altitude-adapted mules. But my most sensitive camera equipment I entrust to Pato Runto, a duck egg–colored mule, aloof but capable, especially on the steep terrain.

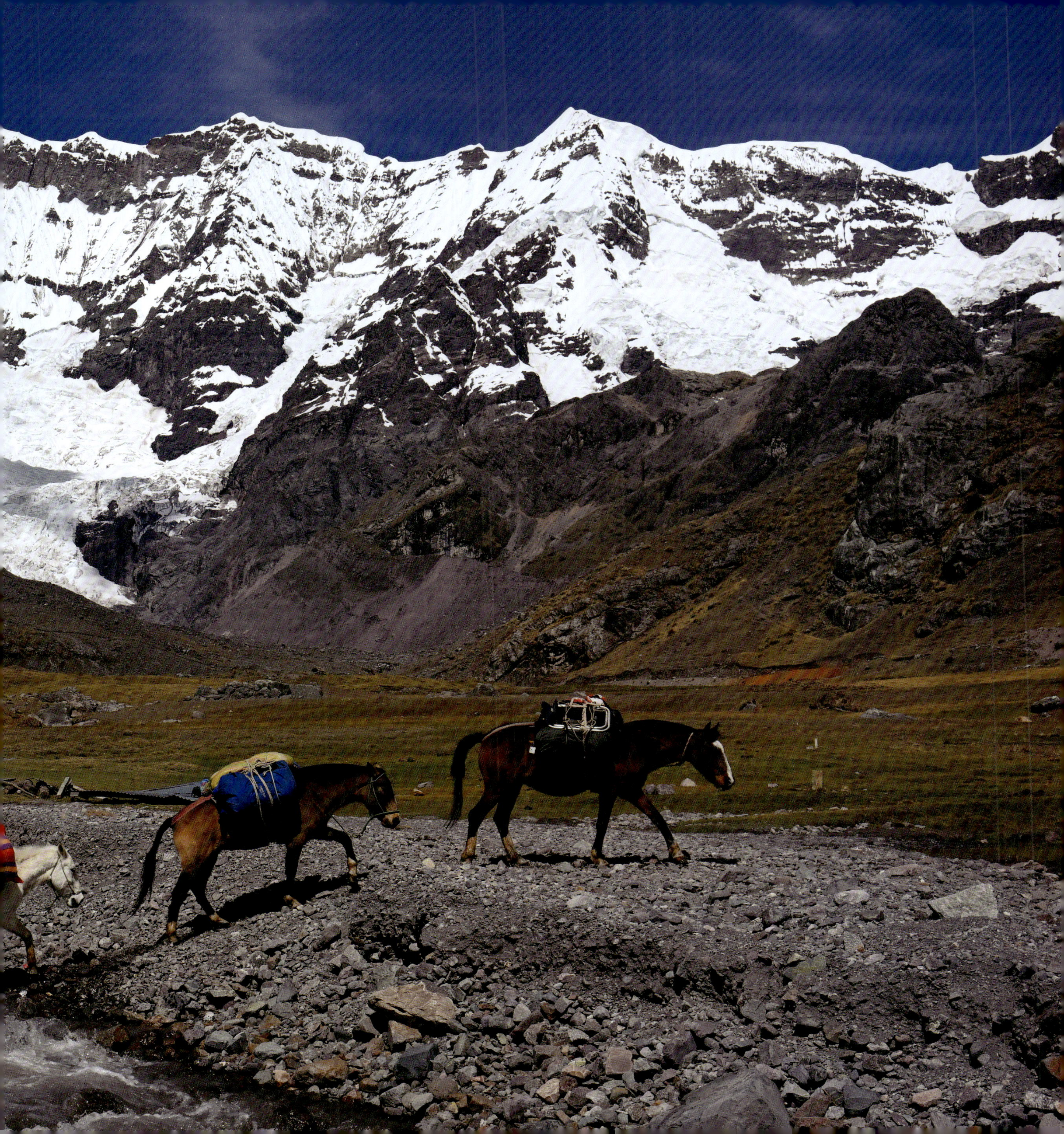

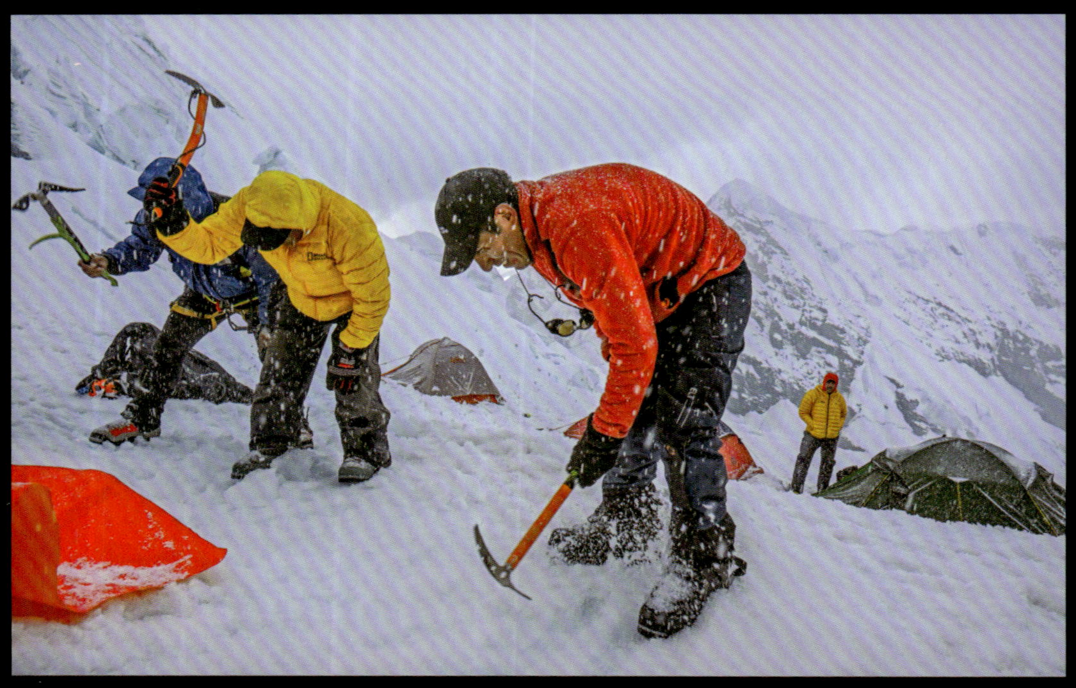

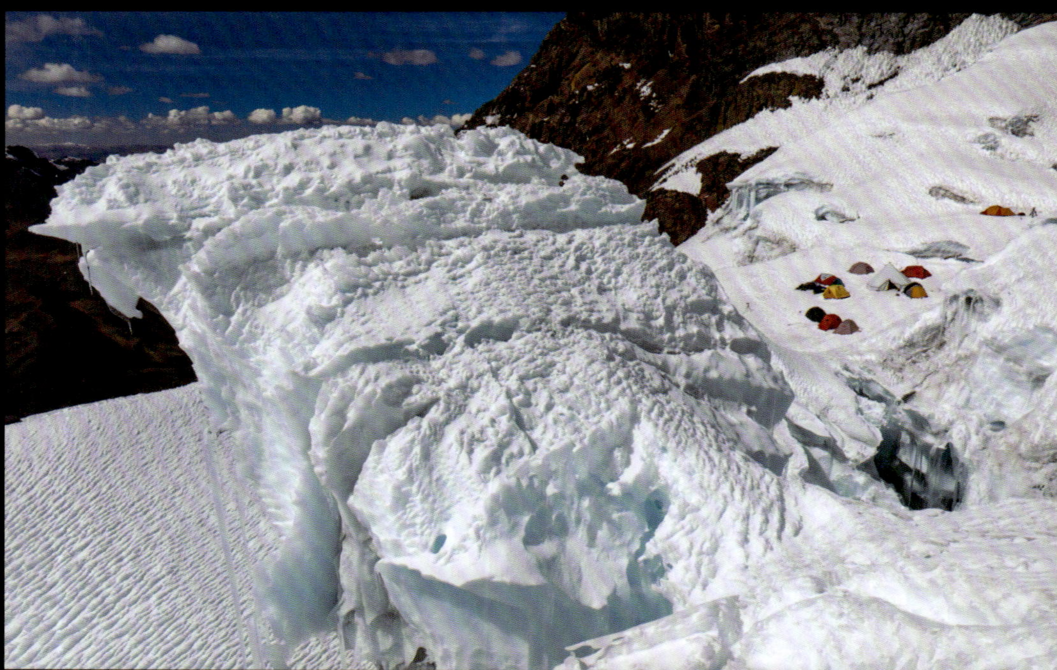

The Climb

Our high camp on Nevado Ausangate is located at just under 19,685 feet (6,000 m), the approach guarded by a steep ice wall that requires crampons and fixed ropes to scale. We have to hack out our tent platforms from the glacier using ice axes, a challenging feat at altitude, with less than half the oxygen available compared to sea level.

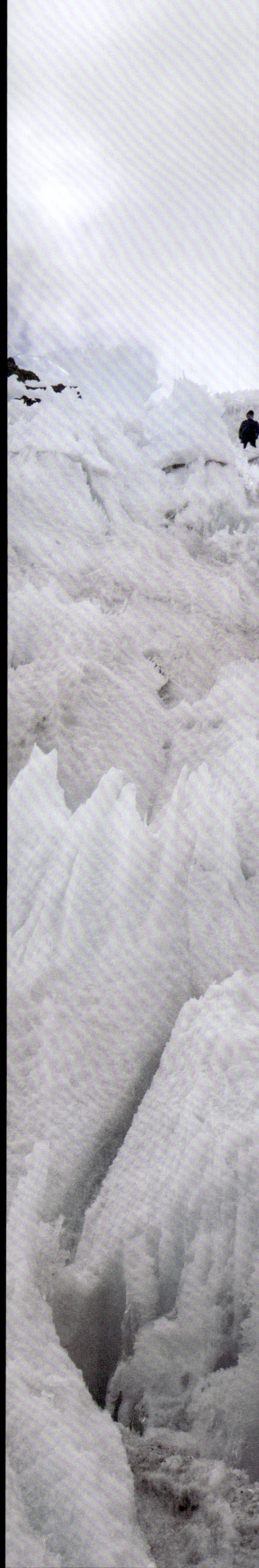

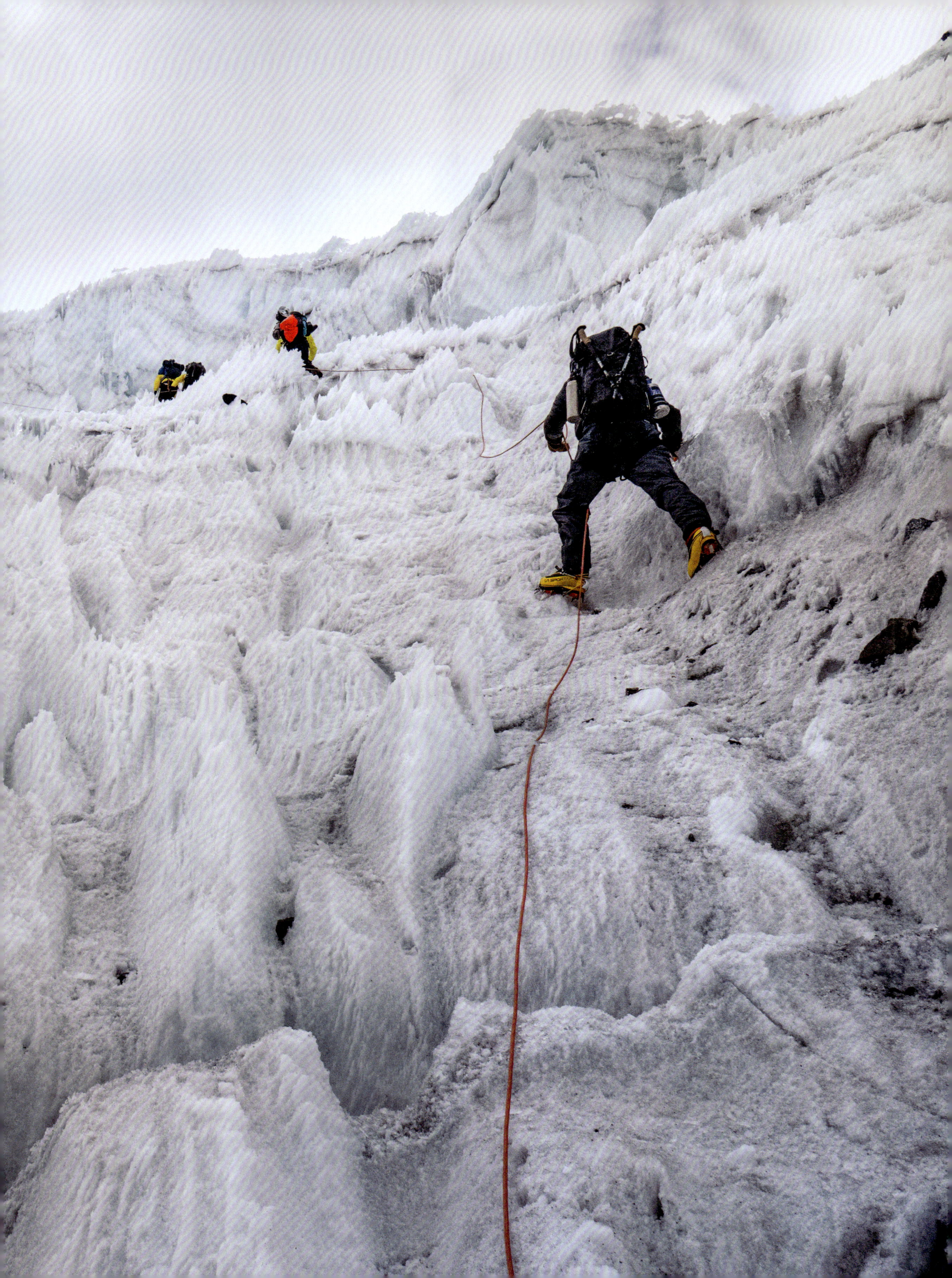

Meeting of the Waters

Our trusty ship, *Vitoria Amazonia,* sails amid the maelstrom where the dark waters of the Rio Negro meet the pale, sandy-colored water of the Amazon River main stem, referred to as the Solimões River in Brazil. For 3.7 miles (6 km), the waters of the two rivers run side by side without mixing, a phenomenon caused by the differences in temperature, speed, and amount of dissolved sediment in the two. I live on this ship for three weeks while photographing pink dolphins in the lakes, flooded forests, and archipelagoes between Manaus and Barcelos.

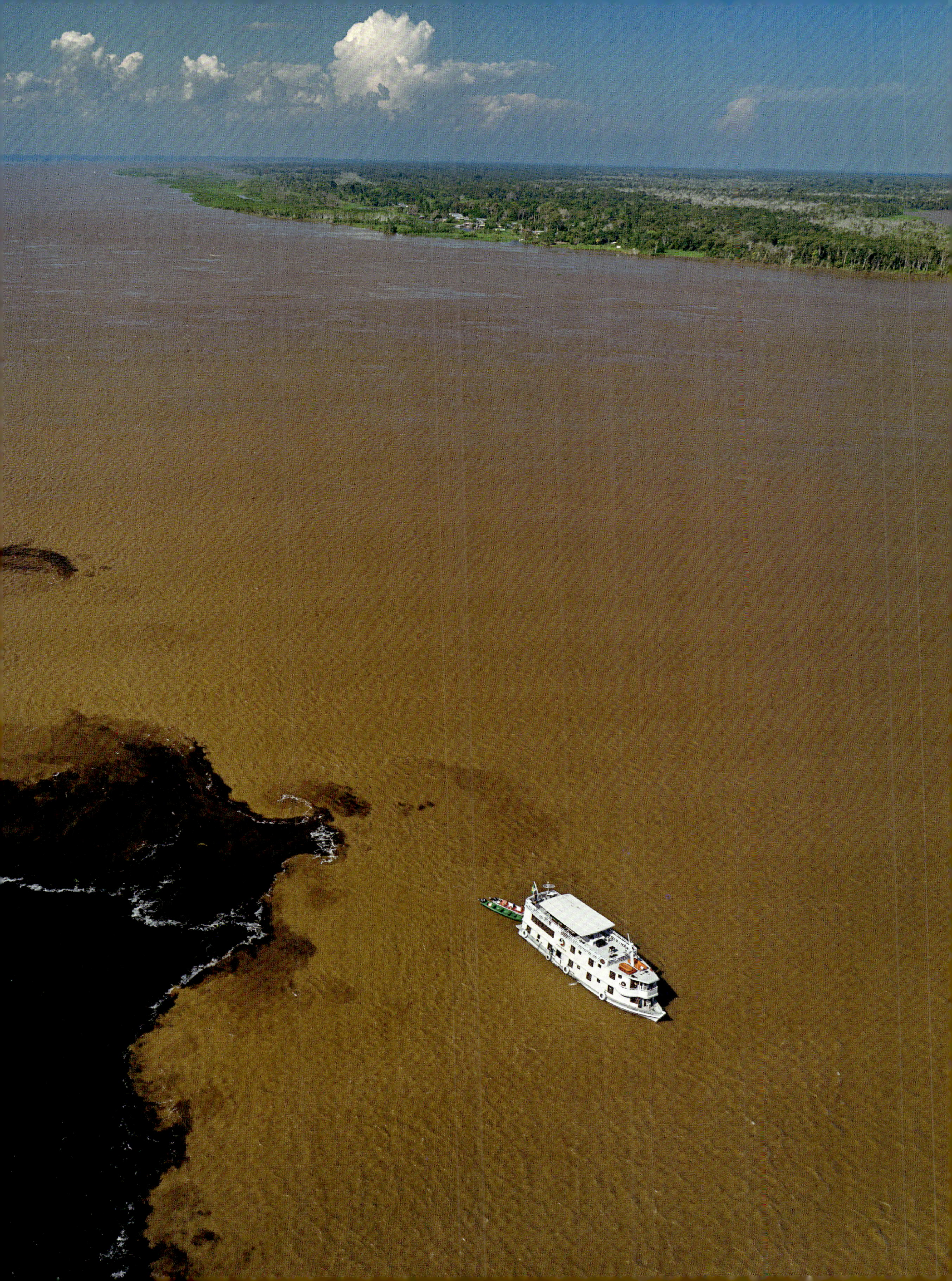

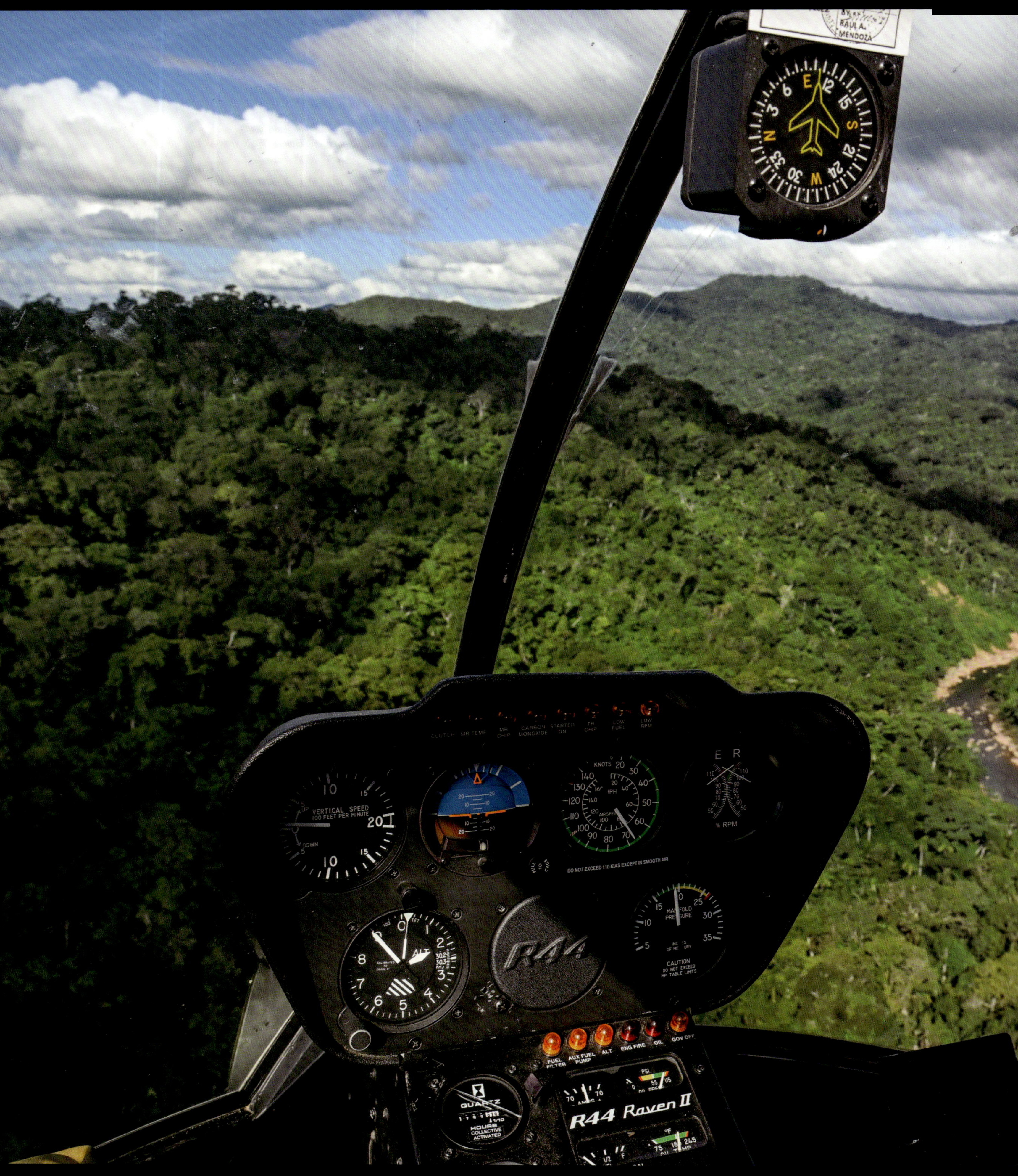
VERTICAL SPEED
100 FEET PER MINUTE
UP
DOWN
KNOTS
MPH
AIRSPEED
DO NOT EXCEED 110 KIAS EXCEPT IN SMOOTH AIR
% RPM
MANIFOLD PRESSURE
CAUTION
DO NOT EXCEED
MP TABLE LIMITS
ALT
R44
FUEL FILTER
AUX FUEL PUMP
ALT
ENG FIRE
OIL
QUARTZ
HOURS
COLLECTIVE
ACTIVATED
R44 Raven II

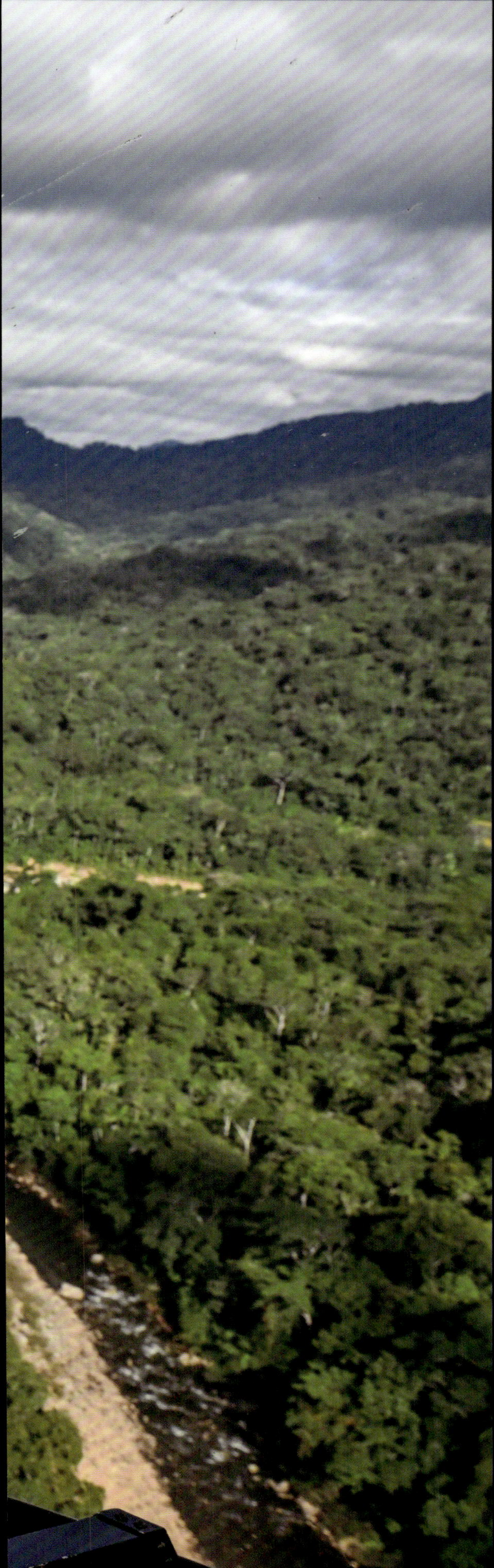

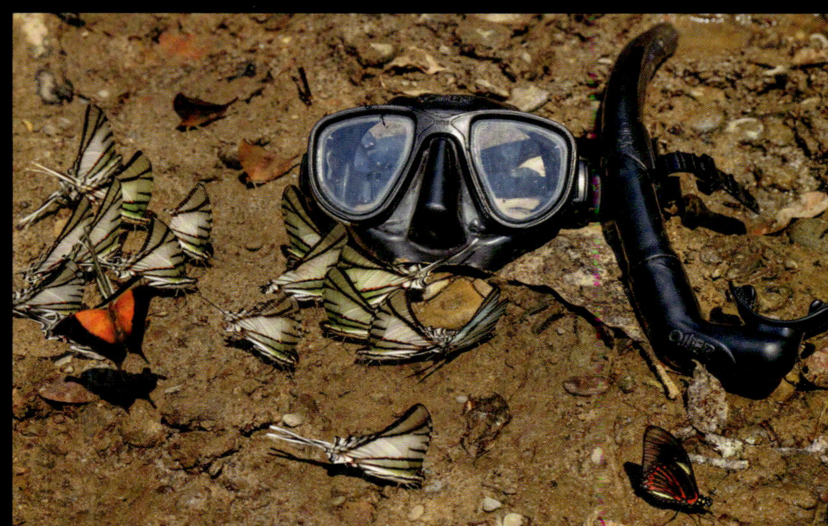

Helicopter Explorations

In 2022, I was privileged to become the first person to dive the remote headwaters of the Pluma and Sécure Rivers in Bolivia's Isiboro Sécure National Park and Indigenous Territory. It is nearly impossible to penetrate the Eva Eva Mountains on foot or by canoe, so a 20-minute helicopter ride was the only way to transport me and my gear to a place where even the Indigenous Tsimané and Yuracaré people have never hunted or fished.

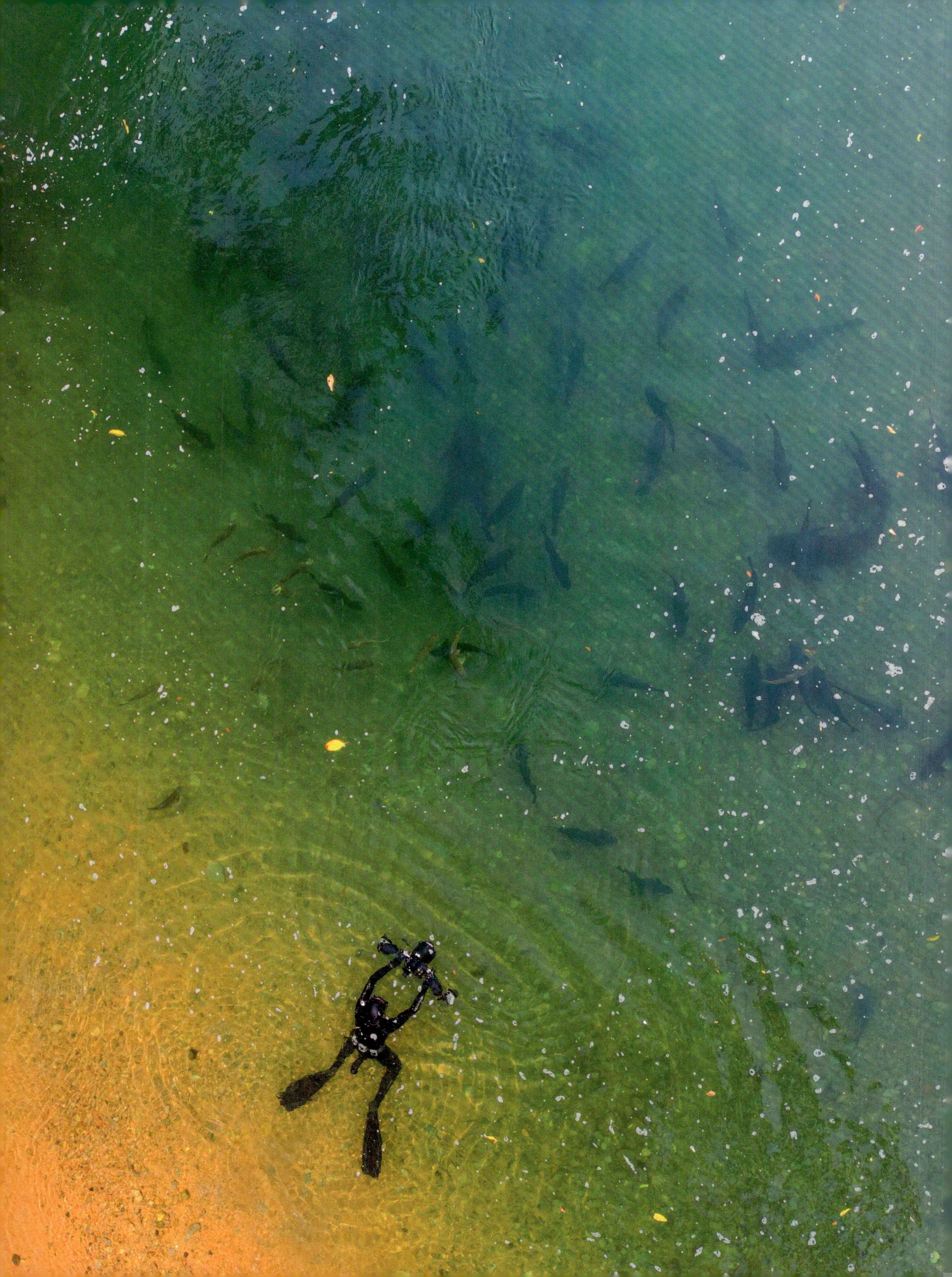

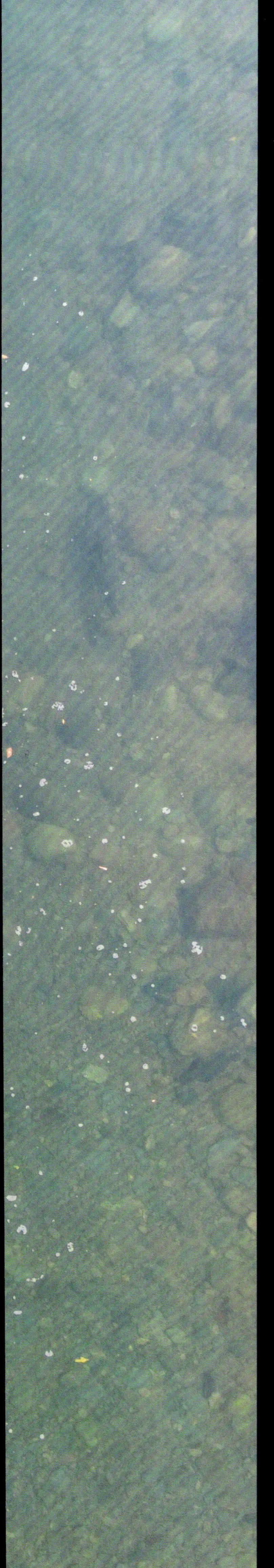

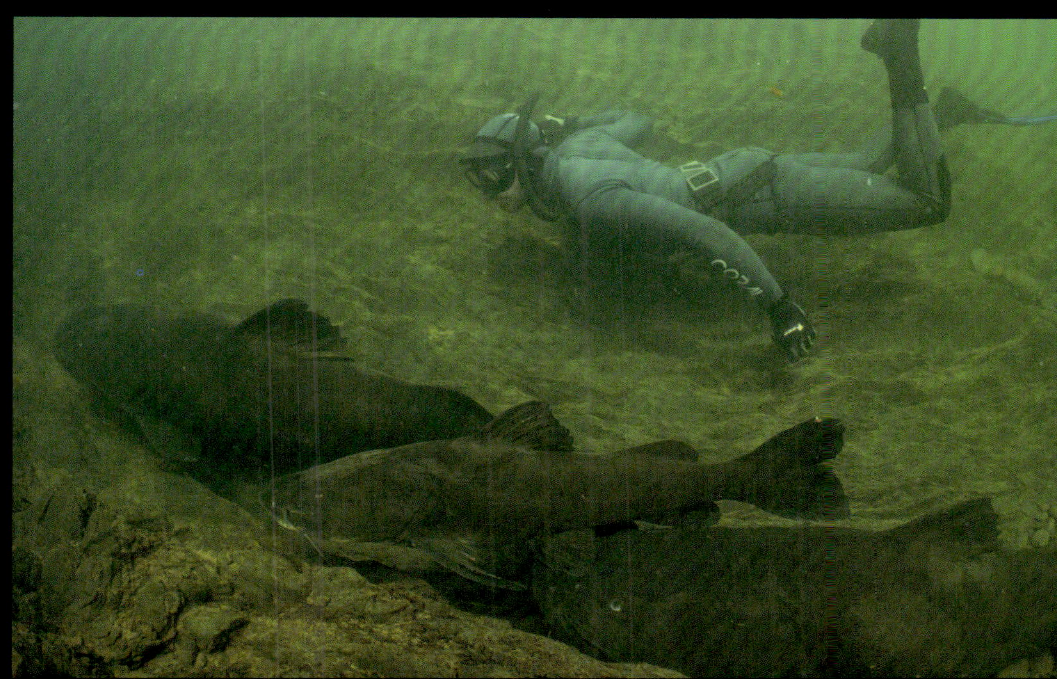

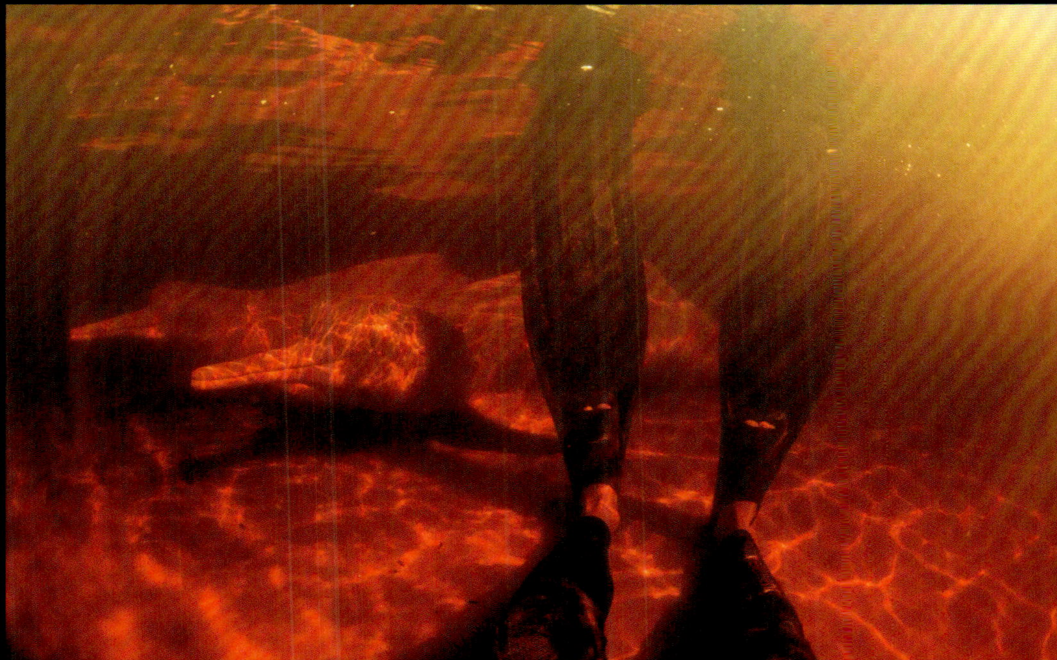

Underwater Explorations

Most of the Amazon Basin has never been explored underwater, so we have no blueprint for where to go and how to do it. Every dive is an adventure into the unknown. Drifting with a school of pacus so dense it blocks out the sun, swimming beneath waterfalls alongside catfish the size of adult humans, and shadowing pink dolphins as they roam flooded forests are just a few of the highlights.

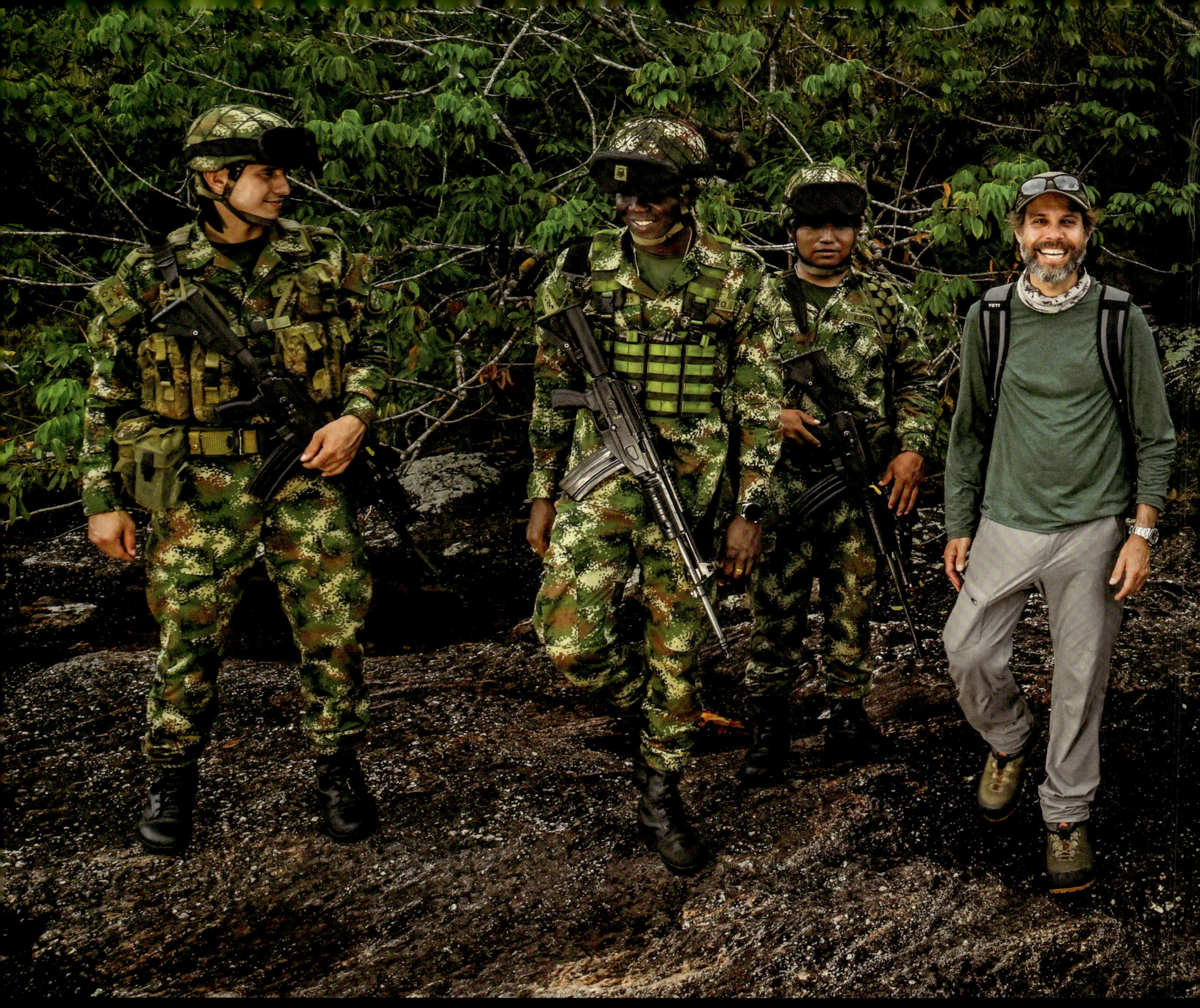

Friends in the Jungle

My explorations are rarely a solo activity, and the humans I meet are as diverse as their environment. I am led by both Western science and Indigenous guides and their knowledge, spending time with biologists, conservationists, park rangers, fly-fishermen, soldiers, pilots, and local village leaders. They all play an important part in making it possible for me to emerge from the Amazon Basin after 396 days, not only with photographs, but also with all my limbs intact.

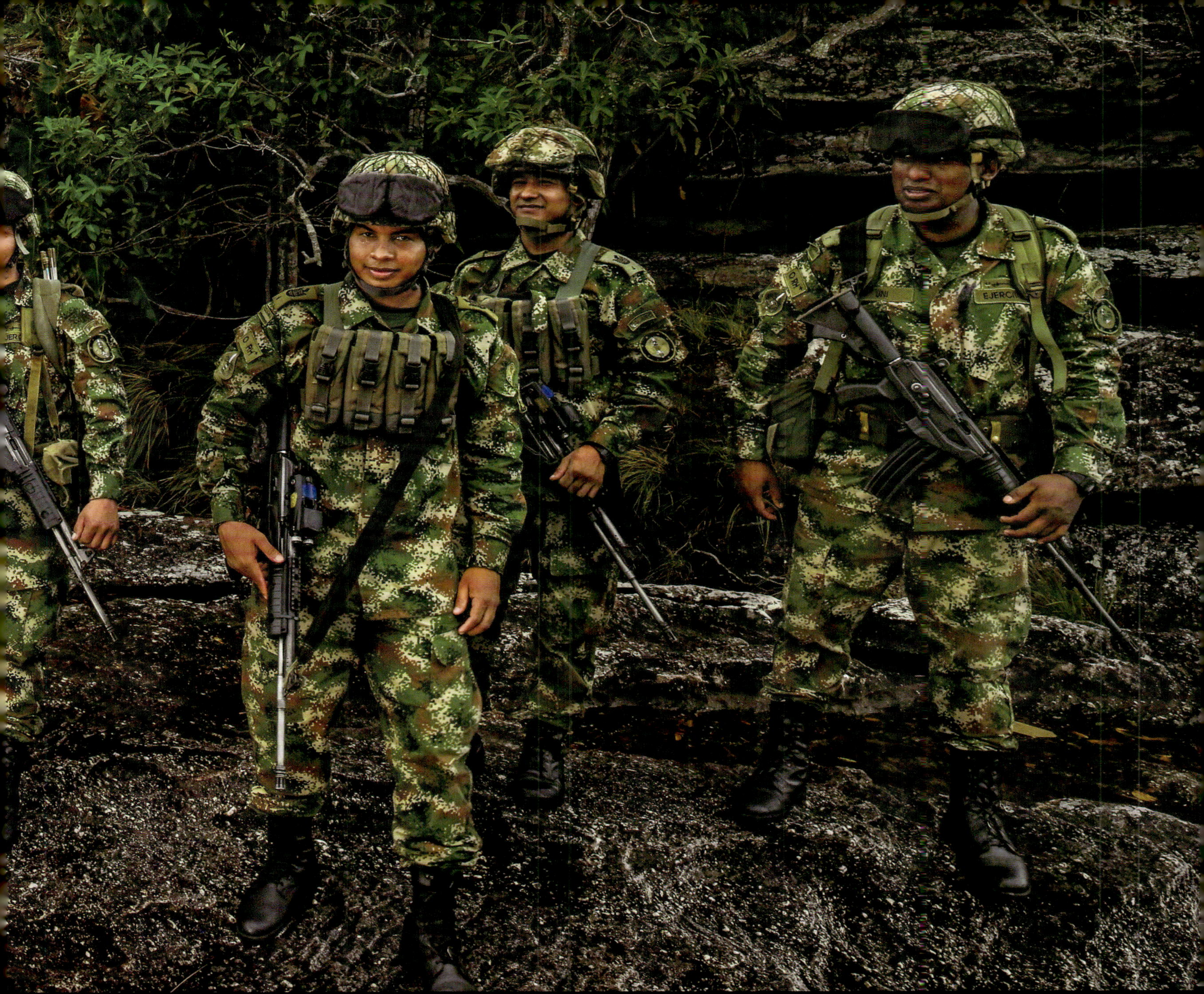

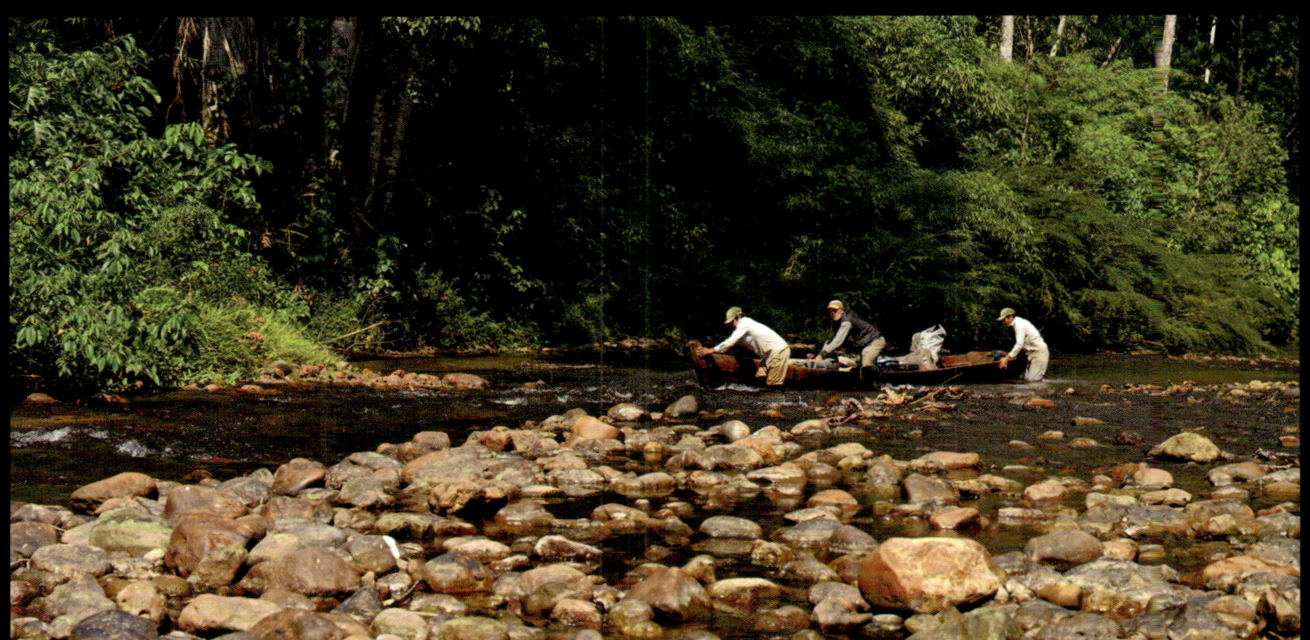

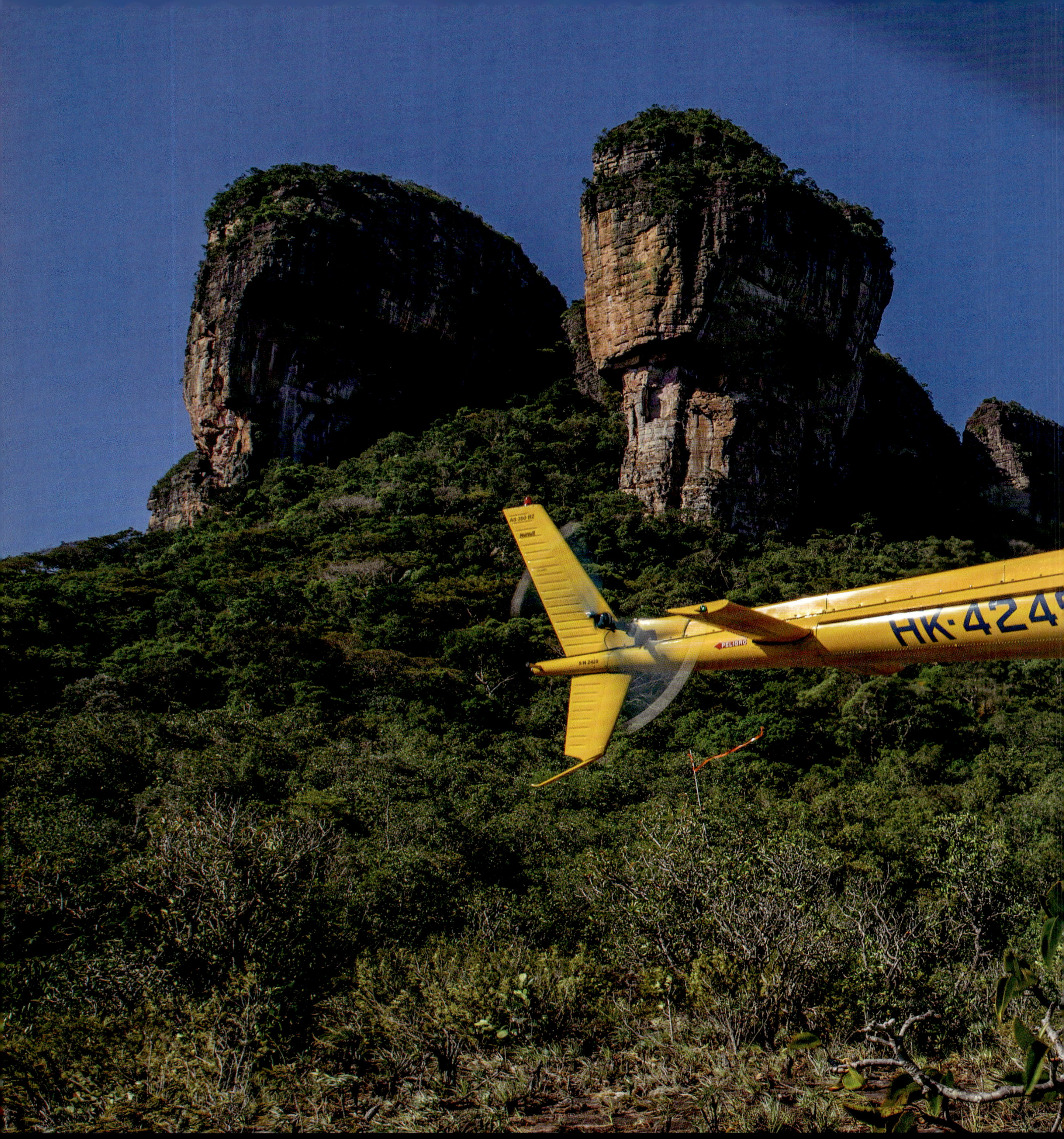

Chiribiquete

Our helicopter takes off from the small airport of San José del Guaviare in south-central Colombia. After a while, an unbroken carpet of pristine rainforest rolls out to the horizon. When the first mountains appear, the pilot descends, and we navigate through canyons so narrow that I can almost reach out and touch them. We land on a tiny patch of uneven rock on top of a *tepui*. The helicopter barely fits, but this is to be our base camp while I explore Chiribiquete National Park.

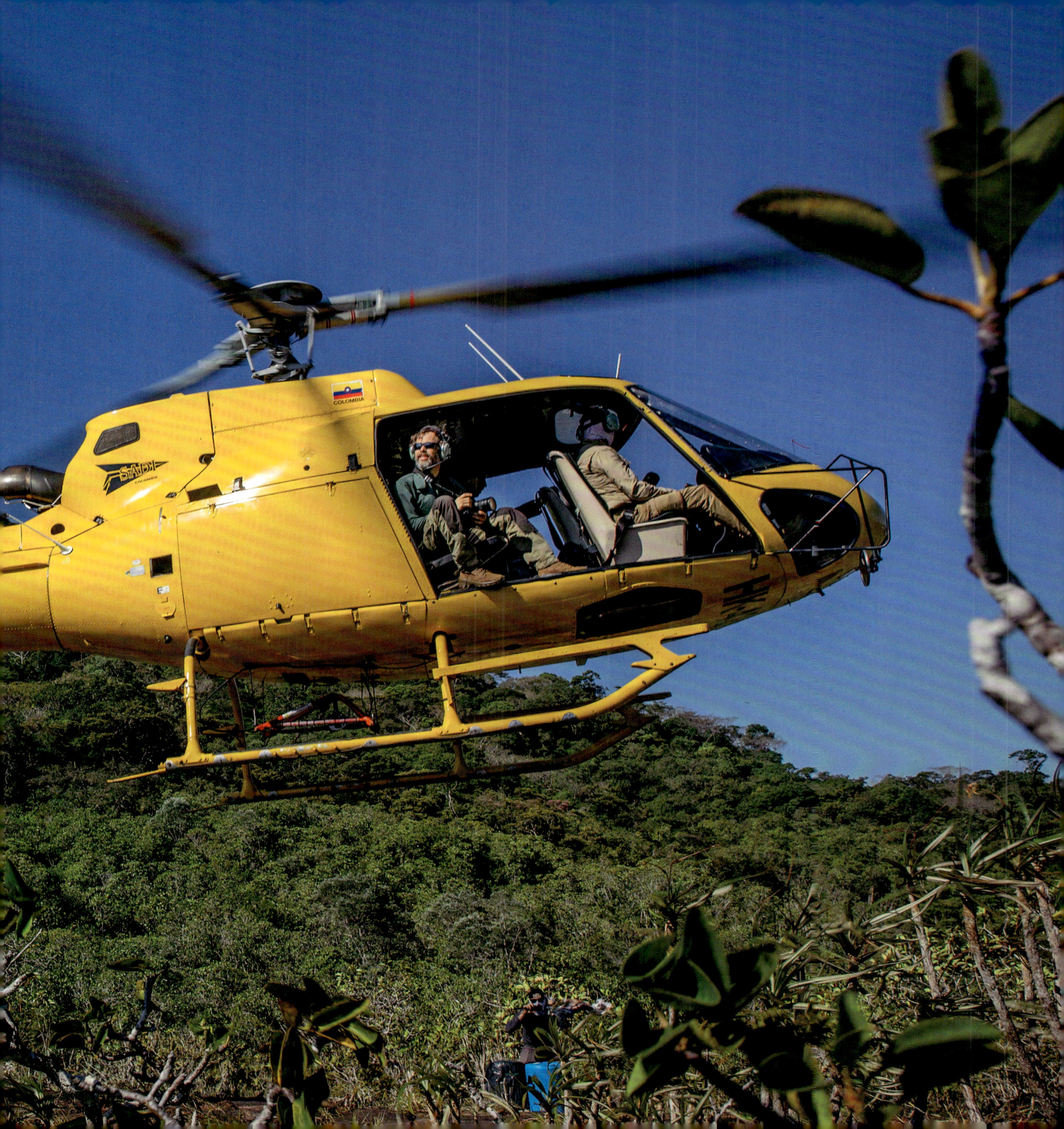
COLOMBIA

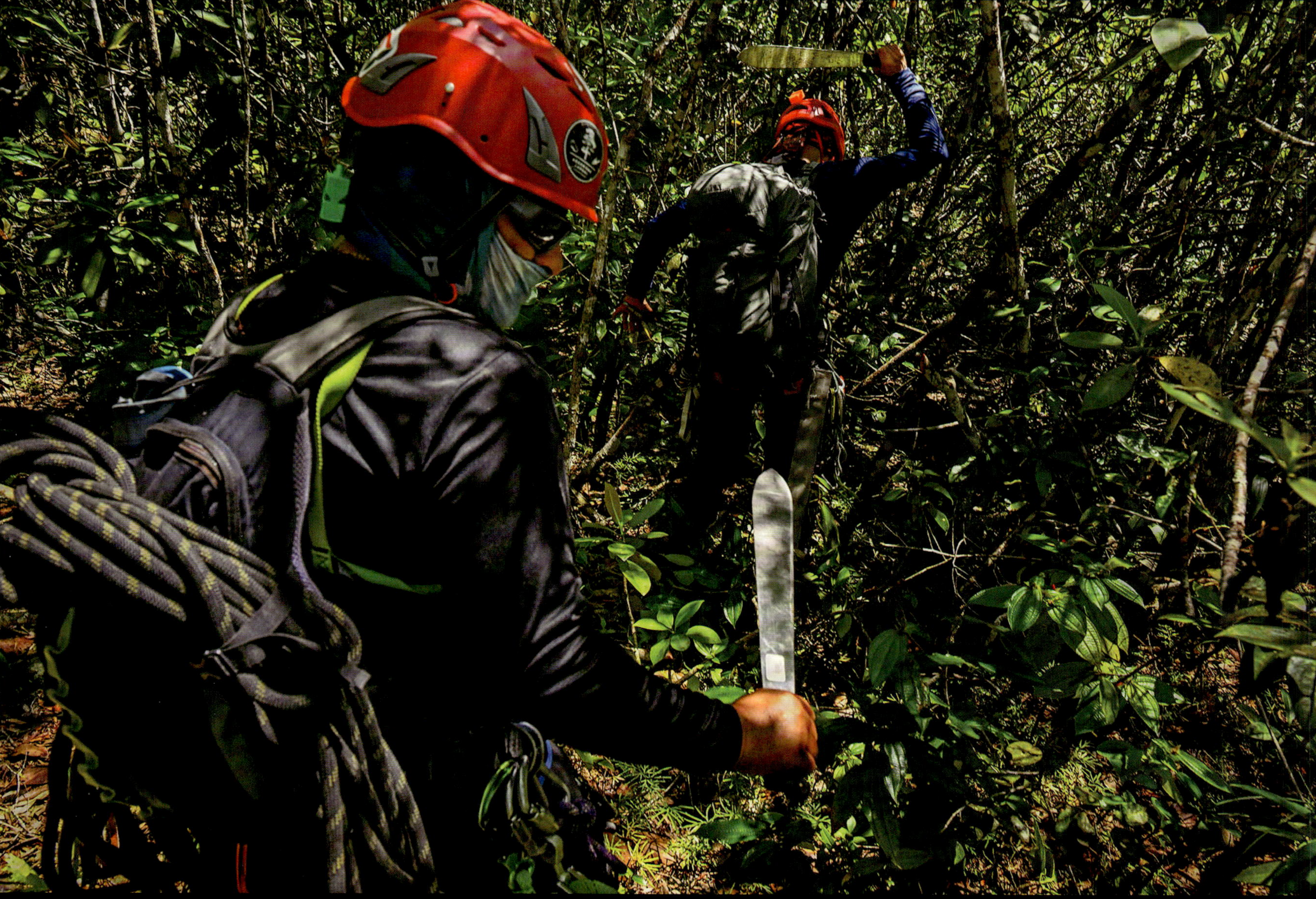

Ancient Stories

Every morning, we set out by helicopter and then on foot, climbing steep and densely forested slopes, rappelling down cliffs, and hauling ladders to navigate dark and damp canyons. The Amazon's first storytellers painted the most ancient visual stories ever found in the Americas in some of the most inaccessible locations. More than 70,000 paintings have been discovered in 58 cave shelters, some dating back 20,000 years. During the day, sweat bees overwhelm our camps, serenading us like tens of thousands of tiny helicopters. Anything left outside is instantly coated in bees, and if they catch us without a head net, they crawl into our noses, eyes, and ears.

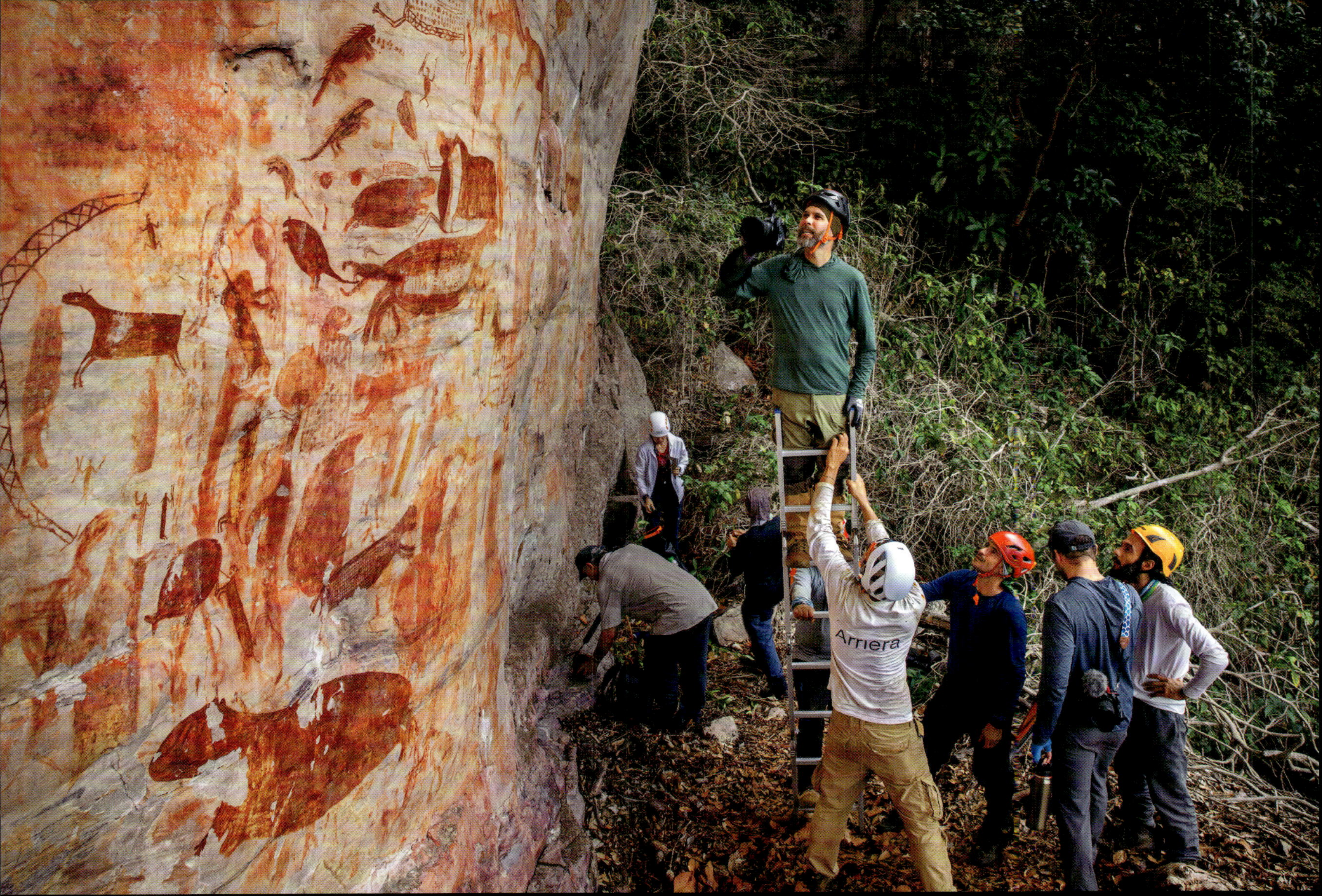

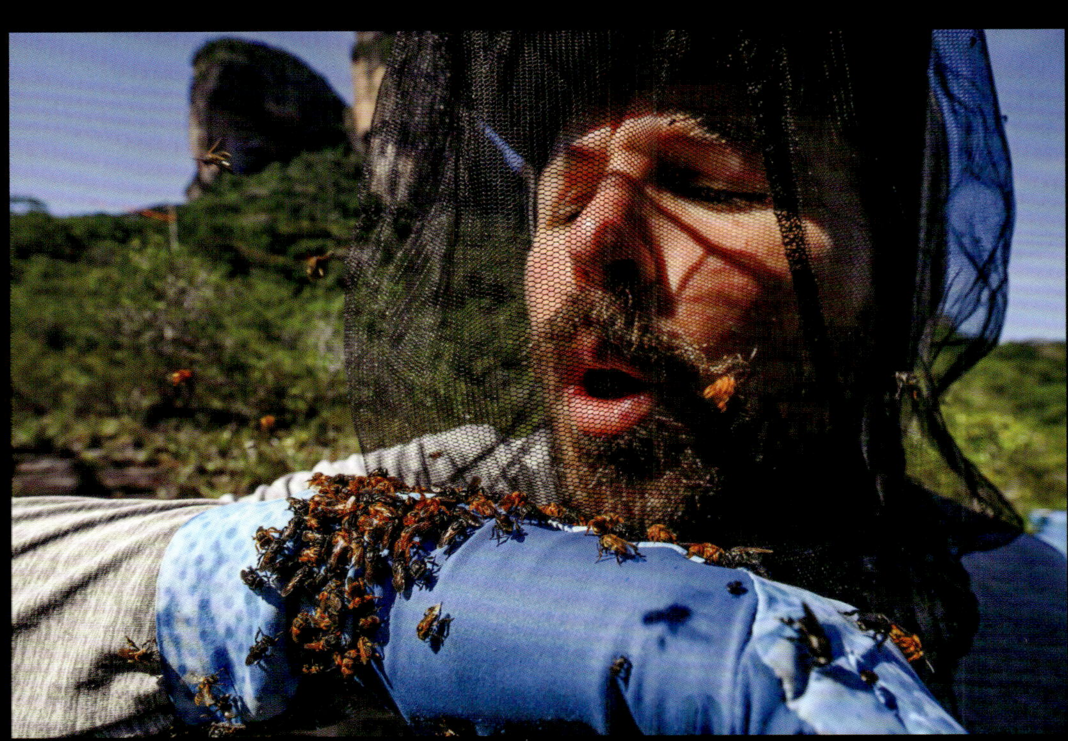

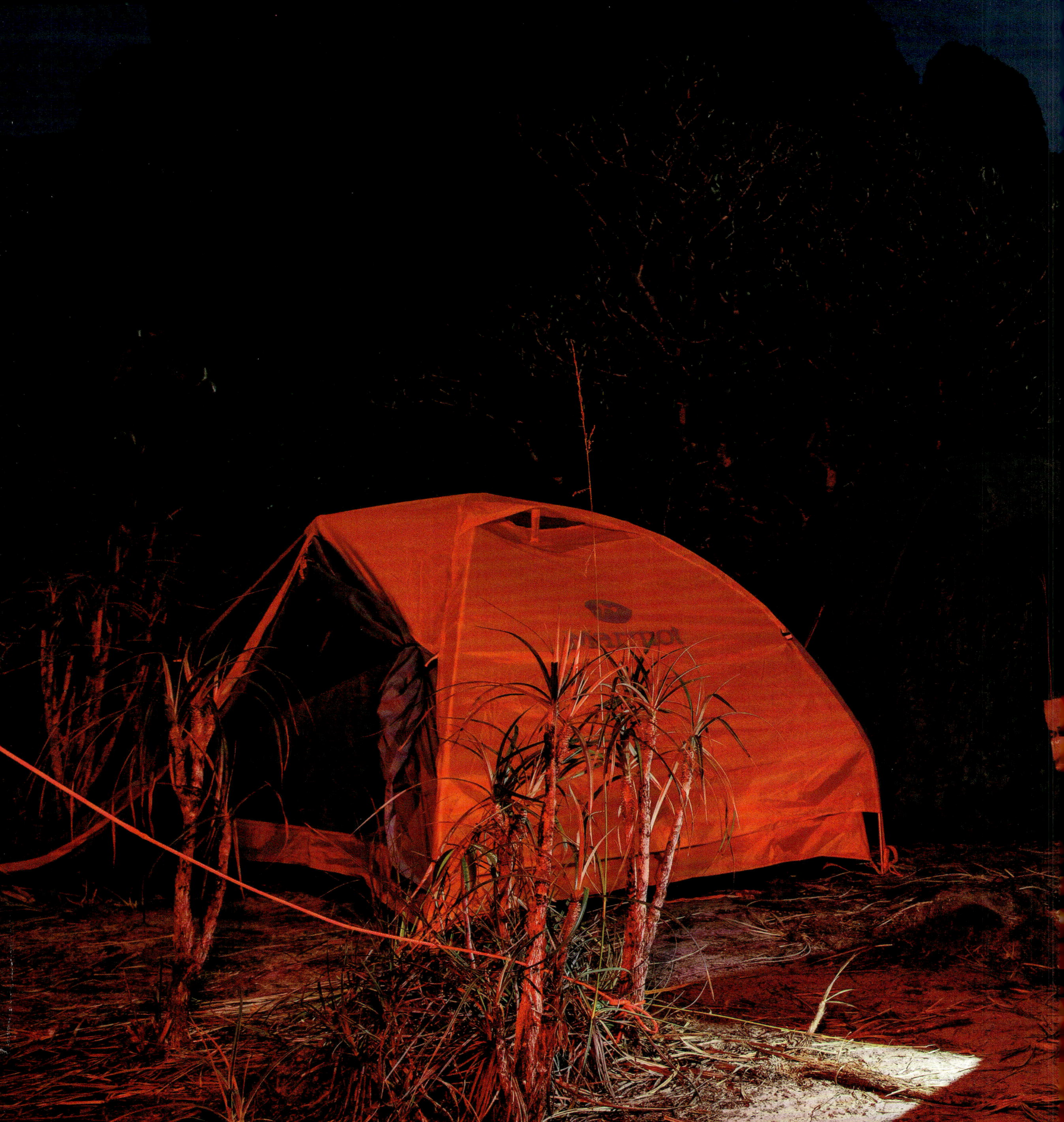

Jungle Nights

We are only the ninth expedition to be granted permission to explore Chiribiquete, Colombia's largest park. While there, only at night did I have the luxury of not wearing a head net. Then, I edit my photographs in relative coolness until the early hours of the morning.

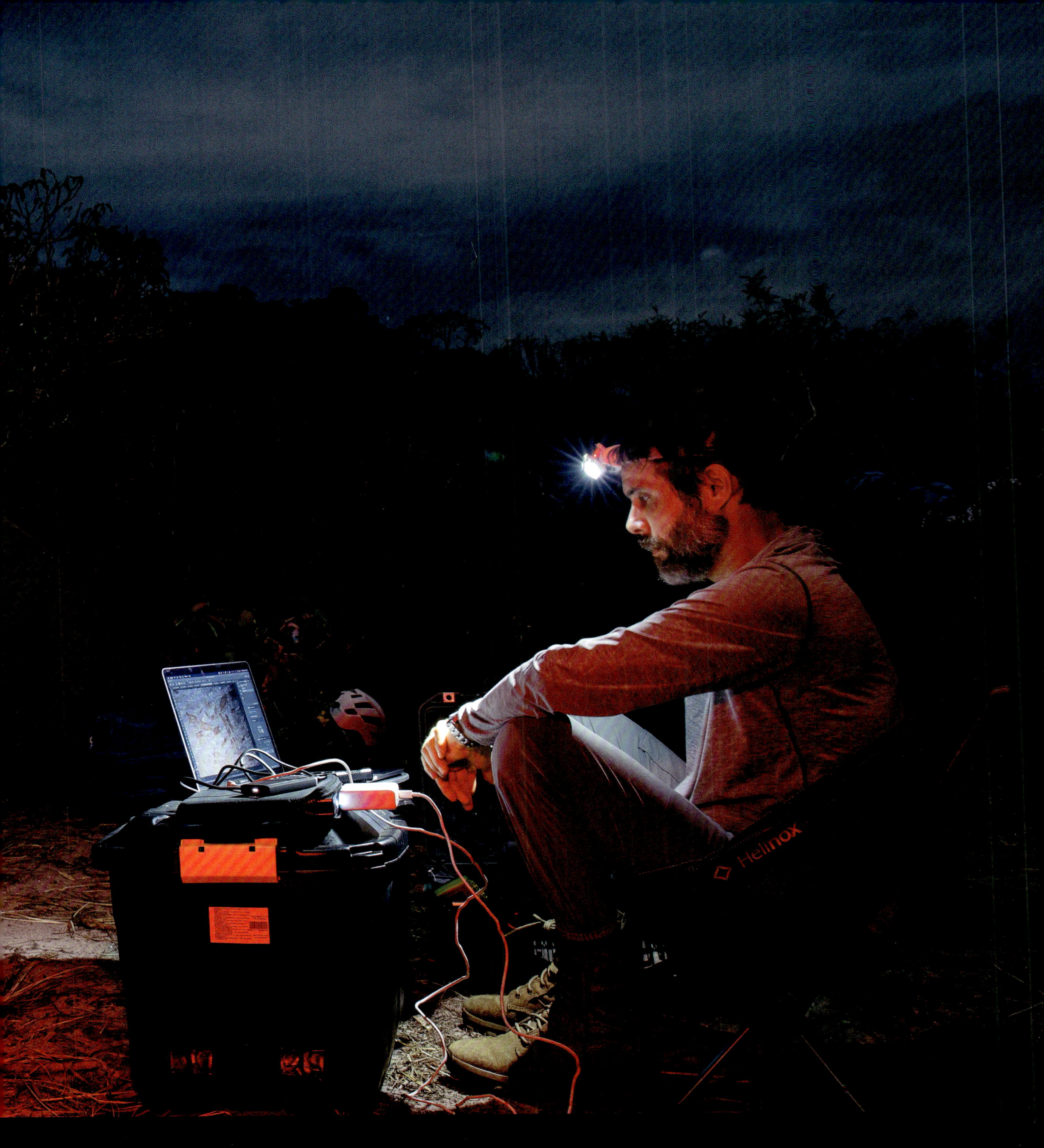
Helinox

ACKNOWLEDGMENTS

I want to thank:

Jill Tiefenthaler, Kaitlin Yarnall, Ian Miller, Kara Ramirez Mullins, Nicole Alexiev, and the entire Amazon team at the National Geographic Society.

Alexa Keefe, Peter Gwin, Cynthia Gorney, Jordan Salama, Sadie Quarrier, Paul Martinez, Nathan Lump, David Miller, and everybody else at *National Geographic* magazine who worked so tirelessly on the special Amazon issue.

Lisa Thomas, Hilary Black, Ashley Leath, Kathy Moran, David Griffin, Adrian Coakley, Nicole Miller Roberts, and Jeremy Goldsmith from National Geographic Books, who helped create and craft the printed volume you are holding in your hands right now.

I want to thank Rolex for their support of the National Geographic and Rolex Perpetual Planet Amazon Expedition.

Fernando Trujillo, João Campos-Silva, Ruthmery Pillco Huarcaya, Angelo Bernardino, Thiago Silva, Baker Perry, Hinsby Cadillo-Quiroz, Tom Matthews, Josh West, Carlos Castaño-Uribe, Julia Tavares, Guido Miranda, Jennifer Angel-Amaya, Mariana Paschoalini Frias, María Jimena Valderrama Avella, and Andrew Whitworth—all fellow seasoned explorers with whom I shared unforgettable adventures across the Amazon Basin.

Marcelo Pérez, Vicente "Chucky" Lorente, Roycer Herbi, Alejandro Gatti, Djokro Kayapó, Bepgogore Kayapó, Rafael Costa, and Rodrigo Salles from Untamed Angling in Bolivia and Brazil.

Carolina Fernandes of Banksia Films; mountain guide extraordinaire Adrian Condor; the Kichwa Añangu community of the Napo Wildlife Center; Sean, Kathleen, and Dutch Robinson of Tobago Dive Experience; and fellow photographer and conservationist Hussain Aga Khan.

Nikon Europe and Daniel Ziegert for providing me with all the cameras and lenses that I needed for my Amazon expedition. It is a real honor to be a Nikon ambassador.

My long-suffering assistant and videographer Otto Whitehead, who was with me every step, paddle, and fin stroke of the way for the entire 396 days I spent in the field.

Lauren van Noort, Steve Benjamin, Ryan Daly, and Lucas Bustamante for providing additional help as assistants at different points along the journey.

My parents for instilling in me the confidence that I could achieve anything I put my mind, heart, and soul into.

Sunnye Collins, who is my most important and essential partner. She is my sounding board and litmus test, my travel companion, and my confidant. In the Amazon, she conducted interviews, recorded audio and video, kept detailed diaries, held lights, and lugged heavy backpacks across difficult terrain.

And to everyone else I couldn't name on the limited real estate of this page, thank you very much.

MAPS CREDITS: 10–11: Main map: Ana P. Barros, University of Illinois Urbana-Champaign; Science for Nature and People Partnership; ESA; NASA/JPL; OpenStreetMap. Inset maps: Ajit Subramaniam, Lamont-Doherty Earth Observatory at Columbia University; Patricia L. Yager, University of Georgia; Angelo Bernardino, Universidade Federal do Espírito Santo; ESA Ocean Colour Climate Change Initiative (Global Chlorophyll-a Data, v. 6); UNEP-WCMC.

ILLUSTRATIONS CREDITS: 84–85, Thomas Peschak and Otto Whitehead; 141, Thomas Peschak and Otto Whitehead; 249, Otto Whitehead; 253, Otto Whitehead; 258, Vicente "Chucky" Lorente; 260–261 (top), Otto Whitehead; 262–263: Andrew Whitworth; 265 (top right), Andrew Whitworth; 266–267, Andrew Whitworth.

ABOUT THE AUTHOR

Thomas Peschak is a National Geographic Explorer and photographer who specializes in documenting the beauty and fragility of the world's oceans, coasts, and wild places. Trained as a marine biologist, he embraced photojournalism after realizing his photographs could have a greater conservation impact than scientific statistics. Peschak has covered some of the most critical conservation narratives of our time, resulting in 20 feature print stories for *National Geographic* magazine. His images and stories have won 18 Wildlife Photographer of the Year and seven World Press Photo Awards. He was also recently awarded National Geographic's Eliza Scidmore Award for outstanding storytelling.

Peschak is a founding director of the Manta Trust and the director of storytelling for the Save Our Seas Foundation. He's spoken numerous times at National Geographic Live events, and his 2015 TED Talk "Dive Into an Ocean Photographer's World" has been viewed more than a million times. As part of the National Geographic and Rolex Perpetual Planet Amazon Expedition, Peschak completed a 396-day exploration of the Amazon River Basin, documenting its wonders and challenges from underwater and topside perspectives. Starting with ice axes and crampons in the icy high Andes and finishing with scuba gear in the Atlantic Ocean, he created a first-of-its-kind comprehensive photographic archive of our planet's most iconic and biodiverse river system. This body of work was published in October 2024, making Peschak only the second person in *National Geographic* magazine's 136-year history to photograph an entire issue.

Since 1888, the National Geographic Society has funded more than 15,000 research, conservation, education, technology, and storytelling projects around the world. National Geographic Partners distributes a portion of the funds it receives from your purchase to National Geographic Society to support their mission to illuminate and protect the wonder of our world.

National Geographic Partners, LLC
1145 17th Street NW
Washington, DC 20036-4688 USA

Get closer to National Geographic Explorers and photographers, and connect with our global community. Join us today at nationalgeographic.org/joinus

For rights or permissions inquiries, please contact National Geographic Books Subsidiary Rights: bookrights@natgeo.com

Financially supported by the National Geographic Society.

ISBN: 978-1-4262-2445-4

The authorized representative in the EU for product safety and compliance is Disney Trading B.V., Asterweg 15S, 1031 HL, Amsterdam, The Netherlands email: DCP.DL-EU.bookscontact@disney.com

Printed in China

26/RRDH/1

Amazon: A River's Journey From the Andes to the Atlantic is the result of National Geographic Explorer and photographer Thomas P. Peschak's nearly 400-day journey photographing the rarely seen aquatic underworld of the largest freshwater ecosystem on Earth. Embedded with fellow Explorers on the National Geographic and Rolex Perpetual Planet Amazon Expedition, a multiyear series of solutions-centered science expeditions spanning the entire Amazon River Basin, Peschak captured the Amazon rainforest's freshwater realm like never before. Peschak's photojournalism has bolstered the Expedition's efforts to ensure the protection, restoration, revival, and survival of this vital ecosystem.

The National Geographic Society is a global nonprofit organization that uses the power of science, exploration, education, and storytelling to illuminate and protect the wonder of our world. Since 1888, the Society has pushed the boundaries of exploration to better understand our world, awarding more than 15,000 grants to National Geographic Explorers—scientists, conservationists, innovators, educators, and storytellers—for work across all seven continents. Today, Explorers are advancing knowledge and leading conservation programs with outsize impact to protect nature, wildlife, historical places, and communities. They're documenting the wonder of our world—including its beauty, its mystery, and the threats it faces—and are inspiring people to care and act on behalf of our planet and its people.

In 2019, the National Geographic Society and Rolex enhanced their long-standing partnership to support expeditions to the planet's most critically important environments, establishing Perpetual Planet Expeditions. By harnessing world-renowned scientific expertise and cutting-edge technology, and revealing new insights about systems vital to life on Earth, these expeditions help scientists, decision-makers, and local communities find solutions for the impacts of climate and environmental change in mountains, rainforests, and the ocean.

For nearly a century, Rolex has supported pioneering explorers pushing the boundaries of human endeavor to help them achieve countless historic feats. Over time, the company has moved from championing exploration for the sake of discovery to protecting the planet. Through their Perpetual Planet Initiative, Rolex stands alongside explorers, scientists, and entrepreneurs, supporting their work to build a better future for all life on Earth. By supporting those who take action and find solutions to today's environmental challenges, Rolex hopes to inspire future generations to strive for a perpetual planet.

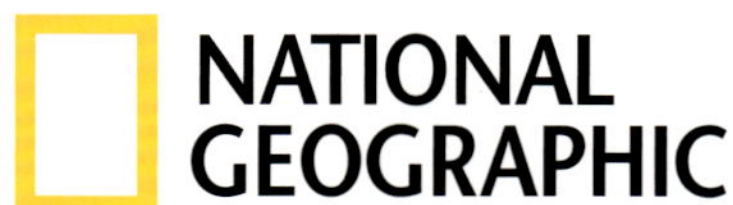

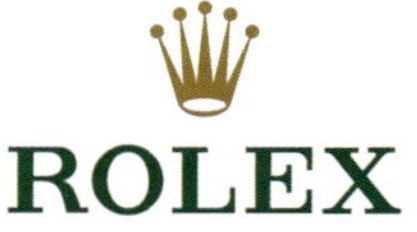

COMMITTED TO A PERPETUAL PLANET